Preachers, Poets, Women, and the Way

Michigan Monograph Series in Japanese Studies
Number 62

Center for Japanese Studies
The University of Michigan

Preachers, Poets, Women, and the Way

Izumi Shikibu and the Buddhist Literature of Medieval Japan

R. Keller Kimbrough

Center for Japanese Studies
The University of Michigan
Ann Arbor, 2008

Published by the Center for Japanese Studies,
The University of Michigan
1007 E. Huron St.
Ann Arbor, MI 48104-1690

Library of Congress Cataloging in Publication Data

Kimbrough, R. Keller, 1968–
Preachers, poets, women, and the way : Izumi Shikibu and the Buddhist literature of medieval Japan / R. Keller Kimbrough
p. cm. — (Michigan monograph series in Japanese studies ; 62)
Translations of some excerpts from the Japanese included.
Includes bibliographical references and index.
ISBN 978-1-929280-47-6 (cloth : alk. paper) — ISBN 978-1-929280-48-3 (pbk. : alk. paper)
1. Buddhist literature, Japanese—History and criticism. 2. Japanese literature—1185–1600—History and criticism. 3. Women authors in literature. 4. Women authors, Japanese—Heian period, 794–1185—Fiction. I. Title.

PL726.33.B8K56 2008
895.6'14099287—dc22

2008037231

This book was set in Palatino Macron.
Kanji set in Hiragino Mincho Pro W3.

This publication meets the ANSI/NISO Standards for Permanence of Paper for Publications and Documents in Libraries and Archives (Z39.48—1992).

Printed in the United States of America

This book is dedicated to
Mary Drew Griffin,
who inspired in me a love of old books.

Contents

Illustrations

Acknowledgments

This book began as a doctoral dissertation, which I first started researching in the early spring of 1997 and completed in the late summer of 1999. In the decade that has passed since then, I have received extraordinary aid and encouragement from a vast number of individuals and institutions, some of whom I would like to acknowledge here. I would like to thank the Japan Foundation for providing me with the financial means to conduct dissertation research in Tokyo in 1997–98; Yale University for a Dissertation Fellowship in 1998–99; the Yale East Asian Council for additional research funding in the summer of 1999; the Sainsbury Institute for the Study of Japanese Arts and Cultures for allowing me to spend the 2002–3 academic year revising my manuscript as a Sainsbury Research Fellow at the School of Oriental and African Studies at the University of London; and the Nanzan Institute for Religion and Culture for permitting me to continue revising my manuscript as a Visiting Research Fellow at Nanzan University in Nagoya in 2005–6 and in the summer of 2007.

I owe my greatest debt of thanks to Edward Kamens, who took me on as his graduate student at Yale in the fall of 1994 and taught me how to write. I will be forever grateful. I would also like to thank Komine Kazuaki for allowing me to study under his guidance at Rikkyō University in 1997–98; Tokuda Kazuo for years of inspiration and advice; Stanley Weinstein for his friendship, wisdom, and enthusiasm, and for teaching me how to make sense of difficult texts; Edwin McClellan for six semesters of graduate seminars; Benjamin Dorman, James Heisig, and Tom Kasulis for their computer wizardry; Bruce Willoughby for his lovely layout and editorial acumen; and Joshua Mostow, Amy Franks, and all of my graduate and undergraduate students at the University of Colorado, Colby College, and the University of Michigan who read and commented on early drafts of the manuscript. In addition, I would like to thank Ogurisu Kenji at the Hyōgo Prefectural Museum of History; Wakasugi Junji at the Kyoto National Museum; Matsuura Masaaki at the Nara National Museum; Minobe Shigekatsu at Nanzan University; Mimi Yiengpruksawan at Yale; John Carpenter at SOAS; Ezawa Yoshiko at Tōyō University; Yuge Shigeru at Gifu University; Tsuda Tetsuei at the Kanazawa Bunko Archives; the priests of Seiganji; and all of the individuals and organizations listed in the following pages who have allowed me to reproduce photographic images of their paintings and manuscripts here. Finally, I would like to thank my mother for her proofreading, little Peggy for her patience, and Eiko for her good sense, encouragement, and tireless support.

Boulder, 2008

Introduction

In the thirteenth year of the Enryaku era (794), the Japanese Emperor Kanmu established the capital city of Heian in what is now the heart of metropolitan Kyoto. The next nearly four hundred years—the Heian period, stretching until Minamoto no Yoritomo's relocation of governmental power to the eastern city of Kamakura in 1185—came to be recalled in later centuries as a golden age in the history of Japan: a time of relative peace and stability, and an era of unprecedented cultural, literary, and artistic achievement among the leisured aristocracy. In regard to literature, the late tenth and early eleventh centuries during the reign of Emperor Ichijō (980–1011) were a particularly brilliant time. It was in and around these years that some of Japan's greatest and most renowned literary works were composed, including *The Tale of Genji, The Pillow Book, A Tale of Flowering Fortunes, The Murasaki Shikibu Diary,* and *The Izumi Shikibu Diary.*[1] Authorship of these texts is attributed to the female writers and poets Murasaki Shikibu, Sei Shōnagon, Akazome Emon, and Izumi Shikibu, ladies-in-waiting in the salons of Empresses Shōshi and Teishi at the turn of the millennium, approximately one thousand years ago.[2]

The accomplishments of these women authors are well known today, both in Japan and abroad. Their compositions have been annotated, translated, and widely reproduced. Yet far less understood are the many fictional and pseudo-biographical texts from the Japanese medieval age—roughly the Kamakura and Muromachi periods (1185–1333 and 1336–1573)—that take as their subject the imagined lives, deaths, and afterlives of these and other Heian literary figures.[3] These works, often overlapping in content and frequently contradictory, form unto themselves a distinct body of literature

[1]*Genji monogatari, Makura no sōshi, Eiga monogatari, Murasaki Shikibu nikki,* and *Izumi Shikibu nikki,* respectively.

[2]Fujiwara no Teishi (976–1000) was appointed *chūgū* (empress) in 990. Fujiwara no Shōshi (988–1074), later known as Jōtōmon'in, was appointed *chūgū* in the second month of 1000, at which time Teishi was promoted to the position of *kōgō* (also translatable as "empress"). Teishi died in childbirth in the twelfth month of 1000; Emperor Ichijō's simultaneous conference of the titles *chūgū* and *kōgō* on two different women was unprecedented.

[3]I use the term "medieval" as a translation of *chūsei,* "middle age." *Chūsei* refers to both a specific period of time (1185–1600) and the feeling of an age: the era of change, uncertainty, and religious and social upheaval following the twelfth-century decline of the Heian Court, and preceding the seventeenth-century rise of Tokugawa hegemony.

spanning the various folkloric, dramatic, poetic, commentarial, and Buddhist traditions. Both reverent and libelous, they represent, in microcosm, the ever-changing worlds of late-Heian, Kamakura, and Muromachi-period fiction. In cataloguing the poets' virtues and vices, their beauty, elegance, vanity and lust, their poetic prowess and sometimes religious devotion (or lack thereof), these works recreated and preserved, however inaccurately, the authors of the Heian court for later generations of audiences to whom they might otherwise have been lost.

Much of medieval Japanese literature, including *setsuwa* (tale literature), *otogizōshi* (short medieval fiction), *jisha engi* (temple and shrine histories), *gunki mono* (martial tales), and some narrative painting (Buddhist didactic picture scrolls and pilgrimage mandala), has its roots in the storytelling, proselytizing, and fund-raising activities of an array of Heian and Kamakura-period preacher-entertainers. Blind minstrel-priests (*biwa hōshi*) traveled throughout Japan in the medieval period chanting *The Tale of the Heike*, the priests of Agui became famous for their enthralling sermons, and Kumano *bikuni*—the so-called "nuns of Kumano"—wandered the provinces with large rolled-up paintings of heavens and hells and the Nachi Kumano Shrine, which they would display at temples and festivals as props for their street-corner sermons and storytelling performances.[4] In many cases, the oral literature of these and other groups of lay and monastic entertainers evolved into the elaborate temple histories, dramas, and works of fiction for which the medieval period is best known today.

As symbols of the elegance, sophistication, and decadence of the Heian court, Izumi Shikibu, Sei Shōnagon, and other Heian women authors became popular subjects for a variety of these temple-based and itinerant preacher-entertainers. Tales of Murasaki Shikibu's rebirth in hell as punishment for writing *The Tale of Genji* were used to discuss the morality of literature, while written and pictorial representations of Ono no Komachi's physical degradation—both in old age and in death—were used to teach the concept of impermanence and to demonstrate the impurity of the human body. Few Heian authors, male or female, were put to as wide or diverse use in medieval Buddhist sources and fictional works as Izumi Shikibu, and this extensive use of her name and her poetry in the thirteenth through sixteenth centuries, as documented in various surviving sermons, tale collections, sutra commentaries, narrative paintings, and quasi-secular literary texts, played a crucial role in her establishment in Japan in the medieval and

[4]For more on these and other medieval preacher-entertainers, see Barbara Ruch, "Medieval Jongleurs and the Making of a National Literature," in *Japan in the Muromachi Age*, ed. John Hall and Toyoda Takeshi (Berkeley: University of California Press, 1977), 279–309.

early-modern periods as a transcendent, or universally recognized, cultural icon.

With the exception of the early twentieth-century folklorist and ethnologist Yanagita Kunio, modern scholars have tended to ignore these accounts because of their obvious fictitiousness. In the early 1930s, Yanagita set about exploring the surviving written and oral accounts of a variety of Nara, Heian, and medieval literary, cultural, and religious figures.[5] He was especially intrigued by the prevalence of nearly identical stories of single individuals in different parts of Japan. To take one example, he identified a group of tales, most often concerning Sei Shōnagon, about a dead Heian woman author's poetic response to the attempted removal or inadvertent desecration of her tomb.[6] The story seems to date from the early-modern period—it is difficult to tell because of its originally oral nature—and it is usually set on the island of Shikoku. The poet and author Ban Kōkei includes a version in his miscellany *Kanden kōhitsu* (The Brush that Tills the Kanden Fields; completed in the winter of 1799), and he lists three places in Shikoku—two in Sanuki province and one in Awa—in which the renowned *Pillow Book* author is said to be buried.[7]

Yanagita explained this and other clusters of accounts by postulating that mendicant women preacher-entertainers, including *miko* (shrine maidens), Kumano *bikuni* (nuns of Kumano), *goze* (minstrels, many of whom were blind), and *yūjo* (singer-performers, later regarded as prostitutes), circulated stories of Buddhas, deities, and Heian women poets throughout Japan in the medieval and early-modern periods. These itinerant singer-storyteller-preacher-entertainers told a range of tales about Sei Shōnagon, Izumi Shikibu, and Ono no Komachi—women who, like themselves, purportedly wandered the provinces reciting poems in the hardship of their latter years—in village after village as they collected donations for the con-

[5]I am referring in particular to Yanagita's "Izumi Shikibu no tabi" (1931) and *Josei to minkan denshō* (1932), in which Yanagita discusses stories of Izumi Shikibu, Ono no Komachi, Sei Shōnagon, Ono no Otsū, Jōruri-hime, Saigyō, Kūkai, and others. "Izumi Shikibu no tabi" (Izumi Shikibu's Travel-Socks; named after a story in which Izumi Shikibu wears *tabi*, Japanese socks, to hide her cloven deer feet) was first published in *Tabi to densetsu* in November 1931, and then in January 1933 as a chapter of Yanagita's *Momotarō no tanjō*. *Josei to minkan denshō* (Women and Folklore) was published in more than sixty installments of the weekly *Fujo shinbun* (Women's Newspaper), and then in its entirety in December 1932. Both works are printed in Yanagita Kunio, *Teihon Yanagita Kunio shū*, vol. 8 (Tokyo: Chikuma Shobō, 1962), 265–88 and 315–447.

[6]Yanagita, "Sei Shōnagon no bōrei," in "Izumi Shikibu no tabi," 283–86. Also see Yanagita, *Josei to minkan denshō*, 339.

[7]Nihon Zuihitsu Taisei Henshūbu, ed., *Nihon zuihitsu taisei: dai ikki*, vol. 18 (Tokyo: Yoshikawa Kōbunkan, 1976), 167. Also see R. Keller Kimbrough, "Apocryphal Texts and Literary Identity: Sei Shōnagon and *The Matsushima Diary*," *Monumenta Nipponica* 57, no. 2 (Summer 2002), 155.

struction of temples, shrines, bridges, and roads.[8] Yanagita speculated that the women adapted the tales to suit the places they told them; for example, if a nun recounted her story in a town named "Ono-mura," she might tell it about Ono no Komachi, or if in a place called "Izumi," about Izumi Shikibu.[9] Similar accounts of different Heian women authors would have been spread about as a result. Yanagita further contended that the storytellers themselves were often identified with their stories, and that after the women died, their graves came to be confused with those of the women in their tales, which would account for Sei Shōnagon's, Izumi Shikibu's, and Ono no Komachi's multiple graves in disparate places.[10]

The present volume seeks to follow in the footsteps of Yanagita's groundbreaking work, addressing issues of religion, gender, and medieval literary production. Unlike Yanagita, I have tended to confine my explorations to textual sources from the Kamakura and Muromachi periods, with only occasional forays into works of Heian and early-modern literature. For the most part, the stories that I discuss tell little about the actual historical figures that they purport to represent. Nevertheless, they shed a great deal of light on the development of medieval Japanese literature and on the processes by which Izumi Shikibu and other aristocratic women, formerly representatives of exclusive Heian literary traditions, came to be embraced in the early-modern and modern periods by Japanese society at large as quintessentially canonical writers of Japan. The reader should therefore understand that while the present book takes as its subject the poems and tales of a Heian woman poet, it has relatively little to do with Heian literature *per se* (other than the history of its reception, that is). Rather, like Yanagita's earlier work, it is a study of medieval Japanese religion, history, and popular literary culture, with a special interest in the problems and possibilities for women in Buddhism in the twelfth through sixteenth centuries.

Preachers, Poets, and Expedient Means

One of the central concerns of this book is to demonstrate the ways in which Izumi Shikibu and other literary and cultural figures were adopted by medieval Buddhist proselytizers for use in raising money and teaching Buddhism, and to explore some of the reasons why. Yanagita may be responsible in the modern period for highlighting this as an issue worthy of investigation, but he was certainly not the first Japanese scholar to identify the dissemination of apocryphal poem-stories with the storytelling activities of

[8]Yanagita, *Josei to minkan denshō*, 346–56 and 412–14.
[9]Yanagita, "Izumi Shikibu no tabi," 279.
[10]Yanagita, *Josei to minkan denshō*, 352 and 356.

medieval and early-modern preacher-entertainers. The outspoken nativist scholar Motoori Norinaga (1730–1801), for example, broaches the subject in his miscellany *Tamagatsuma* (A Jeweled Basket). After discounting the divine attributions of two poems in the fourteenth-century poetic anthology *Fūga wakashū* (Collection of Elegant Verse), one of which pertains to Izumi Shikibu's legendary exclusion from Kumano Shrine (discussed on pp. 208–10, below), Norinaga observes:

> We often hear of poems by such-and-such a deity, or verses composed at such-and-such a shrine, but for the most part these are just made-up sayings by Buddhist priests and their ilk trying to lure people into their religion. This is why these sorts of poems go against the Way of the Gods, and are always Buddhist instead. Since time immemorial, priests have never hesitated to lie to attract people to their faith. In this, they take after that person Shakyamuni's so-called "expedient means."[11]

While Yanagita was most interested in the roles of women in the medieval and early-modern transmission of religion and culture (to the extent that he sought to empower women by educating them about their past),[12] Norinaga wished to disentangle native Shinto belief from what he considered the corrupting influence of centuries of imported Buddhist thought. Yet notwithstanding their differing ideological agendas, both Yanagita and Norinaga recognized the importance of Buddhist preaching to the medieval spread of fabricated (non-historical) tales.

In denouncing the "lies" that preachers tell, Norinaga alludes to the principle of *hōben*, or expedient means. As the "Expedient Means" chapter of the *Lotus Sutra* explains, *hōben* are "words of simile and parable" used to "expound the doctrines for the sake of living beings."[13] Because sentient beings vary in their capacities for the Truth, the Buddha tailors his message to his individual audiences' preferences and abilities, rather than preaching at a level beyond their comprehension. Most simply stated, a *hōben* is an untruth used to bring people to the Truth. In the "Simile and Parable" chapter of the *Lotus Sutra*, the Buddha explains the nature of *hōben* with a *hōben*: the parable of the burning house. According to this most famous of *Lotus Sutra* tales, a wealthy father uses deceit to persuade his obstinate young sons to

[11]NST 40:57. For bibliographic abbreviations, see the first page of the bibliography.

[12]On Yanagita's feminist intentions, see *Josei to minkan denshō*, 438–43. Yanagita's decision to publish his work in a newspaper for women is also suggestive of his desire to speak directly to the women of his time.

[13]TSD 9 (262):7a-b; Burton Watson, *The Lotus Sutra* (New York: Columbia University Press, 1993), 31-32. Translation here by Burton Watson.

leave their burning mansion. He lies, telling them that he has prepared an assortment of toys beyond the front gate. The children rush outside, saved from the conflagration—a metaphor for this world of suffering and delusion—but there are no toys to be found. Instead, the father has given them their lives.[14]

Japanese Buddhist tales attest to the use of *hōben* in Heian and medieval Japan by Buddhas, bodhisattvas, and preachers alike. The early twelfth-century *setsuwa* anthology *Konjaku monogatari shū* (Tales of Times Now Past), for example, contains a story of a young Tendai priest who is so distracted by lust that he is unable to study. The bodhisattva Kokūzō appears as a beautiful young woman and promises to sleep with him if he will first memorize the *Lotus Sutra*. Later, she asks that he study for three more years before sharing her bed. Motivated by the woman's words and his own lascivious desire, the man becomes an eminent priest. However, there are to be no "toys" outside the gate for him, either: the woman disappears, denying him his carnal reward. Later revealing herself (now "himself") in a dream, the bodhisattva explains that [s]he deceived him in order to help him along the Buddhist Path.[15] Again, in the Buddhist tale anthology *Hōbutsushū* (late twelfth century), a Buddhist skeptic by the name of Awata Rokuji is said to have fallen ill and died. Rokuji encounters a priest in the afterworld who urges him to lie to King Enma, the judge of the dead, so that he may receive time to transcribe the *Lotus Sutra* and thereby save himself from hell. Rokuji asks the priest his name, whereupon the duplicitous monk replies that he is none other than a human manifestation of the "Expedient Means" chapter of the *Lotus Sutra*.[16] Indeed, who or what else would so brazenly advise a dead man to lie?

The notion of *hōben* is key to understanding Heian women authors in their medieval representations. Since Yanagita's early explorations, there has been a growing body of evidence to suggest that a variety of institutions and individual proselytizers—both male and female—put to use fictional accounts of Izumi Shikibu, Sei Shōnagon, Murasaki Shikibu, Ono no Komachi, and others as a means of attracting and entertaining audiences while teaching Buddhism and collecting donations. Adhering to the principle of expedient means, late-Heian and medieval preachers adapted their sermons to their patrons. In the case of the educated and elite, from whom they might have hoped to receive their most substantial rewards, they did

[14]TSD 9 (262):12b–13c; Watson, *The Lotus Sutra*, 56–62. The father then presents the children with elaborate jeweled carriages, symbols of the Single Vehicle of the Dharma.

[15]SNKBT 36:59–67 (tale 17:33). The young priest had previously prayed to Kokūzō to help him concentrate on his studies.

[16]SNKBT 40:326–28. Rokuji had once carried the water that was used to make the ink that was used to make the copy of that particular chapter, which is why it appears to him as it does.

this by incorporating tales of famous women poets. Among these larger-than-life literary figures—artistically accomplished and sexually charged celebrities of the court—Izumi Shikibu was the most widely employed. Accounts of her life, death, and spiritual salvation were incorporated into an unusually large number of proselytizing traditions, including (apparently) those of Kumano, Agui, Seiganji Temple in Kyoto, Tennōji Temple in Osaka, Enkyōji Temple near Himeji, several medieval Tendai seminaries, and the Ji sect of Pure Land Buddhism.

One of the most famous of the Murasaki Shikibu tales—the early-medieval rumor that she was suffering torment in hell as karmic retribution for leading readers astray with *The Tale of Genji,* her supposedly wicked web of sex and lies—has demonstrable roots in a late-Heian proselytizing tradition intended to discourage the reading of fiction in favor of strict religious practice. The earliest textual reference to Murasaki Shikibu's perdition is contained in a short Buddhist polemic titled *Genji ipponkyō* (A Sutra for Genji; ca. 1168), composed in Sino-Japanese (*kanbun*) by the Tendai priest Chōken (1126–1203), a famous preacher of Agui.[17] Chōken begins by listing twelve Heian narratives (*monogatari*, including *The Tale of Genji*), which, unlike works of history, "tell us nothing about the good or bad of peoples past, nor explain the doings of old."[18] Rather, Chōken complains, "their intent is to lie," and their chief concern is "the path of men and women's amorous affairs." Chōken contends that because of its extraordinary literary excellence, *The Tale of Genji* is an especially dangerous text:

> Upon reading this work, sheltered young women, as yet unmarried, are secretly moved to lust. Opening the *Tale,* single men in their lonely, chilly beds pine with useless longing. Having planted such sinful roots, both the dead author and all her avid readers are condemned to the cycle of birth and death. Every one of them will fall into the Sword-forest Hell.[19] This is why Murasaki Shikibu's

[17]Agui was an urban monastic center affiliated with Enryakuji Temple on Mount Hiei. Its priests were renowned in the medieval period for their fine preaching and storytelling. Chōken, the most famous among them, is regarded today as the progenitor of the Agui preaching lineage. Agui was destroyed in the fires that ravaged Kyoto in the Ōnin Disturbance of 1467–77.

[18]*Genji ipponkyō* is typeset in Miyakawa Yōko, *Genji monogatari no bunkashiteki kenkyū* (Tokyo: Kazama Shobō, 1997), 226–27; Shigematsu Nobuhiro, *Shinkō Genji monogatari kenkyūshi* (Tokyo: Fūkan Shobō, 1961), 112–13 (note 1); and Gotō Tanji, "*Genji ipponkyō* to *Genji hyōbyaku*," *Kokugo kokubun no kenkyū* 48 (September 1930), 31–32. For a discussion of the work and a list of principal secondary sources, see Ii Haruki, *Genji monogatari chūshakusho, kyōjushi jiten* (Tokyo: Tōkyōdō Shuppan, 2001), 113b–14a.

[19]The Sword-forest Hell (*kenju jigoku*) is one of the sixteen smaller hells. Its trees have daggers for leaves, and these rain down upon people whenever the wind blows. Needless to say, it is a very windy place. Nakamura Hajime, *Kōsetsu Bukkyōgo daijiten*, vol. 1 (Tokyo: Tokyo Shoseki, 2001), 403a.

> ghost appeared in someone's dream in the past and declared the burden of her sin.

Chōken's condemnation is severe, but not without purpose. He goes on to tell of a heroic benefactor-nun by the name of Zenjō, who set out to rescue Murasaki Shikibu and her readers by urging all manner of people to make copies of the *Lotus Sutra*. Zenjō instructed them, he says, to inscribe a chapter title from *The Tale of Genji* at the end[s] of each of the sutra's twenty-eight fascicles in order to ensure their effect. Although the identity of the nun is unclear,[20] Chōken's motive in recounting her story is not: by first condemning Murasaki Shikibu and her readers to hell, and then introducing a method of getting them out—a way of ransoming the damned—Chōken sought to exploit the popularity of Murasaki Shikibu's work as a means of compelling the performance of pious acts.

Further accounts of Murasaki Shikibu's distress survive from the Kamakura period. The tale anthologies *Hōbutsushū* (A Collection of Treasures; late twelfth century) and *Ima monogatari* (Contemporary Tales; ca. 1239–40) report that Murasaki Shikibu had appeared in people's dreams, claiming to have fallen into hell as a result of writing *The Tale of Genji*. In *Hōbutsushū*, an overtly didactic Buddhist treatise by Taira no Yasuyori, Murasaki Shikibu urges that her work be destroyed and copies of the sutras dedicated toward her salvation instead.[21] In *Ima monogatari*, compiled by Fujiwara no Nobuzane, she asks that poems containing the *nenbutsu* (the seven-syllable invocation of Amida Buddha's name) and a name from her work be composed upon each of the chapters of her *Tale*.[22] Personally requesting specific devotional acts, Murasaki Shikibu is made to play the part of a celebrity Buddhist advocate from hell. Whether these later accounts reflect an ongoing proselytizing tradition or were solely inspired by Chōken's twelfth-century

[20]In 1930, Gotō Tanji suggested that the nun was Bifukumon'in no Kaga (d. 1193), mother of Fujiwara no Teika (1162–1241). Kaga seems to have orchestrated a group project to copy the *Lotus Sutra* for Murasaki Shikibu's salvation around the time of Chōken's authorship of *Genji ipponkyō*. Gotō's argument is compelling, but as-yet unproven. Gotō, "*Genji ipponkyō* to *Genji hyōbyaku*," 40–44; Ikeda Kikan, *Monogatari bungaku 1* (Tokyo: Shibundō, 1968), 366–67; Ii Haruki, *Genji monogatari no densetsu* (Tokyo: Shōwa Shuppan, 1976), 173–81.

[21]*Hōbutsushū*, in ZGR 32:2:296b (*Ikkan-bon* textual line). According to the corresponding passage in the second *Nanakan-bon* textual line (SNKBT 40:229), Murasaki Shikibu did not request that her own work be destroyed.

[22]Kubota Jun et al., eds., *Ima monogatari, Takafusashū, Tōsai zuihitsu* (Tokyo: Miyai Shoten, 1979), 156. Both the *Hōbutsushū* and *Ima monogatari* accounts are translated in Thomas Harper, "Motoori Norinaga's Criticism of the *Genji monogatari*: A Study of the Background and Critical Content of his *Genji monogatari tama no ogushi*," Ph.D. dissertation (University of Michigan, 1971), 58 and 50.

oration is unclear. In any case, such mercenary and sensational use of her persona—if only by Chōken—is consistent with the medieval uses of those of her Heian women peers.

For Buddhist preachers, the recitation of stories such as these was an expedient means of teaching Buddhism and encouraging devotion. A latter twelfth-century discourse on the principles and techniques of preaching titled *Tenpōrin hiden (seppō hijō)* (Secret Transmissions on Turning the Dharma Wheel, or Secret Articles on Expounding the Dharma) emphasizes the importance of recounting "parables, stories and the like" as a means of illustrating and enlivening sermons.[23] While a preacher must be well versed in doctrine, the treatise maintains, he must also be an engaging storyteller. Furthermore, he "should possess a heart for Japanese poetry" so that he may speak with grace and ease.[24] The use of poems in preaching is treated within the work as being simply a matter of course. On the basis of internal evidence, Abe Yasurō has suggested that the *Tenpōrin hiden* author was a monk at the Enryakuji Tendai complex on Mount Hiei.[25] If so, he may have been a colleague of Chōken, who employed the story of Murasaki Shikibu in hell from around 1168 as his own expedient means of promoting the performance of pious acts.

Like Izumi Shikibu and Murasaki Shikibu, the ninth-century poet Ono no Komachi seems to have been employed in preaching from as early as the Heian period. In her case, the defining text is the mid-Heian *Tamatsukuri Komachi shi sōsuisho* (The Prosperity and Decline of Tamatsukuri Komachi; hereafter *Sōsuisho*), a two-part work of unknown authorship written in *kanbun*.[26] Because of its strong Pure Land Buddhist flavor, Katagiri Yōichi has suggested that it was composed by a tenth- or early eleventh-century

[23]Mabuchi Kazuo and Taguchi Kazuo, "Honkoku: Daigoji-zō *Tenpōrin hiden (seppō hijō)*," *Daigoji bunkazai kenkyūjo kenkyū kiyō* 18 (2000), 8a; Lorinda Kiyama, "Performative Preaching: The Art and Politics of Persuasion in Medieval Japan," Ph.D. dissertation (Stanford University, forthcoming). Translation by Kiyama. I am grateful to Kiyama for introducing me to this text, and for sharing her translation with me prior to the completion of her dissertation.

[24]Mabuchi and Taguchi, "Honkoku," 12b; Kiyama, "Performative Preaching." Translation here by Kiyama.

[25]Cited in Mabuchi and Taguchi, "Honkoku," 4.

[26]*Tamatsukuri Komachi shi sōsuisho* is annotated and photographically reproduced in Tochio Takeshi, ed., *Tamatsukuri Komachi shi sōsuisho*, Iwanami bunko 570 (Tokyo: Iwanami Shoten, 1994). It is translated in Terry Kawashima, *Writing Margins: The Textual Construction of Gender in Heian and Kamakura Japan* (Cambridge: Harvard University Asia Center, 2001), 306–21, and in Felice Renee Fischer, *Ono no Komachi: A Ninth-Century Poetess of Heian Japan*, Ph.D. dissertation (Columbia University, 1972), 186–205. Translation of the title is by Kawashima. For a detailed discussion of the work in English, see Kawashima, *Writing Margins*, 128–52.

preacher for singing or recitation in sermons.[27] The unnamed narrator tells of his encounter with a filthy, emaciated, barefoot and naked old hag. Although unidentified within the work, the beggar-woman was widely associated with Ono no Komachi in the late-Heian, Kamakura, and Muromachi periods (which is why I refer to her here as Komachi). The woman tells of the luxury and haughtiness of her youth, the bitterness of her fall, and her resulting realization that the gold and jewels of this world are as nothing compared to the jewels of the Buddha's Holy Law. In the second part of the work—a section in verse—the narrator contrasts the wretchedness of the woman's present with the glory of her future rebirth in Amida Buddha's Pure Land Paradise. Her salvation is assured by her humble renunciation of worldly affairs and her whole-hearted turn to the Path of the Buddha. The narrator seems to suggest that if a woman as formerly deluded as Komachi could yet attain salvation, then all women have the Pure Land within their grasp.

In addition to her supposed debasement in life, Ono no Komachi was associated in death with graphic paintings of human cadavers in each of their purportedly nine stages of decay. Known collectively as *kusō-e* ("pictures of the nine aspects"), these macabre artworks were employed as props in centuries of medieval sermons on the topics of impermanence and the horrors of the flesh.[28] As a Buddhist meditative practice, the contemplation of decomposing corpses (*fujōkan* in Japanese) dates back to the early Indian "meditation on foulness," which Liz Wilson writes is "praised by the Buddha of the Pāli canon and discussed at length in doctrinal compendia such as Buddhaghosa's *Visuddhimagga*." Wilson explains:

> According to Buddhaghosa—the fifth-century commentator who

[27]Katagiri Yōichi, *Ono no Komachi tsuiseki* (Tokyo: Kasama Shoin, 1975), 56. *Sōsuisho* is traditionally attributed to Kūkai (774–835), founder of the Shingon sect of Japanese Buddhism. According to *Gyokuden jinpi* (Profound Secret Transmissions), a medieval compendium of secret literary lore from the poetic lineage of Fujiwara no Tameaki (fl. ca. 1263–78), Kūkai composed *Sōsuisho* as one of his prophecies, or *miraiki*, because Ono no Komachi was only four years old when he died. *Tōden gyōhitsu* (fifteenth century) and the Reizei text of *Ise monogatari shō* (Kamakura period; also called *Ise monogatari chū*) contain similar explanations. See Komine Kazuaki, "Chūsei setsuwa no Komachi," *Kokubungaku: kaishaku to kanshō* 60, no. 8 (August 1995): 46–52; Ogawa Toyoo, ed., *Nihon koten gisho sōkan*, vol. 1 (Tokyo: Gendai Shichōshinsha, 2005), 86–87; Katagiri, *Ono no Komachi tsuiseki*, 54–55; and Ichiko Teiji, ed., *Tōden gyōhitsu* (Tokyo: Miyai Shoten, 1992), 198–99.

[28]The most famous of these paintings, the Kamakura-period *Kusōshi emaki*, is reproduced in Komatsu Shigemi, ed., *Gaki zōshi, Jigoku zōshi, Yamai no sōshi, Kusōshi emaki*, Nihon emaki taisei, vol. 7 (Tokyo: Chūō Kōronsha, 1977). Komachi may have been associated with *kusō-e* because of Kūkai's purported authorship of both *Sōsuisho* and a set of nine poems ("Kusōshi") on the nine stages of the body's decay. Kūkai's "Kusōshi" are reproduced in NKBT 71:460–71, and discussed in Nakamura Tanio, "Kusōshi emaki no seiritsu," in *Gaki zōshi, Jigoku zōshi, Yamai no sōshi, Kusōshi emaki*, ed. Komatsu, 166–67. Also see Fusae Kanda, "Behind the Sensationalism: Images of a Decaying Corpse in Japanese Buddhist Art," *The Art Bulletin* 87, no. 1 (March 2005): 24–49, and Kawashima, *Writing Margins*, 190–99.

> is often considered the premier spokesman of monastic Buddhism—the meditator should go to a cremation ground and select a corpse in one of ten stages of decay, from a corpse bloated with putrescence (*uddhumāta*) to a skeleton (*aṭṭhika*). Each of the ten stages has a characteristic foulness that serves as an antidote to the one of ten types of attraction to physical form. For example, the bloated corpse suits those who are particular about the shapes of bodies; discolored corpses are recommended for those who are attentive to the complexion of the skin.[29]

Buddhaghosa further advised that in choosing a corpse, the meditator should take care not to choose one of the opposite sex—especially if it is recently dead—in order to avoid giving rise to "untoward thoughts" (a disturbing thought in itself).[30]

Despite Buddhaghosa's ominous advice, Ono no Komachi came to be identified in Japan with fetishistic paintings of bodily decay from the Kamakura period, when *kusō-e* became a genre independent of *rokudō-e* ("pictures of the six realms").[31] In their earlier, more traditional forms, *kusō-e* tended to constitute large, single-panel tableaux with the deceased woman simultaneously visible in all of her nine (as opposed to Buddhaghosa's ten) stages of putrefaction. The Kamakura-period adaptation of these works to picture scrolls allowed preachers to incorporate a measure of drama into their grisly sermons, permitting them to unroll the scrolls in a cinematic revelation of human decomposition. One of the purposes of such performances was to disenamor men of women—to discourage male sexual desire—and to this end, the initially attractive yet increasingly bloated, maggot-eaten corpse was sometimes identified as that of the formerly beautiful Komachi.

Baseless images and tales of Komachi's degradation, both in life and in death, were thus employed in the Heian and medieval periods as expedient means for teaching Buddhist principles and encouraging righteous behavior (although for whom and within what specific contexts is unknown). Preachers may to have chosen Ono no Komachi for use in this way because of her reputation for beauty.[32] While Murasaki Shikibu tended to be identified with

[29]Liz Wilson, *Charming Cadavers: Horrific Figurations of the Feminine in Indian Buddhist Hagiographic Literature* (Chicago and London: University of Chicago Press, 1996), 16.

[30]Wilson, *Charming Cadavers*, 16.

[31]Hosokawa Ryōichi, "*Kusōshi emaki* to Ono no Komachi," in *Onna no chūsei* (Tokyo: Nihon Editā Sukūru Shuppanbu, 1989), 250.

[32]In his preface to the poetic anthology *Kokin wakashū* (Collection of Poems Past and Present; ca. 905), Ki no Tsurayuki states that Ono no Komachi was of the poetic line of Sotoori-hime (Princess Sotoori), a fifth-century poet famed for her exceptional beauty (SNKBT 5:14). The mytho-history *Nihon shoki* (Chronicles of Japan; 720) reports that Sotoori-hime's loveliness was such that it shone through her robes like rays of light. NKBT 67:440; W.G. Aston, *Nihongi: Chronicles of Japan from the Earliest Times to A.D. 697* (Tokyo: Charles E. Tuttle, 1972 [first published in 1896]), 318.

Fig. 1. The seventh stage of human decomposition. Detail from *Kusōshi emaki* (early fourteenth century). Courtesy of Nakamura Atsuko and the Tokyo National Museum.

The Tale of Genji, and was thus employed in hortative accounts related to her *Tale*, Ono no Komachi's legendary looks naturally invited stories of her later poverty, disfigurement, and degradation. Amy Hollywood has suggested that in the European tradition—in male-authored biographies of high-medieval Christian female saints—"the identification of women with the body demands that their sanctification occur in and through that body."[33] The same is certainly true of Komachi, who is prophesied in *Sōsuisho* to attain her own Buddhist apotheosis as a result of extreme deprivation and bodily humiliation (and who is reputed in several medieval works to have been an incarnation of the bodhisattva Kannon).[34] It is also true of Izumi Shikibu, who was known in her own lifetime for her scandalous affairs with men, and who in one late-medieval tale (discussed in chapter eight) achieves spiritual salvation for herself and her parents by fulfilling a pious vow to sleep with one thousand men.

[33]Quoted in Sharon Farmer, "The Beggar's Body: Intersections of Gender and Social Status in High Medieval Paris," in *Monks & Nuns, Saints & Outcastes: Religion in Medieval Society*, ed. Sharon Farmer and Barbara H. Rosenwein (Ithaca and London: Cornell University Press, 2000), 155.

[34]The *Ise monogatari* commentary *Waka chikenshū* (Kamakura period; spuriously attributed to Minamoto no Tsunenobu [1016–97]) identifies her as Nyoirin Kannon. Katagiri Yōichi, *Ise monogatari no kenkyū: shiryō hen* (Tokyo: Meiji Shoin, 1969), 112a. The identification is repeated in *Komachi no sōshi* and a number of other texts. See NKBT 38:101, headnote 6. The *otogizōshi Tamadasuki* asserts that she was a Buddha rather than a bodhisattva (MJMT 8:561a).

A Literature of Extremes

A second major concern of this book is to examine some of the more significant ways in which the early Buddhist appropriations of Izumi Shikibu's and other Heian women's poetry and personae affected their later representations in medieval works of history, biography, drama, and fiction. The problem is not an easy one, for issues of influence can be devilishly complex. Tales beget other tales, and while Buddhist sermon-stories clearly influenced the composition of certain later works, the opposite is also true. As we will see in chapter six, for example, in composing his own Izumi Shikibu account for use in preaching and temple fund-raising, the unknown author of the sixteenth-century *Rakuyō Seiganji engi* (A History of Seiganji in the Capital) drew upon a number of disparate sources, including an ornate fifteenth-century literary account which was itself based upon an oral anecdote employed in contemporary Tendai preaching.

In the case of Ono no Komachi, the influence of the Heian-period Pure Land Buddhist *Sōsuisho* is readily apparent in numerous texts and images from the Kamakura and Muromachi periods, including a temple history from 1335 that claims that Komachi suffered from leprosy.[35] As Watanabe Hideo has observed, both a fourteenth-century painting of Komachi in the Yōmei Bunko archive and two illustrations of her in Shibukawa Seiemon's early eighteenth-century woodblock-printed text of the late-medieval *otogizōshi Komachi no sōshi* (The Tale of Komachi; figs. 2 and 3) portray her as she is described in the *Sōsuisho* preface, right down to the basket on her arm and the bundle on her back.[36] Watanabe argues that the *Sōsuisho* descriptions of Komachi in her decline are modeled on the descriptions of *gaki* (hungry ghosts) in various sutras, and that this explains her *gaki*-like representation in these later pictorial works.

Tales of Ono no Komachi's poverty and vagrancy, together with her association with painted pictures of corpses employed in Buddhist preaching,

[35]*Iōzan engi*, a Musashi Kokubunji temple history. *Iōzan engi* relates that Komachi prayed to the temple's statue of Yakushi Nyorai for three weeks in 848, whereupon a mysterious boy appeared and advised her to bathe in a nearby pool. With that, her leprosy was cured. The story is cited in Ishihara Shōhei, "Musashino no Narihira/Komachi setsuwa," in *Setsuwa denshō no Nihon, Ajia, sekai*, ed. Setsuwa Denshō Gakkai (Tokyo: Ōfūsha, 1983), 167. Other *Sōsuisho*-related Komachi accounts include *Jikkinshō* 2:4 (dated 1252; SNKBZ 51:116–17); *Kokon chomonjū* 182 (dated 1254; NKBT 84:167–68); and *Sangoku denki* 12:6 (ca. 1407–46).

[36]Watanabe Hideo, *Heianchō bungaku to kanbun sekai* (Tokyo: Benseisha, 1991), 608–9. The Yōmei Bunko painting, titled "Ono no Komachi zo" (dated 1367), is reproduced on p. 57 of Katagiri, *Ono no Komachi tsuiseki*, and on the cover of Tochio, *Tamatsukuri Komachi shi sōsuisho*. The term *otogizōshi* ("companion books") refers to a corpus of over four hundred short fictional works, mostly anonymous, dating from around the Muromachi period (1336–1573).

Fig. 2. Komachi in her ruin. From *Komachi no sōshi* (Shibukawa text, early eighteenth century). Courtesy of the Kyoto Prefectural Library Archives (Kyōto Furitsu Sōgō Shiryōkan).

Fig. 3. Komachi in her ruin. From *Komachi no sōshi* (Shibukawa text, early eighteenth century). Courtesy of the Kyoto Prefectural Library Archives (Kyōto Furitsu Sōgō Shiryōkan).

led to the rumor in the late Heian and medieval periods that she continued suffering after death as an unburied body in the fields. In most versions of the story, a traveler identified as the poet Ariwara no Narihira (825–80) chances upon Komachi's skull in a deserted field. His discovery is prompted by a mysterious voice reciting a *waka* (a Japanese poem) about pain in the eye sockets every time the wind blows.[37] The fifteenth-century miscellany *Tōden gyōhitsu* (Snipe and Carriage Bench Musings at Dawn), attributed to Ichijō Kaneyoshi,[38] contains four versions of the tale. In one, the traveler is Izumi Shikibu:

> As another source explains it, Izumi Shikibu once went to visit Hōrinji Temple, but by the time she got to Sagano the sun had set, so she took lodging there.[39] In the night she heard a voice in the fields reciting that same poem. When she went to have a look in the morning, she found a skull with eulalia grass growing out of its eye sockets. She placed it at the top of a tall tree. A woman spoke to her in a dream that night: "I am [Ono no] Komachi. For the joy you have given me, I will make you a poet unrivalled in all the land." It is said that Izumi Shikibu became famous in the Way of Poetry from that time on.[40]

Izumi Shikibu's poetic abilities are attributed directly to the benevolence of Ono no Komachi's ghost. There are numerous tales of Ono no Komachi and Izumi Shikibu in *setsuwa*, *otogizōshi*, and noh—more than those of all other Heian women authors combined—but they rarely interact within a single story as they do here.

[37]Kawashima discusses different versions of this account in *Writing Margins*, 177–90 and 200–208.

[38]If *Tōden gyōhitsu* is indeed by Kaneyoshi (also read Kanera; 1402–81), it likely dates from ca. 1460–66. On the etymology of the title, see Ichiko, ed., *Tōden gyōhitsu*, 537–38 (opening lines of the "Tales of Mice" [*Nezumi monogatari*] section).

[39]Hōrinji Temple overlooks Togetsu Bridge at the foot of Arashiyama on the western edge of the capital. According to *Shasekishū* (ca. 1280; NKBT 85:488a), Izumi Shikibu once traveled there to seduce her would-be paramour, the priest Dōmyō Ajari. See pp. 43–44, below.

[40]Ichiko, ed., *Tōden gyōhitsu*, 197–98. I am grateful to Shiba Kayono for introducing me to this source. It is most similar to the story as it is cited in *Mumyōzōshi* (ca. 1200; SNKS *Mumyōzōshi*, 108–9), in which Komachi bestows Fujiwara no Michinobu (972–94) with outstanding poetic abilities. Other versions are contained in *Fukurozōshi* (ca. 1157–58; SNKBT 29:160), about an unnamed person; *Mumyōshō* (ca. 1211–16; NKBT 65:96–97), about Ariwara no Narihira; *Kojidan* (ca. 1212–15; SNKBT 41:155–56), about Narihira; *Sangoku denki* 12:6 (ca. 1407–46), about Kūkai; *Komachi no sōshi* (late Muromachi period; NKBT 38:99–100), about Narihira; and *Komachi monogatari* (late Muromachi or early Edo period; MJMT 5:130–41), about Saigyō. In the four versions of the story in *Tōden gyōhitsu*, the traveler is (1) unidentified, (2) Narihira, (3) Izumi Shikibu, and (4) Kūkai.

As these various depictions of Komachi suggest, Heian women authors tend to be represented in medieval sources in a language of extremes. Their lives are characterized by beauty, talent, piety and fame, and by poverty, disfigurement, abandonment and humiliation. There is seldom any middle ground. The two aspects are two sides of a single coin, for in the moral economy of the more didactic accounts—essentially Buddhist cautionary tales—it is the very heights to which the women attain that precipitate their falls. In many cases, whether in their glory or their degradation, the women are made to illustrate and embody the norms of cultural and religious behavior and belief. While the authors of largely secular literary and commentarial works tended to enshrine them as poetic champions of the past—exemplars of a golden age, now lost—morality tales frequently idealize them in their wretchedness for their desperate and unequivocal turns to Buddhism. In the late-Heian and medieval Japanese literary context, the distinction between exemplary and cautionary tales is often murky, for although the former should provide examples to be emulated and the latter, to be avoided, many accounts of the women in their purportedly inevitable and deserved ruin simultaneously celebrate them as models of Buddhist repentance and devotion. In addition to the stories' contents, the sensational tones of their descriptions—both reverential and calumnious—are often indebted to the tendencies of early-medieval preachers who relied on impressive tales to capture and hold their audiences' attention.

The *otogizōshi Koshikibu* (Koshikibu), an anonymous work of prose fiction from the late medieval period, is in some ways representative of the corpus of medieval stories of Izumi Shikibu and her peers.[41] Named after one of its three protagonists (the poet Koshikibu no Naishi, daughter of Izumi Shikibu), *Koshikibu* survives in at least seven manuscripts in three textual lines, suggesting a substantial readership in the sixteenth and seventeenth centuries. Preserved in hand-copied *nara ehon* booklets with colorful hand-painted illustrations,[42] *Koshikibu* purports to tell the life-stories of Murasaki Shikibu, Izumi Shikibu, and Koshikibu no Naishi. If we are to believe the text (which we should not), the three women constitute three generations of Shikibus: mother, daughter, and granddaughter. The asser-

[41]See the appendix of this book for a classification of extant *Koshikibu* manuscripts. *Koshikibu* is translated in the translations section, below.

[42]*Nara ehon* ("Nara picture books") are handwritten manuscripts with colorful and often simple hand-painted illustrations, mass-produced as bound booklets by usually anonymous artists and calligraphers in the late-Muromachi and early-to-mid Edo periods. Some scholars include selected picture scrolls within the category as well. For a discussion in English, see Yutaka Shimizu, *Nara Picture Books*, trans. Richard Zumwinkle (Los Angeles: Dawson's Book Shop, 1960).

Fig. 4. Murasaki Shikibu and her daughter. From *Koshikibu* (Gifu Library text, ca. 1661–73). Courtesy of Yuge Shigeru and the Gifu University Library.

tion is a flagrant misrepresentation of historical fact—comical in its ludicrousness—and in this sense typical of the many ostensibly biographical works of its genre.

Koshikibu opens with a charmingly overblown description of Murasaki Shikibu in her prime (see fig. 5). The passage is nearly identical to one in *Murasaki Shikibu no maki* (Murasaki Shikibu's Scroll), the fourth volume of the early seventeenth-century *otogizōshi Ishiyama monogatari* (Tales of Ishiyama),[43] demonstrating the currency of her hyperbolic characterization in the late-medieval and early-Edo periods:

[43]*Murasaki Shikibu no maki* survives in several copies of a single woodblock-printed text published in 1658, typeset in MJMT 2:241–50, and in Kyōto Daigaku Bungaku-bu Kokugogaku Kokubungaku Kenkyūshitsu, ed., *Kyōto Daigaku-zō Muromachi monogatari*, vol. 9 (Kyoto: Rinsen Shoten, 2003), 393–402 (the manuscript is also photographically reproduced on pp. 281–326).

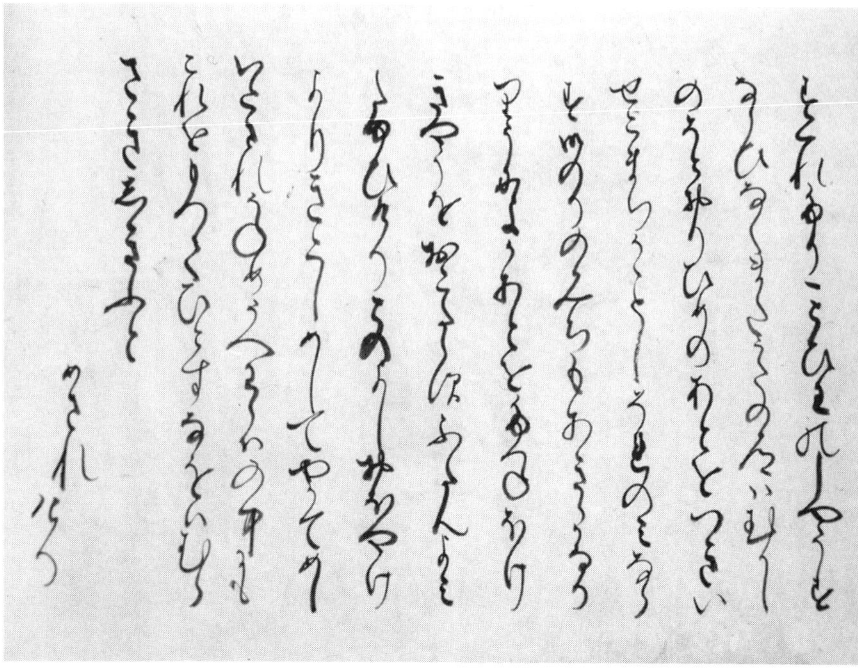

Fig. 5 *(opposite page and above)*. Description of Murasaki Shikibu. From *Koshikibu* (Taku Library text, ca. eighteenth century). Courtesy of the Taku City Archives (Taku-shi Kyōdo Shiryōkan), Saga Prefecture.

In the salon of Empress Shōshi in the not-so-distant past, there was once a woman by the name of Murasaki Shikibu. She was uncommonly beautiful, as graceful as a willow swaying in the wind. Her jade hairpin was as translucent as the wings of a cicada, and the flush of her cheeks, faintly visible at the edges of her slightly mussed hair, was like the moon shining through a thin veil of cloud. Her lips were as lotus petals, her bosom was as if bedecked with jewels, and her loveliness was as that of the plum or cherry, blossoms overflowing in the glow of a garden's evening light.

She was of exceedingly profound mind, superior to the normal run of people, and her skill at playing the *koto* and the *biwa* was without parallel.[44] In the Way of Poetry she took after Princess Sotoori of old, like Ise and Komachi. Not only this, but for her, even the Way of the Dharma was clearly revealed, and thus tracing the path of the Dragon Girl, she recited the *Lotus Sutra* at all times. Hearing such things from the courtiers, the empress had her summoned to the palace. Among all her ladies-in-waiting and high-ranking young attendants, the empress regarded her as

[44]A *koto* is a kind of hollow-bodied harp, and a *biwa* is a sort of lute.

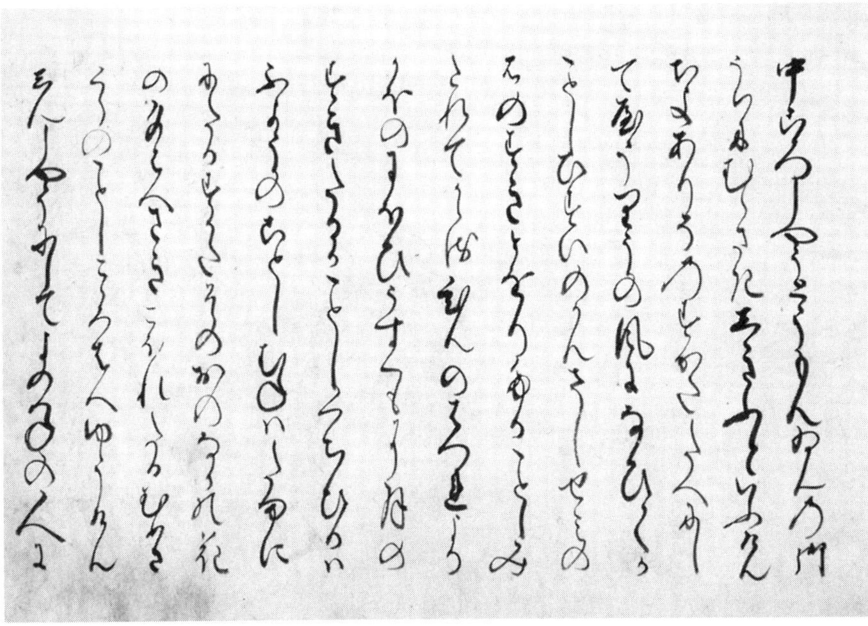

> a flower of perfection, and so she called her Murasaki Shikibu.[45]
> Thus within the court she was premier.[46]

Otogizōshi are not known for their subtlety. Not only is Murasaki Shikibu presented as having been extraordinarily beautiful, she is said to have been a gifted musician and poet (in the tradition of Lady Ise and Ono no Komachi) and an exceedingly devout Buddhist as well. In "tracing the path of the Dragon Girl," she follows in the footsteps of the legendary Dragon King's eight-year-old daughter, who in the "Devadatta" chapter of the *Lotus Sutra* is said to have instantly transformed into a Buddha (after first transforming into a man) in spite of being female. In this, too, Murasaki Shikibu is cast in the role of the outstanding Heian woman poet, bound for spiritual glory.

The *Koshikibu* description of Murasaki Shikibu's piety is consistent with a body of tales composed in reaction to earlier accounts of her suffering in hell. The oldest of these is contained in the historical chronicle *Ima kagami* (Mirror of the Present; ca. 1170, some two years after Chōken's *Genji ippon-kyō*), in which an old nun first disputes the likelihood of Murasaki Shikibu's perdition and then counter-claims that she was probably a manifestation

[45]"Murasaki" is kind of plant, a gromwell (*Lithospermum erythrorhizon*), and "Shikibu" refers to the Ministry of Ceremonial, in which Murasaki Shikibu's father once held a position.

[46]MJMT 5:20–21 (unillustrated Tenri Library manuscript); Shimazu Hisamoto, *Kinko shōsetsu shinsan* (Tokyo: Yūseidō, 1983 [first published by Chūkōkan in 1928]), 233–34.

of Myōon, Kannon, or some other divinity, and that her purpose in writing *The Tale of Genji* was to transmit the Dharma as a means of drawing readers to enlightenment.[47] Several hundred years later, the (probably) Muromachi-period commentary *Genji shō* (Treatise on *The Tale of Genji*) asserted that because women are particularly estranged from the Path of the Buddha, the bodhisattva Kannon took on a temporary female manifestation—that of Murasaki Shikibu—and wrote *The Tale of Genji* in the Japanese vernacular in order to save the women of Japan.[48] Further reactionary accounts of how the brilliant woman author composed her *Tale* at Ishiyama Temple under the divine inspiration of the Ishiyama Kannon (or was herself the Ishiyama Kannon) began to proliferate from around the fourteenth century.[49] These in turn were taken up and reproduced in a wide range of dramatic and fictional works, including *Koshikibu,* throughout the medieval and early-modern periods.

As we can see, Chōken's twelfth-century condemnation and perhaps others like it seem to have had profound and far-reaching effects. In some cases, Murasaki Shikibu's supporters celebrated their Heian woman hero as an exemplar for women—a far cry from castigating her for perverting the young with her "lurid romance." *Menoto no sōshi* (The Nursemaid's Handbook), a fourteenth-century educational tract for women, for example, relates that Murasaki Shikibu wrote her work as a means of instructing women in the rules of propriety and decorum; she had been disturbed, the unidentified narrator explains, by the ill manners of the women of her time.[50] And in *Koshikibu,* Murasaki Shikibu again plays the part of an enlightened tutor, educating her daughter in the finer points of feminine social grace. Her advice includes solemn warnings against jealousy, conceit, gossip, and opening one's mouth too wide when laughing.

Like Ono no Komachi and the dead Murasaki Shikibu, Izumi Shikibu and Sei Shōnagon are said to have endured exceptional hardship in their latter years. Indeed, if there is a theme that runs through many of the medi-

[47]Sakakibara Kunihiko et al., eds., *Ima kagami: honbun oyobi sōsakuin* (Tokyo: Kasama Shoin, 1984), 293–96. The passage is translated in Harper, "Motoori Norinaga's Criticism of the *Genji monogatari,*" 52–55.

[48]Ikeda, *Monogatari bungaku 1,* 359. Ikeda refers to this work as the "Myōzenji-bon *Genji shō.*"

[49]One of the earliest of these stories is contained in the *Genji* commentary *Kakaishō* (1363), by Yotsutsuji Yoshinari. Tamagami Takuya, ed., *Shimeishō, Kakaishō* (Tokyo: Kadokawa Shoten, 1968), 186. In the noh play *Genji kuyō* (earliest recorded performance in 1464), Murasaki Shikibu is herself said to have been a manifestation of the Ishiyama Kannon. See Janet Goff, *Noh Drama and The Tale of Genji* (Princeton: Princeton University Press, 1991), 198–202.

[50]GR 27:229a. *Menoto no sōshi* is of unknown authorship; it should not be confused with the *otogizōshi* of the same name.

eval accounts of Heian women authors, it is that of the formerly proud and beautiful court lady fallen to ruin. In *Koshikibu*, for example, Izumi Shikibu wanders through the countryside, hopeless and forlorn, on a seemingly futile search for her daughter, whom she had abandoned at Tōji Temple in a fit of shame. As the narrator explains, "she was a pitiful sight as her wet nurse, Renzei, led her by the hand, proceeding aimlessly in this direction and that, her wretchedness no less severe than had she been walking the road of death between this life and the next."[51] Again, in the *otogizōshi Little Shikibu* (not to be confused with *Koshikibu*, an entirely different work of the same name), the death of her husband Michisada leaves Izumi Shikibu destitute and forsaken, with "creeping weeds of desolation growing up around her door."[52] Tales of Murasaki Shikibu's rebirth in hell and Ono no Komachi's suffering as the tormented spirit of an unburied body in the fields are extensions of this convention—accounts of the women's hardships and humiliations in the afterlife.

Although next to nothing is known about Sei Shōnagon after the death of Empress Teishi in the twelfth month of 1000, tales of Sei Shōnagon's poverty and humiliation began to be recorded in a variety of sources from around the early thirteenth century. The origins of these stories are all unknown. *Mumyōzōshi* (A Unnamed Account), a work of literary criticism composed between 1198 and 1202, reports that she abandoned the capital for a home in the provinces:

> Perhaps because she had no one to rely upon, Sei Shōnagon went off with the child of a wet nurse to live in the distant countryside. "How they all used to look in their court robes—now that I can't forget," she was once heard to say as she stepped outside to dry some vegetables known as "greens." She was wearing a shabby robe, and her hood was a patchwork of rags—most moving indeed! Truly, how she must have longed for the past.[53]

Sei Shōnagon's description stands in striking contrast to her own animated explanations in *The Pillow Book* of her glorious years at court. Her removal from the capital is metaphoric of her social marginalization after Teishi's

[51]MJMT 5:32b–33a.

[52]Yoshida Kōichi, ed., *Izumi Shikibu zenshū: honbun hen* (Tokyo: Koten Bunko, 1959), 739. *Little Shikibu*, referred to by scholars as "*Koshikibu (beppon)*" (The Other *Koshikibu*), is an *otogizōshi* of unknown date and origin, possibly from the late Muromachi or early Edo period. It survives as a single two-volume *nara ehon* in the former collection of Shimazu Hisamoto (now in the possession of Tōyō University), and is translated in the translations section of this book.

[53]SNKS *Mumyōzōshi*, 110–11. The phrase *aona to iu mono*, "vegetables known as 'greens,'" is subject to varying interpretations. Tanaka Jūtarō suggests that *aona to*, "green vegetables," might be read *ao nado*, "hunting costumes and the like." Tanaka Jūtarō, *Sei Shōnagon Makura no sōshi kenkyū* (Tokyo: Kasama Shoin, 1971), 416.

death; reduced to an object of pity, she can only lament the past. The *setsuwa* anthology *Kojidan* (Tales of Ancient Matters), compiled by Minamoto no Akikane between 1211 and 1215, contains two similarly unfortunate accounts of Sei Shōnagon as an old and impoverished nun. In the first, Sei Shōnagon is ridiculed by several young male courtiers who laugh at her in her ruin; in the second, she is reduced to exposing herself naked to a group of warriors in order to prove that she is not a man.[54]

Stories of Sei Shōnagon's degradation came to be aestheticized in the medieval period, leading to the composition of a fictional illustrated travel journal by the name of *Matsushima nikki* (The Matsushima Diary). Written in a first-person narrative voice and containing a well-known poem by Sei Shōnagon, the work was considered from at least 1462 to recount Sei Shōnagon's lonely journey from her home in the capital to the bay of Matsushima in the north.[55] Setting out as a solitary nun and composing poems on her way, Sei Shōnagon takes to the Path of the Buddha on a spiritual as well as a physical quest. Hamanaka Osamu has observed that in the Heian and medieval literary convention of the fallen court lady, the suffering that a fallen woman endures is typically represented as a kind of ascetic Buddhist practice.[56] This is how Sei Shōnagon sees her own plight in *Matsushima nikki*, and she accepts it as a means of purification, exorcising her of the excesses of her past. As proof of the efficacy of her travails, Amida Buddha appears to her as she stays in a lodging house in Izu province and assures her of her salvation. Like Murasaki Shikibu and Ono no Komachi (and especially Izumi Shikibu, discussed in the following chapters), she is transformed in her distress from a court poet *par excellence* into an exemplary Buddhist devotee, suggesting that *Matsushima nikki*, too, may be ultimately rooted in Buddhist homily (or that it at least draws upon the narrative conventions of works that are).

Women and Buddhism

A third and final concern of this book is to explore the extent to which gender played a determining role in the production, dissemination, and reception of Buddhist tales of Izumi Shikibu and other Heian women poets in medieval Japan. The difficulty of this is hard to overstate, for while the tales

[54]SNKBT 41:190 and 192–93; Kobayashi Yasuharu, ed., *Kojidan*, vol. 1 (Tokyo: Gendai Shichōsha, 1981), 169 and 171.

[55]*Matsushima nikki* is annotated in Chimoto Hideshi, ed., *Nihon koten gisho sōkan*, vol. 2 (Tokyo: Gendai Shichōshinsha, 2004), 27–43, and translated in Kimbrough, "Apocryphal Texts and Literary Identity," 157–64. A colophon from the tenth month of 1462 identifies *Matsushima nikki* with Sei Shōnagon and alludes to its former illustrations, which by that time had been lost.

[56]Hamanaka Osamu, "Chūsei no Komachi zō: kojiki to bosatsu," in *Muromachi monogatari ronkō* (Tokyo: Shintensha, 1996), 226–35.

themselves survive, the contexts of their composition and recitation are now mostly lost to time. Conversely, in the case of Kumano *bikuni*—itinerant nuns affiliated with Kumano Shrine—while the women's painted props survive, the stories that the women told in connection with them do not. Nevertheless, by examining evidence within surviving stories, considering monuments, relics, and relevant icons in the temples associated with those tales, and matching extant textual accounts with scenes in the women's painted props, it is possible to reconstruct the storytelling traditions of a wide range of male and female Buddhist proselytizers who employed accounts of Izumi Shikibu and other prominent women (including but not restricted to Heian women authors) in preaching to women.

Whether by men or women, preaching for women was rarely benign, seeing as how most medieval promises of salvation for women were foregrounded in a misogynistic Buddhist discourse of female sin. The degree to which female proselytizers were complicit in the psychological subjugation of other women to traditional Buddhist conceptions of sanctity and gender has been a subject of recent scholarly debate,[57] and it is an issue that I explore in the following pages as well (in chapter seven, in particular). The reception of such preaching—the extent to which women in the Kamakura and Muromachi periods accepted or resisted preachers' misogynistic characterizations—is also an important issue, but one about which medieval texts have exceedingly little to say. The *Lotus Sutra* commentary *Hokekyō jikidanshō* (Straight Talk on the *Lotus Sutra*), compiled by the Tendai priest Eishin sometime before his death in 1546, contains at least one notable exception: an account of how an old nun stepped out of the audience when the venerable Chinsō Kashō of Gen'ōji Temple was preaching upon the "ten wickednesses of women," and angrily upbraided him for his sexist remarks. The old nun is said to have shouted, "It's not just women who are so evil—you've got plenty of wickedness in you, too!" protesting the hypocrisy of men (or of this particular man) who malign women in the name of the Buddha.[58]

The story of Chinsō and the unidentified nun is relevant to our consideration of Izumi Shikibu in the medieval period because it describes an act

[57]See Barbara Ruch, "Woman to Woman: *Kumano bikuni* Proselytizers in Medieval and Early Modern Japan," in *Engendering Faith: Women and Buddhism in Premodern Japan*, ed. Barbara Ruch (Ann Arbor: University of Michigan Center for Japanese Studies, 2002), 567–75, and Bernard Faure, *The Power of Denial: Buddhism, Purity, and Gender* (Princeton and Oxford: Princeton University Press, 2003), 53 and 78.

[58]*Hokekyō jikidanshō*, vol. 2 (Kyoto: Rinsen Shoten, 1979), 531. "Kashō" (pronounced "Oshō" in the Pure Land and Zen schools) is a monastic title. Chinsō is said to have been preaching at Sakamoto, at the eastern foot of Mount Hiei.

of dissent by an activist nun like those who seem to have employed tales of Izumi Shikibu and other Heian women poets as a means of contesting traditional Buddhist views of women. As a result of her use in medieval preaching, Izumi Shikibu came to be known in the Kamakura and Muromachi periods for her associations with a number of prominent priests, including Dōmyō Ajari (an intendant of Tennōji Temple in present-day Osaka), Shōkū Shōnin (founder of Enkyōji Temple on Mount Shosha), and Ippen Shōnin (founder of the *Jishū*, or "Time Sect" of Pure Land Buddhism).[59] Like her Heian women peers, Izumi Shikibu is most often reported in medieval sources to have eventually overcome her transgressions, attaining salvation in spite of her excessive depravity and delusion. In many of these accounts, some of which are traceable to nuns' proselytizing traditions, she is shown actively confronting male prejudices and prohibitions against women, including *nyonin kinsei* (the institutional exclusion of women from designated holy sites) and the supposedly intrinsic impurity of her sex.[60] By her wit and skill as a poet, Izumi Shikibu triumphs where other women fail, and she is thus very much unlike the dead Ono no Komachi in paintings of the nine stages of human decomposition, in which Komachi is cast as an utterly passive object of a disparaging and typically male gaze. In a few cases, the storytellers—many of whom were women—appear to have raised Izumi Shikibu up as a kind of proto-feminist hero for other women.[61]

In considering Izumi Shikibu's medieval representations, it is important to keep in mind that competition among temples and sects tended to be fierce, and that doctrinal and institutional rivalries were often played out in the realm of seemingly innocuous tales. The *setsuwa* anthology *Sangoku denki* (Tales of Three Countries), compiled by the Tendai priest Gentō in the first half of the fifteenth century, for example, contains an account that is suggestive of some of the more aggressive storytelling practices of the Mu-

[59]Discussed in chapters one through six. In addition, *Kojidan* (ca. 1212–15) records an apocryphal poetic exchange between Izumi Shikibu and the holy man Kūya Shōnin (903–72), who seems to have died before Izumi Shikibu's birth. SNKBT 41:358–59; Kobayashi, ed., *Kojidan*, vol. 1, 302–3.

[60]See chapter seven, below, and R. Keller Kimbrough, "Voices from the Feminine Margin: Izumi Shikibu and the Nuns of Kumano and Seiganji," *Women and Performance* 12, no. 1 (2001): 59–78.

[61]There is a danger of anachronistic interpretation in applying the term "proto-feminist" to the Japanese medieval period. Nevertheless, insofar as there is evidence that some women engaged in preaching and storytelling to other women about women defying and overcoming male Buddhist proscriptions against women, I believe that the use of the term is warranted here (given, that is, that we construe feminism—or "proto-feminism"—in its widest possible sense to include both modern and premodern movements and activities carried out on behalf of women's rights and interests).

romachi period.[62] The account concerns a devotee of the goddess Benzaiten of Amanogawa Shrine who learns that his beloved Benzaiten is in fact a devotee of the famous Pure Land mandala at Taima Temple. As the story is told, Benzaiten appears to the man one night in a dream, and she urges him, for the sake of his future enlightenment, to speak to "Renshin-bō" (a priest named Renshin, the man believes) at Taima Temple. The man travels to Taima, where a "certain person"—presumably a priest—explains that Benzaiten was referring to the silken threads (*renshi*) and fringe (*fusa*, written with the character *bō*) of the Taima Mandala. The priest then tells the man a story of how the former governor of Tsushima province, a lifelong devotee of the Kumano Deity, was similarly persuaded to transfer his faith from the Kumano Deity to the Taima Mandala:

> It happened recently, too, that at the Uda Estate in this very province, there was a person named Tsushima Governor Toshishige who made a monthly pilgrimage to Kumano Shrine. When he had grown old and become unable to walk, he thought to himself, "though the autumn grove will again turn green, grey hair will never turn black."[63] Explaining to the deity that this would be his final visit, he passed the night in prayer in the Hongū Central Hall. An aged priest spoke to him in a dream: "Every time you've come to see me, I've been off worshipping at the soles of [the Buddha's] feet. I visit the Taima Mandala every day at noon. You should go to Taima Temple from now on. It's not only me; great and small, all the deities of the sixty-odd provinces visit there at noon." Thus, from that time forward, Toshishige made his monthly pilgrimage to our temple here. When he attained his cherished wish for rebirth in the Pure Land, purple clouds spread across the sky, and a glorious light fell upon the earth. All the people were overjoyed and came to pay their respects.

If we are to believe the Taima Temple priest, the Kumano Deity, popularly identified as a manifestation of Amida, spends much of his time worshipping the Taima Mandala (an image of Amida in his Pure Land) at Taima Temple. In his annotations to the text, Ikegami Jun'ichi identifies the story as one of "unknown origin." However, there is reason to believe that it was used in preaching in the early fifteenth century at none other than Taima Temple. In addition to its content, which is obviously favorable to Taima at the expense of both the Amanogawa and Kumano Shrines, the story-within-

[62]Ikegami Jun'ichi, ed., *Sangoku denki*, vol. 2 (Tokyo: Miyai Shoten, 1982), 254–55 (tale 11:27: "How a Pauper from Kataoka in Yamato Province Attained Rebirth in the Pure Land").

[63]This is an allusion to a poem in *Shinsen rōeishū* (SKT 2:279c, poem 284), compiled by Fujiwara no Mototoshi ca. 1113–18.

the-story (Toshishige's account) is cited two times in the priest Yūyo Shōsō's *Taima mandara sho* (Commentary on the Taima Mandala; dated 1436), which was based, at least in part, upon a series of Taima Temple sermons.[64] Furthermore, within the *Sangoku denki* account itself, the narrator's attribution of Toshishige's tale to a speaker at Taima suggests that it originated at Taima Temple.

Preachers' use of stories such as these to attract devotees of rival temples and shrines was common in the medieval period.[65] As an essentially medieval fictional character, Izumi Shikibu played leading roles in several tales of this type (discussed in chapters five and six), all of which are traceable to Seiganji Temple in the capital. Like the *Sangoku denki* story of Benzaiten and the Kumano Deity, these accounts attribute various holy men and supernatural beings, including Shōkū Shōnin at Enkyōji Temple, the statue of Shakyamuni at Seiryōji Temple, and the Great Hachiman Bodhisattva at Iwashimizu Hachiman Shrine, with having encouraged Izumi Shikibu to abandon their own institutions for Seiganji. The effects of this widespread use of Izumi Shikibu's and other Heian women authors' poetry and personae in competitive preaching and fund-raising in the Kamakura and Muromachi periods were profound. As temples identified themselves with individual figures—Ishiyama Temple with Murasaki Shikibu, and Seiganji with both Izumi Shikibu and Sei Shōnagon, for example[66]—and drew upon the women's cultural cachet in preaching to all audiences, high and low, educated and illiterate alike, the women and their works came to be known throughout the various social strata of Japan.

[64]*Jōdo-shū zensho*, vol. 13 (Tokyo: Jōdo-shū Shūten Kankōkai, 1910), 60b and 277b (in vols. 8 and 46 of *Taima mandara sho*). On *Taima mandara sho* and Taima Temple preaching, see Tokuda Kazuo, *Otogizōshi kenkyū* (Tokyo: Miyai Shoten, 1988), 370–72. Also see pp. 174–75, below.

[65]As another example, a Hase Temple-related text, *Hase-dera Kannon genki* (Miracles of the Hase Temple Kannon; composed between 1200 and 1209), contains an account in which the wife of an Ōmi provincial official explains that her mother had been a devotee of the Ishiyama Kannon until the Ishiyama Kannon advised her that in order to save her ailing daughter, she ought to pray to the Hase Kannon instead. ZGR 27:2:251b (*Hase-dera reigenki*). Again, in a sixteenth-century Seiganji Temple history (*Rakuyō Seiganji engi*, in the translations section of this book), the principal image of Kurama Temple—a statue of the Buddhist guardian deity Bishamonten—is said to have advised a longtime devotee to give up visiting Kurama Temple and to worship the Seiganji Amida instead.

[66]Ishiyama Temple incorporated the story of Murasaki Shikibu's miraculous composition of *The Tale of Genji* at Ishiyama Temple into volume four of its illustrated history, *Ishiyama-dera engi* (composed in 1324–26), and the temple continues to capitalize on Murasaki Shikibu's reputation to this day. *Ishiyama-dera engi* is photographically reproduced in Kadokawa Shoten Henshūbu, ed., *Ishiyama-dera engi-e*, Nihon emaki-mono zenshū, vol. 22 (Tokyo: Kadokawa Shoten, 1966).

Terry Kawashima has argued that negative portrayals of Ono no Komachi, Sei Shōnagon, and Murasaki Shikibu in late-Heian and medieval literature tended to be marginalizing, constituting "both indirect and straightforward attempts to domesticate the power held by female authors."[67] However, one might say that the opposite was in fact the case: that rather than diminishing or domesticating these women's "sexual and literary powers," as Kawashima would have us believe,[68] all of the apocryphal stories—even the most offensive and demeaning among them—functioned to preserve and enhance those powers by establishing the Heian women authors, together with such male poets as Saigyō and Ariwara no Narihira, as some of the first truly universal literary figures of Japan. Transcending the boundaries of class and time in their later, fictional manifestations, Izumi Shikibu, Ono no Komachi, Murasaki Shikibu, Sei Shōnagon, and Koshikibu no Naishi came to be celebrated as they never had been before.

[67]Kawashima, *Writing Margins*, 291. On the marginalizing of Ono no Komachi, see pp. 123–215 in Kawashima's study; on Sei Shōnagon, p. 151; and on Murasaki Shikibu, p. 215.

[68]Kawashima, *Writing Margins*, 289.

Chapter One
Setsuwa Sources and the Origins of an Affair

Chapters one through three of this book focus on a group of Kamakura- and Muromachi-period tales of Izumi Shikibu and her supposed liaison with the priest and poet Dōmyō Ajari (974–1020), grandson of the so-called "Mother of Michitsuna," author of *The Kagerō Diary*. Stories of Izumi Shikibu and Dōmyō date from as early as the first years of the thirteenth century, and are preserved in a remarkable number and variety of premodern sources, including *setsuwa*, *otogizōshi*, and the noh play *Dōmyō Hōshi*. In this and the following two chapters, we will consider the probable roots of Izumi Shikibu and Dōmyō's association in Kamakura-period preaching and storytelling, as well as the transposition of accounts of their notorious affair into later works of popular fiction, including the *otogizōshi Koshikibu*, *Saru Genji sōshi* (The Tale of Monkey Genji), *Kotohara* (Belly of the Koto), and *Izumi Shikibu*. By doing so, we will explore the influence of Buddhist proselytizing on the development of late-medieval prose works, as well as the resulting impact of those works upon popular medieval conceptions of the Heian past.

Most early accounts of Izumi Shikibu and Dōmyō are preserved in *setsuwa*, a genre of generally short anecdotes of indeterminate origin that were most assiduously collected and compiled into organized anthologies in the late-Heian and Kamakura periods. Both religious and secular and frequently didactic, *setsuwa* differ from works of Heian court fiction (*monogatari*) in many important respects, one of which is that they are invariably presented as having been recorded rather than invented, and are thus, on a purely formal level, always purportedly "true." As written records of comical, dramatic, edifying, or fantastic events about which their authors have either read or heard, *setsuwa* inevitably point back to earlier sources, both textual and oral, which in most cases are ultimately obscure. Insofar as the earliest accounts of Izumi Shikibu and Dōmyō are preserved in *setsuwa* anthologies, these accounts should not, on the whole, be considered "original." Rather, they are traces of older, often oral storytelling traditions, some of which, as we shall see, have been tentatively (and rather tenuously) linked to the proselytizing activities of specific institutions in what is now the Osaka-Himeji region of central Japan.

Fundamental to all medieval tales of Izumi Shikibu and Dōmyō are issues of sexual impropriety. In the wider world of Muromachi fiction, Izumi Shikibu is renowned for her poetry and her sexual exploits, as are many other Heian literary figures, including Ono no Komachi and Ariwara no Narihira. Buddhist accounts of these poets' concomitant sanctity and awesome and indiscriminate promiscuity speak to a universal prurient interest, and one can imagine that they made for excellent storytelling material for a variety of preachers and commentators of a more outrageous inclination. According to the *otogizōshi Komachi no sōshi*, for example, Ono no Komachi was involved with at least one thousand men, and was herself a manifestation of Nyoirin Kannon.[1] Similarly, the Kamakura-period commentary *Waka chikenshū* (Poetic Knowledge Revealed) maintains that Ariwara no Narihira, the reputed author and protagonist of the tenth-century *Tales of Ise*, was an incarnation of Batō Kannon, and that in his limitless compassion he made love to 3,733 women as a means of leading them to enlightenment.[2] (The late Muromachi-period *otogizōshi Isozaki* cheerfully reports that all 3,733 of them attained Buddhahood as a result.)[3]

Narihira's achievement is nearly unrivalled in number—he is only surpassed by Ihara Saikaku's Yonosuke, who in *The Life of an Amorous Man* of 1682 is said to have slept with 3,742 women and 725 boys—but it is no match for Izumi Shikibu's in terms of tragedy and the bizarre.[4] In the two *otogizōshi Izumi Shikibu* and *Jippon ōgi* (Ten Fans), Izumi Shikibu is said to have accidentally slept with her own illegitimate, abandoned children (one of whom is Dōmyō), and in a story within a variant text of the *otogizōshi Jōruri monogatari* (The Tale of Jōruri), she is said to have fulfilled a vow to achieve conjugal intimacy with 1000 men in an attempt to assuage, in part, the spiritually obstructive desires of mankind.[5] Her sexual fiascoes and her heroism are not without consequence; they lead variously to enlightenment, rebirth in Amida Buddha's Pure Land, and the disfiguring effects of a sexually trans-

[1]NKBT 38:88.

[2]Katagiri Yōichi, *Ise monogatari no kenkyū: shiryō hen* (Tokyo: Meiji Shoin, 1969), 108a–10a.

[3]MJMT 2:263a (former Akagi Bunko manuscript). Despite Narihira's salvific intentions (according to *Waka chikenshū*, that is), in his pursuit of women he may have overextended his amorous grace: the *otogizōshi Hamochi Chūjō* (Hamochi the Middle Captain) asserts that "although Narihira was a manifestation of Dainichi Buddha, as punishment for violating the Virgin Priestess of Ise Shrine, he fell into the evil realms [of hell, animals, and hungry ghosts] for a very long time." It would thus seem that even Dainichi, popularly identified with the sun goddess Amaterasu, must avoid transgressing the symbols of Shintō purity. Shimazu Hisamoto, *Kinko shōsetsu shinsan* (Tokyo: Yūseidō, 1983), 168.

[4]*Kōshoku ichidai otoko* (The Life of an Amorous Man), in NKBZ 38:103. The fifty-four episodes of Saikaku's *Life* are allusive to the fifty-four chapters of *The Tale of Genji*, and the number of Yonosuke's lovers is probably allusive to the number of Narihira's as well.

[5]*Izumi Shikibu* and *Jippon ōgi* are discussed in chapter three; *Jōruri monogatari*, in chapter eight.

mitted disease: Izumi Shikibu's own unique fulfillment of the fallen court lady convention.[6] Like Ono no Komachi and Sei Shōnagon in their wandering destitution, Izumi Shikibu is often cast in these tales as an exemplary Buddhist devotee, for it is by her willingness to "tie the lovers' knot" with anyone at all, including a lowly fruit vendor (Dōmyō) in *Izumi Shikibu* and a filthy beggar in *Jōruri monogatari*, that she both achieves her own Buddhahood and rescues her parents from hell.

In addition to the theme of sexual improbity, a second prominent concern in chapters one through three of this book is the likely role of women as consumers and purveyors of accounts of Izumi Shikibu and Dōmyō in the late-Heian through early Edo periods. In the present chapter, I discuss Yamamoto Takashi's theory that didactic tales of Izumi Shikibu and Dōmyō were produced at Tennōji Temple in the twelfth and thirteenth centuries for use in preaching to female courtesan-entertainers (*asobi*, or *yūjo*) at the port towns of Eguchi and Kanzaki, and I explore the implications of this for our understanding of Izumi Shikibu and Dōmyō's posthumous association in Emperor Go-Shirakawa's *Ryōjin hishō* (Secret Notes of Rafter Dust; ca. 1170) and other, later texts. In chapter two I discuss Izumi Shikibu's depiction as a *yūjo* in the *otogizōshi Kotohara*, as well as two late-Heian and Kamakura-period sources that suggest that *asobi* themselves identified personally with the poetry and personae of Izumi Shikibu and Ono no Komachi. In chapter three I discuss the thematic orientation of the *otogizōshi Izumi Shikibu* as a story of and for women, and I discuss the attribution of a related tale in the *otogizōshi Jippon ōgi* to a *yūjo* at the Hashimoto Inn in Tōtōmi. Taken together, these disparate sources provide compelling evidence for the centrality of women to the composition and dissemination of stories about Izumi Shikibu and Dōmyō in the late-Heian and medieval periods.

History to Legend

In the introduction to his translation of *The Izumi Shikibu Diary*, Edwin Cranston writes that "Izumi Shikibu's life was one long scandal. Or so it must have seemed to her contemporaries."[7] Indeed, in addition to her marriages

[6]Izumi Shikibu's disease is described in the noh play *Hokkejiku* (Lotus Bamboo; ca. 1687; also known as *Uta Yakushi* and *Izumi Shikibu*). Although the illness is unnamed within the play, it causes sores on her body and she reasons that she caught it from having had too many lovers. Tanaka Makoto speculates that it was syphilis. Tanaka Makoto, "Izumi Shikibu to yōkyoku," *Kokugo to kokubungaku* (April 1946), 22b. The play is typeset in Tanaka Makoto, ed., *Mikan yōkyokushū*, vol. 7, Koten bunko 231 (Tokyo: Koten Bunko, 1966), 67–70.

[7]Edwin Cranston, *The Izumi Shikibu Diary* (Cambridge: Harvard University Press, 1969), 3.

to Tachibana no Michisada (?–1016) and Fujiwara no Yasumasa (958–1036), Izumi Shikibu is reported in various Heian sources to have carried on scandalous, romantic affairs with the imperial princes Tametaka (977–1002) and Atsumichi (981–1007), the third and fourth sons of Emperor Reizei. The public sensation caused by these liaisons, both of which ended in the princes' untimely deaths, is documented in a number of contemporary (or nearly contemporary) sources, including *Ōkagami* (The Great Mirror; author unknown), Akazome Emon's *Tale of Flowering Fortunes*, Izumi Shikibu's *Izumi Shikibu Diary*, and several poetic anthologies.[8] Izumi Shikibu's indiscretions with Tametaka and Atsumichi were apparently the talk of their time—a delight, it would seem, for many members of the gossip-hungry court. Murasaki Shikibu herself may have had them in mind when she wrote in her diary that Izumi Shikibu's character suffered from a somewhat "unsavory" aspect.[9]

Yet despite Izumi Shikibu's notoriety in her own day for her affairs with Tametaka and Atsumichi, she is far better known in Kamakura-period *setsuwa* and Muromachi *otogizōshi* for her alleged romantic involvement with the Shitennōji (Tennōji) Temple intendant Dōmyō Ajari (Holy Teacher Dōmyō),[10] a son of Fujiwara no Michitsuna (955–1020) and a man remembered in the Kamakura period for his poetry, sutra recitations, and tainted reputation as a fallen monk. Izumi Shikibu and Dōmyō were contemporaries and were active in the same limited court circles—he was a cousin of the empress Shōshi, in whose salon Izumi Shikibu served—but as Yamamoto Takashi and others have argued, that they were ever actually amorously involved is unlikely because no contemporary source contains even a rumor of such an affair.[11] Nevertheless, stories of Izumi Shikibu and Dōmyō are cited in numerous medieval texts, while accounts of Izumi Shikibu and either Tametaka or Atsumichi are almost totally absent from those works.[12] What, then, are the origins of Izumi Shikibu and Dōmyō's notorious, fictional af-

[8]Helen McCullough, *Ōkagami: The Great Mirror* (Princeton: Princeton University Press, 1980), 117 and 165; William and Helen McCullough, *A Tale of Flowering Fortunes*, vol. 1 (Stanford: Stanford University Press, 1980), 255 and 305; Cranston, *The Izumi Shikibu Diary*, 3–18.

[9]NKBT 19:495; NKBZ 18:237. I follow Richard Bowring's translation of *keshikaranu* as "unsavory." Bowring, *The Diary of Lady Murasaki* (New York: Penguin Books, 1996), 53.

[10]Dōmyō was appointed twenty-seventh intendant (*bettō*) of Tennōji Temple in Settsu province (present-day Osaka) in 1016.

[11]Yamamoto Takashi, "Dōmyō to Izumi Shikibu no setsuwa," *Kokugo to kokubungaku* 57, no. 3 (1980), 42a.

[12]Stories of Izumi Shikibu and Dōmyō are contained in the *setsuwa* anthologies *Kojidan*, *Uji shūi monogatari*, *Hōbutsushū*, *Kokon chomonjū*, *Shasekishū*, *Zōtanshū*, and *Tōsai zuihitsu*, in the *otogizōshi Koshikibu*, *Saru Genji sōshi*, *Kotohara*, and *Izumi Shikibu*, and in the noh play *Dōmyō Hōshi*. In contrast, a single story of Izumi Shikibu and Atsumichi (drawn from *The Izumi Shikibu Diary*) is reproduced in *Kohon setsuwa shū* and *Yotsugi monogatari*.

fair, and how did it come to replace Izumi Shikibu's real-life scandals in the popular medieval consciousness?[13]

The *otogizōshi Koshikibu* highlights the importance of this question by demonstrating the influence of *setsuwa* on later fictional reconstructions of Heian history. The *Koshikibu* narrator relates that at a time after Izumi Shikibu's marriage to Hōshō (a Sinified reading of the name of Fujiwara no Yasumasa), baseless rumors began to spread that Izumi Shikibu had taken up with her poetry teacher, the priest Dōmyō.[14] As word of Izumi Shikibu's indiscretion comes to Hōshō's ears, his feelings cool and he abandons her. Akazome Emon hears of Izumi Shikibu's plight, and in sympathy she sends a poem offering advice:

utsurowade	Watch the Forest of Shinoda
shibashi Shinoda no	awhile before changing
Mori wo miyo	the color of your leaves—
kaeri mo zo suru	like the wind that flutters the kudzu,
kuzu no urakaze	he just may come back.[15]

The poem is metaphorical and allusive, but it contains straightforward advice for Izumi Shikibu not to give up hope or give her heart to another. If she will but wait, Akazome Emon suggests, Hōshō may yet return. The verse is contained in several earlier poetic anthologies, including, most notably, *Shinkokin wakashū* (New Collection of Poems Past and Present; ordered compiled in 1201), which attributes it to Akazome Emon with the headnote, "Sent upon hearing that Prince Atsumichi had begun visiting Izumi Shikibu immediately after she was abandoned by Michisada."[16] The import of the poem is essentially the same, but in this, its seemingly original context, the verse is prompted by rumors of Izumi Shikibu and Atsumichi's actual historical affair, rather than those of Izumi Shikibu and Dōmyō's fictional one.

[13]This is an issue raised by Ōshima Tatehiko in "Izumi Shikibu no setsuwa," in *Otogizōshi to minkan bungei* (Tokyo: Iwasaki Bijustsusha, 1967), 124–29, and by Hamanaka Osamu in "Otogizōshi *Izumi Shikibu/Koshikibu* ron," *Kokubungaku: kaishaku to kanshō* 60, no. 8 (August 1995): 119–24.

[14]Actually, "Dōmei." *Koshikibu, Saru Genji sōshi*, and *Izumi Shikibu* all refer to Dōmyō by this alternate reading of his name.

[15]*Utsurowade* is a negative form of the verb *utsurofu*, "to transfer" or "to change," which suggests both a change in the color of autumn leaves and a change of heart. *Kaeri* suggests that the leaves of the kudzu might be turned upright by the wind, as well as that Yasumasa might soon return. The *Koshikibu* narrator explains that the deity of Shinoda Forest in Izumi province is a guardian of the "Way of Men and Women."

[16]SNKBT 11:530, poem 1820. The verse is also contained (with similar headnotes) in *Akazome Emon shū* (SKT 3:1:316b-c, poem 181), *Izumi Shikibu shū* (*seishū* textual line; SKT 3:1:254a, poem 364), and *Shoku shika wakashū* (SKT 2:1:317b, poem 630).

Fig. 6. Izumi Shikibu and Fujiwara no Yasumasa. From *Koshikibu* (Gifu Library text, ca. 1661–73). Courtesy of Yuge Shigeru and the Gifu University Library.

The alteration of the poem's context in *Koshikibu* demonstrates the profound effect of the Izumi Shikibu/Dōmyō association on even preexisting Izumi Shikibu/Atsumichi accounts. Tales of Izumi Shikibu and Dōmyō were not only fabricated in the medieval period, they were also read back onto earlier sources—in this case a relatively well-known, canonical verse—to the effect of altering or rewriting recorded history and its conception.

As an example of the distortion or "medievalization" of Heian literary history, the *Koshikibu* narrator's representation of the Akazome Emon poem is far from unique. The *otogizōshi Little Shikibu* (*Koshikibu [beppon]*), for example, draws upon the poems of both Koshikibu no Naishi (Izumi Shikibu's daughter) and a second Koshikibu (a daughter of Fujiwara no Yoshitada, and a lady-in-waiting in the salon of Princess Yūshi [1038–1105]) in constructing a fanciful (erroneous) poetic biography of Koshikibu no Naishi. In the case of Sei Shōnagon, an account of Sei Shōnagon's supposed exile and destitution in her old age was incorporated into the epilogue of the *Nōin-bon* text of *The*

Pillow Book (the earliest surviving manuscript of which dates from the late fifteenth or early sixteenth century), extending the temporal boundary of that work to a time in the unfortunate future of its elegant, arrogant author, and transforming it into a kind of medieval morality tale cautioning that the proud are sure to fall.[17] As we can see from these and other examples (particularly those of Ono no Komachi and Murasaki Shikibu, discussed in the introduction), fictional yet purportedly historical accounts played a central role in the shaping of literary identity in medieval Japan.

Early Associations

The earliest record of Izumi Shikibu and Dōmyō's association is contained in a fragment of the twelfth-century *Ryōjin hishō* (Secret Notes of Rafter Dust), a collection of *imayō* (modern songs) compiled by Emperor Go-Shirakawa at some time around 1170.[18] *Imayō* is thought to have flourished from near the end of the tenth century; its earliest practitioners may have been *miko* (shamanic shrine-maidens) who sang for their guests. By the twelfth century, it had become the provenance of a wide range of secular courtesan-entertainers—women who made their livings by singing, dancing, storytelling, and prostitution—including *asobi*, known for plying their trade in small boats on the rivers and bays of bustling harbor towns, *kugutsu*, who entertained in the inns of overland travel routes, and *shirabyōshi*, famous for their dancing.[19] Many of these women—*asobi* and *kugutsu* in particular—came to be grouped together under the generic title of *yūjo* (courtesans), a Sinified reading of the characters for *asobi*, from around the Kamakura period. Go-Shirakawa was a great admirer of *imayō* and a dedicated practitioner in his own right, and to the consternation of some at court, he took such women as his instructors and garnered from them many of the songs in his anthology.

[17]NKBZ 11:470. The *Nōin-bon* textual line traces back to the former Sanjōnishi family manuscript, purportedly copied by either Sanjōnishi Sanetaka (1455–1537) or his son Sanjōnishi Kin'eda (1487–1563). Kakitani Yūzō, "Sei Shōnagon densetsu," *Kokubungaku* 12, no. 6 (June 1967), 72.

[18]Most of *Ryōjin hishō* has been lost. Of ten original volumes of songs, only a portion of the first and all of the second volumes survive. *Ryōjin hishō* is translated and discussed in Yung-Hee Kim, *Songs to Make the Dust Dance: The Ryōjin hishō of Twelfth-Century Japan* (Berkeley: University of California Press, 1994).

[19]Amino Yoshihiko and Gotō Toshihiko, eds., "Yūjo, kugutsu, shirabyōshi," *Shūkan Asahi hyakka: Nihon no rekishi* 4 (Chūsei 1), no. 3 (April 1986). In English, see Terry Kawashima, *Writing Margins: The Textual Construction of Gender in Heian and Kamakura Japan* (Cambridge: Harvard University Asia Center, 2001), 27–72; Janet R. Goodwin, "Shadows of Transgression: Heian and Kamakura Constructions of Prostitution," *Monumenta Nipponica* 55, no. 3 (Autumn 2000): 327–68; and Yung-Hee Kim, *Songs to Make the Dust Dance*, 5–17.

Ryōjin hishō contains the following verse, a list of prominent poets. Izumi Shikibu and Dōmyō are coupled at the end:

> Wonderful, outstanding poets are Hitomaro, Akahito, Ono no Komachi, Mitsune, Tsurayuki, Mibu no Tadamine, Henjō, Dōmyō, Izumi Shikibu.[20]

Like Izumi Shikibu, Dōmyō achieved considerable fame as a poet, both in his own lifetime and beyond. His verse is cited and praised in such Heian sources as *A Tale of Flowering Fortunes*, *The Pillow Book*, and *Ōkagami*.[21] As many as fifty-six poems are attributed to him in imperially sponsored anthologies, including sixteen in *Goshūi wakashū* alone (Later Gleanings of Japanese Poetry; compiled in 1086).[22] Whether or not Dōmyō's twelfth-century poetic standing was enough to merit his identification with the likes of Hitomaro, Akahito, and the other poets in the *Ryōjin hishō* song is unclear, however, and the inclusion of his name there has piqued the interest of scholars since the text's rediscovery in the early years of the twentieth century (it had been "lost" for some six hundred years). Okada Yoshio, for example, wrote in 1928 that the situating of Dōmyō's name beside Izumi Shikibu's is almost certainly indicative of a popular association of the two; if such were not the case, he argued, then a greater poet such as Fujiwara no Kintō (966–1041) would have been listed instead.[23] More recently, Shiba Kayono has asserted that the *Ryōjin hishō* song suggests that Dōmyō and Izumi Shikibu were associated in the popular imagination as little as a century after their own time.[24]

Possibly the earliest textual account of Izumi Shikibu and Dōmyō is preserved in *Kojidan* (Tales of Ancient Matters), a *setsuwa* anthology compiled by Minamoto no Akikane after he became a monk in 1211 and before his death in 1215, some forty-five years after Go-Shirakawa's compilation of

[20]SNKBT 56:8; SNKS *Ryōjin hishō*, 18.

[21]*A Tale of Flowering Fortunes* contains two poems attributed to Dōmyō (NKBT 75:394 and 423), *The Pillow Book* contains one (SNKBT 25:328–29), and the *Zōho honkeitō kokatsuji-bon* text of *Ōkagami* (in the *rufubon* textual line) states that "Dōmyō Ajari was an extremely fine poet" (Nemoto Keizō, ed., *Taikō Ōkagami* [Tokyo: Kasama Shoin, 1984], 288).

[22]By comparison, sixty-eight poems are attributed to Izumi Shikibu in *Goshūi wakashū*.

[23]Okada Yoshio, "Izumi Shikibu no ren'ai seikatsu (2)," *Kokugo kokubun no kenkyū* 24 (1928), 31. Enoki Katsurō has observed that all of the poets except for Dōmyō are represented by a poem in Fujiwara no Teika's *Ogura hyakunin isshu* (compiled ca. 1235). The significance of this, however, is unclear. SNKS *Ryōjin hishō*, 18.

[24]Shiba rightly observes that although we can date the compilation of *Ryōjin hishō*, we have no way of dating the songs within it. Shiba Kayono, "*Izumi Shikibu*: Muromachi ki ni okeru monogatari no hirogari," *Kokubungaku: kaishaku to kanshō* 61, no. 5 (May 1996), 53b. Also see Shiba Kayono, "'Dōmyō Izumi Shikibu' kō" *Ryōjin: kenkyū to shiryō* 12 (December 1994): 32–42.

Ryōjin hishō.[25] The story is reproduced in a variety of Kamakura and Muromachi-period texts, including the *setsuwa* anthology *Uji shūi monogatari* (A Collection of Tales from Uji), which likely dates to the first half of the thirteenth century, and thus may or may not precede Akikane's *Kojidan*. The *Uji shūi monogatari* and *Kojidan* accounts are essentially the same, except that the former (quoted below) contains a moral at its end that the *Kojidan* version lacks:

> How Dōmyō Ajari Recited the [*Lotus*] *Sutra* at Izumi Shikibu's Residence and the Fifth Avenue Roadside Deity Came to Listen
>
> In the past there was a lascivious monk by the name of Dōmyō Ajari, a son of the Imperial Tutor [Fujiwara no Michitsuna]. He had taken up with Izumi Shikibu, and his sutra recitations were excellent. He once went to stay with Izumi Shikibu, and awaking beside her in the night, he recited the [*Lotus*] *Sutra* with a tranquil heart. When he had recited all eight scrolls and begun to drift off to sleep in the dawn, he had a sudden sense of someone's presence. "Who's there?" he called out.
>
> "I am an old man from the area around Fifth Avenue and Nishinotōin," someone replied.
>
> "What do you want?" Dōmyō asked.
>
> "In all the worlds and lives to come, I will never forget the sutra recitation I heard tonight."
>
> "But I always recite the *Lotus Sutra*," Dōmyō said. "Why do you say this now?"
>
> "Because when you recite it in a state of purity," the Fifth Avenue Roadside Deity explained, "Brahmā and Indra and others come to listen, and an old man [like me] can't get close enough to hear. But tonight you didn't wash yourself before you began, so Brahmā and Indra didn't come and I had a chance to listen. I'll never forget it."
>
> Thus when you recite—even casually—you should purify yourself first. For as the venerable Eshin admonishes,[26] "In performing the *nenbutsu* or sutra-recitations, one should never break the rules of conduct."[27]

[25]SNKBT 41:291–92; Kobayashi Yasuharu, ed., *Kojidan*, vol. 1 (Tokyo: Gendai Shichōsha, 1981), 249–50 (tale 3:231).

[26]Eshin Sōzu (Genshin; 942–1017) is best known as the author of *Ōjō yōshū* (Essentials for Rebirth in the Pure Land). The "rules of conduct," *shiigi*, are rules governing the behavior of monks and nuns in all situations, whether walking, standing, sitting, or lying down. The quotation here is similar to a passage in *Genshin Sōzu shijūikkajō kishō* (according to SNKBT 42:8, note 2).

[27]SNKBT 42:7–8 (tale 1:1); NKBZ 28:53–54; for an alternate translation, see D.E. Mills, *A Collection of Tales from Uji* (Cambridge: Cambridge University Press, 1970), 135–36. The story is also reproduced in *Zōtanshū* (vol. 7), *Tōsai zuihitsu* (*kōshokurui* section), the *otogizōshi Kotohara*, and the noh play *Dōmyō Hōshi* (Edo period, perhaps).

In medieval Japanese literature, supernatural encounters frequently occur in dreams. Whether or not Dōmyō is asleep when he speaks to the Roadside Deity is uncertain, although in several other versions of the account he clearly is.[28]

Roadside deities, *dōsojin*, are guardians of borders, roads, and mountain passes.[29] Since earliest recorded Japanese history, stone images and memorials to them were erected at crossroads and the edges of towns: liminal sites where they were entrusted with warding off pestilence and harmful spirits.[30] Roadside deities were moreover revered as gods of sexuality and fecundity, a belief manifested in (or perhaps resulting from) their frequent iconographic representation as a man and woman together, sometimes clothed, sometimes naked, and sometimes coupled in coital embrace. *Fusō ryakki* (A Brief Record of Japan), a history compiled between 1094 and 1107, contains an early description of roadside deity sculptures as pairs of wooden statues of men and women set facing each other with their genitals exposed.[31] In some cases they were depicted simply as phalluses or as stone carvings of male and female genitalia, placed side-by-side. This seems to have been the manner in which the roadside deity Hyakudayū, revered among *asobi*, *kugutsu*, and other courtesan-entertainers as a god of love—a kind of patron saint—was frequently represented.[32] Roadside deities were considered vulgar (for obvious reasons) and unlikely to be repelled by human sexual activity, which is perhaps why the Fifth Avenue Roadside Deity in the *Uji shūi monogatari/Kojidan* account is not offended by Izumi Shikibu and Dōmyō's behavior when Brahmā, Indra, and other gods are.

The issue of ritual purity is central to the *Uji shūi monogatari/Kojidan* account, and to other tales of sutras and sutra recitations as well. The Tendai

[28]These include the story as it is cited in *Kojidan*, *Zōtanshū* (1305), and the fifteenth-century *Tōsai zuihitsu*.

[29]The characters for *dōsojin*, "roadside deity," are often read *sae no kami*, "blocking (or preventive) deity." The twelfth-century dictionary *Iroha jiruishō* glosses the characters as *funato*, hence *funato no kami*, or "crossroads deity." Ōshima Tatehiko, "Dōsojin no shinkō to setsuwa," in *Chūsei bungaku no kenkyū*, ed. Akiyama Ken (Tokyo: Tokyo Daigaku Shuppankai, 1972), 58.

[30]See Ōshima's discussion of relevant passages in *Kojiki* (712) and *Nihon shoki* (720), in "Dōsojin no shinkō to setsuwa," 68–69.

[31]The *Fusō ryakki* entry is for the year 939, cited in ibid., 59, and translated in Michael Czaja, *Gods of Myth and Stone: Phallicism in Japanese Folk Religion* (New York: Weatherhill, 1974), 44–45. Czaja's book contains photographs of roadside deity statues in various shapes and forms.

[32]Kim, *Songs to Make the Dust Dance*, 9-10. In a list of an *asobi*'s favorite things, *Ryōjin hishō* names "Hyakudayū, to whom one prays for a man's love" (NKBT 73:412, poem 380); in *Yūjoki* and *Kairaishiki*, Ōe no Masafusa (1041–1111) reports that *asobi* and *kugutsu* were great devotees of Hyakudayū, whom he identifies in *Yūjoki* as a roadside deity (NST 8:155 and 158; Kawashima, *Writing Margins*, 296 and 298; Goodwin, "Shadows of Transgression," 336 and 340). Also see Jane Marie Law, "Of Plagues and Puppets: On the Significance of the Name Hyakudayū in Japanese Religion," *The Transactions of the Asiatic Society of Japan*, series 4, vol. 8 (1993): 107–31.

Lotus Sutra commentary *Hokekyō jikidanshō* (Straight Talk on the *Lotus Sutra*; ca. 1546), for example, contains a story of how a Chinese priest by the name of Huixing was granted a tour of all the Buddhist hells when his life had come to an end. In one place he saw demon torturers binding five thousand priests with red-hot iron chains as punishment "for having handled spotless sutras with dirty hands," or for having otherwise sullied or damaged copies of the scriptures; in another, he saw demon torturers making priests walk across a red-hot iron "garden" as punishment "for having entered temples and cloisters with dirty feet."[33] In the *Uji shūi monogatari/Kojidan* account, Dōmyō's impurity may or may not exceed a case of dirty hands or dirty feet, but it is certainly enough to alienate the gods. The unknown *Uji shūi monogatari* compiler therefore warns that we should all wash before performing our *Lotus Sutra* recitations.

Weak as it may be, the moral at the end of *Uji shūi monogatari* account has led Ōshima Tatehiko to suppose that the *Uji shūi monogatari/Kojidan setsuwa* constitutes the written traces of an account that circulated orally among storytelling-priests in the late-Heian and Kamakura periods.[34] Yamamoto Takashi agrees, and he notes that the ranking of gods in their order of importance, from Brahmā and Indra at the top to a lowly roadside deity at the bottom, is a standard proselytizing technique.[35] Comical, miraculous, and/or frightening stories were often employed in Heian and medieval preaching as a means of attracting and entertaining audiences; as a tale of a dissolute monk, an elegant lady of the court and the power of the *Lotus Sutra* to summon—in most cases—Brahmā, Indra, and an assortment of other deities, the *Uji shūi monogatari/Kojidan* account appears to be one of these.

According to Ōshima and Yamamoto's theory of the didactic origins of the tale, the *Uji shūi monogatari/Kojidan* account is not so much a story of Izumi Shikibu and Dōmyō as it is of the *Lotus Sutra*. There is, in fact, a genre of *setsuwa* about priests who recite the *Lotus Sutra* to a variety of ends. Taira no Yasuyori, for example, includes the following sequence of short accounts (one of which concerns Dōmyō and Izumi Shikibu) in his twelfth-century *Hōbutsushū*:

[33] *Hokekyō jikidanshō*, vol. 3 (Kyoto: Rinsen Shoten, 1979), 243–44. Huixing is said to have been allowed to return to the human world to report what he had seen before going on to the Pure Land.

[34] Ōshima, "Izumi Shikibu no setsuwa," 130–31. Ōshima further argues that within the specific context of *Uji shūi monogatari*, the Buddhist lesson on the importance of maintaining purity in devotional practice is reinforced by the story that follows it: a *setsuwa* in which a priest explains that monks who preach in a state of impurity are reborn as *hiratake* mushrooms—fungi with seemingly phallic connotations.

[35] Yamamoto, "Dōmyō to Izumi Shikibu no setsuwa," 46–47.

> Long ago, a priest by the name of Shūroku pledged to recite the *Lotus Sutra* one thousand times and be reborn in the Pure Land. When he reached eight hundred, he dreamed that he grew wings and flew off to the west. When he finished one thousand, he was reborn in the Pure Land.
>
> The priest Zenjō of Enryakuji Temple caused his mother to be reborn in the Pure Land by performing devotions and reciting the *Lotus Sutra*.
>
> There was a commoner from the Yamada region of Iga province whose mother was reborn as a cow, but by having the *Lotus Sutra* read on her behalf, he rescued her from the animal realm.
>
> Because of Izumi Shikibu, Dōmyō Ajari was an impure, fallen monk. But as a result of reciting the *Lotus Sutra*, he achieved rebirth in the Pure Land.[36]

The *Uji shūi monogatari/Kojidan* account is surely representative of this type of tale. Although Dōmyō is not necessarily redeemed by his recitation as he is in the preceding *Hōbutsushū* passage, he nevertheless attains merit, in the midst of his transgression, by providing the Fifth Avenue Roadside Deity with an opportunity to hear the Holy Law. And that the deity is drawn to Dōmyō, regardless of Dōmyō's defilement, speaks strongly of the power of the *Lotus Sutra*.

Dōmyō's earliest known biography is contained in *Dainihonkoku Hokekyō genki* (Accounts of the *Lotus Sutra* in Great Japan; hereafter *Hokke genki*), a collection of life-histories of devotees of the *Lotus Sutra* compiled by the Tendai priest Chingen between 1040 and 1044, only twenty to twenty-four years after Dōmyō's death and some seventy years before Akikane's compilation of *Kojidan*. Although Dōmyō's *Hokke genki* biography contains no mention of Izumi Shikibu or any roadside deity, it anticipates the *Uji shūi monogatari/Kojidan* account in one of its stories about Dōmyō's miraculous sutra recitations, and in its recorded confession, attributed to Dōmyō after his death, of Dōmyō's sinful disregard for the precepts. The *Hokke genki* biography begins:

> Dōmyō Ajari was the first son of Imperial Tutor and Major Counselor [Fujiwara no] Michitsuna,[37] and a student of the Hiei abbot Senior Archbishop Jie.[38] He took up residence on Mt. Hiei and practiced Buddhist devotions from the time that he was a child. Giving his heart to the *Lotus Sutra*—for him there was nothing

[36]ZGR 32:2:317 (*Ikkan-bon* textual line [*Yasuyori hōbutsushū*]).

[37]Michitsuna was the second son of Fujiwara no Kaneie. He was appointed Major Counselor (*dainagon*) in 997, and Mentor to the Crown Prince (*tōgū no fu*) in 1007.

[38]Jie is the posthumous name of Ryōgen (912–85), appointed eighteenth Hiei Abbot (*Tendai zasu*) in 966 and Senior Archbishop (*daisōjō*) in 981.

> else—he memorized the first volume in a year, and in eight years, he memorized the entire work. He traveled to various sites of miraculous repute, and he accumulated years of Buddhist practice. Above all, his voice was delicate and refined. Without introducing a melody or tempering his intonation, he would allow his voice to lift of its own accord, and all those listening would lend their ears and praise him with joy.[39]

Hokke genki continues with two accounts of the miraculous effects of Dōmyō's *Lotus Sutra* recitations;[40] both were reproduced in the early twelfth-century *Konjaku monogatari shū*, and in the priest Kokan Shiren's *Genkō shakusho* (A History of Buddhism to the Genkō Era; 1322), further contributing to Dōmyō's fame.[41] In the first, a tale that seems likely to have influenced the composition of the *Uji shūi monogatari/Kojidan* account, an old monk at Hōrinji Temple on the western edge of the capital has a dream in which he learns that the Mitake Zaō Bodhisattva and the Kumano, Sumiyoshi, and Matsuo Deities all come to Hōrinji to hear Dōmyō recite the *Lotus Sutra*. In his dream, the old monk overhears a peculiar conversation:

> The Sumiyoshi Deity turned to the Matsuo Deity and spoke:[42] "There are many in Japan who recite the *Lotus Sutra*, but this Ajari is the best. When I hear his recitations, the karmic pains of past lives slip away and good roots flourish. That's why I come here every night from so far away."
>
> "That's right, that's right!" the Matsuo Deity replied. "I live nearby, so I always come to hear him recite, day and night."

The old monk awakens to the sound of Dōmyō reciting the sixth scroll of the

[39]NST 7:164–66 and 551–52. For a full and alternate translation, see Yoshiko Dykstra, *Miraculous Tales of the Lotus Sutra from Ancient Japan: The Dainihonkoku Hokekyōkenki of Priest Chingen* (Honolulu: University of Hawaii Press, 1983), 108–10. In his *Hokke genki* preface, Chingen identifies himself as a monk of Shuryōgon'in on Mount Hiei.

[40]The first account is discussed below. The second is a story of how Dōmyō once recited the *Lotus Sutra* and rescued a woman afflicted by the spirit of her dead husband. By simply hearing Dōmyō recite, the husband escaped his snake incarnation and attained rebirth in a Buddhist heaven.

[41]*Konjaku monogatari shū* 12:36, in SNKBT 35:183–86 and NKBZ 21:332–37; *Genkō shakusho*, in Kuroita Katsumi, ed., *Shintei zōho kokushi taikei*, vol. 31 (Tokyo: Yoshikawa Kōbunkan, 1930), 280–81. *Genkō shakusho* identifies Dōmyō as the founder of the "Way of Sutra Recitation" (p. 432), a religio-aesthetic performative art with established rules and lineages that was popular in the late-Heian and medieval periods. The earliest known reference to sutra recitation as a "Way" is in *Dokyō kuden myōkyōshū*, written by the monk Nōyo in 1284. See Shiba Kayono, "Dokyōdō," *Bungaku* 9, no. 1 (Winter 1998): 124–34.

[42]The deity of Sumiyoshi Shrine in Osaka, and the deity of Matsuo (also read Matsuno'o) Shrine in the western part of the capital. Matsuo Shrine was renamed Great Matsuo Shrine (Matsuo Taisha) in 1950.

Lotus Sutra in a Hōrinji Temple worship hall. Moved to tears by his dream-revelation, he goes to see Dōmyō to pay his respects.

The final section of the *Hokke genki* biography concerns the circumstances of Dōmyō's next-life rebirth. After Dōmyō's death, one of his friends—a monk by the name of Chiin—worries that Dōmyō has been unable to attain rebirth in the Pure Land. After two or three years, Chiin has a dream in which he visits a vast lotus-covered lake. Dōmyō approaches in a boat, and in response to Chiin's concerns, he explains:

> "Although I took to the Way of the Buddha, I neither restrained myself in words, thoughts, and deeds, nor did I keep the precepts. Rather, I committed transgressions however I saw fit. Then when I became intendant of Tennōji, I helped myself to temple property simply as a matter of course. For these sins I was unable to achieve rebirth in the Pure Land. Nevertheless, by the power of the *Lotus Sutra* I was able to escape falling into the Three Evil Realms,[43] and now I live on this lotus-covered lake where I chant the *Lotus Sutra*. I am without suffering in body or mind, and in two or three years, when my karmic debt is paid, I am sure to attain rebirth in Tosotsu Heaven."[44]

Dōmyō does not identify his transgressions as having been of an explicitly sexual nature, as they are represented in the *Uji shūi monogatari*/*Kojidan* account. However, as Shimazu Hisamoto observes, the great number of love poems attributed to Dōmyō in various poetic anthologies is likely to have given that impression to anyone familiar with Dōmyō and the *waka* tradition.[45]

Origins of an Affair

The *Uji shūi monogatari*/*Kojidan* account may be rooted in Dōmyō's *Hokke genki* biography, but the question of how Izumi Shikibu came to be taken up within it remains. Various theories have been advanced, and numerous factors, including Izumi Shikibu and Dōmyō's contemporaneity, their mutually scandalous reputations, and their fame as poets, are likely to have played a part. Ichiko Teiji notes that an association such as theirs could be based on as little as a single suggestive poem, and he cites a likely candidate from Izumi Shikibu's personal poetic anthology, *Izumi Shikibu shū*.[46] Together with its headnote, the poem reads:

[43]The realms of hell, hungry ghosts, and animals.

[44]Tosotsu (Tuṣita) Heaven is the abode of Miroku Bodhisattva, the future Buddha.

[45]Shimazu Hisamoto, *Kinko shōsetsu shinsan* (Tokyo: Yūseidō, 1983 [first published by Chūkōkan in 1928]), 577–79.

[46]Poem 179 in the *seishū* textual line; also *Goshūi wakashū* 1210, attributed to Izumi Shikibu. Ichiko Teiji, *Chūsei shōsetsu no kenkyū* (Tokyo: Tokyo Daigaku Shuppankai, 1955), 118.

Sent to a priest who left his fan after a visit:

hakanaku mo	A poor fan
wasurarenikeru	(a lover's meeting)
afugi ka na	forgotten by its owner—
ochitarikeri to	people will think you dropped it
hito mo koso mire	(and that you broke your vows).

The poem is cleverly playful. First, the word *afugi* (*ōgi*, a fan), contains the verb *afu*, "to meet," which implies a tryst. Next, *ochitarikeri*, a past form of the verb "to fall," suggests both that the fan fell from the unidentified priest's pocket, and that the priest fell from his vows. Context in this case is all-important: the headnote, identifying the addressee as a priest, imbues the verse with its shocking multivalence. Without it, the play on *ochitarikeri* would be lost and the poem would lack its saucy charm.

Like Ichiko Teiji, Shiba Kayono has sought the origins of Izumi Shikibu and Dōmyō's fictional affair in poetry. She proposes that the two Heian poets were associated as a result of their mutual identification with the *Lotus Sutra*: Dōmyō for his recitations, and Izumi Shikibu for a poem attributed to her in the imperial anthology *Shūi wakashū* (Gleanings of Japanese Poetry), compiled around 1005–7.[47] The first three lines of Izumi Shikibu's poem paraphrase a verse in the "Phantom City" chapter of the *Lotus Sutra*, "entering from darkness into darkness":[48]

Composed in the presence of Shōkū Shōnin and offered to him:

kuraki yori	From darkness
kuraki michi ni zo	into a path of darkness
irinubeki	I must enter—
haruka ni terase	shine your light afar,
yama no ha no tsuki	moon on the mountain ridge!

Shōkū Shōnin (910–1007) was a prominent Tendai priest, and the founder, in 966, of Enkyōji Temple on Mount Shosha in Harima province. The poem's headnote is grammatically ambiguous; alternately translated, it might read,

[47]Shiba Kayono, "Chūsei setsuwashū ni egakareta Izumi Shikibu," *Kokubungaku: kaishaku to kanshō* 60, no. 8 (August 1995): 106–11. The poem is *Shūi wakashū* 1342, attributed to "Masamune no musume Shikibu" (Izumi Shikibu).

[48]TSD 9 (262): 22c. Burton Watson translates the larger *Lotus Sutra* passage: "Living beings undergo constant suffering and anguish, / benighted, without teacher or guide, / not realizing there is a way to end suffering, / not knowing how to seek emancipation. / Through the long night increasingly they follow evil paths, / reducing the multitude of heavenly beings; / *from darkness they enter into darkness*, / to the end never hearing the Buddha's name" (italics mine). Burton Watson, *The Lotus Sutra* (New York: Columbia University Press, 1993), 121.

"Composed and sent to Shōkū Shōnin at his abode," although in *setsuwa* sources it is generally not interpreted in this way.

Izumi Shikibu's "darkness into darkness" poem came to be exceedingly well-known from around the late Heian period, and it has been a subject of considerable critical attention since at least that time. Fujiwara no Kintō (966–1041) is said to have belittled it because Izumi Shikibu borrowed its first three lines from the *Lotus Sutra* rather than composing them herself.[49] Some two hundred years later, Kamo no Chōmei (1155?–1216) objected to Kintō's criticism, responding that gold found in the street is treasure all the same.[50] In the modern period, Okazaki Tomoko has argued that Izumi Shikibu wrote her poem in the fourth or fifth month of 1005 and gave it to Kintō to pass on to the holy man when Kintō visited him at his temple in the fifth month of that year.[51] Yoshida Kōichi is of the same opinion, but he proposes that Prince Atsumichi was responsible for the poem's inclusion in *Shūi wakashū*, whereas Okazaki suggests that it was included at the request of Retired Emperor Kazan.[52]

The Buddhist *setsuwa* anthology *Shasekishū* (A Collection of Sand and Pebbles), compiled by the priest Mujū Ichien between 1279 and 1283, some two hundred and forty years after *Hokke genki*, contains a story that suggests that Izumi Shikibu and Dōmyō's association with the *Lotus Sutra* may indeed have played a role in the fabrication of their affair. Of the two poems attributed to Izumi Shikibu in the following *Shasekishū* account, the first alludes to a passage in the "Teacher of the Law" chapter of the *Lotus*, "In desolation, where no man's voice resounds . . .":[53]

> Izumi Shikibu was a beautiful, lascivious woman. Hearing of Dōmyō Ajari's sanctity, she quietly visited his hermitage near Hōrinji Temple one night while he was performing devotions. Intending to upset him from his vows, she knocked on his door. Dōmyō realized what was afoot, however, and he made no sound. Izumi Shikibu called out a poem and left:

[49] According to *Toshiyori zuinō* (ca. 1115; NKBT 65:249b; NKBZ 50:263–64), *Fukurozōshi* (ca. 1157–58; SNKBT 29:77–78), and *Mumyōshō* (ca. 1211–16; NKBT 65:79–82).

[50] *Mumyōshō* (composed between 1211 and 1216), in NKBT 65:81; Hilda Katō, "The *Mumyōshō*," *Monumenta Nipponica* 23, nos. 3–4 (1968), 401–4.

[51] Okazaki Tomoko, "Izumi Shikibu to Shōkū Shōnin: 'kuraki yori' no uta wo megutte" (1959), reprinted in *Heianchō joryū sakka no kenkyū* (Tokyo: Hōzōkan, 1967), 175–92.

[52] Yoshida Kōichi, "Izumi Shikibu no shakkyōka 'kuraki yori' no sakka nendai to *Shūishū* e no nyūshū jijō ni tsuite," *Heian bungaku kenkyū* 28 (June 1962): 35–44.

[53] TSD 9 (262): 32b. Watson translates: "If those who expound the Law / are alone in an empty and silent place, / and *in that stillness where no human voice sounds* / they read and recite this sutra, / at that time I will manifest / my pure and radiant body for them" (italics mine). Watson, *The Lotus Sutra*, 168.

jakumaku no	Though I knock
koke no iwato wo	on the desolate,
tatakedomo	mossy stone door,
muninjō ni te	'tis an uninhabited castle
hito mo oto sezu	and no man's voice resounds.

Dōmyō secluded himself at a mountain temple on Kaseyama (Lending Mountain) and performed devotions. Izumi Shikibu followed. For two or three days she sought him out, and she recited:

miyako idete	Three days from the capital,
kyō Mikanohara	and today, Mikanohara.
Izumigawa	The river breezes of Izumi
kawakaze samushi	(When Shall I See You?) River blow cold.
koromo Kaseyama	Do lend me your robe (Kaseyama)!

Much taken with her poem[s], Dōmyō broke his vows.[54]

Izumi Shikibu is cast in the role of a sexual predator, targeting a reluctant priest sworn to celibacy.[55] Her motive may be spite, or she may simply be inspired by the challenge that Dōmyō poses to her own powers of seduction. Wendy Doniger O'Flaherty has written that in ancient Hindu literature, the celibate ascetic sometimes "becomes an object of desire, in part merely because he is taboo."[56] The same may be true of Dōmyō in *Shasekishū*. In any case, as a famous poet, Izumi Shikibu uses poetry to overcome his defenses: her first verse alludes to the *Lotus Sutra*, obliquely invoking the authority of the sacred scripture, and her second contains a dazzling succession of puns on the poetic place names Mikanohara (Three Day Field), Izumigawa (Izumi [When Shall I See You] River), and Kaseyama (Lending Mountain), stunning Dōmyō into a state of carnal submission. Izumi Shikibu's reference to the *Lotus Sutra* is ironic in that it suggests Dōmyō's defeat, at least in part, by the very sutra to which he is so famously devoted.[57]

[54]NKBT 85:488a-b (Yonezawa text). Mujū Ichien (1226–1312) is also known as Mujū Dōgyō.

[55]Similarly, Tachibana no Narisue's *setsuwa* anthology *Kokon chomonjū* (Remarkable Tales Old and New; dated the tenth month of 1254) contains a story in which Izumi Shikibu challenges Dōmyō to sit facing her in a shared carriage. Dōmyō declines with a poem in which he claims a fear of falling—both from the carriage and from his precepts. NKBT 84:252 (tale 8:318); SNKS *Kokon chomonjū*, vol. 1, 380–81.

[56]Wendy Doniger O'Flaherty, *Śiva: The Erotic Ascetic* (Oxford: Oxford University Press, 1981), 55. O'Flaherty elsewhere writes (p. 56) that "the man of chastity is a good choice by virtue of the sexual powers amassed by his continence."

[57]Other poems based on *Lotus Sutra* passages have been attributed to Izumi Shikibu as well, including the "neither two nor three" poem, discussed in chapter four and attributed to Izumi Shikibu in the twelfth-century *Hōbutsushū* (SNKBT 40:331), and the "*kado no hoka*" poem, attributed to Izumi Shikibu in the noh play *Tōboku* (mid-fourteenth to mid-fifteenth century; SNKBZ

In addition to their shared identification with the *Lotus Sutra*, Izumi Shikibu and Dōmyō may have had a mutual connection to Tennōji Temple. Nagai Yoshinori argues that Izumi Shikibu (rather than the middle daughter of Fujiwara no Naritoki) was the mother of Prince Atsumichi's son Eikaku, and that Eikaku served as thirty-ninth intendant of Tennōji Temple from the second month of 1066 until his death in 1081.[58] Because Dōmyō served as twenty-seventh intendant of Tennōji from 1016 to 1020, Nagai proposes that Izumi Shikibu's connection to Tennōji through Eikaku may have led (or contributed) to her popular association with Dōmyō. *Shasekishū* contains a short account of a "certain priest"—a splendid reciter of the *Lotus Sutra*—who is said to have been Izumi Shikibu and Dōmyō's son.[59] There is no way to know for certain, but in the same way that the *Koshikibu* narrator replaces rumors of Izumi Shikibu and Atsumichi's affair with those of Izumi Shikibu and Dōmyō's, *Shasekishū* may mistakenly identify Izumi Shikibu and Atsumichi's son (if there ever even was such a boy) as Izumi Shikibu and Dōmyō's.

Evidence is lacking, but Ōshima Tatehiko is of the opinion that it was in fact the monks of Tennōji Temple who made up and recited the *Uji shūi monogatari*/*Kojidan* account, and possibly other stories of Izumi Shikibu and Dōmyō as well. In their efforts to proselytize, the monks of Tennōji may have sought to use the comically ignoble reputation of their prominent former intendant, Dōmyō, by pairing him with the infamous Izumi Shikibu (to whom they may also have had a connection through Eikaku) in a bawdy and entertaining tale intended for recitation in Tennōji Temple sermons.[60] Ōshima's theory is intriguing insofar as it offers a reasonable (although as-yet unproven) explanation for why so many stories of Izumi Shikibu and Dōmyō survive from the Kamakura and Muromachi periods, while virtually none of Izumi Shikibu and Tametaka, or Izumi Shikibu and Atsumichi do. Moreover, insofar as the vast majority of early-medieval preaching was carried out independent of aristocratic literary circles, Ōshima's theory sug-

58:255) and in the *setsuwa* collection *Tsuki no karu moshū* (seventeenth century; ZGR 33:1:88b). According to the Yonezawa *Shasekishū* text, Izumi Shikibu's husband Hōshō recited the "*kado no hoka*" poem when Dōmyō rode by Hōshō's house chanting the *Lotus Sutra* (NKBT 85:488b).

[58]Nagai makes a strong case that Eikaku was born to Izumi Shikibu in 1005 and that *Tennōji bettō shidai* (ZGR 4:1:435b–38a) mistakenly records the thirty-ninth intendant as having been Jōkaku instead of Eikaku. Nagai Yoshinori, "Izumi Shikibu no ko: Eikaku Ajari denkō," *Kokubungaku tōsa* (Taishō Daigaku) 7 (March 1963): 1-9.

[59]NKBT 85:488b–89a (Yonezawa text).

[60]Ōshima presents this idea in "Izumi Shikibu no setsuwa" (1967), 134, "Dōsojin no shinkō to setsuwa" (1972), 57, and "*Uji shūi monogatari* daiichiwa to otogizōshi *Izumi Shikibu*," in *Koten no hen'yō to shinsei*, ed. Kawaguchi Hisao (Tokyo: Meiji Shoin, 1984), 253.

gests a reason why most medieval stories about Izumi Shikibu have little basis in the Heian-period texts from which she and her peers are primarily known today.

Yamamoto Takashi endorses Ōshima's theory, and he further suggests that because of Tennōji Temple's proximity to the port towns of Eguchi and Kanzaki—famous as centers for *asobi* and lesser prostitutes—the *Uji shūi monogatari/Kojidan* account and various related tales were likely composed for and used in preaching to women.[61] Tennōji may have been particularly suited to this task, considering that its *honzon*, or "principal image," is a statue of Nyoirin Kannon, popularly associated in medieval Japan with the salvation of women.[62] Yamamoto's hypothesis is moreover intriguing because it would explain the presence of the Fifth Avenue Roadside Deity in the *Uji shūi monogatari/Kojidan* account, for as we have seen, the roadside deity Hyakudayū was revered among *asobi* and other courtesan-entertainers, who may have identified with his overt sexuality and liminal social status. In preaching to the *asobi* of Eguchi and Kanzaki, to whom they would have tailored their sermons in accord with the principle of expedient means, the Tennōji Temple priests may have thought to include a roadside deity in their didactic tale of sex and the *Lotus Sutra*. Notably, Chingen's mid-eleventh-century *Hokke genki* contains an account of how a Tennōji Temple priest by the name of Dōkō once rescued a roadside deity by reciting the *Lotus Sutra*;[63] if not simply coincidental, Dōkō's connection to Tennōji would suggest that multiple tales of Tennōji Temple priests, roadside deities, and the *Lotus Sutra* circulated in the Tennōji Temple community in the mid-to-late Heian period.

Although highly speculative, Yamamoto's theory is also significant to our consideration of the early association of Izumi Shikibu and Dōmyō in

[61]Yamamoto argues that many of the more famous accounts of holy men and promiscuous women, including stories of Izumi Shikibu and Dōmyō, emerged from the proselytizing activities of two temples: Enkyōji on Mount Shosha, and Tennōji in present-day Osaka, which together were near the towns of Muro no Tomari, Eguchi, and Kanzaki, all famous for their courtesan-entertainers. Yamamoto, "Dōmyō to Izumi Shikibu no setsuwa," 44. For a map of early-medieval *asobi* centers in the Tennōji region, see Amino and Gotō, eds., "Yūjo, kugutsu, shirabyōshi," 77.

[62]Nyoirin Kannon is depicted rescuing women from the Blood Pool Hell in numerous extant *Kumano Mind Contemplation Ten Worlds Mandala* (*Kumano kanjin jikkai mandara*), employed by Kumano *bikuni* in preaching to women in medieval Japan (see pp. 214–15, below). *Keiran shūyōshū* (Gathered Leaves from the Mountain-valley Winds), an encyclopedic compendium of Tendai Buddhist lore compiled between 1311 and 1348, identifies the Dragon Girl, widely celebrated as a pioneer of women's enlightenment, as a manifestation of Nyoirin Kannon. TSD 76 (2410): 863c.

[63]NST 7:215–16 and 567b–68a (section 3:128). *Konjaku monogatari shū* 13:34 is a corresponding account (SNKBT 35:256–58; NKBZ 21:437–41). Also see Yamamoto, "Dōmyō to Izumi Shikibu no setsuwa," 45b–46a, and Ōshima, "*Uji shūi monogatari* daiichi wa," 254.

the *imayō* anthology *Ryōjin hishō*. Emperor Go-Shirakawa writes in his memoirs that among his teachers were "*asobi* of Eguchi and Kanzaki," including a Kanzaki woman by the name of Kane.[64] If, as Yamamoto proposes, the monks of Tennōji did in fact spread stories of Izumi Shikibu and Dōmyō among the *asobi* of Eguchi and Kanzaki, then their preaching may have inadvertently led to the listing of Dōmyō's name beside Izumi Shikibu's in the song selected by Go-Shirakawa for inclusion in his twelfth-century compilation. Furthermore, the *Uji shūi monogatari*/*Kojidan* account would represent an early, although apparently not uncommon, use of Izumi Shikibu's name and persona in the medieval Buddhist instruction of women. As we will see in the following chapter, there is evidence to suggest that some *asobi* felt a personal sense of identification with the poems of Izumi Shikibu and Ono no Komachi in the twelfth and thirteenth centuries, lending further credence to Yamamoto's view.

Lovers' Comedy

As their fictional affair became increasingly well known in the Kamakura period, tales of Izumi Shikibu and Dōmyō were taken up in a number of secular, humorous accounts. These were inspired, in large part, by the ludicrous incongruity of Dōmyō and Hōshō (Fujiwara no Yasumasa, Izumi Shikibu's second historical husband) as rivals in love. Like Izumi Shikibu, Ono no Komachi, Ariwara no Narihira, and Saigyō, Hōshō was an exceedingly popular figure in late-Heian and medieval fiction. Celebrated for his bravery and valorous deeds, he is said to have faced down, unarmed, the notorious ruffian Hakamadare,[65] and to have numbered among the small band of warriors that slew the horrible demon Shuten Dōji in Shuten Dōji's mountain-fortress home.[66] Judging from the number and variety of extant *Shuten Dōji* scrolls, the grisly tale of the demon's defeat was among the most popular of all medieval stories; one might even say that the reign of Emperor Ichijō was better known in the Muromachi period for the terror of Shuten Dōji than it was for either Sei Shōnagon's *Pillow Book* or Murasaki Shikibu's *Tale of Genji*. Hōshō's demon-slaying reputation seems to have led

[64]Go-Shirakawa reports this in the tenth volume of *Ryōjin hishō kudenshū* (ca. 1180; NKBT 73:445 and 442). See Yung-Hee Kim, *Songs to Make the Dust Dance*, 17 and 19.

[65]According to *Konjaku monogatari shū* 25:7 (SNKBT 36:514–16; NKBZ 23:469–73) and *Uji shūi monogatari* 1:28 (SNKBT 42:61–63; NKBZ 28:116–18). Hōshō (958–1036) is also known by the name Hirai Yasumasa.

[66]The *otogizōshi Shuten Dōji* (Shibukawa text) is translated by me in Haruo Shirane, ed., *Traditional Japanese Literature: An Anthology, Beginnings to 1600* (New York: Columbia University Press, 2007), 1123-38. Shuten Dōji's story is related in the noh play *Ōe-yama*, and in the *otogizōshi Koshikibu* as well.

to his fictional association with Izumi Shikibu and Dōmyō in a way that Izumi Shikibu's first husband's reputation, or those of the princes Tametaka and Atsumichi, never did.

The Yonezawa text of Mujū Ichien's late thirteenth-century *Shasekishū* contains one such account, a story in which Hōshō catches Dōmyō hiding in a trunk at Izumi Shikibu's residence:

> At a time when Izumi Shikibu was the object of Hōshō's affections but was also receiving visits from her lover Dōmyō, Hōshō once came over suddenly. There was no place for Dōmyō to hide, so he climbed inside a Chinese armor chest, which was quickly put away. Hōshō realized this at once, and he told [his attendants] to hang the armor in the sun. The men pulled out the chest, but sensing that something shameful would come out of it, [Hōshō and Izumi Shikibu] both lost their nerve.
>
> "Don't open it," Hōshō ordered. "Leave it in the sun for a while, and then take it to Gion Shrine. Tell the intendant there that you have a request: that you want this armor presented as an offering to the Deity." Having spoken thus, he sent them off.
>
> The men placed the chest before the altar of the shrine, but the intendant was nowhere to be found. "We can't open it ourselves," the priests and lower administrators explained, waiting. A pitifully forlorn voice emerged from inside the chest: "Just one of you administrators open it." Removing the lid, they found no suit of armor, but their intendant instead![67]

The story is derived from a *Konjaku monogatari shū* account in which an unidentified provincial governor returns home to discover the intendant of Gion Shrine, a priest by the name of Kaishu, paying an inappropriate visit to his wife.[68] Kaishu hides in a chest, which the governor then sends to Gion Shrine as an offering. How or why the governor, the governor's wife, and Kaishu came to be replaced in *Shasekishū* by Hōshō, Izumi Shikibu, and Dōmyō is unclear. Unlike the more subtle alteration of the context of Akazome Emon's poem in *Koshikibu*, the substitution here is unnatural, considering that Dōmyō had no known affiliation with Gion Shrine. It is the nature of storytelling to recycle and recreate, and suffice it to say that Mujū (or some later interpolator) recorded the *setsuwa* as he heard it recounted in the 1270s or early 1280s.

[67]NKBT 85:488b.

[68]SNKBT 37:215–17 (tale 28:11); NKBZ 24:206–8; Marian Ury, *Tales of Times Now Past: Sixty-two Stories from a Medieval Japanese Collection* (Berkeley: University of California Press, 1979), 177–78.

In a story contained within the *otogizōshi Saru Genji sōshi* (The Tale of Monkey Genji), a work of unknown authorship from the late Muromachi period, Dōmyō outsmarts Hōshō with the aid of Izumi Shikibu and his own knowledge of poetry. *Saru Genji sōshi* is the tale of an audacious sardine peddler by the name of Monkey Genji (Saru Genji), who falls in love with an elegant courtesan, Keiga, whose social station far exceeds his own. In his efforts to seduce her, Monkey Genji pretends to be a provincial lord on his first visit to the capital. Keiga succumbs to his deception, but she grows suspicious when he talks in his sleep, calling out, among other things, "Sardines for sale!" Monkey Genji tells the following story to explain why the word *hashi* ("chopstick") was on his mind when he spoke in his sleep:

> Now a man by the name of Hōshō had begun seeing a woman named Izumi Shikibu, and they had become deeply involved. There was also a priest named Dōmyō,[69] and he too had taken up with Izumi Shikibu, pledging vows of love. Hōshō heard tell of this, so he said to Izumi Shikibu, "I want you to write a letter for me, just as I tell you."
>
> "What shall I write?" Izumi Shikibu asked.
>
> "Write, 'Hōshō isn't here now, so come over quickly.' Address it to the priest Dōmyō, and sign it 'Izumi Shikibu.'"
>
> Izumi Shikibu blushed. "But that's outrageous!" she said. She was unable to refuse, however, and she wrote the letter. Nevertheless, at some time or other she managed to break a *hashi*—a chopstick—into five pieces and send them off together with her correspondence.
>
> Dōmyō read her letter, and he thought it most peculiar. "She says for me to come over now," he mused, "but she's broken a *hashi* into five pieces and sent those along too. This is indeed strange. There is a poem that goes,
>
> | | |
> |---|---|
> | yaru hashi wo | If you take this *hashi* |
> | makotobashi shite | for real *hashi* |
> | kibashi shite | and come *hashi* |
> | utarebashi shite | and are struck down *hashi*, |
> | kuyamibashi su na | then don't blame me *hashi*. |
>
> This must be what she meant! Hōshō is surely there." Realizing his situation, Dōmyō stayed at home. That he was thus able to escape grave bodily harm was due to his understanding of the Way of Poetry.[70]

[69]Actually "Dōmei," an alternate reading of the characters in Dōmyō's name.

[70]NKBT 38:182; NKBZ 36:225–26. For an alternate translation, see Edward D. Putzar, "The Tale of Monkey Genji," *Monumenta Nipponica* 18, no. 1 (1963), 309–10.

Izumi Shikibu alludes to a poem with a broken chopstick—a physical representation of what may happen to Dōmyō if he goes to see her as her letter instructs—and because of Dōmyō's excellent knowledge of Japanese poetry, his life is saved. In Heian court literature, oblique poetic allusions by means of objects or deeds are often depicted as acts of the utmost refinement. In *The Pillow Book*, for example, Sei Shōnagon describes how she once had a blind raised as her own charmingly indirect reference to a Chinese verse, and how she was universally praised as a result.[71] In *Saru Genji sōshi*, the chopstick-message episode is farcical, because the poem to which Izumi Shikibu alludes is hardly a poem at all; it is simply a warning with the word "chopstick" inserted five times. Dōmyō's recollection of it is therefore absurd—a comical result of Monkey Genji's attempt to conceal his identity from the gullible Keiga.

Saru Genji sōshi contains an additional tale of Izumi Shikibu and Hōshō, a story that Monkey Genji tells in order to justify his having spoken the word "sardine" in his sleep.[72] Once when Izumi Shikibu was eating a sardine, he explains, Hōshō came by for an unexpected visit. Embarrassed to be caught eating, Izumi Shikibu hid her meal. Hōshō assumed that she was hiding a letter from Dōmyō, and he demanded an explanation. Izumi Shikibu therefore chanted the following poem, an impromptu verse containing the word *iwashi*, "sardine," embedded in the name "Iwashimizu" (of Iwashimizu Hachiman Shrine):

hi no moto ni	Surely there are none
iwawaretamau	who do not visit Iwashimizu
Iwashimizu	(or fail to eat the sardine),
mairanu hito wa	celebrated as it is
araji to zo omou	throughout Japan.

The poem depends for its effect upon the double meaning of the verb *mairu*, "to visit" and "to eat."[73] Like the impecunious Monkey Genji—a fishmonger masquerading as a provincial lord—the poem is a lowly *haikai* (a late-medieval comical verse) passed off as a classical *waka*. Still, Hōshō is said to have

[71]SNKBT 25:321; NKBT 19:310–11; NKBZ 11:427; Ivan Morris, *The Pillow Book of Sei Shōnagon* (New York: Columbia University Press, 1991), 241–42 ("One Day, When the Snow Lay Thick on the Ground"). The story is also contained in *Jikkinshō* (dated 1252; SNKBZ 51:56), *Etsumokushō* (ca. 1317–19; GR 10:695a), and *Mukashi nyōbō no hitokuchi monogatari* (dated 1448; section 5; see footnote 3 in the following chapter).

[72]NKBT 38:185; NKBZ 36:228–29.

[73]Kikuchi Hitoshi notes that the poem is attributed to Murasaki Shikibu in *Shisei zōtanshū* (compiled by Hayashi Jiken and published in 1764). Kikuchi Hitoshi, "Setsuwa denshō to Izumi Shikibu," *Kokubungaku: kaishaku to kyōzai no kenkyū* 35, no. 12 (October 1990), 101a.

been impressed, and realizing the groundlessness of his suspicions, to have quickly apologized.

As the *Saru Genji sōshi* and *Shasekishū* accounts demonstrate, the Izumi Shikibu/Dōmyō association became a subject of seemingly secular humor in the Kamakura and Muromachi periods, transcending its probably didactic origins as it was taken up in medieval fiction and storytelling. Thus, while *otogizōshi* such as *Saru Genji sōshi*, *Kotohara*, and *Izumi Shikibu* (the latter two of which are discussed in the following two chapters) would appear from their content to be derived from the elite literary traditions of the Heian court, they are in fact more directly descended from what seem to have been the *hōben*, or "expedient means," of late-Heian and medieval preacher-entertainers. As medieval writers and storytellers took up these farfetched accounts by earlier (and probably contemporary) proselytizers, who themselves drew upon the poetry and conventions of the Heian court, the Muromachi period saw the emergence of a new, hybrid prose literature with roots in both the didactic Buddhist and the aristocratic literary traditions of the Heian past.

Chapter Two
Mice in the *Koto*: the *Otogizōshi Kotohara*

Among Muromachi-period fictional works that take as their subject Izumi Shikibu and Dōmyō's supposed affair is an *otogizōshi* by the name of *Kotohara*. Although written with the characters for "Belly of the *Koto*" (a *koto* being a musical instrument, a kind of hollow-bodied Japanese harp), the title is homonymic with the word *kotohara*, "a different womb," and it is this latent, secondary meaning that determines the course of events in the first part of the tale. *Kotohara* is of unknown authorship, but it survives in a pristine fifteenth-century *hakubyō* ("white drawing") picture scroll—a medieval form of uncolored court painting—both the text and illustrations of which are traditionally attributed to Emperor Go-Hanazono (1419–70).[1] Go-Hanazono's father, Sadafusa, records in his diary that his son was a skilled painter and calligrapher, as well as an avid purveyor and copyist of picture scrolls.[2] As Go-Hanazono may or may not have reproduced *Kotohara* from an earlier manuscript, the approximate date of the work's original composition is unknown. For scholars of medieval fiction, the emperor's participation in the creation and/or preservation of the *otogizōshi* is significant insofar as it suggests that in the Muromachi period, producers and consumers of such works were to be found among members of even the highest social strata.

In its narrative structure, *Kotohara* comprises two tales of Izumi Shikibu and Dōmyō combined into one. The first is an unusual story of the mysterious birth of mice in the hollow body of a *koto* in an empress's apartments, and a subsequent poem contest, ordered by the emperor, that leads to Izumi Shikibu and Dōmyō's supposed affair. The second is an altered and expanded rendition of the early thirteenth-century *Uji shūi monogatari*/*Kojidan* account

[1]The Go-Hanazono manuscript is photographically reproduced in Ishizuka Kazuo, "Go-Hanazono Tennō shinkan *Kotohara ekotoba*," in *Nihon bungakushi no shin kenkyū*, ed. Kamiya Yoshiyuki (Tokyo: Miyai Shoten, 1984), 116–21, and typeset in Suzuka Sanshichi, *Shinkanshū kaisetsu* (Tokyo: Kunaishō, 1927), 51–60. The Sonkeikaku Bunko archive contains an additional *Kotohara* manuscript, which was hand-copied, without illustrations, from the Go-Hanazono picture scroll in 1707, and which is typeset in MJMT supp. 1:523–28.

[2]According to Suzuka, *Shinkanshū kaisetsu*, 51, and Ishizuka, "Go-Hanazono Tennō shinkan *Kotohara ekotoba*," 115, citing Sadafusa's diary, *Kanmon gyoki*. Prince Sadafusa (1372–1456) is also known as Go-Sukōin.

of Izumi Shikibu, Dōmyō, and the Fifth Avenue Roadside Deity. As for the first account, the only other known version is contained in a short collection of poem-stories titled *Mukashi nyōbō no hitokuchi monogatari* (Bite-size Tales from a Lady of Old), dated 1448, around the same time as Go-Hanazono's *Kotohara* picture scroll.[3] Whether Go-Hanazono drew upon *Hitokuchi monogatari*, the unknown *Hitokuchi monogatari* compiler drew upon *Kotohara*, or both works share a common source is unclear. Despite their disparate origins, the two *Kotohara* sections function together to trace the course of Izumi Shikibu and Dōmyō's affair. They are additionally thematically linked by their concern with the mystical powers of language—both poetry and chanted scripture—to harness, tame, or otherwise subjugate the supernatural.

In an early articulation of the concept of poetry as magic, Ki no Tsurayuki wrote in his preface to the poetic anthology *Kokin wakashū* (Collection of Poems Past and Present; ca. 905) that *waka* (Japanese poetry) has the power to "move heaven and earth, stir feeling in unseen demons and gods, soften relations between men and women, and soothe the hearts of fierce warriors."[4] Purportedly true examples of all these things and more are cited in a variety of Heian and medieval sources. In the twelfth and thirteenth centuries, *waka* came to be widely associated with various aspects of Buddhist thought and practice. In his poetic commentary *Korai fūteishō* (Notes on Styles, Past to Present; 1197), for example, Fujiwara no Toshinari (Shunzei) asserts the concord of poetry and the Three Truths of Tendai Buddhism.[5] The Kamakura-period *Ise* commentary *Waka chikenshū* (Poetic Knowledge Revealed) reports that Japanese poetry "is the source of magical powers, drawing us to enlightenment," and explains that the thirty-one syllables of a *waka* correspond to the thirty-one visible characteristics of a Buddha.[6] In *Shasekishū* (ca. 1280), Mujū Ichien identifies *waka* as the *dharani* (magical Buddhist incantations) of Japan, while an exemplum in *Jikkinshō* (Discourse on Ten Lessons; 1252) suggests that the chanting of *waka* may be substituted

[3]*Hitokuchi monogatari* survives in two known manuscripts, both of which are in the possession of the archives of the Japanese Imperial Household Agency (Kunaichō Shoryōbu). The older of the two is a copy from the early Edo period, and is typeset in Ishizuka Kazuo, "Shiryō shōkai: *Mukashi nyōbō no hitokuchi monogatari*," *Shoryōbu kiyō* 30 (1978): 55–64 (for the *Kotohara*-related account, see p. 63).

[4]SNKBT 5:4. Also see R. Keller Kimbrough, "Reading the Miraculous Powers of Japanese Poetry: Spells, Truth Acts, and a Medieval Buddhist Poetics of the Supernatural," *Japanese Journal of Religious Studies* 32, no. 1 (Spring 2005): 1–33.

[5]NKBZ 50:274 75.

[6]The unknown *Waka chikenshū* author explains that the abstract essence of a poem (its *kokoro*) corresponds to the thirty-second distinguishing characteristic of a Buddha: the Unseen Sign, or *mukenchō-sō*. Katagiri Yōichi, *Ise monogatari no kenkyū: shiryō hen* (Tokyo: Meiji Shoin, 1969), 199b. The poetic commentary *Sangoki* (ca. 1312–17) contains a similar explanation (NKT 4:341).

for that of the *nenbutsu*, the ritual invocation of Amida Buddha's name.[7] Although *Kotohara* is unconcerned with the specifically Buddhist functions or implications of *waka* (or with the larger and more fundamentally contentious issue of the "morality" of secular verse),[8] its preoccupation with the mysterious powers of ritual language, whether that of poetry or sutra recitation, is appropriate to the philosophical tenor of its time.

Omens and the Powers of Words

The *Kotohara* and *Hitokuchi monogatari* account of the emperor's contest to compose poems on the topic of mice born in a *koto* seems to have been inspired by a poem attributed to Fujiwara no Sukemi (died previous to 956) in the poetic anthology *Shūi wakashū* (Gleanings of Japanese Poetry), compiled around 1005–07.[9] Together with its headnote, the poem reads:

> Composed on the topic of a mouse that bore its babies in the body of a *koto:*

toshi wo hete	The passing years
kimi wo nomi koso	I have spent
nesumitsure	with you alone.
kotohara ni ya wa	How could a child of mine
ko wo ba umubeki	be born of another's womb?

The poem is more complex than it appears in translation. While on its surface it is a husband's straightforward reply to his wife's suspicions that he has fathered a child by another woman, it contains the words *nesumi* (a form of the verb *nesumu*, "to live and sleep together") and *kotohara* ("a different womb"), which have alternate significations of "mouse" (*nezumi*) and "hollow body of the *koto*." As a result of these embedded words, the poem is both in keeping with its headnote and classified within *Shūi wakashū* as a *mono no na* (names of things)-type composition. Variants of the verse are contained in the personal poetic anthology of Ki no Tomonori (ca. 856–ca. 905),[10] and in the sixteenth- or seventeenth-century *otogizōshi Chōjū gi-uta-*

[7]*Shasekishū*, in NKBT 85:222–23; *Jikkinshō*, in SNKBZ 51:443–44. *Jikkinshō* 10:53 records that Fujiwara no Ietaka (1158–1237) attained rebirth in the Pure Land after reciting three *waka* at the time of his death, and that a monk by the name of Hōnichi Shōnin achieved Pure Land rebirth after making it his lifelong practice to recite three *waka*, three times a day.

[8]See William R. LaFleur, *The Karma of Words: Buddhism and the Literary Arts in Medieval Japan* (Berkeley and Los Angeles: University of California Press, 1983), and Edward Kamens, *The Buddhist Poetry of the Great Kamo Priestess: Daisaiin Senshi and Hosshin Wakashū* (Ann Arbor: University of Michigan Center for Japanese Studies, 1990).

[9]SNKBT 7:119, poem 421. Also see Ichiko Teiji, *Chūsei shōsetsu no kenkyū* (Tokyo: Tokyo Daigaku Shuppankai, 1955), 112.

[10]*Tomonori shū* (compiled in the tenth or early eleventh century), in SKT 3:1:30c, poem 70.

awase monogatari (Tale of a Playful Poem Contest between Birds and Beasts), which attributes it to Fujiwara no Kiyosuke (1104–77).[11] Although it appears nowhere within *Kotohara* or *Hitokuchi monogatari*, the poem seems to have led to the composition of the fifteenth-century account.

Kotohara begins at an unspecified time during the reign of Emperor Go-Ichijō (r. 1016–36), the first son of Empress Shōshi, in whose salon Izumi Shikibu and Akazome Emon are known to have served (Sei Shōnagon, who is briefly mentioned within the work, served in the salon of the rival empress Teishi [d. 1000]):

> At a time during the reign of Emperor Go-Ichijō, a mouse once bore a litter of babies inside the body of a *koto* in the Empress's apartments.[12] Those in Her Highness's service spoke of it as an ominous sign, and even the emperor inquired among his courtiers as to whether such an event was not of great significance. "One cannot expect mice and the like not to go building nests in objects that have been left lying around," people said, "especially containers that aren't handled very often. But in a case like this, in which Her Highness has been playing the instrument day and night . . ." Thus people gossiped, and feeling rather uneasy, they sought to keep the whole matter quiet.
>
> As for the Uji Chancellor Yorimichi—a person of the time—the incident brought to mind past events.[13] "A mouse once built its nest in the tail of a horse in the Imperial Stables," he said at the palace.[14] "It was in the reign of a certain emperor toward the middle of the Hakuchi era (650–54), or so I've read in a few old books. They say it was an event of some importance; this *koto*, then, must be truly extraordinary."
>
> The emperor later spoke to those in his close service at the palace: "If someone were to compose a really good poem on this strange event, something would surely happen as a result. Such things are not without precedent, you know. Now I want all of you to compose a poem—the very best one you can—and we'll have fun indeed!"

[11]MJMT 9:336b. Because *Shūi wakashū* dates from before Kiyosuke's birth, the attribution of the poem to him in *Chōjū gi-uta-awase monogatari* is obviously incorrect. The "Miraculous Mice" (*Reiso no homare*) section of *Enkyokushō*, a collection of songs compiled by Myōkū ca. 1296, refers to mice having babies in a *koto* as well (ZGR 19:2:135b).

[12]The Empress (*chūgū*) would have been Fujiwara no Ishi (1000–1036), third daughter of Fujiwara no Michinaga; she was appointed *chūgū* in 1018.

[13]Fujiwara no Yorimichi (eldest son of Michinaga) held the post of chancellor (*kanpaku*) from 1019 to 1067. He is best known today for building the Byōdōin Phoenix Hall at Uji in 1052.

[14]This is according to the Sonkeikaku Bunko text. According to the Go-Hanazono Tennō text, the horse was kept in the kitchen (*kuriya*), a likely mistranscription of the character for stable (*umaya*).

Fig. 7. Mice born from the body of a *koto*. From *Kotohara ekotoba* (fifteenth century), in the Higashiyama Go-bunko Archive. Courtesy of the Archives and Mausolea Department of the Japanese Imperial Household Agency (Kunaichō Shoryōbu).

The first *Kotohara* illustration (fig. 7) shows five mice (and a smudge) frolicking beside a *koto* on the floormatting of the empress's chambers. Two women—the empress and a lady-in-waiting, perhaps—look on. Four of the five mice are turned toward the empress, as is a gentleman in formal court attire. In an adjoining room, three ladies sit in conversation. The man in the foreground may be the Uji Chancellor Yorimichi,[15] and he appears to address the empress from his seated position before an open sliding door. The surrounding wall panels are painted with stylized seasonal scenes in an aesthetic, controlled reproduction of the natural world outside. Craggy mountains and forested hills, a river and a waterfall, grasses, trees and bamboo, flying geese and a braying buck—all are visible in static representations. The mice, by contrast, are alive, and the man and two women look on in surprise as if a scene in the paintings had suddenly broken free and come to life. The birth is an unsettling and unnatural event, a crisis of chaos in the calculated order of the painted room.

Mice are known for their mischievous, destructive behavior—chewing holes in walls, undermining the structure of things—so their presence in

[15]According to Miya Tsugio, in Miya Tsugio et al., eds., *Kadokawa emakimono sōran* (Tokyo: Kadokawa Shoten, 1995), 337a.

the empress's apartments is indeed portentous. The Uji Chancellor recalls an ominous incident involving the birth of mice in a horse's tail, but he is mistaken in dating it to the Hakuchi era; according to an account in *Nihon shoki* (720), the mice were born in the first year of Tenji (662), and a diviner interpreted it to mean that there would be an uprising abroad.[16] In *Kotohara*, Go-Ichijō appears to be more amused than concerned, and he turns to poetry in a lighthearted attempt to bring some additional fantastic event to pass. In *Hitokuchi monogatari*, the emperor adopts a more somber tone: "This is the kind of thing that should be set right with a poem," he explains, employing the compound verb *yominaosu*, "to rectify by composing a verse."

The emperor's command in *Hitokuchi monogatari* that his subjects seek protection in the miraculous powers of poetry is not without precedent in Kamakura- and Muromachi-period literature. According to one oft-repeated tale, a Japanese sovereign, sometimes identified as the seventh-century emperor Tenji, sent an envoy to Ise province to drive demons out with a poem (the demons had been "endlessly abducting and eating people, causing terrible grief," the priest Sonshun explains in his *Lotus Sutra* commentary *Hokekyō jurin shūyōshō* [Gathered Leaves of the *Lotus Sutra* from a Grove on Eagle Peak; 1512]).[17] In a discussion of ritual theory, Herbert Plutschow observes that it is by means of ritual that people "seek to control conditions thought to be uncontrollable," and that because of Japanese poetry's inherent order (comprised as *tanka* are of five lines of 5, 7, 5, 7, 7 syllables), it is capable, when ritually inveighed, of restoring order to a disrupted natural environment.[18] Although there is no evidence to suggest that anyone in Heian or medieval Japan understood the powers of Japanese poetry in quite this way, *waka* were widely employed in times of crisis, and it is thus eminently appropriate that the emperor in *Kotohara* and *Hitokuchi monogatari* turns to poetry to counter the implicitly destabilizing effects of the newborn mice.

Kotohara continues:

> The people racked their brains searching for words to capture the essence of what had happened. Among those of fame were Sei

[16]NKBT 68:354–55; W.G. Aston, *Nihongi: Chronicles of Japan from the Earliest Times to A.D. 697* (Tokyo: Charles E. Tuttle, 1972 [first published in 1896]), vol. 2, 277. Also see *Heike monogatari*: SNKBT 44:176, and Helen McCullough, *The Tale of the Heike* (Stanford: Stanford University Press, 1988), 172.

[17]*Hokekyō jurin shūyōshō*, vol. 4 (Kyoto: Rinsen Shoten, 1991), 461–62. The emperor is identified as Tenji in the commentary *Kokin wakashū jo kikigaki sanryūshō* (ca. 1286), quoted in Kamioka Yūji, *Waka setsuwa no kenkyū: chūko hen*, Kasama sōsho, no. 196 (Tokyo: Kasama Shoin, 1986), 194–95.

[18]Herbert Plutschow, *Chaos and Cosmos: Ritual in Early and Medieval Japanese Literature* (Leiden: E.J. Brill, 1990), 31–32.

> Shōnagon, daughter of Kiyohara no Motosuke, Akazome Emon, daughter of the Ōsumi governor Tokimochi, and Izumi Shikibu, daughter of Ōe no Masamune. Other well-known poets were there too, people whose lives would be as fleeting as foam on the water, and they all made terrific efforts to compose a fine and moving verse. Their labor was for naught, however, and their poems—much like those of everyone else—were far from satisfactory. They plumbed the depths of their hearts, but they were unable to express even the haziest sentiment that might set their compositions apart. "For a poet, such times as these are truly humiliating," many thought to themselves.
>
> There was at that time a priest by the name of Dōmyō. He had earned a name for himself composing verse on the morning flowers and the evening moon,[19] and he had access to the imperial palace. He was traveling in the Ise region on matters of love, and meeting with a person from the capital, he heard what was afoot. He seems at length to have had an idea, and word soon reached the capital that he had composed a poem. Izumi Shikibu heard the news back at the palace, and brimming with envy, she decided to lie in wait for Dōmyō at an inn on the road from Ise. Disguising herself as a lurid courtesan, she met with him in the dim light of a certain evening. "Someone from the capital told me you've come up with a poem about that *koto* everyone's talking about," she said. "Won't you tell it to me?"
>
> "I certainly will," he said, "just as soon as I've presented it at the palace."
>
> "But we're so close to the capital as it is," she pressed. "And after you've recited it for the emperor, I'm sure to end up hearing it somehow or other anyway. So just tell me your first line."
>
> "My first line is, 'I once heard tell,'" he said weakly, and he would say no more. Abandoning him as if she had heard the entire verse, Izumi Shikibu immediately returned to the capital.

Under pressure, Sei Shōnagon, Akazome Emon, and Izumi Shikibu are all unable to compose an impressive poem. Their problem is likely to have been a common one in the court, and it brings to mind a *Pillow Book* episode in which Sei Shōnagon describes how she and several other ladies were once hard pressed to come up with a verse on the topic of their fifth-month outing to hear the song of the cuckoo, or *hototogisu*.[20] In *Kotohara* and *Hitokuchi monogatari*, Izumi Shikibu remains undeterred, and she disguises herself as a prostitute in order to steal Dōmyō's composition. Like their fairy-tale counterparts in Europe—the murderous Bluebeard, or the cannibalistic witch in

[19]These are standard topics for poetic composition.

[20]SNKBT 25:127–35; NKBT 19:148–55; NKBZ 11:219–29; Ivan Morris, *The Pillow Book of Sei Shōnagon*, 118–23 ("It Was during the Abstinence of the Fifth Month").

the tale of Hansel and Gretel, for example—characters in *otogizōshi* tend toward outrageous, socially transgressive behavior, whether seducing priests, abandoning babies, slandering their stepchildren, or brutally murdering their rivals. This of course is what makes them so intriguing. Immorality knows no gender bounds in medieval fiction, and Dōmyō's susceptibility to sexual persuasion in *Kotohara* and *Hitokuchi monogatari* is perhaps as scandalous as Izumi Shikibu's underhanded attempt to purloin his poem.

While poetry was understood in premodern Japan to be capable of miraculous effects, it was also thought to pose terrible risks when carelessly composed. In the way that fine poems may move the gods, inappropriate ones may alienate them as well. In his commentary *Kokin joshō* (Notes on the *Kokinshū* Preface; 1264), Fujiwara no Tameie (1196–1275) identifies the Way of Poetry with political governance, and he warns against the reckless composition of verse.[21] Similarly, *Gyokuden jinpi* (Profound Secret Transmissions), a medieval compendium of secret *waka* lore from the poetic lineage of Fujiwara no Tameaki (fl. ca. 1263–78), explains that "the affairs of state depend upon the quality of poems produced."[22] The late Kamakura-period treatise *Jinpi kushō* (Nine Articles of Profound Secrets) goes so far as to propose that Japan suffered the calamity of the Mongol invasions because the imperial poetic anthologies were carelessly compiled.[23]

One of the most outspoken critics of ill-considered composition is the unknown author of the Buddhist poetic commentary *Nomori no kagami* (Mirror of the Watchman of the Fields), dated 1295, a mere fourteen years after the second Mongol incursion. Denouncing the new poetic style of Kyōgoku Tamekane (1254–1332), who had been recently chosen to edit the imperial anthology *Gyokuyō wakashū* (Collection of Jeweled Leaves of Poetry; completed in 1313), the *Nomori no kagami* author argues that if Tamekane's influence should remain unchecked, it will lead to both the death of *waka* and the destruction of Buddhist Truth.[24] In what Ogawa Toyoo has described as a "radical ideology of the powers of poetry,"[25] the anonymous critic invokes Chinese philosophical thought to argue that the security of the very state depends upon the proper maintenance of poetic tradition:

[21]Cited in Ogawa Toyoo, "Katokuron josetsu 2," in *Uta monogatari to waka setsuwa*, ed. Setsuwa to Setsuwa Bungaku no Kai, Setsuwa ronshū, vol. 9 (Osaka: Seibundō, 1999), 244–45.

[22]Ibid., 261.

[23]NKT 4:396. I follow Ogawa Toyoo in interpreting the "national calamity" to be that of the Mongol invasions. Ogawa, "Katokuron josetsu 2," 261.

[24]NKT 4:87; R. Keller Kimbrough, "*Nomori no kagami* and the Perils of Poetic Heresy," *Proceedings of the Association for Japanese Literary Studies* 4 (Summer 2003): 99–114.

[25]Ogawa Toyoo, "Katokuron josetsu," *Kagoshima joshi daigaku kenkyū kiyō* 13, no. 1 (March 1992); reprinted in *Higi to shite no waka*, ed. Watanabe Yasuaki (Tokyo: Yūseidō, 1995), 73.

> It is because *waka* establishes rectitude in music and etiquette that our country is stable and not wracked by outside enemies. That Buddhism is widespread here, excelling countries greater than our own, is also due entirely to the virtues of *waka*. The Song Dynasty is without *waka*, and thus lacking guidance in music and etiquette, their Eight Schools of Buddhism have all disappeared and their country is plundered by foreign traitors. Now considering that the deities of Japan—deities who revere the Holy Law, who protect our nation and love poetry—detest the contemporary style, we are sure to suffer their wrath as a result.[26]

The rhetoric of *Nomori no kagami* is unusually extreme, but it serves to illustrate the perceived dangers of reckless poeticizing in early-medieval Japan. In *Kotohara* and *Hitokuchi monogatari*, although the emperor seeks security (or simply diversion) in the powers of poetry, Izumi Shikibu's attempt to procure a poem by deceit—by seducing a priest, no less—may pose as great a danger as the omen it is meant to counteract.

As *Kotohara* continues, Izumi Shikibu returns to the capital, where she presents her partially stolen verse to Go-Ichijō and the court:

> Izumi Shikibu proceeded to the palace, and stating that she had come up with a poem, she recited the following:

inishie wa	I once heard tell
nesumi kayou to	you'd spend your life
kikishikado	with me,
kotohara ni koso	but a child now grows
ko wa mōkekere	in another's womb.[27]

> The other attendants were vexed, and the emperor was greatly amused.
>
> A certain Lord Sanesuke, son of the former chancellor Kadoyoshi,[28] said that he, too, would compose an excellent verse, and with great fervor he devised the following:

au koto wa	When will we meet,
itsu tamakura no	our arms as pillows
nobe no toko	in our bed in the fields?
ta ga nesumi shite	Who was it (the field mice)
mumaru nadeshiko	who slept there and bore the flowers?

[26]NKT 4:83.

[27]Alternately translated, the poem might read: "I once heard tell / of wandering mice—/ and now / they have borne their young / in the belly of a *koto*."

[28]Fujiwara no Sanesuke (957–1046) was the third son of Commander of the Gate Guards of the Right Fujiwara no Tadatoshi and the grandson of Chancellor (and Regent) Fujiwara no Saneyori. There is no record of a chancellor by the name of Kadoyoshi.

> Such was his poem. It was not well received, however, perhaps because in some respects it was too similar to the earlier composition.
>
> Sometime later Dōmyō returned to the capital from Ise. Explaining that he had written a verse while attending to matters in the provinces, he recited his *koto* poem—and it was identical to the one that Izumi Shikibu had earlier presented at the palace! Their compositions were the same from beginning to end, despite the fact that he had only taught her his first line. This was due entirely to the miraculous powers of the Way of Poetry. Furthermore, it may well have been because of this poem that Emperor Go-Reizei was born of a different imperial womb, a marvelous thing indeed!

According to historical records (which obviously do not include *Kotohara*), the future emperor Go-Reizei (1025–68) was born the son of Go-Ichijō's younger brother, Crown Prince Atsunaga, who himself later became Emperor Go-Suzaku, and Fujiwara no Kishi, a daughter of the eminent Fujiwara no Michinaga. While the *Hitokuchi monogatari* account concludes with the revelation that Izumi Shikibu's and Dōmyō's poems were the same, *Kotohara* goes on to associate this "miracle" with the subsequent birth of Go-Reizei from a "different imperial womb" (*koto-miyabara*)—that of a woman other than Go-Ichijō's Empress Ishi.

But a crucial question remains: Was the unknown, implied calamity of mice in the *koto* thus averted or induced by Izumi Shikibu and Dōmyō's poem? The answer depends upon one's perspective regarding the nature of the imperial succession. In Go-Hanazono's *Kotohara* picture scroll, the *Kotohara* narrator expresses pleasure at the birth of Go-Reizei by the wife of Go-Ichijō's brother, suggesting that the danger was indeed suppressed. However, the narrator's feelings are to be expected, considering that Go-Hanazono's authority was itself contingent upon the legitimacy of the imperial line. As for Izumi Shikibu and Dōmyō's poem, it may be best understood as having channeled the mysterious omen, preempting a true catastrophe by redefining it according to the homonymic possibilities of its semantic signification. Like Fujiwara no Sukemi's verse in *Shūi wakashū*, the poem makes use of the double meanings of *nesumi* and *kotohara*, transforming the living "mice in the hollow body of the *koto*" into an actual "child of a different womb" by the magical powers of poetic wordplay. That the word *nezumi* ("mouse" or "rat") is written with the character for "child" in the Sino-Japanese cyclical calendar may be moreover significant, because it further blurs the distinction between the two.

On a different (non-semantic) level, Izumi Shikibu and Dōmyō's poem may have achieved its effect by the circumstances of its composition. Although Izumi Shikibu borrows Dōmyō's first line in devising her verse, she presents it to the court as her own. Similarly, Dōmyō claims the verse to be his, but according to a statement by Izumi Shikibu in a later part of the tale, he seems to have received it from the deity of Ise Shrine.[29] Finally, in composing his own derivative poem, Lord Sanesuke borrows Izumi Shikibu's pun on *nesumi*, and he is criticized as a result. There is thus a threefold pattern of plagiarism within the work. Since each of the poems is in fact born of another's intellect—a "different womb," so to speak—they may together have precipitated Go-Reizei's birth by the wife of the Crown Prince.

Poets and Prostitutes

When Izumi Shikibu sets out to steal Dōmyō's poem in *Kotohara*, she disguises herself as a courtesan, or *yūkun* (a synonym for *yūjo*, discussed in the preceding chapter). As we have seen, the term *yūjo*, a Sinified reading of the characters for *asobi*, tended to be employed in the medieval period as a generic label for the various groups of courtesan-entertainers plying their trades in the cities, harbors, and highway inns of Kamakura and Muromachi Japan. Izumi Shikibu and Ono no Komachi are in fact identified or described as *yūjo* in a variety of medieval fictional works, and although the reasons for this are a subject of debate, as a pattern of representation—an aspect of Heian women poets' "medievalization" (their representation in post-Heian sources as essentially medieval cultural figures)—the identification of them as courtesans is significant because it provides additional clues as to the origins and transmission of tales of Izumi Shikibu and Ono no Komachi in the centuries after their deaths.

In the early 1930s, Yanagita Kunio argued that in the medieval period the term *yūjo* carried greater connotations of "wandering entertainer" than it did of "prostitute," signifying itinerant women singers, dancers, storytellers and puppeteers.[30] According to this sanitized construction of the term, Izumi Shikibu's and Ono no Komachi's identifications as *yūjo* reflect their accomplishments as poets and entertainers more than their reputations for promiscuity. In the *otogizōshi Koshikibu*, Izumi Shikibu is indeed represented as a kind of female entertainer in that she dances before an audience, both at court and at a shrine (fig. 8, depicting a shrine dance so fine that "the building itself began to tremble").[31] Yanagita's desexualized interpretation is un-

[29]See Izumi Shikibu's *"Ise no kami"* poem in *Kotohara* in the translations section of this book.

[30]Yanagita Kunio, "Ukareme," in *Josei to minkan denshō* (1932), reprinted in *Teihon Yanagita Kunio shū*, vol. 8 (Tokyo: Chikuma Shobō, 1962), 353–55.

[31]Izumi Shikibu is said to have performed the "Dance of the Rainbow Skirt and the Feather Robe" (*Geishōui no mai*), supposedly a dance of Chinese empresses. See *Koshikibu* in the translations, pp. 290–91.

Fig. 8. Izumi Shikibu dancing at the Kyoto Izumoji Dōso Shrine. From *Koshikibu* (Taku Library text, ca. eighteenth century). Courtesy of the Taku City Archives (Taku-shi Kyōdo Shiryōkan), Saga Prefecture.

convincing, however, because it fails to account for the description of Izumi Shikibu's disguise in *Kotohara* as that of a "lurid" (*hashitanaki*) *yūkun*, or Ono no Komachi's description in *Komachi no sōshi* as a "lascivious" (*irogonomi*) *yūjo*.[32] Furthermore, in the aforementioned *Jōruri monogatari* episode in which Izumi Shikibu prostitutes herself for religious merit by fulfilling a vow to sleep with one thousand men, Izumi Shikibu is said to have erected a shack on Kyoto's Fifth Avenue, renowned in the fifteenth and later centuries for its many streetwalkers.[33] Like *asobi*, *kugutsu*, and other entertainers famed for both prostitution and the performing arts, Izumi Shikibu and Ono

[32]NKBT 38:86.

[33]The *Jōruri monogatari* account is discussed in chapter eight. Shiba Kayono cites passages from *Kanmon nikki* (1422), *Shichijūichi-ban shokunin utaawase* (ca. 1500), *Sarugaku dangi* (1430), and other sources identifying Fifth Avenue with prostitution. Shiba Kayono, "Izumi Shikibu: Muromachi-ki ni okeru monogatari no hirogari," *Kokubungaku: kaishaku to kanshō* 61, no. 5 (May 1996), 51b–53a. Also see Gotō Toshihiko, "Tachigimi, tsujigimi: Muromachi jidai kyōraku no yūjo-tachi," in "Yūjo, kugutsu, shirabyōshi," ed. Amino Yoshihiko and Gotō Toshihiko, *Shūkan Asahi hyakka: Nihon no rekishi* 4 (Chūsei 1), no. 3 (April 1986), 86–91.

no Komachi are thus likely to have been identified as *yūjo* for their imagined promiscuity as well as their reputations as poets.

To some extent, Izumi Shikibu and Ono no Komachi may have been predisposed to their medieval designations by their representations in Heian textual sources. The headnote to a poem in Izumi Shikibu's personal poetic anthology, for example, reports that Fujiwara no Michinaga once wrote "the fan of an *ukareme*" (a synonym for *asobi*) on Izumi Shikibu's fan, presumably in reference to her many affairs.[34] Like the verse that inspired the *Kotohara* tale of mice in the *koto*, this incident alone may have led to Izumi Shikibu's later identification as a *yūjo*. Terry Kawashima suggests that Ono no Komachi was associated with *asobi* as early as the mid-Heian-period *Tamatsukuri Komachi shi sōsuisho* (The Prosperity and Decline of Tamatsukuri Komachi), which describes her family's occupation as that of "*shōka*," a term "used for a household whose livelihood is singing and performance, with the women commonly engaged in prostitution."[35] In the late tenth- or early eleventh-century *Yūjoki* (Record of *Asobi*), Ōe no Masafusa (1041–1111) contends that *asobi* are "later manifestations of Sotoorihime," by which he presumably refers to their physical charms.[36] Whether by accident or design, his words echo Ki no Tsurayuki's famous summation of Ono no Komachi as being "of the line of Sotoorihime."[37]

While it is important not to discount the possible influence of Heian-period works on Izumi Shikibu's and Ono no Komachi's later literary identities, it may also have been the case that these Heian women authors were cast as courtesans because their names and poetry were used in preaching and storytelling by and/or to *yūjo*. As we have seen in the introduction, Yanagita Kunio argued that mendicant women singers and storytellers, including *yūjo*, traveled throughout Japan in the medieval period recounting tales of Izumi Shikibu, Ono no Komachi, Sei Shōnagon and others, and that over time, the storytellers came to be identified with the women in their stories. If this was indeed the case, then the inverse effect—that the women in the stories came to be identified with their *yūjo* storytellers—is likely to have occurred as well. Sarah Strong follows a similar train of thought in suggesting that before its written composition, *Komachi no sōshi* may have been performed orally by *azusa miko* ("itinerant female shamans," Strong explains, with whom "the *yūjo* were closely linked"), and that these women may have

[34] *Izumi Shikibu shū* (*seishū* textual line; SKT 3:1:252a, poem 225). The headnote and the poem are discussed in Saeki Junko, *Yūjo no bunkashi* (Tokyo: Chūō Kōronsha, 1987), 63.

[35] Terry Kawashima, *Writing Margins: The Textual Construction of Gender in Heian and Kamakura Japan* (Cambridge: Harvard University Asia Center, 2001), 133.

[36] NST 8:154.

[37] SNKBT 5:14 (from the Japanese preface to *Kokin wakashū*, ca. 905).

identified Ono no Komachi as a *yūjo* within the narrative as a means of establishing a kind of "pro-*yūjo* discourse."[38] Alternately, Yamamoto Takashi has called attention to the possible use of Izumi Shikibu tales by the priests of Tennōji and Enkyōji Temples in preaching to the *asobi* of Eguchi, Kanzaki, and Muro no Tomari.[39] According to this theory, the monks may have chosen to misrepresent Izumi Shikibu and Ono no Komachi as courtesans—*yūjo* of the court, so to speak—as a *hōben*: an expedient means of adapting their tales to suit their audience. Izumi Shikibu's and Ono no Komachi's identifications as *yūjo* in Muromachi fiction, then, might represent a later, residual effect of the women's use in medieval preaching.

In recent years, scholars have argued that there may not have been a great difference between some professional courtesan-entertainers and Heian women of the court, either in life or fiction. Although one can imagine that Sei Shōnagon would have vehemently disagreed, Hitomi Tonomura has written that "there was only a little distance between court ladies—expected to mother aristocratic offspring—and outside entertainers. Both were sexually available to male aristocrats and similarly highly accomplished in literature, the arts, and music."[40] Likewise, Yamamoto Takashi has proposed that "in the world of *setsuwa*, the gap between these two classes of women seems to have been surprisingly narrow," due to perceived similarities in their dress and behavior.[41] Amino Yoshihiko has addressed the issue, and he suggests that as a class of entertainers, *asobi* may have their roots in the *jokan*, cultivated serving women of the early court.[42]

Whatever their origins, *asobi* themselves seem to have identified with Izumi Shikibu and Ono no Komachi (or their poetry, at least) in the late-Heian and early Kamakura periods. As an example, the Buddhist *setsuwa* anthology *Hosshinshū* (Accounts of Awakenings to Faith), compiled by the poet-priest Kamo no Chōmei ca. 1212–16, contains a story of an *asobi* who appeals to a priest for guidance by reciting Izumi Shikibu's "darkness into darkness" poem, much in the way that Izumi Shikibu is said to have appealed to Shōkū Shōnin before her:

[38]Sarah M. Strong, "Reading the 'Court' in Courtesan: The Historicization of the Role of Yūjo in Some Muromachi Tales," *Proceedings of the Midwest Association for Japanese Literary Studies* 4 (Summer 1998), 245–49.

[39]See p. 46, fn. 61.

[40]Hitomi Tonomura, "Re-envisioning Women in the Kamakura Age," in *The Origins of Japan's Medieval World*, ed. Jeffrey P. Mass (Stanford: Stanford University Press, 1997), 160.

[41]Yamamoto Takashi, "Dōmyō to Izumi Shikibu no setsuwa," *Kokugo to kokubungaku* 57, no. 3 (1980), 43b.

[42]Amino Yoshihiko, "Yūjo to hinin/kawaramono," in *Sei to mibun*, ed. Miyata Noboru (Tokyo: Shunshūsha, 1989), 93–128; discussed in Kawashima, *Writing Margins*, 29.

How a *Yūkun* of Muro no Tomari Sang a Salacious Song and Established a Karmic Link with a Holy Man[43]

In the not-so-distant past there was a holy man by the name of Shōshō Hijiri.[44] One night when he happened to be staying in a place called Muro in Harima province, as the moon shone down brightly through a cloudless sky, *asobi* passed by him [in their boats], one after another, singing their songs. "How moving!" the holy man thought, whereupon an *asobi* rowed toward his own vessel. The oarsman angrily shouted: "No, no! This is a priest's boat! You must be confused."

"Of course I see," the *asobi* replied. "Why should I make such a mistake?" Tapping her hand drum, she sang the following song two or three times:

kuraki yori	From darkness
kuraki michi ni zo	into a path of darkness
irinubeki	I must enter—
haruka ni terase	shine your light afar,
yama no ha no tsuki	moon on the mountain ridge!

The woman spoke: "That I have fallen into such a sinful state must be the result of some previous transgression. [For me,] this world looks to end in dreams of darkness.[45] Please, you must save me. With all my heart I join a karmic link to you." The woman rowed away.

"I was overcome with emotion," the holy man later said, "and I wept."

The account is a vivid description of an *asobi* at her trade. Rowing alongside the boats of potential customers, *asobi* would sing and perform sexual favors on the rivers and bays of busy harbor towns. The "customer" in this case is a priest, bound by vows of celibacy, which is why his oarsman rudely attempts to turn her away. Recalling tales, perhaps, of how Izumi Shikibu overcame Shōkū Shōnin's refusal to meet with her by entreating him to

[43]SNKS *Hosshinshū*, 280–81 (account 6:10). The present tale is also contained in Kakunyo's *Shūi kotokuden ekotoba* (within section 7:6), compiled in 1301. Yamamoto Isao, ed., *Kōsō meicho zenshū*, vol. 10 (Tokyo: Heibonsha, 1931), 186. Miki Sumito proposes that "salacious song" (*tei-kyoku*) refers to the manner in which the poem was sung (or that it was sung by an *asobi*), rather than to the poem itself (SNKS *Hosshinshū*, 280, note 4).

[44]Minamoto no Tokinobu, otherwise known as Shōshō Hijiri, "the Lesser-Captain Holy Man." A son of Minamoto no Masanobu (920–93), Tokinobu rose to the position of Junior Fifth Rank, Lower Grade, Lesser Captain of the Right before taking Buddhist vows at the age of 19. In 1013, he founded Shōrin'in Temple in the Ōhara district of the capital.

[45]The *asobi* uses the word *yume* ("dreams") to signify delusion, and *yami* ("darkness") as a form of the verb *yamu*, "to end."

"light her way" (discussed in chapters four and five), the *asobi* chants Izumi Shikibu's "darkness into darkness" poem, enjoining a karmic link to the holy man. *Asobi* are known for composing *waka*—the imperial anthologies *Goshūi wakashū* (Later Gleanings of Japanese Poetry; compiled in 1086) and *Shinkokin wakashū* (New Collection of Poems Past and Present; 1205) contain poems attributed to them[46]—but the *asobi* here sings Izumi Shikibu's verse to the beat of her hand drum as if she were singing an *imayō*.

The tale is of unknown historicity, but if not a complete fabrication, it is significant in that it demonstrates an *asobi*'s familiarity with Izumi Shikibu's "darkness into darkness" composition, and the *asobi*'s seeming identification of her own situation (being turned away from the holy man's boat) with Izumi Shikibu's situation vis-à-vis Shōkū Shōnin at the Enkyōji Temple gate (Izumi Shikibu is said to have been denied entrance because she was a woman). Muro no Tomari is in the Enkyōji Temple vicinity, but whether or not this particular *asobi* (if there ever even was such an *asobi*) heard the tale of Izumi Shikibu and Shōkū Shōnin from the priests of Enkyōji, as Yamamoto Takashi might suggest, is impossible to tell. However, there is substantial evidence that the Izumi Shikibu/Shōkū Shōnin account was used in preaching—probably to women—by both Tendai and Pure Land Buddhist proselytizers in the Kamakura and Muromachi periods, and considering Enkyōji's role in the tale, the priests there likely employed it in their own efforts to preach. There is in fact a stone memorial to Izumi Shikibu on the slope beside the Kaisandō Hall at Enkyōji inscribed with the date "twenty-sixth day of the tenth month of the first year of Tenpuku [1233]," suggesting Izumi Shikibu's importance to Enkyōji Temple in the thirteenth century.[47] Kamo no Chōmei's *Hosshinshū* account, dating to within some twenty years of the Izumi Shikibu memorial, might thus demonstrate the deep impression made by the Enkyōji preachers upon the courtesan-entertainers of their surrounding towns.

A similar story concerning an *asobi* and her recitation of a poem by Ono no Komachi is contained in the poetic anthology *Shinsen rōeishū* (New Selection of Verse to Sing), compiled by Fujiwara no Mototoshi ca. 1113–18. Like the preceding *Hosshinshū* account, it reveals an *asobi*'s seemingly personal identification with the poetry and persona of a famous woman poet of the Heian court:

[46]*Goshūi wakashū* 1197 (SNKBT 8:389), attributed to "the *asobi* Miyagi," and *Shinkokin wakashū* 979 (SNKBT 11:293), attributed to "the *asobi* Tae."

[47]Saijō Shizuo discusses the monument at length in *Izumi Shikibu densetsu to sono koseki*, vol. 3 (Tokyo: Kindai Bungeisha, 1999), 72–75. *Shosha-zan engi* (1644) alludes to it in connection with Izumi Shikibu's "darkness into darkness" poem (DNBZ 117:261b [87:68a]).

> Once when an *asobi* sought to board a merchant vessel, a boatman took up an oar and splashed her with water. Covering her face with a sleeve, she wept and chanted the following poem by Ono no Komachi:

kokoro kara	Since first boarding
ukitaru fune ni	in my heart
norisomete	this wretched, bobbing boat,
hitohi mo nami ni	there is not a day
nurenu hi zo naki	I am not soaked with waves of tears.[48]

The scene is set in an undisclosed part of Japan, and the *asobi*'s name is unknown. The bobbing boat is a metaphor for Komachi's rocky relationship with a man, but for the woman who makes her living on the water, and in this case is drenched by the cruel boatman, the image has a literal significance as well. Shiba Kayono observes that many of Ono no Komachi's poems may have resonated with mendicant *yūjo*, who perhaps perceived in them articulations of the sadness of their own rootless, drifting lives.[49] The number and variety of love poems attributed to Ono no Komachi and Izumi Shikibu are also likely to have contributed to *yūjo*'s identification with the Heian women poets, and the poets' identifications as *yūjo*.

In the early Muromachi-period noh plays *Tōboku* and *Seiganji*, Izumi Shikibu reveals herself to be a human manifestation of Kabu no Bosatsu, the Bodhisattva of Song and Dance.[50] Izumi Shikibu may have achieved this designation as a result of her medieval reputation for poetry and dancing, or she may have been identified as such as a result of her popular association with *yūjo*, for whom "Kabu no Bosatsu" appears to have been a euphemism in the Edo period (and possibly before).[51] The representation might also

[48]GR 12:336a. The poem is also contained in *Gosen wakashū* (poem 779), where it is attributed to "Komachi" with the headnote, "[Composed] when a certain man had come to seem increasingly unkind." It is also contained in *Komachi shū* (SKT 3:1:21b, poem 2). *Ukitaru*, a form of the verb *uku*, "to float," suggests *uki*, "wretched." *Nami* ("waves") is suggestive of *namida* ("tears").

[49]Shiba Kayono, "Ono no Komachi to Izumi Shikibu: yūjo-zō wo megutte," in *Hashi no e: dai yonjū yon kai kōen* (program for a noh performance, Nihon Nōgaku Geijutsu Shinkōkai [Tokyo], December 1994), 4a.

[50]SNKBZ 58:255, and SNKBT 57:551, respectively. *Tōboku* and *Seiganji* have both been attributed to Zeami (1363?–1443?), but in recent years his authorship of the works has come into question. If not by Zeami, the plays at least date from around Zeami's time. See Tanaka Makoto, "Izumi Shikibu to yōkyoku," *Kokugo to kokubungaku* (April 1946), 13a, and Ishiguro Kichijirō, "Yōkyoku to Izumi Shikibu," *Kokubungaku: kaishaku to kyōzai no kenkyū* 35, no. 12 (October 1990), 103–5.

[51]*Nihon kokugo daijiten* lists examples from *Haifū yanagidaru* (vol. 65, which dates from ca. 1799), and from the *kabuki* play *Ukiyogara hiyoku no inazuma* (first performed in 1823). Nihon Daijiten Kankōkai, *Nihon kokugo daijiten*, vol. 5 (Tokyo: Shōgakukan, 1973), 73b.

reflect a common feeling among medieval *yūjo*, who, as a result of various late-Heian and Kamakura-period proselytizing activities, may have looked to Izumi Shikibu as a kind of patron saint of courtesan-entertainers. The designation may be simply coincidental—the male poet Ariwara no Narihira, for example, who has no obvious connection to *yūjo*, is also said to have been a manifestation of Kabu no Bosatsu (which is why, according to a supernatural woman in the noh play *Kakitsubata*, his poetry is capable of causing even grasses and trees to attain Buddhahood)[52]—but if not, it would help to explain the apparent self-identification of the *asobi* in the *Hosshinshū* account with Izumi Shikibu and her "darkness into darkness" poem. Furthermore, it would fit the larger pattern of medieval uses and representations of Izumi Shikibu, Ono no Komachi, and other Heian women authors in the Buddhist instruction of women.

In *Kotohara*, Izumi Shikibu's representation as a *yūjo* extends beyond the description of her initial disguise. As the tale continues, she writes to Dōmyō, coyly revealing her deception at the inn on the road from Ise. Dōmyō is at first perturbed, but he warms to her advances, and the two begin a clandestine affair: "Entrusting her hopes to [the deity at] Sumiyoshi Bay," the narrator explains, "Izumi Shikibu took to frequenting Dōmyō's abode, and in no time at all the two had become a subject of gossip." There is an illustration in Go-Hanazono's picture scroll of four women in a boat—Izumi Shikibu and her attendants—staring out over the water like *asobi* on the lookout for customers (fig. 9). Approaching the shore at Sumiyoshi Shrine, Izumi Shikibu makes her way to Dōmyō at Tennōji Temple. Because a proper lady of the court would receive visits from a man but never make them herself, she is indeed like a *yūjo* in this scene, as she is in the late thirteenth-century *Shasekishū* account of her sexual pursuit of Dōmyō to his Hōrinji Temple hermitage, and to Kaseyama as well (discussed in the previous chapter).

Izumi Shikibu's faith in the "deity at Sumiyoshi" is moreover telling. While the Sumiyoshi Deity is well-known as a god of poetry, Ōe no Masafusa explains in his late tenth- or early eleventh-century *Yūjoki* that the shrine was known in the Heian period as an important site for the worship of the roadside deity Hyakudayū:

> To the south [of Eguchi, Kashima, and Kanzaki] is Sumiyoshi, and to the west, Hirota. These are places where *asobi* pray for help in attracting men. Hyakudayū, whom *asobi* worship in particular, is

[52]SNKBT 57:302–3.

Fig. 9. Izumi Shikibu and her attendants approach Sumiyoshi Shrine. From *Kotohara ekotoba* (fifteenth century), in the Higashiyama Go-bunko Archive. Courtesy of the Archives and Mausolea Department of the Japanese Imperial Household Agency (Kunaichō Shoryōbu).

> a roadside deity. Statues of him are carved in numbers reaching into the hundreds and thousands.[53]

In *Koshikibu,* Izumi Shikibu turns to the roadside deity of Izumoji Dōso Shrine to pray for reconciliation with her husband. In *Kotohara,* she sails into Sumiyoshi Bay with the possible intent of calling on Hyakudayū, venerated among *kugutsu* and *asobi,* for his help in seducing Dōmyō. In this way she sails, both literally and thematically, into the second part of the tale: an alternate and elaborate rendition of the *Uji Shūi monogatari / Kojidan* account of Izumi Shikibu, Dōmyō, and the Fifth Avenue Roadside Deity.

The Wrong Deity?

In its second part, *Kotohara* begins with a curious change of tone. Dōmyō is referred to by the title of *Ajari,* "Esoteric Master," whereas before, in the

[53]NST 8:155. The dictionary *Iroha jiruishō* (ca. 1144–81) lists Hyakudayū as a resident deity of Hirota Shrine; aside from *Yūjoki,* there are no known records of Hyakudayū worship at Sumiyoshi. See NST 8:446a, and Takigawa Masajirō, *Yūjo no rekishi* (Tokyo: Shibundō, 1965), 125–26.

first part of the tale, he had been called simply "Dōmyō," or "Dōmyō *Hōshi*" ("Priest Dōmyō"). The shift occurs precisely at the break between the first and second stories, marked only by a short transitional narrative passage and the illustration of Izumi Shikibu in her boat, suggesting that the *Kotohara* author combined two preexisting accounts without effecting substantial alterations.[54] The tale begins with a brief biographical introduction:

> Now this Dōmyō Ajari was the son of Major Captain of the Right Michitsuna, and the grandson of Higashi Sanjō Chancellor Kaneie.[55] Michitsuna was by his nature a man of utmost refinement, and his son, Dōmyō, was handsome from childhood. After entering the priesthood, Dōmyō was appointed intendant of Tennōji Temple. He was a priest of ability and ideals, far above the usual run of men. He could recite numerous sutras by heart, and as he especially excelled at chanting the scriptures, his sutra-readings were without parallel. However, despite all these of his most excellent capacities, Dōmyō's heart was filled with lust of a most disgraceful sort—such as was not in the least befitting his character.

As its opening lines suggest, the second part of *Kotohara* is more concerned with Dōmyō—both his sins and his sutra chanting—than it is with Izumi Shikibu and the magical potency of Japanese verse. Nevertheless, there is a formal and thematic continuity to the work as a whole, demonstrated in the uniform style of the calligraphy and the illustrations, as well as in the narrator's concern with both the progression of Izumi Shikibu and Dōmyō's affair and the wondrous powers of ritual language:

> Other strange, miraculous events occurred as well. Without fail, Dōmyō would chant the sutras at set times within each six-hour period of the day and night.[56] As he was chanting one night, he was surprised to hear someone moving about in his garden. "Who's there?" he asked.
>
> "I am an old man who lives in the area around Fifth Avenue and Tōin [Road]," someone replied. "I come every night to hear you perform your midnight devotions. Did you not know?"

[54]It is also possible within the context of *Kotohara* that Dōmyō did not receive the title *Ajari* until after presenting his poem at court, but this seems unlikely considering that *Hitokuchi monogatari* never refers to him as *Ajari*, whereas the *Uji shūi monogatari*, *Kojidan*, *Zōtanshū*, and *Tōsai zuihitsu* accounts of Izumi Shikibu, Dōmyō, and the Fifth Avenue Roadside Deity all do.

[55]Fujiwara no Michitsuna (955–1020) was appointed Major Captain in the Office of Bodyguards in the twelfth month of 996. Fujiwara no Kaneie (929–90) was Chancellor for less than one year, in 990.

[56]According to traditional calculations, days were composed of twelve "hours": six in the daytime and six at night.

Fig. 10. The Gojōten Shrine Deity listens to Dōmyō recite. From *Kotohara ekotoba* (fifteenth century), in the Higashiyama Go-bunko Archive. Courtesy of the Archives and Mausolea Department of the Japanese Imperial Household Agency (Kunaichō Shoryōbu).

> Dōmyō was suspicious. "It's a long way from here to the capital," he said. "How could an old man like you come this far every night? And what's your name?"
>
> The old man was none other than the god Sukunahikona, and as there was nowhere he had to be, from that time on he came to listen whenever Dōmyō chanted the sutras. And so although Dōmyō was a man of such shameful inclinations, he must have accumulated a great deal of merit, for his morning and evening devotions never varied and he practiced them unfailingly for years on end. His sutra chanting was as music, and all who heard it were moved to the depths of their hearts. "There are many who chant scripture," people would say, "but none surpass this priest." Perhaps it was for this reason that his chanting could touch even the heart of a god.

The old man is revealed to be Sukunahikona, the deity of Gojōten Shrine at the intersection of Kyoto's Fifth Avenue and Nishinotōin Road.[57] The *Kotohara* illustration (fig. 10) shows him as a well-dressed, whiskered old man

[57]The shrine is presently located at Nishinotōin Matsuhara, immediately to the north of the Fifth Avenue-Nishinotōin intersection.

with drooping eyebrows and a wrinkled face. Holding a fan, he listens with a slightly bowed head as Dōmyō recites from a manuscript by the light of a standing lamp. The painted reeds on the wall of Dōmyō's room mirror the living grasses outside; flowers of an indeterminate variety—lilies, perhaps—bloom by the rocks near where the deity sits.

A map in Tōin Kinkata's mid-fourteenth-century encyclopedia *Shūgaishō* (Gathered Scraps of Notes) shows Gojōten Shrine located directly opposite the shrine of the Fifth Avenue Roadside Deity, and it was perhaps because of the two shrines' proximity that their deities were confused.[58] In most versions of the *Kotohara* account (including those in *Uji shūi monogatari*, *Kojidan*, and the noh play *Dōmyō Hōshi*), Dōmyō's visitor is the Fifth Avenue Roadside Deity; but in Mujū Ichien's *Zōtanshū* (Miscellaneous Tales; 1305), the visitor is identified as Gojō no Tenjin (Sukunahikona), as he is in *Kotohara*.[59] Yamamoto Takashi argues that the deity's original and correct designation is the Fifth Avenue Roadside Deity, because as a god of sexuality, a roadside deity would tie together the two themes of a monk breaking his vows and a deity benefiting from a recitation of the *Lotus Sutra* in a way that an ordinary deity (Sukunahikona) would not.[60] Moreover, within the larger context of the *Kotohara* picture scroll, the appearance of a roadside deity would seemingly resonate with Izumi Shikibu's disguise as a *yūjo* (known for worshipping the roadside deity Hyakudayū), as well as with her visit to Sumiyoshi, where she may have called upon Hyakudayū for his help in seducing Dōmyō.

Kotohara continues:

> One night Dōmyō stayed with Izumi Shikibu in the capital. They talked of various things until the break of dawn, at which time Dōmyō set about his sutra-recitations. After he had been at it for a while, he began to think to himself, "I wonder if that god isn't listening again. I should tell Izumi Shikibu about him and really give her a taste of the fantastic." And so after finishing his routine, Dōmyō called out to the god: "Are you there again tonight?" There was no reply. Dōmyō thought this strange.

[58]The map is reproduced in Yamamoto Takashi, "Dōmyō to Izumi Shikibu no setsuwa," 50a. Earlier evidence of the proximity of Gojōten Shrine and the shrine of the Fifth Avenue Roadside Deity (and the association of the two deities) is contained in *Konjaku monogatari shū* and *Uji shūi monogatari*: in *Konjaku* 20:3 (SNKBT 36:227), the narrator describes a certain location as "the place of the Fifth Avenue Roadside Deity," while in the corresponding *Uji shūi monogatari* account (1:32; SNKBT 42:72), the narrator describes that same location as "the area of Gojō no Tenjin."

[59]Yamada Shōzen and Miki Sumito, eds., *Zōtanshū* (Tokyo: Miyai Shoten, 1980), 233–34. In the fifteenth-century *Tōsai zuihitsu* account (in the *kōshokurui* section), the deity is left unnamed.

[60]Yamamoto Takashi, "Dōmyō to Izumi Shikibu no setsuwa," 49a.

> In the early morning hours of a certain day Dōmyō chanted a *dharani* with exceptional skill.[61] His tone was exquisite, and as time passed he came to have a feeling in his bones that someone was listening. At that most poignant time of day, when the light of the twilight moon shines down through the pines at Suminoe and "moonlit waves of dawn lap against the Golden Shore,"[62] Dōmyō sensed someone moving just beyond his door. He thought that perhaps the god had returned. "Are you there again?" Dōmyō called out after finishing his recitations. In a wondrous voice, the deity replied that he was.
>
> Dōmyō spoke: "The other night when I was with Izumi Shikibu in the capital, I called out to you at dawn and you didn't answer. It seems strange, especially considering how close I was to your shrine. And you say you come here at such a distance every night. How is this?"
>
> "What you say is true," the deity replied. "The closer you are to the capital the better. But when you stay with Izumi Shikibu, the impurity of your wanton deeds is repugnant to me. I do not approach when you engage in such acts, be they ever so infrequent."
>
> Such miraculous events are said to have occurred in the past, and stories of them are told to this day.

With these words, the *Kotohara* picture scroll comes to an end. Because Dōmyō's mysterious visitor is Sukunahikona, he is offended by Dōmyō's defilement in a way that a roadside deity would not have been.

The child psychologist-*cum*-literary critic Bruno Bettelheim maintains that European fairy tales tend to "describe inner states of the mind by means of images and actions." "In fairy tales," Bettelheim explains, "internal processes are translated into visual images. When the hero is confronted by difficult inner problems which seem to defy solution, his psychological state is not described; the fairy story shows him lost in a dense, impenetrable wood, not knowing which way to turn, despairing of finding a way out."[63] The same is often true of *otogizōshi*, many of which function on a symbolic level by depicting inner psychological states and spiritual abstractions as external, concrete phenomena. In the late Muromachi-period *Isozaki* (Isozaki), for

[61]*Dharani* are esoteric Buddhist incantations employed for their practical, magical properties.

[62]This is a slight misquotation of the first two lines of the "Late-night Praise" (*Goyasan*) section of *Gokuraku rokujisan*, a Pure Land hymn attributed to Genshin (942–1017). Takano Tatsuyuki, ed., *Nihon kayō shūsei*, vol. 4 (Tokyo: Tōkyōdō, 1942), 100c. The same two lines are used as the headnote to *Shinkokin wakashū* 1969. "The Golden Shore" (*kogane no kishi*) is the shore of the seven–jeweled lake in Amida Buddha's Pure Land Paradise.

[63]Bruno Bettelheim, *The Uses of Enchantment: The Meaning and Importance of Fairy Tales* (New York: Alfred A. Knopf, 1976), 155.

example, a woman dons a demon mask before bludgeoning her husband's mistress to death; then, after the murder, she finds that she can no longer remove the disguise. Her outer, physical transformation mirrors the psychological transformation wrought within her as a result of her monstrous act. The woman's eventual ability to remove the demon mask—her re-achievement of humanity as a result of her son's Buddhist preaching—similarly suggests her internal spiritual redemption.[64]

In the case of the *Kotohara* account of Dōmyō, Izumi Shikibu, and Sukunahikona (as well as its corresponding *Uji shūi monogatari/Kojidan setsuwa*), the intangible benefits of Buddhist devotional practice (chanting *dharani* and the *Lotus Sutra*) are manifested as the appearance of Sukunahikona. Likewise, the deleterious effects of Dōmyō's violation of his vows, suggested by his recitation of the *Lotus Sutra* in a state of impurity, are concretized as his alienation of the god. Though by contemporary standards the tale is implausibly fantastic, it rings true psychologically, for although Dōmyō senses the presence of the divine when he performs his devotions properly, he loses that sensation when he violates his precepts.

While much of the symbolic significance of the earlier *Uji shūi monogatari/Kojidan* account is preserved in *Kotohara*, a part of it has been lost: because the deity is Sukunahikona, he is repulsed by Dōmyō's defilement, and one of the original Buddhist lessons—that there is always merit in reciting the *Lotus Sutra*, because in even the most sinful of circumstances, a lesser deity might come to listen—is cut from the work. Although it is impossible to say for certain that Sukunahikona is the "wrong deity" in *Kotohara*, his presence in Go-Hanazono's fifteenth-century manuscript probably reflects confusion in the medieval transposition of the tale from its Buddhist-didactic origins to its later, largely secular literary form.[65]

[64] *Isozaki* is typeset and annotated in SNKBZ 63:328–53 (Keiō University manuscript).

[65] Incidentally, several of the *Kotohara* illustrations are closely related to those in the *Shitamoe monogatari* picture scroll, attributed to Tosa Mitsunobu (fl. ca. 1469–1522). The relationship between the two works is unclear. Mitsunobu's *Shitamoe monogatari emaki* is photographically reproduced in *Muromachi monogatari shū* (Tokyo: Nihon Koten Bungakukai, 1990), 9–27.

Chapter Three
Incest and Enlightenment: the *Otogizōshi Izumi Shikibu*

At some time in the late Muromachi period, an anonymous author composed a short work of creative fiction by the name of *Izumi Shikibu*. While in many respects typical of the popular literature of its time, the tale breaks radical new ground in the evolving lore of Izumi Shikibu and her affair with the priest Dōmyō. In this most fanciful of fanciful tales, Dōmyō is reported to have been Izumi Shikibu's long-lost son by a childhood liaison with Tachibana no Yasumasa, an invented lover whose name is a combination of those of Izumi Shikibu's two historical husbands, Tachibana no Michisada and Fujiwara no Yasumasa.[1] Several scholars have proposed explanations for this genealogical misinformation. Yanagita Kunio, for one, has suggested that Izumi Shikibu was identified as Dōmyō's mother because of suppositions, inspired by records of a certain poetic exchange, that she had an affair with Dōmyō's father, Fujiwara no Michitsuna.[2] Alternately, Nagai Yoshinori has observed that the characterization may have resulted from confusion between Izumi Shikibu's (possible) son Eikaku, who was the thirty-ninth intendant of Tennōji Temple, and Dōmyō, who was the twenty-seventh.[3] Yanagita's and Nagai's explanations are logical—reasonable, in fact—but they fail to take into account the irreverent, playful tone of the work as a whole. With this in mind, it seems equally likely that Dōmyō's identification

[1]According to the Shibukawa *Izumi Shikibu* text, that is. The Shimizu text calls him "Tachibana no Hōshō Yasumasa," giving both the Sinified and Japanese readings of his personal name; the Matsui text calls him "Tachibana no Shōshō Yasumasa," Lesser Captain Tachibana no Yasumasa. See the appendix at the end of this book for a list of these and other extant *Izumi Shikibu* manuscripts. In addition to the Shibukawa *Izumi Shikibu* text, *Sangoku denki* 1:27 and the noh play *Izumi Shikibu* (also known as *Shosha*) associate Izumi Shikibu with "Tachibana no Yasumasa."

[2]Yanagita Kunio, *Josei to minkan denshō* (1932), reprinted in *Teihon Yanagita Kunio shū*, vol. 8 (Tokyo: Chikuma Shobō, 1962), 371. The poetic exchange between Izumi Shikibu and Michitsuna is recorded in *Izumi Shikibu shū* (*seishū* textual line; SKT 3:1:252b, poems 237, 238, and 239) and *Mandai wakashū* (Kamakura period; SKT 2:1:440c, poem 2009). The *Izumi Shikibu shū* poems are preceded by an ambiguous headnote, which Okada Yoshio discusses at length in "Izumi Shikibu no ren'ai seikatsu (2)," *Kokugo kokubun no kenkyū* 24 (1928): 21–28.

[3]Nagai Yoshinori, "Izumi Shikibu no ko: Eikaku Ajari denkō," *Kokubungaku tōsa* (Taishō Daigaku) 7 (March 1963), 9.

as Izumi Shikibu's son is simply a willful misrepresentation: a falsehood on a par with the *Koshikibu* narrator's assertion that Izumi Shikibu was Murasaki Shikibu's daughter.

Izumi Shikibu is best known today for its inclusion in *Otogi bunko* (The Companion Library), a box-set anthology of twenty-three works of short medieval fiction published by the Osaka bookseller Shibukawa Seiemon ca. 1716–29.[4] Shibukawa's bookstore and publishing house, the Kashiwara-ya, seems to have specialized in educational texts for women; in the years surrounding his compilation of *The Companion Library*, Shibukawa is attributed with authoring and marketing such standards as *The Women's Writing Primer* (1698), *Elegant Writing for Women* (1721), and *Women's Mirror of Wisdom* (1729).[5] A Kashiwara-ya advertisement dating from around 1764 to 1772, some forty or fifty years after *The Companion Library*'s first publication, advertises the anthology as a "useful guide to women's self-improvement."[6] While it is true, as Barbara Ruch has noted, that many of the tales are of dubious hortative value ("stories of maiden-eating monsters and suicides," to borrow Ruch's characterization),[7] in the case of *Izumi Shikibu*, Shibukawa's interest in producing works for women is useful to bear in mind. With its poetry, simple illustrations, and scandalous plot, *Izumi Shikibu* describes the manner in which even the most heinous of social offenses can lead a woman to Buddhist enlightenment. Indeed, in its orientation and outlook, focused as they are on a woman's sin and salvation, *Izumi Shikibu* might be best described as a tale both of and for women.

Shibukawa Seiemon's *Izumi Shikibu* is an uncolored reproduction of a mid-seventeenth-century *tanrokubon* ("red and green book"), a woodblock-printed manuscript with distinctively red, green, yellow, and blue illustrations, dating from around 1655 to 1658. It begins by introducing Izumi Shikibu as a *yūjo*, or "courtesan." The earliest surviving *Izumi Shikibu* manuscript—the sixteenth-century Shimizu Yutaka *nara ehon*—identifies her as a *nyōbō*, or "court lady," suggesting that late-medieval copyists may have

[4]The term *otogizōshi* (companion books) derives from the name of Shibukawa's *Companion Library*. In 1801, Ozaki Masayoshi used the word in his *Gunsho ichiran* to refer to the tales in Shibukawa's collection. In 1830 and 1847, Kitamura Nobuyo and Santō Kyōzan used it to refer to Muromachi tales in general. See Tokuda Kazuo, ed., *Otogizōshi jiten* (Tokyo: Tōkyōdō Shuppan, 2002), 46 and 53–54; Tokuda Kazuo, *Otogizōshi kenkyū* (Tokyo: Miyai Shoten, 1988), 523; Barbara Ruch, "Origins of *The Companion Library*: An Anthology of Medieval Japanese Stories," *The Journal of Asian Studies* 30, no. 3 (May 1971): 593–610.

[5]*Onna-yō bunshō kōmoku*, *Onna bunshō takamakie*, and *Onna-yō chie kagami*, respectively. Tokuda, *Otogizōshi kenkyū*, 522.

[6]Tokuda, *Otogizōshi kenkyū*, 522; Ichiko Teiji, *Chūsei shōsetsu no kenkyū* (Tokyo: Tokyo Daigaku Shuppankai, 1995), 17.

[7] Ruch, "Origins of *The Companion Library*," 594.

made little distinction between the two. The Shibukawa text begins:

> At a time during the reign of Emperor Ichijō in the not-so-distant past, there was once in the flourishing capital a beautiful courtesan named Izumi Shikibu. Residing in the imperial palace was a man named Tachibana no Yasumasa, and from the time that he was nineteen and she thirteen, Yasumasa and Izumi Shikibu came to pledge wondrous vows of love.[8] They shared a deep affection, and in the spring of her fourteenth year Izumi Shikibu bore a son.
>
> Perhaps in whispered conversations with her lover she felt ashamed, for Izumi Shikibu abandoned her baby on Fifth Avenue Bridge. She wrote a poem on the hem of the baby's iris *kosode* swaddling clothes and left a short unsheathed sword by his side. A townsman adopted the infant, raised him, and later sent him to Mount Hiei to become a monk.[9]

According to the *otogizōshi Fuji no hitoana sōshi* (The Story of the Fuji Cave; Muromachi period), parents who abandon their babies are doomed to spend three million *kalpas* bearing, dismembering, and eating their own children in the realm of hungry ghosts.[10] Nevertheless, unwanted infants are commonly abandoned in Muromachi fiction, usually at temples, shrines, and other public places. In *Koshikibu*, for example, Izumi Shikibu leaves her own daughter at a Tōji Temple gate. In *Izumi Shikibu*, she chooses Fifth Avenue Bridge, but the significance of this is unclear. In addition to its medieval reputation for prostitutes, which both suits and suggests Izumi Shikibu's identification as a *yūjo*, it may represent a connection—being at Fifth Avenue—to the story of Izumi Shikibu, Dōmyō, and the Fifth Avenue Roadside Deity.[11] As Shiba Kayono has observed, the bridge is also propitiously close to the former site of Koyasu no Tō, the "Pagoda of Child Safety" (Taisanji in the Kiyomizu Temple complex), which may be

[8]According to the Shimizu and Matsui texts, Yasumasa was fifteen years old.

[9]This and the following translated passages are from NKBT 38:312–18 and NKBZ 36:384–93. The Shibukawa text is translated in full in the translations section of this book.

[10]MJMT 11:445b (former Akagi Bunko manuscript of 1603). The same punishment is said to be reserved for those who make a living (literally, "feed themselves") by selling older children. A *kalpa* is typically described as the length of time necessary for a heavenly being to wear away a 40-*ri* (hundred-square-mile) rock by brushing it with its silken sleeve once every one hundred years. Three million *kalpas* is thus a very long time.

[11]Several scholars have suggested this possibility. See Ōshima Tatehiko, "Dōsojin no shinkō to setsuwa," in *Chūsei bungaku no kenkyū*, ed. Akiyama Ken (Tokyo: Tokyo Daigaku Shuppankai, 1972), 62; Hamanaka Osamu, "Chūsei no Izumi Shikibu: Eizan no denshō yori," *Bukkyō bungaku* 12 (1988), 55a; Shiba Kayono, "*Izumi Shikibu*: Muromachi-ki ni okeru monogatari no hirogari," *Kokubungaku: kaishaku to kanshō* 61, no. 5 (May 1996), 52. On *yūjo* and Fifth Avenue Bridge, see fn. 33 on p. 63.

meaningful as well.[12] Whatever the significance of Fifth Avenue Bridge, the boy is duly adopted and sent off to Mount Hiei, headquarters of the Japanese Tendai Buddhist sect. In this he is like any number of fictional, abandoned children, including the famous warrior Benkei, the demon Shuten Dōji, and Little Atsumori, the orphaned child of Taira no Atsumori.[13]

As *Izumi Shikibu* continues, Izumi Shikibu's son achieves outstanding success, both at Enryakuji Temple on Mount Hiei and in society at large. His hyperbolic description is typical of the medieval *otogizōshi* style:

> The boy was deeply devoted to his studies—he was a child without peer—and of all the priests, there were none who did not hold him dear to their hearts. His reputation spread throughout all of Mount Hiei. His compassion, too, was of an extraordinary sort. Not only was he celebrated on the holy mountain, but as he diligently pursued the path of the Buddha, his name, Dōmyō Ajari,[14] spread far and wide and he came to be known throughout the land.
>
> When Dōmyō was eighteen years old, he once took part in a performance of the Eight Lectures of the *Lotus Sutra* at the imperial palace. A gusting wind blew up the bamboo blind of an adjoining room two or three times, revealing an elegant court lady of about thirty. Her eyebrows overflowed with charm as she listened to the priests' discussion, obviously engrossed. With but a single glance Dōmyō was overcome; upon returning to his home, ascending the mountain, he was captivated by the alluring image of the woman he had seen. That he could not forget her was the result of a karmic bond from a previous life.

In *The Tale of Genji*, the impetuous and ill-fated young Kashiwagi falls hopelessly in love with the Third Princess with but a single, accidental glance, setting in motion a disastrous chain of events.[15] The story is often repeated in *otogizōshi*—the sardine-monger Monkey Genji in *Saru Genji sōshi*, for example, cites it as a precedent for his own love-at-first-sight[16]—and for some

[12]Shiba, "Izumi Shikibu: Muromachi-ki ni okeru monogatari no hirogari," 52.

[13]See *Benkei monogatari* (SNKBT 55:199–287), *Ibuki Dōji* (SNKBT 54:185–213), and *Ko-Atsumori* (NKBT 38:229–40); also Hamanaka, "Chūsei no Izumi Shikibu," 56a–58a. Mount Hiei is not specifically mentioned in *Ko-Atsumori*, but Hamanaka explains that this is where Hōnen takes the boy to live.

[14]Actually "Dōmei" (an alternate reading of the characters in Dōmyō's name), which, for the sake of consistency, I have changed to "Dōmyō" in this and the following translated passages.

[15]SNKBT 21:296; NKBT 16:307; NKBZ 15:132; Edward Seidensticker, *The Tale of Genji* (New York: Alfred A. Knopf, 1991), 582–83.

[16]NKBT 38:168–69 and NKBZ 36:208–9. The story of Kashiwagi and the Third Princess is also alluded to in the *otogizōshi Jōruri monogatari* and *Kachō Fūgetsu* (MJMT 7:315b [former Akagi Bunko text]; MJMT 3:430a [former Takayasu Rokurō text of 1595]).

Fig. 11. Dōmyō spies Izumi Shikibu at a palace performance of the Eight Lectures of the *Lotus Sutra*. From *Izumi Shikibu* (Shibukawa text, early eighteenth century). Courtesy of the Kyoto Prefectural Library Archives (Kyōto Furitsu Sōgō Shiryōkan).

readers, Dōmyō's sudden fit of affection may have resonated ominously with Murasaki Shikibu's earlier tale. Ironically, Dōmyō's passion is said to have been the result of a karmic link, and indeed it is, but not from a previous life. The woman is Izumi Shikibu, although her identity is withheld from the reader (as well as from Dōmyō) until much later in the tale.[17]

The setting for Dōmyō's awakening to love is a performance of the Eight Lectures of the *Lotus Sutra*, or *Hokke hakkō*, which were something of a fad among the aristocracy in Izumi Shikibu's time.[18] In tenth- and eleventh-century performances, a number of priests (typically eight) would lecture on the eight fascicles of the *Lotus Sutra* over a period of four days. They would be questioned by a group of eight to twenty interrogators, often members of rival sects and institutions, and the ensuing debates would be evaluated by a panel of judges. *Hokke hakkō* were both elaborate ritual ceremonies and important social events; Fujiwara no Michinaga sponsored several himself, and his daughter, the empress Shōshi (in whose salon Izumi Shikibu

[17] In the Shimizu text, the woman is identified as Izumi Shikibu just before she enters Dōmyō's lodgings for the night. In the Shibukawa text, her name is not given until the morning after.

[18] Willa Jane Tanabe, "The Lotus Lectures: *Hokke hakkō* in the Heian Period," *Monumenta Nipponica* 39 (1984): 393–407.

served), is reported to have put on a particularly opulent one in the fifth month of 1026.[19]

The Shibukawa text contains a revealing illustration of the *Hokke hakkō* at which Dōmyō falls in love (fig. 11). The ceremony is a modest one. Four priests sit facing each other reciting from written scrolls. The priest in the bottom right corner—Dōmyō, perhaps—looks up from his sutra in the direction of a well-dressed court lady who listens from behind a screen in an adjoining room. Her long black hair trails over her elaborate robes, shaded red and orange in the colorful seventeenth-century *tanrokubon* text.[20] She is the only audience member visibly present.

Disguise and Persuasion

In the *otogizōshi Izumi Shikibu*, Dōmyō's monastic social status prevents him from easily approaching the woman at court. He thus resorts to subterfuge in order to make his feelings known:

> Dōmyō later returned to the capital. Hoping for a second glimpse of the lady he had seen and adored, he disguised himself as an orange-vendor, proceeded to the palace and set about selling his fruit. A servant-girl emerged from the room of the woman he had seen and asked to buy twenty *sen* worth. Dōmyō counted out twenty oranges and sold them to her, but rather than counting with words, he counted with love poems.

In his fruit-vendor disguise, Dōmyō recites love poems as he produces oranges.[21] Each verse begins with a number, the sound of which is echoed by the first word of each poem's second line (in the following translation, the last word of each poem's first line). As "counting poems" (*kazoeuta*),[22] they allow Dōmyō to both reckon his fruit and proclaim the pain of his unrequited love:

[19] According to *Hyakurenshō* (ca. 1259–74), in Kuroita Katsumi, ed., *Shintei zōho kokushi taikei*, vol. 11 (Tokyo: Yoshikawa Kōbunkan, 1929), 17 (pagination begins anew with the *Hyakurenshō* section in the middle of the volume); also noted in Tanabe, "The Lotus Lectures," 401.

[20] Three of the five *tanrokubon* illustrations are reproduced in color in Yoshida Kogorō, *Tanrokubon: Rare Books of Seventeenth-Century Japan*, trans. Mark A. Harbison (Tokyo: Kodansha International, 1984), 160–62.

[21] Dōmyō's appearance is remarkably similar to that of the fishmonger Monkey Genji in Shibukawa's *Saru Genji sōshi* woodblock illustrations, suggesting the credibility of Dōmyō's disguise. Compare the images in NKBT 38:166 and 315, and NKBZ 36:205 and 389.

[22] The term *kazoeuta* denotes poems that follow a *"hitotsu to ya"*/*"futatsu to ya"*-type enumerative pattern, and (in this case) bears no connection to the *kazoeuta* described by Ki no Tsurayuki in his preface to *Kokin wakashū* (ca. 905) as the second of six poetic styles (SNKBT 5:7).

hitotsu to ya hitori marone no kusamakura tamoto shiboranu akatsuki mo nashi	One is for one who sleeps in his clothes alone, a pillow of grass for his head. No dawn does not find him wringing tears from his sleeve.
futatsu to ya futae byōbu no uchi ni nete koishiki hito wo itsuka mirubeki	Two is for the two-paneled folding screen within which he lies. When will he see her— the one for whom he longs?
mitsu to ka ya mite mo kokoro no nagusamade nado ukihito no koishikaruramu	Three is for he who sees, but in his heart feels no relief. Why must he pine for one so cold?
yotsu to ka ya yobuka ni kimi wo omouramu makura katashiku sode zo tsuyukeki	Four is for his longing in the depths of night— a pillow for one, his sleeve is soaked with dew.

Dōmyō continues reciting poems in this way up to a total of twenty-one. (The servant-girl is so impressed that she presses him for one more orange beyond her original order of twenty.)

Counting poems became increasingly popular in the centuries after *Izumi Shikibu*'s composition, perhaps as a result of Dōmyō's apocryphal verses.[23] As a genre, their origins are obscure. Asano Kenji speculates that *kazoeuta* evolved from ancient enumerative incantations employed in rites for the pacification of spirits and the summoning of deities.[24] Later, in the early Muromachi period, a tradition of singing *kazoeuta* as a means of sum-

[23]*Kazoeuta* of different sorts are cited in numerous Edo-period texts, and variants of the poems in *Izumi Shikibu* are reproduced in *Usuyuki monogatari* (The Tale of Usuyuki; a *kanazōshi* dating from ca. 1615), the noh play *Dōmyō Hōshi* (Edo period, perhaps), and as many as fifteen compilations of Edo-period "dancing songs" (*odoriuta*) from different regions of Japan. Manabe Masahiro maintains that there are two lines of *Izumi Shikibu*-related *kazoeuta*: those corresponding to the *tanrokubon* (Yoshida) and Shibukawa *Izumi Shikibu* texts, and those corresponding to *Usuyuki monogatari*, *Dōmyō Hōshi*, *Chihō yōbunshō* (late Edo period), the aforementioned compilations of dancing songs, and the Matsui *Izumi Shikibu* text (Manabe seems to have been unfamiliar with the Shimizu *Izumi Shikibu* manuscript). Manabe Masahiro, "Fūryū odoriuta kō: katarigusa wo megutte," in *Chūsei/kinsei kayō no kenkyū* (Tokyo: Ōfūsha, 1982), 367–85. Also see Asano Kenji, "Kazoeuta no keifu," *Gengo seikatsu* 266 (November 1973): 25–33; and Asano Kenji, "Kazoeuta," in *Nihon koten bungaku daijiten*, vol. 1 (Tokyo: Iwanami Shoten, 1983), 635.

[24]Asano, "Kazoeuta no keifu," 25–33.

moning good fortune for the coming year was established in New Years' performances of "Daikoku dancing" (Daikoku-*mai*), in which boisterous jongleurs costumed as the Buddhist deity Daikoku—one of seven deities of prosperity—walked from house to house singing, dancing, and begging for alms.[25] The two *otogizōshi Daikoku-mai* (The Dance of Daikoku) and *Umezu no chōja* (The Millionaire of Umezu) contain episodes in which Daikoku himself dances and sings a counting song in ten verses, which Asano suggests is the same as those sung by Daikoku dancers in the Muromachi period.[26] Like Dōmyō's poems in *Izumi Shikibu*, the stanzas are alliterative inasmuch as the first syllable of the second line usually echoes the number of the verse. They are far from being *waka*, however, as we can see from the following example in *Daikoku-mai*:

hitotsu ni,	One,
tawara fumaete,	on a straw bag he steps,
futatsu ni,	Two,
nikko to warafute	he grins and he laughs,
mitsu ni,	Three,
sake tsukurite,	he makes the wine,
yotsu,	Four,
yo no naka yoi yō ni	he makes the world fine,
itsutsu,	Five,
itsumo no gotoku ni	just like it always is,
mutsu,	Six,
mubyō sokusai ni	without illness, in perfect health,
nanatsu,	Seven,
nanigoto nai yō ni	so that nothing goes wrong,
yatsu,	Eight,
yashiki hiromete	enlarging estates,
kokonotsu,	Nine,
kura wo tatenarabe	erecting rows of storehouses,
tō de,	Ten,
tōdo osamaru miyo koso	ensuring a glorious age,
medetakarikere	marvelous indeed![27]

[25]The earliest known reference to a Daikoku dance is contained in *Inryōken nichiroku*, the diary of Kikei Shinzui (1401–69), in an entry for the seventeenth day of the second month of 1466. DNBZ 134:108b (75:289b).

[26]Asano, "Kazoeuta no keifu," 29c–30a. The counting song in *Daikoku-mai* (late Muromachi/early Edo period; also known as *Taietsu monogatari*, A Tale of Great Joy) is contained in SNKBT 55:70 and MJMT 8:395a-b (Kokubungaku Kenkyū Shiryōkan and former Akagi Bunko texts), and the one in *Umezu no chōja* (early Edo period; also known as *Umezu chōja monogatari*) is in MJMT 2:564b (Iwase Bunko text). See the illustration in SNKBT 55:71 of the deity Daikoku dancing as he sings.

[27]SNKBT 55:70 (Kokubungaku Kenkyū Shiryōkan *emaki*).

Fig. 12. Disguised as a fruit vendor, Dōmyō dances for a servant-girl at the palace. From *Izumi Shikibu* (Shibukawa text, early eighteenth century). Courtesy of the Kyoto Prefectural Library Archives (Kyōto Furitsu Sōgō Shiryōkan).

The Shimizu text of *Izumi Shikibu* explains that Dōmyō was "gifted in the way of poetry" from his time on Mount Hiei,[28] so it is perhaps for this reason that he is able to combine what may have been the simple counting songs of jugglers and street entertainers, as represented by the verses in *Daikoku-mai* and *Umezu no chōja*, with the formal conventions of Japanese court poetry, creating a series of *kazoeuta* in the traditional thirty-one-syllable *waka* form.

The Shibukawa *Izumi Shikibu* illustration (fig. 12) shows Dōmyō as a fruit vendor, dancing beside his baskets as the servant-girl looks on. One of his legs and one of his arms are raised in an unusual, off-balance manner, suggesting movement.[29] The servant-girl holds a tray of eleven oranges, and although her body is turned away (in embarrassment, perhaps), she watches Dōmyō with her face turned toward him. Considering the possible origins of counting poems in ancient magical enumerative incantations and their apparent use in medieval Daikoku dancing as a kind of ritual spell for ensuring stability and prosperity, it is appropriate that Dōmyō prances to his own *kazoeuta* in an attempt to "charm" the woman whom he loves.

[28]SNKBZ 63:226; Yoshida Kōichi, ed., *Izumi Shikibu zenshū: honbun hen* (Tokyo: Koten Bunko, 1959), 720.

[29]The demon Ishikuma Dōji is depicted in a similar manner in the illustration of him dancing in the Shibukawa text of the *otogizōshi Shuten Dōji*. See NKBT 38:377 and NKBZ 36:465.

Incest and Enlightenment

As *Izumi Shikibu* continues, Dōmyō returns to his inn for the night. His poems have caused a stir at the palace, and the emperor, having overheard a supposed allusion to a verse by Lady Ise (ca. 875–938), instructs the servant-girl to follow him to see where he goes. The woman whom Dōmyō had seen at the *Lotus Sutra* lectures (his mother) has overheard him as well, and she too is impressed. According to the early thirteenth-century *Kojidan* account of Izumi Shikibu, Dōmyō, and the Fifth Avenue Roadside Deity, when Dōmyō recited the *Lotus Sutra*, "the hearts of all those listening turned to the Path of the Buddha."[30] Similarly, when Dōmyō recites his counting poems in the sixteenth-century *Izumi Shikibu*, the heart of the woman he loves turns toward him:

> Now the woman whom Dōmyō had seen thought long and hard about Dōmyō's profound love for her, and she thought about Ono no Komachi, once adored by men for her youthful beauty. Komachi did nothing to appease the bitter longings of her suitors—an unfathomable sin—and so unable to escape her karma, she became obsessed with the memory of the Fourth Rank Lesser Captain and composed:
>
> | | |
> |---|---|
> | iisutsuru | Would that there were |
> | koto no ha made mo | compassion |
> | nasake aru ya | in your thoughtless words— |
> | tada itazura ni | so meaninglessly, utterly |
> | kuchihatsuru mi wo | have I fallen to ruin. |
>
> Mindful of Ono no Komachi's poem and anxious that she show compassion to all, the woman left the palace with the servant-girl and proceeded to Dōmyō's inn.

Izumi Shikibu recalls the story of Ono no Komachi and her devoted suitor, Fukakusa no Shii no Shōshō, the Fourth Rank Lesser Captain, and from this she is persuaded to act.[31] In Kamakura-period *setsuwa*, Ono no Komachi is remembered as a woman who "looked down on all men with contempt."[32] She proves her cold-hearted reputation in the Muromachi-period noh plays *Sotoba Komachi* and *Kayoi Komachi* by assigning the Fourth-Rank Lesser Captain the onerous task of traveling to her residence for one hundred nights

[30]SNKBT 41:291–92; Kobayashi Yasuharu, ed., *Kojidan*, vol. 1 (Tokyo: Gendai Shichōsha, 1981), 249.

[31]In the Shimizu and Matsui texts, Izumi Shikibu recalls Ono no Komachi and Ariwara no Narihira.

[32]*Jikkinshō* 2:4 (dated 1252; SNKBZ 51:116); *Kokon chomonjū* 5:182 (dated 1254; NKBT 84:167; SNKS 1:239).

before she will meet with him. In *Sotoba Komachi*, the captain dies of pent-up desire on the ninety-ninth night, and his spirit returns to drive Ono no Komachi insane.[33] Tales of Komachi's hard-heartedness, and her resulting ruin, were well known in the medieval period; in *The Tale of the Heike*, for example, Empress Jōsaimon'in cites the legend of Komachi's cruelty in her lecture to the lady Kozaishō about the dangers of spurning men's affections.[34]

Izumi Shikibu, fearful lest she too suffer the consequences of allowing a man's love to remain unrequited, decides to visit Dōmyō in his lodgings that night. Her situation is intertextually absurd in that although a made-up character in a fictional account, she bases her decision upon the imagined suffering of another Heian woman poet in an equally far-fetched set of tales. Her plight as the unwitting object of her pining son's affections is particularly severe. If she should refuse him, she would be guilty of neglect, which is no small matter in Muromachi fiction. (In the Izumi Shikibu tale in *Jōruri monogatari*, for example, Izumi Shikibu's deceased parents are said to have been cast into hell as a result of the unrequited love that their daughter inspired.)[35] But if she were to meet his request, she would both aid a priest in breaking his vows and unknowingly seal a karmic bond with her own son. In the Buddhist tale anthology *Kankyo no tomo* (A Companion in Solitude), compiled by the priest Keisei in 1222, a court lady is said to have escaped a similarly tricky situation by presenting herself to a love-sick priest in a smelly, filthy state, dissuading him of his desire.[36] However, having no such plan, Izumi Shikibu decides to indulge her suitor instead.

[33]*Sotoba Komachi* and *Kayoi Komachi* are attributed to Kan'ami (1333–84) and printed in SNKBT 57:434–40 and SNKBT 57:155–59, respectively. *Sotoba Komachi* is translated in Arthur Waley, *The Nō Plays of Japan* (New York: Grove Press, 1957), 150–60, and *Kayoi Komachi* is translated in Donald Keene, ed., *Twenty Plays of the Nō Theatre* (New York: Columbia University Press, 1970), 52–63. For a discussion of the origins of the story of Ono no Komachi and the Lesser Captain, see Sarah M. Strong, "The Making of a Femme Fatale: Ono no Komachi in the Early Medieval Commentaries," *Monumenta Nipponica* 49, no. 4 (1994): 391–412.

[34]NKBT 33:235 (Kakuichi text); Helen McCullough, *The Tale of the Heike* (Stanford: Stanford University Press, 1988), 324.

[35]See the *Jōruri monogatari* account in the translations section of this book.

[36]SNKBT 40:441–43 (tale 2:9); Rajyashree Pandey, "Women, Sexuality, and Enlightenment: *Kankyo no tomo*," *Monumenta Nipponica* 50, no. 3 (1995), 349–50. In his *History of the Lombards* (ca. 774), Paul the Deacon describes a similar way in which the daughters of Romilda avoided sexual assault by Avar invaders:

> [The noble girls] put the flesh of raw chickens under the band between their breasts, and this, when putrified by the heat, gave out an evil smell. And the Avars, when they wanted to touch them, could not endure the stench that they thought was natural to them, but moved far away from them with cursing, saying that all the Langobard women had a bad smell.

William Dudley Foulke, trans., *History of the Langobards* (Philadelphia: Department of History, University of Pennsylvania, 1907), 183–84.

Fig. 13. Izumi Shikibu visits Dōmyō at his lodgings. From *Izumi Shikibu* (Shibukawa text, early eighteenth century). Courtesy of the Kyoto Prefectural Library Archives (Kyōto Furitsu Sōgō Shiryōkan).

The Shibukawa and *tanrokubon* texts contain an illustration of Izumi Shikibu and the servant-girl as they first encounter Dōmyō in his doorway at the inn (fig. 13). Barefoot and dressed in a blue robe, he extends a hand to greet them. Izumi Shikibu's elaborate robes trail the ground behind her, and she bows her head demurely as the servant-girl stares on from behind. In her formal, stylized appearance, she looks as if she were lifted from a *kasen-e*—books of portraits of poets, produced in large numbers from the Kamakura period on—and dropped in at Dōmyō's door.

After a brief poetic exchange, including an allusion, on Izumi Shikibu's part, to Dōmyō's previous allusion to the supposed poem by Lady Ise, Izumi Shikibu joins Dōmyō in his room. From here, the *otogizōshi* takes a serious turn:

> That night from beneath shared bedcovers they pledged vows of undying love. Night eventually gave way to dawn. As the two were getting dressed, the lady noticed Dōmyō's short sword, and it struck her as odd. "That's a woman's sword," she said. "I've never heard of a man wearing one of those."
>
> "It's special," Dōmyō replied. "You see, I was abandoned on Fifth Avenue Bridge when I was a baby. A man took me in and brought me up, and since this sword was left with me on the bridge, I think of it as my mother—I carry it with me wherever I go."

The woman became anxious. "How old are you?" she asked.

"They say I was left as an infant," Dōmyō replied, "and now I'm grown."[37]

"What about your swaddling clothes?"

"There was a poem on the hem of my iris *kosode*."

"Tell it to me," the woman said. Dōmyō immediately replied:

momo tose ni	Though a hundred years
mata momo tose wa	be piled on
kasanu to mo	a hundred more,
nanatsu nanatsu no	would that the name of a girl of
na wo ba taeji na	seven and seven never disappear.

At the time she abandoned her baby, Izumi Shikibu kept the sheath of the short sword. Because she cherished it as a remembrance of her son, she carried it with her wherever she went. She took the sheath out now and fitted it with the sword; they were without doubt a matching set.

To her horror, Izumi Shikibu realizes that Dōmyō is her own lost son. When she abandoned him as an infant, she inscribed a poem on the hem of his swaddling clothes naming her desire to be known forever as a girl of fourteen ("seven and seven," her age at the time) as her reason for giving him up. The *otogizōshi Koshikibu* and *Jippon ōgi* (Ten Fans) contain similar poems in related accounts, according to which Izumi Shikibu abandoned her child (an unnamed boy in *Jippon ōgi*, and a daughter in *Koshikibu*) so that she might never be known as a woman "of seven days and seven days," an oblique reference to motherhood.[38]

In *Koshikibu* and *Jippon ōgi*, it is the poem alone that allows Izumi Shikibu to recognize her child. In *Izumi Shikibu*, however, the final proof of parentage is provided by the matching of Dōmyō's short sword with Izumi Shikibu's treasured sheath. The *Lotus Sutra* commentaries *Hokekyō jurin shūyōshō* (1512) and *Hokekyō jikidanshō* (ca. 1546) contain a story of a woman who once abandoned her son in the inner tray of an elegant hand-box, and who then identified him years later by fitting the tray into its original box.[39]

[37]In the Shimizu and Matsui texts, Dōmyō claims to be eighteen years old.

[38]See *Koshikibu* in the translations, and *Jippon ōgi*, below. In *Koshikibu*, Izumi Shikibu states that she "will not be called the moon / of seven and seven days," and she explains that as the fifteenth-day moon is called the *mochizuki*, or "full moon," the fourteenth-day moon is called the *ko-mochizuki*, or "little full moon." This in turn is homonymic with *komochizuki*, "moon of motherhood." In the Shimizu text of *Izumi Shikibu*, the final line of the poem reads, "*na wo ba akasu na*," "would that a name [of seven and seven] / not [ever] come to light," which is more in keeping with the poem as it appears in *Koshikibu* and *Jippon ōgi*.

[39]*Hokekyō jurin shūyōshō*, vol. 4 (Kyoto: Rinsen Shoten, 1991), 237–40; *Hokekyō jikidanshō*, vol. 3 (Kyoto: Rinsen Shoten, 1979), 358–61.

Although a variation on a theme, the matching of objects in *Izumi Shikibu* is far more intriguing, for in taking up Dōmyō's dagger with its simultaneously frightening and phallic connotations and inserting it into her scabbard in the sexually charged climax of the tale, Izumi Shikibu symbolically reenacts their outrageous, incestuous act.

In the Buddhist worldview, suffering derives from attachment. It does here, too, for it is their attachments—Dōmyō to the mother he has never known, and Izumi Shikibu to her son—that cause them to carry the sword and the sheath. Without these objects, or the feelings that give them weight, Izumi Shikibu and Dōmyō may never have known their offense. Moreover, in that Izumi Shikibu originally left the blade by Dōmyō's side, she can be seen to have passed her amorous nature on to her son, sowing the seeds of her own later degradation.

As *Izumi Shikibu* continues, the narrator expresses indignation at the nature of Izumi Shikibu and Dōmyō's affair:

> What kind of thing is this, where parent and child, unaware, may tie the lovers' knot? 'Tis because we live in a world of suffering that such things occur! This incident was the seed of Izumi Shikibu's enlightenment, turning her heart to the path of the Buddha.
>
> Izumi Shikibu left the capital in the night. She followed the coast past the bay of Onoe—startled by the sound of the ringing bell—and continued past the Shikama shore.[40] Pushing her way through mist and clouds, she ascended Mount Shosha in Harima province, where she became a disciple of the holy man Shōkū Shōnin. When she attained enlightenment at the age of sixty-one, she wrote a poem on a pillar of the shrine of Mount Shosha's tutelary deity:
>
> | | |
> |---|---|
> | kuraki yori | Born from darkness |
> | kuraki yamiji ni | into a path of darkness |
> | umarekite | in the shade of night— |
> | sayaka ni terase | shine your light down brightly, |
> | yama no ha no tsuki | moon on the mountain ridge! |
>
> As a result of inscribing her poem where she did, "poem pillars" are said to have originated on Mount Shosha in Harima province.

Claude Lévi-Strauss has argued that the "universal prohibition of incest," which he writes is present in some form in "every known society," constitutes the beginning of social organization; it is "a passage from nature

[40]This may be an allusion to a passage in the noh play *Takasago* (attributed to Zeami; 1363?–1443?), which similarly refers to the "ringing bell of Onoe." NKBZ 33:55.

to culture, from animal to human life."[41] By inadvertently transgressing this prohibition, Izumi Shikibu and Dōmyō have lost a part of that which makes them human. Sigmund Freud has explored the social and psychological aspects of taboo (including the incest taboo), and he observes that while "any violation of it produces a fearful sense of guilt which follows as a matter of course and of which the origin is unknown," it stands as a general rule that "the violation of a taboo can be atoned for by a renunciation." Freud further explains that because obedience to a taboo injunction is itself a renunciation, "emancipation from one renunciation is made up for by the imposition of another one elsewhere."[42] In a moment of psychological realism, Izumi Shikibu is made to atone for her transgression by renouncing her secular life in order to become a nun at Enkyōji Temple on Mount Shosha. As for Dōmyō, by breaking his vows and debauching his mother, he has seemingly impregnated her with the seeds of enlightenment—an ironically fortunate result of their most unfortunate affair, and a farcical testament to his persuasive powers as a Buddhist priest. Notably, Dōmyō's own reaction to the startling revelation of the true identity of his lover is left wholly unexplained.

At Mount Shosha, Izumi Shikibu composes a poem. As a variant of her famous "darkness into darkness" verse, its first three lines, "born from darkness / into a path of darkness / in the shade of night," are altered from the *Lotus Sutra*-inspired, "from darkness / into a path of darkness / I must enter." While the difference may be the result of a mistranscription (both the Shimizu and Matsui texts cite the poem in its traditional form), in the Shibukawa and *tanrokubon* texts, the alteration serves to highlight the themes of birth and rebirth that run throughout the tale. For not only is Izumi Shikibu born from a spiritual darkness into a path of delusion, she also gives birth to Dōmyō, who, with no knowledge of his parents, is himself born into a kind of darkness. It is then the darkness of Dōmyō's ignorance that leads him to seduce his mother, impelling her toward a spiritual rebirth.

The Shibukawa and *tanrokubon* texts conclude with the brief and seemingly irrelevant observation that "as a result of Izumi Shikibu inscribing her poem where she did, 'poem pillars' are said to have originated on Mount Shosha in Harima province." The unknown author may have wished to provide some moral justification for the shocking content of the account by transforming it into what Maria Tater has described, in the context of a discussion of the Grimms' fairy tales, as "an etiological story, a tale about

[41]Claude Lévi-Strauss, "The Family," in *Man, Culture, and Society*, ed. Harry Shapiro (London: Oxford University Press, 1971 [first edition from 1956]), 348 and 350.

[42]Sigmund Freud, *Totem and Taboo: Some Points of Agreement Between the Mental Lives of Savages and Neurotics*, trans. James Strachey (London: Routledge and Kegan Paul, 1950), 68 and 34–35.

the origins of creatures and customs."[43] Or, considered from an alternate perspective, the story may be said to be as much about the persuasive powers of poetry and the origins of certain poetic practices as it is about Izumi Shikibu's supposed liaison with her son. Significantly, the Shimizu *Izumi Shikibu* manuscript contains an additional, cautionary passage: "This has been the story of how Izumi Shikibu attained her desire to become a nun. Its meaning (*kokoro*) is not to be made light of."[44] The warning is for the reader to avoid poking fun at any event, however strange, that may lead a person to take religious vows. The import of the story—its *kokoro*, or essence—is that sometimes even the worst of crimes can be a bridge to salvation. The idea is a popular one in late-Heian and medieval fiction: in the twelfth-century *Konjaku monogatari shū*, for example, a hunter kills his mother in her next-life incarnation as a deer, leading him to take holy vows;[45] in the *otogizōshi Isozaki*, a jealous wife murders her husband's concubine, and "three people attained Buddhahood as a result";[46] and in the *otogizōshi Sannin hōshi* (The Three Monks), two men become priests after a woman's murder, demonstrating that "wickedness and goodness are the two sides of a single leaf."[47]

Incest accounts—particularly those concerning siblings—are relatively common in Japanese literature. According to the creation myth in *Kojiki* (Record of Ancient Matters; 712) and *Nihon shoki* (Chronicles of Japan; 720), the Japanese islands were all produced as the result of an incestuous relationship between the sibling deities Izanagi and Izanami.[48] Similarly, *Konjaku monogatari shū* and *Uji shūi monogatari* (twelfth and thirteenth centuries) contain an account of how Imose Island (Brother and Sister Island) in Tosa province came to be populated by the descendents of a brother and sister who were marooned there as children.[49] As many scholars have noted, brother-sister ancestor myths of this kind are common to much of East and Southeast Asia.[50] Even the poet and occasional bodhisattva Ariwara no Narihira is said in the Kamakura-period commentary *Waka chikenshū* to have had sexual

[43]Maria Tater, *Off With Their Heads! Fairy Tales and the Culture of Childhood* (Princeton: Princeton University Press, 1992), 167.

[44]SNKBZ 63:241; Yoshida, ed., *Izumi Shikibu zenshū: honbun hen*, 728.

[45]SNKBT 36:131–33 (tale 19:7).

[46]SNKBZ 63:349; MJMT 2:261b.

[47]MJMT 6:235; Margaret Childs, *Rethinking Sorrow: Revelatory Tales of Late Medieval Japan* (Ann Arbor: University of Michigan Center for Japanese Studies, 1991), 90. Translation here by Childs.

[48]Ōshima, "Dōsojin no shinkō to setsuwa," 67–68; Donald Philippi, *Kojiki* (Tokyo: University of Tokyo Press, 1968), 50–58; W.G. Aston, *Nihongi: Chronicles of Japan from the Earliest Times to A.D. 697* (London: George Allen and Unwin, 1956 [first printing in 1896]), 12–22.

[49]*Konjaku monogatari shū* 26:10 (SNKBT 37:49–51; NKBZ 23:576–79), and *Uji shūi monogatari* 56 (SNKBT 42:112–14; NKBZ 28:176–78).

[50]Ōshima, "Dōsojin no shinkō to setsuwa," 69–73.

relations with his adopted sister (his niece by blood) and to have written about it in *Tales of Ise* in order to demonstrate that in the Way of Love, one should avoid discriminating between near, far, high, and low.[51]

Stories of parent-child transgressions in Japanese literature are somewhat more rare. In *The Tale of Genji*, Genji forces himself upon his stepmother Fujitsubo, and he later weds his adopted daughter Murasaki, but as in the case of Narihira and his adopted sister, the incest is largely symbolic.[52] Murasaki Shikibu may have been loathe to have her protagonist truly violate the taboo and risk offending (or hopelessly offending) her readers' sensibilities. Taira no Yasuyori's late twelfth-century Buddhist *setsuwa* anthology *Hōbutsushū*, on the other hand, is notable for its inclusion of two parent-child incest accounts: a story of a priest who rapes his mother without knowing her identity, and a story of a priest who marries his own daughter. The two tales, presented in *Hōbutsushū* as a single whole, merit consideration for the light that they can shed on the much later *Izumi Shikibu*:

> Myōtatsu Risshi once unknowingly violated his mother; Jungen Hōshi knowingly married his daughter.
>
> Myōtatsu was from Shimotsuke province. When he was a young child he went to live on Mt. Hiei, where he studied and grew to be an adult. One time he decided to leave the mountain to return to his home province and see his mother. His mother, longing for her son on Mt. Hiei, decided at the same time to climb the mountain to visit him. By chance the two met at a travelers' lodge. Not realizing that she was his mother, Myōtatsu forced himself upon her.
>
> Jungen Hōshi contemplated the endless cycle of birth and death and the causes for rebirth in the Pure Land. "Who is there who is neither my mother nor my father?" he thought to himself, and he took his daughter to be his wife. In time these monks both achieved their long-held desires for rebirth in the Pure Land.[53]

Like Dōmyō in *Izumi Shikibu*, Myōtatsu is raised on Mt. Hiei away from his mother. He wishes to be reunited with her, and she with him. Ironically, he succeeds, but not in a way that he had expected. Jungen, on the other hand, appreciates the meaninglessness of the incest prohibition in the face

[51]Katagiri Yōichi, *Ise monogatari no kenkyū: shiryō hen* (Tokyo: Meiji Shoin, 1969), 114a. Also see footnote 70, below, concerning the sibling incest account in *Koyasu monogatari*.

[52]Although Fujitsubo and Murasaki are related to Genji by blood, their connection to him is distant enough (according to the mores of Heian Japan) to avoid categorization as incest. As for a man raising his wife from childhood, Lévi-Strauss writes that among the North American Mohave, "such marriages were thought of as very strong ones, since the natural feelings between husband and wife would be reinforced by the recollection of the parental care bestowed by one of the spouses upon the other." Lévi-Strauss, "The Family," 345.

[53]SNKBT 40:211–12.

of Buddhist Truth. His story is also cited in *Shūi ōjōden* (Gleanings of Pure Land Rebirth Biographies; ca. 1111), in which he is said to have reasoned that "each and every woman is herself both a mother and a child, an older sister and a younger sister. What use is it to distinguish between those who are close and those who are distant, those who are related and those who are not?"[54] Like Narihira who purportedly slept with his own adopted sister, Jungen refuses to discriminate among women when choosing a wife.

Despite the implied wickedness of their deeds (*Shūi ōjōden* records that Jungen was widely criticized for his behavior), both Myōtatsu and Jungen are able to attain rebirth in the Pure Land, which is of course the point of their tales. Remarkably, the fates of Myōtatsu's mother and Jungen's daughter are left totally unexplained. As women, their fortunes were of little apparent concern to Yasuyori, who was a monk at the time of his composition of *Hōbutsushū*. Yasuyori's male-centrism, displayed in these accounts and in the work as a whole, suggests that his intended audience was male and monastic; furthermore, it illuminates, by its striking contrast, the opposing gender bias of *Izumi Shikibu*, which is fundamentally concerned with Izumi Shikibu's sin and salvation to the exclusion of that of either Tachibana no Yasumasa (her lover at the beginning of the tale) or Dōmyō (at the end).[55] In the way that *Hōbutsushū* explains that Dōmyō—a man—was saved by the *Lotus Sutra* in spite of breaking his vows (see p. 39, above), and that Myōtatsu—another man—achieved rebirth in the Pure Land in spite of raping his mother, *Izumi Shikibu* asserts the truth of Izumi Shikibu's enlightenment in spite of (or as a result of) sleeping with her son.

Tokuda Kazuo has observed that in the case of the *otogizōshi Ko-Atsumori* (Little Atsumori), derived from the story of Taira no Atsumori in *The Tale of the Heike*, while *Ko-Atsumori* manuscripts in the so-called "old picture scroll" textual line begin with Atsumori's battle on the beach and end with Atsumori's son's later achievements as a Buddhist priest, the *Ko-Atsumori* text in Shibukawa Seiemon's *Companion Library* begins with Atsumori's wife's lamentations at the death of her husband and ends with her rebirth in the Pure Land. The tale has been altered, Tokuda concludes, to intensify its appeal as a "woman's story."[56] In the case of *Izumi Shikibu*, although it is clear that

[54]NST 7:363–64 and 615b–16a (biography 3:5).

[55]It is worth observing that the hand-copied Matsui manuscript is titled *Dōmei no sōshi* (Dōmyō's Story), which suggests that an unknown copyist may have sought to contest the female orientation of the narrative.

[56]Whether or not Shibukawa himself was responsible for this alteration is unknown. Tokuda Kazuo, "Otogizōshi *Ko-Atsumori* no Kōshōji-bon wo megutte," *Gakushūin Joshi Daigaku kiyō* 4 (2002), 34b. For a discussion of *Ko-Atsumori* in English, see R. Keller Kimbrough, "*Little Atsumori* and *The Tale of the Heike*: Fiction as Commentary, and the Significance of a Name," *Proceedings of the Association for Japanese Literary Studies* 5 (2004): 325–36.

Shibukawa simply reproduced the earlier *tanrokubon* text, his selection of it for inclusion in his anthology is significant. As a specialist in the publication of didactic works for women, he may have chosen *Izumi Shikibu* because of its strong female orientation. Although its Buddhist message is highly conventional—that even the worst of crimes can lead to good results—it is the story of a woman's redemption, told from a woman's point of view.

Setsuwa Connections

In addition to *Izumi Shikibu*, the anonymous and undated *otogizōshi Jippon ōgi* (Ten Fans) contains an unusual, fictional account of how Izumi Shikibu once mistakenly slept with her son. The story is a combination of an oft-repeated tale about a peasant boy (not Dōmyō) who is said to have charmed Izumi Shikibu with a love poem,[57] and a previously unrelated account, contained in both *Koshikibu* and *Izumi Shikibu*, about how Izumi Shikibu discovered her abandoned child by means of her apocryphal "seven and seven" verse. The connection between *Jippon ōgi* and *Izumi Shikibu* is unclear.[58] Ichiko Teiji has argued that *Jippon ōgi* probably dates from before the mid-sixteenth-century demise of the ruling Oda family of Hitachi (an unspecified member of which is the protagonist of the tale),[59] but whether or not this precedes *Izumi Shikibu*'s composition is unknown.

Jippon ōgi tells the tale of a man named Oda of Hitachi, governor of Mikawa province. Returning to his post from the capital, Oda carries with him a set of ten fans painted with scenes inspired by ten famous poems. As Oda travels, he shows his fans to courtesans (*yūkun*) he meets along the way, telling them that the first to properly identify all ten shall be his wife. Such fan-reading contests (*ōgi awase*) may have been popular in the Muromachi

[57]See *Fukurozōshi* (ca. 1157–58; SNKBT 29:165), *Jikkinshō* 10:43 (dated 1252; SNKBZ 51:433–34), *Kokon chomonjū* 201 (dated 1254; NKBT 84:177–78; SNKS *Kokon chomonjū*, vol. 1, 256), and *Shasekishū* (ca. 1279–83; NKBT 85:233–34). Also see the noh play *Inari* (*Izumi Shikibu*; Muromachi period), and the passages from the commentaries *Kokin wakashū Ton'a jochū* (late Kamakura/Muromachi period) and *Ise monogatari shūindan* (dated 1523) in Ishikawa Tōru, *Muromachi monogatari to kochūshaku* (Tokyo: Miyai Shoten, 2002), 193–95.

[58]Hamanaka Osamu has tried to sort out the relationship, but with little success. In a 1988 article, he states without explanation that *Jippon ōgi* appears to be based upon *Izumi Shikibu* and is thus a more recent work. However, in a 1995 article, he writes that *Izumi Shikibu* likely postdates both *Koshikibu* and *Jippon ōgi* because the "seven and seven" poem as it appears in *Izumi Shikibu* (Shibukawa and *tanrokubon* texts) is a corrupted, and thus later, version. The poem in the sixteenth-century Shimizu *Izumi Shikibu* manuscript is similar to the versions in *Koshikibu* and *Jippon ōgi*, however, undermining his 1995 theory. Hamanaka, "Chūsei no Izumi Shikibu: Eizan no denshō yori," *Bukkyō bungaku* 12 (1988), 55b; Hamanaka, "Otogizōshi *Koshikibu*/*Izumi Shikibu* ron," *Kokubungaku: kaishaku to kanshō* 60, no. 8 (August 1995), 120b.

[59]Ichiko Teiji, *Mikan chūsei shōsetsu kaidai* (Tokyo: Rakurō Shoin, 1942), 99.

Fig. 14. Oda of Hitachi shows his fans to a group of courtesans at an inn on the road to Mikawa province. From *Jippon ōgi* (Honokuni Bunko text, mid-to-late seventeenth century). Courtesy of Takemoto Taiichi and the Honokuni Bunko.

period; as a refined recreation, they allowed participants a sense of connecting to the cultural history of the Heian past. (In the *otogizōshi Kachō Fūgetsu* [Kachō and Fūgetsu; composed prior to 1457], this abstract sense of connection is literalized when a group of fourteenth-century Kyoto nobles manages to converse with the ghosts of Genji and Ariwara no Narihira as a result of a dispute that arises in the course of their fan-reading party.[60] Likewise, Oda of Hitachi is able to forge a link to the Heian past as a result of his own fan-reading contest, by marrying a living heiress to ancient poetic fame.)

Although none of the courtesans at the Kagami Inn in Ōmi or the Yahagi Inn in Mikawa can identify the pictures on Oda's fans, an outstandingly beautiful and well-mannered young courtesan at the Hashimoto Inn in Tōtōmi steps forward and names all ten poems after two hundred and forty other women at her establishment have tried and failed. She is later revealed to be a descendant of the legendary Heian poet Sarumaru Dayū,

[60]MJMT 3:420–33 and 434–46 (former Takayasu Rokurō text of 1595, and National Diet Library text, respectively). On the subject of medieval *ōgi awase* in general, see Tokuda Kazuo, "*Ōgi no sōshi* emaki wo megutte," *Kokugo kokubun ronshū* 20 (March 1991): 69–92.

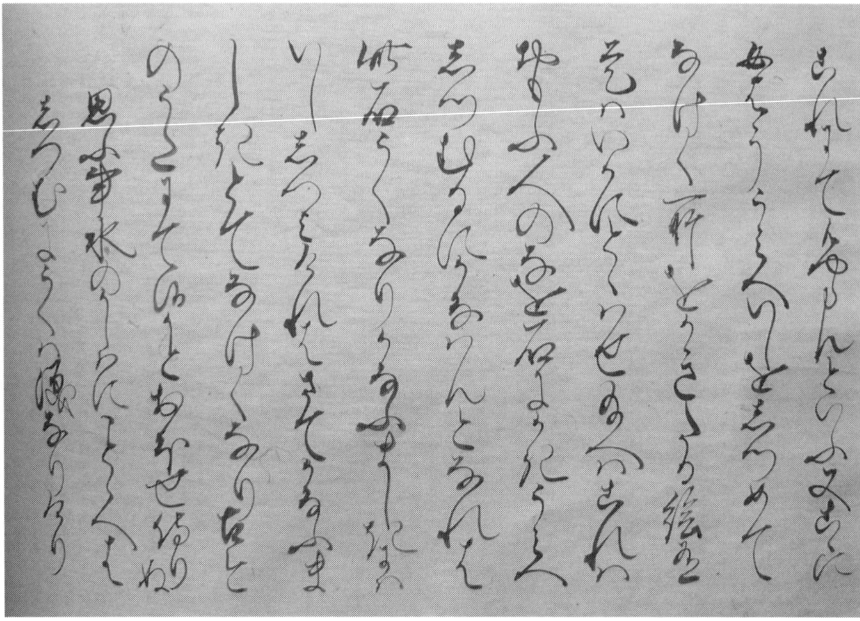

Fig. 15. Explanation of the seventh painted fan. From *Jippon ōgi* (Honokuni Bunko text, mid-to-late seventeenth century). Courtesy of Takemoto Taiichi and the Honokuni Bunko.

immortalized in the Chinese preface to *Kokin wakashū*.[61] That she is identified as a courtesan is significant insofar as it suggests, yet again, the popular association of court ladies with courtesans (and vice-versa), as well as the participation of *yūjo* in the medieval dissemination of Izumi Shikibu lore. The following is her explanation of the eighth fan, which depicts a young man by a mountain shrine in early autumn:[62]

> This one is about Izumi Shikibu when she visited the shrine on Mount Inari. There was a sudden storm on the way, so she approached a peasant hut and had a look inside. She saw a woman

[61]SNKBT 5:344–45. Sarumaru Dayū (dates unknown) was also famed from the mid-Heian period for his inclusion within Fujiwara no Kintō's list of "Thirty-six Poetic Immortals" (*sanjūrokkasen*).

[62]The following translation is from the Honokuni Bunko text (MJMT 7:239b–41a), which in the case of this particular episode is somewhat clearer than the Ichiko text. This account (along with all of the second part of the *otogizōshi*) is absent from the Seikadō Bunko text; it survives in part in the fragmentary Tokuda Kazuo manuscript (Tokuda Kazuo, "Shōkai: otogizōshi *Jippon ōgi* no shinshutsu-bon," *Koten shiryō kenkyū* 3 [June 2001], 7b–8b). For a list and classification of extant *Jippon ōgi* texts, see the appendix at the end of this book.

of about fifty and a fourteen- or fifteen-year-old boy. Taking them to be mother and son, she walked right in and said, "Lend me that thing there—that blue hunting cloak."[63] "But it's been worn," the woman humbly replied. "How can we loan you such a thing?" The boy spoke: "They say that strangers resting in the shade of a single tree or drawing water from a single stream are linked by the bonds of former lives. Of all these houses, that you came to this one is strange indeed." And he loaned her the cloak.

The next day the boy felt as if he had a cold, and the day after that his head ached. As he suffered through the third day, his mother came to his bedside, weeping, and spoke: "I have no children except for you, so I'm counting on you to pray for me when I'm gone. But the way you look now, you're not long for this sad world. If there's anything weighing on your heart, anything at all, you must tell me." The boy raised himself from his pillow. "There is something," he said, "but it's so beyond me, I'm ashamed to say it! I've been in love with Izumi Shikibu since the day I saw her. My heart is in a tumult, and I'm sure I can't live much longer. Please . . . just tell her of my feelings when I'm dead." The boy lay back down.

Struck with pity, the woman hurried off to the palace. She crept in through a back wall and went to see an old acquaintance, a woman who lived in the house of a Major Counselor. She explained everything from beginning to end. Being a kind-hearted person, her friend spoke to Izumi Shikibu on her behalf.[64] "How strange that a lowly peasant boy would be in love with me," Izumi Shikibu said. "It seems unlikely, but if it's true, have him compose a poem on the topic of 'love.' If it's nice, I'll share my pillow with him for a night."

The mother rushed home, pleased. She told her son: "I explained everything to Izumi Shikibu, and she said that if you really do love her, you should compose a poem on the topic of 'love.' She'll see you if it's nice." Overjoyed, the boy rose from his bed. He took out a strip of fine colored paper, ground some ink and wrote:

waga koi wa	My love is
Inari no yama no	the autumn-tinged leaves
usumomiji	of Mount Inari,
awo karishi yori	dyed with longing
omohi someshi ka	since the time they were green
	(ever since you borrowed my cloak).[65]

[63]Izumi Shikibu asks to borrow an "*awo kariginu.*" According to most *setsuwa* versions of the tale, she borrows an "*awo,*" a kind of winter cloak or raincoat.

[64]Much of this sentence is interpolated from the Ichiko text.

[65]The poem depends for its effect upon the double meaning of "*awo karishi yori,*" "since the time [they] were green," and "ever since [you] borrowed [my] cloak."

> "Elegantly composed," Izumi Shikibu said upon reading the poem, and she is reported to have tied the lovers' knot with him for a single night.
>
> "Who are you that you could write a verse like that?" Izumi Shikibu asked as they lay awake in the darkness. The boy replied: "What could I have to hide? I'm not really that woman's child—I am adopted, and I don't know my real parents."
>
> "Were you left with anything when you were abandoned?"
>
> "Only a short sword and a copy of the *Kannon Sutra* in a lacquered lid."[66]
>
> "Your mother must have had her reasons for giving you up," Izumi Shikibu said. "Was there anything on your swaddling clothes?"
>
> "There was a poem:
>
> | | |
> |---|---|
> | itadaki ni | If even seven layers |
> | nanae no shimo wa | of frost should come to rest |
> | kasanu to mo | upon my head, |
> | nanoka nanoka no | would that I not be called a person |
> | mi to wa iwareji | of seven and seven days."[67] |
>
> To say "seven days and seven days" is to use the expression, "fourteen days." In the poem, it means that "even if all my hair turns gray, I would not be called a mother." Izumi Shikibu was startled to learn that this was her own child, whom she had once borne and abandoned—but there was nothing she could do!

Unlike the *Izumi Shikibu* incest account, the *Jippon ōgi* story is seemingly unconcerned with the effects or implications of Izumi Shikibu's transgression, or with the dramatic possibilities inherent in the boy's short sword. That the boy happens to be Izumi Shikibu's son is a final, shocking twist, but it merely serves as an opportunity to include Izumi Shikibu's purported "seven and seven" poem within the courtesan's account. Both Nishimura Tōru and Ishikawa Tōru have suggested that the first part of the tale, concerning the boy's "Mount Inari" poem, is intended to illustrate the persuasive powers of Japanese poetry: it explains how a lowly peasant boy once used a poem to overcome the boundaries of class and custom and achieve a night of love with an elite lady of the court.[68] The unknown author of the di-

[66]According to the Ichiko text, the boy was left in a "lacquered box" (*makie no hako*). In the noh play *Ikuta Atsumori*, attributed to Konparu Zenpō (1454–1532?), the son of Taira no Atsumori was similarly abandoned in the "lid of a handbox" (*tebako no futa*) (NKBT 41:239).

[67]The "seven and seven" poem presumably corresponds to the painting on fan number nine, to which there is no reference in either the Honokuni Bunko or Ichiko text.

[68]Nishimura Tōru, *Uta to minzokugaku* (Tokyo: Iwasaki Bijutsusha, 1966), 52–53; Ishikawa, *Muromachi monogatari to kochūshaku*, 190–97.

dactic moral treatise *Jikkinshō* (Discourse on Ten Lessons), compiled in 1252, seems to have held this view, for he cites the story in order to demonstrate the principle that social mobility—both upward and downward—often depends upon one's proficiency in the arts (or lack thereof).[69] This is clearly the case with Monkey Genji in *Saru Genji sōshi*, and with the winning courtesan in *Jippon ōgi*, both of whom are able to marry above their stations because of their knowledge of poetry.

But why was Izumi Shikibu taken up in incest stories in the first place? As we have seen, Yanagita Kunio suggested that such accounts were possibly derived from suppositions that Izumi Shikibu had an affair with Dōmyō's father, while Nagai Yoshinori proposed that there was confusion between Izumi Shikibu's son Eikaku and Dōmyō, both of whom were intendants of Tennōji Temple. Ōshima Tatehiko has argued for a third possibility: that the Izumi Shikibu/Dōmyō incest accounts resulted from the presence of the Fifth Avenue Roadside Deity in early stories of their fictional affair. Through modern folklore analysis, Ōshima has demonstrated a widespread early-modern association of roadside deities with tales of sibling and parental incest. The appearance of the Fifth Avenue Roadside Deity in the *Uji shūi monogatari/Kojidan* account may have precipitated a view, Ōshima argues, that Izumi Shikibu and Dōmyō were mother and son. Ōshima's theory is highly speculative, and it suffers from a lack of evidence substantiating a Muromachi-period association of roadside deities with incest,[70] but it is important insofar as it highlights *Izumi Shikibu*'s and *Jippon ōgi*'s roots in the Kamakura-period *setsuwa* tradition.

At the end of *Izumi Shikibu*, it is also *setsuwa* that determines Izumi Shikibu's decision to flee to Enkyōji Temple on Mount Shosha. The Tendai priest Shōkū Shōnin (910–1007), founder of Enkyōji in 966, is himself a prominent figure in late-Heian and medieval tales.[71] Accounts of his meeting with Izumi Shikibu (based on the headnote to her "darkness into darkness" poem) were employed in a range of Kamakura and Muromachi-period proselytizing and fund-raising activities, and are preserved today in a variety of medieval

[69]SNKBZ 51:385–87 and 433–34.

[70]As a single medieval example, Ōshima cites the *otogizōshi Koyasu monogatari*, in which a brother and sister (conjoined twins, "like a two-paneled folding screen") bear a daughter who marries an emperor. One of the twins is revealed to be a manifestation of the bodhisattva Jizō, whom Ōshima explains was regarded in a manner similar to that of a roadside deity. Also, of Ōshima's twenty-six examples of early-modern associations of roadside deities with incest, none concern liaisons between mothers and sons. Ōshima, "Dōsojin no shinkō to setsuwa," 60–73. *Koyasu monogatari* is typeset in MJMT 5:142–62 and 163–78.

[71]See Yasuda Takako, "Shōkū Shōnin setsuwa: *Senjūshō* wo chūshin to shite," *Sugiyama kokubungaku* 7 (1983): 15–50, and Hayashi Masahiko, "Shōkū Shōnin setsuwa kō: kitan, kitokudan wo chūshin ni," *Kokugo kokubungaku ronshū* 3 (1974): 35–55.

sources. Two of the earliest of these are *Kohon setsuwa shū* (An Old Collection of Tales; twelfth or thirteenth century) and *Mumyōzōshi* (An Unnamed Account; ca. 1200), according to which Shōkū Shōnin presented Izumi Shikibu with a *kesa*—a kind of surplice or stole—in response to her famous verse. Izumi Shikibu is said to have died soon thereafter, and to have been saved in the afterworld by the inherent virtue of the master's garment.[72]

Hokke genki, Chingen's collection of Buddhist biographies dating from between 1040 and 1044, some thirty-five years after Shōkū Shōnin's death, contains a laudatory history of the holy man, beginning with a story of his miraculous birth:

> The holy man Shōkū of Mount Shosha was from the western part of the Heian capital. His lay name was Tachibana. He was born with his right hand clenched tight, and when his mother and father pried it open, they found a needle inside.

In the world of *setsuwa*, children born grasping needles or relics of the Buddha are invariably bound for spiritual achievement. *Hokke genki* relates that Shōkū Shōnin showed a remarkable devotion to Buddhism from his earliest years, and that as an adult at Enkyōji Temple, he achieved considerable fame:

> Monks and laypeople flocked to see Shōkū Shōnin; rich and poor gathered like clouds. Their name cards accumulated in mounds, and their offerings were enough to fill an ocean. Those who saw the holy man felt as if they had met a Buddha; those who heard him felt as if they had heard a Buddha preach. Those who received a grain of his rice felt as if they had received a relic of a Buddha, and those who received a piece of his robe treasured and revered it as they would the robe of a Buddha.[73]

Among Shōkū Shōnin's eminent guests, the retired emperor Kazan is reported to have visited in the seventh month of 986, and again in the third month of 1002.[74] Fujiwara no Kintō paid Shōkū Shōnin a visit in the fifth month of 1005, at which time he may have presented the holy man with

[72]SNKBT 42:414 (*Kohon setsuwa shū*), and SNKS *Mumyōzōshi*, 114. The account is contained in *Yotsugi monogatari* as well (late twelfth or early thirteenth century; ZGR 32:2:149).

[73]NST 7:109–11 and 533a-b (section 2:45). For a full and alternate translation of Shōkū Shōnin's *Hokke genki* biography, see Yoshiko Dykstra, *Miraculous Tales of the Lotus Sutra from Ancient Japan: The Dainihonkoku Hokekyōkenki of Priest Chingen* (Honolulu: University of Hawaii Press, 1983), 71–72.

[74]According to *Nihon kiryaku* and *Shosha-zan Enkyōji kyūki*, respectively. Cited in Ichiko Teiji et al., eds., *Nihon bunka sōgō nenpyō* (Tokyo: Iwanami Shoten, 1990), 80 and 84.

Izumi Shikibu's "darkness into darkness" poem, and in the same month of that year—on the following day, in fact—Fujiwara no Michinaga held a ceremony in the capital at Shōkū Shōnin's request to dedicate one thousand scrolls of the *Prajñā-pāramitā Sutra*.[75] For Izumi Shikibu to have thus become his disciple at the end of *Izumi Shikibu* is one of the less fantastic aspects of the tale.

In considering *Izumi Shikibu*, it is important to bear in mind the essential constructedness of the narrative. Although less obviously cobbled together than *Kotohara* or the *Jippon ōgi* incest account, *Izumi Shikibu* is also principally formed from two disparate tales: the legend of Izumi Shikibu and Dōmyō's notorious affair, and the "seven and seven" poem-story of Izumi Shikibu's reunion with an abandoned child. Combined with the tale of Ono no Komachi and the Fourth-Rank Lesser Captain, as well as with the story of Izumi Shikibu's meeting with Shōkū Shōnin, these accounts constitute the narrative in its most basic, skeletal form. Like numerous *otogizōshi*, *Izumi Shikibu* is formulated from an array of preexisting *setsuwa*, many of which are rooted in earlier Buddhist proselytizing and storytelling traditions. In tracing the evolution of stories of Izumi Shikibu and Dōmyō's affair, we can thus see that even *otogizōshi* that take Heian court figures as their subjects are in many cases more fundamentally linked to the popular preaching and entertaining of Kamakura and Muromachi-period jongleurs than they are to the elite Heian literary traditions that they purport to represent.

[75]Both Kintō's visit and Michinaga's dedication ceremony are recorded in *Shōyūki*, the diary of Fujiwara no Sanesuke (957–1046). Cited in Okazaki Tomoko, "Izumi Shikibu to Shōkū Shōnin: 'kuraki yori' no uta wo megutte" (1959), reprinted in *Heianchō joryū sakka no kenkyū* (Tokyo: Hōzōkan, 1967), 187–88.

Chapter Four
Tendai Tales: *Sangoku denki* and the *Lotus Sutra* Commentaries

In chapters one through three we explored the development of tales of Izumi Shikibu and Dōmyō Ajari's supposed affair from their probable origins in a late-Heian and early-medieval proselytizing tradition to their incorporation in works of Muromachi fiction, illuminating the influence of Buddhist storytelling on the development of later literary genres. In this and the following two chapters, we will turn to some of the many stories of Izumi Shikibu and Shōkū Shōnin preserved in largely sectarian Buddhist sources—*setsuwa*, Tendai *Lotus Sutra* commentaries, sermon records, and illustrated temple and shrine histories—in order to reflect upon the uses of Izumi Shikibu's poetry and persona (and, to a lesser extent, those of Sei Shōnagon and the eighth-century Chūjōhime) in the medieval marketing of Buddhism to women. In doing so, we will consider aspects of the popular rhetoric of women's sin and salvation, as well as the widespread appropriation of Izumi Shikibu and her peers by a variety of Buddhist sects and institutions as legitimizing and empowering cultural figures to be drawn upon for their celebrity endorsements in preaching and fund-raising.

The status of women in Buddhism has always tended to be inferior to that of men. The *otogizōshi Fuji no hitoana sōshi* (The Story of the Fuji Cave; Muromachi period) is representative of popular medieval Japanese Buddhist thought when it explains that "few men fall into hell, but many women do," and that "only evil-doers are reborn as women"—in effect, that women are women because of their misdeeds in a previous life.[1] At the heart of the traditional Buddhist antipathy toward women is the concept of the "Five Obstructions" (*goshō*). According to the "Devadatta" chapter of the *Lotus Sutra*, women suffer from a fivefold obstruction by which they are naturally

[1]MJMT 11:464b–65a (woodblock-printed *tanrokubon* of 1627). Koyama Issei argues that *Fuji no hitoana sōshi* is derived from the storytelling traditions of medieval *yamabushi* (mountain ascetics) and (possibly) mendicant *miko* from the Fuji mountain region, and that because of its particular emphasis on women's sins and punishments in hell, it was intended for a largely female audience. Koyama Issei, *Fuji no hitoana sōshi: kenkyū to shiryō* (Tokyo: Bunka Shobō Hakubunsha, 1983), 38, 48–50, and 55. Also see R. Keller Kimbrough, "Translation: The Tale of the Fuji Cave," *Japanese Journal of Religious Studies* 33, no. 2 (online supplement, 2006): 1–22.

precluded from five forms of rebirth: that of a Brahmā God King, that of Śakra, that of Māra, that of a Wheel-turning King, and, most importantly, that of a Buddha.[2] As a result of this fifth and last preclusion, women are denied the prospect of attaining Buddhahood simply because they are women. In his commentary *Fahuajing yaojie* (Essential Interpretations of the *Lotus Sutra*; dated 1127), the Song priest Jiehuan summarily explains that "while a Brahmā King is pure, Śakra has few desires, Māra is steadfast, a Wheel King is benevolent, and a Buddha possesses myriad virtues, a woman has many defilements, she has many desires, she is infirm, she is jealous, and she is rife with delusion."[3]

In Japan, the Five Obstructions have often been equated with the Confucian and Brahmanic concept of the "Three Obediences" (*sanjū*, a woman's obligation to obey her father, her husband, and finally her son), and the two together—the Five Obstructions and the Three Obediences—are frequently cited in late-Heian and medieval sources as a metaphor for women and the problems supposedly inherent to their gender.[4] In describing the exclusion of women from Mount Hiei, headquarters of the Japanese Tendai Buddhist sect, for example, Hōnen, progenitor of the Japanese Pure Land sect, writes in his *Muryōjukyō shaku* (Commentary on *The Sutra of Infinite Life*; ca. 1190):

> The mountain peak of the Single Vehicle stands high; the clouds of the Five Obstructions do not gather. The valley of the Single Truth is deep; the waters of the Three Obediences do not flow there.[5]

The "Single Vehicle" is the Single Vehicle of the Dharma, and the "Single Truth" is the Single Truth of Buddhism. Hōnen opposes these to the Five Obstructions and the Three Obediences, emblematic of women. Thus, according to Hōnen, Mount Hiei's sanctity is linked to its gender exclusivity.

In the Kamakura and Muromachi periods, elaborate accounts of how Izumi Shikibu visited Shōkū Shōnin at his temple on Mount Shosha and

[2]TSD 9 (262): 35c; Burton Watson, *The Lotus Sutra* (New York: Columbia University Press, 1993), 188. It is worth noting that although the *Lotus Sutra* propounds the Five Obstructions, it simultaneously subverts their importance by including the tale of the eight-year-old Dragon Girl, discussed below.

[3]*Fahuajing yaojie* (*Hokekyō yoge*), in *Wan xucangjing* (*Manji zoku zōkyō*), vol. 47 (Taibei: Xinwenfeng, 1977), 631.

[4]On the Five Obstructions and the Three Obediences, see Paul Groner, "Vicissitudes in the Ordination of Japanese 'Nuns' during the Eighth through the Tenth Centuries," in *Engendering Faith: Women and Buddhism in Premodern Japan*, ed. Barbara Ruch (Ann Arbor: University of Michigan Center for Japanese Studies, 2002), 73–74; and Nagata Mizu, "Transitions in Attitudes toward Women in the Buddhist Canon: The Three Obligations, the Five Obstructions, and the Eight Rules of Reverence," trans. and adapted by Paul B. Watt, in *Engendering Faith*, 279–81.

[5]NST 10:55 and 247a.

there composed her "darkness into darkness" poem, based on a verse in the "Phantom City" chapter of the *Lotus Sutra*, were disseminated by both Tendai proponents of the *Lotus Sutra* and strictly Pure Land-oriented advocates of Amida Buddha in a range of didactic, promotional, and fund-raising activities. Members of Tendai instructional centers, or *dangisho*, cited the stories to illustrate and enliven their explications of the *Lotus Sutra*, while Pure Land preachers—specifically those affiliated with Seiganji Temple in the capital—employed alternate versions to promote the sacred statue of Amida at Seiganji (the Seiganji Amida) and the practice of the *nenbutsu*, the ritual invocation of Amida Buddha's name. As accounts of Izumi Shikibu and Shōkū Shōnin were manipulated and revised by competing groups with conflicting ideological and economic agendas, they became a textual locus in the sectarian Buddhist struggles of the medieval period, with Izumi Shikibu, a lay literary figure of an earlier age, cast in a leading role at the center of the debate.

Sangoku denki and a Solution for Women

At some time in the first half of the fifteenth century, an otherwise unknown author by the name of Gentō compiled an anthology of stories—mostly Buddhist—concerning India, China, and Japan.[6] He named it *Sangoku denki* (Tales of Three Countries), and included within it an unusually elaborate rendition of the Izumi Shikibu/Shōkū Shōnin account. According to Gentō's narrative frame, introduced in his prologue, the anthology consists of alternating tales related by an Indian priest (Bongobō), a Chinese layperson (Kanjirō), and a Japanese renunciant (Wa'ami) at Kiyomizu Temple on the seventeenth night of the eighth month of 1407.[7] Although nothing is known of Gentō aside from his compilation of the work, internal evidence suggests that he was a Tendai priest in the Shinazaki region of Ōmi province in what is now Shiga Prefecture. Kobayashi Naoki speculates that he studied at or was otherwise affiliated with the Kashiwabara *dangisho* (seminary), a major Tendai instructional center at Jōbodai'in Temple in the Sakata region of Ōmi,

[6]Ikegami Jun'ichi concludes that *Sangoku denki* probably dates from the late 1420s to the early 1440s; the years 1407–46, however, are more certain. Ikegami Jun'ichi, "Kaisetsu," in *Sangoku denki*, vol. 1 (Tokyo: Miyai Shoten, 1982), 19.

[7]"Bongobō," "Kanjirō," and "Wa'ami" might be translated, "Sanskrit Priest," "Chinese Guy," and "Japanese Devotee," respectively. The narrative conceit is modeled on that of the "Account of the All-night Conversation at Kitano Shrine" (*Kitano tsuya monogatari no koto*) section of *Taiheiki* (fourteenth century; NKBT 36:316–35). Ikegami argues that the identification of two of the storytellers in *Sangoku denki* as non-Japanese reflects the increased levels of international trade allowed under the rule of the *shōgun* Ashikaga Yoshimitsu (1358–1408). Ikegami, "Kaisetsu," 5–6.

where he likely had access to his numerous *Sangoku denki* sources, both written and (probably) oral.[8]

Many of the *Sangoku denki* tales, including the story of Izumi Shikibu and Shōkū Shōnin, are of unknown origin. Kobayashi posits that Gentō drew these untraceable accounts from various oral traditions circulating in the *dangisho* at the time.[9] Slightly alternate renditions of the Izumi Shikibu/Shōkū Shōnin *setsuwa* are contained in several late-medieval Tendai *Lotus Sutra* commentaries (discussed in the following section), themselves products of the various *dangisho*, suggesting that Kobayashi's theory is correct and that Gentō likely based his Izumi Shikibu account upon an unwritten source used to teach the *Lotus Sutra* at Tendai institutions in the fifteenth century. Because the tale is fundamentally concerned with the problem of women's enlightenment—the possibility of women attaining Buddhahood, in spite of their gender—it would have constituted natural storytelling material for the Buddhist instruction of women. Kobayashi observes that *Sangoku denki* was likely used as a sermon source book,[10] and if this was indeed the case, then Gentō's Izumi Shikibu/Shōkū Shōnin account or some earlier version of it may well have been used in preaching to women; at the very least, his story is emblematic of the kinds of tales that were. Considering Kamo no Chōmei's account of the *asobi* who recited Izumi Shikibu's "darkness into darkness" poem for the holy man Shōshō Hijiri,[11] women may have been told the tale of Izumi Shikibu's meeting with Shōkū Shōnin from as early as the first years of the thirteenth century.

The *Sangoku denki* account begins as follows, with a largely hagiographic introduction to Shōkū Shōnin:[12]

> Wa'ami spoke:
>
> In the reign of Emperor Ichijō, there was a venerable sage by the name of Shōkū Shōnin on Mount Shosha in Harima province. Although the four walls surrounding the dais upon which he recited the *Lotus Sutra* were thin, the eight winds did not easily penetrate,[13] and although, having attained a state of purity of the

[8]Kobayashi suggests that the Kashiwabara *dangisho* at Jōbodai'in was engaged in *Hokke jikidan* (direct explication of the *Lotus Sutra*) from the late fourteenth century. Kobayashi Naoki, "*Sangoku denki* no seiritsu kiban: *Hokke* jikidan no sekai to no kōshō," in *Chūsei setsuwashū to sono kiban* (Osaka: Izumi Shoin, 2004), 153.

[9]Ibid., 153–54.

[10]Ibid., 121.

[11]Contained in *Hosshinshū*, ca. 1212–16. See p. 66, above.

[12]The following translation is based on Ikegami Jun'ichi's annotated edition of *Sangoku denki* in the woodblock-printed textual line. Ikegami, ed., *Sangoku denki*, vol. 2 (8:21), 108–10.

[13]The "eight winds" (*happū*) are eight elements that disturb or incite the human heart: profit, sorrow, slander, fame, praise, censure, suffering, and pleasure.

> six senses, his mind was empty as a single gourd, his meditative practice was naturally profound. Therefore he realized that the splendor of Knowledge of Universal Oneness is without gap between front and rear, and he understood that interior and exterior are without separation in the infinite emptiness and tranquility of the Buddha's physical form.[14]

In the poverty of his thin-walled dwelling, Shōkū Shōnin is free of the metaphorical Eight Winds, and in the profundity of his meditative practice, he is enlightened to the seminal Tendai truth of nonduality, according to which all things are essentially the same. Gentō's emphasis on this aspect of Shōkū Shōnin's understanding lends the passage a particularly Tendai tone, reflecting the larger Tendai bias of *Sangoku denki* as a whole.

As the account continues, the narrator turns to Jōtōmon'in (Empress Shōshi), in whose salon Izumi Shikibu served:

> In order to meet with Shōkū Shōnin and confess her sins, Jōtōmon'in once secretly left the capital and ascended to the temple on Mount Shosha. Shōkū Shōnin knew of this in advance, and one evening he said to his disciples, "Eight demons will come here tomorrow at noon. All those within the temple should flee." No one doubted his words, and everyone ran and hid. "You should say I've gone off to Kyūshū to preach," Shōkū Shōnin instructed, and he entered a meditation hall to hide. "How are we to face such demons that frighten even the Master?" the disciples cried. Shōkū Shōnin replied: "As long as I am in here, you need have no great fear."
>
> The Empress and eight ladies-in-waiting, including Izumi Shikibu, soon alighted from their palanquins and entered the temple precincts. The beauty of their features was like the evening waves on Lake Furong,[15] and their lithesome gait was as the swaying of a willow in an evening storm. As coquettish as Li Furen and made up like Yang Guifei,[16] their appearance was truly wondrous. The disciples looked upon them in fear. "These must be the demons of which the Master spoke," they thought, "—monsters in disguise."

[14]"Knowledge of Universal Oneness" (*byōdōshōchi*) is the wisdom by which one comprehends the nondual nature of reality. It allows one to perceive the essential sameness (and therefore inseparable nature) of all things. According to this principle, front and rear are like two sides of a single coin—separate yet the same. "The Buddha's physical form" (*sōgō*) refers to the thirty-two major and eighty minor distinguishing characteristics of a Buddha.

[15]Lake Furong lies at the base of Mount Furong in China's Shandong province.

[16]Li Furen (Lady Li) and Yang Guifei are two Chinese imperial consorts immortalized in poems by Bai Juyi: *Li Furen* and *Chang hen ge* (The Song of Everlasting Sorrow). Li Furen lived in the first century B.C.E., during the Early Han period, and Yang Guifei lived in the first half of the eighth century, during the Tang. Yang Guifei is traditionally blamed for precipitating the calamity of the An Lushan Rebellion in 755.

> The disciples explained that the Master was away in Kyūshū. Hearing this, the Empress felt as if the moon over Mt. Gaya had suddenly set, as if in an instant the blossoms of the *śāla* grove had shriveled.[17] "I face grave karmic obstructions," she said, "and for these I regret my sins. Now just when I have come to see the Master, he happens to be away. When I think of pushing on through the long road ahead . . . I have the will, but not the strength. In this too there is nothing so hateful as the body of a woman!"

Endowed with supernatural powers by the profundity of his religious practice, Shōkū Shōnin foresees Jōtōmon'in's arrival; warning his disciples of "demons," he advises them all to run away. The dangers of women—to celibate men, that is—have long been recognized in the Buddhist tradition. For example, in the Indian *Anguttara Nikāya*, a compendium of discourses of the Buddha, Shakyamuni himself warns his monastic disciples to be on their guard against women: "Have a conversation with a man holding a sword in his hand," he explains, "or with a demon, or sit down next to a snake whose bite is fatal, but never have a conversation alone with a woman!"[18] The *Theragāthā*, a compilation of verses attributed to monks of the early Indian Buddhist order, similarly identifies women as "razor blades" slathered with honey.[19] In the *Sangoku denki* account, Shōkū Shōnin's warning to his disciples brings to mind an oft-quoted Japanese Buddhist proverb frequently misattributed to the *Kegon* and *Nirvana* sutras, to the effect that "women are the servants of hell; they stamp out the seeds of the Buddha. On the outside they are as bodhisattvas, while on the inside they are as devils."[20] This conflicted view of women as beautiful monsters—dangerous mantraps in the lovely and alluring guise of bodhisattvas—appears to stem from a mixture

[17]Mt. Gaya (in India) is the legendary site of the Buddha's enlightenment; when the Buddha died in a grove of *śāla* trees, the blossoms there are said to have turned white and scattered.

[18]Cited in Liz Wilson, *Charming Cadavers: Horrific Figurations of the Feminine in Indian Buddhist Hagiographic Literature* (Chicago and London: University of Chicago Press, 1996), 71.

[19]Ibid., 71.

[20]The earliest known citation of this adage is in the twelfth-century *Hōbutsushū*, which mistakenly attributes it to the *Nirvana Sutra* (SNKBT 40:212). The *Lotus Sutra* commentary *Hokekyō jikidanshō* (ca. 1546) alludes to it in explaining Shōkū Shōnin's hostility to women. *Hokekyō jikidanshō*, vol. 2 (Kyoto: Rinsen Shoten, 1979), 285. Bernard Faure follows Kasahara Kazuo in following Zonkaku's *Nyonin ōjō kikigaki* (1324) in attributing the adage to Vasubandhu's *Yuishikiron* (ca. fifth century), but the editors of the SNKBT *Hōbutsushū* volume assert that the proverb is not to be found in that source either (SNKBT 40:212, note 3). Bernard Faure, *The Power of Denial: Buddhism, Purity, and Gender* (Princeton and Oxford: Princeton University Press, 2003), 60 (Faure's fn. 21 should cite p. 52 rather than p. 199 of Kasahara's 1983 book; the misattributed passage is also cited on p. 199 of Kasahara's *Nyonin ōjō shisō no keifu* [Tokyo: Yoshikawa Kōbunkan, 1975], but this is not the work that Faure cites in his note).

of displaced male fear and desire: the projected emotions of celibate priests perceiving women as tantalizing threats to monastic purity. Thus, because she is a woman, even the Empress is a devil inside.

In the Muromachi-period noh play *Izumi Shikibu*, Izumi Shikibu is turned away at the Enkyōji Temple gate because of a rule forbidding entrance to women after dark. The monks tell her to go away and come back in the morning.[21] Such restrictions, referred to as *nyonin kinsei*, "prohibitions of women," seem to have been common in Japan from around the ninth century.[22] As institutional exclusions—misogynistic proscriptions intended to keep dangerous maneaters at bay—they appear to have been enacted both in response to the imagined impurity of women and to the perceived threat that women posed to monks in their Buddhist practice. In Gentō's *Sangoku denki* account, Shōkū Shōnin's disciples look on in horror as Jōtōmon'in and her lovely entourage arrive at their temple: with swaying hips and faces made up like the infamous Chinese beauties Li Furen and Yang Guifei, the Empress and her ladies represent a full-blown sexual menace, violating the sacred space of the all-male mountain enclave. The scene is at once comical and, for the women, deadly serious. The monks lie about their master's whereabouts, prompting Jōtōmon'in to exclaim in frustration that "in this too there is nothing so hateful as the body of a woman," demonstrating her own internalization of the monks' misogynistic views. The story continues:

> Tearfully Jōtōmon'in turned to leave, whereupon her attendant, Izumi Shikibu, wrote out a poem and fixed it to a temple pillar, thinking that Shōkū Shōnin might see it there:

kuraki yori	From darkness
kuraki michi ni zo	into a path of darkness
irinubeki	I must enter—
haruka ni terase	shine your light afar,
yama no ha no tsuki	moon on the mountain ridge!

[21]Paul Groner writes that "according to the *Regulations for Monks and Nuns* (*Sōniryō*), men were not to spend the night at nunneries, and women were not to spend the night at monasteries. This pattern was adopted at a number of monasteries during the early Heian period, including some of those that required monks to be sequestered. For example, Zenrinji, which was founded by Kūkai's disciple Shinshō, required its monks to be sequestered for six years but permitted women to visit as long as they did not stay the night." The situation at Enkyōji, as described in the noh play *Izumi Shikibu*, may have been analogous. Groner, "Vicissitudes in the Ordination of Japanese 'Nuns,'" 77. Tanaka Makoto dates *Izumi Shikibu* to around the fifteenth century. Tanaka Makoto, "Izumi Shikibu to yōkyoku," *Kokugo to kokubungaku* (April 1946), 14. *Izumi Shikibu* (also known as *Shosha*) is printed in Yoshida Kōichi, ed., *Izumi Shikibu zenshū: honbun hen* (Tokyo: Koten Bunko, 1959), 772–76.

[22]Miyake Hitoshi, "Nyonin kinsei," in *Kokushi daijiten*, vol. 11 (Tokyo: Yoshikawa Kōbunkan, 1990), 265a.

The women set out on their return.

Shōkū Shōnin saw the poem, and he must have been moved, for although the women had gone some distance, he had them called back and met with them. The tranquil light of Universal Form emanated from his long, silvery eyebrows, frosted with age and years of devoted practice, and gray hair like the snow of three winter months of ritual incantation rested upon his head, replete with accumulated merit and cognizance of the True Reality.[23] Such was his most venerable appearance.

"Faced with the Five Obstructions, what practices might a woman perform to escape suffering?" the Empress inquired, whereupon Shōkū Shōnin presented her with the *Lotus Sutra*. On the lid of the sutra box, the following poem was inscribed:

futatsu naku	As it expounds the Dharma
mitsu naki nori to	of which there are
toku yue ni	neither two nor three,
itsutsu no sawari	the Five Obstructions, I think,
araji to zo omou	will surely not obstruct.

The Empress grasped the truth of this sutra, which in life upon life, world upon world is but rarely encountered, in innumerable aeons is but seldom heard, and in tears she returned to the capital.

Recognizing Izumi Shikibu's allusion to the *Lotus Sutra* verse, Shōkū Shōnin agrees to allow the Empress and her party inside. According to the *Lotus Sutra* commentary *Hokekyō jikidanshō* (ca. 1546) and an alternate *Sangoku denki* text, Shōkū Shōnin happened to be chanting the identical *Lotus Sutra* passage at the moment that Izumi Shikibu composed her verse.[24] For women, the *Lotus Sutra* opens all doors, the holy man explains, and in this case, it opens his own as well. Paradoxically, it is Izumi Shikibu's knowledge of the *Lotus Sutra*, combined with her skill as a poet, that gives her access to Shōkū Shōnin and the *Lotus Sutra*.

In her conversation with the holy man, Jōtōmon'in brings up the troublesome issue of the Five Obstructions. Shōkū Shōnin's answer is the *Lotus Sutra*, and he presents a copy to Jōtōmon'in in a box with a poem on the lid. Like Izumi Shikibu's "darkness into darkness" verse, which alludes to a passage in the "Phantom City" chapter of the *Lotus Sutra*, Shōkū Shōnin's poem alludes to a passage in the chapter on "Expedient Means": "In the Buddha lands of the ten directions / there is but a single vehicle, / there

[23]"Universal Form" (*shinnyo*) and "True Reality" (*jisso*) are synonyms. Both refer to *tathatā* (Thusness, Suchness, The Essence of All Things).

[24]*Hokekyō jikidanshō*, vol. 2, 284; Nagoya Sangoku Denki Kenkyūkai, ed., *Sangoku denki*, vol. 2, Koten bunko 436 (Tokyo: Koten Bunko, 1983), 354 (*Sangoku denki "hiragana-bon"*).

are neither two nor three."[25] The poem works as a kind of mathematical equation: the Dharma of which there are neither two nor three functions to cancel out the Five Obstructions in the way that negative two plus negative three plus five equals zero.[26] In its mathematical perfection, the poem both nullifies the Five Obstructions and elucidates the fundamental Tendai truth of nonduality, according to which all of the many teachings of the Buddha are one. Martin Heidegger has described poetry as a kind of "illuminating projection"—what he elsewhere terms "one mode of the lighting projection of truth"—and his conception, in this case, is apt, for as "the moon on the mountain ridge," Shōkū Shōnin shines down his light of Buddhist Truth—the promise of the *Lotus Sutra*—by means of a Japanese verse.[27]

The *Sangoku denki* account concludes with a final declaration of hope incorporating references to two exemplary women in the *Lotus Sutra*: Mahāprajāpatī (Shakyamuni's maternal aunt and the first woman admitted to the Buddhist order, prophesied in the "Encouraging Devotion" chapter to attain Buddhahood and lead six thousand other nuns to enlightenment),[28] and the eight-year-old Dragon Girl, reported in the "Devadatta" chapter to have heard the bodhisattva Mañjuśrī preach the *Lotus Sutra*, and, as a result, to have overcome the Five Obstructions and attained instant and full enlightenment before the eyes of a group of doubting men:[29]

> Mahāprajāpatī received the prophecy at the assembly on Sacred [Eagle] Peak, and the Dragon Girl attained enlightenment in the Immaculate World. For this reason the Five Obstructions and the Three Obediences are as yesterday's clouds, and the Ten Elements

[25]TSD 9 (262): 8a; Watson, *The Lotus Sutra*, 35. Variants of the poem are attributed to Izumi Shikibu, Ono no Komachi, and Empress Shōshi (Jōtōmon'in), respectively, in *Hōbutsushū* (twelfth century; SNKBT 40:331), *Jigenshō* (1510; GR 17:289b), and *Hokekyō jikidanshō* (ca. 1546).

[26]As suggested by Edward Kamens in "Dragon-Girl, Maidenflower, Buddha: The Transformation of a Waka Topos, 'The Five Obstructions,'" *Harvard Journal of Asiatic Studies* 53, no. 2 (December 1993), 431–33. The poem constitutes an example of what Susan Klein has described as a "numerological homology," prevalent in esoteric medieval Buddhist and poetic commentaries. Susan Blakeley Klein, *Allegories of Desire: Esoteric Literary Commentaries of Medieval Japan* (Cambridge: Harvard University Asia Center, 2002), 37–40 and 117–18.

[27]Martin Heidegger, *Poetry, Language, Thought*, trans. Albert Hofstadter (New York: Harper and Row, 1971), 72 and 75.

[28]TSD 9 (262): 36a; Watson, *The Lotus Sutra*, 191–92. Mahāprajāpatī is also known by the names Gautamī and, in Japanese, Daiaidō.

[29]As her tale is told, the daughter of the *nāga* dragon king had nearly attained enlightenment as a result of hearing Mañjuśrī expound the *Lotus Sutra*. When Śāriputra questioned her ability to attain Buddhahood, faced as she and all other women are with the Five Obstructions, she presented Shakyamuni with a priceless jewel. "Was that not quickly done?" she asked, whereupon with even greater speed she transformed into a man, carried out all of the bodhisattva practices, and then became a Buddha. TSD 9 (262): 35c; Watson, *The Lotus Sutra*, 187–88.

> and the Single Vehicle are as tonight's moon. Those [women] born into heaven or the world of mortals shall receive sublime comfort; those appearing before the Buddha shall spontaneously come into existence upon a lotus. [For women,] there is indeed a way!

As Shōkū Shōnin explains, the *Lotus Sutra* will sweep away the obscuring clouds of delusion (the Five Obstructions to a woman's rebirth and the Three Obediences that a woman owes to her father, husband, and son), thereby allowing the bright moon of Tendai Truth to shine forth (as represented by the Ten Aspects of all Elements and the Single Vehicle of the Dharma). Gentō uses this account of Jōtōmon'in, Izumi Shikibu and Shōkū Shōnin to present the *Lotus Sutra* as a true female-liberating text, capable not only of freeing women from the Buddhist preclusions of the Five Obstructions, but of releasing them from their subservience to men (as represented by the Three Obediences) as well.

Shōkū Shōnin's recommendation of the *Lotus Sutra* as the solution to the "problem" of being a woman is not without scriptural foundation. In addition to its inclusion of the stories of Mahāprajāpatī's prophecy and the Dragon Girl's enlightenment, the *Lotus Sutra* contains in its "Medicine King" chapter the following promise:

> If there is a woman who hears this chapter on the Former Affairs of the Bodhisattva Medicine King and is able to accept and uphold it, that will be her last appearance in a woman's body and she will never be born in that form again. If in the last five hundred year period after the Thus Come One has entered extinction there is a woman who hears this sutra and carries out its practices as the sutra directs, when her life here on earth comes to an end she will immediately go to the world of Peace and Delight where the Buddha Amitayus [Amida] dwells surrounded by the assembly of great bodhisattvas and there will be born seated on a jeweled seat in the center of a lotus blossom.[30]

It is by means of the *Lotus Sutra*, then, that women may escape the curse of their female form and be reborn in the Pure Land Paradise of Amida Buddha, there to attain enlightenment.[31] The painted frontispiece to the "Medecine King" chapter of the *Heike nōkyō*, a sumptuous set of *Lotus Sutra* scrolls commissioned by Taira no Kiyomori and other members of the Taira clan ca. 1164, depicts a woman in elegant robes gazing out across a lotus pond

[30]TSD 9 (262): 54b; Watson, *The Lotus Sutra*, 287. Translation here by Watson.

[31]The *Jizō Bosatsu hongankyō* (Sutra on the Original Vow of the Bodhisattva Jizō) similarly promises salvation from the female form. See Hank Glassman, "The Nude Jizō at Denkōji: Notes on Women's Salvation in Kamakura Buddhism," in *Engendering Faith*, 400.

at Amida Buddha in his Pure Land; the words of the preceding passage are reproduced within the image itself, suggesting the passage's importance for women in twelfth-century Japan.[32]

Because of their achievements as women (or females, at least), Mahāprajāpatī and the reptilian Dragon Girl are likely to have been staple figures in preaching to women in the medieval period.[33] In Gentō's *Sangoku denki* account, insofar as *nyonin kinsei* proscriptions are metaphoric of women's spiritual exclusion from the Way, Izumi Shikibu's admittance to Enkyōji Temple by means of her "darkness into darkness" poem suggests her own attainment, as a Heian woman poet, of the True Path of the Buddha—both for herself and for the women around her. *Keiran shūyōshū* (Gathered Leaves from the Mountain-valley Winds), an encyclopedic compendium of Tendai lore compiled by the priest Kōsō between 1311 and 1348, explains that in the way that the Dragon Girl presented the Buddha with a precious jewel, and the second Zen patriarch Huike (487–593) offered Bodhidharma his severed arm, Dharma transmissions should be "purchased according to one's ability."[34] For Izumi Shikibu, this is her skill as a poet, and it is thus with a poem that she secures Shōkū Shōnin's instruction. Like Mahāprajāpatī and the Dragon Girl before her, she transcends the imposed limitations of her gender, pioneering a path for other women to tread.

Izumi Shikibu and the Medieval *Lotus Sutra* Commentaries

Whether Gentō did in fact base his rendition of the Izumi Shikibu/Shōkū Shōnin account on a story he heard in an early fifteenth-century Tendai *dangisho* is unknown. It seems probable, however, considering that similar yet apparently unrelated accounts appear in a number of *Lotus Sutra* commentaries from the late-fifteenth and sixteenth centuries, including *Ichijō*

[32]The *Heike nōkyō* frontispiece is reproduced in numerous sources, including Willa J. Tanabe, *Paintings of the Lotus Sutra* (New York and Tokyo: Weatherhill, 1988), plate 8 (see Tanabe's discussion of the image on pp. 65–66). Also see Nicole Fabricand-Person, "Demonic Female Guardians of the Faith: The *Fugen Jūrasetsunyo* Iconography in Japanese Buddhist Art," in *Engendering Faith*, 368–69. A picture of the Dragon Girl presenting Shakyamuni with a jewel is painted as a frontispiece to the "Devadatta" chapter of the *Heike nōkyō* as well.

[33]Mahāprajāpatī is a somewhat ambivalent figure in Buddhism. While she is celebrated on the one hand for opening the monastic order to women, she is also blamed for having reduced the period of the True Law from 1000 to 500 years as a result. See Etienne Lamotte, *History of Indian Buddhism: From the Origins to the Śaka Era*, trans. Sara Webb-Boin (Louvain: Peeters Press, 1988), 192–98; Diana Y. Paul, *Women in Buddhism: Images of the Feminine in Mahāyāna Tradition* (Berkeley: Asian Humanities Press, 1979), 83–84. Also see footnote 34 in chapter six, below.

[34]TSD 76 (2410): 540c; Jacqueline Stone, *Original Enlightenment and the Transformation of Medieval Japanese Buddhism* (Honolulu: University of Hawaii Press, 1999), 145. Translation by Stone.

shūgyokushō (Gathered Jewels of the Single Vehicle), *Hokekyō jurin shūyōshō* (Gathered Leaves of the *Lotus Sutra* from a Grove on Eagle Peak), *Hokekyō jikidanshō* (Straight Talk on the *Lotus Sutra*), and *Jikidan innenshū* (Straight Talk on Causes and Conditions).[35] Known collectively as *jikidan* ("straight talk")-type works because of their self-stated aims of explaining the *Lotus Sutra* in an unambiguous, forthright manner, these texts eschew difficult, complex, or overly abstract discussions in favor of concrete examples from the everyday realms of lay and monastic society.[36] As a result, they constitute troves of late-medieval *setsuwa*, providing snapshots of the evolving world of Muromachi tale literature as well as insights into the role of Tendai preaching in the dissemination of literary and popular culture in the fifteenth and sixteenth centuries.

Part seminary and part scholastic center, Tendai *dangisho* were hotbeds of scholarship and textual production in the late-Kamakura and Muromachi periods. Ogami Kanchū has identified references in medieval manuscripts to as many as sixty-one *dangisho* throughout the various provinces; three were located in Ōmi,[37] where Gentō seems to have made his home. In addition to sponsoring *jikidan*-type sermons for lay audiences and providing doctrinal training for Tendai monks, the *dangisho* hosted numerous visiting scholar-priests engaged in a variety of pedagogical and textual enterprises, including the reproduction of Buddhist and secular literary works and the compilation and dissemination of sutra commentaries, literary commentaries, and (purportedly) secret oral transmissions. The earliest recorded reference to a *dangisho* dates from the fourth month of 1276; Hirota Tetsumichi, by far the most prolific scholar on the subject, maintains that such centers

[35]The first three of these works are discussed below. As for the Izumi Shikibu/Shōkū Shōnin account in the fourth (the surviving manuscript of which was copied out by the priest Shun'yū in 1585), see Abe Yasurō et al., eds., *Nikkō tenkaizō Jikidan innenshū: honkoku to sakuin* (Osaka: Izumi Shoin, 1998), 102–3. Izumi Shikibu's "darkness into darkness" poem is cited in two additional related works: *Tetsujinshō* (1526, by the priest Jikkai), and *Hokke yakuwashū* (*Yakuwashū*; also by Jikkai). Hirota Tetsumichi, *Tendai danjo de Hokekyō wo yomu* (Tokyo: Kanrin Shobō, 1997), 141.

[36]In *Jurin shūyōshō* (1512), the priest Sonshun writes that "[the characters for] *jikidan* should be simply read, 'to directly explain': to plainly convey the message of the *Lotus Sutra* without taking up the explications of the commentaries or engaging in interpretive exegesis." In *Jikidanshō* (ca. 1546), Eishin adds that as Shakyamuni spoke in an idiom that was readily understood, "*jikidan* means explaining things frankly, just like the Buddha preached." *Hokekyō jurin shūyōshō*, vol. 1 (Kyoto: Rinsen Shoten, 1991), 9; *Hokekyō jikidanshō*, vol. 1, 32. Hirota Tetsumichi cites a similar explanation from *Ichijō shūgyokushō* (1488) in his *Chūsei Bukkyō bungaku no kenkyū* (Osaka: Izumi Shoin, 2000), 108.

[37]Ogami's work is cited in Hirota, *Chūsei Hokekyō chūshakusho no kenkyū* (Tokyo: Kasama Shoin, 1993), 39. The information in this paragraph is drawn from this and another of Hirota's books, *Chūsei Bukkyō bungaku no kenkyū*, 78–144. For a further discussion of the *dangisho* in English, see Stone, *Original Enlightenment*, 148–50.

enjoyed their heyday in the hundred-year period from approximately 1450 to 1550, the century in which they produced their many *jikidan*-style texts.

The earliest surviving *jikidan*-type *Lotus Sutra* commentary is *Ichijō shūgyokushō*, compiled by the priest Eikai in 1488, approximately fifty years after Gentō's compilation of *Sangoku denki*, at Kōryūji Temple in the Yoshiki region of Suō province in present-day Yamaguchi Prefecture. Exceedingly little is known about Eikai or his composition of the work. His temple is reported to have flourished in the latter part of the fifteenth century under the patronage of the regional military commander Ōuchi Masahiro (1446–95), a generous sponsor of scholarship, religion and the arts. From 1482 to 1490, Kōryūji was engaged in producing a woodblock-printed edition of the *Lotus Sutra*, a major publishing project to which Eikai's compilation of *Ichijō shūgyokushō* was likely related.[38] Eikai moved east—to the other side of the country, so to speak—in the years after his completion of the work. At some time in or around the early 1490s, he became an active and later leading member of Yakuōin Temple in Hitachi province, an important Tendai center among the various *dangisho* of the eastern Kantō region.[39] *Ichijō shūgyokushō* survives in a single known manuscript hand-copied by the priest Denkai in Hitachi in 1493, indicating that Eikai took his commentary with him when he moved.[40]

From a literary perspective, one of the most interesting aspects of *Ichijō shūgyokushō* is its exceptionally broad use of Izumi Shikibu tales and poems (many of them apocryphal) to fill out its discussions of passages and ideas from the *Lotus Sutra*. Nakano Maori has counted more than thirty *waka* attributed to Izumi Shikibu in *Ichijō shūgyokushō*—roughly twenty percent of all poems cited within the text[41]—indicating that Eikai and probably the Kantō *dangisho* as a whole made especially liberal use of Izumi Shikibu's name and reputation in their efforts to teach. In reciting stories about Izumi Shikibu, Tendai preachers may have thought to enliven their sermons and sutra explications by appealing to native traditions and sensibilities. Employing funny, strange, or moving accounts with which a lay audience might themselves identify, these priests could have appealed to a greater

[38]Nakano Maori, *Ichijō shūgyokushō no kenkyū* (Kyoto: Rinsen Shoten, 1998), 41–42.

[39]Yakuōin is in the present-day city of Mito in Ibaraki Prefecture. Nakano Maori, "*Hokekyō* chū: ishi wo atsumete tama wo toru," in *Chūsei no chi to gaku: chūshaku wo yomu*, ed. Mitani Kuniaki and Komine Kazuaki (Tokyo: Shinwasha, 1997), 222–23; revised and reprinted in Nakano, *Ichijō shūgyokushō no kenkyū*, 5–6.

[40]Denkai's manuscript (minus the "Expedient Means" chapter and the first part of the "Simile and Parable" chapter, which have been lost) is photographically reproduced in *Ichijō shūgyokushō: eiin* (Kyoto: Rinsen Shoten, 1998).

[41]Nakano, *Ichijō shūgyokushō no kenkyū*, 261–63.

number and variety of people than they might otherwise have done. Like their Tennōji Temple counterparts, who Ōshima Tatehiko suggests recounted tales of Izumi Shikibu and Dōmyō Ajari, Eikai and his peers put to use Izumi Shikibu stories as a kind of *hōben*: an expedient means of teaching, in this case, the *Lotus Sutra*. As a prolific author of Buddhist poetry and a scandalous symbol of the Heian court, Izumi Shikibu would have been ideally suited to her medieval role, inspiring interest in audiences high and low alike.

In *Ichijō shūgyokushō*, Eikai cites the story of Izumi Shikibu and Shōkū Shōnin in the "Phantom City" chapter of his commentary, in conjunction with his explanation of the *Lotus Sutra* verse, "from darkness into darkness."[42] He denigrates the traditionally simplistic (what he terms "Hīnayāna") reading of the *Lotus Sutra* passage in favor of a more profound interpretation inspired by medieval Tendai Original Enlightenment thought:[43]

> "From darkness into darkness." In Hīnayāna Buddhism, this means to enter from darkness into darkness. In the *Lotus Sutra*, however, this also means the darkness of Original Enlightenment. Acquired Enlightenment reveals delusion and understanding to be the same; Original Enlightenment reveals that delusion is delusion, and that the cycle of birth and death is the cycle of birth and death. This is the true meaning of "from darkness into darkness." For this reason the extinction of the myriad Buddhas is itself extinct.[44]

Original Enlightenment (*hongaku*) is enlightenment of which all sentient beings are naturally, and usually unknowingly, possessed, while its lesser counterpart, Acquired Enlightenment (*shikaku*), is enlightenment attained as a result of Buddhist practice. According to Eikai's explanation, Acquired Enlightenment reveals the Tendai truth of nonduality: that as all things are essentially one, delusion and understanding are the same. However, Original Enlightenment reveals a more subtle truth: that although delusion is understanding, delusion is also delusion. The phrase "from darkness into darkness," rather than the more obvious "from darkness into light," is therefore suggestive of this deepest of medieval Tendai truths, for although

[42]TSD 9 (262): 22c; Watson, *The Lotus Sutra*, 121.

[43]The following quotations are from *Ichijō shūgyokushō: eiin*, 351. I am grateful to Komine Kazuaki for his help in deciphering Denkai's handwritten text.

[44]This final sentence is unclear. It appears to read *shobutsu no metsu wo taetaru yue nari*, in which case it may suggest that by the principle of nonduality, the death of the Buddhas (by which the Buddhas cease to exist) itself ceases to exist.

darkness equals light, according to the logic of nonduality, darkness also equals darkness.[45]

Ichijō shūgyokushō continues:

> There is a story. During the time of Emperor Ichijō, there was a courtesan (*yūjo*) named Izumi Shikibu. She went to see Shōkū Shōnin on Mount Shosha, where she hoped to meet with the master and attain Buddhahood. However, when she arrived, the holy man refused to see her. "The master won't meet with me because I am a woman," Izumi Shikibu said, and she sent him a poem:
>
> | | |
> |---|---|
> | kuraki yori | From darkness |
> | kuraki michi ni zo | into a path of darkness |
> | irinubeki | I must enter— |
> | haruka ni terase | shine your light afar, |
> | yama no ha no tsuki | moon on the mountain ridge! |
>
> The holy man was impressed, and he met with her. At that time Izumi Shikibu asked: "What part of the *Lotus Sutra* is about a woman's attainment of Buddhahood in this very body?"
>
> "'There are neither two nor three,'" the holy man replied, and he explained at length.[46] Izumi Shikibu composed a poem:
>
> | | |
> |---|---|
> | futatsu naku | When I hear the Dharma |
> | mitsu naki nori to | of which there are |
> | kiku toki wa | neither two nor three, |
> | itsutsu no sawari | the Five Obstructions, I think, |
> | araji to zo omou | will surely not obstruct. |

Compared to Gentō's elaborate and highly polished *Sangoku denki* account, Eikai's story is spare. Notably, among *Sangoku denki* and the various *Lotus Sutra* commentaries, only *Ichijō shūgyokushō* refers to Izumi Shikibu as a *yūjo*,

[45]Citing Tamura Yoshirō's understanding of the concept, Jacqueline Stone explains that Original Enlightenment thought consists "in two philosophical moves":

> First, the Mahāyāna idea of nonduality is pushed to its ultimate conclusion. All existents, being empty of independent self-nature, are seen as interpenetrating and mutually identified. This move negates any ontological difference whatsoever between the ordinary person and the Buddha, the mundane world and the pure land, self and other, and so on. All conventional distinctions of the phenomenal world are thus collapsed in a breakthrough into an undifferentiated, nondual realm. Second, based on this insight into absolute nonduality, one "returns," as it were, to the phenomenal world, affirming its relative distinctions, just as they are, as expressions of ultimate nondual reality or original enlightenment.

Stone, *Original Enlightenment*, 50.

[46]"He explained at length" is a free translation of *unnun*, "and so on."

or "courtesan."

Eikai recounts the story of Izumi Shikibu and Shōkū Shōnin within his work for the obvious reason that Izumi Shikibu's "darkness into darkness" poem is based upon the "darkness into darkness" passage of his sutra explication. As an evidentiary example, however, the tale is far from convincing, because it fails to support Eikai's contention that darkness equals darkness in the "Phantom City" verse in the way that darkness equals light. The darkness of Izumi Shikibu's poem is the darkness of ignorance and delusion, a very different thing from the light of understanding that she calls on Shōkū Shōnin—the moon on the mountain ridge—to shine down to light her way. Darkness does not equal light in the poem, nor does Izumi Shikibu invoke the principle of nonduality. Eikai's use of the *setsuwa* is thus an excellent example of what Jacqueline Stone has described as "*kanjin* [mind contemplation]-style hermeneutics," a type of interpretive scholarship characterized by willful misreadings, fabricated citations, and the often wildly creative use of magical associations and numerological and linguistic play, prevalent in medieval Tendai doctrinal discourse.[47]

While Izumi Shikibu's "darkness into darkness" poem may fail to validate Eikai's reading of the "Phantom City" verse (and to be fair, Eikai never claims that it does), the second part of the tale, concerning Izumi Shikibu's meeting with Shōkū Shōnin, skillfully supports the medieval Tendai Original Enlightenment perspective. Unlike the Empress in *Sangoku denki*, who inquires as to how a woman might overcome the dreaded Five Obstructions and escape suffering, Izumi Shikibu asks after the part of the *Lotus Sutra* that explains how a woman might attain Buddhahood in her own body, as a woman. (The Dragon Girl, it will be recalled, transformed into a man before becoming a Buddha; similarly, in the "Medicine King" chapter of the *Lotus Sutra*, women are promised rebirth in the Pure Land in a male form.) "There are neither two nor three," Shōkū Shōnin replies, reciting the passage from the "Expedient Means" chapter concerning the nondual nature of the Dharma. As an absolute extension of the concept of nonduality, Original Enlightenment thought maintains that all phenomena are one—undifferentiated and interpenetrating. As Eikai would have us understand the story, then, Shōkū Shōnin suggests that because all things are the same (including male and female, and delusion and enlightenment), women are

[47]Stone explains: "Rather than taking classic texts as the basis of interpretation, *kanjin*-style hermeneutics first establishes a normative principle (in this case, the premise of original enlightenment) and then seeks textual passages to support it, deriving these where necessary from the invention of proof texts, out-of-context quotation, or imaginative repunctuating of Chinese sources." Stone, *Original Enlightenment*, 65 (also see pp. 156–67).

already Buddhas, just as they are.[48] At the end of the account, Izumi Shikibu is attributed with composing the "neither two nor three" poem, and thus, within Eikai's commentary (and within medieval Tendai preaching, it would seem), she is made to endorse the Tendai doctrine of nonduality by which the Five Obstructions cease to obstruct.

Nakano Maori has demonstrated that Eikai borrowed heavily from Mujū Ichien's Buddhist *setsuwa* anthology *Shasekishū* (compiled between 1279 and 1283) in composing *Ichijō shūgyokushō*,[49] and it is of course not impossible that Eikai drew upon *Sangoku denki* as well. The differences between Eikai's and Gentō's versions of the Izumi Shikibu/Shōkū Shōnin account make that seem unlikely, however, at least in the case of this particular tale. The messages of the stories are at odds, for while Gentō concludes his account by presenting the *Lotus Sutra* as the solution for women, Eikai contextualizes his story within a discussion of Acquired vs. Original Enlightenment, demonstrating that according to his reading of the *Lotus Sutra*, there is in fact no problem to be solved. Like Gentō before him, Eikai would thus seem to have drawn his tale from a didactic oral tradition circulating in the *dangisho* at the time—a possibility further suggested by the inclusion of yet alternate renditions of the Izumi Shikibu/Shōkū Shōnin account in other medieval Tendai *Lotus Sutra* commentaries.

One such work, *Hokekyō jurin shūyōshō*, was completed in 1512 at Senmyōji Temple in Hitachi province (contemporary Ibaraki Prefecture) by the Tendai priest Sonshun (1451–1514), a native of Tomobe in the central region of Hitachi.[50] Like Eikai, Sonshun recounts the tale within his discussion of

[48]Sonshun makes this point in his commentary *Mongu ryaku taikō shikenmon* (Private Record of Lectures on an Abbreviated Outline of the *Wen ju*), in which he writes that while from the standpoint of Acquired Enlightenment there are no female Buddhas, from the perspective of Original Enlightenment, there are. DNBZ 18:131a (5:195c); Stone, *Original Enlightenment*, 346–47 (translation of the title is by Stone). In the Muromachi-period *kōwakamai* (ballad-drama) libretto *Tokiwa mondō* (Tokiwa's Debate), Lady Tokiwa similarly explains that "although in the face of delusion there is male and female, in the face of enlightenment, there is no such distinction." SNKBT 59:292; Agō Toranoshin, ed., *Kōwaka bukyoku kenkyū*, vol. 1 (Tokyo: Miyai Shoten, 1979), 234.

[49]Nakano, "*Hokekyō* chū: ishi wo atsumete tama wo toru."

[50] Establishing an exact date for *Jurin shūyōshō* is problematic. A prologue by the priest Jikkai gives the year 1510, while in the woodblock-printed text (dating to 1650), Sonshun gives the years 1511 and 1512. Nagai Yoshinori speculates that Sonshun wrote *Jurin shūyōshō* and sent a copy to Jikkai, who wrote the prologue in 1510, and that copies of this manuscript circulated and became the first textual line; Sonshun made changes to the work in 1511 and 1512, and this became the second textual line, represented by the woodblock-printed edition photographically reproduced in Nagai's book and typeset in Nakano Tatsue, ed., *Nihon daizōkyō*, vol. 13 (Tokyo: Nihon Daizōkyō Hensankai, 1917). Nagai Yoshinori, "Kaidai," in *Hokekyō jurin shūyōshō*, vol. 4, 547–49.

the "darkness into darkness" passage in the "Phantom City" chapter, and his interpretation is similarly informed by Original Enlightenment thought: "For all beings who have realized their Original Enlightenment," Sonshun begins by explaining, "Supreme Truth is fully revealed." He concludes his introductory remarks by stating that "delusion is enlightenment, birth and death are nirvana; this is the meaning of 'from darkness into darkness.'"[51] Sonshun's version of the Izumi Shikibu/Shōkū Shōnin account is relatively close to the one contained in *Ichijō shūgyokushō*, but there are differences between the two, suggesting that Sonshun based his own rendition upon some source other than *Sangoku denki* or Eikai's earlier treatise.

The commentary *Hokekyō jikidanshō*, compiled by the priest Eishin in the years immediately preceding his death in 1546, approximately thirty years after *Jurin shūyōshō* and fifty years after *Ichijō shūgyokushō*,[52] also includes the Izumi Shikibu/Shōkū Shōnin account in its discussion of the "Phantom City" chapter, but it avoids explicating the passage "from darkness into darkness," shunning the earlier commentaries' discussions of Original vs. Acquired Enlightenment and the principle of nonduality. This in itself may represent an oblique affirmation of the Original Enlightenment perspective, which, as Stone explains, holds that "there is no truth behind, or above, or underlying actual phenomena; truth is what one sees with one's own eyes."[53] In other words, Eishin may have intended the Izumi Shikibu/Shōkū Shōnin account to speak its own truth—of and for itself—rather than to illustrate an ulterior doctrinal abstraction. However, this may be reading too much into the text. Ikeyama Issaien suggests that Eishin composed *Jikidanshō* as a simplified version of *Jurin shūyōshō*, to be used as a kind of primer or source book for teaching the *Lotus Sutra* to lay audiences at *dangisho* throughout the provinces. Ikeyama supposes that it was for this reason that Eishin cut back on difficult explanations and increased the number and prominence of tales in his work—approximately 380 in all—composing a commentary with the characteristics of an "easy sermon text": one that reads effortlessly like a *setsuwa* anthology, but functions to familiarize audiences with the *Lotus Sutra*.[54]

[51] *Hokekyō jurin shūyōshō*, vol. 2, 549; Nakano, ed., *Nihon daizōkyō*, vol. 13, 369.

[52] Eishin was a member of Sugaoji Temple in the Sakata region of Ōmi province when he composed *Jikidanshō*. Sugaoji was a branch temple of Jōbodai'in, the Kashiwabara *dangisho* with which Kobayashi Naoki speculates Gentō was affiliated when he wrote *Sangoku denki*. Although it no longer exists, Sugaoji was located in what is now Sugawa village in Shiga Prefecture.

[53] Stone, *Original Enlightenment*, 172.

[54] Ikeyama Issaien, "Kaidai," in *Hokekyō jikidanshō*, vol. 1, 6–7, 10, and 12. *Jikidanshō* contains more *setsuwa* than *Jurin shūyōshō*, but fewer *waka* (142 by Hirota Tetsumichi's count, compared to 199 in *Jurin shūyōshō*). Around ninety *waka* are common to both *Jurin shūyōshō* and *Jikidanshō* (Hirota, *Chūsei Hokekyō chūshakusho no kenkyū*, 245), and approximately one hundred are common to both *Jurin shūyōshō* and *Ichijō shūgyokushō* (Nakano, *Ichijō shūgyokushō no kenkyū*, 63).

Eishin cites the Izumi Shikibu/Shōkū Shōnin account in connection with the entire second verse section of the "Phantom City" chapter of the *Lotus Sutra*. He begins his tale with a miraculous account of Shōkū Shōnin's supernatural powers, attained, it seems, as a result of the *Lotus Sutra*:

> The [second] verse passage is a *kokige*.[55] It is in praise of Daitsū Buddha's attainment of enlightenment.[56] Take it just as it is written.
>
> There is a story about the line, "from darkness into darkness." A long time ago there was a poor monk in the Takao area [of the capital], and one night he was bitterly chilled. "Ah, it's so cold," he said. "Why is it that Shōkū Shōnin on Mount Shosha in Harima has so much Harima paper? He must wear it as a robe when he chants the *nenbutsu*." Early the next morning a lone priest arrived with paper. He gave it to the poor monk and vanished into the sky. This was all because Shōkū Shōnin had attained a state of purity of the six senses and was able to hear [the poor monk] from Mount Shosha.

News of this strange event reaches Empress Shōshi, and she sets out with a party of women to visit the holy man. The story proceeds as it usually does, with the exception that Izumi Shikibu recites her "darkness into darkness" poem in a non-standard form.[57] Shōkū Shōnin meets with the Empress and her ladies, and "summing up the message of the *Lotus Sutra*," he explains:

> "When this sutra says that 'In the Buddha lands of the ten directions [there is but a single vehicle], there are neither two nor three,' it means that even women, even evil sinners, even grasses, trees, and earth—all will attain Buddhahood." Taking in his meaning, the Empress composed a poem:

futatsu naku	When I hear the Dharma
mitsu naki nori to	of which there are
kiku toki wa	neither two nor three,
itsutsu no sawari	the Five Obstructions, I think,
aran to zo omou	will surely not obstruct.

> Hearing that even grasses and trees would attain Buddhahood, Izumi Shikibu thought of the [Enkyōji] principal image, [a statue

[55]A *kokige* (or *kada*) is a verse section in a sutra that expresses meaning independent of its preceding prose passage (unlike a *giya*, which repeats the contents of the prose).

[56]According to the "Phantom City" chapter, Daitsū Buddha (Daitsūchishō Nyorai) once preached the *Lotus Sutra* over a span of eight thousand kalpas.

[57]The second line reads "into blackest darkness" (*kuraki yami ni zo*) instead of "into a path of darkness" (*kuraki michi ni zo*). If not a mistake, the change may have been intended to bring the poem more into line with the original *Lotus Sutra* passage, which makes no mention of a path or road.

of] Kannon [carved] from a living cherry tree,[58] and she recited:

kusa mo ki mo	So the mountain cherry
hotoke ni naru to	shows the truth of the Dharma
toku nori no	that holds that
makoto arawasu	even grasses and trees
yamazakura ka na	will become Buddhas.[59]

Playfully poeticizing on the master's words, the Empress and Izumi Shikibu compose two final *waka*, artfully rearticulating Shōkū Shōnin's Tendai summation of the *Lotus Sutra*. The possibility of grasses and trees attaining Buddhahood—the topic of Izumi Shikibu's "mountain cherry" verse—is a seminal concept in Original Enlightenment thought, and Sonshun and Eishin discuss it within both the "Expedient Means" and "Parable of Medicinal Herbs" chapters of their respective commentaries.[60] Doctrinally speaking, the Buddhahood of non-sentient beings is guaranteed by the notion of nonduality; as Jacqueline Stone explains, "because self and the outer world are nondual, when the practitioner manifests Buddhahood, so will that person's environment."[61] Nichiren (1222–82), the radically outspoken founder of the Nichiren *Lotus Sutra* sect, pursues this line of thought in his *Kanjin honzon shō* (On the Contemplation of the Mind and the Object of Worship; 1273) when he posits that the worship of wooden images is efficacious for the sole reason that plants and trees are inherently imbued with the "Buddhaseed."[62] As a later corollary to the doctrine of the enlightenment of plants, the *otogizōshi Fuji no hitoana sōshi* actually includes a description of the torment in hell for those who wantonly abuse grasses and trees: such people are to have their limbs hacked off with an adze.[63]

[58]According to *Shosha-zan engi* (A History of Enkyōji Temple on Mount Shosha [also *Banshū Shoshazan engi*]; dated 1644), Shōkū Shōnin built the Enkyōji Nyoirin Hall in the first year of Tenroku (970) in order to house an image of Nyoirin Kannon that he had carved from a living cherry tree. He had seen the tree repeatedly worshipped and praised by a heavenly being. DNBZ 117:259a-b (87:67a-b).

[59]*Hokekyō jikidanshō*, vol. 2, 283–85 (woodblock-printed text). Also see the Myōhōin, Kondaiin, and Sochiku texts in *Hokekyō jikidanshō: koshahon shūsei*, vols. 2, 2, and 3 (Kyoto: Rinsen Shoten, 1989), 451–52, 583–85, and 522–23.

[60]On the treatment of *sōmoku jōbutsu* (the Buddhahood of grasses and trees) in *Jikidanshō* and *Jurin shūyōshō*, see Hirota Tetsumichi, *Chūsei Bukkyō setsuwa no kenkyū* (Tokyo: Benseisha, 1987), 382–84. On *sōmoku jōbutsu* in general, see William R. LaFleur, "Saigyō and the Buddhist Value of Nature, Part I," *History of Religions* 13, no. 2 (November 1973): 93–128; and Donald H. Shively, "Buddhahood for the Nonsentient: A Theme in Nō Plays," *Harvard Journal of Asiatic Studies* 20 (1957): 135–61.

[61]Stone, *Original Enlightenment*, 29 (also see pp. 202–3).

[62]Ibid., 276–77; Philip B. Yampolsky, ed., *Selected Writings of Nichiren* (New York: Columbia University Press, 1990), 152. Translation of the title is by Stone.

[63]MJMT 11:445a (former Akagi Bunko manuscript of 1603).

In discussing the structure and devices of the medieval *Lotus Sutra* commentaries, Hirota Tetsumichi notes that the authors of these works sometimes employ Japanese poems and tales as evidence in support of a particular scriptural interpretation, and sometimes as a means of illustrating the larger truth of an individual passage. And unlike *setsuwa*, Hirota observes, *waka* are often cited because they encapsulate, in verse form, the overall meaning or message of a particular chapter or sutra section.[64] In the cases of *Ichijō shūgyokushō* and *Jurin shūyōshō*, although the Izumi Shikibu/Shōkū Shōnin account is seemingly ineffective in affirming Eikai's and Sonshun's Original Enlightenment interpretations of the "darkness into darkness" passage, it does speak strongly of the efficacy of the *Lotus Sutra*, whether as Izumi Shikibu's means of overcoming male prejudice and effecting a meeting with Shōkū Shōnin (through her "darkness into darkness" poem), or as every woman's means of eliminating the obstacles to Buddhahood (through the arithmetic of the "neither two nor three" poem).

Perhaps most interesting are the ways in which the Izumi Shikibu/Shōkū Shōnin accounts in *Sangoku denki* and the *Lotus Sutra* commentaries represent a larger blending of secular literary traditions (represented by the poems and persona of Izumi Shikibu) and *Lotus Sutra*-centered Tendai Buddhism. More than didactic tales of laywomen's encounters with an eminent Tendai priest, they are stories of Buddhist *waka*: two—and in the case of *Jikidanshō*, three—poems inspired by the *Lotus Sutra*. Such verses are themselves not uncommon in the Heian and medieval literary traditions,[65] but their liberal use in Tendai preaching in the fifteenth and sixteenth centuries suggests a degree of exchange between the worlds of literature and Buddhism that, in both the plenitude of its practice and its circular intensity (i.e., explanations of the *Lotus Sutra* were based upon made-up stories of poems based upon the *Lotus Sutra*), may have been previously unknown. As we have seen in the introduction, the Tendai author of *Tenpōrin hiden (seppō hijō)*, a latter twelfth-century discourse on preaching, wrote that "a preacher ought by all means to have a heart for *waka*" in order to speak with grace and ease.[66] Considered

[64]Hirota, *Chūsei Hokekyō chūshakusho no kenkyū*, 213–30.

[65]For example, from around the mid Heian period, poets wrote sequences of *waka* on specific passages from each of the twenty-eight chapters of the *Lotus Sutra*. Known as "Poems on the Twenty-eight Fascicles" (*nijū happon no uta*), the sequences were composed as devotional and literary exercises by such poets as the Great Kamo Priestess Senshi (Senshi Naishinnō; 964–1035), Fujiwara no Kintō (966–1041), and Akazome Emon (active ca. 964–1041). Edward Kamens, *The Buddhist Poetry of the Great Kamo Priestess: Daisaiin Senshi and "Hosshin Wakashū"* (Ann Arbor: University of Michigan Center for Japanese Studies, 1990), 36–37.

[66]Mabuchi Kazuo and Taguchi Kazuo, "Honkoku: Daigoji-zō *Tenpōrin hiden (seppō hijō)*," *Daigoji bunkazai kenkyūjo kenkyū kiyō* 18 (2000), 12b; Lorinda Kiyama, "Performative Preaching: The Art and Politics of Persuasion in Medieval Japan," Ph.D. dissertation (Stanford University, forthcoming).

together, the surviving *Lotus Sutra* commentaries and assorted monuments and memorials to Izumi Shikibu on Mount Shosha and Mount Hiei intimate that Tendai proselytizers maintained this tradition, making especial use of Izumi Shikibu's poetry and persona throughout the medieval period.[67]

[67]Regarding the memorial on Mount Shosha, see p. 67, above. For a short list of Izumi Shikibu monuments on Mount Hiei, see Nakano, *Ichijō shūgyokushō no kenkyū*, 263–64.

Chapter Five
The Pure Land Proselytizing Traditions of Seiganji Temple

In discussing the textual history of *Sangoku denki*, Ikegami Jun'ichi observes that the woodblock-printed *Sangoku denki* text contains strong Pure Land Buddhist elements that the hand-copied National Library manuscript does not. As a single example, the National Library manuscript includes an account of a person by the name of Shōtai who saves his mother from hell by making a copy of the *Lotus Sutra*, while in the woodblock-printed text he saves her by copying out the three Pure Land sutras, the *Jōdo sanbukyō*, instead.[1] Ikegami concludes that these types of discrepancies—substitutions of specifically Pure Land-related symbols and practices for those of a more Tendai-*Lotus* orientation (such as Amida Buddha for Shakyamuni, the three Pure Land sutras for the *Lotus Sutra*, and chanting of the *nenbutsu* for copying out the *Lotus Sutra*)—are the result of a later, pro-Pure Land copyist's attempt to subvert the largely Tendai-*Lotus* tone of the anthology.[2] In its various textual lines, *Sangoku denki* therefore reflects a kind of Tendai-*Lotus*/Pure Land conflict: a sectarian struggle played out among the surviving manuscripts of a single fifteenth-century collection of tales.

Sectarian rivalry was of course not relegated to written works alone. Some hundred and seventy or eighty years before Gentō's compilation of *Sangoku denki*, in the seventh month of the first and only year of Bun'ō (1260), Nichiren presented his menacing treatise *Risshō ankoku ron* (Establishment of the Legitimate Teaching for the Protection of the Country) to the former regent Hōjō Tokiyori (1227–63). In it he rails against members of the Pure Land sect who he says were mutilating Buddhist statues—"cutting off the fingers of the images of Shakyamuni and refashioning them to form the

[1]Account 7:8 in Ikegami's printing of the *Mukanki hanpon* woodblock-printed text. Ikegami Jun'ichi, ed., *Sangoku denki*, vol. 2 (Tokyo: Miyai Shoten, 1982), 39–41. According to the *hiragana-bon* text (account 10:16), Shōtai made a copy of the *Jōdo sanbukyō* as well. Nagoya Sangoku Denki Kenkyūkai, ed., *Sangoku denki*, vol. 2, Koten bunko 436 (Tokyo: Koten Bunko, 1983), 236–39.

[2]Ikegami, "Kaisetsu," in *Sangoku denki*, vol. 2, 3–8. According to the *Sangoku denki* account of Izumi Shikibu and Shōkū Shōnin in both the National Library and woodblock-printed texts, Shōkū Shōnin gives the Empress a copy of the *Lotus Sutra*. Shōkū Shōnin's popular association with the *Lotus Sutra* may have precluded a *Jōdo sanbukyō*-type substitution.

gesture appropriate to Amida"—in order to make them icons of the growing Pure Land movement.[3] Aspects of this larger ideological contest naturally manifested themselves in preaching as well, and they came to feature in conflicting sermon-stories of Izumi Shikibu's meeting with Shōkū Shōnin. Exactly when the members of Tendai *dangisho* began using the tale of Izumi Shikibu and her "darkness into darkness" poem to explain the "Phantom City" chapter of the *Lotus Sutra* is unclear, due to the oral nature of such instruction. However, a Kamakura-period manuscript with the double title *Izumi Shikibu ōjō no koto* (An Account of Izumi Shikibu's Rebirth in the Pure Land) and *Seiganji Amida no koto* (An Account of the Seiganji Amida) reveals that an alternate account of Izumi Shikibu and Shōkū Shōnin, as well as an unrelated tale about Sei Shōnagon, were put to use in promoting specifically Pure Land-oriented practices and institutions—especially Seiganji Temple in the capital—from as early as around the thirteenth century, the time of Nichiren's complaint.

An Account of Izumi Shikibu's Rebirth in the Pure Land

Izumi Shikibu ōjō no koto survives in a single handwritten *masugatabon*, a small square booklet of a kind carried by itinerant monks and nuns as they preached.[4] Considering its content, format, and related sources, it appears to be the text of a Seiganji Temple sermon or performative appeal. The characters *Taishi yō* ("Taishi use") appear on the cover, indicating that it may have been employed in a festival or religious service for Shōtoku Taishi (574–622), the legendary founder of Buddhism in Japan, although the work's connection Shōtoku Taishi is unclear.[5] The two poems within the text (Izumi Shikibu's "darkness into darkness" verse, and Sei Shōnagon's "What can I say?" poem, in the second part) are abbreviated to their opening lines, suggesting that *Izumi Shikibu ōjō no koto* constitutes a rough outline (or pair of outlines) rather than a polished sermon-story in and of itself. The first part of the work, concerning Izumi Shikibu's meeting with Shōkū Shōnin and her circuitous trek to Seiganji, reads as follows:

[3]TSD 84 (2688): 207b; Philip B. Yampolsky, ed., *Selected Writings of Nichiren* (New York: Columbia University Press, 1990), 35–36. Translation by Yampolsky. I am grateful to Todd Brown for bringing this passage to my attention.

[4]*Izumi Shikibu ōjō no koto / Seiganji Amida no koto* is in the possession of the Kanazawa Bunko archive. The manuscript is typeset and photographically reproduced in Kanagawa Kenritsu Kanazawa Bunko, ed., *Bukkyō setsuwa* (Yokohama: Kanazawa Bunko, 1997), 27–29. The Izumi Shikibu-related portion is also typeset in Tsukudo Reikan, *Fukko to jojishi*, in *Tsukudo Reikan chosaku shū*, vol. 1 (Tokyo: Serika Shobō, 1976), 319–20.

[5]Kanagawa Kenritsu Kanazawa Bunko, ed., *Bukkyō setsuwa*, 27.

Izumi Shikibu was a daughter of Echizen Governor [Ōe no] Masamune during the reign of Emperor Ichijō. She had mastered the styles of Japanese [poetry] and earned a reputation as an amorous woman, and her mind was turned only toward spring blossoms, autumn leaves, misguided thoughts and frivolous conversations. Through moonlit evenings and snowy mornings she passed her days in the unending cycle of birth and death.

In time she reached the age of fifty, and regretting the misdeeds of her past, she set out for Mount Shosha to see Shōkū Shōnin and confess her transgressions. Shōkū Shōnin knew of this in advance. "Today at noon eight demons will come," he told the monks of his temple. "You should tell them all I've gone away, and explain [to them] how women are sinful devils."[6]

Now at noon of that day eight women arrived, including Izumi Shikibu. Facing the monks, she spoke: "I have come to see the master to learn how to leave this illusory world behind." The monks explained that their master was away on Mount Tōnomine in Yamato [province]. Izumi Shikibu was disappointed, but as there was no use staying [on at Mount Shosha], she recited,

kuraki yori	From darkness
kuraki michi ni zo	into a path of darkness

and turned to leave.

Shōkū Shōnin heard her words, and thinking that this woman had grasped the essence of the *Lotus Sutra*—that she was close to the Way—he called her back. "The principles of Buddhism are beyond my understanding," he said, "but the [statue of] Shakyamuni at Saga is a living manifestation of the Buddha. You should go there and pray."[7] Izumi Shikibu therefore secluded herself [in the temple] at Saga, and as she prayed, the Saga Shakyamuni appeared and said, "You should pray to the Amida Buddha at the rear of Kōryūji Temple in Uzumasa."[8]

Izumi Shikibu therefore secluded herself in the Amida Hall [at Kōryūji Temple], and as she prayed, the Kōryūji Buddha appeared and said, "At the Kawasaki Kannon Hall, Amida Buddha himself comes to preach the Dharma on every vernal and autumnal equinox. The various Buddhas of the three worlds all come as well, as do the bodhisattvas of the ten directions. At that time your

[6]"Explain how women are sinful devils" is written in somewhat smaller characters than the surrounding text. It is possible that this line is not a part of Shōkū Shōnin's instructions at all, but rather an interlinear note directing the preacher to extemporize here.

[7]Seiryōji Temple on the Saga plain, on the western outskirts of Kyoto.

[8]On the western side of Kyoto, somewhat to the east of Seiryōji. The Amida to which the Saga Shakyamuni refers is probably the wooden statue of Amida (dating from the Heian period) in the Kōryūji Lecture Hall. The current Lecture Hall was rebuilt in 1165, after a fire in 1150.

> present-life rewards, your next-life rebirth in the Pure Land and all the wishes in your heart will be perfectly achieved. You ought therefore visit [Kannon Hall] on the equinox and listen to Amida's explication of the Law."[9]
>
> Now Izumi Shikibu came to Kawasaki, and as she prayed, the [Kawasaki] Kannon appeared and said, "Amida Buddha of Seiganji Temple travels to the Pure Land three times a day. You should go to Seiganji."[10] Izumi Shikibu therefore built a hut at Seiganji, and placing her faith in Amida, she prayed fervently for rebirth in the Pure Land. They say that on her last evening, at the time of her death, music rang in the sky and a wondrous scent filled her room. Kannon came to greet her and she attained rebirth in the perfect tranquility of the Pure Land.

As her tale begins, Izumi Shikibu sets out at the age of fifty to see Shōkū Shōnin on Mount Shosha. Her reason for choosing him is left unexplained, and although he miraculously foresees her visit, he lamely admits that the principles of Buddhism are beyond his understanding. His description is a far cry from his later hagiographic representations in *Sangoku denki* and the *Lotus Sutra* commentaries. Rather than citing the "neither two nor three" passage from the "Expedient Means" chapter of the *Lotus Sutra* to espouse the liberating Tendai truth of nonduality, Shōkū Shōnin's "solution" is to send Izumi Shikibu off to Seiryōji Temple at the western edge of the capital to seek guidance from the famed Seiryōji Shakyamuni instead.[11] As a philosophical concept, nonduality (in its most radical extension) is largely incompatible with mainstream Pure Land Buddhist thought. While in Japanese Original Enlightenment discourse this most central of Tendai principles serves to affirm the sanctity of the phenomenal realm by teaching that all things are the same—identical and interpenetrating—Pure Land ideology takes as a basic premise the notion that this world and the Pure Land are *not* the same: that one ought to shun this defiling realm for the immaculate pu-

[9]The Kawasaki Kannon Hall was located on the west bank of the Kamo river in Kyoto, just to the south of what is now the Kawaharachō and Imadegawa Avenue intersection. It was an important temple from the Heian period on, but it fell into decline after fires in 1467 and 1531. The Kannon Hall became a part of Seiwain Temple in the 1650s, and following the Pacific War its famous statue of Kannon was sold.

[10]By the time of *Izumi Shikibu ōjō no koto*, Seiganji had presumably moved to its location at what is now the Moto-Seiganji and Ogawa Avenue intersection, directly to the west of the Kawasaki Kannon Hall. Seiganji moved again (to its present location) in 1591.

[11]In an alternate version of the tale in the Kamakura-period *Seiganji shin engi* (A True History of Seiganji), Shōkū Shōnin sends Izumi Shikibu to see the statue of Amida at Kōryūji Temple. The Kōryūji Amida appears to her in a dream and sends her on to see the Seiganji principal image. Yutani Yūzō, "*Seiganji engi* kankei shiryō," *Fukakusa kyōgaku* 19 (1999), 322.

rity of Amida Buddha's Western Paradise.[12] The unknown author/preacher of *Izumi Shikibu ōjō no koto* thus denigrates Shōkū Shōnin by quoting him as admitting to his own incomprehension of the Dharma.

In accord with the holy man's instruction, Izumi Shikibu travels to Seiryōji Temple, popularly known as the Saga Shakadō ("Saga Shakyamuni Hall") for its life-size statue of Shakyamuni Buddha. Documents discovered within the body of the image in February 1954 reveal that the Seiryōji Shakyamuni was carved in 985 in Kaifeng in Song China at the request of the Japanese priest Chōnen (938–1016), who brought it back with him to Japan in the following year.[13] The statue has been an important object of worship among both Tendai proponents of the *Lotus Sutra* and Pure Land Buddhist advocates of the *nenbutsu* from the time of the late-Heian and Kamakura-period popularization of the Pure Land faith;[14] as the illustrated six-scroll *Seiryōji engi* (A History of Seiryōji Temple; ca. 1515) explains, "this wondrous sandalwood image is unlike any ordinary wooden statue: to behold it is like to encounter a Buddha in the living flesh."[15] Indeed, in its hollow central cavity the icon has been found to contain a full set of vital organs, woven in silk, including a heart, lungs, liver, stomach, kidneys, gall bladder, and intestines.[16] *Seiryōji engi* describes the Seiryōji Shakyamuni as a great supporter of the Pure Land faith, granting numerous worldly benefits and personally securing for his devotees rebirth in Amida Buddha's Pure Land Paradise. In *Izumi Shikibu ōjō no koto*, however, rather than guaranteeing Izumi Shikibu's rebirth in the Pure Land, the Seiryōji Shakyamuni sends her forward on her

[12]However, the two perspectives (dual and nondual) are not necessarily exclusive in the Pure Land thought of the medieval Tendai sect. In discussing the Tendai Pure Land treatise *Shinnyo kan* (The Contemplation of Suchness), dating from around the twelfth century and traditionally (mis)attributed to Genshin (942–1017), Jacqueline Stone writes that "*The Contemplation of Suchness* on one hand speaks of birth after death in Amida's pure land as a real event and yet, on the other, urges the necessity of realizing that oneself and the Buddha are nondual in essence. This dual perspective is not altogether uncommon in the Tendai Pure Land writings of this period, which may describe the pure land as both a real place in the western part of the universe and immanent in this world, and Amida, as both a transcendent Buddha and identical to one's own mind." Jacqueline Stone, "The Contemplation of Suchness," in *Religions of Japan in Practice*, ed. George J. Tanabe, Jr. (Princeton: Princeton University Press, 1999), 203.

[13]Gregory Henderson and Leon Hurvitz, "The Buddha of Seiryōji: New Finds and New Theory," *Artibus Asiae* 19, no. 1 (1956): 5–55.

[14]Heibonsha Chihō Shiryō Sentā, ed., *Jiin jinja daijiten: Kyōto, Yamashiro* (Tokyo: Heibonsha, 1997), 372c.

[15]DNBZ 117:471b (83:288c); ZGR 27:1:395b. *Seiryōji engi* (also known as *Shakadō engi*) is photographically reproduced in Nara Kokuritsu Hakubutsukan, ed., *Shaji engi-e* (Tokyo: Kadokawa Shoten, 1975), 275a–309a.

[16]Henderson and Hurvitz write that "the custom of inserting textile intestines into the bodies of precious Buddhas seems to have been common." Henderson and Hurvitz, "The Buddha of Seiryōji," 25.

wandering, pilgrimage-like quest, leading first to Kōryūji and the Kawasaki Kannon Hall, and later to Seiganji in the central part of the capital.

Of the various temples that Izumi Shikibu visits on her way, Seiganji is the best because, as the Kawasaki Kannon explains, the Seiganji Amida travels to and from the Pure Land three times a day. Temple histories explain that Seiganji's wooden statue of Amida—its *honzon*, or "principal image," destroyed in a temple fire in 1864—was a creation of the Great Kasuga Deity. As the story is related in *Rakuyō Seiganji engi* (A History of Seiganji in the Capital; *Sankan-bon* textual line, dating from ca. 1565–95),[17] the statue was carved in the seventh century by Kenmonshi and his son Keshikoku, human manifestations of the bodhisattvas Jizō and Kannon.[18] The *engi* explains that as the Great Kasuga Deity is a native Japanese incarnation of Jizō and Kannon, it was the Great Kasuga Deity himself, in a double human manifestation, who carved the famous Amida.[19] The original Seiganji was built in Nara by order of Emperor Tenji (626–71) to house the miraculous image; in 667, the eminent priest and Pure Land advocate Eon was appointed the first temple intendant.[20] Like all important icons in Japan, the Amida at Seiganji has been credited with various miraculous deeds and appearances, and it therefore comes as little surprise—especially in the context of what was probably a Seiganji Temple sermon-story—that the Kawasaki Kannon in *Izumi Shikibu ōjō no koto* recommends Izumi Shikibu to go there.

Rakuyō Seiganji engi contains the following explanation of the history of Pure Land Buddhism in Japan, as well as Seiganji's own Pure Land orientation:

[17]See the appendix of this book for a classification of *Seiganji engi* texts and textual lines. All subsequent references to *Rakuyō Seiganji engi* are to the Jingū Bunko manuscript in the *Sankan-bon* textual line, typeset in ZGR 27:1:206–43 and DNBZ 117:340–72 (83:148–62).

[18]Hase-dera temple legend similarly maintains that the great statue of Jūichimen ("Eleven-headed") Kannon at Hase-dera was carved by two human manifestations of Jizō and Kannon (Fukūkenjaku Kannon). For a painted illustration of them at work, see the early Muromachi-period *Hase-dera engi*, photographically reproduced in Nara Kokuritsu Hakubutsukan, ed., *Shaji engi-e*, 262c. Also see Susan Tyler, *The Cult of Kasuga Seen through its Art* (Ann Arbor: University of Michigan Center for Japanese Studies, 1992), 142–44.

[19]ZGR 27:1:210b–11a; DNBZ 117:343b–44a (83:149b-c).

[20]ZGR 27:1:213b; DNBZ 117:346b (83:150c). According to *Rakuyō Seiganji engi*, Emperor Kanmu ordered that Seiganji be moved to the Otokuni region of Yamashiro province (site of the new Nagaoka capital) in 784 (ZGR 27:1:215a; DNBZ 117:348a [83:151b]). Yutani Yūzō argues that this account is apocryphal, however, and that the temple did not move from Nara until between ca. 1150 and 1209. Seiganji must have moved to Kyoto (either from Nara or Nagaoka) by 1209, because *Hyakurenshō* (entry for the ninth day of the fourth month of 1209) reports that Seiganji and Gyōganji Temple burned on the same day of that year, indicating their mutual proximity. Yutani, "*Seiganji engi* kankei shiryō," 308–9. Heibonsha Chihō Shiryō Sentā, ed., *Jiin jinja daijiten: Kyōto, Yamashiro*, 407c.

As for the ten schools of Buddhism in Japan, each is suited to the abilities and circumstances [of its adherents], and thus none are the same. Among these, the Pure Land school has been known since the time of Shōtoku Taishi, when Buddhism was first introduced [in our land]. Twenty years after Shōtoku Taishi's death, on the fifth day of the fifth month in the summer of the twelfth year of Emperor Jomei [640], the priest Eon was summoned to the palace, where he lectured on *The Sutra of Infinite Life* (*Muryōjukyō*) with the priest Eshi posing questions.[21] From that time eminent priests from the various schools have turned to the way of the Pure Land, and those same priests have gone on to spread the Pure Land teachings. Countless written sources attest to the fact that they carried out practices for their own benefit while guiding others to the Way, with rebirth in Paradise their principal aim.

Nevertheless, until the time of Hōnen Shōnin the Pure Land-school name had not yet been established, nor had the profound significance of the *nenbutsu* of the Original Vow been brought to light. But once in the Jōan period [1171–74] when Hōnen was staying at Seiran [Temple] in Yoshimizu,[22] the Great Teacher Shandao appeared in Hōnen's dream,[23] and displaying his mysterious half-golden hue, he carefully explained the fundamentals of Pure Land [thought]. Since then the Pure Land school—brought from India, through China, and on to Japan—has flourished and spread throughout our country. More than half of Japan now adheres to its teachings.

Our temple was constructed by order of Emperor Tenji, and since the distant past of our founder, the priest Eon, we have been solely dedicated to illuminating the teachings of the Western Paradise. In his illustrious, meritorious practice, Hōnen Shōnin came and stayed with us from time to time. As our link [to him] was not shallow, the intendant Zōshun Shōnin [put his faith in the principles of the Pure Land school, and from that time forward acclaimed Hōnen Shōnin][24] as the founder of our sect. Then one after

[21]According to *Nihon shoki* (720), Eon lectured at the palace on the *Muryōjukyō* on the fifth day of the fifth month of 640, as well as on the fifteenth through twentieth days of the fourth month of 652. It was in this latter year, 652, that Eshi served as Eon's questioner. NKBT 68:234–35 and 318–19.

[22]The text actually reads "at a lotus in Yoshimizu." *Renge* ("lotus") seems to be a mistake for "Shōren," the characters for which are easily confused. Shōren'in is a temple near Chion'in in the Yoshimizu part of Kyoto; Hōnen is known as the Yoshimizu Master for having lived in the area.

[23]Shandao (613–81) was an important formulator of Chinese Pure Land thought.

[24]This bracketed passage is interpolated from *Rakuyō Seiganji honzon engi* and the six-scroll *Seiganji engi*, two alternate manuscripts in the *Sankan-bon* textual line, typeset in Kikuchi Masakazu, "Kyōhō hachinen-sha *Rakuyō Seiganji honzon engi*," in *Shōdō bungaku kenkyū: dai san shū*, ed. Fukuda Akira and Hirota Tetsumichi (Tokyo: Miyai Shoten, 2001), 383, and in Yutani Yūzō, "*Seiganji engi* rokkanbon no kaidai to honkoku," *Dōhō Daigaku Bukkyō bunka kenkyūjo kiyō* 18 (1998), 92b. Zōshun Shōnin (1104–80) was the twenty-first intendant of Seiganji; Hōnen is counted as the twenty-second.

> another, Shōkū Shōnin and Enkū Shōnin continued to spread the Pure Land teachings from here at Seiganji.[25]

As the *engi* explains, although Seiganji did not become a temple of the Pure Land sect until the twelfth century (the Pure Land sect did not exist before then), it was nevertheless a center for Pure Land faith and Amida-worship from the time of its founding in the seventh. This is relevant to *Izumi Shikibu ōjō no koto* because, although *Izumi Shikibu ōjō no koto* promotes the cult of Amida and the Western Pure Land, it contains no reference to the *nenbutsu*, the principal devotional practice in the centuries after Hōnen (1133–1212). This absence is consistent with the work's early composition, and it may indicate that *Izumi Shikibu ōjō no koto* predates Seiganji's acceptance of Hōnen and his doctrine of the sole practice of the *nenbutsu* (*senju nenbutsu*) in the late twelfth century as the one and only means of attaining rebirth in the Pure Land. More significantly, rather than instructing audiences in the abstractions of either pre- or post-Hōnen Pure Land thought, *Izumi Shikibu ōjō no koto* seems to have been written (and hence performed) to praise the Seiganji Amida. It would thus, in turn, have served to celebrate the temple itself.

Sei Shōnagon at Seiganji

In addition to relating the celebrity story of Izumi Shikibu's encounter with Shōkū Shōnin, her faith in the Seiganji Amida and resulting Pure Land rebirth, *Izumi Shikibu ōjō no koto* contains an account of Sei Shōnagon's own supposed salvation at Seiganji. The tale is derived—one might say plagiarized—from a similar poem-story in both Sei Shōnagon's *Pillow Book* and the poetic anthologies *Senzai wakashū* (Japanese Poems of a Thousand Years; completed in 1187) and *Sei Shōnagon shū* (The Sei Shōnagon Collection).[26] According to these works, Sei Shōnagon composed her verse when she was visiting a temple "named Bodai" to attend a performance of the Eight Lectures of the *Lotus Sutra*. In her *Pillow Book* she explains:[27]

> Once when I had gone to a temple named Bodai to hear the Eight Lectures for establishing karmic links, someone sent a message:

[25]ZGR 27:1:232a–32b; DNBZ 117:362b–63a (83:157c–58a). Shōkū Shōnin (1177–1247; not the Shōkū Shōnin of the Izumi Shikibu/Shōkū Shōnin account) was a disciple of Hōnen; Enkū Shōnin (Ryūshin; 1213–84) became Shōkū's student at the age of fifteen.

[26]The poem-story is contained in the *Sankan-bon*, *Nōin-bon*, and *Maeda-ke-bon* texts of *The Pillow Book*, but not in the *Sakai-bon*. The poem is *Senzai wakashū* 1206 (attributed to Sei Shōnagon), and *Sei Shōnagon shū* 18 (SKT 3:1:228a).

[27]The following translation is from the *Sankan-bon* textual line (SNKBT 25:42). Also see Ivan Morris, *The Pillow Book of Sei Shōnagon* (New York: Columbia University Press, 1991), 55.

> "Come back soon. Things are terribly dull here." I wrote my reply on a lotus petal and sent it off:
>
> | | |
> |---|---|
> | motomete mo | Beckon as you may, |
> | kakaru hachisu no | the dew has come to rest |
> | tsuyu wo okite | upon the lotus. |
> | ukiyo ni mata wa | So how could I return |
> | kaeru mono ka wa | to this world of sorrow? |
>
> Truly, it was all so noble and moving that I felt like staying on forever. But one mustn't forget the impatience of Xiang Zhong's family [waiting for him] at home.[28]

To whom Sei Shōnagon sent her reply is unknown. As Tanaka Jūtarō observes, it could not have been the Empress, considering that the original message contains an honorific verb.[29] Inscribing her verse upon a paper lotus petal, Sei Shōnagon playfully protests that because "the dew has lit upon the lotus (a lotus such as this)"—that because she has joined a karmic link to the Buddha as a result of the lectures she has heard—she cannot simply leave it behind now and return.

Although the Bodai Temple to which Sei Shōnagon refers is unknown,[30] there is no reason to think that it was Seiganji. Rather, Seiganji proselytizers appear to have appropriated the *Pillow Book* episode as a means of promoting their own temple in the Kamakura and Muromachi periods, transforming the earlier poem-story, which Ikeda Kikan proposes was suggestive of a desire on Sei Shōnagon's part to take religious vows,[31] into a fictional account of an illustrious court lady who gave up her wicked ways at Seiganji. That the priests (and possibly nuns) of Seiganji would have done this is easy to understand; for the proselytizer-entertainers of Heian and medieval Japan, historical accuracy was far less important than spiritual and financial results. The twelfth-century *Tenpōrin hiden (seppō hijō)* actually advises preachers against employing old poems and anecdotes without adapting them first. As its author explains, if one can inspire devotion, "it does not matter much what you preach."[32] This is the nature of *hōben*: the notion that

[28]A likely allusion to a story in volume 6 of *Lie xian zhuan*, according to which Xiang Zhong once became so caught up in his reading that he lost way his home. Ibid., 286 (note 93).

[29]Tanaka Jūtarō, *Makura no sōshi zen chūshaku*, vol. 4 (Tokyo: Kadokawa Shoten, 1972), 317b.

[30]Tanaka, *Makura no sōshi zen chūshaku*, vol. 4, 316b–17b.

[31]Ikeda Kikan notes that Sei Shōnagon could only have stayed on at the temple by taking vows. Quoted in Tanaka, *Makura no sōshi zen chūshaku*, 316a.

[32]Mabuchi Kazuo and Taguchi Kazuo, "Honkoku: Daigoji-zō *Tenpōrin hiden (seppō hijō)*," *Daigoji bunkazai kenkyūjo kenkyū kiyō* 18 (2000), 12b and 12a; Lorinda Kiyama, "Performative Preaching: The Art and Politics of Persuasion in Medieval Japan," Ph.D. dissertation (Stanford University, forthcoming). Translation here by Kiyama.

an untruth can serve the ultimate purpose of bringing people to the Truth. And it was this kind of willingness to alter poems and biographical accounts that led to the spread in the late Heian and medieval periods of diverse, overlapping, and often conflicting tales of Sei Shōnagon, Izumi Shikibu, Ono no Komachi, and other women poets.

On its last two pages, *Izumi Shikibu ōjō no koto* relates:

> Sei Shōnagon, daughter of the governor of Higo, [Kiyohara no] Motosuke, was a lady-in-waiting to Empress Teishi. Her appearance was enticingly lovely, her mind subtle and profound. She, too, achieved rebirth in the Pure Land while she was at this temple. Once when she was appointed lady chamberlain and received a summons from the Empress, [she recited,]

asamashi ya[33]	What can I say?
kakaru [hachisu] no	The dew has come to rest
tsuyu wo oki, unnun	upon the [lotus], etc.

Compared to the tale of Izumi Shikibu at Seiganji, the account is brief, seemingly appended as an afterthought—a possibility further suggested by the work's title, *An Account of Izumi Shikibu's Rebirth in the Pure Land*. Sei Shōnagon's poem is both altered and incomplete, and she sends it, in this case, to the Empress.

The character for *hachisu* ("lotus") in the verse's second segment is illegible, but it can be interpolated from a more elaborate rendition of Sei Shōnagon's story in the institutional histories *Seiganji shin engi* (A True History of Seiganji), which Yutani Yūzō dates to between 1209 and 1288,[34] and *Seiganji engi* (A History of Seiganji) in the Sonkeikaku Bunko textual line, which Yoshida Kōichi argues was composed for use in a fund-raising campaign for temple reconstruction after a devastating fire in the fifth month of 1467.[35] Elaborate mytho-histories (*engi*) of these sorts were widely and creatively composed throughout the Heian and medieval periods as a means of asserting the relative merits of the icons, temples and shrines that they purported to describe. As "official" (temple-sponsored) records of the legendary origins, saintly founders, later miracles, and aristocratic patronage of their sacred statues and institutions, these works were employed in centuries of

[33]"*Asamashi ya*" is an exclamation of surprise. Sei Shōnagon seems to imply that the summons has left her speechless.

[34]Yutani, "*Seiganji engi* kankei shiryō," 303 (the Sei Shōnagon account is typeset on p. 321).

[35]Although Yoshida has traced the Sonkeikaku Bunko textual line to ca. 1477, the Sonkeikaku Bunko manuscript itself dates from ca. 1680. Yoshida Kōichi, "*Seiganji engi* to *Izumi Shikibu engi*," *Bungaku ronsō* (May 1966), 6b–8b.

preaching and fund-raising as documentary evidence of the importance of providing continued devotional and financial support.

In the endless and occasionally bitter inter-institutional struggle to secure parishioners and funds from a limited pool of potential sponsors and devotees, exaggeration and outright fabrication of historical traditions seems to have been the norm. Neither *Seiganji shin engi* nor the Sonkeikaku Bunko *Seiganji engi* are exceptions in this regard, and like the Tendai *Lotus Sutra* commentaries of the fifteenth and sixteenth centuries, much of their contents, including the following Sei Shōnagon account, was likely drawn from oral tales circulating in their temple communities at the time. The impact of these typically apocryphal tales was sometimes profound; the woodblock-printed *Kyō warabe* (Child of the Capital), a popular illustrated guide to famous places in and around Kyoto published in 1658, for example, reports that Sei Shōnagon is buried at Seiganji.[36] The fifteenth-century Sonkeikaku Bunko *Seiganji engi* explains:

> Sei Shōnagon, granddaughter of Kiyohara no Fukayabu and daughter of Higo governor Kiyohara no Motosuke, was lady-in-waiting to an empress of Emperor Ichijō. Devoting her days to the passions of love, she gave not a thought to the fleeting nature of the present life. Taking pleasure in the flowers of spring, she turned her thoughts to the autumn moon and exhausted her heart in frivolous, elegant pursuits.
>
> She was without the slightest aspiration to the Path of the Buddha, but oddly enough she came to stay at our temple, and from that time forward she never again stained her heart in this dusty, filthy realm. She came to loathe this life and wish only for an end; her desire for rebirth in the Pure Land was far from shallow. And although she had until but recently taken pride in the favor shown to her at court, she now turned to the Dharma practice hall, where she cut off her glossy hair and became a nun, a woman of pure belief. This was because her desire for the Way was strong. She erected a hut beside our temple hall and lived there as a practitioner of the *nenbutsu-zanmai*, [always chanting Amida's name].
>
> Once when she received a summons from the court, she sent back a single poem in reply:

asamashi ya	What can I say?
kakaru hachisu no	The dew has come to rest
tsuyu okite	upon the lotus.
ukiyo no chiri ni	So how could I soil myself
ikaga kegaren	in the dust of this world of sorrow?

[36]Takemura Toshinori, ed., *Kyōto no maki* 1, vol. 7 of *Nihon meisho fūzoku zue* (Tokyo: Kadokawa Shoten, 1979), 9b. *Kyō warabe* was followed by a sequel (*Kyō warabe atooi*, "Pursuing the Child of the Capital") in 1667, suggesting its popularity at the time.

> This is how she composed her poem. She did not return to the palace, and in the end she passed away at our temple.[37]

Unlike her descriptions in *Izumi Shikibu ōjō no koto* and *Seiganji shin engi*, Sei Shōnagon is here identified as a devotee of the *nenbutsu-zanmai*, the "contemplative practice of the *nenbutsu*." The change is suggestive of Hōnen's influence on Seiganji, as well as the generally increasing prominence of doctrines of single, exclusionary devotional practices in medieval Japanese Buddhist thought. The *Pillow Book* reference to the Eight Lectures of the *Lotus Sutra*—Sei Shōnagon's original reason for visiting Bodai Temple—is in this way replaced by her anachronistically single-minded dedication to the *nenbutsu*. Like the statues of Shakyamuni that Nichiren complains were being mutilated to "make them Amida," Sei Shōnagon's *Pillow Book* poem-story is transformed into a tale of Seiganji and the Pure Land faith.

While Sei Shōnagon's rebirth in the Pure Land is merely implied in the *Seiganji engi* account, in *Izumi Shikibu ōjō no koto* it is reported as fact. As for Izumi Shikibu, her tale in *Izumi Shikibu ōjō no koto* concludes with the revelation that at the time of her death, miraculous music rang in the sky and a wondrous scent filled her room—sure signs of her spiritual salvation in the *ōjōden* (Pure Land-rebirth biography) *setsuwa* genre. Beginning with Yoshishige no Yasutane's *Nihon ōjō gokuraku ki* (Records of Japanese Reborn in the Pure Land; ca. 987), the Heian and medieval periods witnessed a succession of *ōjōden* anthologies cataloging the circumstances and identities of all native Pure Land practitioners known to have attained rebirth in the Western Paradise.[38] Whether for reading, reference, or use in preaching, these works were intended to inspire faith and hope by providing proof of the possibility of Pure Land rebirth in contemporary times. Many of these collections contain accounts of women,[39] but none of them include a single tale of Izumi Shikibu or Sei Shōnagon. Although Izumi Shikibu's and Sei Shōnagon's *ōjōden* (as recorded in *Izumi Shikibu ōjō no koto* and *Seiganji engi*) were clearly used in preaching, authors of purportedly "serious" *ōjōden* anthologies may have recognized their fictionality and thus excluded them from their evidentiary collections of Pure Land rebirth tales.

[37]Yoshida, "*Seiganji engi* to *Izumi Shikibu engi*," 4–5. For the Sei Shōnagon account in the sixteenth-century *Rakuyō Seiganji engi* (in which Sei Shōnagon's poem appears as it does in *The Pillow Book*), see the translations section of this book.

[38]For a comprehensive discussion of *ōjōden* in English, see Frederick Kotas, "Ōjōden: Accounts of Rebirth in the Pure Land," Ph.D. dissertation, University of Washington, 1987.

[39] For translations of some of these, see William E. Deal, "Women and Japanese Buddhism: Tales of Birth in the Pure Land," in *Religions of Japan in Practice*, ed. George J. Tanabe, Jr. (Princeton: Princeton University Press, 1999), 176–84. Also see the biography of the woman from Mutsu on pp. 233–34, below.

The *Seiganji engi* Hanging Scrolls

The *Izumi Shikibu ōjō no koto* Izumi Shikibu account is recorded in an alternate form in the thirteenth-century *Seiganji shin engi*, but it is strangely absent from the fifteenth-century Sonkeikaku Bunko textual line.[40] However, there is additional evidence that both the Izumi Shikibu and Sei Shōnagon Pure Land rebirth tales were employed in Seiganji temple preaching and fund-raising throughout the Kamakura and Muromachi periods: there is a pair of large painted-silk *Seiganji engi* hanging scrolls on permanent loan from Seiganji to the Kyoto National Museum, and they can be seen to incorporate the Sei Shōnagon and Izumi Shikibu/Shōkū Shōnin *setsuwa* in their elaborate pictorial representations of Seiganji temple history.[41] Lavish painted *engi* of this sort were produced in great numbers in the Kamakura and Muromachi periods for use as visual aids in preaching and storytelling. Miya Tsugio and other scholars have listed dozens of extant examples,[42] and in the case of the *Seiganji engi* hanging scrolls, there are records of the scrolls' use as props in fifteenth- and sixteenth-century *etoki* "picture explaining" performances by Seiganji priests.

The *Seiganji engi* hanging scrolls comprise two colorful paintings of a width and length of approximately five by eight feet each, with no written explanatory text. The first of the two tableaux contains five scenes depicting important events in the early history of the temple, including the carving of the Seiganji Amida by Jizō and Kannon. The second (fig. 16) contains seven scenes, including those of Izumi Shikibu and Sei Shōnagon. It has been proposed that the organized layout of episodes in the two paintings is suggestive of the influence of an earlier picture scroll,[43] although no such work has been found. Like all narrative paintings of their kind, the *Seiganji engi* hanging scrolls are known to have been "read," but in what way (or ways) is now unclear. Fortunately, there is an extant seventeenth-century picture-scroll

[40]As Yutani Yūzō has observed, since the Sonkeikaku Bunko manuscript comprises eleven scrolls, some of which are dedicated to individual accounts, a scroll containing the Izumi Shikibu story may simply have been lost. Yutani, "*Seiganji engi* rokkan-bon no kaidai to honkoku," 73.

[41]The hanging scrolls have been designated "Important Cultural Properties" by the Agency for Cultural Affairs; they are photographically reproduced in Nara Kokuritsu Hakubutsukan, ed., *Shaji engi-e*, 45–46 (the Kamakura-period attribution is from p. 135). There is an additional Edo-period *Seiganji engi* hanging scroll attributed to Kaihō Yūsetsu (1598–1677), which is also in the possession of the Kyoto National Museum (see *Shaji engi-e*, 47).

[42]Miya Tsugio, "Shaji engi-e no shosō," in *Etoki: shiryō to kenkyū*, ed. Hayashi Masahiko et al. (Tokyo: Miyai Shoten, 1989), 344–58. Also see Nara Kokuritsu Hakubutsukan, ed., *Shaji engi-e*, and Osaka Shiritsu Hakubutsukan, ed., *Shaji sankei mandara* (Tokyo: Heibonsha, 1987).

[43]Nara Kokuritsu Hakubutsukan, ed., *Shaji engi-e*, 136. The width and length of the paintings are identified as 243 by 150.7 centimeters in *Shaji engi-e*,135.

Fig. 16. The second of two Kamakura-period *Seiganji engi* hanging scrolls. Courtesy of Seiganji Temple and the Kyoto National Museum.

known as the *Seiganji engi emaki*—a three-fascicle history of Seiganji from within the *Sankan-bon* textual line—and because many of its illustrations are close reproductions of scenes in the original *Seiganji engi* hanging scrolls, it can be tentatively employed to decipher the stories in the two Kamakura-period paintings.[44] Although the *Seiganji engi emaki* is apparently based upon an earlier picture scroll composed some three centuries after the *Seiganji engi* hanging scrolls,[45] and is thus representative of a later version of Seiganji temple history, its identification of scenes within the hanging scrolls is likely to be at least generally consistent with earlier oral traditions.

In the bottom left corner of the second hanging scroll (fig. 17), a woman in black robes and *geta* (wooden elevated sandals) is shown approaching the steps of the Seiganji central hall. With a rosary in her hand and a large hat on her back, she looks over her shoulder at a young woman (or servant girl, perhaps) who is leading an older woman toward those same temple stairs. Inside the central hall, three monks and two nuns—all in patterned gray robes—perform devotions before the Seiganji Amida, which in this particular scene is concealed from view. Distinctive purple clouds trail above the roof as a sign of someone's impending Pure Land rebirth. Although both Yutani Yūzō and the editors of *Shaji engi-e* identify this scene as depicting Izumi Shikibu's arrival at Seiganji, the *Seiganji engi emaki* reproduces it in the context of its Sei Shōnagon account, indicating that the woman in black (brown in the seventeenth-century picture scroll) is most likely Sei Shōnagon, and that the purple Pure Land clouds are for her.[46] The scene may be two-part, showing Sei Shōnagon first arriving at Seiganji, and later performing devotions in the central hall. The *Seiganji engi emaki* is particularly suggestive in this regard, insofar as it shows the costume of the woman at the steps to be nearly identical to those of the nuns inside.

In the bottom right corner of the same painting (fig. 18), six women in sandals and elegant blue, pink, and white robes are shown gathered before a closed temple gate in craggy autumn mountains, shaded yellow and a brilliant bluish-green. Red and orange-tinted leaves brighten the trees around them, and grazing deer are visible on a patch of yellow mountain slope behind. One of the women knocks on the wooden doors of the gate, two others stand talking, two hold fans, and one crouches on the ground, seemingly in

[44]On the *Seiganji engi emaki*, see ibid., 137–38. Like the *Seiganji engi* hanging scrolls, the *emaki* is on permanent loan to the Kyoto National Museum.

[45]See the appendix of this book for a discussion of the *Seiganji engi emaki* within the corpus of *Seiganji engi* texts and textual lines. As for "some three centuries," this is a rough calculation based upon Yoshida Kōichi's dating of the *Sankan-bon* textual line to 1565–95.

[46]Yutani, "*Seiganji engi* kankei shiryō," 303; Nara Kokuritsu Hakubutsukan, ed., *Shaji engi-e*, 136. Because the *Shaji engi-e* identifications are based upon the illustrations in *Seiganji engi emaki*, "Izumi Shikibu" is most likely a misprint for "Sei Shōnagon." Yutani provides no explanation for his own interpretation. He seems to have read the hanging scrolls in light of the unillustrated *Seiganji shin engi*, choosing to disregard the identifications in the *Seiganji engi emaki*.

Fig. 17. Sei Shōnagon at Seiganji Temple. Detail from the second *Seiganji engi* hanging scroll (Kamakura period). Courtesy of Seiganji Temple and the Kyoto National Museum.

tears. A lady's hat lies at their feet. A lone priest with an oddly misshapen head—a sure sign of his sagacity—stands listening from the other side of the gate.[47] In a connected scene immediately above and to the right, the women are shown seated before the priest in an elevated temple hall. A teapot rests on the open porch, and the women listen deferentially, their heads bowed slightly as the holy man appears to speak.

[47]As an apparent testimony to their sanctity, Ippen's and many of his followers' heads are similarly misshapen in *Ippen Hijiri e* (1299), in Kadokawa Shoten Henshūbu, ed., *Ippen Hijiri e*, Nihon emaki-mono zenshū, vol. 10 (Tokyo: Kadokawa Shoten, 1960).

Fig. 18. Izumi Shikibu at Enkyōji Temple. Detail from the second *Seiganji engi* hanging scroll (Kamakura period). Courtesy of Seiganji Temple and the Kyoto National Museum.

The *Seiganji engi emaki* reproduces this two-part scene in the context of its Izumi Shikibu/Shōkū Shōnin account, indicating that the women are Izumi Shikibu and a party of ladies from the court, and the priest, Shōkū Shōnin. In the first (lower) part of the picture, the holy man has barred the women from entering his temple precincts simply because they are women. The scene is an apt and moving statement of the traditionally sorry plight of women in Buddhism, a situation in which women have often found themselves "locked out"—both literally and metaphorically—by men. The scene is also one of triumph and redemption, for in its second (upper) part, Izumi Shikibu and her companions are shown to have overcome Shōkū Shōnin's recalcitrance, effecting a meeting with the holy man as a result of Izumi Shikibu's "darkness into darkness" poem. Although the *Seiganji engi emaki* suggests that the hanging scrolls contain no further illustrations of Izumi Shikibu,[48] based upon the evidence of *Izumi Shikibu ōjō no koto* and the Izumi Shikibu/Shōkū Shōnin account in *Seiganji shin engi* (as well as the fact that the painted scene is included within a pictorial history of Seiganji, rather than Enkyōji), we may suppose that the story represented here did not end with Izumi Shikibu's meeting with Shōkū Shōnin. Records of Seiganji *etoki* performances provide little information, however, and because the tales depicted in the hanging scrolls clearly changed with time, it is impossible now to say exactly how they were recounted by different generations of Seiganji preachers.

One of the few surviving records of a medieval Seiganji *etoki* performance is contained in *Sanetaka-kō ki* (Records of Lord Sanetaka), the diary of the courtier Sanjōnishi Sanetaka (1455–1537). In an entry for the fourteenth day of the eighth month of the ninth year of Bunmei (1477), Sanetaka writes that "His Majesty [Emperor Go-Tsuchimikado] viewed the *Seiganji engi* painting(s), and a fascicle of the *engi* was read to him."[49] *Nobutane-kyō ki* (Records of Lord Nobutane), the diary of the courtier Nakamikado Nobutane (1442–1525), contains a second important notation. In an entry for the third day of the fourth month of the second year of Bunki (1502), some twenty-five years after Sanetaka's entry, Nobutane writes that "a Seiganji priest came with *Seiganji engi* paintings in two scrolls. He hung them up and read a fascicle of the *engi*. It was an admirable performance, bound to increase [people's] faith."[50] Picture-based sermon-performances of this kind were common in Japan (and Eurasia as a whole) throughout the premodern period.[51] Yoshida Kōichi has

[48]In a scene slightly above and to the left, a woman in travel robes is shown walking toward the steps of Seiganji, the main hall of which is thronged with priests and courtiers in tall *eboshi* hats. Uemura Etsuko has taken the woman to be Izumi Shikibu, but because the *Seiganji engi emaki* reproduces the scene in conjunction with the story of Emperor Daigo's visit to Seiganji in 903, the woman is probably someone else. Uemura reproduces the illustration of the woman as a frontispiece to her book, *Ōchō joryū sakka no kenkyū* (Tokyo: Kasama Shoin, 1975). Yutani Yūzō identifies the scene with Empress Shōshi's visit to Seiganji after her father's death in 1027, again with no explanation.

[49]Ōta Tōshirō, ed., *Sanetaka-kō ki*, vol. 1 (Tokyo: Taiyōsha, 1931), 237.

[50]Zōho Shiryō Taisei Kankōkai, ed., *Zōho shiryō taisei*, vol. 45 (Kyoto: Rinsen Shoten, 1965), 20a. The *Sanetaka-kō ki* and *Nobutane-kyō ki* entries are also quoted in Yoshida, "*Seiganji engi* to *Izumi Shikibu engi*," 7a.

[51]Victor Mair, *Painting and Performance: Chinese Picture Recitation and its Indian Genesis* (Honolulu: University of Hawaii Press, 1988); Ikumi Kaminishi, *Explaining Pictures: Buddhist Propaganda and Etoki Storytelling in Japan* (Honolulu: University of Hawaii Press, 2006).

written that in this particular case, the tableaux described by Sanetaka and Nobutane are the *Seiganji engi* hanging scrolls, and the one-fascicle *engi* may have been a manuscript from the Sonkeikaku Bunko *Seiganji engi* textual line, at that time but recently composed.[52] Although Yoshida's identification of the one-fascicle *engi* is problematic—the contents of the Sonkeikaku Bunko manuscript are not closely matched to the contents of the *Seiganji engi* hanging scrolls—his identification of the paintings as the *Seiganji engi* hanging scrolls would appear to be correct.[53]

As Yoshida has also observed, the timing of these *etoki* performances is revealing. Two of the Seiganji Temple buildings burned on the twenty-fourth day of the fifth month of 1467,[54] but thanks to the fund-raising efforts of the *kanjin* (fund-raising) priest Jūkoku Shamon,[55] they were reconstructed in the sixth month of 1477. The *etoki* performances for the emperor and for Nobutane were probably a part of this larger capital campaign, indicating that the stories of Izumi Shikibu's and Sei Shōnagon's Pure Land rebirths, as well as unrelated accounts of Emperor Tenji's order to found Seiganji in the seventh century, Emperor Daigo's visit to Seiganji in 903, and Empress Shōshi's performance of a memorial service at Seiganji for her late father, Fujiwara no Michinaga (d. 1027), were likely used in soliciting donations from the emperor and his urban aristocracy. In addition to providing the appearance of a kind of state-sanctioned institutional legitimacy, the preponderance of court-related tales in the *Seiganji engi* hanging scrolls and in later textual renditions of the Seiganji temple-history may reflect the shrewd fund-raising instincts of the Seiganji authorities, who would have appealed to the court (or to aspirants to the prestige of the court) for their most substantial donations.

Although Nobutane indicates in his diary that it was a priest (or priests) who gave the *etoki* performance with the hanging scrolls, Yanagita Kunio speculates that it was the nuns of Seiganji who were largely responsible for

[52]Yoshida, "*Seiganji engi* to *Izumi Shikibu engi*," 7b.

[53]Yutani Yūzō has alternately proposed that the one-fascicle *engi* was the one-scroll *Seiganji shin engi*, which he says is nearly identical in its contents and the order of those contents to the contents and layout of the two *Seiganji engi* hanging scrolls (Yutani, "*Seiganji engi* kankei shiryō," 302–3). Yutani's logic is circular, however, in that he appears to have first read the hanging scrolls according to *Seiganji shin engi*, and then to have identified the *engi* with those scrolls on the basis of their purported similarity.

[54]The Okudō and Komidō halls, according to a *Daijōin jisha zōjiki* entry for the twenty-ninth day of the fifth month of 1467. Cited in Heibonsha Chihō Shiryō Sentā, ed., *Jiin jinja daijiten: Kyōto, Yamashiro*, 408a.

[55]According to an entry for the twenty-sixth day of the sixth month of 1477 in *Nagaoki-sukune ki* (the diary of Ōmiya Nagaoki [also Ozuki Nagaoki; 1412–99]), Jūkoku Shamon led fund-raising efforts with a temple solicitation book written by Ichijō Kaneyoshi (Ichijō Kanera; 1402–81). *Nagaoki-sukune ki*, in Kondō Keizō, ed., *Kaitei shiseki shūran*, vol. 24 (Tokyo: Kondō Shuppanbu, 1903; 3rd ed. 1932), 596. The relevant entry is also cited in the woodblock-printed *Ekotoba yōryaku Seiganji engi* (An Abridged History of Seiganji in Words and Pictures), from 1792, in DNBZ 117:385a (83:168a).

the dissemination of Izumi Shikibu legends in the medieval period.[56] As we have seen in previous chapters, Yanagita has written persuasively of the role of mendicant storytelling nuns in the spread of Buddhism and folklore, of women who traveled the provinces entertaining audiences with accounts of Ono no Komachi, Izumi Shikibu, Sei Shōnagon, and others while preaching and raising funds for the maintenance and construction of temples, shrines, bridges and roads. Yanagita identifies Seiganji as a center of such proselytizing activity—a hub from which storytelling women set out to teach, solicit, and sell various wares manufactured in the Seiganji temple community. Yanagita's theory remains unsubstantiated, however, and due to the paucity of surviving records, it is difficult to gauge the character of Seiganji in the thirteenth through sixteenth centuries. Nevertheless, there do seem to have been nuns at Seiganji for much of the medieval period: two of them are shown worshipping at Seiganji in the Sei Shōnagon scene in the Kamakura-period *Seiganji engi* hanging scrolls; Sei Shōnagon and Izumi Shikibu are both reported in *Seiganji engi* (Sonkeikaku Bunko and *Sankan-bon* textual lines) to have lived as nuns at Seiganji; a fourteenth-century memorial to Izumi Shikibu at Seiganji bears the inscribed names of six nuns; and the *Lotus Sutra* commentary *Ichijō shūgyokushō* (1488) describes Izumi Shikibu as a "Seiganji *bikuni*" (a Seiganji nun).[57] Furthermore, the Uesugi *Rakuchū rakugai-zu* (screen paintings of scenes in and around the capital), painted by Kanō Eitoku ca. 1560–70, provides a colorful, tantalizing glimpse of Seiganji as it might have stood in the middle years of the sixteenth century (fig. 19), and it shows a number of nuns, priests, and lay people—men, women, and begging children alike—gathered in and around the temple at its old location at what is now the Moto-Seiganji and Ogawa Avenue intersection, immediately to the east of the Imperial Palace.[58]

In addition to the pictures of nuns in the *Seiganji engi* hanging scrolls, the existence of *Izumi Shikibu ōjō no koto* may be a sign that women were gathering at Seiganji and engaging in preaching and storytelling (as Yanagita proposes) from as early as the Kamakura period. In that *Izumi Shikibu ōjō no koto* relates stories of Izumi Shikibu's and Sei Shōnagon's Pure Land rebirths,

[56]Yanagita Kunio, *Teihon Yanagita Kunio shū*, vol. 8 (Tokyo: Chikuma Shobō, 1962), 282–83 and 361–62.

[57]On the memorial to Izumi Shikibu, see pp. 167–68, below; on the *Ichijō shūgyokushō* account, see p. 198.

[58]The paintings are known as the "Uesugi screens" because they were purportedly presented to the feudal lord Uesugi Kenshin by Oda Nobunaga in 1574. See Matthew P. McKelway, "The Partisan View: Rakuchū Rakugai Screens in the Mary and Jackson Burke Collection," *Orientations* 28, no. 2 (February 1997), 52–53; Henry D. Smith and Matthew P. McKelway, "Digitalizing Japanese Art," *Monumenta Nipponica* 57, no. 4 (Winter 2002), 511–14. Although the screens are believed to depict Kyoto as it was in the 1550s during the military rule of the Ashikaga *shōgun* Yoshiteru (McKelway, "The Partisan View," 52), the accuracy of their representation of Seiganji in particular is unknown.

Fig. 19. Seiganji Temple in the sixteenth century. Detail from the Uesugi *Rakuchū rakugai-zu* (screen paintings of scenes in and around the capital; ca. 1560–70). Courtesy of the Yonezawa City Uesugi Museum, Yamagata Prefecture.

and thus deals specifically with issues of women in Buddhism, it would constitute natural storytelling material for women preaching to other women. Moreover, the text's description of Izumi Shikibu's meandering progress from her abode at the palace to her eventual home at Seiganji is not unlike the travels of the mendicant nuns whom Yanagita argues were spreading her tales. If *Izumi Shikibu ōjō no koto* is indeed the surviving manuscript of a sermon preached by women, it would thus not only have promoted the worship of the Seiganji Amida, but also—by the natural association (in audiences' minds) of the storytellers with their stories—lent a kind of glamour and legitimacy to the lives of the wandering nuns themselves.[59]

[59]Sarah Strong makes much the same point in her writing on medieval *yūjo*'s possible performances of tales of Ono no Komachi. Strong additionally observes that "the audience in turn, however humble its actual social rank, would have enjoyed, for the duration of the performance, elevated status as consumers of the elite culture embodied by the Komachi performer." Sarah Strong, "Performing the Courtesan: In Search of Ghosts at Zuishin-in Letter Mound," *Women and Performance: A Journal of Feminist Theory* 12:1, no. 23 (2001), 91.

Chapter Six
Writing Redemption: *A History of Seiganji in the Capital*

Seiganji burned in the fourth month of 1573, but by order of the warlord Toyotomi Hideyoshi in the second month of 1591, the temple was moved and rebuilt at its present location along Shinkyōgoku Avenue in central Kyoto.[1] Construction began in the fifth month of 1591, and the finished temple was dedicated nearly six years later, in the third month of 1597. It seems to have been at some time in or before these years that a new history of Seiganji (*Rakuyō Seiganji engi*, "A History of Seiganji in the Capital") was composed in what is now known as the *Sankan-bon* textual line.[2] In its sprawling city compound—now greatly reduced—the new Seiganji contained as many as eighteen buildings and subsidiary halls, including those devoted to Amida, Shakyamuni, Kannon, Jizō, Yakushi Nyorai, and the Great Kasuga Deity. The temple was counted among the largest and grandest institutions of the city, and although the earlier *Seiganji engi* (the parent text of the Sonkeikaku Bunko manuscript) was probably lost in the fire of 1573, it was soon replaced by an expanded version, a picture scroll of a length and magnificence appropriate to Seiganji's newfound prominence and prosperity.[3]

As a legitimizing, temple-sponsored institutional history, *Rakuyō Seiganji engi* reveals the extent to which Seiganji identified itself with Izumi Shikibu in the sixteenth century and sought to use her as a means of pro-

[1]Much of the information in this paragraph is drawn from Heibonsha Chihō Shiryō Sentā, ed., *Jiin jinja daijiten: Kyōto, Yamashiro* (Tokyo: Heibonsha, 1997), 406–9, and Mochizuki Shinkō, *Bukkyō daijiten*, vol. 3 (Kyoto: Sekai Seiten Kankō Kyōkai, 1954), 2891–92.

[2]Yoshida Kōichi argues that the *Sankan-bon* (what he called the "second textual line," since he was apparently unaware of the Kamakura-period *Seiganji shin engi*) dates from between 1565, when Yamashina Tokitsugu (1507–79) records having being shown a Seiganji manuscript corresponding to an older version of the *engi* (*Tokitsugu-kyō ki*, tenth day of the twelfth month of 1565), and 1595, when Tokitsugu's son Tokitsune (1543–1611) alludes to a section from the *Sankan bon* textual line in an entry on the noh play *Seiganji* in the noh commentary *Utaishō* (Notes on the Noh). Yoshida Kōichi, "*Seiganji engi* to *Izumi Shikibu engi*," *Bungaku ronsō* (May 1966), 13a.

[3]Ibid., 8a and 13a. Although the original *emaki* of the *Sankan-bon* textual line has been lost, a copy (the *Seiganji engi emaki*) survives.

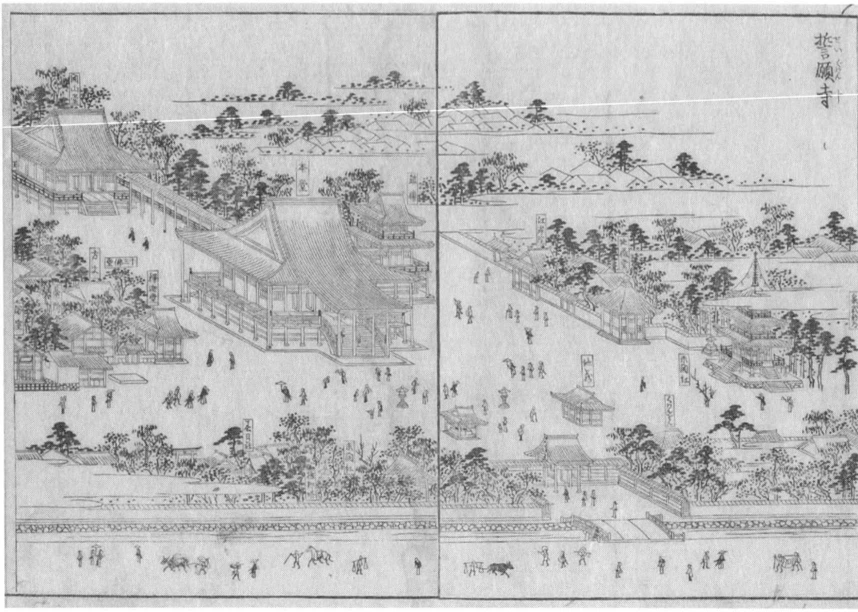

Fig. 20. Seiganji Temple in the eighteenth century. From *Pictures of Famous Places in the Capital* (*Miyako meisho zue*; 1780), reprinted edition of 1786. Courtesy of the International Research Center for Japanese Studies (Kokusai Nihon Bunka Kenkyū Sentā).

moting itself and the practice of the *nenbutsu* in the seventeenth. A full third of the enlarged *engi* comprises stories in which Izumi Shikibu plays a part (as opposed to Sei Shōnagon, who is the subject of only one short account). These include tales of her meetings with Shōkū Shōnin on Mount Shosha, with the Great Hachiman Bodhisattva at Iwashimizu Hachiman Shrine, and with an unusual female manifestation of the Seiganji Amida. In addition, the *engi* chronicles Izumi Shikibu's later ghostly appearances at Seiganji with the legendary Chūjōhime (an exemplary woman in Buddhism famed in medieval and early-modern Japan for having received a Pure Land mandala from a female Amida at Taima Temple in the sixth month of 763), and with Ippen Shōnin (1239–89), the charismatic and controversial founder of the *Ji* ("Time") sect of Pure Land Buddhism. Taken together, these stories are an indication of Seiganji's concern with issues of women in Buddhism in the sixteenth century, and they reveal the extent to which the temple (or some members of the temple community) sought to promote Seiganji through its revised and expanded history as a premier institution for women in the Pure Land faith.

Izumi Shikibu and Shōkū Shōnin

The story in *Rakuyō Seiganji engi* of Izumi Shikibu's meeting with Shōkū Shōnin and subsequent trek to Seiganji is a far cry from the Kamakura-period *Izumi Shikibu ōjō no koto* and *Seiganji shin engi* accounts. As a polished literary work, *Rakuyō Seiganji engi* contains numerous speeches, poems, and scriptural and poetic allusions in its long and carefully crafted version of the tale. In its first part, various phrases and passages are borrowed from Gentō's fifteenth-century *Sangoku denki* account, indicating that the *engi* author drew upon sources other than those originating at Seiganji.[4] The course of Izumi Shikibu's journey is altered and simplified, and while its pilgrimage-like quality remains, its doctrinal import (the certainty of women's Pure Land rebirth by the sole practice of the *nenbutsu*, rather than a more general faith in the Seiganji Amida) is updated in accord with Hōnen's sectarian Pure Land Buddhist thought.

Following the story of Sei Shōnagon's rebirth in the Pure Land from her abode at Seiganji, the *Rakuyō Seiganji engi* narrator introduces Izumi Shikibu as a skilled poet and an amorous lady of the court, a woman of worldly concerns, mired in delusion. Her decadence is represented by her frivolous devotion to the ways of love and poetry. As a woman intent on "leading men's hearts astray"[5]—making herself attractive to men, thereby distracting them from the path of the Buddha—she poses a hazard to all men. Her beauty inevitably fades, and at the age of thirty-five she loses her daughter, Koshikibu no Naishi, to illness. Akazome Emon's eleventh-century historical chronicle, *A Tale of Flowering Fortunes*, records that Koshikibu died after bearing a child in the eleventh month of 1025, and although it also reports that Izumi Shikibu composed a poem at the sight of her daughter's children,[6] *Rakuyō Seiganji engi* describes Koshikibu's demise as a kind of spectacular literary event: on

[4]The correction of Sei Shōnagon's "What can I say?" ("Beckon as you may") poem in *Seiganji shin engi* and the Sonkeikaku Bunko textual line is a further indication of the *Rakuyō Seiganji engi* author's familiarity with outside literary sources.

[5]This and the following *Rakuyō Seiganji engi* translations are from the Jingū Bunko manuscript, typeset in ZGR 27:1:206–43 and DNBZ 117:340–72 (83:148–62). See the translations section of this book for a full rendition of the Izumi Shikibu/Shōkū Shōnin account.

[6]NKBT 76:250; William and Helen McCullough, *A Tale of Flowering Fortunes*, vol. 2 (Stanford: Stanford University Press, 1980), 702–3. The relevant passage is also translated in the introduction to Edwin Cranston, *The Izumi Shikibu Diary* (Cambridge: Harvard University Press, 1969), 16–17.

the verge of death at the age of fourteen, Koshikibu composes a movingly filial verse, and her mother, though overwhelmed with grief, produces an immediate and tasteful reply.[7]

The *engi* explains that in the face of personal tragedy, Izumi Shikibu awoke to the nature of Buddhist Truth:

> Izumi Shikibu thought deeply about the impermanence of this world of suffering, that death must come to young and old alike, that all must suffer the pain of separation from loved ones. Who can escape the fate of our inconstant bodies, like so many leaves blowing in the wind? She may have lost Koshikibu today, but tomorrow the end would bear down on her as well, and she understood the certain futility of losing one's heart to this transient dream, this dreamlike world. She came to loathe earthly splendors, fleeting as a morning mist, and she recognized the spiritual guidance afforded her in the death of her beloved child, the flower on whom she doted. She turned to the path of enlightenment, praying in her heart to meet a wise or holy man from whom she might seek a means of leaving the world behind.

In an unusual coupling of poetic and Buddhist tropes, Izumi Shikibu recognizes the death of her *nadeshiko* (her beloved child, "the flower on whom she doted") to be a *zenchishiki* (a "dharma companion"), drawing her toward salvation.[8] The association implies a fusion, in Izumi Shikibu's mind, of the Ways of Buddhism and Poetry. Her newly pious thoughts, recreated and transcribed for Seiganji audiences in the late sixteenth century, suggest the *engi* author's principally didactic intent.

As in all other versions of her tale, Izumi Shikibu sets out to see Shōkū Shōnin at Enkyōji Temple on Mount Shosha. Her journey is a metaphor for her inner spiritual quest: struggling over desolate mountain roads, she treads the figurative Buddhist Path. Foreseeing her arrival, the holy man warns his disciples of "demons," and he enters a meditation hall to hide. Later lurking behind his fastened temple gate, he overhears Izumi Shikibu's

[7]In most related Koshikibu deathbed accounts in *setsuwa* and *otogizōshi*, Koshikibu's life is said to have been spared when a demon was so moved by her poem that he granted her a reprieve. See *Little Shikibu* in the translations section of this book. The version of events in the noh play *Izumi Shikibu* (*Shosha*; ca. fifteenth century) is closest to that in *Rakuyō Seiganji engi*, in which Izumi Shikibu goes to see Shōkū Shōnin as a result of Koshikibu's death. Yoshida Kōichi, *Izumi Shikibu zenshū: honbun hen* (Tokyo: Koten Bunko, 1959), 772.

[8]A *nadeshiko* is a flower (a wild pink), but because of its alternate meaning of "beloved child," or "child upon whom one dotes," it is a conventional poetic metaphor for a young woman. The term *zenchishiki* is usually reserved for people and other sentient beings who lead one to the path of the Buddha, but it is also sometimes used to signify related occurrences or events. See supp. note 9 (on *zenchishiki*) in NKBT 33 (*Heike monogatari*, vol. 2): 457–58.

"darkness into darkness" poem, and recalling his own vow to save sentient beings, he reluctantly opens the door.

The seventeenth-century *Seiganji engi emaki* contains a colorful illustration of the scene (fig. 21) that is closely based on the one in the second Kamakura-period *Seiganji engi* hanging scroll. Izumi Shikibu stands outside the locked temple gate with a group of women from the court, while Shōkū Shōnin listens from the other side. Next, in the upper right-hand corner, Izumi Shikibu and the women meet with the holy man in a small temple hall. As a picture scroll, the *Seiganji engi emaki* unwinds from right to left in an unbroken narrative progression. However, because the illustration here is faithful to the original hanging scroll, it shows Izumi Shikibu and her companions moving backwards from the temple gate (from left to right, to meet with Shōkū Shōnin) as they move forward in time, resulting in their transgression of the internal temporal-narrative flow—the silent current of the painted scroll.

As the tale continues, Izumi Shikibu confesses her wickedness and begs the holy man's instruction, pleading with him to reveal to her a means of escaping the Five Obstructions. Shōkū Shōnin responds with the following advice:

Fig. 21. Izumi Shikibu at Enkyōji Temple. From *Seiganji engi emaki* (seventeenth century). Courtesy of Seiganji Temple and the Kyoto National Museum.

> "In truth the three worlds are as a dream, a mirage, and the six roads are to be abandoned.[9] To be born in human form is rare. Should you pass your life for naught, then when might you hope to escape the cycle of birth and death? But if you immediately set about performing the Buddhist austerities with unwavering devotion, you'll quickly leave birth and death behind—such is without doubt.
>
> "Now in Buddhism there are as many as 84,000 gates through which one may enter the Way, for as each person's aptitude and circumstances are unique, benefits are conferred according to individual capacities. The gate of which you inquire is that of rebirth in the Pure Land. In addition to my other devotions, I too have undertaken the practices of the Western Paradise for many years. But as comprehension of the Absolute is a fundamental aim, the benefits of Amida's teaching are not yet entirely revealed to me either.
>
> "The Great Bodhisattva on Mount Hachiman to the south of the capital is a native manifestation of Lord Amida of the Pure Land. He conceals his brilliance and mingles with the filth of this world in order to establish innumerable links to sentient beings. You should visit his shrine and single-mindedly pray for his will. If you lay bare your true heart, you'll surely receive a response."

Rather than sending Izumi Shikibu off to Seiryōji Temple to seek the famous Saga Shakyamuni as he does in *Izumi Shikibu ōjō no koto* (or to see the Kōryūji Amida, as he does in *Seiganji shin engi*), Shōkū Shōnin recommends that she visit the Great Hachiman Bodhisattva, whom he identifies with Amida Buddha, at Iwashimizu Hachiman Shrine on Mount Otoko near the southwestern edge of the capital.

Izumi Shikibu and the Great Hachiman Bodhisattva

Although he is a native Shintō deity, the Great Hachiman Bodhisattva was granted the honorific title "Great Bodhisattva" (*dai-bosatsu*) in the year 781 in recognition of his protection of Buddhism and the state.[10] According to *Iwashimizu Hachimangū Gokokuji ryakki* (A Short Record of Gokokuji Temple and Iwashimizu Hachiman Shrine), composed in the first month of 863 by Gyōkyō, a priest of Daianji Temple in Nara, the Bodhisattva appeared to Gyōkyō as Gyōkyō performed devotions at Usa Hachiman Shrine on the

[9] The three worlds (*sangai*) are the three worlds of delusion in which sentient beings dwell. The six roads (*rokushu*; also *rokudō*) are the six planes of existence through which sentient beings transmigrate according to their karma.

[10] Nakano Hatayoshi, "Hachiman shinkō," in Kokushi Daijiten Henshū Iinkai, ed., *Kokushi daijiten*, vol. 11 (Tokyo: Yoshikawa Kōbunkan, 1990), 611.

southern island of Kyūshū on the fifteenth night of the seventh month of the first year of Jōgan (859).[11] At that time, the Bodhisattva requested that arrangements be made for him to be moved to an appropriate site near the capital so that he might offer his protection there. The Bodhisattva appeared to Gyōkyō again on the twenty-fifth day of the eighth month of that same year, and he asked that a shrine be built to him on Mount Otoko. It was thus, with the permission of the emperor, that Iwashimizu Hachiman Shrine came to be constructed. According to an account in the *setsuwa* anthology *Zoku kojidan* (More Tales of Ancient Matters; ca. 1219), an Amida Triad (Amida and his two attendants, Kannon and Seishi) shone upon Gyōkyō's robes at the time of his first encounter with the deity.[12] The Great Hachiman Bodhisattva is traditionally identified with the legendary Emperor Ōjin of the early fifth century, but as *Zoku kojidan* and other sources indicate, he came to be identified with Amida from an early time as well.[13]

The Great Hachiman Bodhisattva has enjoyed a large and dedicated following since at least the early eighth century, but why Shōkū Shōnin chooses to send Izumi Shikibu to him in particular (within the context of a Seiganji temple history, that is) is unclear. However, as a bridge between Shōkū Shōnin and Seiganji—a bridge between the late-medieval Tendai and Pure Land Buddhist sects—the Bodhisattva is an excellent choice, considering his popular identification with Amida and the fact that both Saichō and Kūkai, the late eighth- and early ninth-century founders of the Japanese Tendai and Shingon sects, are said to have beseeched him for protection.[14] Furthermore, for the author(s) of Seiganji's new temple history, the Bodhisattva's considerable fame would have made his subsequent endorsement of the Seiganji Amida all the more desirable.

[11]GR 1:498–500; Shimura Kunihiro et al., eds., *Hachiman jinja kenkyū* (Tokyo: Sōbunsha, 1989), 202–4. Three deities are enshrined at Iwashimizu Hachiman Shrine: Honda Wake no Mikoto, Hime Ōkami, and Okinagatarashi Hime no Mikoto. The most prominent of these, Honda Wake no Mikoto, is recognized as the Great Hachiman Bodhisattva. There was a temple on Mount Otoko previous to the establishment of Iwashimizu Hachiman Shrine, and in 863, its name was changed from Iwashimizu Temple to Gokokuji. Heibonsha Chihō Shiryō Sentā, ed., *Jiin jinja daijiten: Kyōto, Yamashiro*, 82-83.

[12]SNKBT 41:721; GR 17:679. Also see *Konjaku monogatari shū* 12:10 (twelfth century; SNKBT 35:116; NKBZ 21:234) and *Chōya gunsai* (ca. 1116; Kuroita Katsumi, ed., *Shintei zōho kokushi taikei*, vol. 29:1 [Tokyo: Yoshikawa Kōbunkan, 1938], 394), in which an unspecified triad is reported to have appeared on Gyōkyō's robes. According to an alternate tradition, the figures were those of a Shakyamuni Triad. Murayama Shūichi, *Honji suijaku* (Tokyo: Yoshikawa Kōbunkan, 1974), 68; Shimura Kunihiro, "Iwashimizu Hachimangū no setsuwa," in *Hachiman jinja kenkyū*, 20–23.

[13]In addition, *Zoku honchō ōjōden* 16 (ca. 1100; NST 7:240 and 575) and *Shiju hyaku innenshū* 9 (1257; DNBZ 148:160b [92:204c–205a]) state explicitly that the Great Hachiman Bodhisattva is a manifestation of Amida.

[14]Nakano, "Hachiman shinkō," 611c.

As *Rakuyō Seiganji engi* continues, Izumi Shikibu arrives at Iwashimizu Hachiman Shrine and immediately begins to pray:

> For seven days and seven nights Izumi Shikibu kept a vigil before the inner shrine of the Great Bodhisattva. Unsurpassed in devotion, she prayed for a means of achieving rebirth in the Pure Land. It was then the middle of the eighth month, and in the clear light of the moon a bell rang forth in the deep stillness of early morning. As dawn began to break, an eighty-year-old monk suddenly appeared from within the shrine.
>
> "At Seiganji Temple in the capital," he said, "the principal image, carved by the Great Kasuga Deity, Bodhisattva of Myriad Acts of Compassion, is Buddha of the Western Paradise. In accord with his Great Transcendent Vow, he expediently appears at Seiganji in order to lead sentient beings to the Pure Land. He greets the dying and guides them on to Paradise, traveling without fail once every day to the Western Pure Land and back.
>
> "You should put your faith in this image at Seiganji, pay obeisance, chant Amida's name, and set your mind on being cured.[15] Even men and women turned upside-down with delusion are included in the Vow. How then could you not be saved? Now hurry to Seiganji and pray for a straight path to the Pure Land." The old monk vanished without a trace.

Like Shōkū Shōnin (and the Seiryōji Shakyamuni and the Kōryūji Amida), the Great Hachiman Bodhisattva urges Izumi Shikibu on her way, and he encourages her to take heart in the saving power of Amida's Great Transcendent Vow, the eighteenth of his forty-eight Original Vows.[16]

[15]According to two alternate manuscripts in the *Sankan-bon* textual line (*Rakuyō Seiganji honzon engi* and the six-scroll *Seiganji engi*), Izumi Shikibu should put her faith in the Seiganji Amida, pay obeisance, chant Amida's name, and *look forward to the end of her life* (italics mine). Kikuchi Masakazu, "Kyōhō hachinen-sha *Rakuyō Seiganji honzon engi*," in *Shōdō bungaku kenkyū: dai san shū*, ed. Fukuda Akira and Hirota Tetsumichi (Tokyo: Miyai Shoten, 2001), 373; Yutani Yūzō, "*Seiganji engi* rokkanbon no kaidai to honkoku," *Dōhō Daigaku Bukkyō bunka kenkyūjo kiyō* 18 (1998), 88a.

[16]A similar story of Izumi Shikibu's meeting with the Great Hachiman Bodhisattva is contained in the "Tales of Hachiman" subsection of the "Deities" chapter of a Muromachi-period Shintō text by the name of *Kingyoku yōshū* (An Essential Collection of Golden Jewels) in the Naikaku Bunko archive, but its relationship to *Rakuyō Seiganji engi* is unclear:

> Izumi Shikibu . . . journeyed to Iwashimizu Hachiman Shrine, where for seven days and seven nights she secluded herself in prayer. Before long the seven days had passed, and at dawn of the morning she was to return, [the Great Hachiman Bodhisattva appeared to her] and spoke: "The principal image at Seiganji Temple in the capital is a living manifestation of Amida. By the power of his Transcendent Vow he saves all sentient beings, good and bad. You should go there and pray." Taking the deity's

According to Shakyamuni's explanation in *The Sutra of Infinite Life* (*Muryōjukyō*), the Original Vows are a set of promises made by the renunciant-king Dharmākara, later to become Amida Buddha, countless eons in the past.[17] Together, they stipulate the conditions and attributes of a wondrous Pure Land Paradise to be established in the west, as well as the means by which sentient beings may attain rebirth there. Dharmākara swears in each of his vows to refuse enlightenment if his pledge should remain unfulfilled; that he did attain enlightenment some ten ages ago (according to *The Sutra of Infinite Life*) is taken among Pure Land devotees as proof of their efficacy. The eighteenth and most celebrated of Dharmākara's vows guarantees rebirth in the Western Paradise to all people who call on his name (the name Amida Buddha) even ten times, excluding those who commit the Five Evil Deeds.[18] This "Great Transcendent Vow," as the Great Hachiman Bodhisattva and others have called it, constitutes the scriptural basis for the doctrine of the sole practice of the *nenbutsu*: the ritual invocation of Amida's name as the one and only means of attaining rebirth in the Pure Land.

The *Seiganji engi emaki* depicts Izumi Shikibu's encounter with the Great Hachiman Bodhisattva in a painted scene absent from the Kamakura-period *Seiganji engi* hanging scrolls (fig. 22). The illustration shows Izumi Shikibu dozing in an open hall of the Iwashimizu Hachiman Shrine, her head resting upon the sleeve of her folded right arm. A barefoot old priest—the Great Hachiman Bodhisattva—stands before her in plain brown robes, his head partially obscured, gazing down at her as she sleeps. A second, unknown woman sleeps where she sits upon the veranda at the front of the hall. In sculpture, the Great Hachiman Bodhisattva is commonly represented as a Buddhist priest in what is known as the Sōgyō Hachiman ("Priest-pattern

---

> revelation to heart, Izumi Shikibu traveled to Seiganji Temple beyond First Avenue and secluded herself there for forty-eight days. Eventually she achieved rebirth in the Pure Land. Though a woman of the Five Obstructions, her faith was true, and thus the Great Bodhisattva deigned to speak with her and appear to her in just such a manner.

Quoted in Itō Masayoshi, "*Seiganji* kaidai," in SNKS *Yōkyokushū*, vol. 2, 461. Because Seiganji is described as being beyond (literally, "above") First Avenue, *Kingyoku yōshū* probably dates from before 1591, when the temple was moved to Shinkyōgoku, between Third and Fourth Avenues.

[17]For a list of the Original Vows, see TSD 12 (360): 267c–69b, and Hisao Inagaki, *The Three Pure Land Sutras* (Kyoto: Nagata Bunshodō, 1995), 241–49.

[18]The Five Evil Deeds (*go gyakuzai*) are matricide, patricide, murdering an arhat, causing a disruption in the monastic order, and injuring the body of a Buddha. Ishida Mizumaro, *Reibun Bukkyōgo daijiten* (Tokyo: Shōgakukan, 1997), 294c–95a. The significance and validity of the vow's final exclusionary clause has long been a subject of controversy.

Fig. 22. Izumi Shikibu at Iwashimizu Hachiman Shrine. From *Seiganji engi emaki* (seventeenth century). Courtesy of Seiganji Temple and the Kyoto National Museum.

Hachiman") iconographic convention;[19] it is a tradition with which his depiction here is in accord. Although the circumstances of his revelation are unspecified within the written text, from the illustration he would appear to bestow his oracle in a dream, as indeed most oracles are bestowed in Heian and medieval literature.

A far more elaborate version of the Izumi Shikibu/Hachiman account is contained in an *otogizōshi* with the unusual title *Izumi Shikibu engi* (A History of Izumi Shikibu). Loosely based upon the Izumi Shikibu sections of *Rakuyō Seiganji engi* or some other closely related source, *Izumi Shikibu engi* is a didactic Buddhist tale of Izumi Shikibu's life, death at Seiganji, and afterlife encounter with Ippen Shōnin. According to a colophon dated the tenth month of 1643 in the two-scroll Seishin'in Temple manuscript, the Seishin'in intendant of the time (Mimuro Kakuyū; d. 1660) had the work reproduced from

[19]Christine Guth Kanda, *Shinzō: Hachiman Imagery and Its Development* (Cambridge: Harvard University Press, 1985), 46–47. Prominent images in the Sōgyō Hachiman style include those at Tōdaiji and Yakushiji temples.

an older, deteriorating text,[20] although what that might have been is now unknown. The Seishin'in scrolls contain a total of thirteen colorful hand-painted illustrations executed in the style of the Tosa school and seemingly uninfluenced by either the Kamakura-period *Seiganji engi* hanging scrolls or the seventeenth-century *Seiganji engi emaki.*[21] Considering its connection to Seishin'in, a small Shingon temple in central Kyoto traditionally associated with both Izumi Shikibu and Seiganji (Seishin'in was formerly a sub-temple of Seiganji), *Izumi Shikibu engi* may have been employed by the members of Seishin'in in their own Pure Land preaching in the late Muromachi and early Edo periods.

Among Seiganji-related texts, *Izumi Shikibu engi* is unique for its description of a poetic exchange between Izumi Shikibu and the Great Hachiman Bodhisattva. As the tale unfolds (or unrolls, in this case), Izumi Shikibu passes seven days and seven nights praying before the inner sanctuary at Iwashimizu Hachiman Shrine. Toward the break of dawn on her final, seventh night, a "mysterious voice" emerges from within the sacred sanctum, reciting a cryptic verse:[22]

yo no naka wa	The world is wind and
kaze hagi no ha no	the dew at the tips of the
sue no tsuyu	bush-clover leaves
kiekaerite mo	vanishes into nothing—
aru wa aru ka wa	so it seems, or so it seems.

The Great Hachiman Bodhisattva is not especially well known for his *waka*. Nevertheless, the poetic anthology *Shinkokin wakashū* (New Collection of Poems Past and Present; ordered compiled in 1201) contains a single verse attributed to him,[23] and *Sangoku denki* relates an account of how he once recited a poem in the dreams of two *nenbutsu*-devotees, revealing that he had nothing to teach them other than that they ought to recite the

[20]The colophon is signed Kaijuan (Prince Ryōjun). The Seishin'in manuscript is typeset (with illustrations) in Ōhashi Kiyohide, *Izumi Shikibu nikki no kenkyū* (Tokyo: Shoon Shobō, 1961), 529–41. In regard to Kaijuan's colophon, see Yoshida, "*Seiganji engi* to *Izumi Shikibu engi*," 8–9. (Yoshida misprints Kakuyū's name as "Kakuu." See Akamatsu Toshihide et al., eds., *Sennyūji shi: honbun hen* [Kyoto: Hōzōkan, 1984], 352 and 677–79.) The second half of *Izumi Shikibu engi* is also preserved in a manuscript titled *Ippen Shōnin Izumi Shikibu monogatari*, in the possession of Tōhokuin Temple (formerly affiliated with Seishin'in).

[21]Tokuda Kazuo, ed., *Otogizōshi jiten* (Tokyo: Tōkyōdō Shuppan, 2002), 153; Sawai Taizō, "Nara ehon to otogizōshi: Izumi Shikibu," *Kokubungaku: kaishaku to kyōzai no kenkyū* 35, no. 12 (October 1990), 107a.

[22]This and the following *Izumi Shikibu engi* translations are from Ōhashi, *Izumi Shikibu nikki no kenkyū*, 533–34.

[23]SNKBT 11:542 (poem 1863). Also see *Fukurozōshi* (SNKBT 29:143–44) and *Jikkinshō* 6:38 (SNKBZ 51:277).

nenbutsu.[24] According to the thirteenth- or fourteenth-century war chronicle *Genpei jōsuiki* (An Account of the Prosperity and Decline of the Minamoto and Taira Clans), there have been few revelations by any of the Sumiyoshi, Tamatsushima, Ise, Iwashimizu, Kamo, and Kasuga deities that were not bestowed as poems.[25] (This would of course not include the Great Hachiman Bodhisattva's speech in the sixteenth-century *Rakuyō Seiganji engi*.) In *Izumi Shikibu engi*, although it is Izumi Shikibu's devotion to the ways of love and poetry that are at the heart of her delusion, the Bodhisattva chooses poetry as his means of communicating the truth of impermanence. Such is the nature of expedient means, for how might he better tailor his message to a poet than with a poem? The *Izumi Shikibu engi* narrator explains:

> The Bodhisattva's poem urges us to immediately abandon our love of the world. Truly, though in morning we may be flush with youth and achieve glory in worldly paths, come evening we are but bleached bones moldering in the dewy grass of the fields. And then although in the night we may sport with the clear light of the moon, from that too we are yet hidden by the parting clouds of dawn. On what should we set our hearts in a fleeting realm such as this? Of the dew on the leaves and the drops on the stalk, though one may disappear before the other, neither yet remains for long. Izumi Shikibu understood this to be the meaning of the Great Hachiman Bodhisattva's poem, and taking it very much to heart, she composed the following verse in the same venerable tone:

gokuraku no	I myself
michi no shirube wa[26]	am the guide
waga mi nari	on the path to Paradise—
kokoro hitotsu no	if my single heart, that is,
naoki nariseba	be true.

As Ōshima Yukio has observed, variants of Izumi Shikibu's poem are attributed to the bodhisattva Jizō in the early twelfth-century *Konjaku monogatari shū* (Tales of Times Now Past), and to the Shintō deity Jūzenji, identified as a native manifestation of Jizō, in *Kokon chomonjū* (Remarkable Tales Old

[24]*Sangoku denki* 8:30, in Ikegami Jun'ichi, ed., *Sangoku denki*, vol. 2 (Tokyo: Miyai Shoten, 1982), 120–21. There is also an oft-repeated tale of a young woman who once composed a poem at Iwashimizu Hachiman Shrine that induced the Great Hachiman Bodhisattva to grant her a husband. See *Kokon chomonjū* 5:173 (NKBT 84:159–60), *Jikkinshō* 10:12 (SNKBZ 51:399–400), *Shasekishū* 5:1 (NKBT 85:227), and *Sangoku denki* 9:30 (Ikegami, ed., *Sangoku denki*, vol. 2, 162–63).

[25]Matsuo Ashie, ed., *Genpei jōsuiki*, vol. 2 (Tokyo: Miyai Shoten, 1993), 38.

[26]Actually *shirushibe* (a mistranscription of *shirube*) in Ōhashi's typesetting of the text.

and New; dated 1254).[27] That the verse exists in at least four different versions (including the one in *Izumi Shikibu engi*), all of which are cited within miraculous tales of a deity or a bodhisattva, suggests its use in centuries of preaching, as well as the influence of preaching on the composition of *Izumi Shikibu engi*.

As *Izumi Shikibu engi* continues, the narrator urges audiences to place their faith in Amida's saving vows:

> In truth, Hachiman's holy teachings are an expedient means of sparking enlightenment in sentient beings. If we but take the sword of Buddhist faith and sever the fetters binding us to the Three Worlds, then the path of Pure Land rebirth will be ours. We ought to foster truth in our hearts, abandon all doubt and single-mindedly call on Amida's Original Vows. If our faith is not weak, we can depend on those vows, for they are without flaw. With the merit of one or ten invocations of the Name, the five or ten evils are joyfully erased.
>
> Realizing the certainty of her Pure Land rebirth by means of the Compassionate Vow of Reciting the Name, Izumi Shikibu drenched her sleeves in happy tears. The Great Bodhisattva later spoke to her in a dream: "In my original state I am [Amida Buddha,] founder of the Pure Land Realm of Nourishing Tranquility. Since dimming my brilliance to mingle with the filth of this world, I have lost my way in paths of manifest forms and forgotten the means of escaping delusion. But at a place called Seiganji in the capital, the principal image is a true incarnation of Amida Buddha, carved by the Kasuga Deity. By the power of his Transcendent Vow he guides all living beings to salvation. You should go there and pray."

The Great Hachiman Bodhisattva directs Izumi Shikibu to Seiganji as he does in other versions of the tale, but *Izumi Shikibu engi* is unusual for the disparaging statement that it attributes to him: he confesses that in the natural course of saving sentient beings, he has become lost and can no longer find his way back to the Pure Land. It is a damning admission for a figure of such popular religious belief. His defamation in this case is reminiscent of that of Shōkū Shōnin in *Izumi Shikibu ōjō no koto*, in which the holy man is

[27]In *Konjaku monogatari shū* 17:29 (SNKBT 36:54), Jizō teaches a slight variant of the poem to the third daughter of Taira no Masayuki before bringing her back from the dead. In *Kokon chomonjū* 1:7 (NKBT 84:53), Jūzenji recites another variant in answer to a question by Tokishige as to how one might escape the cycle of birth and death. A third version of the poem is cited in *Konjaku monogatari shū* 17:32 (SNKBT 36:58), which is again the story of Tokishige and Jūzenji. See Ōshima Yukio, "*Izumi Shikibu engi*: Amida shinkō no shujinkō," *Kokubungaku: kaishaku to kanshō* 60, no. 8 (August 1995), 128–29.

said to have admitted to his own incomprehension of the Dharma, and that of the Kumano Deity in *Sangoku denki* (discussed on pp. 24–26, above), in which the Deity is said to have explained that he is usually absent from his shrine because he spends his time worshipping at Taima Temple. However, considering that the Great Hachiman Bodhisattva is himself a manifestation of Amida, his admission is logical—and thus perhaps desirable from the point of view of the *Izumi Shikibu engi* author—insofar as it provides a legitimate reason for him to send Izumi Shikibu on to see the living statue of Amida at Seiganji.

Although the roots of Izumi Shikibu's folkloric association with the Great Hachiman Bodhisattva are obscure, that there was such an association in the Muromachi period is further implied by an entry in the shrine record *Iwashimizu Hachimangū narabi ni Gokurakuji engi no koto* (An Account of the History of Iwashimizu Hachiman Shrine and Gokurakuji Temple), which bears a date of 1452.[28] In the "question and answer" section of the work, an imaginary interlocutor asks:

> Question: As for Izumi Shikibu always coming to stay at Hachiman Shrine—please explain.
>
> Reply: We are unclear of this here at the shrine-temple. Ajari Hokkyō Kenshō's *Ōnen sōdan* (Discussions of Years Past), however, records that Lord Kiyosuke once came here toward the end of the tenth month.[29] As Kiyosuke spent the night performing devotions in the western sutra hall, he recalled the governor of Settsu's sleeves. Amused at how the pines [of Sumiyoshi] had become "signaling cypress," he rushed over to [our] Sumiyoshi [branch-shrine] and performed a devotional offering.[30]
>
> As he turned off the main path to enter a sutra hall, the shrine pheasants began to cry at last, and the lingering morning moon began to disappear in a faint glow of light. Stirred by the loneliness of the dawn, Kiyosuke hurried around to the southern gate-tower.

[28]According to a two-part colophon to the text, the extant manuscript dates from 1633, when it was copied and revised by the priest Kyōjō from a manuscript copied by the priest Jūgen in 1452. The following account is printed in *Iwashimizu Hachimangū shiryō sōsho*, vol. 2 (Kyoto: Iwashimizu Hachimangū Shamusho, 1976), 167–68.

[29]*Ōnen sōdan* is unknown. The priest and poet Kenshō (also called Suke no Ajari; 1130?–1209?) was given the title *hokkyō* in 1207. Fujiwara no Kiyosuke (1104–77) was Kenshō's older brother-in-law, and he is best known today as the author/compiler of various works of poetic lore, including *Ōgishō* and *Fukurozōshi*.

[30]This is perhaps an allusion to a story in *Fukurozōshi* about Settsu governor Mibu no Tadami (SNKBT 29:107–8). Having been summoned to court for a poetry contest in 960, Tadami arrived in the capital without the proper attire. He therefore improvised a pair of sleeves by putting his arms through his *kobakama*, or "shortened trousers." Returning to Settsu before the night was through, Tadami excused his early departure with the following poem:

Gazing through the fence of the inner shrine at the dim light of the fire-offering, he thought of Izumi Shikibu's poem, "Shine your light afar."

"You light of the moon," he beseeched, "dimming your brilliance to take on this native form . . . reflect in the dew of my evanescent body and lead me, by this link that I join to you through the Eight Righteous Practices, to the Single Buddha Land." He then softly chanted: "Praise be the Great Hachiman Bodhisattva in his three manifestations; with a tranquil heart in my time of dying, may I attain rebirth in the Pure Land Paradise."

He turned his gaze to the south and saw a dark, strangely elongated cloud hovering over a building known as the "Iidonoya." The cloud passed straight down through the roof-beams, and as Kiyosuke watched, wondering what it could be, a lady in white five-layered robes and crimson trousers flew out from the mist and stood at the gate-tower railing. Kiyosuke was amazed. "Who are you?" he asked.

"I am Izumi Shikibu," the woman replied. "I manifest as the Tamatsushima Deity.[31] On the outside I receive festival celebrations twice a year, but on the inside I suffer horribly from the Three Burning Torments.[32] This is because I broke men's hearts with passions of love and told fancy lies with flowers [of poetry]. Indeed, poetry may provoke responses in Buddhas and inspire gods to lend their aid, but lies of love and flowers—[what we call poetry]—will also waste people's hearts. It is for this that I am punished. Yet thanks to you remembering my "moon on the mountain ridge," I have occasion to rest from time to time. I have come here for a while because you set your heart on the moon at the southern gate-tower."

Sumiyoshi no	Faintly I hear
matsu to honoka ni	the pines of Sumiyoshi
kikishikaba	awaiting my return.
michi kishi oki ya	Like the incoming tide at its peak,
yoru kaeri nan	tonight I must withdraw.

The word *matsu* is used in the poem to signify both "pine trees" and "wait"; *yoru* means both "to draw near" (hence "incoming") and "night." "Signaling cypress" refers to the cypress trees at Iwashimizu Hachiman Shrine and alludes to a poem in *Shūi wakashū* (486), which in turn alludes to *Kokin wakashū* 982.

[31]The deity of Tamatsushima Shrine (in the present-day city of Wakayama) is popularly revered as a god of poetry, and has been identified with the poet Sotoori-hime since at least the Heian period. See Susan Blakeley Klein, *Allegories of Desire: Esoteric Literary Commentaries of Medieval Japan* (Cambridge: Harvard University Asia Center, 2002), 198–204, and Heibonsha Chihō Shiryō Sentā, ed., *Jiin jinja daijiten: Yamato, Kii* (Tokyo: Heibonsha, 1997), 538b.

[32]The Three Burning Torments (*sannetsu*) are three agonies that snakes, dragons and the like are said to suffer in the animal realm.

> Thus the story is told. The year is not recorded. It all seems rather dubious.

As Kiyosuke gazes through the shrine fence at the sacred fire offering, he remembers Izumi Shikibu's "darkness into darkness" poem, composed for Shōkū Shōnin in the century before. Staring in at the holy fire, he calls on the moon—the Great Hachiman Bodhisattva, in this case—to light the way for him to the Pure Land. Living on through her poetry (which has also condemned her in the next life to the Three Burning Torments), Izumi Shikibu is summoned by the allusion to her famous verse. Her strange revelation brings to mind the twelfth- and thirteenth-century tales of Murasaki Shikibu, similarly reported to have returned from the dead and admitted to suffering torment for writing *The Tale of Genji*.

Interesting as Kiyosuke's account may be, the question that prompts it is more revealing. "As for Izumi Shikibu always coming to stay at Hachiman Shrine," the unidentified interrogator states, "please explain." The shrine authorities can neither confirm nor deny this, but the existence of such hearsay—if that is indeed what it represents—implies that stories of Izumi Shikibu at Iwashimizu Hachiman Shrine were circulating in the shrine community previous to the work's composition prior to 1452. Takigawa Masajirō has observed that according to the Kamakura-period *Gūji enjishō* (Notes on the History of the Iwashimizu Hachiman Shrine-Temple), there was a subshrine to the roadside deity Hyakudayū within the Iwashimizu Hachiman shrine complex.[33] This suggests the presence of *kugutsu* and other courtesan-entertainers—women who, as we have seen, are believed to have told tales of Izumi Shikibu, Ono no Komachi, and other cultural and religious figures as they traveled. If Izumi Shikibu stories were indeed spread by women at Iwashimizu Hachiman Shrine, they may have been picked up by the mendicant nuns (or monks) of Seiganji, and thus have made their way—altered in the form of the Izumi Shikibu/Hachiman account—into the sixteenth century *Rakuyō Seiganji engi*.

Izumi Shikibu and the Seiganji Amida

Following Izumi Shikibu's encounter with the Great Hachiman Bodhisattva, *Rakuyō Seiganji engi* reports that Izumi Shikibu felt as if she were "the nun Mahāprajāpatī when she received the prophecy at the assembly on Sacred [Eagle] Peak," or as if she were "the eight-year-old Dragon Girl when she attained enlightenment in the Immaculate World to the south." The unknown

[33] Takigawa Masajirō, *Yūjo no rekishi* (Tokyo: Shibundō, 1965), 148.

engi author was apparently inspired by the rhetoric of Gentō's fifteenth-century *Sangoku denki* account. By citing such illustrious examples from the history of women and Buddhism, the author both hints at Izumi Shikibu's approaching Buddhahood and elevates her, within popular Buddhist lore, to the status of a Japanese Buddhist exemplar for women—a native counterpart to Mahāprajāpatī and the Dragon Girl.[34]

As *Rakuyō Seiganji engi* continues, Izumi Shikibu makes her way to Seiganji, where for forty-eight days—a number allusive to Amida's forty-eight Original Vows—she remains within the temple grounds, chanting Amida's name and praying for rebirth in the Pure Land:

> Late one night when the temple had grown quiet and the lamplight dim, Izumi Shikibu dozed for a short while. An old nun of more than seventy suddenly stepped down from within the altar. Drawing near Izumi Shikibu's side, she spoke:
>
> "The intent with which you call on me is true. Entrust your rebirth to the Transcendent Vow.
>
> "The Pure Land teachings and practices have nothing to do with supplications that strain the heart or mortify the flesh. If you but chant 'Hail Amida Buddha' with unwavering faith and a desire to be saved, you will be received in the beneficent light of salvation, illuminating the lightless gloom of delusion.
>
> "Women's Pure Land rebirth in particular is taken up in my thirty-fifth Original Vow. Lady Vaidehī witnessed the Miraculous Reception with her own eyes, and that she attained supreme enlightenment just as she was, without having her filthy femininity transformed, was thanks to the wonder of that Original Vow.[35]

[34]Both Mahāprajāpatī's and the Dragon Girl's suitability as role models for women have been subjects of debate. In "A Voice from the Silence: The Buddha's Mother's Story" (*History of Religions* 33 [1994]: 358–79), Jonathan Walters discusses Mahāprajāpatī (also known as Gotamī) as a "female counterpart to the Buddha" (p. 373). Walters writes that "the arhatship of women is not dependent on Gotama, but on Gotamī: it was she who founded the nuns' order, it was her *parinibbāna* that cleared the way for nuns to reach the goal" (p. 378). In *Charming Cadavers* (Chicago: University of Chicago Press, 1996), Liz Wilson takes up Walters's argument and counters that "Gotamī renounced the world at the death of her husband and became a disciple of her son. In her immediate transition from being Suddhodana's chief queen to being Gotama's chief female disciple, we see a pattern of female subservience like that idealized in Brahminical culture" (p. 144). As for the Dragon Girl, she first transforms into a man before becoming a Buddha, and this has been seen to compromise her legitimacy as a model for women. In *Rakuyō Seiganji engi,* Mahāprajāpatī and the Dragon Girl are mentioned simply as women who achieved Buddhahood, and in this very basic sense they are both treated within the *engi* as female exemplars.

[35]According to the *Visualization Sutra* (*Kanmuryōjukyō*), Shakyamuni appeared before Queen Vaidehī (Idaike) when she was imprisoned by her evil son Ajātaśatru. At that time, Shakyamuni taught her several meditative practices by which she could visualize Amida's Pure Land. The Miraculous Reception (*raigō*) is the term for Amida's appearance with a host of bodhisattvas when he comes to greet dying devotees to lead them on to the Pure Land.

> You shouldn't think it was because of anything that Vaidehī did herself. Explicitly, the vow proclaims:
>
> When I am to become a Buddha, if in the innumerable, wondrous, various Buddha Lands of the ten directions there is a woman who hears my name, whose heart is turned to the Dharma in joyous faith, who despises her female body and who, when her life has come to pass, is yet reborn in the female form, then I shall not accept enlightenment.[36]
>
> "If women of the Latter Age appeal to my Original Vows and wholeheartedly recite the *nenbutsu*, they may enjoy the same rewards as Vaidehī. Their Pure Land rebirth is guaranteed. Now put aside all other vows and practices—simply keep me in your heart and single-mindedly chant my name."

In a gesture of solidarity with women, the Seiganji Amida appears before Izumi Shikibu in the form of an old nun and assures her of the possibility of women's rebirth in the Pure Land by means of the *nenbutsu*, guaranteed by the Original Vows. Because she addresses a woman, she recites her thirty-fifth Original Vow promising salvation from the female form. Her words are simultaneously disparaging and empowering of women, and in this sense they are reminiscent of both the *otogizōshi Izumi Shikibu*, which attests to the possibility of a woman achieving Buddhahood in spite of her wicked inclinations, and Gentō's *Sangoku denki* account, which emphasizes women's ability to attain enlightenment in the face of the Five Obstructions.

As Terry Kawashima observes, Hosokawa Ryōichi has argued that the Pure Land Buddhism of the Heian period "attempted to implant in women the notion of their inherent impurity and sinfulness and thereby co-opt them into its religious paradigm by offering redemption."[37] The same can be said of the Pure Land and Tendai Buddhism of later centuries, as we have seen in this and the previous chapters. In a discussion of Minamoto Junko's views on women and Pure Land Buddhist doctrine, Kawashima further explains:

> Although some scholars have claimed that Hōnen's and Shinran's views empowered women, Minamoto insists that, in fact, they

[36]This is the thirty-fifth Original Vow as it is cited in *The Sutra of Infinite Life* (*Muryōjukyō*), in TSD 12 (360): 268c. For an alternate translation, see Inagaki, *The Three Pure Land Sutras*, 246–47.

[37]Terry Kawashima, *Writing Margins: The Textual Construction of Gender in Heian and Kamakura Japan* (Cambridge: Harvard University Asia Center), 129, citing Hosokawa Ryōichi, *Onna no chūsei* (Tokyo: Nihon Editā Sukūru Shuppanbu, 1989), 218–80.

> were highly oppressive. As for the Pure Land rhetoric of "everyone will be saved, even the lowest of the low," that very phrase succeeds in positioning certain people as "the lowest of the low" even as it hides this manipulating move by emphasizing that they, too, will be saved; in other words, the religious rhetoric constructs social stratification. In the case of women, their sinfulness (*tsumibukasa*) was emphasized in order to show that Pure Land belief would save even the most sinful.[38]

While Minamoto's observations ring true, one might also argue that individual works like *Rakuyō Seiganji engi* (or *Izumi Shikibu* or the *Sangoku denki* account, for that matter) are pro-woman within a misogynistic context; that they function to liberate as they inadvertently oppress. For although Amida's thirty-fifth vow requires women to despise their female bodies, and although, in *Rakuyō Seiganji engi*, the Seiganji Amida celebrates Queen Vaidehī as a woman who attained enlightenment without having her "filthy femininity" transformed, the Seiganji Amida appears before Izumi Shikibu as a woman and, in that unusual manifestation, assures her of the possibility of all women, as women, attaining rebirth in the Pure Land.[39]

Toward the end of her speech, the Seiganji Amida-nun declares the certainty of Pure Land rebirth for "women of the Latter Age," an anachronism suggestive of the *engi*'s true intended audience of sixteenth-century women. The "Latter Age," *mappō*, is the third and final era of the Dharma, a degenerate period of ten thousand years in which individuals are said to be incapable of attaining enlightenment by their own efforts. It is a fundamental concept in Hōnen's and Shinran's Pure Land Buddhist thought, which maintains that in this final epoch, sentient beings can attain salvation only by relying on the "other power" (*tariki*) of Amida's eighteenth vow. According to traditional Japanese calculations, *mappō* was believed to begin in 1052, two thousand years after the death of Shakyamuni.[40] *Rakuyō Seiganji engi* reports that Izumi Shikibu passed away in the third month of the third year of Chōwa (1014), thirty-eight years before the advent of *mappō*. Although salvation in the Latter Age is thus unlikely to have been a crucial concern for

[38]Kawashima, *Writing Margins*, 18, note 30, citing Ōgoshi Aiko and Minamoto Junko, *Kaitai suru Bukkyō: sono sekushuaritī kan to shizen kan* (Tokyo: Daitō Shuppanbu, 1994), 140, 92, and 96.

[39]The notion of Pure Land rebirth without sexual transformation was relatively common in medieval Japan. In *Guanki hensatsu*, a defense of Shinran's Jōdo Shinshū Pure Land sect, for example, the priest Nyodō (1253–1340) writes that "the woman, even as woman, will be ushered into Pure Land (*raikō*) if she chants [the *nenbutsu*]." Cited in James Dobbins, *Jōdo Shinshū: Shin Buddhism in Medieval Japan* (Bloomington and Indianapolis: Indiana University Press, 1989), 127. Translation by Dobbins.

[40]Nakamura Hajime, *Bukkyōgo daijiten*, vol. 2 (Tokyo: Tokyo Shoseki, 1975), 1284b.

Izumi Shikibu (unless, of course, her concern was for the *approach* of *mappō*), it was a fundamental issue for medieval *engi* audiences—"women of the Latter Age," to borrow the Seiganji Amida's phrase—which may explain the nun's somewhat premature assurances.

Like the Great Hachiman Bodhisattva, the Seiganji Amida-nun presents Izumi Shikibu with a poem:

> Not the least bit aware that she was dreaming, Izumi Shikibu wept tears of joy. "Oh, thank you," she cried, and reverently pressed her palms together in obeisance. The old nun chanted a single verse:
>
> | | |
> |---|---|
> | Amida-bu to | At Naniwa in Settsu |
> | iu yori hoka wa | one should gather reeds— |
> | tsu no kuni no | other than saying |
> | naniwa no koto mo | "Amida Buddha," |
> | ashikarinubeshi | all deeds are wrong. |
>
> "If you keep this poem in mind and call on me with earnest intent," the nun explained, "I will certainly come to greet you and lead you on to the Pure Land in accord with your invocation of my name. You should abandon every single doubt, devote yourself to the *nenbutsu* and await my host of bodhisattvas coming to receive you."

The *waka* here attributed to the Seiganji Amida is in fact attributed to Hōnen in the poetic anthology *Fuboku wakashō* (Collected Poems of Japan; compiled by Fujiwara no Nagakiyo, a devotee of the Ji sect of Pure Land Buddhism, ca. 1310).[41] As Yanagita Kunio wryly observes, the Seiganji Amida borrows it from Hōnen more than a hundred years before Hōnen's birth.[42] *Rakuyō Seiganji engi* contains the following explanation in half-size print beside the poem:

> In what seems to have been the Kenkyū era [1190–98], Master Hōnen once stayed at our temple after completing his *Senchakushū* (Passages on the Selection).[43] Hearing how this poem by our principal image had moved Izumi Shikibu to enlightenment, he declared it to be in perfect accord with his treatise. He is said to have recited it with great feeling.

[41]The poem is *Fuboku wakashō* 16386 (SKT 2:1:837a), attributed to Genkū Shōnin (Hōnen).

[42]Yanagita Kunio, *Josei to minkan denshō* (1932), reprinted in *Teihon Yanagita Kunio shū*, vol. 8 (Tokyo: Chikuma Shobō, 1962), 364.

[43]The full title of this work is *Senchaku hongan nenbutsu shū*, "Passages on the Selection of the *Nenbutsu* in the Original Vow." See *Senchakushū* English Translation Project, ed., *Hōnen's Senchakushū* (Honolulu: University of Hawaii Press, 1998).

Yanagita supposes that accounts of the Seiganji Amida reciting Hōnen's "Amida Buddha" poem circulated orally for some time before the written *engi* was produced. When *Rakuyō Seiganji engi* was composed, Yanagita writes, the author probably knew of the poem's original attribution and felt it necessary to provide the preceding explanation.[44]

As an expedient means of transmitting the Dharma, the Seiganji Amida's (Hōnen's) verse employs conventional poetic language and techniques to promote the sole practice of the *nenbutsu*. The words *tsu no kuni no* ("of the province of Settsu") function as a pillow phrase (*makura kotoba*) for the poetic place name "Naniwa," a pivot word (*kakekotoba*) that serves in this and many other poems both as a proper noun (Naniwa) and as a part of the expression *naniwa no koto mo* ("everything"). The word *ashi* signifies both "reeds" (associated with Naniwa) and "bad," and is used within the construction *ashikarinubeshi* to mean "one should gather reeds" and "would certainly be bad." Thus, in its layered expression of poetic and Buddhist truths (at Naniwa in Settsu one should gather reeds; other than chanting the *nenbutsu*, all deeds are wrong), the poem represents a perfect fusion of the Ways of Buddhism and Poetry.

Paradoxically, while it is Izumi Shikibu's devotion to poetry that is at the heart of her delusion in *Rakuyō Seiganji engi*, it is poetry that pushes her ever forward on the Buddhist path: Koshikibu's death-bed verse awakens her to a realization of impermanence and a desire for salvation; her own "darkness into darkness" poem convinces Shōkū Shōnin to meet with her and send her onward; the Great Hachiman Bodhisattva's "world is wind" poem (in *Izumi Shikibu engi*) confirms her in her Buddhist belief; and the Seiganji Amida's "Amida Buddha" poem instructs her in Pure Land sectarian practice.

Upon awaking from her miraculous dream-revelation, Izumi Shikibu renounces the vanity of her former life. The *Rakuyō Seiganji engi* narrator explains:

> In her days at the palace Izumi Shikibu had passed her time before an elegant mirror, forever making up her lovely face and combing out her glossy hair, preening and dressing in the finest robes—and though this is the kind of woman she had been, in an instant she swept away the impurities of this floating world, cut the bonds tying her to the endless cycle of birth and death, turned to the path of enlightenment and became a pure, precept-minding nun.

The decadence of Izumi Shikibu's youth is epitomized by her attention to her looks. In the *otogizōshi Chōhōji yomigaeri no sōshi* (Back from the Dead at

[44] Yanagita, *Josei to minkan denshō*, 364.

Chōhōji Temple; composed prior to 1513), King Enma, the judge of the dead, explains that mirrors should be used to inspire in us an awareness of advancing years and the inevitable approach of death, encouraging our aspiration to enlightenment; those who use mirrors to make themselves more attractive, he observes, will have copper needles thrust into their eyes in hell.[45]

In *Rakuyō Seiganji engi*, Izumi Shikibu abjures her previously sinful ways with a single decisive act. By cutting her hair, a symbol of her femininity and all the impediments that it entails, she cuts her ties to the world; by exchanging her robes for the dark raiment of the clergy, she adopts the asexual identity of a renunciant. In this way she is more like the Dragon Girl than Vaidehī, for she chooses to abandon her femininity before attaining Buddhahood. At the time of her death on "the twenty-second day of the third month of the third year of Chōwa [1014]," purple clouds are said to have trailed from the temple eaves, music to have rung in the sky, and a wondrous scent to have filled the air—sure signs of her salvation in the *ōjōden* Pure Land-rebirth *setsuwa* genre.

After her meeting with the Seiganji Amida (and before her Pure Land rebirth), Izumi Shikibu is said to have taken up residence at Seiganji, first in a brushwood shack beside the main temple hall, and later in a "one-room building constructed by the Midō Chancellor [Fujiwara no] Michinaga called the Komidō" (Small Buddha Hall). *Rakuyō Seiganji engi* explains that Michinaga gave the Komidō to Izumi Shikibu, and that thus making her permanent home within the Seiganji temple compound, "she accumulated great merit over many years of reciting Amida's name." Sometime later—presumably after Izumi Shikibu's death—the Komidō came to be known as Seishin'in, a small Sennyūji-branch Shingon temple presently located off Shinkyōgoku Street, immediately to the south of Seiganji.[46] Although Seishin'in's early history is not well understood, Seishin'in tradition holds that it was originally constructed by Michinaga as a part of Tōhokuin Temple (itself a part of Hōjōji Temple) near Ichijō Avenue and the western bank of the Kamo river, and that it was later moved to a location within the former Seiganji compound at Ichijō-Ogawa. How and when Seishin'in came to be affiliated with

[45]SNKBZ 63:431 (Chōhōji scroll of 1513). *Chōhōji yomigaeri no sōshi* is also known as *Hirano yomigaeri no sōshi*. According to the *otogizōshi Fuji no hitoana sōshi* (The Story of the Fuji Cave), women who seek to make themselves more attractive to men will have the skin of their faces peeled back and burning oil dripped on the flesh underneath. MJMT 11:439a (hand-copied manuscript of 1603).

[46]The proper Buddhist reading of the temple name is "Jōshin'in," under which it is listed in most Japanese reference works. However, with a sign at its entrance, the temple identifies itself by the popular reading of "Seishin'in," which is why I do, too. According to *Izumi Shikibu engi* (the two-scroll manuscript of which is in the possession of Seishin'in), the principal image in the Komidō was a statue of Amida, "the Buddha whose praises are sung in the six directions," carved by Kūkai, founder of the Shingon sect. Ōhashi, *Izumi Shikibu nikki no kenkyū*, 535a.

Seiganji is unclear, but when Hideyoshi had Seiganji moved to its present location in 1591, Seishin'in moved with it.[47]

Yanagita Kunio observes that up until the 1780s or 1790s, the area around Seishin'in was known as "Izumi Shikibu Town" because of Seishin'in's prominent self-identification with Izumi Shikibu.[48] To this day Seishin'in possesses a number of Izumi Shikibu-related artifacts, including the two-scroll *Izumi Shikibu engi*; a painting of Izumi Shikibu attributed to Kanō Takanobu (1571–1618); a folding screen made from a robe supposedly given to Izumi Shikibu by Empress Shōshi; and a small wooden statue of Izumi Shikibu as a middle-aged nun, set at a place of honor near the inner altar.[49] In the Seishin'in cemetery there is a large stone memorial to Izumi Shikibu dated the fifth month of 1313 (eighty years after the Izumi Shikibu memorial at Enkyōji Temple), bearing the inscribed names of six nuns (*bikuni* Myōshō, *bikuni* Hōa, *bikuni* Kakushō, *bikuni* Gyōa, *bikuni* Dōen, and *bikuni* Myōa) and five monks (*sō* Sen'en, *sō* Rengon, *shami* Zengan, *sō* Yuinen, and *kanjin-sō* [fund-raising priest] Jōshin).[50] If the monument's date is indeed reliable, then

[47]Heibonsha Chihō Shiryō Sentā, ed., *Jiin jinja daijiten: Kyōto, Yamashiro*, 354, and Yoshida, "*Seiganji engi* to *Izumi Shikibu engi*," 2. If the Komidō was indeed located either beside or within Tōhokuin until after Izumi Shikibu's death, the *Rakuyō Seiganji engi* and *Izumi Shikibu engi* accounts of Izumi Shikibu residing in the Komidō at Seiganji are anachronistic. But as there are no known Seishin'in-related historical records predating the *Sankan-bon* textual line of *Seiganji engi* (*Rakuyō Seiganji engi*, composed more than five hundred years after Izumi Shikibu's demise), it is impossible to know. Complicating matters still, Seiganji's own late tenth-/early eleventh-century location is in question. As for Hōjōji and its subsidiary, Tōhokuin, Hōjōji became defunct in the Nanbokuchō period (1336–92); Tōhokuin (of the Tendai sect) also fell into decline at that time, but in 1560 it was revived as a Pure Land institution of the Ji sect. Tōhokuin moved to its present location in the Sakyō-ku district of Kyoto in 1693, after a fire in 1692. Heibonsha Chihō Shiryō Sentā, ed., *Jiin jinja daijiten: Kyōto, Yamashiro*, 524–25, and Umetani Shigeki, "Kyōto Tōhokuin-zō *Ippen Shōnin Izumi Shikibu monogatari* ni tsuite," in *Chūsei yūgyō hijiri to bungaku* (Tokyo: Ōfūsha, 1988), 321–22.

[48]Yanagita, *Josei to minkan denshō*, 324.

[49]Cranston, *The Izumi Shikibu Diary*, 23. Both Ōhashi Kiyohide and Uemura Etsuko provide photographs of the statue as frontispieces to their books, *Izumi Shikibu nikki no kenkyū* and *Ōchō joryū sakka no kenkyū* (Tokyo: Kasama Shoin, 1975). The nun holds a rosary in one hand and a scroll in the other; neither the image's date nor its sculptor are known. Yanagita suggests that it originally represented someone other than Izumi Shikibu, although there is no way now to tell. Yanagita, *Josei to minkan denshō*, 361.

[50]The names are transcribed in Gorai Shigeru, *Jisha engi kara otogibanashi e*, Shūkyō minzoku shūsei 6 (Tokyo: Kadokawa Shoten, 1995), 190; and in Saijō Shizuo, *Izumi Shikibu densetsu to sono koseki*, vol. 2 (Tokyo: Kindai bungeisha, 1999), 56. The memorial is a *hōkyōintō*, which Edwin Cranston describes as "an elaborate structure with a square base and middle sections, and a cylindrical spire on top, erected in Buddhist graveyards in memory of the dead." Cranston, *The Izumi Shikibu Diary*, 206, note 107. Ōhashi reproduces a photograph of the memorial in *Izumi Shikibu nikki no kenkyū*. A woodblock-printed illustration of the monument is included in *Kyō warabe* (1658), reproduced in Takemura Toshinori, ed., *Kyōto no maki* 1, vol. 7 of *Nihon meisho fūzoku zue* (Tokyo: Kadokawa Shoten, 1979), 10a.

the memorial was intended to commemorate the three hundredth anniversary of Izumi Shikibu's death at Seiganji. Although Yanagita doubts that it is quite so old, it was certainly constructed in or before the mid-fifteenth century, because the noh play *Seiganji* (ca. 1464) contains references to it.[51] Gorai Shigeru argues that the monument does in fact date from the early fourteenth century, and that it was likely constructed with donations raised by proselytizers of the Ji sect—the monks and nuns whose names are inscribed upon it, it would seem—who spread the story of Izumi Shikibu's encounter with Ippen Shōnin on which the noh play *Seiganji* was later based.[52]

Hank Glassman, Gorai Shigeru, and others have written about the prominent use of statues and reliquary objects in Buddhist preaching. To paraphrase Glassman's words, the ritual exhibition of relics (including statues) often served as the principal context for the recitation of tales.[53] Gorai maintains that "medieval preaching was more than simply speaking from a dais; it required personal relics, likenesses, sutra scrolls, calligraphy, picture scrolls, and other remnant objects to prove the truth and the reality of its stated claims."[54] It was these objects that gave strength to the sermons, allowing audiences a sense of connection to the figures and events of the legendary past. When considered in conjunction with the plethora of Izumi Shikibu-related Seiganji textual sources (including *Izumi Shikibu ōjō no koto*, *Seiganji shin engi*, the *Seiganji engi* hanging scrolls, *Rakuyō Seiganji engi*, etc.), the grave marker, the statue, the portrait, and other Izumi Shikibu-related artifacts at Seishin'in suggest the presence of a thriving cult of Izumi Shikibu at Seishin'in/Seiganji throughout the medieval period. The monks and nuns there may have sought to enshrine Izumi Shikibu as a kind of patron saint—a Pure Land woman-hero, perhaps, for the many women who seem to have been gathering at Seiganji at the time.

Chūjōhime and a Seiganji/Taima Temple Connection

That the Seiganji Amida appears to Izumi Shikibu in *Rakuyō Seiganji engi* in the form of an old nun—a woman—is best explained in terms of *hōben*, "expedient means." Amida is usually depicted or described as either male

[51]Yanagita, *Josei to minkan denshō*, 324 and 361–62. For the *Seiganji* references, see SNKBT 57:549–50.

[52]Gorai, *Jisha engi kara otogibanashi e*, 189–91.

[53]Hank Glassman, "'Show Me the Place Where My Mother Is!' Chūjōhime, Preaching, and Relics in Late Medieval and Early Modern Japan," in *Approaching the Land of Bliss: Religious Praxis in the Cult of Amitabha*, ed. Richard K. Payne and Kenneth K. Tanaka (Honolulu: University of Hawaii Press, 2004), 154.

[54]Gorai, *Jisha engi kara otogibanashi e*, 102. Also see Glassman, "Show Me the Place," 155.

Fig. 23. Stone memorial to Izumi Shikibu (upper right) at Seiganji Temple. Detail from the Burke *Rakuchū rakugai-zu* (screen paintings of scenes in and around the capital; ca. 1629). Courtesy of the Mary and Jackson Burke Foundation. Photo by Sheldan Comfert Collins.

or androgynous,[55] but in appealing to a woman troubled with the Five Obstructions, Amida here chooses a specifically female manifestation likely to inspire faith and trust. In adapting his gender to his audience, Amida is not alone. According to the "Wonderful Sound" chapter of the *Lotus Sutra*, the bodhisattva Myōon "changes himself into a woman's form and preaches this sutra" for the sake of women at the royal palace, and the bodhisattva

[55]Diana Y. Paul, *Women in Buddhism: Images of the Feminine in Mahāyāna Tradition* (Berkeley: Asian Humanities Press, 1979), 285 and 307–8.

Kannon is said to do the same.[56] That the Seiganji Amida chooses to reveal himself to Izumi Shikibu as an aged nun may be additionally significant, because in appearing as a woman of over seventy, he disassociates himself from the overt feminine sexuality that a younger manifestation might suggest. The *Seiganji engi emaki* contains an illustration of the scene (fig. 24), but except for a part of her brown robes, her white *kesa*, and a single pale foot, the Seiganji Amida-nun is entirely hidden from view. While not uncommon in paintings of deities, such concealment is unusual for a Buddha,[57] and it functions in this case to increase the aura of mystery surrounding the Seiganji Amida's unusual feminine form.

In the Japanese Buddhist tradition, Amida's most famous manifestation as a woman is in the oft-repeated tale of Chūjōhime and the miraculous weaving of the Taima Mandala. The mid-to-late thirteenth-century *Taima mandara engi emaki* (Picture Scroll of the History of the Taima Mandala) records that on the twentieth day of the sixth month of the seventh year of Tenpyō-hōji (763), Amida Buddha appeared to the daughter of Yokohagi no Otodo (the young Chūjōhime) at Taima Temple in the Nara valley.[58] Taking the form of a nun, Amida instructed Chūjōhime, who was herself then a nun, to collect one hundred horse loads of lotus stems. Amida spun these into a thousand spools of thread and dyed them five colors. Kannon, also appearing in a female manifestation, erected a loom in a corner of the temple hall, and there, with the dyed lotus thread, wove the Taima Mandala. In an archetypal act of *etoki* "picture explaining," Amida expounded upon the contents of the new Pure Land tableau. (In medieval *etoki* performances of the Chūjōhime legend, this would have constituted an *etoki* within an *etoki*.) Amida disappeared with Kannon into the west, and twelve years later, in 775, Chūjōhime attained rebirth in the Pure Land.

[56]TSD 9 (262): 56a and 57b; Burton Watson, *The Lotus Sutra* (New York: Columbia University Press, 1993), 295 and 302. Translation here by Watson.

[57]Susan Tyler writes that as an artistic convention, the faces of deities in Japanese paintings are sometimes obscured, while those of their *honji*—their original Buddhist forms—are not. Susan Tyler, *The Cult of Kasuga Seen Through its Art* (Ann Arbor: University of Michigan Center for Japanese Studies, 1992), 90.

[58]*Taima mandara engi emaki* (in the possession of Kōmyōji Temple) is the earliest illustrated account of Chūjōhime and the Taima Mandala. It is reproduced in Komatsu Shigemi, ed., *Taima mandara engi, Chigo Kannon engi*, Nihon emaki taisei, vol. 24 (Tokyo: Chūō Kōronsha, 1979). The textual portions of the *engi* are typeset and annotated in NST 20:29–35, and translated in Elizabeth ten Grotenhuis, *The Revival of the Taima Mandala* (New York: Garland Publishing, 1985), 156–64. The text of *Taima mandara engi emaki* is similar to that of *Yamato-kuni Taima-dera engi* (the unillustrated Ninnaji-*bon* manuscript of 1253). Other closely contemporaneous accounts are contained in *Kokon chomonjū* (dated 1254; account 2:36, NKBT 84:72-74), and *Shiju hyaku innenshū* (dated 1257; account 7:4, DNBZ 148:121a–24a [92:187b–88c]).

Fig. 24. Izumi Shikibu at Seiganji Temple. From *Seiganji engi emaki* (seventeenth century). Courtesy of Seiganji Temple and the Kyoto National Museum.

In this, its earliest form, the story of Chūjōhime is the story of the Taima Mandala, a woven representation of the Pure Land Paradise of Amida Buddha as described by Shakyamuni Buddha to Queen Vaidehī in the *Visualization Sutra* (*Kanmuryōjukyō*) and interpreted by Shandao (613–81) in his commentary on that work.[59] Contemporary scholars believe that the original, so-called "Konpon" Taima Mandala, a silk tapestry nearly four meters square, was woven in China in the eighth century and only later imported to Japan. Although now severely degraded, it survives in several copies (fig. 25), one of which (the "Bunki Mandala," dating from the Bunki era, 1501–4) is revered today as the principal image of Taima Temple. In its central court, the mandala depicts the various physical features of the Pure Land, including, at its center, a seated Amida flanked by the bohisattvas Kannon and Seishi. The spectacle is framed on three sides by a series of small panels depicting scenes from the *Visualization Sutra*: on the left is a pictorial representation of the story of Queen Vaidehī's imprisonment by her son, Ajātaśatru, and her subsequent encounter with Shakyamuni; on the bottom and on the right are

[59]I am indebted to Elizabeth ten Grotenhuis for my knowledge of the Taima Mandala. In particular, see her *Japanese Mandalas: Representations of Sacred Geography* (Honolulu: University of Hawaii Press, 1999), and "Rebirth of an Icon: The Taima Mandala in Medieval Japan," *Archives of Asian Art* 36 (1983): 59–87.

Fig. 25. The Cleveland *Taima mandala*. Japan, Kamakura period, 1185–1333. Hanging scroll; ink, color and gold on silk, 140 x 134.8 cm. © The Cleveland Museum of Art, Severance and Greta Millikin Purchase Fund, 1990.82.

the sixteen meditative practices Shakyamuni teaches Vaidehī as a means of visualizing the Pure Land.[60]

The legends of the Taima Mandala—both those of Vaidehī and Chūjōhime—are fundamentally concerned with the issue of women's salvation. It was to an imprisoned woman (Vaidehī) that Shakyamuni chose to describe the attributes of Amida's Pure Land, and it was to a self-impris-

[60]The first thirteen meditative practices are shown on the right. The remaining three, subdivided into nine divisions of Pure Land rebirth according to Shandao's *Commentary on the Visualization Sutra* (*Guan jing shu*), are displayed at the bottom.

oned woman (Chūjōhime, who had pronounced a vow to remain within Taima Temple until she had met Amida in a living manifestation) that Amida revealed an image of that land. As Tokuda Kazuo has observed, in the similarity of their tale patterns, Chūjōhime fulfills the role of a "Japanese Vaidehī."[61] In its symbolic importance for women, however, Chūjōhime's legend exceeds that of her Indian counterpart, for unlike Shakyamuni, Amida appears before Chūjōhime in the body of a nun. Chūjōhime's story, like Vaidehī's, came to be woven into the mandala itself, taking the form of a 414-character inscription in the lower horizontal court of the sixteenth-century Bunki Mandala. Whether or not similar inscriptions were contained within earlier copies of the tapestry is unknown, as they are all abraded in their corresponding lower sections.[62] In any case, by at least the early sixteenth century the mandala and its legends were one.

The Taima Mandala has been employed in preaching by institutions of the Seizan branch of the Pure Land sect, including both Seiganji and Taima Temple, since its early thirteenth-century "discovery" at Taima Temple by Zennebō Shōkū, a disciple of Hōnen and the twenty-third intendant of Seiganji.[63] Shōkū sparked a revival of interest in the Taima Mandala that came to be of enormous benefit to the Taima Temple community from around that time. Evidence of Taima's use of the story of Chūjōhime and the weaving of the mandala in its preaching and fund-raising campaigns in the thirteenth century survives in various forms, including a Taima Temple history from 1253 (*Yamato-kuni Taima-dera engi*, "A History of Taima Temple in Yamato Province," also known as the "Ninnaji Variant") which contains the Chūjōhime account and which was itself employed as a registration book for the solicitation of funds for a repair of the Taima Mandala Hall;[64] a pair of Kamakura-period

[61]Tokuda Kazuo, "Etoki: toku ni 'Kangyō-hen' to Chūjōhime setsuwa wo megutte," in *Sōden, jisha engi, emaki, eden*, ed. Itō Hiroyuki et al., Bukkyō bungaku kōza 6 (Tokyo: Benseisha, 1995), 384–85. Hank Glassman has similarly equated Chūjōhime with Vaidehī. Glassman, "Show Me the Place," 150.

[62]ten Grotenhuis, "Rebirth of an Icon," 81–82. ten Grotenhuis writes: "Many of the earlier mandalas, such as the Chion-ji and Zenrin-ji paintings, have abraded inscriptions of short length that are almost impossible to read. It seems possible that this abrasion could have resulted from the paintings being struck by pointers as *etoki* (picture explainer) priests expounded their meanings by gesticulating forcefully."

[63]Zennebō Shōkū (1177–1247) is more commonly known as Shōkū Shōnin (not the Shōkū Shōnin of the Izumi Shikibu/Shōkū Shōnin account). He is perhaps best known today as the founder of the Seizan branch of the Pure Land sect. On his role in the revival of the Taima Mandala, see ten Grotenhuis, "Rebirth of an Icon," 67–70.

[64]Tokuda Kazuo, *Otogizōshi kenkyū* (Tokyo: Miyai Shoten, 1988), 373–74; Elizabeth ten Grotenhuis, "Chūjōhime: The Weaving of Her Legend," in *Flowing Traces: Buddhism in the Literary and Visual Arts of Japan*, ed. James H. Sanford et al. (Princeton: Princeton University Press, 1992), 184. Translation of *kanjin-chō* as "registration book for solicitation of funds" is by ten Grotenhuis.

Taima mandara engi hanging scrolls, one of which is entirely devoted to the story of Chūjōhime and the Taima Mandala (and which was undoubtedly used in *etoki*);[65] and *Ippen Hijiri e* (Pictures of the Holy Man Ippen; 1299), the illustrated biography of the priest Ippen, which notes that when Ippen visited Taima Temple in 1286, the monks there presented him with a copy of the *Shōsan Pure Land Sutra* in Chūjōhime's own hand.[66] As a treasured relic, the gift suggests Chūjōhime's importance to the temple at that time.

One of our most detailed sources of information on preaching at Taima Temple in the Muromachi period is a text by the name of *Taima mandara sho* (Commentary on the Taima Mandala), compiled by the priest Yūyo Shōsō in 1436.[67] As Tokuda Kazuo has demonstrated, parts of this work, including those concerning Vaidehī, Chūjōhime, and the weaving of the Taima Mandala, are apparent transcriptions of *etoki* sermon-performances given at Taima Temple over a series of days. Of particular interest is the use in these lectures of previously unrecorded tales of Chūjōhime's childhood, including stories of her mistreatment at the hands of an evil stepmother and her repeated abandonment (two times in two sermons) in the wilds of Mount Hibari and Mount Katsuragi. The influence of this or related preaching was profound, leading to the production of the noh plays *Hibariyama* and *Taema*, both of which contain accounts of Chūjōhime's abandonment,[68] and to the composition and widespread circulation of the *otogizōshi Chūjōhime no honji* (Chūjōhime in Her Original Form), a melodramatic tale of Chūjōhime's beauty, piety, near-beheading, and eventual rebirth in the Pure Land.[69] One

[65]See the color photographs in Matsushima Ken and Kawahara Yoshio, *Taima-dera*, Nihon no koji bijutsu 11 (Osaka: Hoikusha, 1988), frontispieces 12 and 13, and the black-and-white photos in Nara Kokuritsu Hakubutsukan, ed., *Shaji engi-e* (Tokyo: Kadokawa Shoten, 1975), 26 and 27. Another Kamakura-period *Taima-dera engi* painting (in the possession of Shōjōshin'in on Mount Kōya) is notable as well. See Matsushima and Kawahara, *Taima-dera*, 178–79.

[66]Kadokawa Shoten Henshūbu, ed., *Ippen Hijiri e*, Nihon emaki-mono zenshū, vol. 10 (Tokyo: Kadokawa Shoten, 1960), 75b; ten Grotenhuis, "Chūjōhime: The Weaving of Her Legend," 187. On Chūjōhime and the *Shōsan Pure Land Sutra* (*Shōsan jōdokyō*, Xuanzang's translation from 650 of the *Smaller Sukhāvatīvyūha sūtra*, better known in Japan by Kumārajīva's translation of 402, titled *Amidakyō*), see Glassman, "Show Me the Place," 157–59.

[67]*Taima mandara sho*, in *Jōdo-shū zensho*, vol. 13 (Tokyo: Jōdo-shū Shūten Kankōkai, 1910); Tokuda, *Otogizōshi kenkyū*, 370–72.

[68]*Hibariyama* and *Taema* (an alternate reading of "Taima") are traditionally attributed to Zeami (1363?–1443?), although in the case of *Hibariyama*, the attribution is suspect. See ten Grotenhuis, "Chūjōhime: The Weaving of Her Legend," 188–92. In *Taema*, the story of Chūjōhime's abandonment is recounted in the *kyōgen*.

[69]The composition of *Chūjōhime no honji* was in fact further mediated by the production of the three-scroll *Taima-dera engi* (also known as the "Kyōroku-bon") of 1531, which was itself influenced by Shōsō's *Taima mandara sho*. Monika Dix has translated the Kyōroku-bon in "Writing Women into Religious Histories: Re-reading Representations of Chūjōhime in Medieval Japanese Buddhist Narratives," Ph.D. dissertation (University of British Columbia, 2006), 82–134. The

of the most intriguing aspects of Shōsō's commentary is its emphasis on the importance of Vaidehī, Chūjōhime, and the Taima Mandala to women's salvation in general,[70] suggesting that the preaching recorded in Shōsō's work was directed, in large part, toward women.

The members of Seiganji were of course aware of Chūjōhime and her significance for women in Buddhism. Her charisma was so great, in fact, that both she and the Taima Mandala came to be taken up in Seiganji temple storytelling traditions—now preserved only in *Rakuyō Seiganji engi*—that seem to have been intended to capitalize on her fame by linking her and the Mandala to Izumi Shikibu and the Seiganji Amida. According to *Rakuyō Seiganji engi*, the Seiganji Amida (the wooden statue, that is) lacks a *nikkei*, the fleshy protuberance on the top of the head that constitutes one of the thirty-two distinguishing characteristics of a Buddha.[71] The *engi* explains that although the Seiganji Amida in fact possesses this and every other distinguishing characteristic, in his great compassion he chooses to hide his *nikkei* until such time as all sentient beings have attained enlightenment. The text then explains:

> Only the principal image at the center of the Taima Mandala—the Amida and the Kannon who manifested themselves as a nun and a [lay] woman—and our own principal image, carved by Jizō and Kannon in their human forms, do not display the distinguishing characteristic of the *nikkei*.

Insofar as their *nikkei* remain hidden, the Seiganji and Taima principal images alone are united in their expressions of sympathy for unenlightened beings. There is a problem with this iconographic interpretation, however, inasmuch as the Amida at the center of the Taima Mandala (the original, Konpon Mandala) does in fact appear to display a *nikkei*.[72]

Kyōroku-bon is photographically reproduced in the hardcover edition of Komatsu, ed., *Taima mandara engi, Chigo Kannon engi*; an Edo-period copy is photographically reproduced in Nara Kokuritsu Hakubutsukan, ed., *Shaji engi-e*, 213–36. See Tokuda, *Otogizōshi kenkyū*, 360–413, and Shibahara Mika, "Chūsei shōsetsu *Chūjōhime* no denbon keitō ni tsuite—*Taima mandara sho* to no hikaku wo chūshin ni," *Kokugo to kyōiku* 15 (1990): 61–72. *Chūjōhime no honji* is printed in SNKBZ 63:396–416, and translated by me in Haruo Shirane, ed., *Traditional Japanese Literature: An Anthology, Beginnings to 1600* (New York: Columbia University Press, 2007), 1138–50.

[70]In particular, see the passages quoted in Tokuda, *Otogizōshi kenkyū*, 372.

[71]ZGR 27:1:211b; DNBZ 117:344b (83:150a). The entire section describing the physical appearance of the Seiganji Amida is absent from the *Seiganji engi emaki*, and in the *emaki* illustrations, the Seiganji Amida is in fact painted with a *nikkei*. Because the Seiganji Amida was lost in a temple fire in 1864, it is impossible to verify whether or not it actually displayed a *nikkei*

[72]See the black-and-white photograph in ten Grotenhuis, "Rebirth of an Icon," 62, and the color photograph in Nara Kokuritsu Hakubutsukan, ed., *Jōdo mandara: Goku-raku Jōdo to raigō no roman* (special exhibition catalogue, April 24-May 29, 1983), 25.

In a later section of the *engi*, Zennebō Shōkū (Shōkū Shōnin), the priest who was largely responsible for the thirteenth-century revival of the Taima Mandala as a major Pure Land icon, preaches a sermon in which he also alludes to the Seiganji and Taima principal images' lack of a *nikkei*. His words help to clear up the confusion:

> In the spring of 1236, the Kujō Minister Michiie engaged seven days of Buddhist services at our temple. For the sake of enjoining a karmic link, he [acclaimed Shōkū Shōnin his teacher and][73] invited him to conduct daily lectures on the Way. One of the master's sermons concerned the *Visualization Sutra* "Kannon meditation," the following lines from which he cited:
>
> > Of all other physical characteristics Kannon is possessed; he is without difference from a Buddha. Only the *nikkei* on the top of the head and its unseen apex—in these he is not equal to a Buddha.[74]
>
> "Although Kannon is unequal to a Buddha in two of his physical characteristics," the master explained, "thus demonstrating that unlike his mentor, his vow to attain enlightenment is not yet fulfilled, bodhisattvas on the path of enlightenment do possess a red *nikkei*. But our own principal image lacks even this,[75] which is truly wonderful!" The master explained that the principal image at the center of the Taima Mandala is [also] woven without a *nikkei*,[76] and he praised the profound benefits of Amida Buddha's Original Vow of Great Compassion. All those at the temple were extraordinarily moved. Everyone listening—clergy and laity alike—wept with emotion.[77]

[73]This bracketed passage is interpolated from *Rakuyō Seiganji honzon engi* and the six-scroll *Seiganji engi*, in Kikuchi, "Kyōhō hachinen-sha *Rakuyō Seiganji honzon engi*," 383, and in Yutani, "*Seiganji engi* rokkanbon no kaidai to honkoku," 93a. Kujō Michiie (1193–1252) was appointed Minister of the Left (*sadaijin*) in 1218, Regent (*sesshō*) in 1221, and Chancellor (*kanpaku*) in 1228.

[74]This is a passage from the *Visualization Sutra* (*Kanmuryōjukyō*) describing the appearance of the bodhisattva Kannon (from contemplation 10). TSD 12 (365): 344a; Inagaki, *The Three Pure Land Sutras*, 335.

[75]There was confusion either before or at the time the Jingū Bunko *Rakuyō Seiganji engi* manuscript was typeset, because both the ZGR and DNBZ editors have added a "not" in brackets, altering the text to read that the principal image is *not* without such a characteristic. This would be inconsistent with the earlier *engi* passage, and it would render Shōkū's speech meaningless. In addition, it is inconsistent with *Rakuyō Seiganji honzon engi* and the six-scroll *Seiganji engi*. Like the previous *engi* passage explaining the Seiganji Amida's lack of a *nikkei*, this entire section is absent from the *Seiganji engi emaki*.

[76]According to *Rakuyō Seiganji honzon engi* and the six-scroll *Seiganji engi*, that is. In the ZGR and DNBZ typesetting of the Jingū Bunko text, the negative compound-verb *ori-arawasazaru* ("not woven to display") is rendered as a passive, *ori-arawasaruru* ("is woven to display").

[77]ZGR 27:1:232b–33a; DNBZ 117:363a-b (83:158a).

Shōkū uses the term "red *nikkei*," probably referring to the so-called "*nikkei* jewel," a red dot at the base of the *nikkei* that became a standard feature of Japanese Amida iconography, both in sculpture and in painting, from around the early eleventh century.[78] Because of the Taima Mandala's age, the Amida at its center is without one, and this may have been its supposed connection to the Seiganji Amida. Shōkū was an expert on the Taima Mandala, and according to his influential commentary on the work (*Taima mandara chū*, dated 1223), the Amida at its center lacks a red *nikkei* because Amida takes the form of a monk and conceals his distinguishing characteristics when he helps people who rely upon their own good deeds rather than upon the *nenbutsu*.[79]

As the *Rakuyō Seiganji engi* account continues, one of Shōkū's disciples has a mysterious encounter with Izumi Shikibu and Chūjōhime at Seiganji on the very night of Shōkū's lecture. They had come to hear Shōkū preach:

> One of the master's disciples, the monk Shōtatsu,[80] spent the night performing devotions before the temple altar. In the midnight hour, when people had grown quiet and Shōtatsu's heart serene—a clear pool of water such as to harbor the Buddha's light—Shōtatsu quietly chanted the *nenbutsu*. From among a large group of devotees that had arrived sometime in the night, two old and unusually dressed nuns approached. They were talking amicably. Wondering what they were saying, Shōtatsu listened.
>
> "Today's sermon was especially wonderful," one of the nuns remarked. The other spoke: "Back when I received the Pure Land mandala at Taima Temple, that woman—the temporary human manifestation—explained about all the distinguishing characteristics of the figures in the image. And the master's explanation today didn't differ from hers in the least. Of course, that weaver-woman was actually a manifestation of the Great Kasuga Deity—the bodhisattva to the left of the Western Founder.[81] The master here is also a manifestation of Kannon, so who wouldn't believe

[78]According to Matsuura Masaaki at the Nara National Museum, the *nikkeishu* (*nikkei* jewel) began to appear in Japan from around the time of the sculptor Jōchō (?–1057). Personal communication, June 1999.

[79]The people whom Amida comes to help are *jōsan no ki*, those who rely upon meditative and non-meditative practices. Their problem is that they rely upon their own power, *jiriki*, instead of upon Amida's power, *tariki*. *Taima mandara chū*, in Seizan Zenshū Kankōkai, ed., *Seizan zensho*, vol. 2 (Kyoto: Bun'eidō Shoten, 1973), 109b; also in DNBZ 63:109b (51:103b). Recent scholarship has questioned Shōkū's authorship of the commentary; it may actually date from the early Muromachi period. See ten Grotenhuis, "Rebirth of an Icon," 86, note 23.

[80]Shōtatsu (dates unknown) was a disciple of Shōkū and the founder of Chionji Temple in modern Saga Prefecture.

[81]The "Western Founder" is Amida; the bodhisattva to Amida's left is Kannon, of whom the Great Kasuga Deity is identified as a native manifestation.

> his explanation of the Buddhas and bodhisattvas in their various incarnations?"
>
> The women talked at length about the weaving of the [Taima] Mandala, and night eventually gave way to dawn. After paying their respects to the principal image, the two nuns bid farewell to their companions and exited the temple building. Shōtatsu thought this all rather strange, and rushing out from the inner sanctum, he asked the two nuns who they were and where they came from. Identifying themselves as Shōren and Sen'i, they vanished into the air.[82] Shōtatsu thought for a while, and remembering that Chūjōhime had been known as Shōren and that Sen'i was Izumi Shikibu's Buddhist name, he was all the more amazed. Searching for a trace of the two, he saw them disappear into the mist of the western sky. What a marvelous encounter to have had!

The *Seiganji engi emaki* contains an illustration of the scene (fig. 26), although, strangely, it lacks the corresponding textual account. The two women are painted as ghosts—apparitional nuns without legs or feet—and they drift away from the temple, talking, as Shōtatsu and two other men look on. A similar scene is painted into the third *Seiganji engi* hanging scroll, and there as well the two women taper off mysteriously at the waist.[83] Chūjōhime's presence in these works suggests her use, like Sei Shōnagon and Izumi Shikibu, in Seiganji preaching and fund-raising in the sixteenth and seventeenth centuries.

At the heart of Chūjōhime's fame is her wondrous encounter with the female Amida, and it is to this that she alludes in her *Rakuyō Seiganji engi* conversation some 461 years after her Pure Land rebirth. In her discussion with Izumi Shikibu, Chūjōhime identifies the weaver-woman of the Taima Mandala as a manifestation of the Great Kasuga Deity, who she says is a manifestation of Kannon. As we have seen in an earlier section of *Rakuyō Seiganji engi*, the Seiganji Amida is also said to have been carved by the Kasuga Deity, who in that passage is identified as a single manifestation of both Kannon and Jizō.[84] The Seiganji and Taima principal images thus share a common creator, which may account for their (supposedly) identical lack

[82]According to *Rakuyō Seiganji honzon engi* and the six-scroll *Seiganji engi*, the women departed through the western gate. Kikuchi, "Kyōhō hachinen-sha *Rakuyō Seiganji honzon engi*," 384; Yutani, "*Seiganji engi* rokkanbon," 93a-b.

[83]This third *Seiganji engi* hanging scroll dates from the Edo period. It is traditionally attributed to Kaihō Yūsetsu (1598–1677), and it depicts several accounts in *Rakuyō Seiganji engi* that are absent from the Kamakura-period paintings, but which correspond to accounts in the third scroll of the *Seiganji engi emaki*. Nara Kokuritsu Hakubutsukan, ed., *Shaji engi-e*, 47 and 135–37 (52).

[84]ZGR 27:1:210b–11a; DNBZ 117:343b–44a (83:149b-c).

Fig. 26. The ghosts of Izumi Shikibu and Chūjōhime at Seiganji Temple. From *Seiganji engi emaki* (seventeenth century). Courtesy of Seiganji Temple and the Kyoto National Museum.

of a *nikkei* jewel. In a further endorsement of Seiganji, Taima Temple, and the Taima Mandala, Chūjōhime identifies Zennebō Shōkū as a manifestation of Kannon, which must have been a surprise for Shōtatsu, his disciple.

It seems likely that the *Rakuyō Seiganji engi* author was interested in establishing links between Seiganji and Taima Temple for the purpose of enhancing Seiganji's reputation, particularly among women. As we have seen, Seiganji was not above "borrowing" a good story (Sei Shōnagon at Bodaiji) or sometimes slandering its rivals (Shōkū Shōnin and the Great Hachiman Bodhisattva) as a means of self-promotion. However, what is perhaps most interesting about the inclusion of the Chūjōhime account within *Rakuyō Seiganji engi* is that rather than attempting to compete with or overcome Taima's famous legend of Chūjōhime and the Taima Mandala, the *engi* author sought to appropriate it by linking it to Izumi Shikibu and the Seiganji principal image. The same might be said of the female Amida, appearing as she did in early accounts of Chūjōhime at Taima Temple and only later in *Rakuyō Seiganji engi*. By writing Chūjōhime (and the female Amida) into its history in the late medieval period, the Seiganji temple authorities sought to profit from her celebrity, making it their own. Indeed, although Chūjōhime had been a mainstay of Taima Temple proselytizing and fund-raising activities since at least the thirteenth century, the Seiganji community may have felt a right to her, seeing as it was their own Zennebō Shōkū who inspired the revival of the Taima Mandala, and thus, by association, of Chūjōhime herself.

As *Rakuyō Seiganji engi* surely reflects the written and oral traditions circulating in and around the temple at the time of its composition, and as both the Izumi Shikibu and Chūjōhime accounts were natural storytelling material for women in Pure Land Buddhism, it may well have been the nuns of Seiganji—devotees of both the Taima Mandala and the Seiganji Amida—who first established the connection between the Seiganji and Taima principal images, and between Izumi Shikibu and Chūjōhime. Even today, Chūjōhime is venerated by the nuns of Seirenji, a Pure Land "women's temple" (*amadera*) in Nara Prefecture, although when she came to be associated with that institution is unclear.[85] In any case, by the late Muromachi or early Edo period, Chūjōhime had taken on the role of a mystical guardian of women. According to the *otogizōshi Asagao no tsuyu* (Dew of the Morning Glories), Chūjōhime's ghost once appeared to a girl by the name of Asagao after Asagao had been abandoned in the mountains: "My stepmother hated me too, just like you," Chūjōhime explains, and for three years she looks after Asagao in the wilds.[86] Like Izumi Shikibu, Chūjōhime seems to have found her place in the popular imagination through the medieval marketing of Buddhism to women.

Amida's Emissary: Izumi Shikibu and Ippen Shōnin at Seiganji

Immediately after the tale of Izumi Shikibu and Chūjōhime at Seiganji, *Rakuyō Seiganji engi* presents an account of the holy man Ippen Shōnin (1239–89), founder of the Ji sect of Pure Land Buddhism,[87] and his miraculous meeting with Izumi Shikibu at Seiganji. The two stories—those of Izumi Shikibu and

[85]In the Taishō period (1912–26), Seirenji adopted a wooden statue of Chūjōhime as its principal image. Before then, the Chūjōhime image had been a "guest Buddha" (*kyakubutsu*), used in preaching. Gorai Shigeru writes that Seirenji was already a "women's temple" by the early Edo period (Gorai, *Jisha engi kara otogibanashi e*, 90). Based upon the illustrations in a book about an early nineteenth-century touring exhibition of Taima Temple treasures, Hank Glassman has observed that "nuns were exclusively responsible for displaying and explaining the personal effects and bodily relics of Chūjōhime." Glassman, "Show Me the Place," 156.

[86]MJMT 1:413a–14b (former Akagi Bunko manuscript); also cited in Tokuda, *Otogizōshi kenkyū*, 367–68 (Yūzankaku Bunko manuscript).

[87]As Sybil Thornton has shown, the actual founding of the *Jishū* as an independent religious order is perhaps best attributed to Ippen's disciple Taamidabutsu Shinkyō. S.A. Thornton, *Charisma and Community Formation in Medieval Japan: The Case of the Yugyō-ha (1300-1700)* (Ithaca: Cornell University East Asia Program, 1999), 44.

Chūjōhime, and Izumi Shikibu and Ippen—are connected by the figure of Shōtatsu, the disciple of Zennebō Shōkū who is said to have spoken with the ghosts of Izumi Shikibu and Chūjōhime on the night of Shōkū's lecture on the Taima Mandala. *Rakuyō Seiganji engi* explains that although Ippen at first studied the doctrines and practices of the Tendai sect, he later rejected them for Hōnen's Pure Land teachings and became, at the age of eighteen, a student of Shōtatsu.[88] *Ippen Hijiri e*, composed in 1299, a mere ten years after Ippen's death, similarly identifies Shōtatsu as Ippen's instructor, and it explains that Ippen spent twelve years studying Pure Land Buddhist doctrine with Shōtatsu in Dazaifu in Kyūshū.[89]

As the progenitor of the *Jishū*, what James Foard has described as "the largest order of medieval itinerants, and perhaps the largest Pure Land movement until the middle of the Muromachi period,"[90] Ippen exerted a profound influence upon the practice and conception of Pure Land Buddhism in early-medieval Japan. Though revered by his followers, he was bitterly resented by many members of the older Buddhist sects, for whom his popularity was construed as a threat. Ippen was known as the "Wandering Holy Man" (Yugyō Shōnin) for his travels throughout Japan visiting holy sites, teaching the *nenbutsu* and distributing *nenbutsu fuda* (paper talismans inscribed with Amida's name, along with the phrase "Assured Rebirth of the 600,000"). In his own lifetime, he was perhaps most famous for propagating the *odori nenbutsu*, the "dancing *nenbutsu*," which, according to *Ippen Hijiri e*, Ippen took up as a life-long practice in Shinano province in 1279.[91] One of his contemporary critics, the unknown author of the Buddhist poetic commentary *Nomori no kagami* (Mirror of the Watchman of the Fields; 1295), acridly complains:

> The priest Ippen misunderstands the principle of the *nenbutsu*. Because he thinks the phrase "skip and dance with great rejoicing" (*yuyaku kangi*) means one ought to dance, he prances about as a kind of *nenbutsu* practice, waving his head and lifting his feet.[92]

[88]ZGR 27:1:233b–34a; DNBZ 117:364a (83:158b). The ZGR edition of the Jingū Bunko text mistakenly reads "Shōren"; the DNBZ edition of the same text, as well as *Rakuyō Seiganji honzon engi*, the six-scroll *Seiganji engi*, and the *Seiganji engi emaki*, read "Shōtatsu."

[89]Komatsu Shigemi, ed., *Ippen Shōnin eden*, Nihon no emaki, vol. 20 (Tokyo: Chūō Kōronsha, 1988), 2–3 (also see the modern-Japanese translation on p. 357).

[90]James H. Foard, "*Seiganji*: The Buddhist Orientation of a Noh Play," *Monumenta Nipponica* 35, no. 4 (1980), 440.

[91]Kadokawa Shoten Henshūbu, ed., *Ippen Hijiri e*, 68 and 40–41; Dennis Hirota, *No Abode: The Record of Ippen* (Honolulu: University of Hawaii Press, 1986 [rev. ed. 1997]), xxxix.

[92]The phrase "joyful dancing" (*yuyaku kangi*) appears in *The Sutra of Infinite Life* (*Muryōjukyō*; TSD 12 [360]: 273a).

> Moreover, he thinks the expression, "the True Heart is the Pure Land" (*jikishin soku jōdo*), means that one should avoid lying or holding anything back. Thus, he does not cover himself when he is naked, and just like a crazy person, he speaks his mind against those he dislikes without the least restraint. People esteem this as the epitome of righteousness, and rich and poor alike, they flock to him. Their number is greater than that of a thriving market.[93]

Fukuda Hideichi, Kobayashi Chishō, and others have identified the *Nomori no kagami* author's conservative doctrinal orientation as Tendai-mikkyō,[94] according to which Ippen was guilty of disseminating illegitimate, heterodox views.

The author of *Tengū zōshi* (The Book of Tengu), a satiric picture scroll dating from 1296, one year after *Nomori no kagami*, provides a similarly critical description of Ippen and his sect:

> When they practice the *nenbutsu*, they wave their heads, shake their shoulders and dance, just like wild horses. The way they carry on, they're no different from mountain monkeys. Neither the men nor the women hide their genitals. Eating with their bare hands, reveling in their impropriety, they act like beasts from the animal realm.[95]

In addition to its prose passages, *Tengu zōshi* contains painted illustrations of Ippen and his followers in a variety of vulgar situations, including one in which Ippen is shown urinating into a bamboo tube in order to provide medicine for his devotees. "What a lot of pee!" one onlooker exclaims in an inscribed caption. "It's a cure for all that ails you," another remarks. A blind nun declares her intention to wash her eyes out in it, and a lay woman says that she wants to drink some to cure a stomach ailment, of all things.[96]

The earliest textual account of Ippen's encounter with Izumi Shikibu's ghost is contained in the noh play *Seiganji*, first known to have been per-

[93]NKT 4:68. Also see R. Keller Kimbrough, "*Nomori no kagami* and the Perils of Poetic Heresy," *Proceedings of the Association for Japanese Literary Studies* 4 (Summer 2003): 99–114.

[94]Fukuda Hideichi, "*Nomori no kagami* ni tsuite no kōsatsu," in *Chūsei waka shi no kenkyū* (Tokyo: Kadokawa Shoten, 1972), 628–30; Kobayashi Chishō, "*Nomori no kagami* kō," in *Hōgo bungaku no sekai* (Tokyo: Kasama Shoin, 1975), 208.

[95]Komatsu Shigemi, ed., *Tsuchigumo sōshi, Tengu zōshi, Ōeyama ekotoba*, Zoku Nihon emaki taisei, vol. 19 (Tokyo: Chūō Kōronsha, 1984), 56b and 168b.

[96]Ibid., 59b and 168c-d; Kimbrough, "*Nomori no kagami* and the Perils of Poetic Heresy," 105–7. In *Genkō shakusho* (1322), the Zen priest and author Kokan Shiren also disparages the dancing *nenbutsu*, although he does not mention Ippen by name. Kuroita Katsumi, ed., *Shintei zōho kokushi taikei*, vol. 31 (Tokyo: Yoshikawa Kōbunkan, 1930), 434.

formed on the tenth day of the fourth month of 1464.[97] The Izumi Shikibu/ Ippen story is absent from the early Ippen biographies, including *Ippen Hijiri e* and *Ippen Shōnin eshiden* (The Illustrated Life of Ippen Shōnin), suggesting that it dates from the fourteenth or early fifteenth century.[98] The textual relationship between *Seiganji* and *Rakuyō Seiganji engi* is unclear, opinions being divided as to whether *Seiganji* is based on an early version of *Seiganji engi*, or whether the *Rakuyō Seiganji engi* Izumi Shikibu/Ippen account is based upon *Seiganji*.[99] The two views are not necessarily incompatible, for although it seems likely that the play ultimately derives from a Seiganji-affiliated proselytizing tradition, the author(s) of *Rakuyō Seiganji engi* may well have drawn upon the play in composing the sixteenth-century history of Seiganji. According to entries in the diaries *Chikanaga-kyō ki* (Records of Lord [Kanroji] Chikanaga) and *Sanetaka-kō ki* (Records of Lord [Sanjōnishi] Sanetaka), a *kanjin* (fund-raising) *sarugaku* performance was held at Seiganji on the twenty-second day of the fourth month of 1478.[100] Whether or not this included a staging of *Seiganji* is unknown; if it did, it would demonstrate Seiganji's use of the Izumi Shikibu/Ippen account in temple fund-raising as early as the fifteenth century.

Because Seiganji Temple claims Ippen as one of its own—a student of Shōtatsu, disciple of Shōkū, the twenty-third intendant of Seiganji–*Rakuyō Seiganji engi* speaks only positively of the thirteenth-century holy man. *Rakuyō Seiganji engi* explains that in his early years, Ippen was seized with a desire to travel the provinces and promote the practice of the *nenbutsu*. After securing the permission of his master, Shōtatsu, he set out on his journey, making his way first to Kumano Shrine, the principal deity of which

[97]As noted in *Tadasugawara kanjin sarugaku nikki*, in GR 19:720a. Although *Seiganji* is attributed to Zeami (1363?–1443?) in *Nōhon sakusha chūmon* (1524) and *Nihyakujūban utai mokuroku* (1765), Nishino Haruo, editor of the recent SNKBT *yōkyoku* volume, identifies it as "author unknown." See Sanari Kentarō, ed., *Yōkyoku taikan*, vol. 3 (Tokyo: Meiji Shoin, 1931), 1549, and SNKBT 57:546. *Seiganji* is translated in Foard, "*Seiganji*: The Buddhist Orientation of a Noh Play," 445–56.

[98]*Ippen Shōnin eshiden* is dated 1307 in a postscript to the Muromachi-period Konrenji manuscript. The Ippen Shōnin/Izumi Shikibu account is contained in *Ippen Shōnin nenpuryaku* (ZGR 9:1:215b), but this work is now believed to date from the Edo period. Imai Masaharu, *Ippen jiten* (Tokyo: Tōkyōdō Shuppan, 1989), 45b.

[99]Yoshida Kōichi is of the latter opinion, because, as he explains, although the Sonkeikaku Bunko text of *Seiganji engi* (which Yoshida dates to ca. 1477) includes an account of how the Kumano Deity sent Ippen to Seiganji to distribute *nenbutsu fuda*, it contains no mention of Izumi Shikibu. Yoshida, "*Seiganji engi* to *Izumi Shikibu engi*," 11b. Also see SNKBT 57:546, and Sanari, ed., *Yōkyoku taikan*, vol. 3, 1551.

[100]Zōho Shiryō Taisei Kankōkai, ed., *Zōho shiryō taisei*, vol. 42 (Kyōto: Rinsen Shoten, 1965), 12a; Ōta Tōshirō, ed., *Sanetaka-kō ki*, vol. 1 (Tokyo: Taiyōsha, 1931), 280. The term *sarugaku* now refers to a theatrical genre that predates noh; in the fifteenth century, it was often employed as a synonym for noh.

has been identified with Amida since the late Heian period.[101] Ippen spends seven days and seven nights at the Hongū, the central shrine in the three-shrine Kumano complex at the southern edge of the Kii peninsula, praying and reciting the *nenbutsu*. On the final morning at dawn, the Kumano Deity appears to him in the form of a white-haired mountain ascetic—a *yamabushi*—and delivers the following oracle:

> "I am the progenitor of the Western Pure Land. In order to bestow compassion on the living beings of this sordid world, I dim my brilliance and mingle with the fleeting dust. I manifest on this mountain to be near the many sentient beings in whom I cause my vow to be fulfilled. I establish links with the noble and the lowly so that I may eventually lead them to the Jeweled Land Untainted.
>
> "Your desire to spread the *nenbutsu* is profound; you do my will and aid me in my cause. You are a true latter-age teacher, a *nenbutsu*-friend of the Dharma. Quickly make your way to Seiganji Temple in the capital and distribute *nenbutsu fuda* to everyone, whether they have faith or not, and [we] shall surely bring to pass the merciful vow by which everyone, together, may attain rebirth." Having spoken thus, the deity recited a verse in four lines:
>
> The six-character name is the single Dharma;
> The beings and abodes of the ten worlds are a single body.
> The myriad practices, freed from thought, evidence the one;
> Among people, a perfect excellent lotus.

The poem is a famous one, variously attributed to Ippen and the Kumano Deity.[102] Each of its first three lines contains the word "single" or "one" (*ippen*), and it is from this that Ippen takes his name. Although enigmatic, the verse has been understood to constitute a concise statement of *Jishū* doctrine, according to which the moment of Amida's enlightenment in the distant past is fused with the immediate present in the single utterance of the *nenbutsu*. In that utterance, distinctions between the enlightened and the unenlightened, between this world and the Pure Land, disappear. Thus, as

[101]Heibonsha Chihō Shiryō Sentā, ed., *Jiin jinja daijiten: Yamato, Kii*, 239c. According to *Ippen Hijiri e*, Ippen visited a number of other holy sites, including Zenkōji, Sugō, Shitennōji, and Kōya-san, before making his way to Kumano. *Ippen Shōnin nenpuryaku* alternately explains that in the year 1275 the Great Hachiman Bodhisattva at Iwashimizu Hachiman Shrine appeared to Ippen in a dream and told him to go to Kumano (ZGR 9:1:212a).

[102]The poem is cited in *Ippen Shōnin goroku* (NST 10:309), *Ippen Hijiri e* (Komatsu, ed., *Ippen Shōnin eden*, 77), *Izumi Shikibu engi* (Ōhashi, *Izumi Shikibu nikki no kenkyū*, 537a), and the noh play *Seiganji* (SNKBT 57:548). In *Ippen Hijiri e* and *Ippen Shōnin eshiden*, the poem is attributed to Ippen; in *Seiganji*, *Rakuyō Seiganji engi*, and *Izumi Shikibu engi*, it is attributed to the Kumano Deity.

the poem explains in its first two lines, the six-character name, the *nenbutsu*, is itself the single Dharma, and the multitudinous beings of the ten worlds are ultimately one. In its third line, the verse has been read to declare that of the myriad Buddhist practices, it is the practice that is free from misguided thought and attachment to self—the *nenbutsu*, that is—that evidences the identity (the simultaneous oneness) of Amida's enlightenment and the rebirth of living beings in his Pure Land.[103] The fourth line proclaims that those who recite the *nenbutsu* are like a perfect, excellent lotus—a symbol of purity and enlightenment—rising not from the proverbial mud, but from among their fellow human beings.

In *Ippen Hijiri e*, the encounter with the Kumano Deity is a defining moment for Ippen because it allows him to resolve his doubts regarding the efficacy of distributing *nenbutsu* talismans. The deity quells Ippen's anxiety by telling him to hand out *fuda* to everyone, regardless of their faith.[104] In *Rakuyō Seiganji engi*, the Kumano Deity is said to have given Ippen similar advice, with the additional request that he proceed immediately to Seiganji:

> Following the deity's instructions, the master hurried to the capital. It was then the spring of 1276. Taking up residence at Seiganji, he performed Pure Land devotions in the six periods of day and night, single-mindedly chanting the *nenbutsu*. He distributed *nenbutsu fuda* among the various people, and he urged that they too chant the Name. Carrying out holy practices and inspiring others to do the same, his manner was most venerable. Men and women, lay and monastic alike, from both the city and the country, near and far, gathered in great numbers day and night. Pressing shoulder to shoulder and heel to heel, they received *nenbutsu fuda* and established links to the Pure Land.
>
> One day an elegant woman pushed her way through the crowd and appeared before the master. "This talisman that you gave me," she said, "—it reads, 'Assured Rebirth of the 600,000.' But what of all other living beings—are they to be denied the benefits of salvation?"
>
> The master spoke: "Amida's compassion is without bounds; it spans the breadth of the ten directions and the height of the three worlds, saving all sentient beings, good and bad, including those who suffer in the three evil realms. His limitless vow is vast and great. How, then, could salvation be limited to 600,000? The words

[103]Imai, *Ippen jiten*, 313a. Alternately, *Rakuyō Seiganji engi* explains that we should read "the myriad practices, freed from thought" (*mangyō rinen*) as "the *nenbutsu*, freed from thought" (*nenbutsu rinen*), because "although the *nenbutsu* is a single practice within the myriad practices, the myriad practices are inherent in the *nenbutsu*." ZGR 27:1:235b; DNBZ 117:365b (83:159a).

[104]See Dennis Hirota, "The Illustrated Biography of Ippen," in *Buddhism in Practice*, ed. Donald Lopez (Princeton: Princeton University Press, 1995), 569–70.

> on the talisman are the first characters of the four lines of the [Kumano] Deity's verse; they are there but to testify [to the certainty of rebirth in the Pure Land]. You need only cultivate unwavering faith, and then if you perform the *nenbutsu* without distraction, by means of the Original Vows your Pure Land rebirth will quickly follow."
>
> The woman wept tears of joy. "So rebirth in the Pure Land is certain," she said, "even for deeply sinful women such as myself. What marvelous benefit!" The woman pressed her palms together before the holy man and recited the *nenbutsu*.

As Ippen explains, the phrase "600,000 people" (*roku-jū-man-nin*), printed on his *nenbutsu fuda* together with the *nenbutsu*, is made up of the first character of each of the four lines of the Kumano Deity's verse. Rather than representing a definite (limited) number of devotees who will attain Pure Land rebirth, it is symbolic of all living beings. As James Foard has observed, the number sixty furthermore suggests the sixty-odd provinces of Japan, and the number ten thousand, the multitude of living creatures in each of those provinces.[105] Six hundred thousand would therefore indicate all Japanese—hence everyone.

> After a while, the woman again spoke: "There is a Seiganji placard at the front of this temple. Please, master, in your own hand write out the six-character name and place it beside it. This is not my wish; it is the august instruction of the principal image." The master thought this wondrously strange. "Where do you come from?" he inquired. "And what is your name?"
>
> "The worship hall that you see there is named the [Hall of] Eight Mandalas," the woman explained. "It is also called the Komidō, because it was built by the Midō Chancellor [Michinaga]. It was from there that I attained rebirth in the Pure Land." Having spoken thus, the woman vanished into the air.
>
> The holy man was struck with realization. "That woman must have been Izumi Shikibu," he thought, "appearing here from the Pure Land as a messenger of the Buddha!" In accord with her request, he reverently wrote out the six-character name and had it raised up beside the temple placard.[106] He earnestly paid his respects and passed several hours reciting the *nenbutsu*.
>
> The hall was suddenly suffused with a wondrous smell, and mysterious clouds hovered near the eaves. Amid the faint sounds of music, a strange light shone from above. A golden Amida stood within the clouds, surrounded by bodhisattvas and all his heav-

[105]Foard, "*Seiganji*: The Buddhist Orientation of a Noh Play," 440; James H. Foard, "Prefiguration and Narrative in Medieval Hagiography: The *Ippen Hijiri-e*," in *Flowing Traces*, 89–90.

[106]In the noh play *Seiganji*, Ippen replaces the Seiganji placard with his own (SNKBT 57:550).

> enly host. Izumi Shikibu was with him as well. All those at the temple threw themselves to the ground. There were none who did not wet their sleeves with tears of joyous adulation.

The *Seiganji engi emaki* contains an illustration of the scene (fig. 27). Ippen is one of two priests and an acolyte standing on the Seiganji Temple balcony. He and several laypeople—six women, one man, and a child—gaze up at a cloud bearing Izumi Shikibu, now with long hair and elegant robes, as she floats down to greet them. One of her accompanying musicians plays a *biwa*, and another beats a large drum or gong. Strangely, Amida is nowhere to be seen—at least, not in an appearance or stature sufficient to set him apart from the members of his host. Izumi Shikibu is the single largest figure on the cloud, having seemingly replaced the Pure Land founder as the object of Ippen and the six women's religious veneration. (In medieval Japanese literature, such inconsistencies between text and illustration are not uncommon.) The scene is one of total, final redemption, for although the *Seiganji engi emaki* previously showed Izumi Shikibu locked out of Enkyōji Temple, denied access to the Way, it now depicts her returning through the sky, free of her austere nun's robes and deified as a female emissary from the Pure Land.

Unlike *Rakuyō Seiganji engi*, the *otogizōshi Izumi Shikibu engi* contains a long didactic passage at its end, a *Jishū* sermon that Izumi Shikibu delivers from her cloud. Umetani Shigeki argues that the passage was drawn largely from the *mondō* ("question and answer") section of *Ippen gishū* (Collected Principles of Ippen), a *Jishū* treatise attributed Taa Chiren and dating from between 1497 and 1513.[107] By assigning Chiren's rhetoric to Izumi Shikibu some 260 years after her rebirth in the Pure Land, the unknown *Izumi Shikibu engi* author both enlivens and invests it with an air of infallibility. In the process, the author appropriates Izumi Shikibu's celebrity to the cause of the *Jishū*, much as the authors of the medieval *Lotus Sutra* commentaries, *Izumi Shikibu ōjō no koto*, and *Rakuyō Seiganji engi* did to their own.

Dennis Hirota has written that in some scenes in *Ippen Hijiri e*, nearly half of Ippen's followers appear to be nuns.[108] Likewise, Umetani argues that Ippen possessed a fascination for women, both in his own lifetime and beyond, and he seconds Yanagita Kunio in supposing that the Izumi Shikibu/Ippen account circulated orally among the nuns of Seiganji before it

[107] Umetani, "Kyōto Tōhokuin zō *Ippen Shōnin Izumi Shikibu monogatari* ni tsuite," 326–27. Umetani actually discusses the passage as it appears in *Ippen Shōnin Izumi Shikibu monogatari*.

[108] Hirota, *No Abode*, xxxvii.

Fig. 27. Ippen Shōnin and Izumi Shikibu at Seiganji Temple. From *Seiganji engi emaki* (seventeenth century). Courtesy of Seiganji Temple and the Kyoto National Museum.

was recorded in *Rakuyō Seiganji engi* or some other text in the *Sankan-bon* textual line.[109]

Although there is no direct evidence to demonstrate that it was indeed the nuns of Seiganji or the *Jishū* who were responsible for spreading the story of Izumi Shikibu and Ippen, there is proof that the story was used in preaching to women. There is a temple solicitation scroll (*kanjin-chō*) dated the twenty-first day of the third month of 1537—some thirty-to-sixty years before the composition of *Seiganji engi* in the *Sankan-bon* textual line—and it contains the full Izumi Shikibu/Ippen account, as well as a substantial story of the legendary carving of the Seiganji Amida. The solicitation scroll, approximately the last fourth of which is translated below, explains the circumstances of the fund-raising campaign for which it was composed. In its final passage, it alludes to the female audience to which it makes its appeal:

> In the latter part of the seventh month of last year, 1536, there was an unexpected disturbance in the capital. A fire that was set to some houses spread to Seiganji, where the Central Hall and the priests' quarters all burned to the ground. However, the principal image emerged unharmed, perhaps because of Amida's desire to bestow the benefits of his single teaching on sentient beings in these Latter

[109]Umetani, "Kyōto Tōhokuin zō *Ippen Shōnin Izumi Shikibu monogatari* ni tsuite," 325. Umetani also speculates that Ippen and Izumi Shikibu came to be associated because of their mutual links to Shōkū Shōnin at Enkyōji Temple. *Ippen Hijiri e* contains an account of how Ippen came to Enkyōji in the spring of 1287 and was moved to tears at the thought of Shōkū Shōnin. Komatsu, ed., *Ippen Shōnin eden*, 250–53.

> Days. The Seiganji Amida has now returned to its former place, but the fine timbers of our temple hall are reduced to ash and dirt. Thus we have housed our reverend image with its 84,000 distinguishing characteristics in a simple thatch-roofed shelter with pillars of bamboo. Those who see it there weep at the sight, and those who hear of it burn inside. The people make donations as they see fit, begrudging neither the treasures in their storehouses nor the clothes on their backs, neither the short swords at their waists nor the great swords in their hands. As for the poor without a scrap of paper or half a coin to their names, the women cut their hair, and the men, their topknots, enjoining a karmic link.
>
> Believing that because ours is a large temple its reconstruction will not be so easily achieved, the younger priests roam the ignorant, roadless provinces, far from the emperor's sway, spreading their sleeves and clasping their hands in supplication before fishermen on the roiling seas and hunters in the mountains. They do this not out of stupid greed; it is only the rebuilding of our temple that they so fervently desire.
>
> The lives of those who establish links with a bit of iron, a piece of wood, a scrap of paper, or half a coin will be extended like that of Xi Wangmu, "Queen Mother of the West";[110] the bounty of their storerooms will be as that of Sudatta.[111] Then, in a hundred years to come, they shall be received by Amida's Pure Land host, sit with crossed legs on a seven-jeweled dais, and in a single moment arrive in the Pure Realm of Non-Regression. There they may feast upon the hundred delicacies, just as they like, and they may joyfully wade through the fragrant waters of the [Lake of] Eight Virtues, just as they please. The deluding clouds of the Five Obstructions shall instantly disappear, allowing the brilliant moon of the Five Wisdoms to shine its perfect light. The deluding mists of the Three Obediences shall immediately vanish, allowing the Buddhist sun of the Three-Bodies Myriad Virtues to shine its dazzling rays.[112]

The Seiganji solicitation scroll of 1537 is a fascinating document in several respects. First, its description of the plight of the Seiganji Amida, unavoidably housed in a shoddy, makeshift structure, suggests the turbulence of the times, as well as the unflagging efforts of those who worked on the statue's behalf. (A Seiganji solicitation scroll from the eighth month of 1574 actually describes the devastating Kyoto fire of 1573 as a *hōben*—an expedient means for allowing myriad people to establish karmic

[110]Xi Wangmu (Seiōbo) is one of the legendary Daoist immortals. She is said to have lived on the mythical Mount Kunlun in Western China.

[111]Sudatta (Sudatsu) was a man of great wealth and charity in the age of Shakyamuni.

[112]Yutani Yūzō, "*Seiganji engi* kankei shiryō," *Fukakusa kyōgaku* 19 (1999), 348–50.

links by making contributions to Seiganji's reconstruction.)[113] Second, the scroll's reference to the "young priests" (*kozō*) who travel the provinces collecting temple donations suggests the process by which stories of Izumi Shikibu, Ono no Komachi, Sei Shōnagon, and others were spread through the provinces, although not, as Yanagita would have us believe, by nuns. Third, the scroll intimates the gender of its intended audience: by promising donors the Five Wisdoms of Amida Buddha in exchange for the Five Obstructions, and the Three-Bodies Myriad Virtues (the virtues adhering to the metaphysical, physical, and manifested bodies of the Buddhas) in exchange for the Three Obediences, it appeals unambiguously to women. The story of Izumi Shikibu and Ippen Shōnin was thus employed in an early sixteenth-century Seiganji fund-raising campaign directed, at least in part, toward women.

[113]Yutani, "*Seiganji engi* kankei shiryō," 336. The solicitation scroll explains that reconstructing Seiganji "is the same as ornamenting the Pure Land."

Chapter Seven
Climbing the Forbidden Mountain: *Nyonin kinsei* and the Gendered Proselytizing Traditions of Medieval Japan

As we have seen in chapters four through six, Izumi Shikibu stories were put to an exceptionally wide use in the medieval period for a variety of overtly religious purposes. They were employed as a means of illustrating and explaining the *Lotus Sutra*, of promoting the Seiganji Amida and the practice of the *nenbutsu*, of raising funds for Seiganji Temple, and of advocating *Jishū* Pure Land doctrine. In the various accounts, Izumi Shikibu is made to discover, and thereby endorse, the truths of the groups and institutions recounting her story. Cast in the role of a celebrity spokesperson, she is made to lend her seemingly neutral voice to the causes and beliefs of those recreating her past. Izumi Shikibu is of course not the only Heian woman author whose poetry and persona were put to such use in medieval preaching, but in the frequency and degree of their appropriation, she is unique.

Although many of the Izumi Shikibu accounts discussed in the previous three chapters conflict in their details and ideological orientations, those that pertain to Izumi Shikibu's associations with Shōkū Shōnin, Chūjōhime, and Ippen Shōnin are all concerned with issues of women in Buddhism. Izumi Shikibu's problems are universal and unchanging; it is only the solution to those problems—the *Lotus Sutra*, the Seiganji Amida, or the practice of the *nenbutsu*—that differs from one story to the next. In the majority of her tales, including those that we have seen and those to be examined in this and the following chapter, Izumi Shikibu is shown to have overcome the many obstacles in her path, uncovering ways in which all women can attain Buddhahood. She does this most often by her skill as a poet, using *waka* to protest the physical, doctrinal, and psychological barriers emplaced against women, including the supposedly intrinsic impurity of her gender. In an unusual account within the *otogizōshi Jōruri monogatari* (discussed in chapter eight), she uses her own sexuality as a means of transcending the impediments of her femininity, demonstrating that a woman can achieve rebirth in the Pure Land without sublimating or denying her bodily nature.

In medieval Japan, the Buddhist marginalization of women was most concretely manifested as the institutional exclusion of women from designated holy sites, a practice known as *nyonin kinsei*, "prohibition of women." As we have seen in chapter four, *nyonin kinsei* proscriptions appear to have become common from around the ninth century.[1] Although the reasons for their propagation are not entirely clear, they seem to have been enacted both in response to the imagined impurity of women and, as evidenced by the stories of Izumi Shikibu's meeting with Shōkū Shōnin at Enkyōji Temple (and a variety of other sources), to the perceived threat that women posed to monks in their Buddhist practice.[2] In Buddhist discourse, mountains are often employed as metaphors for enlightenment—Shakyamuni Buddha is said to have preached the *Lotus Sutra* at an assembly on Eagle Peak, for example—so it follows that in addition to constituting regimens of actual, tangible discrimination, *nyonin kinsei* restrictions are metaphoric of women's metaphysical exclusion from the Way.

In many cases, *nyonin kinsei* rules came to be supported by a body of tales, presumably spread by men, of women who suffered divine punishment for attempting to violate the sanctity of all-male spaces. Nevertheless, despite the efforts of some monks to frighten women into compliance with these injunctions, an opposing corpus of accounts can be seen to have flourished. Comprising subversive stories of prominent female figures—Izumi Shikibu, Lady Tokiwa, Chūjōhime, and others—challenging and overcoming *nyonin kinsei* proscriptions laid down by men and gods alike, these accounts are of largely indeterminate origin. Still, there is reason to believe that many of them were propagated by diffuse groups of women preachers and performers, including Kumano *bikuni* (the mendicant, picture-explaining "nuns of Kumano"), who seem to have actively resisted women's segregation by means of their own proselytizing and storytelling traditions.

Challenging *Nyonin kinsei*

In Muromachi fiction, *nyonin kinsei* exclusions tend to be as well-known for their violation as they are for being maintained, and though evidence is scarce, many accounts of their contestation seem to have emerged from the

[1] Miyake Hitoshi, "Nyonin kinsei," in *Kokushi daijiten*, vol. 11, ed. Henshū Iinkai (Tokyo: Yoshikawa Kōbunkan, 1990), 265a; Miyazaki Fumiko, "Female Pilgrims and Mt. Fuji: Changing Perspectives on the Exclusion of Women," *Monumenta Nipponica* 60, no. 3 (Autumn 2005), 340–43.

[2] Gaynor Sekimori has succinctly explained that "scholars such as Nishiguchi Junko and Taira Masayuki see female exclusion as deriving ultimately from fears of blood pollution, while Hori Ichirō and Ushiyama Yoshiyuki ascribe it to temple regulations demanding separation of male and female clergy." Gaynor Sekimori, "Shugendō: The State of the Field," *Monumenta Nipponica* 57, no. 2 (Summer 2002), 217.

storytelling of women. One especially famous and presumably fictional incident is described in the *kōwakamai* libretto *Tokiwa mondō* (Tokiwa's Debate), dating from around the sixteenth century. *Kōwakamai*, or "ballad-drama," emerged as a distinct performance genre in the fifteenth or early sixteenth century. It evolved out of *kusemai* (a popular form of dance), many of the early practitioners of which were women.[3] Almost nothing is known about how *kōwakamai* was performed in the period of its greatest popularity, the late sixteenth and early seventeenth centuries, and to what degrees dialogue, mimicry, and dance were employed are all unclear. James Araki, author of the most comprehensive English-language study of the genre, writes that while *kōwakamai* and noh "seem to have been equally prized by the samurai of the late sixteenth century," whether or not *kōwakamai* can be classified "as a form of staged drama," like noh, is difficult to say.[4]

Tokiwa mondō is a tale of the twelfth-century Lady Tokiwa (Tokiwa-gozen, b. 1137), the mother of the Minamoto general and folk hero Yoshitsune. Strong-willed and courageous, she is a popular figure in *kōwakamai*, with as many as four libretti bearing her name.[5] Muroki Yatarō has suggested that her prominence in the genre may result from the absorption within *kōwakamai* of the oral repertoires of earlier women raconteurs, for whom stories of Lady Tokiwa are likely to have been staple features.[6] If correct, Muroki's supposition would indicate that *Tokiwa mondō* is itself derived from a medieval women's performance tradition—a plausible conjecture, considering the pro-woman content of the work.

In *Tokiwa mondō*, Lady Tokiwa travels alone to Kurama Temple in the mountains north of the capital. She makes her way to the Kurama worship hall, where she blithely steps inside the barrier grating, climbs atop the priests' elevated dais, and begins to perform her religious devotions. The abbot Tōkō discovers her there, and infuriated by the presence of a woman, he demands that she remove herself at once. "Though human like men," Tōkō rails, "women are beset by many obstacles, and they are forbidden to

[3]James T. Araki, *The Ballad-Drama of Medieval Japan* (Berkeley and Los Angeles: University of California Press, 1964), 69–70.

[4]Ibid., 7–8. All the *kōwakamai* libretti that survive today, including *Tokiwa mondō*, are written without musical or stage notation, allowing for little insight into how they were actually performed.

[5]*Fushimi Tokiwa* (Tokiwa at Fushimi), *Nabiki Tokiwa* (Tokiwa's Submission), *Tokiwa mondō* (Tokiwa's Debate), and *Yamanaka Tokiwa* (Tokiwa at Yamanaka). For synopses, see Araki, *The Ballad-Drama of Medieval Japan*, 125–28.

[6]Muroki Yatarō, *Zōtei katarimono (mai, sekkyō, ko-jōruri) no kenkyū*, 2d rev. ed. (Tokyo: Fūkan Shobō, 1992), 30.

tread upon pure, sacred ground."[7] Lady Tokiwa refuses to budge, and after listening to Tōkō expound upon the life of Shakyamuni and the sutras that he preached (none of which, as Tōkō explains, instruct a woman to mount a temple dais), she engages him in debate. Employing the kind of *kanjin*-style hermeneutics that we have seen in chapter four, Lady Tokiwa argues that because the first character in the title of the *Lotus Sutra* (the *myō* 妙 in *Myōhō rengekyō*, according to Kumārajīva's fifth-century Chinese translation) contains the element for woman 女, and because the *Lotus Sutra* is superior to all other sutras, women enjoy a place at the forefront of Buddhism. Furthermore, she says, insofar as there is no sutra that specifically prohibits women from mounting a temple dais, Tōkō has no right to request that she step down. Tōkō angrily responds:

> "Well said, lady. But as a certain sutra explains, 'the combined delusion of men in all the three thousand worlds equals the karmic obstructions of but a single woman.'[8] This means that if we were to assemble all the delusion of all the men in the three thousand worlds, it would be equal to the karmic obstructions faced by one woman alone. That's why hell is in women, and nowhere else. People say that when a woman is born, a servant of hell has appeared, and that the Buddhas of the three ages all curl their tongues in dread.
>
> "In far-off China, women don't climb the peak of Mount Tiantai, and they're not permitted on Mount Yuwang, Mount Moli, or Mount Qingliang either. Over here in Japan, women can't look upon the gratings of the inner sanctums at Enryakuji, Mount Kōya, Hase and Oka Temples, Taima Temple, or Mount Tōnomine, which is why they pray from a distance. Women are insufficiently pious—that's the reason they're born as women. In their profound stupidity, they slander the True Law, and they're deeply jealous as well. Their misunderstanding knows no end.
>
> "You are polluting the worship hall, so go on and get out. If you won't, I'll tell the lower-ranking priests, and they'll throw you out."[9]

Lady Tokiwa replies that "those who know nothing should shut up," and invoking the principal of non-duality, she explains that in the face of enlightenment, men and women are the same. She goes on to accuse Tōkō

[7]SNKBT 59:288; Agō Toranoshin, ed., *Kōwaka bukyoku kenkyū*, vol. 1 (Tokyo: Miyai Shoten, 1979), 222.

[8]This is an aphorism of unknown origin. In Kamakura and Muromachi-period texts, it is variously misattributed to the *Kegon* and *Nirvana* sutras. Agō, ed., *Kōwaka bukyoku kenkyū*, vol. 1, 232, note 1.

[9]SNKBT 59:291–92; Agō, ed., *Kōwaka bukyoku kenkyū*, vol. 1, 231.

of ingratitude toward his mother, and after lambasting him for his ignorance and delusion, she declares victory in the debate upon hearing that the temple was originally constructed to serve as an imperial lady's tomb. Insofar as the principal image is a statue of the guardian deity Bishamonten, whose sister and disciple, the goddess Kichijōten, is said to stand at his side, Lady Tokiwa furthermore declares her right to remain. "Truly," she says in the final passage of the *kōwakamai*, "if it is decided that women are to be expelled from this temple, then expel Kichijōten and the imperial lady's tomb. I'll go with them, and we'll take up residence in some other temple. What do you think about that, you priest?" Lady Tokiwa's words are withering, and not for Tōkō alone; as Muroki observes, "they undoubtedly dealt a furious counterblow to the misogyny of their time."[10]

Tōkō's list of Japanese Buddhist sites proscribed to women is a strange one, considering that among those that he identifies, only Enryakuji (on Mount Hiei), Mount Kōya, and Mount Tōnomine are known to have maintained *nyonin kinsei* restrictions. Tōkō's inclusion of Taima Temple is particularly odd when one takes into account the temple's medieval self-identification with Chūjōhime and the female Amida. Nevertheless, there are at least two manuscripts of the *otogizōshi Chūjōhime no honji* (Chūjōhime in Her Original Form) that describe how Chūjōhime was once reprimanded for praying before the central altar at Taima Temple after she had taken holy vows. "However much of a nun you may become," a priest explains in an early Edo-period *Chūjōhime* text, "you'll still be a woman, so it's inconceivable that you should take a place before the Buddha. You should pray from somewhere outside the main gate."[11] Like Lady Tokiwa, Chūjōhime argues with the priest, explaining that "before the Buddha, there is neither male nor female," and eventually she is allowed to stay. While there is no historical evidence of a *nyonin kinsei* exclusion at Taima, either formal or informal, the

[10]Muroki, *Zōtei katarimono no kenkyū*, 173. The archetype of this and other tales of women debating priests is the *Vimalakīrti Sutra* account of a goddess's confounding of the monk Śāriputra at Vimalakīrti's house. In the course of their discussion, the goddess transforms Śāriputra into herself, and herself into Śāriputra, in order to demonstrate the insubstantiality of gender. Robert A. F. Thurman, *The Holy Teaching of Vimalakīrti: A Mahāyāna Scripture* (University Park and London: The Pennsylvania State University Press, 1976), 58–63. Thurman bases his English translation on a ninth-century Tibetan translation. In Japan, the *Vimalakīrti Sutra* was best known by Kumārajīva's fifth-century Chinese translation.

[11]Quoted in Abe Yasurō, "Chūjōhime monogatari no seiritsu," in *Chūjōhime setsuwa no chōsa kenkyū hōkoku sho*, ed. Gankōji Bunkazai Kenkyūjo (Nara: Gankōji Bunkazai Kenkyūjo, 1983), 72b. The two *Chūjōhime* texts alluding to *nyonin kinsei* at Taima Temple are the Murakami Bunko manuscript, titled *Chūjōhime monogatari*, and a *nara ehon* titled *Chūjōhime* (quoted above), in the possession of Abe Yasurō. I am grateful to Hank Glassman for introducing me to these works.

late-medieval ascription of one in fiction is useful—within the context of Chūjōhime's tale, that is—insofar as it provides an additional obstacle that Chūjōhime can be shown to overcome.

In the *otogizōshi Komachi monogatari* (The Tale of Komachi; late Muromachi or early Edo period), and, to a lesser extent, the noh play *Sotoba Komachi*, Ono no Komachi engages in a similar debate with a priest.[12] In *Komachi monogatari*, an aged Komachi seals her victory in an argument at Seki Temple by citing the examples of the eight-year-old Dragon Girl and Shakyamuni's mother, Māyā, as women who attained Buddhahood, thereby demonstrating that enlightenment may be attained by women as well as men. Following Akegawa Tadao, Sarah Strong has suggested that this and other Komachi debates were performed in the Muromachi period by "*bikuni-hijiri* couples, quasi-Buddhist religious, who, according to Akegawa, told Komachi's story to medieval audiences as a husband and wife team."[13] Although Strong's theory suffers from a lack of evidence, it is intriguing for its imputation of the origins of the Komachi debates (and, by extension, the related tales of Lady Tokiwa and Chūjōhime) to a male-female performance tradition.

Yet another counter-*nyonin kinsei* account that may have its origins in women's storytelling is contained in the poetic anthology *Shinsenzai wakashū* (New Japanese Poems of a Thousand Years), compiled by Nijō Tamesada in 1359. According to a headnote in that anthology, Izumi Shikibu once composed a verse when she encountered a priest carrying an *ominaeshi*, a "maidenflower," for the *nenbutsu* altar on Mount Hiei.[14] Because "*ominaeshi*" 女郎花 contains the word "*omina*" 女 ("girl," or "maiden") and is written with the characters for "*jorō*" 女郎 ("young woman"), it has been used in Japanese poetry as a metaphor for women since at least the early Heian period.[15] As the

[12]The debate in *Komachi monogatari* is in MJMT 5:136b–39a (woodblock-printed text of ca. 1688–1710). *Sotoba Komachi* is translated in Arthur Waley, *The Nō Plays of Japan* (New York: Grove Press, 1957), 150–60.

[13]Sarah Strong, "Reading the 'Court' in Courtesan: The Historicization of the Role of *Yūjo* in Some Muromachi Tales," *Proceedings of the Midwest Association for Japanese Literary Studies* 4 (1998), 249. Also see Sarah Strong, "Performing the Courtesan: In Search of Ghosts at Zuishin'in Letter Mound," *Women and Performance: A Journal of Feminist Theory* 12:1, no. 23 (2001), 90.

[14]The poem is *Shinsenzai wakashū* 894; it is also contained in the *Matsui-bon* text of *Izumi Shikibu shū* (compiled after 1439; NKBT 80:177, poem 256). As *Shinsenzai wakashū* was compiled some three hundred years after Izumi Shikibu's death, the poem is likely apocryphal. Yanagita Kunio argues against its authenticity on grammatical and stylistic grounds as well. Yanagita Kunio, *Josei to minkan denshō* (1932), in *Teihon Yanagita Kunio shū*, vol. 8 (Tokyo: Chikuma Shobō, 1962), 336.

[15]Katagiri Yōichi, *Utamakura utakotoba jiten* (Tokyo: Kadokawa Shoten, 1983), 459–60. According to the *waka* treatise *Nōin utamakura*, compiled by the poet-priest Nōin (b. 988), "[the word] *ominaeshi* should be employed [in poetry] as a metonym for women." NKT 1:72 and 106 (*ryaku-hon* and *kō-hon* textual lines).

headquarters of the Tendai Buddhist sect, Mount Hiei was officially closed to women from the fourth month of 822, toward the end of its founder's, the priest Saichō's, life, until an act of the Meiji government in 1872.[16] Thus, in her poem, Izumi Shikibu expresses envy of the so-called "maidenflower" that climbs the mountain while she herself cannot:

> A priest once passed in front of [Izumi Shikibu's] house carrying a maidenflower. "Where are you going?" [Izumi Shikibu] asked. "I'm taking this for the *nenbutsu* altar on Mount Hiei," the priest replied. Izumi Shikibu attached a poem:

na ni shi owaba	Though by its name
itsutsu no sawari	it faces
aru mono wo	the Five Obstructions,
urayamashiku mo	enviably
noboru hana kana	this flower yet ascends the mount.[17]

Unlike Lady Tokiwa and Chūjōhime, who employ reason and erudition to overcome *nyonin kinsei*, Izumi Shikibu composes a clever verse—a *waka* containing a play on the words "*ura yama*" ("back mountain," or "mountain interior") and "*urayamashiku*" ("envious")—which she affixes to the stem of the priest's *ominaeshi* as a kind of devotional offering. By having the maidenflower deliver her poem for her, she symbolically circumvents the female exclusion. Moreover, inasmuch as the poem calls attention to Izumi Shikibu's unhappiness at Mount Hiei's institutional prohibition of women, it serves as a sort of protest-message as well. Sending it up with her silent sister, the maidenflower, to decorate the altar of the Enryakuji *nenbutsu* hall, Izumi Shikibu lodges her complaint with the very Buddhas and deities of the mountain itself.

Izumi Shikibu's maidenflower poem seems to have been well-known in Tendai circles in the Muromachi period, as we can see from its inclusion in the *Lotus Sutra* commentaries *Ichijō shūgyokushō* and *Hokekyō jurin shūyōshō*. In the first of these, compiled in 1488, Eikai cites the poem in conjunction

[16]Paul Groner, *Saichō: The Establishment of the Japanese Tendai School* (University of California at Berkeley, 1984), 158–59. The *nyonin kinsei* proscription on Mount Hiei was not always strictly enforced. The Jesuit missionary Luis Frois (1532–97) reports that when Oda Nobunaga razed the temple complex and massacred it inhabitants in 1571, he murdered numbers of women and children there as well. Michael Cooper, ed., *They Came To Japan* (Ann Arbor: University of Michigan Center for Japanese Studies, 1995), 98–99; Nishiguchi Junko, *Onna no chikara* (Tokyo: Heibonsha, 1987), 119.

[17]SKT 1:1:618b-c, poem 894. Also see Edward Kamens, "Dragon-Girl, Maidenflower, Buddha: The Transformation of a Waka Topos, 'The Five Obstructions,'" *Harvard Journal of Asiatic Studies* 53, no. 2 (December 1993), 425–30.

with his explanation of the Three Obediences in the "Devadatta" chapter of his commentary:

> As for the Three Obediences, the first is a young woman's duty to her parents, the second is a grown woman's duty to her husband, and the third is an old woman's duty to her children. This is explained in the *Agongyō* [sutras].[18]
>
> Regarding this: At a time when Izumi Shikibu had taken holy vows and become a nun at Seiganji Temple, she once saw a mountain priest climbing [Mount Hiei] with a maidenflower for the *nenbutsu* altar. It was toward the eighth month. She composed a poem:

na ni shi owaba	Though by its name
itsutsu no sawari	it ought to face
arubeki ni	the Five Obstructions,
urayamashiku mo	enviably
noboru hana kana	this flower yet ascends the mount.[19]

Eikai's renditions of the poem and its headnote differ from those in *Shinsenzai wakashū*, indicating that Eikai probably drew his passage from some source other than Nijō Tamesada's anthology. In *Jurin shūyōshō*, completed in 1512, Sonshun cites the account in conjunction with his explanation of the Five Obstructions rather than the Three Obediences, and his poem matches the one in *Shinsenzai wakashū*.[20] The use of different versions of the maidenflower poem-story in separate but related contexts (the Three Obediences vs. the Five Obstructions) suggests that the Izumi Shikibu story circulated orally in and among the Tendai instructional centers in the fifteenth and sixteenth centuries, and that it was upon this oral tradition that Eikai and Sonshun based their written accounts.

What is perhaps most intriguing about the *Ichijō shūgyokushō* passage is the statement that Izumi Shikibu encountered the priest at a time after she had become a nun at Seiganji. This may be a clue that the tale did not originate in the Tendai *dangisho* at all, but rather in an earlier Seiganji proselytizing tradition. Like many of the *Rakuyō Seiganji engi* accounts, the *Ichijō shūgyokushō* story may represent a fragment of the oral repertoire—now largely lost—of the mendicant, storytelling nuns of Seiganji. That those nuns would

[18]The *Agongyō*, or *Āgamas*, are the four major collections of Hīnayāna sutras in the East Asian Buddhist canon; they correspond roughly to the five Pali *Nikāyas*.

[19]*Ichijō shūgyokushō: eiin* (Kyoto: Rinsen Shoten, 1998), 494–95.

[20]The *Jurin shūyōshō* headnote simply reads: "There is a story. Izumi Shikibu once saw a mountain priest pluck a maidenflower and carry it up Mount [Hiei]. [She composed] a poem." *Hokekyō jurin shūyōshō*, vol. 3 (Kyoto: Rinsen Shoten, 1991), 294.

have recited a tale about Izumi Shikibu and Mount Hiei's *nyonin kinsei* restriction is easy to imagine, considering the stories that they likely spread about Izumi Shikibu's triumph over her exclusion from Enkyōji Temple on Mount Shosha by means of her "darkness into darkness" verse. The use of the maidenflower account in early-medieval proselytizing (whether that of Seiganji, the Tendai instructional centers, or both) would moreover help to explain the *Shinsenzai wakashū* compiler Nijō Tamesada's fortuitous discovery of a "new" Izumi Shikibu poem in the mid-fourteenth century.

Divine Enforcements

In protesting the *nyonin kinsei* exclusion of women from Mount Hiei (and in literally overcoming the exclusion in accounts of her journey to see Shōkū Shōnin on Mount Shosha), Izumi Shikibu challenges a frightful and entrenched taboo. On Mount Hiei in the Heian period, *nyonin kinsei* was believed to have been enforced by the Sannō Gongen, the protective deity of Enryakuji Temple.[21] In a diary entry for the ninth day of the ninth month of 1020, Minamoto no Tsuneyori records the distress of the Enryakuji monks at the deity's non-response to a recent female intrusion:[22]

> I climbed Mount [Hiei]. People were saying that a crazy woman had ascended the mountain and had been walking the corridors of the Dharani Hall,[23] and that the monks had tied her up and sent her down. The older monks lamented, "Since our mountain's founding there has never been anything like this that we've heard of. Years ago a woman lost her way and climbed up near the peak, and the sky began to crash with thunder and rain. The weather was unprecedented—it was the Sannō Deity reproaching the woman for her ascent. But this time there was no thunder and no rain. Are the Deity's miracles at an end?" That the Deity did not reproach the woman is extraordinary. The holy mountain must be going to ruin.[24]

[21]The Sannō Gongen is enshrined at Hie Shrine at the eastern foot of Mount Hiei.

[22]From *Sakei ki*, in Zōho Shiryō Taisei Kankōkai, ed., *Zōho shiryō taisei*, vol. 6 (Kyoto: Rinsen Shoten, 1965), 104 (entry for Kannin 4.9.9). The passage was reproduced nearly two hundred years later by Minamoto no Akikane (1160–1215) in *Kojidan*: SNKBT 41:477; Kobayashi Yasuharu, ed., *Kojidan*, vol. 2 (Tokyo: Gendai Shichōsha, 1981), 104.

[23]*Kuin bukkakushō* (ca. fourteenth century) lists the *Sōjiin*, the "Dharani Hall," as one of nine original temple buildings on Mount Hiei. Groner, *Saichō: The Establishment of the Japanese Tendai School*, 111.

[24]This last sentence is ambiguous. Alternately translated, it might read, "[The Deity] must have disappeared from (abandoned) the temple-mountain."

Tsuneyori's and the monks' surprise at the Sannō Deity's inaction demonstrates a deep-seated and seemingly widespread belief in the divine enforcement of *nyonin kinsei*, even in cases of unintentional violations. The deity's disregard of the crazy woman in 1020 is the exception that proves the rule.

Later literature and folklore abounds in tales of the failure of women to overcome *nyonin kinsei*. Yanagita Kunio has documented numerous accounts of women—often *miko* and nuns—who were turned to stone for attempting to scale forbidden mountains.[25] Mount Ōmine in Nara Prefecture, Mount Hakusan in Ishikawa Prefecture, and Mount Tateyama in Toyama Prefecture all have boulders that are identified as the petrified remains of nuns who sought to violate the *nyonin kinsei* of those places. Yanagita speculates that such accounts were circulated by men as a means of discouraging women from climbing mountains prohibited to them.[26] The message that these stories must have conveyed to women in the medieval and early-modern periods—"stay out or else"—was sure to have been frighteningly clear.

A late Kamakura-period account of the nun Toran-ni's ill-fated ascent of Mount Ōmine (also known as Mount Kinbu) is contained in Kokan Shiren's *Genkō shakusho* (A History of Buddhism to the Genkō Era; completed in 1322), an encyclopedic collection of biographies and sundry information relating to the history of Buddhism in Japan. In *Genkō shakusho*, Toran-ni is said to have been a powerful sorceress, and although in this version of her story she is not turned to stone for violating the *nyonin kinsei* exclusion, the mountain reacts unfavorably to her attempt:

> The nun Toran-ni was from the province of Yamato. She was accomplished in Buddhism, and she had studied the mystic arts of the mountain ascetics in the foothills of the Yoshino range.[27] People say that Mount Kinbu is made of gold, and that it is guarded by the bodhisattva Kongō Zōō, who does not allow women to enter its precincts.[28] Toran-ni spoke: "My body is that of a woman, but I

[25]Yanagita Kunio, "Rōjo kaseki dan" (1916), in *Imōto no chikara*, reprinted in *Yanagita Kunio zenshū*, vol. 11 (Tokyo: Chikuma Shobō, 1998), 371–79. Also see Yanagita, *Josei to minkan denshō*, 416, and Suzuki Masataka, *Nyonin kinsei* (Tokyo: Yoshikawa Kōbunkan, 2002), 82–88.

[26]Yanagita, "Rōjo kaseki dan," 376.

[27]The Yoshino Mountains are in the central part of modern Nara Prefecture. They were famous in the medieval period for their cherry blossoms and as a center of *shugendō*, the magico-religious practice of *yamabushi* (mountain ascetics). The "mystic arts of the mountain ascetics," *senjutsu*, is a kind of sorcery practiced by *sennin*, "Daoist immortals."

[28]Mount Kinbu is a prominent peak in the Yoshino range. Its *nyonin kinsei* was widely recognized—both in Japan and China—as early as the tenth century. In *Yichu liutie* (*Giso rokujō*, compiled in 975), Yichu (Giso) records that women are forbidden from ascending Mount Kinbu, and that the Kongō Zōō Bodhisattva resides at its summit. Quoted in Miyake Hitoshi, *Ōmine shugendō no kenkyū* (Tokyo: Kōsei Shuppansha, 1988), 390.

> maintain the precepts and enjoy mystical response. How am I like a lay-woman?" Thus she set out to climb the mountain.
>
> The sky suddenly turned dark, and lightning and thunder began to strike. Toran-ni lost her way. She threw down her staff, whereupon it rooted itself in the earth and grew into a great tree. Toran-ni conjured up a dragon. She mounted it and flew up the mountain, but when she had reached only as far as the spring, she became unable to proceed any higher. Furious, she stamped on the rocky ridge, crushing and rending it entirely.
>
> The pond that supported her dragon is located beneath the rocks. Even now, two footprints remain. People say that [Toran-ni] was adept in the Way of Longevity, and no one knows where she met her end.[29]

Max Moerman has observed that Toran-ni bases her challenge to *nyonin kinsei* upon "a claim for exceptionalism rather than egalitarianism"; she is shown to assert "not women's equality with men but her own superiority to ordinary women."[30] Nevertheless, not even she is capable of defying the *nyonin kinsei* of Mount Kinbu, which seems to be the point of the account. Significantly, the numerous references to mountain landmarks suggest that the tale circulated orally on Mount Ōmine before it was incorporated into *Genkō shakusho*; it is not hard to imagine a fourteenth-century priest entertaining visitors with this and other fantastic stories as he led them up the mountain slope, pointing out the tree, the spring, the rocky ridge, and the footprints along the way.[31]

Women were likewise prohibited from entering the precincts of Mount Kōya, headquarters of the Japanese Shingon Buddhist sect, founded by Kūkai in the early years of the ninth century. A story of Kūkai's own mother's failure to ascend Mount Kōya is contained in the *sekkyō-bushi* sermon-ballad *Karukaya*. Also known as *sekkyō* and *sekkyō jōruri*, *sekkyō-bushi* flourished in the Muromachi period as an oral literature spread by itinerant preacher-entertainers, lay "priests" who typically performed their didactic,

[29]*Genkō shakusho*, in Kuroita Katsumi, ed., *Shintei zōho kokushi taikei*, vol. 31 (Tokyo: Yoshikawa Kōbunkan, 1930), 260–61. For an alternate translation, see Marian Ury, "Nuns and Other Female Devotees in *Genkō shakusho* (1322), Japan's First History of Buddhism," in *Engendering Faith: Women and Buddhism in Premodern Japan*, ed. Barbara Ruch (Ann Arbor: University of Michigan Center for Japanese Studies, 2002), 193. An earlier and somewhat simpler version of Toran-ni's story is contained in Ōe no Masafusa's *Honchō shinsenden* (ca. 1098). NST 7:260 and 581.

[30]D. Max Moerman, *Localizing Paradise: Kumano Pilgrimage and the Religious Landscape of Premodern Japan* (Cambridge and London: Harvard University Asia Center, 2005), 205.

[31]Ōsumi Kazuo similarly suggests that the account circulated among the mountain ascetics of the Yoshino region. Ōsumi Kazuo, "Bukkyō to josei: *Genkō shakusho* no ni'nyoden ni tsuite," *Rekishi hyōron* 395 (1983), 7a.

melodramatic tales for small audiences at temples, shrines, street corners and crossroads, usually to the rhythmic sound of a *sasara*, a notched bamboo scraper.[32] The earliest surviving *Karukaya* manuscript is a hand-copied, illustrated text dating from around the Keichō era (1596–1615),[33] but as with all works of its genre, the tale predates its transcription. Scholars agree that like the *Genkō shakusho* account, which may have first circulated among the monks of Mount Ōmine, *Karukaya* emerged from the medieval storytelling of the Kōya *hijiri*, the mendicant, pseudo-monastic priests of Mount Kōya.[34]

Karukaya is the story of Katōzaemon Shigeuji, a provincial lord who abandons his daughter and pregnant wife to become a disciple of Hōnen (1133–1212) in the eastern part of the capital. Thirteen years after leaving his family, Shigeuji's wife, Akō, and son, Ishidōmaru, whom Shigeuji has never seen, set out on a journey to find him. Sensing their approach, Shigeuji flees to Mount Kōya, where he takes refuge in the local *nyonin kinsei* exclusion. (In *The Tale of the Heike*, the Takiguchi Novice similarly seeks sanctuary from his former love, Yokobue, in the *nyonin kinsei* of Mount Kōya, demonstrating the mountain's medieval reputation as a haven for men-on-the-run.[35]) Akō and Ishidōmaru follow him there. They soon arrive at the foot of the mountain, but when Akō declares her intention of meeting her husband, an innkeeper informs her of the local *nyonin kinsei* proscription. In a woodblock-printed *Karukaya* text published in Kyoto in 1631, he explains to her that Mount Kōya is a place from which all females—plant and animal alike—are strictly prohibited:

> The mountain is a seven-league precinct of non-discriminatory self-practice, and thus while male trees grow on the mountain peak, female trees grow in the valley below. Male birds fly up at the ridge; female birds fly in the valley. Bucks graze on the mountainside; does graze in the valley. Trees, reeds, grasses, fowl, and

[32]Muroki Yatarō, "Sekkyō jōruri," in *Nihon koten bungaku daijiten*, vol. 3 (Tokyo: Iwanami Shoten, 1984), 613–14; Susan Matisoff, "Holy Horrors: The Sermon-Ballads of Medieval and Early Modern Japan," in *Flowing Traces: Buddhism in the Literary and Visual Arts of Japan*, ed. James Sanford, William LaFleur, and Masatoshi Nagatomi, 234–61 (Princeton: Princeton University Press, 1992).

[33]The attribution of the manuscript to the Keichō era is by Muroki Yatarō ("*Karukaya*," in *Nihon koten bungaku daijiten*, vol. 2, 36a). The *Karukaya* story is also preserved in the noh play *Karukaya*, which is of unknown date and origin.

[34]Muroki Yatarō, "*Karukaya*," in *Nihon koten bungaku daijiten*, vol. 2, 35–36; Muroki, *Zōtei katarimono no kenkyū*, 330–41; Sakaguchi Hiroyuki, "Sekkyō *Karukaya* to Kōya denshō," *Kokugo to kokubungaku* 71, no. 10 (October 1994): 1–18; Susan Matisoff, "Barred from Paradise? Mount Kōya and the *Karukaya* Legend," in *Engendering Faith*, 465.

[35]SNKBT 45:227 (Kakuichi text); Helen McCullough, *The Tale of the Heike* (Stanford: Stanford University Press, 1988), 342.

> beasts—all that are male may enter, and all that are female may not. Absolutely no women are allowed.[36]

The innkeeper's explanation presents Mount Kōya's *nyonin kinsei* as a kind of natural law, a rule of nature beyond the powers of ordinary men and women to dispute or overcome. Even plants and animals adhere to its intent.

In the illustrated *Karukaya* manuscript of ca. 1596–1615, Akō protests that the venerable Kūkai himself was "born of a wretched woman," and that even if she had to debate Kūkai on the *nyonin kinsei* issue for seven days and seven nights (like Lady Tokiwa and Chūjōhime, it would seem), she would surely win.[37] In the woodblock-printed text of 1631, the innkeeper launches into a lengthy lecture on the life of Kūkai. His monologue constitutes an independent section of the work, the so-called "*Kōya no maki*" (Kōya Scroll), which likely circulated orally and independently of the main *Karukaya* narrative.[38] Toward the end of his speech, the innkeeper explains that despite the *nyonin kinsei* injunction, Kūkai's eighty-three-year-old mother once decided to visit her son on Mount Kōya. Because she was a woman, the ground shook and lightning struck as she climbed. Kūkai came down to greet her, and explaining that positively no women are allowed—neither human, bird nor beast—he asked her to turn back. Kūkai's mother argued, accusing her son of ingratitude (again, like Lady Tokiwa), but to no avail. The innkeeper relates:

> Kūkai took off his seven-paneled surplice—his *kesa*—and spread it over a rock. "Step over this," he said. As the *kesa* was her son's, the woman was unconcerned. She boldly stepped across, whereupon the blood of her monthly obstruction began to fall in tiny drops. It had ceased when she was forty-one, but now, at the age of eighty-three, it began anew. The *kesa* burst into flame and flew up into the sky.[39]

In medieval Buddhist literature, menstruation is often equated with the problems and spiritual defects associated with women.[40] The most frequently

[36]SNKS *Sekkyōshū*, 43. In the illustrated manuscript of ca. 1596–1615, the innkeeper simply explains that Mount Kōya is prohibited to women. SNKBT 90:281.

[37]SNKBT 90:281. In the text of 1631, Akō says nothing about debating Kūkai.

[38]The "*Kōya no maki*" section is absent from the earlier, illustrated *Karukaya* manuscript, but Sakaguchi Hiroyuki argues that it was originally included within it. Sakaguchi proposes that the "*Kōya no maki*" section was simply dropped (as a time-saving measure, perhaps) from the particular oral performance upon which the illustrated *Karukaya* manuscript was based. Sakaguchi, "Sekkyō *Karukaya* to Kōya denshō," 11.

[39]SNKS *Sekkyōshū*, 54; SNKBT 90:289. In the SNKBT typesetting of the illustrated *Karukaya* manuscript, the "*Kōya no maki*" section is interpolated from the woodblock-printed text of 1631.

[40]Nishiguchi Junko argues that the Japanese Buddhist abhorrence of menstruation emerged in the late Heian and early medieval periods under the influence of Shintō conceptions of ritual purity and pollution. Nishiguchi, *Onna no chikara*, 29–36.

used term for menstruation, *tsuki no sawari*, "monthly obstruction," is itself reminiscent of the phrase "Five Obstructions," *itsutsu no sawari*, and the former is commonly associated with the latter. One point of the *Karukaya* "*Kōya no maki*" story of Kūkai's mother seems to be that although the menopausal old woman has shed the outward signs of her female impurity, when she steps over her son's *kesa*, an act symbolic of her violation of Mount Kōya's *nyonin kinsei*, her true nature is revealed. Her "monthly obstruction" begins to flow as a physical reminder that she and all women, young and old, face the karmic obstructions of their gender. For the innkeeper and for medieval *sekkyō-bushi* audiences, the moral of the story was surely that the forces of nature permit no woman, not even Kūkai's mother, from climbing the mountain. If the monks of Mount Kōya were indeed responsible for circulating this account—and Shinno Toshikazu, for one, proposes that they were[41]—then it should be understood as a kind of male monastic propaganda intended to keep women at bay.[42]

While the *Karukaya* innkeeper's story of Kūkai's mother is the tale of one woman's failure to overcome *nyonin kinsei*, his telling of it results in a second woman's failure as well. The innkeeper asks Akō how she could possibly think of climbing a mountain that "the Master's mother could not even climb,"[43] and she is indeed discouraged from trying. Ishidōmaru proceeds by himself, and Akō, marginalized and demoralized, dies alone at the foot of the mountain awaiting his return. Thus with the aid of their fictional accomplice, the innkeeper, the monks of Mount Kōya appear to have succeeded in one of their probable aims: that of dissuading women—even a fictional one like Akō—from violating the sacred male space of the mountain.

Against this background of threatening *nyonin kinsei* lore, Izumi Shikibu's, Lady Tokiwa's, and Chūjōhime's purported defiance of female exclusions is all the more remarkable. In the maidenflower poem-story, Izumi Shikibu merely voices her dissatisfaction with the *nyonin kinsei* of Mount Hiei, but in the tales of her encounter with Shōkū Shōnin at Enkyōji Temple,

[41]Shinno maintains that both the main *Karukaya* narrative and the independent "*Kōya no maki*" section are likely rooted in the preaching and storytelling of Kōya *hijiri*. Shinno Toshikazu, "Kōbō Daishi no haha: Akoya-gozen no denshō to Shikoku reijō engi," in *Kōbō Daishi shinkō*, ed. Hinonishi Shinjō (Tokyo: Yūzankaku Shuppan, 1988), 96.

[42]It is unclear how effective this propaganda may have been, especially among urban audiences in later centuries. In Ejima Kiseki's *Seken musume katagi* (Sketches of Worldly Young Women), published in 1717, a female character proposes climbing Mount Kōya to tease the monks there; it would be fun, she tells her husband, because they are all so woman-shy. SNKBT 78:399; Howard Hibbett, *The Floating World in Japanese Fiction* (London: Oxford University Press, 1959), 106.

[43]SNKS *Sekkyōshū*, 55; SNKBT 90:290.

she uses her skill as a poet to persuade the holy man to open his temple gate and allow her inside. Thus, though neither a sorceress nor a nun, Izumi Shikibu triumphs where Toran-ni and Kūkai's own mother supposedly failed. Moreover, in that as a result of her disobedience she learns from Shōkū Shōnin that she and other women may circumvent the Five Obstructions by means of the *Lotus Sutra*, her victory constitutes a victory for all women who encounter her tale.

A Hero at Kumano Shrine

To plainly assert that men spread stories of women who were turned to stone for violating *nyonin kinsei* while women spread stories of women challenging *nyonin kinsei* would be overly simplistic. Susan Matisoff, for example, has demonstrated that Kumano *bikuni* may have participated in the dissemination of accounts of Kūkai's mother's preclusion from Mount Kōya (although whether or not this can be traced back as far as the Muromachi period is unclear),[44] and as we have seen in chapter four, the monastic Tendai *dangisho* employed tales of Izumi Shikibu's encounter with Shōkū Shōnin in their efforts to teach the *Lotus Sutra*. Still, it does seem possible to draw some broad gender-based distinctions among storytelling traditions, particularly considering that the Kumano *bikuni* appear to have propagated a tale from at least the sixteenth century of Izumi Shikibu's liberation of women from a misogynistic restriction at the entrance to their own Nachi Kumano Shrine.

Exceedingly little is known about Kumano *bikuni* in the medieval period. According to one of our earliest textual sources of information, Asai Ryōi's *Tōkaidō meishoki* (Record of Famous Places along the Eastern Sea Road; ca. 1661), mendicant nuns (*bikuni*) who made it their practice to visit the Ise and Kumano shrines and perform austerities at those places were called Kumano *bikuni*. Among their ranks were some who raised funds by singing, and some who performed *etoki* picture explaining using "so-called 'Kumano paintings' of hells, heavens, and all the other features of the six realms of existence."[45] The paintings that Asai describes are apparently *Kumano Mind Contemplation Ten Worlds Mandala* (*Kumano kanjin jikkai mandara*), approximately fifty copies

[44]Matisoff, "Barred from Paradise?" 480–83.

[45]Asakura Haruhiko, ed., *Tōkaidō meishoki*, vol. 1, Tōyō bunko 346 (Tokyo: Heibonsha, 1979), 139. Barbara Ruch has translated the larger *Tōkaidō meishoki* passage in "Woman to Woman: *Kumano bikuni* Proselytizers in Medieval and Early Modern Japan," in *Engendering Faith*, 547. As Ruch has shown, not all of the women identified in the seventeenth and later centuries as Kumano *bikuni* were *etoki bikuni*, with which I am concerned here.

of which are known to survive today.[46] A famous scene within the twofold screen painting *Festival at Sumiyoshi Shrine* (*Sumiyoshi Jinja sairei-zu*; ca. 1615–44) in the Freer Gallery of Art in Washington, D.C., depicts a Kumano *bikuni* performing *etoki* upon just such an image (fig. 28).[47] The woman is dressed in traditionally gray clerical robes, and she uses a straw-like pointer to indicate and explain the different scenes in her mounted picture, approximately half of which is devoted to the tortures of hell, to an audience of women and children at a bustling shrine festival. A young assistant sits on the ground beside her, staring up at the painting and holding a *hishaku*, a kind of ladle used for collecting alms.

In addition to preaching upon *Kumano Mind Contemplation Ten Worlds Mandala*, Kumano *bikuni* are believed to have employed *Nachi Pilgrimage Mandala* (*Nachi sankei mandara*) as props in their medieval sermons. These paintings, which Elizabeth ten Grotenhuis maintains became prominent "from the sixteenth century on,"[48] constitute colorful and elaborate representations of the Nachi shrine-complex at Kumano. They contain a multitude of human and mythical figures in a variety of settings and situations, and though distances are not painted to scale, they tend to be reasonably accurate in their portrayal of the physical layout of the shrine. Because these mandala detail the path of a seemingly hypothetical pilgrim-couple through the various sites of the mountain complex and incorporate dramatic scenes from the legendary history of the shrine—the twelfth-century priest Mongaku, for example, immortalized in *The Tale of the Heike* for his performance of winter austerities in the Nachi waterfall, and Retired Emperor Kazan (968–1008) receiving a wish-fulfilling jewel from a dragon deity in the Ichinose River—they seem to have been designed with *etoki* in mind.[49]

[46]Color photos are reproduced in Ikumi Kaminishi, *Explaining Pictures: Buddhist Propaganda and Etoki Storytelling in Japan* (Honolulu: University of Hawaii Press, 2006), plate 8, and in Moerman, *Localizing Paradise*, plate 10. As of November 27, 2005 (the date of a *Kumano kanjin jikkai mandara* conference at the Okayama Library and Prefectural Museum), 49 different *Kumano kanjin jikkai mandara* had been identified; Ogurisu Kenji lists 42 of these in "*Kumano kanjin jikkai mandara* no seiritsu to tenkai," *Hyōgo kenritsu rekishi hakubutsukan kiyō: jinkai* 15 (2004), 133. For a discussion of the mandala in English, see Kuroda Hideo, "The *Kumano kanshin jikkai mandara* and the Lives of the People in Early Modern Japan," in *Practicing the Afterlife: Perspectives from Japan*, ed. Susanne Formanek and William R. LaFleur (Vienna: Osterreichische Akademie der Wissenschaften, 2004), 101–20, and R. Keller Kimbrough, "Preaching the Animal Realm in Late-Medieval Japan," *Asian Folklore Studies* 65, no. 2 (Autumn 2006): 179–204.

[47]Barbara Ruch discusses this and many similar painted scenes in "Woman to Woman," 557–75; Hayashi Masahiko discusses the Sumiyoshi scene in *Zōho Nihon no etoki*, 139 and 144.

[48]Elizabeth ten Grotenhuis, *Japanese Mandalas: Representations of Sacred Geography* (Honolulu: University of Hawaii Press, 1999), 167.

[49]ten Grotenhuis discusses the Mongaku scene in *Japanese Mandalas*, 178-79; Moerman discusses the Kazan scene in *Localizing Paradise*, 174–75.

Fig. 28. A Kumano *bikuni* performing *etoki*. From the *Festival at Sumiyoshi Shrine* screen paintings (*Sumiyoshi Jinja sairei-zu*; ca. 1615–44). Courtesy of the Freer Gallery of Art, Smithsonian Institution, Washington DC. Gift of Charles Lang Freer, F1900.25 (detail).

Tokuda Kazuo has identified a scene in most extant examples of the *Nachi Pilgrimage Mandala* as a pictorial representation of a Muromachi-period story about Izumi Shikibu's sorrow at once having been unable to visit Kumano Shrine because of her menstrual period.[50] Although different versions of the mandala differ in their details, in its overall aspects the painted scene is generally always the same (fig. 29). A woman (Izumi Shikibu) stands beside a cherry tree at Ninose Bridge, just below the confluence of the Ichinose and

[50]The mandala survives in at least 29 copies, 22 of which Tokuda was able to investigate. Of these, 18 (including the oldest three, dating from the late sixteenth century) contain the scene that Tokuda associates with the Izumi Shikibu account. Tokuda Kazuo, "Kumano ni mōderu Izumi Shikibu," *Nihon no bigaku* 25 (1997), 78. Eight of the mandala (six of which contain the apparent Izumi Shikibu scene) are reproduced in Osaka Shiritsu Hakubutsukan, ed., *Shaji sankei mandara*, plates 1–5 and 7–9.

Nachi rivers at the entrance to Nachi Kumano Shrine.[51] As Tokuda explains it, the river functions within the painting as a natural boundary between the sacred inner precincts of the shrine-complex and the profane world outside, and Izumi Shikibu hesitates to cross over into the holy grounds because of the sudden onset of her "monthly obstruction."[52]

The earliest textual rendition of this Izumi Shikibu account is contained in the poetic anthology *Fūga wakashū* (Collection of Elegant Verse), completed in the second month of 1349 by retired emperor Kōgon, some ten years before *Shinsenzai wakashū* (which, as we have seen, contains the Izumi Shikibu "maidenflower" poem-story).[53] The account is cited within an explanatory note to poem 2099, attributed to the Kumano Deity:

> When Izumi Shikibu visited Kumano, she was unable to present her offering to the deity because of her [monthly] obstruction. She recited a poem:
>
> | | |
> |---|---|
> | hareyaranu | The sad, drifting clouds |
> | mi no ukigumo no | of my body |
> | tanabikite | trail the sky, unlifting, |
> | tsuki no sawari to | now obstructing the moon. |
> | naru zo kanashiki | How sad! |
>
> It is said that in her dream that night, [the Kumano Deity] recited this poem in reply:
>
> | | |
> |---|---|
> | moto yori mo | By my nature |
> | chiri ni majiwaru | I am a god |
> | kami nareba | who mingles with the dust. |
> | tsuki no sawari mo | What could bother me about |
> | nani ga kurushiki | the monthly obstruction?[54] |

[51]Some exceptions include a mandala in the possession of Shōgakuji Temple in Wakayama Prefecture, in which the woman is accompanied by a maidservant; a mandala in the former collection of Kibitsu Shrine in Okayama Prefecture, in which the woman sits instead of stands; and a mandala in the Ōshajō Art Museum, in which the cherry tree is replaced by a cedar. Tokuda, "Kumano ni mōderu Izumi Shikibu," 78 and 80.

[52]In a mandala in the possession of the Takehisa family in Okayama Prefecture, the woman is shown standing on the far side of the first bridge, where she has already crossed the river. Osaka Shiritsu Hakubutsukan, ed., *Shaji sankei mandara*, plate 5.

[53]The compilation of *Fūga wakashū* was traditionally attributed to Emperor Hanazono (1297–1348), but it is now thought to have been largely compiled by Kōgon (1313–64) under Hanazono's supervision. Tsugita Kasumi, "*Fūga wakashū*," in *Koten bungaku daijiten*, vol. 5, 214–15.

[54]Tsugita Kasumi and Iwasa Miyoko, eds., *Fūga wakashū* (Tokyo: Miyai Shoten, 1974), 395. I have reversed the order of the two poems for the sake of clarity. In *Fūga wakashū*, the Kumano Deity's verse is cited first and the explanatory note (containing Izumi Shikibu's poem) follows.

Fig. 29. Izumi Shikibu (right) at the entrance to Nachi Kumano Shrine. Detail from the Kokugakuin *Nachi Pilgrimage Mandala Scroll* (*Nachi sankei mandara emaki*; sixteenth century). Courtesy of Kokugakuin University.

The *Fūga wakashū* story, which presumably corresponds to an oral tradition of the Kumano *bikuni*, suggests that had Izumi Shikibu not been suffering from her monthly obstruction, she would have been able to visit the shrine and present her offering to the deity. Her visit is not prevented by a *nyonin kinsei* rule *per se*, but rather by a related Shintō taboo against menstruation (according to medieval Japanese syncretic thought, there seems to have been little difference between the two).[55] In her poem, Izumi Shikibu draws upon the double meanings of *uki* ("sad" and "drifting") and *tsuki no sawari* ("monthly obstruction" and "moon obstruction," i.e., "clouds") to state that the "sad, drifting clouds" of her femininity gather densely every month, becoming her monthly obstruction and blocking the light of the moon—a

[55]The Shintō view of menstruation as a source of ritual pollution may have existed by the early eighth century, or it may have developed later, in the early-to-mid Heian period. Donald Philippi, *Kojiki* (Tokyo: University of Tokyo Press, 1968), 245, note 5; Nishiguchi Junko, *Onna no chikara*, 29–31; Karen Smyers, "Women and Shinto: The Relation Between Purity and Pollution," *Japanese Religions* 12, no. 4 (July 1983): 7–18.

traditional metaphor for Buddhist Truth. Because it prevents her from visiting Kumano Shrine, her monthly obstruction is a true moon obstruction, darkening her way on the Path of the Buddha.

The compiler of the *setsuwa* anthology *Kohon setsuwa shū* (An Old Collection of Tales; twelfth or thirteenth century) observes that "whether reverent or base, people's prayers are effective when they are most heartfelt,"[56] and indeed, Izumi Shikibu's poem impels a response. The Kumano Deity, commonly identified as a manifestation of Amida,[57] appears to her in a dream that night, and in a verse of his own he explains that because he is descended from the heavens to "mingle with the dust"—to associate freely with sentient beings in order to lead them to salvation—the impurity of her monthly obstruction causes him no offense. And even if it should gather like clouds and obstruct the moon, he seems to ask, how could it block his own light when he himself is descended to earth? In this way the Kumano Deity declares the monthly obstruction to be no obstruction at all; thanks to Izumi Shikibu, he disavows the menstrual taboo at Kumano Shrine while simultaneously affirming all women's spiritual potential.

A variant of the Izumi Shikibu/Kumano poem-story is contained in the mid-to-late fourteenth-century *Shintō shū* (A Shintō Compendium), a collection of Shintō doctrines, histories of shrines, and biographies of Japanese deities compiled at around the same time as *Fūga wakashū*.[58] The anthology is marked by a prominent Shintō-Buddhist syncretism characteristic of medieval religious thought, and it seems to have been produced at the Agui monastic center in Kyoto (affiliated with Enryakuji Temple on Mount Hiei) from both written and oral sources. Kishi Shōzō has argued that *Shintō shū* was intended for use as a sermon sourcebook for the priests of Agui, who were renowned in the medieval period for their fine preaching and storytelling.[59] This would suggest that the Kumano poem-story was employed by male as well as female proselytizer-entertainers in medieval Japan.

In the following version of the story (*Shintō shū* 5:26), the female protagonist is identified as a daughter of Emperor Takakura (r. 1168–80), rather than Izumi Shikibu. Compared to their renditions in *Fūga wakashū*, the poems are

[56]SNKBT 42:463.

[57]*Fūga wakashū* does not state which of the three main Kumano deities appeared in Izumi Shikibu's dream. By default, it was probably Ketsumiko no Mikoto, deity of the Hongū central shrine, who is associated with Amida.

[58]The *Shintō shū "kohonkei"* textual line contains dates corresponding to the years 1354 and 1358, and the work is thought to have been compiled soon after that. Murakami Manabu, "*Shintō shū*," in *Nihon koten bungaku daijiten*, vol. 3, 499.

[59]Kishi Shōzō, "Kaisetsu," in *Shintō shū*, Tōyō bunko 94 (Tokyo: Heibonsha, 1967), 300–9. Agui burned in the Ōnin Disturbance of 1467–77 and was never rebuilt.

different as well, suggesting that the account circulated orally before it was recorded in either (or both) of these fourteenth-century works:

> A daughter of [Emperor] Takakura once set out for Kumano. When she reached a place called Fujishiro,[60] she began having her monthly period, as women are wont to do. In deep sorrow she recited:

moto yori mo	The fivefold clouds
itsue no kumo no	lay thick from the start,
atsukereba	and now
tsuki no sawari to	they obstruct the moon.
naru zo kanashiki	How sad!

> An old monk appeared beside her pillow as she slept that night, and he replied:

amakudari	Descended from the heavens
chiri ni majiwaru	I am
ware nareba	to mingle with the dust.
tsuki no sawari wa	What could bother me about
nani ga kurushiki	the monthly obstruction?

> Her menstruation suddenly ceased, and with no further hindrance she was able to visit the shrine.[61]

In her poem, the unnamed daughter of Emperor Takakura equates her monthly obstruction with the Five Obstructions by referring to it as a "five-layered cloud." As in the corresponding *Fūga wakashū* account, the Kumano Deity responds with a verse disclaiming the menstrual taboo. In addition

[60]Fujishiro is now a part of Kainan City in modern Wakayama Prefecture, near the central (Hongū) Kumano Shrine.

[61]Shintō Taikei Hensankai, ed., *Shintō taikei: bungaku hen 1: Shintōshū* (Tokyo: Shintō Taikei Hensankai, 1988), 148 (Akagi Bunko manuscript in the *kohonkei* textual line). Tokuda notes that the *Fūga wakashū* and *Shintō shū* accounts may be related to the following story in *Fukurozōshi*, compiled by Fujiwara no Kiyosuke ca. 1157–58. Otonashi River runs near the main Kumano Shrine:

Otonashi no	Though Otonashi River
kawa no nagare wa	runs shallow,
asakeredo	by the depth
tsumi no fukasa ni	of my transgressions
e koso watarane	I am unable to cross.

> A woman went to visit Kumano, but she was turned back at Otonashi River. In tears she recited this poem, after which she was allowed to proceed.

In the Tsukuba University Library text (upon which the SNKBT *Fukurozōshi* volume is based), the third line of the poem reads "*mizu no fukasa ni*," "by the depth of the water" (SNKBT 29:157). "*Tsumi no fukasa ni*" ("by the depth of [my] transgressions") is from the National Diet Library text, reproduced in Ozawa Masao et al., eds., *Fukurozōshi chūshaku*, vol. 1 (Tokyo: Hanawa Shobō, 1974), 472, and quoted in Tokuda, "Kumano ni mōderu Izumi Shikibu," 81a.

(and somewhat paradoxically), he puts an end to her period, metaphorically curing her of her spiritual impediments. The contrast with the story of Kūkai's mother in the sermon-ballad *Karukaya* could not be more striking: whereas the elderly woman begins to menstruate when she violates the *nyonin kinsei* of Mount Kōya, Takakura's daughter is miraculously relieved of her menstrual cycle and allowed to proceed.

In the Heian period, clouds came to be employed in *waka* as a conventional metaphor for the Five Obstructions; poems that speak of "five," "fivefold," or "five-layered" clouds, while signifying those same obstructions, tended to be more explicit.[62] Edward Kamens has described the "literary language of poetic figuration" in traditional court poetry as a kind of metonymic "code," an elaborate system in which "things are so often represented by other things, where one word is so often not only substituted for another but also made to *be* another (at least contingently) even while it is still itself."[63] As likely remnants of a fourteenth-century storytelling/proselytizing tradition, the *Fūga wakashū* and *Shintō shū* Kumano accounts allow us to indirectly observe the dissemination of this elite literary language—this privileged poetic code—to society at large by medieval preacher-entertainers. Exactly who these storytellers were is a subject of speculation. Some possibilities include the monks and nuns of the Ji sect, whom Tokuda posits were responsible for associating Izumi Shikibu with a preexisting version of the Kumano account;[64] the preachers of Agui, in whose anthology a non-Izumi Shikibu version is reproduced; and the Kumano *bikuni*, assuming that Tokuda is correct in identifying the Kumano poem-story with the scene in the *Nachi Pilgrimage Mandala*.

But how, we might ask, is Tokuda able to identify these early Kumano accounts with the painting of the woman in the sixteenth- and seventeenth-century *Nachi Pilgrimage Mandala*? Tokuda cites a passage from *Hokishō* (Notes on a Votive Urn), a late Muromachi-period commentary on calendrical science, to demonstrate the story as it may have circulated in the years in which the mandala was most widely reproduced. According to *Hokishō*, the woman at Kumano was an unnamed "lady of the palace." Her poem and the deity's response are generally the same as in the earlier versions of their tale, but in *Hokishō*, the woman composes an additional verse:

sakuraki no	Is it because
sono inishie wo	it does not forget its past

[62]Kamens, "Dragon-Girl, Maidenflower, Buddha," 405–10.

[63]Edward Kamens, *Utamakura, Allusion, and Intertextuality in Traditional Japanese Poetry* (New Haven and London: Yale University Press, 1997), 39.

[64]Tokuda, "Kumano ni mōderu Izumi Shikibu," 82.

wasurezu wa	that the cherry,
sugi ni narite mo	now turned to cedar,
hana ya sakuran	blossoms anew?[65]

The significance of the poem—the meaning of the cherry-turned-to-cedar—is unknown. However, the inclusion of the verse in the *Hokishō* Kumano account (and in another textual source from 1721, in which the woman is explicitly identified as Izumi Shikibu)[66] suggests a connection between this later version of the story and the painted image of the woman beside the cherry tree (in one version of the mandala, a cedar) in the *Nachi Pilgrimage Mandala*.

Little is known with any certainty about Kumano *bikuni* and the circumstances of their *etoki* performances, but based on evidence from a variety of textual and pictorial sources, including paintings employed by the nuns themselves, scholars tend to agree that Kumano *bikuni* preached largely to audiences of women.[67] If it is indeed true that the painted scene in the *Nachi Pilgrimage Mandala* was interpreted for medieval audiences as depicting Izumi Shikibu (or some other woman) exchanging poems with the Kumano Deity, then it would suggest that women—Kumano *bikuni*—were telling tales to other women about how a woman (Izumi Shikibu) once used a poem to overcome her monthly obstruction and gain access to Nachi Kumano Shrine.[68] Al-

[65]Quoted in Tokuda, "Kumano ni mōderu Izumi Shikibu," 83b. The third line of the poem actually reads "*imarezu wa*" ("does not abhor"). I follow Tokuda's supposition that *imarezu* is a mistake for *wasurezu* ("does not forget").

[66]The source is *Kumano sōsō yurai zasshō* (Miscellaneous Notes on the History of Early Kumano), cited in Tokuda, "Kumano ni mōderu Izumi Shikibu," 84b.

[67]Hagiwara Tatsuo goes so far as to write that Kumano *bikuni*'s audiences were "overwhelmingly female." Hagiwara Tatsuo, *Miko to Bukkyō shi: Kumano bikuni no shimei to tenkai* (Tokyo: Yoshikawa Kōbunkan, 1983), 60. Also see Kuroda Hideo, "*Kumano kanjin jikkai mandara* no uchū," in *Bukkyō to Nihonjin, vol. 8: sei to mibun*, ed. Miyata Noboru (Tokyo: Shunjūsha, 1989), 252–62; and Hayashi, *Zōho Nihon no etoki*, 138–41.

[68]There is further evidence that Kumano *bikuni* employed Izumi Shikibu's name and poetry in their medieval *etoki* performances. Hagiwara Tatsuo describes a surviving *Kumano Mind Contemplation Ten Worlds Mandala* with paper slips—apparent *etoki* reminder notes—pasted to individual scenes. One of these reads, "Izumi Shikibu saw a transformation-tableau painting of hell (*jigoku hensō e*). Sensing [the nature of] karma, she composed a poem:

asamashi ya	How frightening!
tsurugi no eda no	[Tortured] until
tawamu made	the sword-branches bend—
nani no ko no mi no	from what tree's seed (what karma?)
nareru naruramu	could such things arise?"

Hagiwara writes that although this paper slip is now attached to the top of the mandala, it seems to have been formerly affixed to the image of the Sword-forest Hell. Hagiwara, *Bukkyō to Nihonjin*, 87. The poem is a variant of *Kinyō wakashū* 644, attributed to Izumi Shikibu with the headnote, "Composed when she saw a person impaled upon branches of swords in a painting of hell." SNKBT 9:190.

though it would be naive to simply assume women's agency in a premodern discourse of women's liberation, insofar as Izumi Shikibu (or the daughter of Emperor Takakura) surmounts the seemingly insurmountable obstacle of her femininity in every recorded version of the account, invariably prompting the Kumano Deity to liberate all women from the misogynistic restriction against menstrual pollution at Kumano Shrine, she is likely to have been portrayed in *etoki* as a true hero for women.

Reconstructing the oral storytelling traditions of such groups of women proselytizer-entertainers as the Kumano *bikuni* (and, even more problematically, the nuns of Seiganji) is fraught with difficulty. Because their *etoki* sermons have been lost to time, the best that we can do is to identify scenes in their painted props with contemporary written accounts, and hope that the differences are not too extreme. Nevertheless, it is possible by such methods to extrapolate some parts of what were likely the performance repertoires of these women raconteurs, and the reconstructions are intriguing. To cite but one example, Barbara Ruch has observed that in depictions of the Blood Pool Hell in *Kumano Mind Contemplation Ten Worlds Mandala*, Nyoirin Kannon is shown rescuing women from the notorious bloody lake. Ruch argues that this suggests that Kumano *bikuni* innovated upon existing accounts of the Blood Pool Hell in order to emphasize women's salvation, rather than their damnation, "providing women listeners with compassion, comfort, and immediate remedy."[69]

Though convincing, Ruch's argument is a tricky one, because, as Bernard Faure rightly observes, "even if they simultaneously preached deliverance from these hells and rebirth in the Pure Land, [Kumano *bikuni*] were nonetheless instrumental in spreading the fear of the Blood Pond Hell among women."[70] By promising salvation from the Blood Pool Hell rather than denying its existence or ignoring it altogether, Kumano *bikuni* would have unwittingly enforced prevailing notions of female sin, and thus, in Faure's words, "contributed to the subjection of women to Buddhist male ideology."[71] Faure makes an important point, but it should be kept in mind that rather than simply depicting the Blood Pool Hell, *Kumano Mind Contemplation Ten Worlds Mandala* show women being *rescued* from that hell (fig. 30). Like *nyonin kinsei*, the Blood Pool Hell is a common motif in late-medieval fiction (as we shall see in the following chapter), demonstrating its signifi-

[69]Ruch, "Woman to Woman," 574. For more on the Blood Pool Hell, see pp. 230–33, below.

[70]Bernard Faure, *The Power of Denial: Buddhism, Purity, and Gender* (Princeton and Oxford: Princeton University Press, 2003), 78.

[71]Ibid., 78. Also see Moerman, *Localizing Paradise*, 230–31.

Fig. 30. Nyoirin Kannon rescuing women from the Blood Pool Hell. Detail from the Rokudō Chinnōji *Kumano Mind Contemplation Ten Worlds Mandala* (*Kumano kanjin jikkai mandara*; seventeenth century). Courtesy of Ogurisu Kenji and Rokudō Chinnōji Temple.

cance as a topic in the popular religious discourse of the sixteenth and seventeenth centuries. Just as Kumano *bikuni* appear to have raised the specter of women's exclusion from Kumano Shrine for the sake of denying it (in the case of their apparent preaching upon the Izumi Shikibu scene in the *Nachi Pilgrimage Mandala*, that is), the painted scene of women's salvation from the Blood Pool Hell suggests that Kumano *bikuni* preached upon the Blood Pool Hell as a means of diminishing it.

While Kumano *bikuni* and other female proselytizers were obviously and perhaps unavoidably complicit in propagating aspects of traditional Buddhist misogyny, they were simultaneously engaged in its subversion. Their message—a mixed message, from our contemporary point of view—is not unlike that of the Seiganji Amida in *Rakuyō Seiganji engi*, who celebrates Lady Vaidehī's achievement of Pure Land rebirth "without having her filthy femininity transformed." Like the Seiganji Amida (and the narrator of the *Sangoku denki* Izumi Shikibu account, for that matter), Kumano *bikuni* were pro-woman within an overwhelmingly misogynistic context; if we are to judge them for their service to the cause of women in Buddhist ideology, then we need to do so with an appropriately historical consideration of their place within the larger discourse of the time. As we have seen, while men in some monastic orders may have propounded tales intended to intimidate or demoralize women in Buddhism, Kumano *bikuni* and other groups of women and men seemingly resisted with their own stories of Izumi Shikibu and other female figures who were able to overcome gender proscriptions and live on, in legend, as proto-feminist, poetic champions of medieval Japan.

Chapter Eight
Sex and Salvation: Izumi Shikibu and *The Tale of Jōruri*

According to an account in Kokan Shiren's *Genkō shakusho* (A History of Buddhism to the Genkō Era; completed in 1322), the eighth-century Empress Kōmyō, a devout patron of Buddhism renowned for the construction of the Hokkeji, Tōdaiji, and Kokubunji temples, once erected a bathhouse and pronounced a vow to wash the dirt from the bodies of one thousand men.[1] The empress's heroic deed, undertaken in response to a miraculous command from the sky, is best understood as a metaphor for her efforts to cleanse the people of their intangible spiritual impurities. A putrid leper is said to have appeared before her as her final, one-thousandth guest, and to have requested that she first bathe him and then suck the pus from his many festering sores. The empress's consternation is likely to have been severe, considering that the symptoms of lepromatous leprosy include facial disfiguration, crippling deformations, and stinking ulcerations in the mouth and mucous membranes; as Catherine Peyroux explains, in its final stages the disease's effects on the body suggest "walking death, or life animating a rotting corpse."[2] Still, the empress is said to have agreed to her repulsive visitor's bizarre request, demonstrating the depth of her compassion and her commitment to her vow.

The story of Empress Kōmyō and the leper was well known in medieval Japan. As a native counterpart to Indian *jātaka* tales of the self-sacrifices of the Buddha Shakyamuni in his former lives, it was employed in preaching and fund-raising and reproduced in numerous written texts and Tōdaiji

[1]Kuroita Katsumi, ed., *Shintei zōho kokushi taikei*, vol. 31 (Tokyo: Yoshikawa Kōbunkan, 1930), 261. The account is translated in Marian Ury, "Nuns and Other Female Devotees in *Genkō shakusho* (1322), Japan's First History of Buddhism," in *Engendering Faith: Women and Buddhism in Premodern Japan*, ed. Barbara Ruch (Ann Arbor: University of Michigan Center for Japanese Studies, 2002), 194–95; and in Marian Ury, "*Genkō shakusho*: Japan's First Comprehensive History of Buddhism," Ph.D. dissertation (University of California at Berkeley, 1971), 313–15.

[2]Catherine Peyroux, "The Leper's Kiss," in *Monks & Nuns, Saints & Outcastes: Religion in Medieval Society*, ed. Sharon Farmer and Barbara H. Rosenwein (Ithaca and London: Cornell University Press, 2000), 177.

temple paintings from the Kamakura period on.[3] A most unusual recreation of the story—one that literalizes the latent erotic implications of the *Genkō shakusho* account—is contained within a single manuscript of the *otogizōshi Jōruri monogatari* (The Tale of Jōruri) in the former collection of the Akagi Bunko archive.[4] Rather than Empress Kōmyō, it concerns Izumi Shikibu and her fulfillment of a vow to achieve sexual union with one thousand men, the last of whom, as in the case of the former empress, is said to have posed a particular challenge. Considering Izumi Shikibu's widespread use in Buddhist proselytizing and storytelling, as well as her popular medieval reputation for lasciviousness, she seems to have been ideally suited to the tale.

Jōruri monogatari, the performative recitations from which the early-modern *jōruri* puppet theater takes its name, is rooted in the fifteenth- and sixteenth-century storytelling activities of a variety of monks, nuns and other entertainers, including *biwa hōshi* (mendicant *biwa*-playing priests), some of whom sang it in addition to *The Tale of the Heike*.[5] Although of questionable didactic content, the Izumi Shikibu account may have been recited by medieval proselytizer-entertainers as an independent narrative, which was only later incorporated into the larger frame of the *otogizōshi*. A caustic speech by a dirty beggar midway through the account suggests as much, because of its striking similarity, both in structure and content, to late-medieval polemics on the sorry plight of women in Buddhism. Rajyashree Pandey has observed that the story may contain "traces of the heretic [Shingon] Tachikawa teachings, which held sex as the highest form of Buddhist practice,"[6] but there is no way now to tell.

[3]Pictorial representations are contained in the late Kamakura-period *Tōdaiji engi* hanging scrolls (the relevant section of which is reproduced in Ury, "Nuns and Other Female Devotees in *Genkō shakusho*," 195), and in the Muromachi-period *Daibutsu engi*, in Nara Kokuritsu Hakubutsukan, ed., *Shaji engi-e* (Tokyo: Kadokawa Shoten, 1975), 323b. Abe Yasurō discusses the use of the Kōmyō account in medieval preaching and fund-raising, and he traces the tale to an early rendition in *Kenkyū gojunreiki*, composed in 1191. Abe Yasurō, "Yuya no kōgō: Kōmyō Kōgō yusegyō no monogatari wo megurite," *Bungaku* 54–55, nos. 11 and 1 (1986 and 1987): 76–87 and 79–92.

[4]*Jōruri monogatari* (also known as *Jōruri-gozen monogatari*, *Jūnidan sōshi*, and simply *Jōruri*) survives in numerous manuscripts and textual lines. The Izumi Shikibu account is contained within the three-scroll Akagi Bunko *emaki* (titled *Jōruri*), which dates from the late Muromachi period, in MJMT 7:316–19, and in Mori Takenosuke, *Jōruri monogatari kenkyū* (Tokyo: Inoue Shobō, 1962), 36–41.

[5]Shinoda Jun'ichi, "*Jōruri-gozen monogatari*," in *Koten bungaku daijiten*, vol. 3, ed. Nihon Koten Bungaku Daijiten Henshū Iinkai (Tokyo: Iwanami Shoten, 1984), 398–99.

[6]Rajyashree Pandey, "Poetry, Sex and Salvation: The 'Courtesan' and the Noblewoman in Medieval Japanese Narratives," *Japanese Studies* 24, no. 1 (May 2004), 77. On the history of the Tachikawa sect, see Susan Klein, *Allegories of Desire: Esoteric Literary Commentaries of Medieval Japan* (Cambridge and London: Harvard University Asia Center, 2002), 150–53.

Though seemingly absurd, the Izumi Shikibu story is in fact emblematic of a larger body of Japanese Buddhist works, principally from the Tendai and esoteric traditions, that seek to equate the sacred and the profane. Despite frequent Buddhist pronouncements against lasciviousness—Taira no Yasuyori, for example, states in his twelfth-century Buddhist *setsuwa* anthology *Hōbutsushū* (A Collection of Treasures) that for a man to sleep but once with a woman is to be condemned to the cycle of birth and death for five hundred ages[7]—the association in medieval literature of promiscuity and the divine is a common one. As we have seen in chapter one, Ono no Komachi is reported in the *otogizōshi Komachi no sōshi* to have been involved with at least one thousand men and to have been a manifestation of Nyoirin Kannon, and Ariwara no Narihira is said in the *Ise monogatari* commentary *Waka chikenshū* to have slept with 3,733 women and to have been Batō Kannon. Strange as they may sound, such assertions are not without doctrinal foundation. As Ryuichi Abe has observed, chapter ten of the *Greater Prajñā-pāramitā Sutra* itself "illustrates the intrinsic purity of all things by radically describing such acts of passion as lovemaking as pure stages of Bodhisattva practice."[8] Though a lurid and facetious work of Muromachi fiction, the Izumi Shikibu account is thus notable for its jumbled and highly imaginative revelation of truths expressed in more "serious" (orthodox) Buddhist texts.

Izumi Shikibu's Vow

The Izumi Shikibu account is a story within a story, a tale told by the fifteen-year-old Minamoto no Yoshitsune (1159–89) in his efforts to seduce the lovely Jōruri-hime, the fourteen-year-old daughter of the governor of Mikawa province.[9] Although the historical Yoshitsune is best remembered for his daring in the twelfth-century Genpei War, the fictional Yoshitsune of *Jōruri monogatari* is here overcome with love. He creeps into Jōruri-hime's mansion in the night, where, with the aid of a maidservant, he discovers her asleep. He wakes her and tells her of his feelings, but Jōruri-hime asks him to leave. Undaunted, Yoshitsune presses his suit by citing numerous examples of lovers, and love refused, from the past. In a passage immediately preceding his

[7]SNKBT 40:205.

[8]Ryuichi Abe, *The Weaving of Mantra: Kūkai and the Construction of Esoteric Buddhist Discourse* (New York: Columbia University Press, 1999), 248.

[9]Yoshitsune's and Jōruri-hime's ages are given according to traditional Japanese calculations, by which a child is considered one year old at birth. Age subsequently increases by one at the start of each calendar year. For a synopsis of *Jōruri monogatari* in English, see Helen McCullough, *Yoshitsune: A Fifteenth-Century Japanese Chronicle* (Stanford: Stanford University Press, 1966), 47–50.

Izumi Shikibu account, he threatens Jōruri-hime with the possibility that she will become a blue demon in this life and wander lost on Mount Tsurugi (a mountain of swords in hell) in the next if she continues to deny him.[10] Still, the young woman resists:

> The young master's heart was drawn to her all the more, and he spoke on without pause:
>
> You know of course that the Way of Love has never expired, not in all the past until now. An outstanding woman was once born into the world, a great beauty and a poet by the name of Izumi Shikibu. Countless men lost their hearts to her, and she became the wife of the master of the Kyōgoku Estate.[11] The adoration of those around her was quite beyond words.
>
> Izumi Shikibu once visited the Tōdaiji and Kōfukuji temples in order to perform memorial services for her late mother and father. She spent one week at each praying for her parents' enlightenment, and in the early morning twilight of the final day, her mother and father appeared before her where she slept. "You have diligently performed these many services so that we might attain enlightenment," they said, "but Buddhahood remains beyond our reach. This is because you were born an outstanding beauty and a poet, and countless men have lost their hearts to you. You spurned their love and we have fallen into hell as a result. We implore you to take a vow to love all men, without distinction, from the highest to the lowest. Should you do this, it is without doubt that we and you both will attain Buddhahood in this very existence."
>
> Izumi Shikibu awoke. "The karma from my past must be wretched," she thought to herself. "After all the services I performed . . . how awful that my parents haven't achieved Buddhahood!" Deciding to abandon her feminine charms so that she might better pray for their enlightenment, she set about cutting her luxuriant hair. Amida Buddha was touched with pity, and so at that very moment, just as Izumi Shikibu was on the verge of making the first cut, he appeared to her in the form of an eighty-year-old monk. "Here you are about to change your looks for your parents' sake," he said, "but it will be to no avail. If you want to help them, you should take a vow to love all men, without distinction, from the highest to the lowest. If you do this, it is without doubt that both you and your parents will attain Buddhahood in this very existence." The monk vanished into the air.

[10]MJMT 7:316a; Mori, *Jōruri monogatari kenkyū*, 36.

[11]"Kyōgoku Estate" (*Kyōgoku-dono*) refers to one of several mansions facing East Kyōgoku Avenue in the Heian capital. The most famous of these, the Tsuchimikado Kyōgoku-dono, belonged to Fujiwara no Michinaga (966–1027), in whose daughter's salon Izumi Shikibu served as a lady-in-waiting.

As Izumi Shikibu's dead mother and father explain to her in a dream, by unwittingly winning the affections of innumerable men and leaving their desires unfulfilled, Izumi Shikibu has committed a terrible transgression. Her sin is a common one in medieval literature, in which women are frequently held accountable for male desire and its consequences—most notoriously, as we have seen in chapter three, in the tale of Ono no Komachi and Fukakusa no Shii no Shōshō, the Fourth-Rank Lesser Captain. According to a version of their story in the *otogizōshi Komachi monogatari* (The Tale of Komachi), Ono no Komachi caused the deaths of 18,099 of her suitors, including the Fourth-Rank Lesser Captain, by callously ignoring their love. Together with the accumulated grief of the families of the 18,099 murdered men, the Captain's angry spirit attached itself to Komachi and drove her insane.[12] In the *otogizōshi Izumi Shikibu*, Izumi Shikibu decides to sleep with Dōmyō based upon what she had heard of Komachi, and in the noh play *Inari* (composed prior to 1518), it is Izumi Shikibu's own refusal to sleep with a lovesick peasant boy that causes the boy's death and postmortem attack, as a disembodied spirit, on Izumi Shikibu's daughter Koshikibu.[13]

In *Jōruri monogatari*, Yoshitsune is careful to remind Jōruri-hime of Komachi's madness and the reason for it.[14] Within his story, Izumi Shikibu finds herself confronted with the devastating effects of her own good looks, and she decides to take drastic action to aid her parents. With the stated intention of abandoning her female charms, she sets about cutting her hair. In Heian and medieval society, a woman's hair was the symbol of both her beauty and her ties to the secular world, and in her readiness to cut her own locks, Izumi Shikibu demonstrates her willingness to perform the symbolic act of self-mutilation necessary to become a nun. By this act of ritual disfigurement, Izumi Shikibu would render herself unattractive to men, thereby releasing them from her spell. The logic is universal. Medieval Christian hagiography abounds in tales of women's self-mutilation—whether by gouging out their eyes, lacerating their faces, or cutting off their noses and upper

[12]MJMT 5:135b–36a; Sarah Strong, "Komachi at the Crossroads: Elements of Popular Female Performance in Two Nō Plays," *Proceedings of the Midwest Association for Japanese Literary Studies* 3 (Summer 1997), 135–36. *Komachi monogatari* (also known as *Shinpan Komachi no sōshi*) survives in several copies of a single woodblock-printed text produced by the Urokogataya publishing house in Edo ca. 1688–1710.

[13]Yoshida Kōichi, ed., *Izumi Shikibu zenshū: honbun hen* (Tokyo: Koten Bunko, 1959), 762–64 (Yoshida refers to *Inari* by its alternate title, *Izumi Shikibu*).

[14]MJMT 7:312b (Akagi Bunko manuscript); SNKS *Otogizōshi*, 47 (Tōdai Library *kokatsuji hanpon* text). In *The Tale of Genji*, the frustrated Genji similarly threatens Fujitsubo by suggesting that her denial of his love will cause his death and then become an obstacle on his path to salvation. And for this, he warns, Fujitsubo will be to blame. NKBZ 13:104; Edward Seidensticker, *The Tale of Genji* (New York, Alfred A. Knopf, 1976), 197–98.

lips—all for the purpose of discouraging male desire. While Izumi Shikibu's intended act is less extreme, it is nonetheless an example of what Jane Schulenburg has described, in the context of medieval European traditions, as "the heroics of virginity."[15]

Moved to pity by Izumi Shikibu's noble intentions (or so Yoshitsune would have us believe), Amida Buddha appears in the form of an eighty-year-old monk. Unlike the Seiganji Amida in *Rakuyō Seiganji engi*, who merely councils Izumi Shikibu to recite the *nenbutsu*, this Amida urges Izumi Shikibu to take the vow suggested by her parents to "love all men, without distinction, from the highest to the lowest," in order to rescue her parents from hell. Although Amida's rationale is left unexplained, logic would suggest that in order to undo the wickedness of having aroused and then ignored the spiritually obstructive desires of mankind, Izumi Shikibu would need to assuage those desires, or at least make a good-faith effort to do so. However, this course of action is a strange one for Amida to suggest, if for no other reason than that Izumi Shikibu would be relying upon *jiriki*, "self-power," rather than *tariki*, "Amida's power" (literally, "other power"), to achieve Buddhahood for her parents and herself. Still, self-sacrifice is the bodhisattva way, and in this sense Izumi Shikibu's task is not without precedent. According to an account in the thirteenth-century *Shinran muki* (A Record of Shinran's Dream), the Kannon of Rokkakudō Temple once appeared in the dream of Shinran (1173–1262), progenitor of the Shin sect of Pure Land Buddhism, and promised to take on the form of a beautiful woman in order to satisfy the carnal cravings of devotees distracted by sexual desire.[16] Similarly, the *setsuwa* anthologies *Nihon ryōiki* (Record of Miracles in Japan; ca. 787) and *Konjaku monogatari shū* contain a story of how, during the reign of Emperor Shōmu (r. 724–49), a clay statue of the goddess Kichijōten at a mountain temple in Izumi province gave herself to a man who prayed that he might lie with a woman.[17]

As the *Jōruri monogatari* account continues, Izumi Shikibu takes leave of her husband and relocates to Fifth Avenue, well known in the late medieval

[15]Jane Tibbetts Schulenburg, "The Heroics of Virginity: Brides of Christ and Sacrificial Mutilation," in *Women in the Middle Ages and the Renaissance: Literary and Historical Perspectives*, ed. Mary Beth Rose (Syracuse: Syracuse University Press, 1986).

[16]*Shinran muki* was composed by Shinran's disciple Shinbutsu (1209–58). It is translated in James Dobbins, *Jōdo Shinshū: Shin Buddhism in Medieval Japan* (Bloomington: Indiana University Press, 1989), 24; and in Endō Hajime, "The Original Bōmori: Husband and Wife Congregations in Early Shin Buddhism," trans. James Dobbins, in *Engendering Faith*, 506.

[17]*Nihon ryōiki* 2:13 (SNKBT 30:81); *Konjaku monogatari shū* 17:45 (SNKBT 36:87–88). The man is said to have slept with the goddess in a dream, and to have later discovered her image stained at the skirt.

period for its many prostitutes.[18] As in *Kotohara*, the *otogizōshi Izumi Shikibu* and other medieval sources, Izumi Shikibu is again cast in the role of a *yūjo*. But rather than selling herself for money, she exchanges sex for Buddhist merit with which to save her parents:

> Izumi Shikibu took leave of the Kyōgoku Estate, erected a shack on Fifth Avenue in the capital, and hung out a placard proclaiming her intention to achieve intimacy with one thousand men. As she was truly very beautiful, in three years and three months she had entertained nine hundred ninety-nine men who had loved her from before. "Tonight my vow comes to an end," she thought on the thousandth night, the final night. "I don't know who my master will be this evening, but I'll put a light outside and wait." She placed a faint light in front of her shack, spread out her brocade bedding and bid her time, thinking to herself how late it had grown.
>
> In the dead of night she heard a sound at her south door. Opening it to take a look, she saw the old mute who lived on Kiyomizu Hill. Leaning on a bamboo cane as he always did, his body wrapped in reddish-brown rags, the man seemed to exude sickness from his very core. He was endlessly frightening, and with one look Izumi Shikibu felt dazed. Her heart seemed to stop. "If I had known it would come to this," she thought, "I never would have made that vow. Even if my parents and I both tumble down into the Three Evil Realms,[19] the horror of making love to a seedy old mute is more than I can bear." She decided to turn him away with a lie. "Listen here," she said, "Izumi Shikibu's shack is much farther to the south. Go on and see her there."
>
> Taking in her meaning, the old mute spoke: "I am from the eastern edge of the city, and I have come because I heard you took a certain vow. But as you say I have the wrong door, my trip is for naught. Now if your vow to sell your body is a true vow[20]—a vow to love all men, without distinction, from the highest to the lowest—then you are sure to enter the True Path. This is despite the fact that women are despised by the myriad Buddhas of the Three Ages.[21] Women are the seeds of hell, for as the *Kegon Sutra* explains, 'Women are the servants of hell; they stamp out the seeds of the Buddha. On the outside they are as bodhisattvas, while on the inside they are as devils.'"

[18]See fn. 33 on p. 63, above.

[19]The Three Evil Realms are the realms of hell, hungry ghosts, and animals.

[20]The text describes Izumi Shikibu's vow as a "vow to sell [your] body," but the implication is that she is selling herself for Buddhist merit rather than monetary compensation.

[21]The Three Ages are the past, present, and future.

Despite the fact that he can speak, Izumi Shikibu's visitor is described as an *iwazu*, a "mute," lending a surrealistic quality to his speech. His criticism of women—only the first part of which is quoted here—is severe.[22] Voices such as his are not uncommon in *setsuwa* and *otogizōshi*; in preaching to female audiences, medieval proselytizers appear to have used these sorts of denunciations as dramatic prefaces to their promises of salvation for women. The *otogizōshi Daibutsu kuyō monogatari* (An Account of Services for the Great Buddha at Tōdaiji), for example, composed by the priest Kyōsen in 1485, contains a sermon that Hōnen supposedly delivered to the wife of Minamoto no Yoritomo and others at a Tōdaiji Temple dedication ceremony in 1195.[23] Hōnen first rails against women, citing the familiar passages about women resembling bodhisattvas on the outside and demons within (and about the combined delusion of all men in all the three thousand worlds equaling the delusion of a single woman, etc.), after which he delivers his happy news that regardless of the Five Obstructions, women are guaranteed the possibility of rebirth in the Pure Land by the saving grace of Amida's thirty-fifth vow.[24] Although a work of fiction, *Daibutsu kuyō monogatari* provides a clear indication of what such preaching must have been like in the fifteenth century. The old mute's speech in *Jōruri monogatari* is apparently modeled on this type of sermon, suggesting that his harsh words bode well for Izumi Shikibu and her eventual salvation.

Like the storyteller Yoshitsune, the old mute takes advantage of the weak position of women in Buddhism in his efforts to seduce, and in the end Izumi Shikibu is browbeaten into spending the night with her offensive guest:

> During the course of the old mute's exhortation, Izumi Shikibu experienced a change of heart. "If my parents, at least, can attain Buddhahood as a result," she thought, "then I'll sleep with this

[22]Yoshitsune's Izumi Shikibu story is translated in full in the translations section of this book.

[23]*Daibutsu kuyō monogatari*, also known as *Nanto Daibutsu kuyō monogatari*, *Nara daibutsu kuyō*, and *Daibutsu kuyō*, survives in numerous manuscripts in at least two textual lines. According to a postscript dated 1537 in the Taishō University text, the work was composed by the priest Kyōsen in the fifth month of 1485. The Akagi Bunko manuscript (early Edo period) contains an illustration of Hōnen performing his sermon for a small audience of men and women. The image is reproduced as a frontispiece to MJMT 8.

[24]MJMT 8:409b–11a (Tenri Library text, dated 1531), and DNBZ 121:64a–65b (49:157b–58a) (Taishō University text, dated 1537). The fourteenth- or fifteenth-century *Soga monogatari* attributes a similar sermon to Hōnen, but without Hōnen's exposition upon the salvific power of Amida's thirty-fifth vow. NKBT 88:420–23; Thomas J. Cogan, *The Tale of the Soga Brothers* (Tokyo: University of Tokyo Press, 1987), 290–93.

> man. And if I later turn into a mute like him, then so be it." Poor Izumi Shikibu! Taking hold of his sleeve, she led him inside to her single bed. As the night eventually gave way to dawn, the old mute spoke: "Do you think that I am really an old mute? I am the Kannon of Kiyomizu Temple, and I have appeared in this form to test the strength of your filial resolve. It is now without doubt that both you and your parents will attain Buddhahood in this very existence."
>
> The old mute departed, enveloped in the shining light of his great compassion. In deepest gratitude Izumi Shikibu accompanied him as far as Kiyomizu Temple, where he did in fact withdraw into the inner sanctum.

The old mute reveals himself to be the Kiyomizu Kannon, the living wooden statue of the bodhisattva Kannon at Kiyomizu Temple. His sudden revelation is not unlike that of the blind beggar who shows himself to be a guardian deity in the famous *jātaka* tale of King Śibi, after he has persuaded Śibi to give him both of his eyes,[25] nor is it unlike that of the leper in *Genkō shakusho*, who, having had the pus sucked from his sores, reveals himself to Empress Kōmyō to be an incarnation of Ashuku Buddha. The frequency of this tale type, both in Japan and abroad, suggests that the sensational and seemingly malicious testing of virtue was a universally popular theme.[26] While the difficulty of Izumi Shikibu's vow is physically embodied in the old mute's nightmarish presence, the mute's outward transformation implies Izumi Shikibu's inner spiritual change. By embracing him in the intimacy of her bed (for the sake of her parents, no less, evincing her filial piety), Izumi Shikibu embraces the True Path of the Buddha, literalized here in the figure of the Kiyomizu Kannon. As we have seen in so many other tales, Izumi Shikibu triumphs, yet again, over the dreaded Five Obstructions. However, her success in this case is unique, for rather than sublimating or denying her sexuality as she does in *Rakuyō Seiganji engi* when she shaves her head and becomes a nun, she uses it as her very means of overcoming the obstacles of her gender. Thus, in her seeming victimization by men, including the male

[25]Peter Khoroche, *Once the Buddha Was a Monkey: Ārya Śūra's Jātakamālā* (Chicago: University of Chicago Press, 1989), 10–17. This particular story of King Śibi was known in Japan through the sutra *Senjū hyakuenkyō* (TSD 4 [200]: 218). The guardian deity is Śakra (J., Taishakuten).

[26]According to a story in Caesarius of Heisterbach's early thirteenth-century *Dialogus Miraculorum*, a leper once requested that a certain bishop lick the rotting flesh of his nose. As Catherine Peyroux explains, "the bishop applied his tongue to the leper's diseased face, and miraculously received a precious gem from the nostrils of him who had seemed to be a leper but who was now revealed to be Christ, ascending to heaven in glory." Peyroux, "The Leper's Kiss," 184–85. Also consider the story of Abraham's near sacrifice of his son Isaac at God's behest in the Old Testament of the Bible (Gen. 24–28).

Amida and the libidinous mute/Kiyomizu Kannon, she paradoxically affirms her own femininity, demonstrating that the impediments of her sexuality are no impediment at all.

The story ends as follows:

> Flush with happiness, Izumi Shikibu composed the following poem:
>
> | | |
> |---|---|
> | aki no ta no | I feel as though I've |
> | karisomebushi no | slumbered, |
> | kokochi shite | like the wild geese in autumn fields. |
> | makoto no michi ni | What joy now |
> | iru zo ureshiki | to tread the True Path! |
>
> "That she composed this verse was also because of the Way of Love," the young master said. "So what do you think of that?"

In her joy at having slept with the old mute, thus fulfilling her vow and delivering her parents from hell, Izumi Shikibu composes a verse with Buddhist and erotic overtones. The word *karisomebushi*, "a nap," works as a hinge for *aki no ta no kari*, "the wild geese of autumn fields," and *karisomebushi no kokochi shite*, "the feeling of a short sleep."[27] "I feel as though I've slumbered," she seems to say on the one hand, comparing her former delusion to a dream; "It feels as though it were but a short autumn night—those years it took me to sleep with all one thousand of them," she also seems to say, celebrating her attainment of the Way through sex.[28]

The story ends where it begins, with Yoshitsune attempting to seduce Jōruri-hime in her apartments. The implications of his tale are clear: while on the one hand he suggests that Jōruri-hime's parents, too, may fall into hell if she should continue to refuse him, on the other he implies that both she and her parents will attain rebirth in the Pure Land (or attain some comparable state of grace) if she should acquiesce. Yoshitsune's narration imbues the story with an ironic complexity, for while within the tale itself Izumi Shikibu's salvation of her parents appears to constitute a kind of victory for women, affirming as it does the beneficial nature of female sexuality, Yoshitsune's telling of it is purely exploitative. The true degree of his ruth-

[27] *Aki no ta no kari* can also mean "harvest of autumn fields." The last two lines of the poem are identical to those of a verse attributed to the Takiguchi Novice in *The Tale of the Heike*. SNKBT 45:227 (Kakuichi text); Helen McCullough, *The Tale of the Heike* (Stanford: Stanford University Press, 1988), 342.

[28] Izumi Shikibu's promiscuity is not without consequence; as we have seen in chapter one, the noh play *Hokkejiku* (ca. 1687) reports that she eventually came to suffer the disfiguring effects of a sexually transmitted disease.

lessness is only apparent in light of the *otogizōshi*'s larger narrative frame. In declining Yoshitsune's advances, Jōruri-hime states that she must maintain her ritual purity in order to carry out religious services for her late father;[29] if Yoshitsune is thus aware of Jōruri-hime's father's death at the time that he tells his tale, he would appear to tell it as an act of emotional blackmail: an attempt to associate Jōruri-hime's chastity in this world with her father's possible perdition in the next, rendering her sexual abstention a despicable act of filial impiety.

Women and the Blood-Pool Hell

Yoshitsune's Izumi Shikibu story may be best understood as a tale of two genders: an account of the relations of power between the sexes, of disharmony and the restoration of unmitigated male authority. As Izumi Shikibu's parents reveal to her in a dream, Izumi Shikibu's beauty has bestowed her with an inadvertent power over men. Her crime is her latent sexual domination of men, which, within the context of Yoshitsune's account, can only be undone by means of her own sexual domination *by* men. Izumi Shikibu's utter physical and psychological submission to men, as demonstrated by her fulfillment of the command that she "love all men, without distinction," is therefore necessary to reestablish the traditional gender hierarchy, set askew by her exceptional desirability. Without rectifying the imbalance of male-female sexual power, Izumi Shikibu would be unable to save her parents from hell, as even Amida Buddha is reported to have explained. The implications of this for women in Buddhism are severe, for it suggests that within Yoshitsune's story, women's Pure Land salvation is predicated upon their subordination to men.

In his disguise as a mute, the Kiyomizu Kannon plays a leading role in effecting Izumi Shikibu's sexual and psychological degradation. His speech is particularly demeaning, and insofar as it deprives Izumi Shikibu of her remaining dignity, it succeeds in subjugating her to even the lowest of men.[30]

[29]Jōruri-hime is especially clear on this point in the Tōdai Library *kokatsuji hanpon* text, which does not contain the Izumi Shikibu account (SNKS *Otogizōshi*, 45). In the Akagi Bunko manuscript, she makes this excuse immediately *after* Yoshitsune tells her his Izumi Shikibu story (MJMT 7:319b–20a).

[30]Though a common figure in Muromachi fiction, the Kiyomizu Kannon is not always known for his compassion. In the late-medieval sermon-ballad *Shintokumaru*, for example, he blinds the boy Shintokumaru—his special ward—and afflicts him with a horrible skin disease at the request of the boy's stepmother. Later, he tells Shintokumaru's future wife, Otohime, not to take offense; various people ask him to do various things, for which he cannot be held to blame. SNKS *Sekkyō shū*, 202; Haruo Shirane, ed., *Traditional Japanese Literature: An Anthology, Beginnings to 1600* (New York: Columbia University Press, 2007), 1180.

After explaining the notion that women are deceivers—that they appear as bodhisattvas on the outside, but are demons within—the old mute/Kiyomizu Kannon launches into a learned and misogynistic lecture, intended, it would seem, to break Izumi Shikibu's will:

> "Consider even the lotus blossom of the heart: in the case of men, it unfolds properly in eight leaves, and numbers of Buddhas and deities manifest themselves there for the men's protection. In the hearts of women, however, the blossom has only seven leaves. One leaf is lacking. The lotus stem is folded over, broken at the base, and since the leaves are sunken low, the Buddhas and deities materialize upside-down.
>
> At the base of the lotus is a four-inch snake.[31] Though the woman may eat various foods, the snake is held back by the blossom, and because it cannot eat at once, it cries bitterly in frustration. As its red tears accumulate, they become the woman's monthly obstruction. Should she cleanse herself in clear water, she faces the reproach of the water deity, or if in the earth, the reproach of the deities of the soil. And should she enter the sunlight, Dainichi will chastise her severely.
>
> "As it is explained in the Devadatta chapter, 'First, a woman may not be reborn as a Brahmā God King; second, as Śakra; third, as Māra; fourth, as a Wheel-turning King; fifth, as a Buddha. How then is it possible for a woman to swiftly attain Buddhahood?'[32] Though you may escape the Five Torments through recitation of this scripture, the Three Torments you cannot escape.[33] As the Buddha explains, 'in the Three Worlds there are no fences, in the Six Realms there are no barriers, and for a woman, there are no three dwellings.'[34] Now I, too, implore you—uphold your vow of love and enter the True Path!"

[31]"*San sun no kuchinawa*," a snake of three *sun* (about four inches). *Keiran shūyōshū* (compiled between 1311 and 1348) also contains a reference to such a snake inside the human body (TSD 76 [2410]: 864a and 792a).

[32]These are the Five Obstructions, the five forms of rebirth listed in the Devadatta chapter of the *Lotus Sutra* as prohibited to women (TSD 9 [262]: 35c).

[33]The Five Torments (*goku*) are the suffering of birth, illness, old age, death, and separation from loved ones. The Three Torments (*sanku*) are the suffering of facing things one dislikes, losing things one likes, and experiencing change in all things. Nakamura Hajime, *Bukkyō-go daijiten*, vol. 1 (Tokyo: Tokyo Shoseki, 1975), 358a and 460b.

[34]The Three Worlds (*sangai*) are the worlds of desire, form, and non-form. The Six Realms (*rokudō*) are those of heaven, hell, hungry ghosts, animals, *asuras*, and humans. To say that there are no fences or barriers within the Three Words/Six Realms is to say that sentient beings move freely, according to their karma, amid the various planes of existence. The statement, "for a woman, there are no three dwellings," may be a misquotation of the aphorism, *sangai ni ie nashi*, "in the three worlds there is no dwelling" (i.e., there is no place that is truly secure). *Wada sakamori*, a *kōwakamai* libretto dating from the Muromachi period, contains a nearly identical passage. See SNKBT 59:480, and Fukuda Akira and Manabe Masahiro, eds., *Kōwaka bukyoku kenkyū*, vol. 8 (Tokyo: Miyai Shoten, 1994), 261–63.

In the esoteric Tendai (*taimitsu*) tradition, the human heart is frequently depicted or described as a closed lotus blossom. Through devotional practice it opens up into eight leaves, resembling the eight-leaved lotus at the center of the Taizō Mandala. Dainichi Nyorai sits at the center, where he is surrounded by four Buddhas and four bodhisattvas, each upon a single leaf.[35] According to explanations in *Jōruri monogatari* and other sources, the lotus in the hearts of women is malformed, bent or broken at the stem.[36] Drawing on traditional Chinese conceptions of sentient worms in the body, the author of *Shintō shū* (A Shintō Compendium; ca. fourteenth-century) explains that while the worms (*shichū*) in the chests of men are able to eat their fill, the worms in the chests of women, in which the lotus is sunken low, cannot. As they starve, they cry the tears that become a woman's menstrual blood.[37]

In the *otogizōshi Komachi monogatari*, composed some two or three hundred years after *Shintō shū* (much closer to the time of *Jōruri monogatari*), a fictional priest at Seki Temple further explains:

> Within a woman's body there are two mountains, called Suisan and Saisan. At the foot of these mountains is a lake named Toku. There is an eight-leaved lotus growing on this lake. Now this lotus is different from any ordinary lotus; it is bent at the stem and buds upside-down. There are worms that live at its base, and gathered there, they raise their voices in sorrow. "How sad!" they cry. "Though we were fortunate to be born, we live within the body of a woman rather than the belly of a man. And though there are foods that we would eat, the lotus blocks our way and we starve. How sad!" These creatures cry seven times at night and seven times in the day, wriggling up, down, and side to side. Their accumulated tears become the woman's monthly flow.[38]

In the context of *Komachi monogatari*, the priest belittles Ono no Komachi by attributing her menses to the innate damage in her heart, a metaphor for her

[35]Sawa Ryūken et al., eds., *Mikkyō jiten* (Kyoto: Hōzōkan, 1975), 566b (entry for "*hachiyō nikudanshin*"); Nakamura, *Bukkyō-go daijiten*, vol. 2, 1107a (entry for "*hachiyō renge*"); Kuroda Toshio, "The Discourse of the 'Land of Kami' (*Shinkoku*) in Medieval Japan," trans. Fabio Rambelli, *Japanese Journal of Religious Studies* 23, nos. 3–4 (1996), 366.

[36]*Dainichikyōsho*, a commentary by Śubhākarasiṃha (J., Zenmui [637–735]) on the *Dainichi* (*Mahāvairocana*) *Sutra*, similarly states that the eight-leaved lotus blossom faces up in the hearts of men and down in the hearts of women (TSD 39 [1796]: 623a). As Bernard Faure has shown, *Keiran shūyōshū* and *Hokekyō jikidanshō* contain similar explanations as well. Bernard Faure, *The Power of Denial: Buddhism, Purity, and Gender* (Princeton and Oxford: Princeton University Press, 2003), 102–3.

[37]Shintō Taikei Hensankai, ed., *Shintō taikei: bungaku hen 1: Shintōshū* (Tokyo: Shintō Taikei Hensankai, 1988), 152–53.

[38]MJMT 5:138 (woodblock-printed text of ca. 1688–1710).

and all other women's purported spiritual impairment. As in many works of medieval fiction that reproduce such conceits, his rhetoric achieves its authority through its analytically objective tone.

Unlike Hōnen's sermon in *Daibutsu kuyō monogatari* or the Seki Temple priest's harangue in *Komachi monogatari*, the old mute/Kiyomizu Kannon's speech in *Jōruri monogatari* reveals the additional influence of the *Blood Bowl Sutra* (*Ketsubonkyō*) and its late-medieval cult. According to Takemi Momoko, the *Blood Bowl Sutra* was imported to Japan from China in the late-fourteenth or fifteenth century.[39] Though a short apocryphal work of only four hundred and twenty-odd characters, it came to play an important role for women in Buddhism in late-medieval Japan, so much so that even Chūjōhime is reported to have carved a *Blood Bowl Sutra* printing block for the salvation of women to come.[40] Chinese and Japanese versions of the scripture explain how women who pollute the earth and the water with blood shed in childbirth will offend the deities of earth and water and be reborn in a vast pool of blood in hell; the sutra then describes how women may avoid the blood pool (or be rescued from it after death) by means of the *Blood Bowl Sutra*. In some Japanese redactions, menstruation is identified as an additional offense for which women will be reborn in the blood pool, and it is to this belief in particular that the old mute alludes in *Jōruri monogatari* when he speaks of women facing the reproach of the deities of water and soil. The preacherly narrator of the *otogizōshi Isozaki*, dating from the late Muromachi period, explains:

> The *Blood Bowl Sutra* is a savior of women, and as it, too, reveals, if at the time of her menstrual period a woman spills blood on the ground, the deity of earth will mourn. Or, if she releases blood

[39]Takemi Momoko, "'Menstruation Sutra' Belief in Japan," trans. W. Michael Kelsey, *Japanese Journal of Religious Studies* 10, nos. 2–3 (1983), 238. Michel Soymié has suggested that the *Ketsubonkyō* was imported to Japan ca. 1250–1350, but Matsuoka Hideaki sides with Takemi in dating its importation to the early Muromachi period. Michel Soymié, "Ketsubonkyō no shiryōteki kenkyū," in *Dōkyō kenkyū*, ed. Yoshioka Yoshitoyo and Michel Soymié (Tokyo: Shōrinsha, 1965), 137–38; Matsuoka Hideaki, "Waga kuni ni okeru *Ketsubonkyō* shinkō ni tsuite no ichikōsatsu," in *Nihon josei ronshū 5: Josei to shūkyō*, ed. Sōgō Joseishi Kenkyūkai (Tokyo: Yoshikawa Kōbunkan, 1998), 257 and 276 (note 1). Also see Duncan Ryūken Williams, *The Other Side of Zen: A Social History of Sōtō Zen Buddhism in Tokugawa Japan* (Princeton and Oxford: Princeton University Press, 2005), 50–58 and 125–28, and D. Max Moerman, *Localizing Paradise: Kumano Pilgrimage and the Religious Landscape of Premodern Japan* (Cambridge and London: Harvard University Asia Center, 2005), 221–31.

[40]Hank Glassman, "'Show Me the Place Where My Mother Is!' Chūjōhime, Preaching, and Relics in Late Medieval and Early Modern Japan," in *Approaching the Land of Bliss: Religious Praxis in the Cult of Amitabha*, ed. Richard K. Payne and Kenneth K. Tanaka (Honolulu: University of Hawaii Press, 2004), 160.

> in a river, the deity of water will suffer. As women's menses and parturition blood accumulate, they become the Blood Pool Hell, 80,000 *yojanas* deep and wide.[41] Upon falling into this boiling lake of blood, women are tortured by demons who shout, "It's blood from your own bodies, so drink it all up!" Though a woman may feel remorse, it will have no effect, and though she may have children, they will do her little good.[42]

The *Blood Bowl Sutra* and its story of the Blood Pool Hell was a popular subject in medieval preaching to women, and it came to be touted by a variety of temple-based instructors and itinerant proselytizer-entertainers, including Kumano *bikuni,* who enhanced their sermon-stories with grisly paintings incorporating scenes of women wallowing in the bloody lake.[43] As we have seen in the previous chapter, the paintings still survive. In some cases, the preachers' tales may have too, for they were apparently set down in works of medieval fiction purporting to describe the pleasures of paradise and the torments of hell.

In the *otogizōshi Tengu no dairi* (Palace of the Tengu; late Muromachi period), for example, Minamoto no Yoshitsune embarks upon a fantastic tour of the underworld and various Pure Lands at the age of thirteen (two years before his fictional meeting with Jōruri-hime), during the course of which he and his *tengu* (demon) guide come upon the lake of blood in hell (fig. 31). Drawing upon the rhetoric of the *Blood Bowl Sutra,* the *tengu* explains that women fall into this place because their menstrual and parturition blood pollutes the water of the world; then, when that water is used to make offerings to the Buddhas, the Buddhas are likewise defiled. The *Tengu no dairi* narrator describes the ghastly scene, which Sawai Taizō, noting the passage's distinctly oral tone, has suggested is a transcription of a medieval fund-raising nun's street-corner sermon:[44]

> There is an iron cable over the lake of blood. Five demons appear in five different colors, and they goad women out over the lake.

[41]One *yojana* equals approximately seven or nine miles, depending upon the interpretation.

[42]SNKBZ 63:350 (Keiō University manuscript [early Edo-period *nara ehon*], photographically reproduced in Matsumoto Ryūshin, ed., *Eiin: Muromachi monogatari,* vol. 4 [Tokyo: Kyūko Shoin, 1971], 229–57).

[43]Kōdate Naomi, "Aspects of *Ketsubonkyō* Belief," in *Practicing the Afterlife: Perspectives from Japan,* ed. Susanne Formanek and William R. LaFleur (Vienna: Osterreichische Akademie der Wissenschaften, 2004), 121–43; Barbara Ruch, "Woman to Woman: *Kumano bikuni* Proselytizers in Medieval and Early Modern Japan," in *Engendering Faith,* 567–75; Hayashi Masahiko, *Zōho Nihon no etoki: shiryō to kenkyū* (Tokyo: Miyai Shoten, 1984), 126–55.

[44]Sawai Taizō, "Otogizōshi *Isozaki* kō: otogizōshi to sekkyō no sekai," in *Koten no hen'yō to shinsei,* ed. Kawaguchi Hisao (Tokyo: Meiji Shoin, 1984), 326.

Fig. 31. Yoshitsune and the Great Tengu (left) pass by the Blood Pool Hell and into the realm of hungry ghosts. From *Tengu no dairi* (Katei Bunko text, seventeenth century). Courtesy of the Tokyo University General Library.

> "Cross the cable!" they shout. But the women lose their footing before they even reach the center, and they fall in with a splash. Their bodies sink below, while their long hair floats on the surface like duckweed. When they try to rise, the demons push them back down with iron rods. The women's anguished cries are thinner than a spider's thread. "It's your punishment for the crimes you committed in the human realm!" the demons shout, their voices echoing all around, "so don't blame us!"[45]

Yoshitsune asks his guide how a woman might avoid the torments of the Blood Pool Hell, to which the *tengu* replies that a woman may proceed directly to the Pure Land if she prays for a favorable rebirth in the next life while either reciting the *nenbutsu* or possessing one hundred thirty-three

[45]From the British Library *Tengu no dairi emaki* (two illustrated scrolls dating from the late Muromachi period), in Tsuji Eiko, *Zaigai Nihon emaki no kenkyū to shiryō*, Kasama sōsho, no. 328 (Tokyo: Kasama Shoin, 1999), 361a. For a further discussion of *Tengu no dairi*, see R. Keller Kimbrough, "Tourists in Paradise: Writing the Pure Land in Medieval Japanese Fiction," *Japanese Journal of Religious Studies* 33, no. 2 (Autumn 2006): 280–86.

copies of the *Blood Bowl Sutra*. According to traditional conceptions of Amida's Pure Land, the woman will be reborn there upon a lotus in the Lake of Eight Virtues—a sacred and immaculate reservoir standing in direct contraposition to the bloody lake in hell.

Although the old mute/Kiyomizu Kannon in *Jōruri monogatari* does not allude directly to the *Blood Bowl Sutra* or its notorious pool, his fiery oration, culminating in a recitation of the Five Obstructions and a demand that Izumi Shikibu uphold her vow of love and "enter the True Path," derives from the same late-medieval proselytizing milieu. With its visually suggestive descriptions of seven and eight-leaved lotus blossoms—some standing upright and some broken at the stem—and the snake at the base of the lotus whose tears become a woman's menstrual blood, the Kiyomizu Kannon's speech may itself be borrowed from the text of a late-medieval *etoki* performance. Whether or not a corresponding painting can be found remains to be seen. In any case, at the very least the Kiyomizu Kannon's sexist tirade demonstrates that the roots of Yoshitsune's Izumi Shikibu account lie in the popular proselytizing of the Muromachi period.[46]

The Compassion of a Bodhisattva

Although Izumi Shikibu's vow in Yoshitsune's *Jōruri monogatari* account is an unusual one, it is not exceptionally so. *Goshūi ōjōden* (Later Gleanings of Pure-Land Rebirth Biographies), a collection of Pure Land rebirth tales compiled by the Heian literatus Miyoshi Tameyasu in the early twelfth century, contains the biography of a woman who is also said to have slept with any man who wanted her, and to have attained rebirth in the Pure Land as a possible (or partial) result:

> There was a woman from the province of Mutsu who was beautiful and amorous in her youth. She was without any definite husband, and many men would come to see her. She never refused anyone—she allowed them all to have their way. After a while not a single man would visit, and she passed her years alone. A friend asked her why this was so.

[46]Like much of the oral didactic literature of late-medieval Japan, the Izumi Shikibu account seems to have been taken up in the early-modern theater, surviving in a *kabuki* play titled *Izumi Shikibu sennin otoko* (Izumi Shikibu and the Thousand Men; first performed in 1709). See *Kokusho sōmokuroku* (Hotei-ban), vol. 1 (Tokyo: Iwanami Shoten, 1989), 190c. In addition, Tokue Gensei describes an Ise festival dance ("Shikibu *odori*") in which Izumi Shikibu is said to achieve intimacy with one thousand men for the sake of her parents' enlightenment. Tokue Gensei, "Otogizōshi: *Izumi Shikibu*," *Kokubungaku: kaishaku to kyōzai no kenkyū* 19, no. 4 (March 1974), 77b.

> "I've heard that it's the way of the bodhisattva to accede to the feelings of others," the woman replied, "so I've never turned away a man who came to see me. I've also heard that lust fuels the cycle of birth and death, so when I was with a man, I let not the slightest attachment arise in my heart. I would snap my fingers [in disgust] and shut my eyes to the sight of impurity. When a person indulges his desire, the desire increases all the more. For this reason the men became ashamed and stopped coming to see me."
>
> The woman later became a nun and took up the practice of the *nenbutsu*. In the sickness of her final hour she closed her eyes, and it is said that the sky filled with golden Buddhas like stars on a clear night.[47]

Like Izumi Shikibu in *Jōruri monogatari*, the woman from Mutsu demonstrates a willingness in her youth to sleep with anyone at all. Typically, this would be considered a source of sin. According to the *otogizōshi Fuji no hitoana sōshi* (The Story of the Fuji Cave), the punishment in hell for women with multiple male lovers is to have nails pounded into the bones of their hips; the number of the nails—objects with brutally phallic connotations—is said to be equal to the number of sexual partners that the women have had in the course of their lives.[48] The woman from Mutsu, however, is motivated by an aspiration to total, passive compliance—a kind of ascetic self-abasement—rather than lust. She engages in sex with neither passion nor pleasure, and thus, though outwardly wanton, maintains what Wendy Doniger O'Flaherty has described in a discussion of ancient Hindu literature as an "elusive chastity of the mind."[49]

In her refusal to choose among men, the woman from Mutsu fulfills the bodhisattva ideal of nondiscrimination (*mushabetsu*). According to this concept, a bodhisattva shows equal compassion to all, without distinguishing between high and low, rich and poor, or young and old. Likewise, this is the principle behind Izumi Shikibu's parents' instruction that Izumi Shikibu take a vow "to love all men, without distinction, from the highest to the lowest."[50] The application of the ideal to sex is not original to Japan. The Pali

[47]NST 7:669a. For a modern Japanese translation, see Kasahara Kazuo, *Nyonin ōjō shisō no keifu* (Tokyo: Yoshikawa Kōbunkan, 1975), 72.

[48]MJMT 11:468a (woodblock-printed *tanrokubon* of 1627).

[49]Wendy Doniger O'Flaherty, *Śiva: The Erotic Ascetic* (Oxford: Oxford University Press, 1981), 81. O'Flaherty elsewhere writes that "this is the philosophy behind much of the Tantric sexuality of the later Purāṇas: [that] one may perform the *act* of sexual intercourse without losing one's purity, as long as the *mind* remains uninvolved." Ibid., 79 (italics by O'Flaherty).

[50]We have also seen the principle at work in the twelfth-century *Hōbutsushū* and *Shūi ōjōden* accounts of Jungen Hōshi, who, because of his refusal to discriminate among women, takes his own daughter to be his wife (discussed on pp. 92–93).

Buddhist treatise *Milindapañha* (The Questions of King Milinda), which Nakamura Hajime dates to no later than the middle of the first century B.C.E.,[51] contains a story of the prostitute Bindumatī, who, because of her willingness to sleep with anyone who can pay, acquires a supernatural power by which she causes the Ganges to temporarily reverse its flow. Through her absolute refusal to discriminate among men (on the bases of looks or status, that is), Bindumatī attains perfection in her role as prostitute, and by this, she is able to achieve what would otherwise be impossible.[52] Izumi Shikibu similarly fulfills the ideal, albeit reluctantly, when she agrees to sleep with the old mute. And like Bindumatī, she too achieves a miraculous feat: the salvation of her parents from hell.

Tales of Buddhas and bodhisattvas in disguise (like those of Empress Kōmyō and Ashuku Buddha, or Izumi Shikibu and the Kiyomizu Kannon) are relatively common in *setsuwa* and *otogizōshi*. In one of the most famous of these accounts, an *asobi* (courtesan) of Kanzaki reveals herself to the priest Shōkū Shōnin (the Shōkū Shōnin to whom Izumi Shikibu is said to have presented her "darkness into darkness" poem) to be a living manifestation of the bodhisattva Fugen. The following version is from Minamoto no Akikane's *setsuwa* anthology *Kojidan* (Tales of Ancient Matters), compiled between 1212 and 1215:

> How Shōkū [Shōnin] Saw the Living Fugen Bodhisattva
>
> The holy man of Mount Shosha prayed that he might see Fugen in a living manifestation, and in a dream-revelation he was told, "If you wish to view the living Fugen, you should look upon the head courtesan of Kanzaki." Overjoyed, the holy man set out for Kanzaki, where he inquired after the head courtesan's abode. A group of lower-ranking officials happened to be there at the time, engaged in boisterous feasting and dancing. The head courtesan sat at the front, where with a hand drum she kept time for the dance. In her song she sang:

Suō Murozumi no	In the hand-washing shallows
naka naru mitarai ni	in Murozumi in Suō,

[51]Nakamura Hajime et al., eds., *Shin butten kaidai jiten* (Tokyo: Shunjūsha, 1966), 76b.

[52]T.W. Rhys Davids, *The Questions of King Milinda*, vol. 1 (1890; reprint, Delhi: Motilal Banarsidass, 1965), 182–84; I.B. Horner, *Milinda's Questions*, vol. 1 (London: Luzac & Company, 1969), 170–71. W. Norman Brown writes that Bindumatī "followed unchastity without slipping into affection or dislike for any customer and was thus the perfect prostitute." W. Norman Brown, "The Metaphysics of the Truth Act (*Satyakriyā*)," in *Melanges d'Indianisme à la Memoire de Louis Renou* (Paris: Editions E. de Boccard, 1968), 172. The *Milindapañha* was known in Japan through an incomplete Chinese translation titled *Nasenbikukyō* (TSD 32 [1670A and B]: 694–719), which corresponds up to p. 89 of the Pali Text Society text (p. 136 in Rhys Davids 1890).

kaze wa fukanedomo	little waves ripple,
sasaranami tatsu	though the wind doesn't blow.

The holy man had a strange feeling, and when he closed his eyes and put his palms together, the head courtesan appeared before him as Fugen. Riding on a white elephant with six tusks and emitting light from between the eyebrows—illuminating all the people, lay and monastic alike—Fugen explained in a marvelous voice:

jissō muro no ōumi ni	In the Great Ocean
gojin rokuyoku no	of Truth Untainted,
kaze wa fukazu to mo	fleeting waves ripple always,
zuien shinnyo no	though the winds of dust
nami tatanu toki nashi	and desire do not blow.[53]

The holy man paid reverent obeisance and brushed joyous tears from his eyes. When he opened them, there was the woman as she was before, performing the song about Murozumi in Suō, and when he closed them, there again was the bodhisattva, expounding the Holy Law. After paying his respects several times, the holy man set out on his return, weeping all the while. The head courtesan suddenly stood up, and by way of a side road she caught up with the holy man.

"You shouldn't speak of this to others," she said, and immediately died. People say that a mysterious fragrance filled the air, and that at the moment of her death, the party fell suddenly quiet.[54]

The *asobi* is a bodhisattva, and her *imayō* (song), the Holy Law. Buddhas and bodhisattvas appear in many guises for the sake of sentient beings, and this is apparently one of them. As Fugen explains in the song, the water (Ultimate Reality) is itself immutable, but the waves (phenomenal reality) dance in accord with fluctuating causes and conditions. In other words, while the water of the ocean is unchanging, its appearance—as waves—is forever shifting as it constantly takes on new forms and manifestations. Thus a courtesan is a bodhisattva, the Kiyomizu Kannon is a dirty beggar, and, as

[53]Actually, the "Five Dusts" and the "Six Desires." The Five Dusts (*gojin*) are five elements that pollute or delude the human heart, and the Six Desires (*rokuyoku*) are six kinds of craving that obstruct proper understanding.

[54]SNKBT 41:359–61; Kobayashi Yasuharu, ed., *Kojidan*, vol. 1 (Tokyo: Gendai Shichōsha, 1981), 303. Other versions of the story are contained in *Jikkinshō, Senjūshō, Shiju hyaku innenshū, Sangoku denki, Tōsai zuihitsu*, the *otogizōshi Suzuriwari* (Naikaku Bunko manuscript), the noh play *Eguchi*, and the *Lotus Sutra* commentaries *Hokekyō jurin shūyōshū* and *Hokekyō jikidanshō*. On the account and its use in the *Lotus Sutra* commentaries, see Sakaguchi Kōtarō, "Jikidan kōkyō ni mieru Shōkū Shōnin Fugen kankendan," *Bungaku ronsō* 67 (February 1993): 86–96.

all things are essentially the same, the Way of Earthly Love is the Way of the Buddha. For this reason Izumi Shikibu's sinful liaison with her son in *Izumi Shikibu* is itself the precious seed of her enlightenment, and her uncompromising dedication to the Way of Love in *Jōruri monogatari* is her means of rescuing her parents and attaining rebirth in the Pure Land.

In the *Lotus Sutra* commentary *Hokekyō jurin shūyōshū* (1512), Sonshun writes that one of his acquaintances, the priest Genkyō of Myōjōin Temple, frequently said that he himself had awakened to the truth of *zuien shinnyo* (the notion of ultimate unchanging reality manifesting in ever fluctuating forms) when he heard the courtesan/Fugen's song chanted throughout the night at an inn in Murozumi in Suō province.[55] Genkyō had been on his way to China, but he immediately gave up his journey and returned to live on Mount Hiei, headquarters of the Tendai sect. Why did he need to travel to China, he seems to have thought, when he could learn about Buddhism in Japan? Genkyō's testimony demonstrates the mysterious power of the courtesan/Fugen's *imayō* (or stories of the *imayō*, such as the one translated above) to transmit the Dharma in the centuries after its composition. Many works of popular medieval fiction, though similarly humble in form, are also illustrative of the highest of Buddhist truths and thus likewise functioned to transmit the Dharma. As the *asobi* of Kanzaki—the living Fugen—might explain, Izumi Shikibu, Ono no Komachi, Sei Shōnagon, Murasaki Shikibu and their Heian women peers are all bodhisattvas, and the made-up, often appalling stories of their glorious, scandalous, and sometimes wretched lives are themselves the *hōben*, or expedient means, of the Buddha.

[55]*Hokekyō jurin shūyōshō*, vol. 4 (Kyoto: Rinsen Shoten, 1991), 504. Also cited in Nagai Yoshinori, "Kaidai," in *Hokekyō jurin shūyōshō*, vol. 4, 553.

Epilogue
Popular Preaching and the Dissemination of Culture

According to an entry in the fourteenth-century *Record of the Special Kasuga Festival of 1349*, two *miko* (shamanesses, or shrine maidens) played the roles of Murasaki Shikibu and Izumi Shikibu in a performance of *sarugaku*—a forerunner of noh—at a Kasuga Wakamiya Shrine festival on the tenth day of the second month of 1349. Of two dramas staged that day by the *miko* of Kasuga, the first concerned an episode in the life of Saigyō. The *Record* describes the second as follows:

> The second *sarugaku* concerned Murasaki Shikibu's visit to Izumi Shikibu when she was ailing. Murasaki Shikibu was played by Songiku-gozen, and Izumi Shikibu by Tsuruju-gozen. The two blossoms were played by Harutsuru-gozen and Hōju-gozen. The bonding-deity was played by Mumeō-gozen.[1]

The entry is enigmatic. Iura Yoshinobu has noted the possibility of a connection between the *sarugaku* and an episode in the *otogizōshi Koshikibu*, in which Murasaki Shikibu laments her daughter Izumi Shikibu's illness. In *Koshikibu*, Izumi Shikibu composes a poem that so moves a demon that he deigns to save her life, and Iura proposes that the *sarugaku* at Kasuga Shrine may have been a reenactment of some earlier version of this account.[2]

Kinoshita Motoichi has suggested a different possibility. Kinoshita argues that the *sarugaku* was indeed related to an account in *Koshikibu*, although not the one about Izumi Shikibu's illness. In a later part of the *otogizōshi*, Izumi Shikibu becomes estranged from her husband Hōshō (Fujiwara no Yasumasa) because of rumors of an affair with the poet-priest Dōmyō. Akazome Emon visits Izumi Shikibu in her despair, and in a poem she warns Izumi Shikibu to "watch the Forest of Shinoda awhile" before giving up on

[1]*Jōwa gonen Kasuga rinji saireiki* (also titled *Jōwa gonen nigatsu tōka haiden rinjisai shidai*, "Proceedings of the Worship-Hall Special Festival on the Tenth Day of the Second Month of Jōwa 5 [1349]"), cited in Matsuoka Shinpei, "Nō ni egakareta Izumi Shikibu," *Kokubungaku: kaishaku to kanshō* 60, no. 8 (August 1995), 112b–13a. Also see P.G. O'Neill, "The Special Kasuga Wakamiya Festival of 1349," *Monumenta Nipponica* 14, no. 3/4 (October 1958–January 1959), 415–16.

[2]Iura Yoshinobu, *Nihon engeki shi* (Tokyo: Shibundō, 1963), 796–800.

her spouse. The *Koshikibu* narrator explains that of the two guardian deities of Shinoda Forest, one "takes the form of the camphor," and the other, "the form of the kudzu."[3] Izumi Shikibu travels to Izumoji Shrine (Izumo Shrine in the Tenri Library manuscript) to petition the deity—a "bonding deity"—for help in restoring relations with her husband.[4] Kinoshita proposes that if one were to substitute the name Akazome Emon for Murasaki Shikibu, the *sarugaku* would match the *Koshikibu* account. Akazome Emon would visit Izumi Shikibu in her sorrow, the "two blossoms" played by Harutsuru-gozen and Hōju-gozen would be the deities of Shinoda Forest, and the "bonding deity" played by Mumeō-gozen would be the deity of Izumoji Shrine.[5] Matsuoka Shinpei has additionally suggested that the *sarugaku* concluded with Izumi Shikibu's shrine dance, the climax of which would have been her recitation of her "mighty gods" ("*chihayaburu kami*") poem and her reconciliation with Hōshō.[6]

Intriguing as Kinoshita and Matsuoka's reconstruction of the Kasuga *sarugaku* performance may be, it is perhaps more important here to simply note that *miko* are reported to have enacted tales of Saigyō, Murasaki Shikibu, and Izumi Shikibu, whatever they may have been, at a shrine festival in Nara in 1349. It is a further confirmation of Yanagita's speculations from the early 1930s that female religious, including *miko*, *yūjo*, Kumano *bikuni* and other proselytizer-entertainers, were engaged in the spread of stories of Heian women poets and other cultural and literary figures in the medieval and early-modern periods. As we have seen in the course of this book, men were also active in the Kamakura and Muromachi periods in disseminating accounts of Izumi Shikibu and her peers, a fact that Yanagita tends to downplay in his work. To greater or lesser extents, the priests of Tennōji, Enkyōji, Seiganji, Agui, and the medieval Tendai *dangisho* all appear to have drawn upon Izumi Shikibu's imagined life and poetry in their preaching and fundraising, suggesting that Yanagita, in his efforts to address society's ignorance of women's roles in the Buddhist and cultural history of Japan, may have overstated the relative importance of women in the spread of these fictional and pseudo-biographical accounts.

[3]MJMT 5:29a (Tenri Library manuscript); MJMT supp. 1:513b–14a (Ono manuscript).

[4]Alternate versions of this account are contained in *Shasekishū* (ca. 1280; NKBT 85:446), *Sangoku denki* (ca. 1407–46; 1:27), *Ichijō shūgyokushō* (1488), the noh play *Kibune* (attributed to Kanze Nobumitsu [1435–1516]), and *Tsuki no karu moshū* (seventeenth century; ZGR 33:1:92–93). The *Ichijō shūgyokushō* version is typeset in Nakano Maori, *Ichijō shūgyokushō no kenkyū* (Kyoto: Rinsen Shoten, 1998), 14–15.

[5]Kinoshita Motoichi, "Yōkyoku to denshō no Saigyō," *Kanze* 51, no. 12 (1984), 6a–7b.

[6]Matsuoka, "Nō ni egakareta Izumi Shikibu," 113b–14b. Matsuoka notes, however, that the *sarugaku* record contains no mention of either a *miko* or a husband. For Izumi Shikibu's "mighty gods" poem, see *Koshikibu* in the translations, p. 291.

While the present study has attempted to illuminate some of the influences of Buddhist proselytizing upon the formation and transmission of medieval literary culture, the reader should be aware that the dissemination of apocryphal tales of Heian poets did not result from the activities of Buddhist preacher-entertainers in isolation. As Susan Klein has shown in her work on early-medieval literary commentaries and what she describes as the "*waka* initiation pedagogical system," spurious stories of Ono no Komachi, Ariwara no Narihira and others also appear to have been manufactured in the Kamakura period by teachers of poetry for sale as articles of privileged information: purportedly secret transmissions serving an economic need for marketable esoteric knowledge.[7] Klein and Ishikawa Tōru have demonstrated that the so-called "secret" lore from the early-medieval commentaries was often reproduced, as well as parodied, in *otogizōshi*,[8] indicating the inadvertent influence of one or more of the Kamakura-period poetic houses—the principal purveyors of that formerly proprietary information—upon the contents of late-medieval fiction. To take but one example, the *otogizōshi Kachō Fūgetsu* (Flowers and Birds, Wind and Rain; composed prior to 1457), which takes its name from its two female protagonists, the *miko* sisters Kachō and Fūgetsu, is fundamentally rooted in the medieval commentarial tradition, displaying the characteristic commentarial preoccupation with the technical and biographical "facts" of its subjects: the lives, loves, and tales of Ariwara no Narihira and Hikaru ("Shining") Genji.[9]

In her book on temple fund-raising campaigns in Heian and medieval Japan, Janet Goodwin has emphasized the late-Heian decline of the *shōen* (estate) system, together with the simultaneous rise of extramonastic movements of *hijiri* and other popular preachers, for their roles in precipitating an increase in evangelistic proselytizing and public solicitation in late Heian- and Kamakura-period society.[10] Whatever their motivations, be they principally economic, pietistic, or, as Goodwin suggests, a combination of the two, Buddhist sects and institutions took up tales of their sacred icons,

[7]Susan Klein, *Allegories of Desire: Esoteric Literary Commentaries of Medieval Japan* (Cambridge and London: Harvard University Asia Center, 2002).

[8]Ibid., 295; Ishikawa Tōru, *Muromachi monogatari to kochūshaku* (Tokyo: Miyai Shoten, 2002).

[9]Tokue Gensei has demonstrated a specific *Kachō Fūgetsu*-commentarial link by showing that Fūgetsu's conversation with Narihira's ghost is closely related to a passage in *Ise monogatari kuden shidai* (An Assemblage of Oral Transmissions on *Tales of Ise*), attributed to a secret Hamuro family tradition. Tokue Gensei, *Muromachi geinō-shi ronkō* (Tokyo: Miyai Shoten, 1984), 24–30. *Kachō Fūgetsu* is translated by me in Haruo Shirane, ed., *The Tale of Genji Reader* (New York: Columbia University Press, forthcoming).

[10]Janet R. Goodwin, *Alms and Vagabonds: Buddhist Temples and Popular Patronage in Medieval Japan* (Honolulu: University of Hawaii Press, 1994), 12–14.

former benefactors, and celebrity devotees as they never had before, putting them to use in their efforts to preach and expand their bases of support. Heian women authors, with their legendary beauty, poetry, decadence and refinement, are likely to have impressed high and low audiences alike, and it was from around this time—the late-Heian and Kamakura periods—that they came to be employed as staple figures in preaching and entertaining.

The implications of this long-term, widespread use of Izumi Shikibu's, Ono no Komachi's, Sei Shōnagon's, and Murasaki Shikibu's poetry and personae in medieval proselytizing and entertaining are profound. As a variety of temple-based monastics, mendicant *hijiri*, *bikuni*, *miko*, secular *yūjo*, and other settled and itinerant preachers and performers spread tales of Izumi Shikibu, Ono no Komachi and their peers, they succeeded in familiarizing a range of audiences with the names, works, and reputations of these Heian women authors. It was thus that the women came to be reconstituted, in their later manifestations, as poets and heroes of the Kamakura and Muromachi periods, rather than the Heian. In transcending their historical roles as rarefied representatives of an elite court society, they achieved a new and lasting place in the popular imagination, culminating in the women's elevation to the status of national cultural icons in the early-modern and modern periods. (Murasaki Shikibu's portrait, for example, has graced the back of the 2,000 yen bill since July of 2000.)

Today, the Heian court and its accomplishments are regarded in Japan as the cultural inheritance of all Japanese. It is ironic that the origins of this conception, as well as the canonical literary status of some of Japan's most famous writers, may ultimately lie in the panoply of medieval fabrications and creative misrepresentations—"expedient means," to use a more charitable term—that characterizes the ubiquitous proselytizing and storytelling of the Japanese medieval world.

Translations

A History of Seiganji in the Capital (Excerpt)[1]

Sei Shōnagon, grandchild of Kiyohara no Fukayabu, daughter of the governor of Higo, Kiyohara no Motosuke, was a serving-woman to an empress of Emperor Ichijō. Devoting her days to the passions of love, thinking not of the brevity of this transient life, her heart was filled with lascivious desire. Unaware of the frightful future in store for her, merely taking pleasure dallying in the flowers of spring, she turned her thoughts to the autumn moon and exhausted her heart on frivolous banquets and entertainments. Basking in the glory of the favor of her empress, she had not the slightest aspiration to the Buddhist austerities.

By some karmic link she once came to our temple. Offering prayers to the [Seiganji] Buddha, she was swept with feelings of sorrow and joy, and a desire for Buddhahood mysteriously welled up within her. Later cutting off her glossy hair before the Buddha, she became a nun, and she erected a hut beside the temple hall. Doing nothing other than carry out the Buddhist practices and going nowhere other than the temple hall, she became a practitioner of the perpetual *nenbutsu*, always chanting Amida Buddha's name.

Once when she received a summons from the court, she sent back a single poem in reply:

motomete mo	Beckon as you may,
kakaru hachisu no	the dew has come to rest
tsuyu okite	upon the lotus.
ukiyo ni mata wa	So how could I return
kaeru mono ka wa	to this world of sorrow?[2]

[1]The following sections are translated from the Jingū Bunko text in the *Sankan-bon* textual line (ca. 1565–95), in ZGR 27:1:218a–32a, and in DNBZ 117:350b–62b (83:152c–57c). They correspond to the end of the first and all of the second scroll of the three-scroll *Seiganji engi emaki* (seventeenth century).

[2]This is a slightly alternate version of *Senzai wakashū* 1206, attributed to Sei Shōnagon. The headnote reads: "Once when the lectures for establishing karmic links were being held at a temple named Bodai, [Sei Shōnagon] went to listen. Someone sent a message for her to return at once, and she sent the following poem in reply." The same poem appears in *Sei Shōnagon shū* (poem 14), and in the *Sankan-bon*, *Nōin-bon*, and *Maeda-ke-bon* textual lines of *The Pillow Book* (SNKBT 25:42; NKBT 19:76; NKBZ 11:115–16).

Fig. 32. Sei Shōnagon at Seiganji. From *Seiganji engi emaki*. Courtesy of Seiganji Temple and the Kyoto National Museum.

This is how she composed her verse, and she never returned to the palace.

Sei Shōnagon spent her days reciting the *nenbutsu*, and her devotion deepened all the more. In her dying hour she chanted Amida's name in an especially strong voice. Omens appeared of their own accord, and it was from here at our temple that she achieved her cherished desire for rebirth in the Pure Land. While one may say that her religious aspiration blossomed over time, with either time or the aid of the Buddha, it was a wonderful, marvelous thing indeed!

Izumi Shikibu was a serving-woman to Jōtōmon'in, empress of sixty-sixth emperor Ichijō. She was a daughter of Echizen governor Masamune and the wife of Izumi governor Tachibana no Michisada, from whose title she came to be known as Izumi Shikibu. From youth she excelled in the way of poetry. She was exceedingly lascivious, her amorous attachments were deep, and dawn and dusk she occupied herself solely in leading men's hearts astray. She spent her years composing upon the occasional feelings that would come to her on flowering spring mornings and moonlit autumn evenings, and before she knew it, the blossom of her beauty had passed its full bloom.

Until the age of thirty-five Izumi Shikibu had given no thought, even in dreams, to enlightenment in the afterworld. But when her beloved daughter Koshikibu no Naishi fell gravely ill, she grieved and prayed to the gods and Buddhas to prolong her little girl's life. There was not the least effect, however, and Koshikibu began to slip away. Just when her time had seemed to have come, she took hold of her mother's hand, weeping, and with a look of sadness at their imminent parting, chanted a single verse:

ika ni semu	What shall I do?
yukubeki kata mo	Not knowing the path
omohoezu	one takes before a parent,
oya ni sakidatsu	I cannot imagine
michi wo shiraneba	the way I am to go.

Such was her poem, yet even without it, "though a parent's heart be not mired in darkness, 'tis the way of the world to wander lost on paths of concern for a child."[3] Izumi Shikibu was not unlike an aged cow licking her calf, or a distraught monkey crying out for its child, and at the sound of her daughter's loving verse, her heart throbbed all the more. Breaking down in tears, she replied:

koashi ni te	On little feet
tadori yukuran	you'll wander forward,
shide no yama	lost on that road, you say,
michi shiranu to te	through the Mountains of Death.
kaeri koyo ka shi	Oh do come back!

How moving that we may know the feelings in her heart, strung together like this in a poem! But as is the way of this world in which there is no weir

[3]This is a slightly alternate version of *Gosen wakashū* 1102/3, attributed to Fujiwara no Kanesuke (877–933). According to *Yamato monogatari* (*dan* 45), Kanesuke composed the poem out of concern for his daughter's fortunes at court:

hito no oya no	A parent's heart
kokoro wa yami ni	is not mired in
aranedomo	darkness,
ko wo omou michi ni	yet I wander lost
madoinuru kana	on paths of concern for my child.

to hold back final partings,[4] alas, at the age of fourteen Koshikibu no Naishi passed away.

Izumi Shikibu thought deeply about the impermanence of this world of suffering, that death comes to young and old alike, that all suffer the pain of separation from loved ones. Who can escape the fate of our inconstant bodies, like so many leaves blowing in the wind? She may have lost Koshikibu today, but tomorrow the end would bear down on her as well, and she understood the certain futility of losing one's heart to this transient dream, this dreamlike world. She came to loathe earthly splendors, fleeting as a morning mist, and she recognized the spiritual guidance afforded her in the death of her beloved child, the flower on whom she doted. She turned to the path of enlightenment, praying in her heart to meet a wise or holy man from whom she might seek a means of leaving the world behind.

Now at that time there was a venerable priest by the name of Shōkū Shōnin on Mount Shosha in Harima province. Of legendary virtue, he is said to have attained a state of purity of the six senses through his recitations of the *Lotus Sutra*. Izumi Shikibu was eager to meet him, receive the mysterious teachings of the Dharma and embark upon the blissful path of the Buddha. And so putting her desire for enlightenment above all else, in the fall of her thirty-fifth year she slipped out of the palace in the dark of night and set out for Mount Shosha, accompanied by eight court ladies with similar aspirations to the Way.

Izumi Shikibu and her companions emerged from the palace grounds. As it was then mid-autumn, the surrounding mountains were desolate. Insects seemed to plead with the women as they walked, and the sleeves of their travel-robes, soaked from the dewy grasses, were without a chance to dry. The days passed and in a short time they arrived at Mount Shosha.

Because Shōkū Shōnin had attained a state of purity of the six senses through his many years of reciting the *Lotus Sutra*, he knew that the women would be coming from the capital. "When eight demons come looking for me tomorrow evening," he told his disciples, "tell them I've gone off to

[4]This is an allusion to *Kokin wakashū* 836, attributed to Mibu no Tadamine. The headnote reads, "Composed on the death of his sister":

se wo sekeba	Dam them up
fuchi to narite mo	and rushing waters
yodomikeri	become a deep pool, unmoving—
wakare wo tomuru	yet there is no weir
shigarami zo naki	to hold back final partings.

Chinzei to preach."[5] He then secluded himself within a meditation hall. The disciples trembled with fear. "How are we to face such demons that frighten even the master?" they clamored among themselves, wondering what to do. "There is no great danger as long as I am in this room," Shōkū Shōnin announced, quieting them with his words.

Now Izumi Shikibu had beautiful features and the graceful bearing of a willow, but the dew and frost of the roadside had taken their toll and her appearance was somewhat disheveled as she approached Shōkū Shōnin's rustic abode. Calling out that she had something to say, she knocked on his brushwood door. But Shōkū Shōnin had given his instructions, and his disciples merely gathered together and stared at the ladies outside. It was beyond imagination, the disciples thought, for women such as these to have made their way into such deep mountains so far from civilization, and they truly took them to be demons in disguise. "Our master went off toward Tsukushi,"[6] they said. "Please go away now."

Regrettably, the doors of the temple gate were shut tight, barring the women's way. Izumi Shikibu felt as if the moon over Mount Gaya had suddenly set, as if in an instant the blossoms of the *śāla* grove had shriveled.[7] The women lingered for a while outside the barrier, but the sun was already disappearing behind the western ridge, and with its every ring the evening temple bell echoed the impermanence of all.[8] A howling wind on the mountain peak gusted forth the truth of ephemerality—scattered blossoms and falling leaves—and the forlorn wailing of the deer and the sad cries of hedge-insects filled Izumi Shikibu's heart with a quiet calm.

It was then that she heard a wondrous voice emanating from Shōkū Shōnin's still hermitage, "in desolation, where no man's voice resounds, reading and reciting this sutra."[9] Once more she approached the gate and knocked. But there was no reply, and she turned back, defeated. Soaking her sleeve in a dew of tears, she gazed up at the moonlight filtering through the pines and intoned a single verse:

[5]Chinzei is an alternate name for Kyūshū. It is curious that Shōkū Shōnin would give the number of demons as eight, when including Izumi Shikibu there were nine women coming to see him.

[6]Tsukushi is another old name for Kyūshū.

[7]Mount Gaya (in India) is the legendary site of the Buddha's enlightenment. When the Buddha died in a grove of *śāla* trees, the blossoms there are said to have turned white and scattered.

[8]This may be an allusion to the opening passage of *The Tale of the Heike*, "The bells of Gion Shōja echo the impermanence of all."

[9]This is a quotation from the "Teacher of the Law" chapter of the *Lotus Sutra*. TSD 9 (262): 32b; Burton Watson, *The Lotus Sutra* (New York: Columbia University Press, 1993), 168.

kuraki yori	From darkness
kuraki michi ni zo	into a path of darkness
irinu beki	I must enter—
haruka ni terase	shine your light afar,
yama no ha no tsuki	moon on the mountain ridge!

"I've come to meet with the master to ask him of the afterworld and sweep away the darkness of this floating realm," Izumi Shikibu lamented in frustration. "That's why I've traveled these tens of leagues, never minding the distance. To go back now for nothing is hard indeed. I've heard that women are rife with sin—the Five Obstructions and the Three Obediences—and I've heard that they're despised by the various Buddhas and bodhisattvas and excluded from the eighty-thousand benefits of the Teaching. That the master is away now, too, must be because a group of wicked women has come."

Thus Izumi Shikibu lingered, her voice choked with tears. Shōkū Shōnin had been listening from the other side, and from her single poem he realized that her desire to seek the Way was not shallow.[10] Recalling his own vow to save sentient beings and thinking that to exclude this woman would not be in accord with that vow, he had the gate opened at last and met with her face to face. Izumi Shikibu was overjoyed. She felt as if she had received an *udonge* flower,[11] and chanting, "Praise be the Most Exalted One," she bowed three times in obeisance.

"I am Izumi Shikibu," she said, "daughter of Echizen governor Masamune and lady-in-waiting to Jōtōmon'in, empress of Emperor Ichijō. Though I am ashamed to say it, until reaching this age I passed my days for nothing, without the least interest in the Buddhist practices. But recently I lost my darling daughter. Her death was for me a karmic link to enlightenment, causing me to despise the filth of this floating world. This is why I left the capital and came all this way—in hopes of receiving your instruction and being saved for eternity.

"Though I am a woman like all others, my wickedness is especially profound. Please, Master, show compassion. Teach me the True Law by which I can instantly sweep away the Five Obstructions, the Three Transgressions, the clouds and mists of illusion and attachment in the cycle

[10]Perhaps because Izumi Shikibu's verse alludes to a passage in the "Phantom City" chapter of the *Lotus Sutra*, "From darkness into darkness" (TSD 9 [262]: 22c; Watson, *The Lotus Sutra*, 121).

[11]Because the *udonge* (*ficus glomerata*) is said to bloom once every three thousand years, it is employed as a metaphor for that which is extremely precious.

Fig. 33. Izumi Shikibu at Enkyōji. From *Seiganji engi emaki*. Courtesy of Seiganji Temple and the Kyoto National Museum.

of birth and death, and by which I can be reborn in the jeweled paradise of non-regression."[12]

She threw herself to the ground and confessed her sins. Shōkū Shōnin listened closely. Greatly moved by her fervent intent, and wringing tears from his priestly sleeves, he stood silent for a while. Eventually, he spoke:

"In truth the three worlds are as a dream, a mirage, and the six roads are to be abandoned.[13] To be born in human form is rare. Should you pass your life for naught, then when might you hope to escape the cycle of birth and death? But if you immediately set about performing the Buddhist austerities with unwavering devotion, you'll quickly leave birth and death behind—such is without doubt.

"Now in Buddhism there are as many as 84,000 gates through which one may enter the Way, for as each person's aptitude and circumstances are

[12]The Pure Land is described as a paradise of non-regression because once rebirth is attained there, the achievement is permanent.

[13]The three worlds are the worlds of delusion in which sentient beings dwell. The six roads are the six planes of existence through which sentient beings transmigrate according to their karma.

unique, benefits are conferred according to individual capacities. The gate of which you inquire is that of rebirth in the Pure Land. In addition to my other devotions, I too have undertaken the practices of the Western Paradise for many years. But as comprehension of the Absolute is a fundamental aim, the benefits of Amida's teaching are not yet entirely revealed to me either.

"The Great Bodhisattva on Mount Hachiman to the south of the capital is a native manifestation of Lord Amida of the Pure Land. He conceals his brilliance and mingles with the filth of this world in order to establish innumerable links to sentient beings. You should visit his shrine and single-mindedly pray for his will. If you lay bare your true heart, you'll surely receive a response." Having spoken thus, Shōkū Shōnin offered no further advice.

Izumi Shikibu proceeded to Mount Hachiman as she had been instructed. For seven days and seven nights she kept a vigil before the inner shrine of the Great Bodhisattva. Unsurpassed in devotion, she prayed for a means of achieving rebirth in the Pure Land. It was then the middle of the eighth month, and in the clear light of the moon a bell rang forth in the deep stillness of early morning. As dawn began to break, an eighty-year-old monk suddenly appeared from within the shrine.

"At Seiganji Temple in the capital," he said, "the principal image, carved by the Great Kasuga Deity, Bodhisattva of Myriad Acts of Compassion, is Buddha of the Western Paradise. In accord with his Great Transcendent Vow,[14] he expediently appears at Seiganji in order to lead sentient beings to the Pure Land. He greets the dying and guides them on to Paradise, traveling without fail once every day to the Western Pure Land and back. You should put your faith in this image at Seiganji, pay obeisance, chant Amida's name, and set your mind on being cured. Even men and women turned upside-down with delusion are included in the Vow. How then could you not be saved? Now hurry to Seiganji and pray for a straight path to the Pure Land."

The old monk vanished without a trace. Izumi Shikibu felt as if she were the nun Mahāprajāpatī when she received the prophecy at the assembly on Eagle Peak to become Buddha-Gladly-Seen-by-All-Living-Beings,[15] or as if she were the eight-year-old Dragon Girl when she attained enlightenment

[14]The "Great Transcendent Vow" is the eighteenth of Amida's forty-eight Original Vows, the one in which he promises rebirth in his Pure Land to all who invoke his name.

[15]According to the "Encouraging Devotion" chapter of the *Lotus Sutra*, Shakyamuni Buddha prophesied at the assembly on Eagle Peak that his aunt and adoptive mother Mahāprajāpatī (Gautamī; also Daiaidō) would attain enlightenment in the company of six thousand other women (TSD 9 [262]: 36a; Watson, *The Lotus Sutra*, 191–92). I have borrowed the translation "Gladly-Seen-by-All-Living-Beings" from Watson, *The Lotus Sutra*, 191.

Fig. 34. Izumi Shikibu and the Great Hachiman Bodhisattva. From *Seiganji engi emaki*. Courtesy of Seiganji Temple and the Kyoto National Museum.

in the Immaculate World to the south as a result of Mañjuśrī's teaching.[16] Unable to restrain her tears, she wept into her sleeves and proceeded to Seiganji.

Thus Izumi Shikibu came to our temple. For forty-eight days she stayed within the temple grounds, exercising unparalleled devotion; constantly chanting Amida's name, she earnestly prayed for rebirth in the Pure Land. Late one night when the temple had grown quiet and the lamplight dim, she dozed for a short while. An old nun of more than seventy suddenly stepped down from within the altar. Drawing near Izumi Shikibu's side, she spoke:

"The intent with which you call on me is true. Entrust your rebirth to the Transcendent Vow.

"The Pure Land teachings and practices have nothing to do with supplications that strain the heart or mortify the flesh. If you but chant 'Hail

[16]According to the "Devadatta" chapter of the *Lotus Sutra*, the Dragon Girl attained instant enlightenment before the eyes of a group of doubting men by first transforming into a man and then into a Buddha (TSD 9 [262]: 35c; Watson, *The Lotus Sutra*, 188).

Amida Buddha' with unwavering faith and a desire to be saved, you will be received in the beneficent light of salvation, illuminating the lightless gloom of delusion.

"Women's Pure Land rebirth in particular is taken up in my thirty-fifth Original Vow. Lady Vaidehī witnessed the miraculous reception with her own eyes, and that she attained supreme enlightenment just as she was, without having her filthy femininity transformed, was thanks to the wonder of that Original Vow.[17] You shouldn't think it was because of anything that Vaidehī did herself. Explicitly, the vow proclaims:

> When I am to become a Buddha, if in the innumerable, wondrous, various Buddha Lands of the ten directions there is a woman who hears my name, whose heart is turned to the Dharma in joyous faith, who despises her female body and who, when her life has come to pass, is yet reborn in the female form, then I shall not accept enlightenment.[18]

"If women of the Latter Age appeal to my Original Vows and wholeheartedly recite the *nenbutsu*, they may enjoy the same rewards as Vaidehī. Their Pure Land rebirth is guaranteed. Now put aside all other vows and practices—simply keep me in your heart and single-mindedly chant my name."

Not the least bit aware that she was dreaming, Izumi Shikibu wept tears of joy. "Oh, thank you," she cried, reverently pressing her palms together in obeisance. The old nun chanted a single verse:

Amida-bu to	At Naniwa in Settsu
iu yori hoka wa	one should gather reeds—
tsu no kuni no	other than saying
naniwa no koto mo	"Amida Buddha,"
ashikarinubeshi	all deeds are wrong.

"If you keep this poem in mind and call on me with earnest intent," the nun explained, "I will certainly come to greet you and lead you on to the Pure Land in accord with your invocation of my name. You should abandon every single doubt, devote yourself to the *nenbutsu* and await my host of bodhisattvas coming to receive you."

[17]According to the *Visualization Sutra* (*Kanmuryōjukyō*), Shakyamuni appeared before Queen Vaidehī (Idaike) when she was imprisoned by her evil son Ajātaśatru. The "miraculous reception" (*raigō*) is the term for Amida's appearance with a host of bodhisattvas when he comes to greet dying devotees to lead them on to the Pure Land.

[18]This is the thirty-fifth Original Vow as it is cited in *The Sutra of Infinite Life* (*Muryōjukyō*), in TSD 12 [360]: 268c. That Amida did accept enlightenment is taken as proof of its reliability.

Fig. 35. Izumi Shikibu and the Seiganji Amida. From *Seiganji engi emaki*. Courtesy of Seiganji Temple and the Kyoto National Museum.

Izumi Shikibu awoke.[19] She knew in her heart that the nun had been a manifestation of Amida Buddha. She was deeply grateful and revered Amida's vow to save all living beings, abandoning none, even more than she had before. In her days at the palace she had passed her time before an elegant mirror, forever making up her lovely face and combing out her glossy hair, preening and dressing in the finest robes—and though this is the kind of woman she had been, in an instant she swept away the impurities of this floating world, cut the bonds tying her to the endless cycle of birth and death, turned to the path of enlightenment and became a pure, precept-minding nun.

[19]The text contains a note here written in half-size characters:

> In what seems to have been the Kenkyū era [1190–98], Master Hōnen once stayed at our temple after completing his *Senchakushū*. Hearing how this poem by our principal image had moved Izumi Shikibu to enlightenment, he declared it to be in perfect accord with his treatise. He is said to have recited it with great feeling.

According to one tradition, Hōnen composed *Senchakushū* (*Senchaku hongan nenbutsushū*, "Passages on the Selection of the Nenbutsu in the Original Vow") in 1198, at the age of 66.

Taking the name Sen'i, she wrapped herself in the dark robes of the clergy and began carrying a rosary of one hundred and eight beads.[20] She submitted offerings of holy water and *shikimi* flowers, and with purity of words, thoughts, and deeds, she devoted herself to the sacred practices day and night. She erected a brushwood shack beside our temple and made her home within it.

There was a one-room building constructed by the Midō Chancellor Michinaga called the *Komidō*, or "Small Buddha Hall."[21] Michinaga gave it to Izumi Shikibu. She thereupon took up residence in the temple compound itself, remaining at most times within this hall. Other than going out to pay her respects to the principal image in the mornings and evenings, she never left her room at all. Thus over many years of reciting Amida's name, she accumulated great merit.

At the time of her death, purple clouds trailed from the building's eaves, music rang in the sky, and a wondrous fragrance filled the air all around. Amida and his heavenly host came to receive her. Facing toward the Western Paradise, she sat erect with her palms pressed together, continuously reciting the *nenbutsu*. Then, on the twenty-second day of the third month of the third year of Chōwa in the reign of Sanjō, sixty-seventh mortal emperor of Japan, Izumi Shikibu achieved her fundamental desire for rebirth in the Pure Land.[22]

In the reign sixty-sixth emperor Ichijō, there was a ruffian in the western provinces. His lay name is unknown.[23] He led a band of five hundred evil criminals. He would accost passenger boats on the ocean and seize merchants' wealth and wares, and he would hold up travelers in mountain villages and take their gold and silver. In his thievery and piracy, he was just like Zhou Chu of old.[24] Word spread, and because the people felt uneasy, traffic along the post roads all but ceased.

[20]For the one hundred and eight types of human delusion (*hyakuhachi bonnō*).

[21]Fujiwara no Michinaga (966–1027) is known as the Midō *Kanpaku* (Buddha Hall Chancellor) for having constructed Hōjōji Temple in 1020.

[22]According to *Rakuyō Seiganji honzon engi* and the six-scroll *Seiganji engi*, Izumi Shikibu achieved rebirth in the Pure Land on the *twenty-first* day of the third month of Chōwa 3 (1014). Kikuchi Masakazu, "Kyōhō hachinen-sha *Rakuyō Seiganji honzon engi*," in *Shōdō bungaku kenkyū: dai san shū*, ed. Fukuda Akira and Hirota Tetsumichi (Tokyo: Miyai Shoten, 2001), 375; Yutani Yūzō, "*Seiganji engi* rokkanbon no kaidai to honkoku," *Dōhō Daigaku Bukkyō bunka kenkyūjo kiyō* 18 (1998), 89a.

[23]This sentence appears to be an interpolated note. It is written in half-size characters within the text.

[24]Zhou Chu was a famous miscreant of the Jin Dynasty (265–420) who eventually came to mend his ways.

Fig. 36. Izumi Shikibu in her latter years at Seiganji. From *Seiganji engi emaki*. Courtesy of Seiganji Temple and the Kyoto National Museum.

One time the ruffian came to the capital to steal some valuables, and he stopped at our temple. Because he lacked the least bit of goodness in his heart, he did not think to pay his respects to the principal image. But when he wandered inside the temple hall and gazed upon the Seiganji Amida, his hair stood on end and faith welled up within him. Renouncing his crimes with heartfelt regret and giving up his wicked ways, he became a practitioner of the single-minded *nenbutsu*. He wished to return to his home province to tell his wife and children, but because he lamented parting from the principal image, he had a two-inch likeness of it cast in metal. He kept it on his person, revering it at all times.

One of the ruffian's former companions was later captured in connection with an unrelated affair, and in the process of interrogation, he identified the ruffian as the leader of the thieves. Emperor Ichijō therefore commanded Fujiwara no Yasumasa to apprehend the man.[25] Yasumasa gathered a group of warriors and quickly set out. He seized the ruffian without difficulty and delivered him to the capital. It was the fifth year of the Kankō era [1008]. He led the ruffian to the Seventh Avenue Riverbed,[26] but when he tried to cut off

[25]Fujiwara no Yasumasa (958–1036) was Izumi Shikibu's second historical husband.

[26]*Shichijōgawara*, where the man was to be executed.

Fig. 37. The near-execution of a ruffian at the Seventh Avenue Riverbed. From *Seiganji engi emaki*. Courtesy of Seiganji Temple and the Kyoto National Museum.

the man's head, his long sword snapped in two. Because the man remained unharmed, people asked him why.

"After abandoning evil," the ruffian explained, "I placed all of my faith in the Buddha at Seiganji. For this reason I had a two-inch metal statue cast in its image. I always wear it around my neck and single-mindedly chant the *nenbutsu*. There's nothing more to it. So, the image must have protected me." The constables were amazed, and when they took out the ruffian's icon, they saw that it was true. Lay and monastic, everyone who saw or heard tell of these events was struck with wonder. Yasumasa informed the emperor of all that had transpired. The emperor listened, and he decided that since the ruffian had given up his evil ways, and since he had also received an act of supernatural protection, he ought not to be executed. The emperor thus absolved him of his crimes.

Because the ruffian had indeed received divine protection, his faith increased all the more. He returned to our temple, where he shaved his head, adopted priestly robes, and took the name Jōkyō Shōnin. Giving up silk and cotton and the five grains, he clothed himself in coarse cloth and sustained his life on fruit and grasses. He became a mendicant holy man, passing years in the performance of painful austerities. Urging everyone to contribute, he raised money for the casting of our temple bell. You can read all about it in the bell's inscription. Not only that, but recalling his own former wickedness

Fig. 38. Jōkyō Shōnin carves an image of Tamonten. From *Seiganji engi emaki*. Courtesy of Seiganji Temple and the Kyoto National Museum.

and reasoning that evil arises from poverty, he set out to alleviate the people's destitution by carving a statue of Tamonten.[27] Every time he swung his hatchet, he bowed down three times in obeisance, praying that the wishes of all sentient beings be fulfilled. The image was finally completed after three years, and it was enshrined in the outer sanctuary of our temple hall.

In the reign of Emperor Ichijō, Jōtōmon'in, daughter of the Midō Chancellor Fujiwara no Michinaga, a twelfth generation descendant of Chief Minister Kamatari,[28] transcribed the three Pure Land sutras in her own hand for the sake of her late father. She passed a week performing spirited services at our temple, ceaselessly chanting sutras and invoking the name, praying with all her heart that Amida Buddha might reveal to her the place of her father's rebirth. As she dozed near dawn on the final day of her devotions, a man

[27]Bishamonten, one of four Buddhist guardian deities. Bishamonten (Tamonten) is revered in Japan as a deity of wealth.

[28]Chief Minister (*taishokan*) Fujiwara no Kamatari (614–69) was the founder of the Fujiwara clan.

Fig. 39. Jōtōmon'in at Seiganji. From *Seiganji engi emaki.* Courtesy of Seiganji Temple and the Kyoto National Museum.

in a standing court cap and a priestly stole appeared to her in a dream and presented her with a letter. Jōtōmon'in asked him where he had come from, and the man replied, "I am a messenger of the Seiganji Buddha." Jōtōmon'in quickly opened the letter. Written in an elegant hand, it read, "Your late father has attained rebirth in the lower grade, lower rank."[29]

"Why was he reborn in the lower grade?" Jōtōmon'in inquired. The messenger replied: "During his lifetime, your father was firm in his aspiration for rebirth in the Pure Land, so he was destined for rebirth in the upper rank of the upper grade. But because he wavered in his purpose, he was reborn in the lower grade. And even this was due to the magnificent power of the Buddha's vow." Awaking from her dream, Jōtōmon'in wept with grief. Praying all the more for her father, she gathered devotees of every kind and paid them to perform diligent services for his rebirth in the upper grade.

The lay priest Ennō was a man of Fushimi Village in the Soekami district of Yamato province.[30] He ascended Mount Shigi at the age of eighteen, and

[29]According to the *Visualization Sutra* (*Kanmuryōjukyō*), there are three grades of Pure Land rebirth (Higher, Middle, and Lower), each of which is divided into an additional three grades (Higher, Middle, and Lower), for a total of nine grades of Pure Land rebirth.

[30]Ennō's story is also contained in *Honchō shinshū ōjōden* (1151; NST 7:692b–93b), and in *Genkō shakusho* (1322), in Kuroita Katsumi, ed., *Shintei zōho kokushi taikei,* vol. 31 (Tokyo: Yoshikawa Kōbunkan, 1930), 282–83. For a discussion of Ennō's tale, see R. Keller Kimbrough, "Tourists in Paradise: Writing the Pure Land in Medieval Japanese Fiction," *Japanese Journal of Religious Studies* 33, no. 2 (Autumn 2006): 269–96.

although he spent days and years reading and studying, he had difficulty learning because he was dim-witted by birth. Nevertheless, he was righteous at heart. Constantly placing his trust in Amida, he devoted himself solely to the practices of the Western Pure Land.

One time Ennō heard a teacher lecture on the *Yakushi Sutra* passage, "If a person should call upon the name of World-Honored Yakushi, Lapis Lazuli Buddha of Light, eight bodhisattvas will come flying through the air at the moment of death in order to show the way."[31] Ennō thought, "If I concentrate on Yakushi, he'll show me the way to the Pure Land. Fortunately the sixteen-foot Yakushi at Kōbun'in Temple is known for its miracles.[32] I'll pray to it and then bow down before Amida."

Ennō began a hundred-day course of pilgrimages to the temple, prostrating himself three thousand times a day in prayer that he might pay his respects to the living Yakushi and Amida in this present life. Before long it was the ninety-sixth day. Ennō set out for the temple. Appearing in the very flesh, Yakushi filled the sky over an open field beside the road. The living Amida and his Pure Land host were there too, all at the same time. Ennō bowed. Brimming with joy, he pressed his face to the ground in reverent supplication, his faith strengthened all the more. The Buddhas later disappeared into our temple. Ennō venerated the principal image all through the day, never pausing in his invocation of Amida's name.

Three years passed in this way until the last day of the third month of the second year of Kyūan [1146], when, at the age of fifty-seven, Ennō suddenly died. A crowd of priests gathered to see, but as the warmth had not yet left his breast, they held off burying him, keeping a close watch for two weeks in case he might revive. However, in the end he did not revive, so with little choice they left his body in a field. Lay and monastic believers went to pray over him every day, and they saw that birds and animals left him completely untouched. The days and nights passed, and Ennō's corpse remained intact. Many people looked and talked, thinking it most peculiar. Then, on the fourth day of the fifth month of that same year, Ennō awoke. He said little at first, but after three years he was able to speak as he had before, and facing the other priests, he explained:

"I was on my way to the Dark Land after I died that year,[33] when six priests called out to me and led me through the air. As I went with them, I asked, 'What is this place?' 'We're headed to King Enma's palace,' one of

[31] *Bussetsu Yakushi rurikō nyorai hongan kudoku kyō* (Yakushi Sutra), TSD 14 (450): 406b.

[32] On the location and history of Kōbun'in, see Yutani Yūzō, "*Seiganji engi* kankei shiryō," *Fukakusa kyōgaku* 19 (1999), 304–9.

[33] The Dark Land (*meido*) is the world of the dead.

them explained. I protested, saying, 'I've been performing the Pure Land practices for a long time so that I could be reborn in the Western Paradise. So what are we doing going to see Enma?' 'First we're going to the King's palace to show you the karmic torments for living beings,' the priest said, 'and then we're going to take you to Paradise.' But when I refused, the priest said, 'In that case, we'll let you pay homage to the Pure Land first.'

"The priests seemed to lead me onward, and in a moment we were at the eastern gate of Paradise. We passed through the barrier and gazed upon the many palace halls, each of which was lavishly adorned with the seven kinds of jewels. They cast a myriad forms of sparkling light, and the buildings stood upon the water. Thinking this strange, I wondered whether it was the doing of some heavenly being, or an example of the Buddhas' miraculous power. 'It's unheard of!' I cried. One of the priests spoke: 'This is lapis lazuli, not water.' I felt the ground with my hand. It was indeed hard, and my hand was not wet in the least.

"When I gazed out upon the Lake of Eight Virtues, I saw great jeweled lotus blossoms with tall buildings on each. Bodhisattvas and the Heavenly Host and countless divine protectors played music and praised the virtues of the Buddhas. The marvelous cries of swans and peacocks were softened by the waves of the jeweled lake, and the air was filled with chanted meditations on the Buddhas and the Sangha. The seven-jeweled trees were adorned with seven-layered nets of gems. There were palace halls among the trees, mixing their radiance in a dazzling display. Bodhisattvas beyond number rained wondrous flowers from the sky as they flew back and forth in homage to the Buddhas. I worshiped each and every aspect of the realm's virtue and magnificence every moment I was there.

"I asked the six priests, 'Which is the hall where Amida Buddha abides?' One of them replied, 'I'll go first and see.' He entered one of the palace halls and then returned. He led me and the other five priests into the hall, and then he spoke: 'This is the Amida Buddha of Seiganji. Since you have been at that temple for so many years single-mindedly chanting the *nenbutsu* and paying reverent obeisance, he has deigned to appear here now.' When I prayed to Amida, he shone a brilliant reddish light from each of his distinguishing Buddha marks,[34] illuminating the ten directions. The majesty of it was beyond words to describe.

"I asked the priests to let me stay in that palace hall, but one of them said, 'You are to hurry back to the human world and transcribe the five Mahāyāna sutras. If you continue paying your respects and chanting the

[34]*Sanjūni-sō*, the thirty-two distinguishing characteristics of a Buddha.

Fig. 40. Ennō in the Pure Land. From *Seiganji engi emaki*. Courtesy of Seiganji Temple and the Kyoto National Museum.

Name, you are sure to be reborn here. Have you made a vow to copy the sutras?' I replied that I had not. 'Well, I'll show you Enma's palace,' the priest said.

"The priest began to lead, and in a moment we arrived at the King's abode. Enma also asked if I had made a vow to transcribe the five Mahāyāna sutras, and again I replied that I had not. One of the priests spoke: 'All those years you used to sit with people when they copied the sutras, and you felt joy in your heart when you thought that someday you, too, might make copies, just like them.' Catching the priest's meaning, I replied that in fact I had. 'Just so,' the priest said. 'And since your allotted years are not yet through, you are to return now to your former land, transcribe the sutras, and be reborn in the Paradise World.'

"The priest then invited me on a tour of hell. Words cannot describe the plight of all those beings suffering the torments of the eight freezing and eight burning realms. After we emerged, the six priests spoke: "Do you recognize us? We are the six Jizō from the outer sanctuary of the Seiganji Temple Hall. We have come here to teach you the causes and effects of good and bad behavior.' No sooner had they spoken than I revived, as if awaking from a dream."

Ennō quickly encouraged lay and monastic priests and nuns to transcribe the five Mahāyāna sutras in gold ink, and he enshrined them on Mount Kinbu. He passed three years at our temple invoking the *nenbutsu* with even more ardor. Then, in the reign of Konoe, seventy-sixth human emperor, at the hour of the horse on the twenty-fourth day of the first month of the first year of Ninpei [1151],[35] Ennō announced that his life was through. He bathed and donned a priestly stole. Sitting cross-legged with his head bowed and his palms together, revering the Buddha and bodhisattvas' miraculous reception, he met his end reciting the *nenbutsu* with right concentration. Music rang in the sky and a wondrous scent filled the room. The priests left him as he was for more than ten days so that the people of the capital could pay their respects. When they went to bury him on Mount Funaoka, the road was lined with devotees of every kind playing music and establishing karmic links to the Pure Land.

Our temple hall was destroyed in a sudden fire on the ninth day of the fourth month of the third year of the Jōgen era [1209] in the reign of eighty-third human emperor Tsuchimikado. Miraculously, the principal image remained unharmed. The temple community was overjoyed, and its members immediately built a temporary hall in which to house the image.

At that time there was an Ise provisional governor by the name of Tameie. He had suffered the pains of poverty for many years, living in a wretched dwelling, frustrated in his desires. Day and night he lamented his sorry state, thinking only of how he might acquire material wealth. For some years he had been traveling to Kurama Temple in the northern part of the capital to pray. One day as he was passing by our temple gate on his way to Kurama, a drizzling rain began to fall. He took shelter for a while in the outer sanctum of our central hall, and perhaps because he was tired from walking, he dozed off to sleep. Tamonten appeared to him in a dream and spoke:

"Why do you travel such a distance to the north? I am Tamonten of Kurama.[36] In one of my manifestations, I reside in the outer sanctum of this temple hall in order to protect this place from harm. From now on you should come to this temple hall and venerate the principal image with single-minded devotion. For sentient beings who worship Amida, I bestow my constant, joyful protection, putting their lives at ease. And it's not only me who does this—Bonten, Taishakuten, and all the other deities do too."

Tameie awoke. Unsettled by his dream, he asked a resident priest to explain. "This is an image of Tamonten," the priest said, showing him a

[35]The hour of the horse spans from 11:00 a.m. to 1:00 p.m.

[36]Tamonten (Bishamonten) is the principal image of Kurama Temple. The tale of his former life as a supernatural "Golden Prince" in India is told in the *otogizōshi/sekkyō-bushi Bishamon Tennō no honji* (a variant of *Bishamon no honji*), in Yokoyama Shigeru, ed., *Muromachi jidai monogatari shū*, vol. 2 (Tokyo: Inoue Shobō, 1962), 109–26 (see page 126b for the Golden Prince/Bishamonten's identification with Mount Kurama).

Fig. 41. Ise Governor Tameie at Seiganji. From *Seiganji engi emaki*. Courtesy of Seiganji Temple and the Kyoto National Museum.

statue, and he related how Jōkyō Shōnin had carved it in the distant past by revering it three times every time he cut.[37] Because Tameie had received a divine revelation, his faith deepened to his very bones. Following the deity's advice, from that day forward he ceased traveling to Kurama, visiting only our own temple instead.[38] His belief bore fruit in the end, and he achieved wealth and prosperity just as he had wished.

Now Tameie was deeply distressed at the effects of our temple fire. "That I've attained such prosperity is due entirely to Tamonten and the Seiganji Amida," he thought to himself. "So how could I forget my debt of gratitude at this time and not give my wealth to aid the temple's reconstruction?"

[37]Jōkyō Shōnin is the rehabilitated ruffian apprehended by Fujiwara no Yasumasa in a preceding part of the *engi*, translated above.

[38]This and the second part of the preceding sentence are interpolated from *Rakuyō Seiganji honzon engi* and the six-scroll *Seiganji engi*, in Kikuchi, "Kyōhō hachinen-sha *Rakuyō Seiganji honzon engi*," 382, and Yutani, "*Seiganji engi* rokkanbon no kaidai to honkoku," 92a.

Fig. 42. Tameie's reconstruction of Seiganji. From *Seiganji engi emaki*. Courtesy of Seiganji Temple and the Kyoto National Museum.

Tameie made a great vow and informed the emperor of his intention. In addition to entrusting him with additional funds, the emperor decreed that Tameie should do his best to rebuild the temple hall. Donating his own resources, Tameie engaged himself in the construction. He personally directed the work, and the temple was eventually restored to its former state. For this reason Tameie, Tametada, and generations of their descendents have been benefactors of our institution. Their house has prospered for a very long time.

Shakyamuni opened the Pure Land gate for Vaidehī in the royal palace, causing Taishakuten, Bonten, and the other world-protecting deities to appear in the sky and rain down heavenly flowers in obeisance. And when Ryōnin Shōnin promoted the interpenetrating *nenbutsu*, Tamonten and all the deities and functionaries of the afterworld proclaimed that they, too, would join him.[39] That there should be miracles such as these is wonderful indeed!

[39]Ryōnin Shōnin (1073–1132) was the founder of the Yūzū Nenbutsu (Interpenetrating Nenbutsu) sect. According to *Kokon chomonjū* 53 (dated 1254; NKBT 84:90), the Kurama Bishamonten (Tamonten) and numerous other Buddhas and deities appeared before Ryōnin and pledged their support for his Pure Land Buddhist movement.

Izumi Shikibu[1]

At a time during the reign of Emperor Ichijō in the not-so-distant past, there was once in the flourishing capital a beautiful courtesan named Izumi Shikibu. Residing in the Imperial Palace was a man named Tachibana Yasumasa,[2] and from the time that he was nineteen and she thirteen, Yasumasa and Izumi Shikibu came to pledge wondrous vows of love. They shared a deep affection, and in the spring of her fourteenth year Izumi Shikibu bore a son.

Perhaps in whispered conversations with her lover she felt ashamed, for Izumi Shikibu abandoned her baby on Fifth Avenue Bridge. She wrote a poem on the hem of the baby's iris *kosode* swaddling clothes and left a short unsheathed sword by his side. A townsman adopted the infant, raised him, and later sent him to Mount Hiei to become a monk.

The boy was deeply devoted to his studies—he was a child without peer—and of all the priests, there were none who did not hold him dear to their hearts. His reputation spread throughout all of Mount Hiei. His compassion, too, was of an extraordinary sort. Not only was he celebrated on the holy mountain, but as he diligently pursued the path of the Buddha, his name, Dōmei Ajari, spread far and wide and he came to be known throughout the land.

When Dōmei was eighteen years old, he once took part in a performance of the Eight Lectures of the *Lotus Sutra* at the Imperial Palace.[3] A gusting wind blew up the bamboo blind of an adjoining room two or three times, revealing an elegant court lady of about thirty. Her eyebrows overflowed with charm as she listened to the priests' discussion, obviously engrossed. With but a single glance Dōmei was overcome; upon returning to his home, ascending the mountain, he was captivated by the alluring image of the

[1]The following translation is based upon the Shibukawa *Otogi bunko* text, published ca. 1716–29, in NKBT 38:312–18 and NKBZ 36:385–93.

[2]"Tachibana Yasumasa" is a combination of the names of Izumi Shikibu's two historical husbands, Tachibana no Michisada (?–1016) and Fujiwara no Yasumasa (958–1036).

[3]The Eight Lectures of the *Lotus Sutra* (*Hokke hakkō*) is a ceremony in which priests read and discuss the eight fascicles of the *Lotus Sutra*, mornings and evenings, over a period of four days.

Fig. 43. Dōmyō is sent to live on Mt. Hiei. From *Izumi Shikibu* (Shibukawa text, early eighteenth century). Courtesy of the Kyoto Prefectural Library Archives (Kyōto Furitsu Sōgō Shiryōkan).

woman he had seen. That he could not forget her was the result of a karmic bond from a previous life.

Dōmei later returned to the capital. Hoping for a second glimpse of the lady he had seen and adored, he disguised himself as an orange-vendor, proceeded to the palace and set about selling his fruit. A servant-girl emerged from the room of the woman he had seen and asked to buy twenty *sen* worth. Dōmei counted out twenty oranges and sold them to her, but rather than counting with words, he counted with love poems:

hitotsu to ya	One is for one
hitori marone no	who sleeps in his clothes alone,
kusamakura	a pillow of grass for his head.
tamoto shiboranu	No dawn does not find him
akatsuki mo nashi	wringing tears from his sleeve.
futatsu to ya	Two is for the two-paneled
futae byōbu no	folding screen
uchi ni nete	within which he lies.
koishiki hito wo	When will he see her—
itsuka mirubeki	the one for whom he longs?
mitsu to ka ya	Three is for he
mite mo kokoro no	who sees, but in his heart

Fig. 44. Dōmyō spies Izumi Shikibu at the palace. From *Izumi Shikibu* (Shibukawa text, early eighteenth century). Courtesy of the Kyoto Prefectural Library Archives (Kyōto Furitsu Sōgō Shiryōkan).

nagusamade
nado ukihito no
koishikaruramu

feels no relief.
Why must he pine for
one so cold?

yotsu to ka ya
yobuka ni kimi wo
omouramu
makura katashiku
sode zo tsuyukeki

Four is for
his longing
in the depths of night—
a pillow for one,
his sleeve is soaked with dew.

itsutsu to ya
ima ya ima ya to
matsu hodo ni
mi wo kagerō ni
nasu zo kanashiki

Five is for the waiting,
his life disappearing
all the while.
"Does she come now?" he thinks,
"or now?" How sad!

mutsu to ka ya
mukai no nobe ni
sumu shika mo
tsuma yue ni koso
nakiakashikere

Six is for the buck
who lives in the fields
across the way—
he too cries through the night
for his mate.

nanatsu to ya
naki na no tatsu mo

Seven is for a name:
victim to groundless rumors,

tsurakaraji
kimi yue nagasu
waga na narikeri

yet no hardship to bear.
'Tis for my darling
this gossip spreads my name.

yatsu to ka ya
yayoi no tsuki no
hikari wo ba
omowanu kimi ga
yado ni todomeyo

Eight is for the light
of the Third Month Moon—
may it linger
on the dwelling
of one who thinks not of me.

kokonotsu ya
koko de awazu wa
gokuraku no
mida no jōdo de
au yo aru beshi

Nine is for Paradise.
If in this world
we are not to meet,
then in Amida's Pure Land
we shall surely share a night.

tō to ka ya
toya wo hanareshi
arataka wo
itsuka waga te ni
hikisuete min

Ten is for a fledgling hawk,
flown from the coop
and unused to the touch of man.
When shall I bring her
to rest upon my hand?

jūichi ya
ichido makoto no
aru naraba
hito no koto no ha
ureshikaramashi

Eleven is for sincerity,
for if but once such a thing
you should know,
how happy I might be
upon hearing your words!

jūni to ya
nikushi to hito no
omouran
kanawanu koto ni
kokoro tsukuseba

Twelve is for you
who must think it
hateful—
how I waste my heart
on that which I cannot attain.

jūsan ya
sa nomi nasake wo
furisute so
nasake wa hito no
tame ni araneba

Thirteen is for compassion:
don't throw it away
just like that.
Compassion, you know,
is not for others alone.[4]

jūshi to ya
shi nan inochi mo
oshikarazu
kimi yue nagasu
waga mi nariseba

Fourteen is for
death or life—
neither would I begrudge
if for you
I should drift away.

[4]The poem alludes to an aphorism, *nasake wa hito no tame narazu*, "compassion is not for others alone." (Good deeds benefit the doer as well as the receiver.)

jūgo to ya gose no sawari to nari ya sen mi no hakanaku mo awade hatenaba	Fifteen is for the obstacle it would be in the world to come, if our fleeting lives should end without us once having met.
jūroku ya rokuji no hodo wo suguru ni mo kimi ni kokoro wo tsurete koso yuke	Sixteen is for the six lands through which I pass, carrying you with me in my heart all the while.
jūshichi ya shichido mōde no tabi tabi mo kimi ni au yo to inori koso sure	Seventeen is for the seven pilgrimages I perform, praying every time for a world (a night!) in which we can meet.
jūhachi ya hazukashinagara iu koto wo kokorozuyoku mo awanu kimi ka na	Eighteen is for my bashful darling, who with hardhearted words refuses me still.
jūkyū to ya kurushi yo goto ni machikanete sode itazura ni kuchi ya hatemashi	Nineteen is for every torturous night I wait in teary longing— Shall my sleeve rot through for naught?
nijū to ya nikushi to hito no omouran ware naranu mi wo hito no kōreba	Twenty is for you who must think it hateful, for a love-sick man to be so enamored of you.

"Oranges aren't something to be greedy for," the servant-girl said, "but your poems are so lovely, I think I'll have one more!" Dōmei gave her another orange and recited:

nijūichi to ichido no nasake komen to te ōku no kotoba kataritsukushitsu	Twenty-one is for the singleness of my love, which in so many words I've tried to express, running out of things to say.

The servant-girl stared hard at Dōmei. "How can you be so refined and selling fruit?" she asked.

Fig. 45. Dōmyō dances for a servant-girl at the palace. From *Izumi Shikibu* (Shibukawa text, early eighteenth century). Courtesy of the Kyoto Prefectural Library Archives (Kyōto Furitsu Sōgō Shiryōkan).

"'The rain,'" Dōmei replied, "'—falling, falling.'" His meaning was lost upon her.

The emperor had been listening all the while. "Watch this vendor and see where he goes," he commanded, sending the servant-girl out after him. Dōmei exited the palace grounds. "The sun has set today," he thought to himself, "but there's still tomorrow!" He took lodging at an inn. The servant-girl took note of his boarding house and returned to report what she had seen.

"I'm sure you didn't know it," the emperor said, "but the words of that vendor—they were from a poem by Lady Ise when she was in love with Prince Genji:[5]

kimi kōru	Drenched
namida no ame ni	in a rain of tears
sode nurete	of love for you—
hosan to sureba	I spread my sleeves to dry,
mata wa furi furi	but again the rain—falling, falling.

This is what he meant."

[5]Lady Ise (ca. 875–938) was a prominent woman poet. That she would have loved Genji, a character in a fictional work written after her death, is extremely unlikely.

Now the woman whom Dōmei had seen thought long and hard about Dōmei's profound love for her, and she thought about Ono no Komachi, once adored by men for her youthful beauty. Komachi did nothing to appease the bitter longings of her suitors—an unfathomable sin—and so unable to escape her karma, she became obsessed with the memory of the Fourth Rank Lesser Captain and composed:[6]

iisutsuru	Would that there were
koto no ha made mo	compassion
nasake aru ya	in your thoughtless words—
tada itazura ni	so meaninglessly, utterly
kuchihatsuru mi wo	have I fallen to ruin.

Mindful of Ono no Komachi's poem and anxious that she show compassion to all, the woman left the palace with the servant-girl and proceeded to Dōmei's inn. Rapping softly on Dōmei's door, she recited:

idete hose	Come out this night
koyoi bakari no	in the light of the moon
tsukikage ni	and dry love's sleeves—
furi furi nurasu	drenched as they are
koi no tamoto wo	in the falling, falling rain.

Hearing the poem from inside his room, Dōmei felt as if he were dreaming. He opened his front door but did not emerge. With a pained, love-sick expression he recited:

idezu to mo	Though I don't come out,
kokoro no araba	you morning moon,
kage sashite	shine your light
yami wo ba terase	if you have a heart
ariake no tsuki	and illuminate this darkness!

Dōmei appeared dazed. The court lady was by her nature deeply compassionate, so she went inside. That night from beneath shared bedcovers they pledged vows of undying love.

Night eventually gave way to dawn. As the two were getting dressed, the lady noticed Dōmei's short sword, and it struck her as odd. "That's

[6]In the noh plays *Sotoba Komachi* and *Kayoi Komachi*, Ono no Komachi gives Fukakusa no Shii no Shōshō, the Fourth Rank Lesser Captain, the onerous task of traveling to her residence one hundred nights before she will meet with him. In *Sotoba Komachi*, the Captain dies on the ninety-ninth night. SNKBT 57: 434–40 and 155–59.

Fig. 46. Izumi Shikibu visits Dōmyō at his lodgings. From *Izumi Shikibu* (Shibukawa text, early eighteenth century). Courtesy of the Kyoto Prefectural Library Archives (Kyōto Furitsu Sōgō Shiryōkan).

a woman's sword," she said. "I've never heard of a man wearing one of those."

"It's special," Dōmei replied. "You see, I was abandoned on Fifth Avenue Bridge when I was a baby. A man took me in and brought me up, and since this sword was left with me on the bridge, I think of it as my mother—I carry it with me wherever I go."

The woman became anxious. "How old are you?" she asked.

"They say I was left as an infant," Dōmei replied, "and now I'm grown."

"What about your swaddling clothes?"

"There was a poem on the hem of my iris *kosode*."

"Tell it to me," the woman said. Dōmei immediately replied:

momo tose ni	Though a hundred years
mata momo tose wa	be piled on
kasanu to mo	a hundred more,
nanatsu nanatsu no	would that the name of a girl of
na wo ba taeji na	seven and seven never disappear.[7]

[7]"Seven and seven" is fourteen, Izumi Shikibu's age when she bore her son.

Fig. 47. Izumi Shikibu at Enkyōji. From *Izumi Shikibu* (Shibukawa text, early eighteenth century). Courtesy of the Kyoto Prefectural Library Archives (Kyōto Furitsu Sōgō Shiryōkan).

At the time she abandoned her baby, Izumi Shikibu kept the sheath of the short sword. Because she cherished it as a remembrance of her son, she carried it with her wherever she went. She took the sheath out now and fitted it with the sword; they were without doubt a matching set.

What kind of thing is this, where parent and child, unaware, may tie the lovers' knot? 'Tis because we live in a world of suffering that such things occur! This incident was the seed of Izumi Shikibu's enlightenment, turning her heart to the path of the Buddha.

Izumi Shikibu left the capital in the night. She followed the coast past the bay of Onoe—startled by the sound of the ringing bell—and continued past the Shikama shore.[8] Pushing her way through mist and clouds, she ascended Mount Shosha in Harima Province, where she became a disciple of the holy man Shōkū Shōnin. When she attained enlightenment at the age of sixty-one, she wrote a poem on a pillar of the shrine of Mount Shosha's tutelary deity:

kuraki yori	Born from darkness
kuraki yamiji ni	into a path of darkness

[8]This may be an allusion to a passage in the noh play *Takasago* (attributed to Zeami; 1363?–1443?), which similarly refers to the "ringing bell of Onoe." NKBZ 33:55.

umarekite
sayaka ni terase
yama no ha no tsuki

in the shade of night—
shine your light down brightly,
moon on the mountain ridge![9]

As a result of inscribing her poem where she did, 'poem pillars' are said to have originated on Mount Shosha in Harima Province.

[9]This is an alternate version of Izumi Shikibu's famous "darkness into darkness" poem, *Shūi wakashū* 1342:

kuraki yori	From darkness
kuraki michi ni zo	into a path of darkness
irinu beki	I must enter—
haruka ni terase	shine your light afar,
yama no ha no tsuki	moon on the mountain ridge!

"Izumi Shikibu's Vow" (excerpt from *The Tale of Jōruri*)[1]

The young master's heart was drawn to her all the more, and he spoke on without pause:[2]

You know of course that the Way of Love has never expired, not in all the past until now. An outstanding woman was once born into the world, a great beauty and a poet by the name of Izumi Shikibu. Countless men lost their hearts to her, and she became the wife of the master of the Kyōgoku Estate.[3] The adoration of those around her was quite beyond words.

Izumi Shikibu once visited the Tōdaiji and Kōfukuji temples in order to perform memorial services for her late mother and father. She spent one week at each praying for her parents' enlightenment, and in the early morning twilight of the final day, her mother and father appeared before her where she slept. "You have diligently performed these many services so that we might attain enlightenment," they said, "but Buddhahood remains beyond our reach. This is because you were born an outstanding beauty and a poet, and countless men have lost their hearts to you. You spurned their love and we have fallen into hell as a result. We implore you to take a vow to love all men, without distinction, from the highest to the lowest. Should you do this, it is without doubt that we and you both will attain Buddhahood in this very existence."

Izumi Shikibu awoke. "The karma from my past must be wretched," she thought to herself. "After all the services I performed . . . how awful that my parents haven't achieved Buddhahood!" Deciding to abandon her feminine

[1]The following translation is from the three-scroll, sixteenth-century Akagi Bunko manuscript of the *otogizōshi Jōruri monogatari* (The Tale of Jōruri), in MJMT 7:316–19 and Mori Takenosuke, *Jōruri monogatari kenkyū* (Tokyo: Inoue Shobō, 1962), 36–41.

[2]The young master is Minamoto no Yoshitsune (1159–89), famed for his later daring in the Genpei War. He speaks to the fourteen-year-old Jōruri-hime in her apartments one night.

[3]"Kyōgoku Estate" (*Kyōgoku-dono*) refers to one of several mansions facing East Kyōgoku Avenue in the Heian capital. The most famous of these, the Tsuchimikado Kyōgoku-dono, belonged to Fujiwara no Michinaga (966–1027), in whose daughter's salon Izumi Shikibu served.

charms so that she might better pray for their enlightenment, she set about cutting her luxuriant hair. Amida Buddha was touched with pity, and so at that very moment, just as Izumi Shikibu was on the verge of making the first cut, he appeared to her in the form of an eighty-year-old monk. "Here you are about to change your looks for your parents' sake," he said, "but it will be to no avail. If you want to help them, you should take a vow to love all men, without distinction, from the highest to the lowest. If you do this, it is without doubt that you and your parents both will attain Buddhahood in this very existence."

The monk vanished into the air. "If my parents, at least, can attain Buddhahood as a result," Izumi Shikibu thought, "then what can be so hard about fulfilling such a vow?" She took leave of the Kyōgoku Estate, erected a shack on Fifth Avenue in the capital, and hung out a placard proclaiming her intention to achieve intimacy with one thousand men. As she was truly very beautiful, in three years and three months she had entertained nine hundred ninety-nine men who had loved her from before. "Tonight my vow comes to an end," she thought on the thousandth night, the final night. "I don't know who my master will be this evening, but I'll put a light outside and wait." She placed a faint light in front of her shack, spread out her brocade bedding and bid her time, thinking to herself how late it had grown.

In the dead of night she heard a sound at her south door. Opening it to take a look, she saw the old mute who lived on Kiyomizu Hill. Leaning on a bamboo cane as he always did, his body wrapped in reddish-brown rags, the man seemed to exude sickness from his very core. He was endlessly frightening, and with one look Izumi Shikibu felt dazed. Her heart seemed to stop. "If I had known it would come to this," she thought, "I never would have made that vow. Even if my parents and I both tumble down into the Three Evil Realms,[4] the horror of making love to a seedy old mute is more than I can bear." She decided to turn him away with a lie. "Listen here," she said, "Izumi Shikibu's shack is much farther to the south. Go on and see her there."

Taking in her meaning, the old mute spoke: "I am from the eastern edge of the city, and I have come because I heard you took a certain vow. But as you say I have the wrong door, my trip is for naught. Now if your vow to sell your body is a true vow[5]—a vow to love all men, without distinction, from the highest to the lowest—then you are sure to enter the True Path. This is despite the fact that women are despised by the myriad Buddhas of

[4]The Three Evil Realms are the realms of hell, hungry ghosts, and animals.

[5]The text describes Izumi Shikibu's vow as a "vow to sell [your] body," but the implication is that she is selling herself for Buddhist merit rather than monetary compensation.

the Three Ages.[6] Women are the seeds of hell, for as the *Kegon Sutra* explains, 'Women are the servants of hell; they stamp out the seeds of the Buddha. On the outside they are as bodhisattvas, while on the inside they are as devils.'[7] This means that while women appear in the bodies of bodhisattvas, on the inside they are as devils—what we speak of as the demons of this world.

"Consider even the lotus blossom of the heart: in the case of men, it unfolds properly in eight leaves, and numbers of Buddhas and deities manifest themselves there for the men's protection.[8] In the hearts of women, however, the blossom has only seven leaves. One leaf is lacking. The lotus stem is folded over, broken at the base, and since the leaves are sunken low, the Buddhas and deities materialize upside-down. At the base of the lotus is a four-inch snake. Though the woman may eat various foods, the snake is held back by the blossom, and because it cannot eat at once, it cries bitterly in frustration. As its red tears accumulate, they become the woman's monthly obstruction. Should she cleanse herself in clear water, she faces the reproach of the water deity, or if in the earth, the reproach of the deities of the soil. And should she enter the sunlight, Dainichi will chastise her severely.

"As it is explained in the Devadatta chapter, 'First, a woman may not be reborn as a Brahmā God King; second, as Śakra; third, as Māra; fourth, as a Wheel-turning King; fifth, as a Buddha. How then is it possible for a woman to swiftly attain Buddhahood?'[9] Though you may escape the Five Torments through recitation of this scripture, the Three Torments you cannot escape.[10] As the Buddha explains, 'in the Three Worlds there are no fences, in the Six Realms there are no barriers, and for a woman, there are no three dwellings.'[11] Now I,

[6]The Three Ages are the past, present, and future.

[7]This is an oft-repeated passage of unknown origin. It has been wrongly attributed to the *Kegon Sutra*, the *Nirvana Sutra*, and other sources; its earliest known citation is in the twelfth-century *Hōbutsushū* (SNKBT 40:212).

[8]In *mikkyō*, the esoteric Buddhist tradition, the human heart is sometimes described as a closed lotus blossom. Through devotional practice it opens up into eight leaves, resembling the eight-leaved lotus blossom at the center of the Taizō Mandala. Dainichi Nyorai sits at the center, where he is surrounded by four Buddhas and four bodhisattvas, each upon a single leaf.

[9]These are the Five Obstructions (*goshō*), the five forms of rebirth listed in the Devadatta chapter of the *Lotus Sutra* as prohibited to women.

[10]The Five Torments are the suffering of birth, illness, old age, death, and separation from loved ones. The Three Torments are the suffering of facing things one dislikes, losing things one likes, and experiencing change in all things.

[11]The Three Worlds are the worlds of desire, form, and non-form. The Six Realms are those of heaven, hell, hungry ghosts, animals, *asuras*, and humans. To say that there are no fences or barriers within the Three Words/Six Realms is to say that sentient beings move freely, according to their karma, amid the various planes of existence. The statement, "for a woman, there are no three dwellings," is perhaps a misquotation of the aphorism, *sangai ni ie nashi*, "in the three worlds there is no dwelling" (i.e., there is no place that is truly secure).

too, implore you—uphold your vow of love and enter the True Path!"

During the course of the old mute's exhortation, Izumi Shikibu experienced a change of heart. "If my parents, at least, can attain Buddhahood as a result," she thought, "then I'll sleep with this man. And if I later turn into a mute like him, then so be it." Poor Izumi Shikibu! Taking hold of his sleeve, she led him inside to her single bed. As the night eventually gave way to dawn, the old mute spoke: "Do you think that I am really an old mute? I am the Kannon of Kiyomizu Temple, and I have appeared in this form to test the strength of your filial resolve. It is now without doubt that both you and your parents will attain Buddhahood in this very existence."

The old mute departed, enveloped in the shining light of his great compassion. In deepest gratitude Izumi Shikibu accompanied him as far as Kiyomizu Temple, where he did in fact withdraw into the inner sanctum. Flush with happiness, Izumi Shikibu composed the following poem:

aki no ta no	I feel as though I've
karisomebushi no	slumbered,
kokochi shite	like the wild geese in autumn fields.
makoto no michi ni	What joy now
iru zo ureshiki	to tread the True Path![12]

"That she composed this verse was also because of the Way of Love," the young master said. "So what do you think of that?"[13]

[12]The True Path is the path of the Buddha. The word *karisomebushi* works in the poem as a hinge for *aki no ta no kari* ("the wild geese of autumn fields" and "harvest of autumn fields") and *karisomebushi no kokochi shite* ("I feel as though I've slumbered"). *Karisomebushi no kokochi shite* can also be read, "It was like a short nap—[those years it took to sleep with them all]."

[13]The story ends where it begins, with Yoshitsune attempting to seduce Jōruri-hime.

Koshikibu[1]

In the salon of Empress Shōshi in the not-so-distant past, there was once a woman by the name of Murasaki Shikibu. She was uncommonly beautiful, as graceful as a willow swaying in the wind. Her jade hairpin was as translucent as the wings of a cicada, and the flush of her cheeks, faintly visible at the edges of her slightly mussed hair, was like the moon shining through a thin veil of cloud. Her lips were as lotus petals, her bosom was as if bedecked with jewels, and her loveliness was as that of the plum or cherry, blossoms overflowing in the glow of a garden's evening light.

She was of exceedingly profound mind, superior to the normal run of people, and her skill at playing the *koto* and the *biwa* was without parallel.[2] In the Way of Poetry she took after Princess Sotoori of old, like Ise and Komachi. Not only this, but for her, even the Way of the Dharma was clearly revealed, and thus tracing the path of the Dragon Girl, she recited the *Lotus Sutra* at all times.[3] Hearing such things from the courtiers, the empress had her summoned to the palace. Among all her ladies-in-waiting and high-ranking young attendants, the empress regarded her as a flower of perfection, and so she called her Murasaki Shikibu.[4] Thus within the court she was premier.

One night Murasaki Shikibu had a mysterious dream and she became pregnant. When her time had come, she gave birth to a daughter like a jewel, a child unlike that of any normal person, of such beauty as is difficult to comprehend or express with words. This daughter grew rapidly, and soon reaching the age of six, her beauty was beyond description.

[1]The following translation is from the unillustrated Tenri Library manuscript (with some corrections from the Ono, Gifu University, and Taku Library texts), in MJMT 5:20–38 and Shimazu Hisamoto, *Kinko shōsetsu shinsan* (Tokyo: Yūseidō, 1983 [first published by Chūkōkan in 1928]), 233–54.

[2]A *koto* is a kind of hollow-bodied harp, and a *biwa* is a sort of lute.

[3]According to the "Devadatta" chapter of the *Lotus Sutra*, the eight year-old Dragon Girl attained instant enlightenment before the eyes of a group of doubting men.

[4]"Murasaki" is kind of plant, a gromwell (*Lithospermum erythrorhizon*), and "Shikibu" refers to the Ministry of Ceremonial, in which Murasaki Shikibu's father once held a position.

"Now listen," Murasaki Shikibu told her, fondly combing her hair, "you really must learn to compose poetry." "How can I learn to compose poetry?" her daughter asked in a grown-up tone. "More than anything," her mother said, "you have to see what's interesting about the old verses and use those as your model. You should study the poems of Ise and Komachi with your whole heart, every day and every night. If you like them, you're bound to succeed." Her daughter giggled and replied:

haha ya hashi	Darling Mother,
konomeba uta no	if she likes it,
yomaruru ni	this leaf-bud composes poems.
suriko no hachi ni	Now give me the mortar,
sara soete tabe	together with a plate![5]

Her words were endearingly childish, and explaining that her guardian and her wet nurse had carried on like this about plates, her mother burst out laughing and loved her all the more.

Later, Murasaki Shikibu spoke: "I have a vow from a previous life, so I need to visit the Ishiyama Kannon. I'll be obliged to seclude myself there for three weeks. While I'm away, you are to do just as your governess says. Don't give her any trouble." "Why do I have to wait three weeks? Do hurry back!" her daughter said. "It should be about ten days, then," Murasaki Shikibu replied.

The little girl stayed with her governess, and because she was so innocent and beautiful, the woman was not troubled in the least. A certain person took a trip to Ise and brought back small earthenware pots as souvenirs. Having two children of her own, the governess gave the pots to them, without giving any to Murasaki Shikibu's daughter.[6] The little girl wept with longing. As she cried, she listened to a warbler singing beneath the bamboo eaves. Tearfully she intoned:

uguisu yo	Oh warbler,
nado sa wa naku zo	why do you cry so?
chi ya hoshiki	Do you want your wet nurse?
konabe ya hoshiki	Do you want a little pot?
haha ya koishiki	Do you miss your mother?

[5]*Konome* is a tree-leaf bud, and *konomeba* means, "if [I] like it." *Konome* is also a name for the buds of the *sanshō* pepper plant, which is ground up in a mortar—hence the second part of the poem. In the Ono, Gifu, and Taku texts, the first line of the poem reads *haha ya haha*, "Mother oh Mother."

[6]According to the Ono, Gifu, and Taku texts, there were only two pots to give.

The governess was touched. She took back one of the pots that she had given to her own children and gave it to Murasaki Shikibu's daughter instead.[7]

Murasaki Shikibu composed *The Tale of Genji* in sixty chapters at Ishiyama Temple, writing it out on the back of an Ishiyama copy of the *Great Wisdom Sutra*.[8] She summoned an artist from the capital and had him paint her portrait, and then building a hermitage, she had it installed as the principal image. With her parting words she asked that holy services be performed. She endowed the hermitage with lands and returned to the capital. Even today the *Lotus Sutra* is recited there without cease. Returning from Ishiyama and seeing her daughter again, she asked about all that had taken place in her absence. She was impressed by her girl's good manners, and she was pleased with the governess's kindness as well.

The years and months passed by, and Murasaki Shikibu's daughter grew increasingly beautiful, such as one who is not of this world. With her lotus-blossom eyes and bejeweled breast—she excelled the likes of Yang Guifei of the Tang, Li Furen of the Han, or even Ono no Komachi and the Nijō empress. Her *biwa* playing was finer than that of the daughter of Chōanshō, such as might bring to mind the "Riding Song of Wang Zhaojun," or that verse from when the Ise Priestess awesomely strummed her jewel-studded *biwa* and intoned:

koto no ne ni	It blows in the sound of the *koto,*
mine no matsukaze	that wind in the pines
kayourashi	on the mountain ridge.
izure no o yori	From what hills—what strings—
shirabe someken	does such tone pour forth?[9]

Murasaki Shikibu's daughter continued to grow, but in the spring of her thirteenth year she fell suddenly ill, and it soon seemed as if her end were

[7]Related *setsuwa* are contained in *Toshiyori zuinō* (NKBZ 50:78), *Fukurozōshi* (SNKBT 29:165), *Saikō danshō* (*Saigyō Shōnin danshō*, in Hisamatsu Sen'ichi, ed., *Karonshū* [Tokyo: Miyai Shoten, 1971], 111), *Kohon setsuwa shū* (SNKBT 42:421–22), the Ikkanbon text of *Hōbutsushū* (ZGR 32:2:195a), and the *otogizōshi Hanyū no monogatari* (MJMT 10:568–69). *Saikō danshō* (ca. 1227) attributes the poem to Ki no Tsurayuki's daughter at the age of nine, while *Hanyū no monogatari* attributes it to Koshikibu at the age of 5.

[8]*Greater Prajñā-pāramitā Sutra* (*Daihannyakyō*), translated in 600 volumes by Xuanzang in the seventh century.

[9]This is *Shūi wakashū* 451, attributed to Saigū no Nyōgo (Kishi Joō; 929–85). The headnote reads: "Composed on the topic of 'an evening *koto* in the wind in the pines,' when the Ise Priestess [Kishi] passed a *kōshin* day at Nomiya." (A *kōshin* day came once every sixty days; it was often an occasion for poetry contests, music, and other entertainment.) The Ise Priestess Kishi was the daughter of Kishi Joō (Saigū no Nyōgo), herself a former Ise Priestess and the author of the poem. In her verse, the word *o* is used to mean both "foothills" and "strings."

near. The director of the Bureau of Divination was called in to divine. "A terrible spirit is to blame," he said, "and our prayers are unlikely to help." The man turned and left. Murasaki Shikibu's strength quite disappeared. She made vow upon vow to the deities of Sumiyoshi and Kitano, and pronounced oath upon oath inside her heart. "Take my life instead," she cried, but her daughter's illness grew only worse. Certain that the end was now at hand, she pressed her face to her daughter's cheek, lamenting, "What shall I do?" As it was then the fourth month, a lone cuckoo could be heard singing outside the palace. With some effort, Murasaki Shikibu's daughter raised herself up, and in a faint voice she intoned:

hototogisu	Guide me through
shide no yamabe no	the Mountains of Death,
shirube seyo	you cuckoo—
oya ni sakidatsu	for I know not the path
michi wo shiraneba	one takes before a parent.[10]

Her mother's and her wet nurse's feelings were beyond compare.

Just then a frightening voice thundered down from above, and a red, five-horned, three-headed demon ripped apart the ceiling. "How touching!" he roared, shedding tears like white jewels. "Your time had come, and I was just about to take you down the road of death, but then, this poem! The Ten Kings of the Underworld and the gods all weep, moving me even more! I will release you this time. You shall be summoned to the palace in the fall, there to receive the favor of your lord. Well, I'll be going now." The demon rose up and out through a gable. Murasaki Shikibu's daughter quickly recovered, becoming just as she had been before.[11]

[10]This is a variant of *Shoku shika wakashū* 439 (compiled ca. 1165). The poem and its headnote read: "A woman who had been ill for some time suddenly passed away. Her mother and father pleaded with Lord Taizan [a deity of the afterworld] that he might take their lives instead, whereupon the daughter came back to life and recited:

shide no yama	Not knowing the path
koyubeki kata mo	one takes before a parent,
omohoezu	I cannot imagine
oya ni sakidatsu	the way across
michi wo shiraneba	the Mountains of Death.

A more common variant (traditionally attributed to Koshikibu no Naishi) is cited in *Little Shikibu*, below.

[11]Related *setsuwa* appear in *Jikkinshō* 10:14 (SNKBZ 51:401), *Kokon chomonjū* 175 (NKBT 84:160), *Shasekishū* (NKBT 85:227), *Mumyōzōshi* (SNKS *Mumyōzōshi*, 112), and *Little Shikibu*. In all of these it is Koshikibu no Naishi rather than Izumi Shikibu who avoids death through the excellence of her verse.

Hearing of these events, Empress Shōshi had the girl summoned to court, where she provided her with robes of the permitted colors and crimson-layered trousers. Her Majesty further presented her with a drape-sash, a jeweled chaplet, a charm-necklace, figured-cloth slippers and a brocade skirt. Then, she named her Izumi Shikibu.[12] All the other ladies-in-waiting and high-ranking young attendants were filled with envy. Nevertheless, Izumi Shikibu was later allowed to perform the Dance of the Rainbow Skirt and the Feather Robe, the dance of such empresses as Yang Guifei, Li Furen, and Yu Meiren. As for the permitted colors, they were crimson and purple. In this way she was splendidly favored, and there was no one to whom she could be compared.

Now around this time a frightful demon had begun venturing into the capital disguised as a beautiful child. Every night he would abduct people and eat them. His name was Shuten Dōji, and the commotion he caused in the city was beyond description. The emperor ordered the generals Raikō and Hōshō to have him slain.[13]

Shuten Dōji's fortresses were located on the three mountains of Nishiyama, Atago, and Oi, and the generals reasoned that as he possessed supernatural powers, he was likely to run away to China if they approached with an army of men. Should they allow him to flee, their mission would be for naught. Raikō thus arranged for the peerlessly valorous Tsuna to accompany him alone; Hōshō arranged for just Hitori Musha—the "Single Warrior"—to accompany him as well.[14] Knowing Shuten Dōji's fondness for liquor, they filled a bamboo flask with *sake,* and disguising themselves as mountain ascetics, they went off to his mountain for three days and three nights.

Abducting another person and returning to his fortress, Shuten Dōji noticed a scent of *sake* in the air. Thinking it strange, he looked around and saw four or five mountain ascetics approaching with a bamboo flask. He transformed into his usual child disguise and went outside. His beauty was beyond words, in no way inferior to that of Lord Meitōkanki when he was a child, and it radiated forth such that Raikō and Hōshō were unable to get a very good look at him. The two generals danced, sang, and drank with the

[12]This sentence is interpolated from the Ono, Gifu, and Taku texts.

[13]Raikō and Hōshō are Minamoto no Yorimitsu (948–1021) and Fujiwara no Yasumasa (958–1036; also known as Hirai Yasumasa). The following is a highly condensed version of the story of Shuten Dōji, related in such sources as the *otogizōshi Shuten Dōji* and the noh play *Ōe-yama*.

[14]Watanabe no Tsuna (953–1025) and Hitori Musha (literally, "single warrior"). According to the noh play *Ōe-yama,* Hitori Musha was one of Hōshō's retainers; according to the noh play *Tsuchigumo,* he was one of Raikō's. Sanari Kentarō, ed., *Yōkyoku taikan,* vols. 1 and 3 (Tokyo: Meiji Shoin, 1930–31), 569 and 2064.

boy, and they became exceedingly drunk. The child became drunk as well, and they all fell asleep on the ground.

When Hōshō awoke, he saw that Shuten Dōji had changed back into a demon—a horrible creature with eight heads, nine legs, and sixteen eyes. Spitting breath like fire, Shuten Dōji made a grab for the men, but the generals pulled their swords and set upon him. Against such blades as Whisker Cutter and Kamakura Genta, Shuten Dōji's own sword shattered, and the generals cut off his heads. It was thanks to the protection of the Sumiyoshi Deity, manifesting as an old man, that they were able to accomplish their feat.

The men returned to the capital. Appearing before the emperor, they related all that had taken place. Declaring that he would give them the world, the emperor bestowed Raikō with incalculable estates, and he commanded Hōshō to name his desire. "Though it is much to ask," Hōshō replied, "I wish to have Izumi Shikibu for my wife." The emperor was reluctant, but as a ruler's words are not to be withdrawn,[15] he eventually gave his consent. He further decreed that Hōshō be made a palace courtier. Hōshō returned to his lodgings exceptionally pleased. Daytime service at the palace became his principal concern, and he looked after his lord with the greatest care.

Hōshō was deeply devoted to his wife; there was nothing for which they lacked. Around this time in the capital there was a famous poet by the name of Dōmei Hōshi. As he would occasionally instruct Izumi Shikibu in the essentials of poetry, they soon became a target of vulgar suspicions. Rumors came to Hōshō's ears and his feelings for Izumi Shikibu cooled. The days and years passed by, and such gossip reached Murasaki Shikibu as well. Summoning her daughter, she explained in full all there is to know about the proper behavior of a lady—secret teachings of the utmost importance, not to be shared with anyone. In her own words, she said:

> Social interactions are of primary importance. Now listen closely. You think that because you enjoy the great favor of your lord, you can go about with a conceited look on your face, never incurring the ill will of your rivals. But just look at how they slander you behind your back.
>
> When you're among people, don't stare. And don't look at them with your head held up high. People will think you're spiteful if you're always looking them in the eye. But then again, you shouldn't be looking at the ground all the time, either.
>
> If something funny happens and people laugh, you should relax a bit and laugh with them. But when you do, you mustn't open your mouth too wide.

[15]Actually, "as a ruler's words are like sweat" (*ringen, ase no gotoku nareba*). A ruler's words are like sweat in that once spoken, they cannot be withdrawn.

When people start telling stories about others, even if they're saying bad things, you shouldn't give knowing looks or say anything yourself.

If someone asks you something, you should speak a bit. People will think you're ignorant if you never say anything. You should always be careful not to talk too much, but if you speak too little, people will think you're ill-tempered, and that's very bad.

When you're with your husband, you should be careful not to look overly assured, but you should also take care not to be too distrusting either. It's best to remain aloof. Then again, if you appear utterly unconcerned, he's likely to grow suspicious of you instead. There are many examples of this from the past. For instance, there was once a person called the Middle Captain Ariwara [no Narihira]. He was the fifth son of Prince Abo, and his mother was known as Princess Itō.

This Narihira was exceedingly lascivious, and he was also extraordinarily handsome. He radiated such exquisite, dazzling beauty that people never tired of looking at him, and as he was naturally redolent with the musky fragrance of orchids, the places through which he passed were filled with a lovely smell. In the Way of Music he was a master of the deepest mysteries—he was especially good at playing the flute—and in the Way of Poetry he shone with an even greater brilliance. His disposition was most excellent, superior among men and women, and his pedigree was not to be spoken of lightly, for he was superior among the gods as well. Whether princesses, ladies of the court, or even the most lowly, wretched of women, there were none whose hearts were not stirred with longing for him. You can read all about it in *Tales of Ise*.

Although it is difficult to say of which divinity Narihira was a manifestation, one should not make light of his vow to lead to salvation, by means of karmic links, those women who loved him in their hearts and those who sought to draw physically near. It would be impossible to give accounts of all his many lovers. He once had a wife in a town called Akishino, and a mistress in the province of Kawachi.[16] He would travel back and forth between the two places every night. Always seeing him off on his way, his wife never appeared to be particularly jealous. Narihira thought this strange, and he imagined her engaging in some untoward behavior in his absence.

One evening he lied, saying, "I'm off to Kawachi," and he hid in the shrubs on the south side of their house. It grew increasingly late as he watched his wife. The people of the neighborhood

[16]Variations of the following poem-story are contained in *Tales of Ise* (*dan* 23; SNKBZ 8:155–58), *Kokin wakashū* (poem 994; SNKBT 5:298), and *Yamato monogatari* (*dan* 149; SNKBZ 8:395–97). The version cited here is most closely related to that in *Yamato monogatari*.

settled in for the night, and the moon came into glimmering view. The woman rolled up a reed blind and began playing her *koto*. She played "Sōfuren"—a song about a woman longing for her lover—over and over again. Narihira thought this suspicious. Then, in a beautiful voice she intoned:

kaze fukeba	When blowing winds
okitsu shiranami	lash up
Tatsuta-yama	white-crested waves,
yowa ni ya kimi ga	do you cross Mount Tatsuta
hitori yukuran	alone in the night?[17]

In an attempt to soothe her smoldering, burning heart, she filled a *sake* pot with water and placed it on her chest. The water immediately began to boil. Mount Tatsuta is flush with bandits, and she composed her poem out of anxiety for her husband, traveling over it alone. Narihira was overjoyed, and he rushed in from the garden. From then on he made no more visits to Kawachi.

Now Narihira had liaisons with 3,733 women. Among these, there were twelve about whom he chose to write in *Tales of Ise*, including Ise and Komachi and many other princesses and ladies of the court. But it was the selfless intentions of which I have just spoken that pleased him most, and it was therefore this account that he wrote out first. You should read *Tales of Ise* for the details.

Thus Murasaki Shikibu explained many things, and saying that she would visit Ishiyama Temple again, she left. Of the sixty chapters of *The Tale of Genji*, she took out five and carefully hid them away. There are many stories in the *Genji* chapter "Concealed by Clouds,"[18] and this is one of them. It is a great secret text and should not be shown to others lightly. Those who flaunt this warning are sure to suffer the retribution of the Ishiyama Kannon, for it is written that this chapter is truly awesome and must be concealed. There are secret oral transmissions explaining why this is so. For various reasons, they have not been written down. One should learn all about the sacred scriptures, and about poetry, too. This is Izumi Shikibu's story.[19]

[17]*Tatsu* functions as a pivot word within the poem, acting as a part of the place name "Tatsuta-yama" (Mount Tatsuta) and the phrase *shiranami tatsu*, "white waves crest [upon the ocean]."

[18]"Concealed by Clouds" (*Kumo ga kure*) is the most famous of the supposedly "lost" chapters of *The Tale of Genji*.

[19]"Izumi Shikibu's Story" (*Izumi Shikibu no monogatari*) is the name of an independent *otogizōshi* that closely corresponds to the second half of *Koshikibu*, which, in the cases of the Ono and Gifu texts, begins here. (The second part of the Taku text begins after Izumi Shikibu's reconciliation with Hōshō at Izumoji Shrine.) The Tenri text contains only this single indistinct indication of a mid-story break. I hereafter refer to *Izumi Shikibu no monogatari* as the Togawa text.

Now even among the men and women of the court, Izumi Shikibu was preeminent, such as is truly beyond words. But around this time rumors were spreading as to her involvement with the priest Dōmei, and nothing seemed to go as she wished. Distraught over how she might continue facing those around her, she took leave of Hōshō and began to drift, like "the floating grass—should the water invite."[20] Thus she suffered great mental anguish.

There was a poet by the name of Akazome Emon in the capital at that time, and inquiring as to the feelings in Izumi Shikibu's heart, she sent a poem:

utsurowade	Watch the Forest of Shinoda
shibashi Shinoda no	awhile before changing
mori wo miyo	the color of your leaves—
kaeri mo zo suru	like the wind that flutters the kudzu,
kuzu no urakaze	he just may come back.[21]

Izumi Shikibu read the poem. "And I had thought our worlds the same,"[22] she said, and sent the following reply:

toshi fu to mo	Do their colors change
kawaran mono ka	with the passing years,
Izumi naru	those leaves of

[20]This is an allusion to *Kokin wakashū* 938, attributed to Ono no Komachi. Together with its headnote, the poem reads, "Composed in reply to Fun'ya no Yasuhide's invitation to visit him at his post when he was made a third-ranking official of Mikawa Province:"

wabinureba	Soaked with misery—
mi wo ukikusa no	like the floating grass
ne wo taete	I would cut my roots
sasou mizu araba	and float away,
inamu to zo omou	should the water invite.

[21]This is *Shinkokin wakashū* 1820, attributed to Akazome Emon. The headnote reads: "Sent upon hearing that Prince Atsumichi had begun visiting Izumi Shikibu immediately after she was abandoned by Michisada." *Utsurowade* suggests both a change in the color of autumn leaves and a change in heart. *Kaeri* suggests that the leaves of the kudzu might be turned upright by the wind, as well as that Michisada might soon return.

[22]Izumi Shikibu's statement is unclear. Following the Ono, Togawa, Gifu, and Taku texts, we might read it as a garbled allusion to *Fūyō wakashū* 547, attributed to Hamamatsu no Chūnagon on his return to Japan from China (also in *Hamamatsu Chūnagon monogatari*, NKBT 77:237):

onaji yo no	To think that
shibashi no hodo to	for a time
omou dani	our worlds were the same—
wakare tefu na wa	how sad indeed,
ikaga kanashiki	this thing called "parting."

Shinoda no mori no	the thousand-branched camphor
chie no kusu no ha	in Shinoda Forest in Izumi?[23]

The Shinoda Forest of Izumi Shikibu's poem is in Izumi Province. Its deity is a guardian of the Way of Men and Women, and takes the form of the camphor. As a kind of evergreen, its color is unchanging. The Shinoda Forest in Akazome Emon's poem is in Owari Province. Its deity takes the form of the kudzu, and is the spouse of the Shinoda Deity in Izumi. There are secret oral teachings regarding these places. They are forests of the Way of Love, and one ought to learn of them.

The days and months passed by. Izumi Shikibu summoned a medium from Yasaka Shrine and asked her to divine. The medium called out: "You god who settles matters between human husbands and wives in the capital on the first night of spring—present yourself! We will visit your shrine on the first night of spring and pay homage to you there." The medium took her leave. On the appointed night, the two women traveled together to the deity's abode. Hōshō had heard what was afoot, and he lay in wait in the shadows of Izumo Shrine.[24] Unaware of his presence, Izumi Shikibu and the medium arrived late in the night.

As it was then the first night of spring, the shrine was crowded with supplicants. Pushing aside the people in front of the altar, the medium asked Izumi Shikibu to perform the Dance of the Rainbow Skirt and the Feather Robe. Izumi Shikibu stepped forward. She wore a patterned gauze jacket over a rich purple robe, and treading softly on the extended cuffs of her crimson trousers, she danced with placid, exquisite poise, concealing her face behind a dark red fan and gently waving her silken sleeves. A charm

[23]This is the version of Izumi Shikibu's poem as it appears in the Togawa, Gifu, and Taku texts. (In the Tenri text, the first two lines read, *toshi furu to kawaran mono wa,* "that which changes with the passing years . . .") The first two lines constitute a rhetorical question; they are identical to the first two lines of Niou's poem to Ukifune in the Ukifune chapter of *The Tale of Genji* (NKBZ 17:142). The last three lines allude to the anonymous *Kokin rokujō* 1049/*Fuboku wakashō* 10093. In *Shinkokin wakashū,* Izumi Shikibu's reply (poem 1821) is reported to have been:

akikaze wa	Though the weary winds
sugoku fukedomo	of autumn blow fierce,
kuzu no ha no	the underside of the kudzu—
uramigao ni wa	my own bitter face—
mieji to zo omou	is not likely to be seen.

[24]According to the Ono, Togawa, Gifu, and Taku texts, Hōshō hid in the shadows of a different shrine: Kyoto's Izumoji no Yashiro (Izumoji Dōso Shrine), the deity of which is a protector of men and women's relations. For the legend of the Izumoji Deity, see *Soga monogatari,* NKBT 88:116.

necklace of gold brocade on a red backing dangled from her crimson drape-sash, and with her jeweled chaplet, socks of figured cloth and embroidered slippers, her beauty and charm were truly beyond expression. Her appearance was as that of a heavenly being in temporary human form, and the shrine was filled with such purity that the building itself began to tremble. Hōshō gazed on in wonder, forgetting himself entirely.

The medium wrote Izumi Shikibu's and Hōshō's names on a wooden card, and at the climax of the dance, she told Izumi Shikibu to face in the direction of the deity, open her robe at the chest and rub the wooden card between her breasts. Izumi Shikibu meekly accepted the card. The elegant movement of her steps as she danced was like the swaying of a willow in a spring breeze. Hearing the medium's words, Hōshō wondered how he might endure such a sight. Thinking that his wife was now to perform her mortifying act, he covered his eyes and listened. Waving her sleeves, Izumi Shikibu held up the wooden card. Crying out in a piteous voice, gracefully dancing her finale, she intoned:

chihayaburu	What shame I'd feel
kami no miru me mo	in the eyes
hazukashi ya	of the mighty gods.
mi wo omou to te	For love of myself
mi wo ya sutemashi	shall I throw myself away?

"You gods have heard their malicious lies," Izumi Shikibu shouted.[25] "Now sweep them away!" Perhaps because he pities those unfairly maligned, the deity accepted her plea. The shrine quaked with a tremendous force, and everyone was stirred to tears. Hōshō was overcome with emotion. Rushing out from the shadows, he embraced his wife, took her home and loved her with an unwavering heart, the result, everyone said, of her having enacted such devotions.[26]

Izumi Shikibu returned to the capital and served in the palace. The emperor was impressed. He bestowed her with many favors, and in the spring of her seventeenth year she came to know the pains of pregnancy.[27] Before

[25]This sentence is problematic. Whereas the Ono and Taku texts read *sanken* (or *zangen*, "malicious lies"), the Tenri and Gifu texts read *sanke* (possibly *zange*, "confession"). The entire passage is absent from the Togawa text.

[26]Related *setsuwa* are contained in *Shasekishū* (NKBT 85:446), *Sangoku denki* (1:27), *Ichijō shūgyokushō*, the noh play *Kibune* (attributed to Kanze Nobumitsu; 1435–1516), and *Tsuki no karu moshū* (ZGR 33:1:92–93).

[27]Although the Tenri text implies that the emperor is the father, the Ono, Togawa, Gifu, and Taku manuscripts are less clear on the matter.

long she gave birth to a daughter—a child of exquisite beauty, a veritable jewel. "I'll be so ashamed if people laugh at me for having become a mother so soon," Izumi Shikibu thought. "And just when I was mixing with all these people at the court! I'll never be able to keep it a secret, not even with guardians and wet nurses." And so although it pained her deeply, she decided to abandon her baby before anyone might find out.

Izumi Shikibu assembled a jeweled handbox and inlaid the edges with silver and gold. Having it lacquered, she had a poem inscribed on the lid. Lining the box with various robes, she wrapped her baby inside and set out for the Tōji Temple gate.[28] There, on a pillar-stone, she heartlessly abandoned her child. Returning home and thinking back on her desperate act, she shed silent, endless tears. How moving to imagine the feelings in her heart!

At around this time an old man and woman had come to Kiyomizu Temple from the province of Kawachi. For three weeks they had prayed for a child, an heir to perform devotions for them after they died, but their prayers had gone unanswered. As they set off for home, they decided to pass by Tōji Temple on their way. Praying here and there, they paused to rest at the temple gate. There they found a splendid handbox. Picking it up, they smelled an exceptional fragrance. They removed the lid and discovered a baby girl like a jewel, all wrapped up in layers of robes. So lovely that she sparkled, she had been placed in the box and abandoned. Wondering whose child she was, they asked all around, but no one knew a thing. They decided that this was the doing of Kiyomizu, and in their joy they revered the Kiyomizu [Kannon] even more than they had before.

The old man and woman carried the baby home. In the burning heat of summer they spread a thin bed of moss for her, fanning her all the while, and in the snowy cold of winter they piled high their blanketing robes, cherishing her like a lotus in the mud. For them this daughter was everything, such that they forgot their own advancing years. Vowing to see her to adulthood, they raised her with the utmost care. She was unlike the child of any person of this world, and as she grew, her beauty increased beyond the power of words to describe. She was exceptionally kind-hearted, and day and night she looked after the old man and woman with unstinting devotion.

In her free time, without ever having been taught, the girl composed poetry, chanted *renga* and the like, and as the days passed she gave her heart entirely to thoughts of blossoms and the moon.[29] But as hers was an iso-

[28]Tōji Temple is a large Shingon institution on Kyoto's Ninth Avenue. It contains two prominent gates, Rengemon and Nandaimon.

[29]These are standard topics for poetic composition. *Renga* is a kind of linked verse.

lated mountain village, there was no one from whom she could learn of such things. Gathering firewood and edible plants and roots from time to time, she attended to her adoptive parents' every need. Unknowing in their hearts how close they ought to draw, the old man and woman loved her with boundless affection. And so the years passed, and before long she was eleven years old.

From around this time Izumi Shikibu began to ponder. "I've aged so quickly," she thought. "I'll be thirty soon. But looking back on my life until now, it seems like only two or three days. When I think of the months and years gone by, they're like an illusion or a dream. And who knows how old I'll be when I reach my end. Of all the famous people from the past, are there any who still survive? Even the likes of Dong Fangshuo, Xi Wangmu, and Tao Yuanming—only their names remain. It'll be the same for me, too. And who's to pray for me when I'm gone? I may yet bear an heir, but then again, I may not. To think that my child, whom I abandoned at the Tōji Temple gate, probably hates me . . . oh, to find my baby girl!"

Izumi Shikibu asked Hōshō for his leave. After making suitable, careful preparations, he saw her off in a palanquin with attendants. Upon arriving at Hase Temple, Izumi Shikibu sent back all of her servants except for one—a woman by the name of Renzei, with whom she secluded herself to pray. No one knows what revelation she received, but emerging in the garb of a mendicant, she left Hase Temple and set out upon her search, drifting like a cloud in the desolate sky. Wandering lost through the mountains of Kawachi, unused to the hardships of travel, her body grew tired and her feet swelled. She was indeed a pitiful sight as her wet nurse, Renzei, led her by the hand, proceeding aimlessly in this direction and that, her wretchedness no less severe than had she been walking the road of death between this life and the next.

Drawing near a lowly peasant dwelling in the mountains, Izumi Shikibu begged lodging for the night. An old woman stepped outside. Staring Izumi Shikibu up and down, she spoke: "My, how beautiful! You don't look to be of this world at all. What brings you to a place like this?" In a voice cracked with suffering, Izumi Shikibu replied: "There's someone for whom I pine. I left the capital thinking to live in some deep mountain recess, but now I drift about in despair. When strangers meet, it's always because of vows from a previous life. So please let me stay the night."

The old woman and her husband were sympathetic. They opened their grimy brushwood door, and laying out a coarse straw sleeping-mat, they invited their guest inside. But unused to the pains of travel, Izumi Shikibu was unable to sleep. Gazing up at the moonlight filtering through the eaves, she chanted the following verses:

miyako nite	Though it is
minareshi tsuki to	the same moon that
omoedomo	I knew in the capital,
kusa no makura ni	does it now take its rest
yadorinuru kana	on a pillow of grass?

yamazato wa	The mountain village
nerarezarikeri	was unable to sleep—
yomosugara	startled by the wind
matsu fuku kaze ni	in the pines
odorokasarete	all through the night.

Thus Izumi Shikibu set her heart at rest.

"What wonderful poems!" the old man and woman exclaimed. "Though covered by clouds, the moon indeed shines down on these wretched eaves. It's so mysteriously elegant, and yet here it is, lodging in a squalid little place like ours! Fantastic!"

"Honey," the old man and woman called out to their daughter, "did you hear this traveling-woman's poems? She's chanting *renga* or poetry or something right here in front of your ignorant old mother and father. How should we answer?" A small child replied: "I heard her poems. They were funny, dreadful even. I couldn't keep from laughing inside." Izumi Shikibu heard her words. "How strange!" she thought. "No one laughs at my poems in the capital. And such a little child as this . . . it's certainly odd for her to be so amused!"

"Now see here," Izumi Shikibu said, "how is it that you have a child like this? Let's hear her reply!" The old woman pressed the girl for an answer, and so in her childish voice she explained, "There's nothing for which you can blame the mountain winds:

yamazato ni	What do you mean you
nenu to wa ikani	couldn't sleep in the mountain town?
nureba koso	It's because you slept
matsu fuku kaze no	that you were startled
odorokasuran	by the wind in the pines."[30]

"She's right," Izumi Shikibu thought. "How embarrassing to be laughed at for my mistake!" Izumi Shikibu blushed. "Let me see this child of yours,"

[30]The girl's poem is logical. But grammatically speaking, the last line should end with *rame,* not *ran,* a mistake befitting a child raised in the mountains. Related *setsuwa* are contained in *Little Shikibu, Sangoku denki* (6:21), and the Keiō University text of *Wakan rōeishū wadanshō* (typeset in Kuroda Akira, "*Sangoku denki* to *Wakan rōeishū wadanshō,* pt. 2," *Kokubungaku* [Kansai Daigaku] 59 [1982]: 9–10). In the *Sangoku denki* and *Wadanshō* versions of the story, the poet-priest Saigyō is corrected by the ghost of Hitomaro (whose poem ends with "*rame*").

she said, but the old man and woman were ashamed: "How could we present her to you in such shabby robes?" "You needn't be so reserved," Izumi Shikibu pressed; "just bring her out." And so, as is the custom with mountain folk, the old man lit a pine torch and carried his daughter into the room.

The girl was strikingly beautiful, not at all like the child of such humble mountain-dwellers. And even though the old man and woman were well along in years, she was still quite young—nothing, in fact, like her parents. Izumi Shikibu inquired as to the meaning of this. "She was abandoned on a pillar-stone at the Tōji Temple gate in the capital," the old couple explained. "We found her on our way back from Kiyomizu. We brought her home and now we're raising her up."

"How old is she?" Izumi Shikibu asked. They replied that she was eleven.

"When did you find her—and in what manner was she abandoned?"

"She was in a beautiful lacquered box, all wrapped in robes." Izumi Shikibu grew increasingly suspicious. "We still have the box," the old couple added.

"There was a poem on the lid, wasn't there?" Izumi Shikibu asked. The old man and woman replied that there was. "Well then, there's no doubt. This is my child—I abandoned her myself. You can give her back now, if you don't mind."

The old man and woman laughed. "The capital is an awfully big place," they said. "Who knows how many people abandon their children there. We're not convinced. Why don't you tell us the poem before we show you the box?" Izumi Shikibu recited a poem, and this is what she said:

mina kami ni	If the frost of a hundred nights
momo yo no shimo wa	should fall upon my head,
furaba fure	well, then, let it fall!
nanuka nanuka no	I will not be called the moon
tsuki to iwareji	of seven and seven days.[31]

The old man and woman brought out the box, and comparing the two poems, they found them to be without the slightest difference.

"But what does it mean?" they asked. Izumi Shikibu explained: "It means that even if my hair should turn white, I would not have people laugh at me for being a *komochi*, a mother. Now seven and seven days is

[31]This is the version of the poem as it appears in the Ono, Togawa, Gifu, and Taku texts. In the Tenri manuscript, the first three lines read, *mina kami ni kotoyo no shimo wa furanedomo* ("though the frost / of a different night / shall not fall upon my head").

fourteen days. The fifteenth-day moon is called the *mochizuki*, or 'full moon.' The fourteenth-day moon is therefore called the *ko-mochizuki*, or 'little full moon' [also, 'mother moon'].[32] You see, it's for this very child that I've been wandering lost. If it's just as well with you, give her back now, and I'll take her to the capital."

"This is incredible!" the old man and woman cried, loathe to give up their daughter. "If this is your intention, then why don't you ask the girl."

The little girl spoke: "It's beyond imagination! For what sin—from what hatred—did you leave me like that? The old man and woman didn't know me at all, but they pitied me, picked me up and raised me with love. What could have made you abandon me so cruelly? It's because of them that I didn't end up as food for some bird or animal. And now to forget what they've done for me all these months and years, and go off with you, just like that? I wouldn't dream of it!" The child wept with resentment.

Izumi Shikibu found herself both hated and humiliated, and she knew, to her shame, that her daughter was right. There was nothing she could say. "I've pinned all my hopes on this journey," she thought to herself, "so again, I'll call upon the grace of Kannon." She bent down and prayed in the direction of Hase Temple.

After sending news to the capital, Izumi Shikibu received word that she should bring everyone back together with her. The old man and woman were sent new clothes, and they all traveled to the city as a group. The emperor was deeply moved when he heard of these events, and he granted the old man and woman the Yosa region in Tango Province. They soon took up residence there, passing their days in wealth and prosperity.

Later, when the emperor traveled to Sumiyoshi, he brought Izumi Shikibu along as an attendant. As they walked around the shrine they saw plovers, sea gulls, and a myriad other birds bobbing in the waves. The emperor was delighted, and he commanded his retainers to shoot the floating birds. Numbers of men took their bows and strode into the surf. The emperor looked on with pleasure as they began to take aim, and he commanded Izumi Shikibu to compose a poem on the scene at hand.

"There's nothing novel about my poems," Izumi Shikibu said. "Perhaps you should summon my daughter and have her compose one instead." "Bring her forth!" the emperor agreed. The girl was summoned and given her charge. Bashfully she stepped forward. "Hurry up now," people urged.

[32]Izumi Shikibu's poem plays on the words *ko-mochi*, "woman with child," and *ko-mochizuki*, "little full moon" (derived from *mochizuki*, "full moon"). Kitamura Kigin explains the pun in an alternate context in his poetic treatise *Yama no i* (The Mountain Well), published in 1648. See Katsumine Fufū, ed., *Nihon haisho taikei*, vol. 14 (Tokyo: Shunshūsha, 1971), 443.

She glanced over at her father,[33] and in an exceedingly thin voice, intoned, "*Chihayaburu . . .*"[34]

"What's that?" her mother scolded, interrupting.

"Why do you stop her?" the emperor asked.

"*Chihayaburu* is what one says of the gods," Izumi Shikibu explained. "But the topic here is birds, which is why I spoke."

"That's true, of course, but she's so very young, what could be the harm? Let's hear her poem."

"Alright, give us your poem," Izumi Shikibu said, and her daughter replied:

chihayaburu	Though not within
kami no igaki ni	the sacred fence
aranedomo	of the mighty gods,
nami no ue ni mo	these birds—a Shinto archway—
torii tachikeri	yet alight upon the waves.[35]

The emperor and all of his higher and lower-ranking nobles were touched. The girl was immediately bestowed with robes of the permitted colors, and she was given the name Koshikibu no Naishi.[36] Exulting in her splendor, she was thus appointed Handmaid at the age of thirteen.

Later, thinking to visit Kusenoto, Izumi Shikibu requested several days' leave from her duties at court. Arriving at her destination, she reverently gazed upon the sacred lantern.[37] She had heard that those upon whom its light once falls will not lose their way on the dark path of death. She erected a stone monument for her future rebirth and endowed it with lands. Services are performed there still.

One of the emperor's beloved young pines suddenly withered, and His Majesty was filled with deepest sorrow. "Even gods and plants bend to the Way of Poetry," he declared. "Send for Izumi Shikibu and have her compose a verse in prayer for my tree!" But as the province of Tango was so very

[33]The Ono, Togawa, and Taku texts read "mother," for which this is probably a mistake (the passage is absent from the Gifu text). Another possibility is that the emperor is her father, as the Tenri text elsewhere seems to suggest.

[34]*Chihayaburu* is a pillow word for *kami*, "the gods." In the poem below, I have translated *chihayaburu kami* as "mighty gods."

[35]The poem plays upon the words *torii*, "Shinto archway," and *tori*, "birds." Despite her mother's apprehensions, the girl's use of *chihayaburu* is without fault.

[36]"Little Shikibu the Handmaid." Members of the Handmaids' Office were personal attendants to the emperor. The permitted colors were light shades of crimson and purple.

[37]The Dragon Lantern of the Kusenoto Monju (or simply the "Monju Lantern") at Chionji Temple (Monju Hall) at Ama no Hashidate. The legend of the lantern is related in *Sangoku denki* (6:3), and in the noh play *Kusenoto* (Sanari, ed., *Yōkyoku taikan*, vol. 2, 924).

far away, Koshikibu no Naishi suggested that she first compose a poem instead. "Very well then, do it quickly," the emperor agreed, and Koshikibu intoned:

kotowari ya	How right that
karete wa ika ni	you should wither,
himekomatsu	you dear little pine,
chiyo wo ba kimi ni	if you think to leave His Highness
yuzuru to omoeba	your one thousand years!

The pine trembled violently, and within moments it was thriving again. Deeply impressed, the emperor granted Koshikibu numerous robes. Someone slandered her, however, saying that a person had arrived from Tango the day before, and that Izumi Shikibu had composed the poem and sent it to her. The emperor asked Koshikibu if this was true.

"A number of things did arrive from Tango last night," Koshikibu explained, "but I was busy with your summons and didn't read any messages." She then intoned:

Ōe-yama	The road to Mount Ōe
Ikuno no michi no	and Ikuno is long—
tōkereba	I have neither crossed the bridge
mada fumi mo mizu	of Ama no Hashidate,
Ama no Hashidate	nor have I heard from my mother.[38]

Greatly impressed, the emperor sent a messenger to Izumi Shikibu, who, upon seeing her daughter's verse, composed a poem of her own about Ama no Hashidate:

Yosa no umi ya	The moon shines clear
tsuki sumiwataru	upon the Yosa sea—
urakaze ni	in ocean breezes,
kumo mo kawaranu	clouds are unchanging
Ama no Hashidate	in the skies of Ama no Hashidate.[39]

[38]This is *Kinyō wakashū* 550, attributed to Koshikibu no Naishi. The headnote reads: "There was once a poetry contest at court when Izumi Shikibu was in Tango with Yasumasa, and Koshikibu no Naishi was chosen as a contestant. Lord Sadayori came by her quarters. 'What will you do for a poem?' he teased. 'Did you send someone off to Tango? You must be awfully anxious if your messenger hasn't returned yet.' Seizing Sadayori where he stood, Koshikibu recited: . . ."

[39]In the Ono text, the fourth line reads *kumo mo kakaranu*, "clouds do not form," which makes more sense. The *ama* of Ama no Hashidate functions as a hinge for *kumo mo kawaranu ama*, "sky of unchanging clouds" (or *kumo mo kakaranu ama*, "cloudless sky"), and the place name Ama no Hashidate.

Such was her poem, and she recited it in prayer to the bodhisattva Monju. Soon returning to the capital, Izumi Shikibu basked in endless glory and prosperity. It was thus excellent indeed to have said, "Above all, one should devotedly pursue the Way of Poetry."[40] Excellent indeed, excellent indeed!

[40]This may refer to Murasaki Shikibu's advice to Izumi Shikibu in the first part of the story.

Kotohara[1]

At a time during the reign of Emperor Go-Ichijō, a mouse once bore a litter of babies inside the body of a *koto* in the empress's apartments.[2] Those in Her Highness's service spoke of it as an ominous sign, and even the emperor inquired among his courtiers as to whether such an event was not of great significance. "One cannot expect mice and the like not to go building nests in objects that have been left lying around," people said, "especially containers that aren't handled very often. But in a case like this, in which Her Highness has been playing the instrument day and night . . ." Thus people gossiped, and feeling rather uneasy, they sought to keep the whole matter quiet.

As for the Uji Chancellor Yorimichi—a person of the time—the incident brought to mind past events.[3] "A mouse once built its nest in the tail of a horse in the imperial stables," he said at the palace.[4] "It was in the reign of a certain emperor toward the middle of the Hakuchi era (650–54), or so I've read in a few old books. They say it was an event of some importance; this *koto,* then, must be truly extraordinary."

The emperor later spoke to those in his close service at the palace: "If someone were to compose a really good poem on this strange event, something would surely happen as a result. Such things are not without precedent, you know. Now I want all of you to compose a poem—the very best one you can—and we'll have fun indeed!"

The people racked their brains searching for words to capture the essence of what had happened. Among those of fame were Sei Shōnagon, daughter of Kiyohara no Motosuke, Akazome Emon, daughter of the Ōsumi governor Tokimochi, and Izumi Shikibu, daughter of Ōe no Masamune. Other well-known poets were there too, people whose lives would be as

[1]The following translation is from the fifteenth-century Go-Hanazono Tennō picture scroll, in Suzuka Sanshichi, *Shinkanshū kaisetsu* (Tokyo: Kunaishō, 1927), 51–60. The title *Kotohara* (Belly of the *Koto*) is homonymic with the word *kotohara,* "a different womb."

[2]Emperor Go-Ichijō (r. 1016–36) was the first son of Fujiwara no Michinaga's daughter Shōshi. The empress (*chūgū*) would have been Fujiwara no Ishi, third daughter of Michinaga; she was appointed *chūgū* in 1018.

[3]Fujiwara no Yorimichi (eldest son of Michinaga) held the post of chancellor (*kanpaku*) from 1019 to 1067. He is best known today for building the Byōdōin Phoenix Hall at Uji in 1052.

[4]This is according to the Sonkeikaku Bunko text (MJMT supp. 1:524a). According to the Go-Hanazono Tennō text, the horse was kept in the kitchen (*kuriya*) rather than the stable (*umaya*).

Fig. 48. Mice born from the body of a *koto*. From *Kotohara* (Go-Hanazono Tennō *emaki*). Courtesy of the Archives and Mausolea Department of the Japanese Imperial Household Agency (Kunaichō Shoryōbu).

fleeting as foam on the water, and they all made terrific efforts to compose a fine and moving verse. Their labor was for naught, however, and their poems—much like those of everyone else—were far from satisfactory. They plumbed the depths of their hearts, but they were unable to express even the haziest sentiment that might set their compositions apart. "For a poet, such times as these are truly humiliating," many thought to themselves.

There was at that time a priest by the name of Dōmyō. He had earned a name for himself composing verse on the morning flowers and the evening moon,[5] and he had access to the imperial palace. He was traveling in the Ise region on matters of love, and meeting with a person from the capital, he heard what was afoot. He seems at length to have had an idea, and word soon reached the capital that he had composed a poem.

Izumi Shikibu heard the news back at the palace, and brimming with envy, she decided to lie in wait for Dōmyō at an inn on the road from Ise. Disguising herself as a lurid courtesan, she met with him in the dim light of a certain evening. "Someone from the capital told me you've come up with a poem about that *koto* everyone's talking about," she said. "Won't you tell it to me?"

[5]These are standard topics for poetic composition.

Fig. 49. Dōmyō encounters a man from the capital. From *Kotohara* (Go-Hanazono Tennō *emaki*). Courtesy of the Archives and Mausolea Department of the Japanese Imperial Household Agency (Kunaichō Shoryōbu).

"I certainly will," he said, "just as soon as I've presented it at the palace."

"But we're so close to the capital as it is," she pressed. "And after you've recited it for the emperor, I'm sure to end up hearing it somehow or other anyway. So just tell me your first line."[6]

"My first line is, 'I once heard tell,'" he said weakly, and he would say no more. Abandoning him as if she had heard the entire verse, Izumi Shikibu immediately returned to the capital. She proceeded to the palace, and stating that she had come up with a poem, she recited the following:

inishie wa	I once heard tell
nesumi kayou to	you'd spend your life
kikishikado	with me,
kotohara ni koso	but a child now grows
ko wa mōkekere	in another's womb.[7]

The other attendants were vexed, and the emperor was greatly amused.

[6]Actually, "your first five syllables."

[7]Alternately translated, the poem might read: "I once heard tell / of wandering mice—/ and now they have borne their young / in the belly of a *koto*." The verse depends for its effect upon the double meanings of *nesumi/nezumi* as "mouse" and "living and sleeping together," and *kotohara* as "belly of the *koto*" and "another's womb."

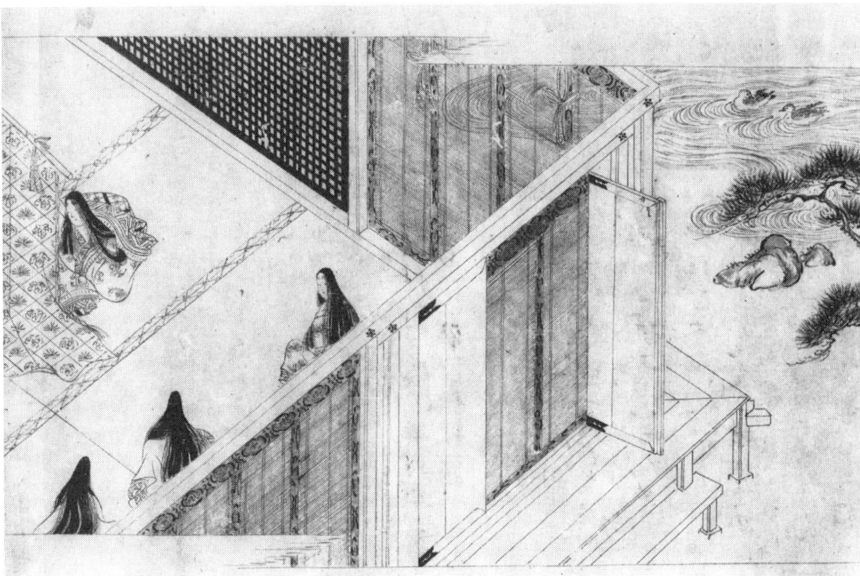

Fig. 50. Izumi Shikibu at the palace. From *Kotohara* (Go-Hanazono Tennō *emaki*). Courtesy of the Archives and Mausolea Department of the Japanese Imperial Household Agency (Kunaichō Shoryōbu).

A certain Lord Sanesuke, son of the former chancellor Kadoyoshi,[8] said that he, too, would compose an excellent verse, and with great fervor he devised the following:

au koto wa	When will we meet,
itsu tamakura no	our arms as pillows
nobe no toko	in our bed in the fields?
ta ga nesumi shite	Who was it (the field mice)
mumaru nadeshiko	who slept there and bore the flowers?

Such was his poem. It was not well received, however, perhaps because in some respects it was too similar to the earlier composition.

Sometime later Dōmyō returned to the capital from Ise. Explaining that he had written a verse while attending to matters in the provinces, he recited his *koto* poem—and it was identical to the one that Izumi Shikibu had earlier presented at the palace! Their compositions were the same from beginning to end, despite the fact that he had only taught her his first line. This was

[8]Fujiwara no Sanesuke (957–1046) was the third son of Commander of the Gate Guards of the Right Fujiwara no Tadatoshi and the grandson of Chancellor (and Regent) Fujiwara no Saneyori. There is no record of a chancellor by the name of Kadoyoshi.

Fig. 51. Lord Sanesuke composes a poem. From *Kotohara* (Go-Hanazono Tennō *emaki*). Courtesy of the Archives and Mausolea Department of the Japanese Imperial Household Agency (Kunaichō Shoryōbu).

due entirely to the miraculous powers of the Way of Poetry. Furthermore, it may well have been because of this poem that Emperor Go-Reizei was born of a different imperial womb, a marvelous thing indeed![9]

Hearing of Dōmyō's return to the capital, Izumi Shikibu sent him a message. At the bottom she wrote:

Ise no kami	It was impressive indeed,
kakete tazuneshi	that, "in the past
inishie wa	the mice would travel"
kayou nesumi no	that you asked of the god of Ise—
anakashiko naru	and I asked of you.[10]

[9]Go-Reizei (1025–68) was the son of Emperor Go-Ichijō's younger brother, Crown Prince Atsunaga (later to become Emperor Go-Suzaku) and Fujiwara no Kishi, daughter of Michinaga. Go-Ichijō's Empress Ishi bore only daughters. *Kotohara* suggests that it was miraculous for the new crown prince (Go-Reizei) to have been born to Atsunaga and Kishi rather than to Go-Ichijō and Ishi. The text reads *"kotomiyabara,"* "a different Imperial womb," which echoes both the poem and the title of the story.

[10]The translation is more explicit than the original poem, in which it is unclear exactly who does the asking of whom. Also, the double meaning of *nesumi/nezumi* is again suggestive; the last part of the poem could be read, "it was impressive indeed, our night together." The word *ana* functions within the *waka* as a hinge for *nezumi no ana* ("the mouse hole") and *anakashiko* ("impressive indeed").

Fig. 52. Izumi Shikibu and her attendants approach Sumiyoshi Shrine. From *Kotohara* (Go-Hanazono Tennō *emaki*). Courtesy of the Archives and Mausolea Department of the Japanese Imperial Household Agency (Kunaichō Shoryōbu).

As a result of this poem, Dōmyō realized that the woman he had seen so briefly in Ise was in fact Izumi Shikibu, and he was extremely annoyed. But later the two became very close, and as their hearts were filled with the longing of Mount Shinobu in the far north, [Izumi Shikibu] traveled—despite the distance—to Tennōji in Settsu, thinking as she passed the channel markers of Naniwa, "What can come of exhausting this body of mine?" Entrusting her hopes to [the deity at] Sumiyoshi Bay, she took to frequenting [Dōmyō's] abode, and in no time at all the two had become the subject of gossip.[11]

Now this Dōmyō Ajari was the son of Major Captain of the Right Michitsuna, and the grandson of Higashi Sanjō Chancellor Kaneie.[12] Michitsuna was by his nature a man of utmost refinement, and his son, Dōmyō, was handsome from childhood. After entering the priesthood, Dōmyō was appointed intendant of Tennōji Temple. He was a priest of ability and ideals, far above the usual run of men. He could recite numerous sutras by heart, and as he especially excelled at chanting the scriptures, his sutra readings

[11]This paragraph is more compact in the original as a result of the lyrical, layered syntax of *"kokoro no oku no shinobu yama"* and *"naniwa naru mi wo tsukushi."* Also, the text is unclear as to who is doing the traveling. According to the illustration, it is Izumi Shikibu.

[12]Fujiwara no Michitsuna (955–1020) was appointed Major Captain in the Office of Bodyguards in the twelfth month of 996. Fujiwara no Kaneie (929–90) was chancellor for less than one year, in 990. *"Ajari"* is a title used to refer to priests of a certain rank.

Fig. 53. The Gojōten Shrine Deity listens to Dōmyō recite. From *Kotohara* (Go-Hanazono Tennō *emaki*). Courtesy of the Archives and Mausolea Department of the Japanese Imperial Household Agency (Kunaichō Shoryōbu).

were without parallel. However, despite all these of his most excellent capacities, Dōmyō's heart was filled with lust of a most disgraceful sort—such as was not in the least befitting his character.

Other strange, miraculous events occurred as well. Without fail, Dōmyō would chant the sutras at set times within each six-hour period of the day and night.[13] As he was chanting one night, he was surprised to hear someone moving about in his garden. "Who's there?" he asked.

"I am an old man who lives in the area around Fifth Avenue and Tōin [Road],"[14] someone replied. "I come every night to hear you perform your midnight devotions. Did you not know?"

Dōmyō was suspicious. "It's a long way from here to the capital," he said. "How could an old man like you come this far every night? And what's your name?"

The old man was none other than the god Sukunahikona, and as there was nowhere he had to be, from that time on he came to listen whenever

[13]According to traditional calculations, days were composed of twelve "hours": six in the daytime and six in the night.

[14]The old man is referring to the area around the intersection of Kyoto's Fifth Avenue and Nishi no Tōin Road, the vicinity of the former Gojōten Shrine.

Fig. 54. Izumi Shikibu and a nun. From *Kotohara* (Go-Hanazono Tennō *emaki*). Courtesy of the Archives and Mausolea Department of the Japanese Imperial Household Agency (Kunaichō Shoryōbu).

Dōmyō chanted the sutras. And so although Dōmyō was a man of such shameful inclinations, he must have accumulated a great deal of merit, for his morning and evening devotions never varied and he practiced them unfailingly for years on end. His sutra chanting was as music, and all who heard it were moved to the depths of their hearts. "There are many who chant scripture," people would say, "but none surpass this priest." Perhaps it was for this reason that his chanting could touch even the heart of a god.

One night Dōmyō stayed with Izumi Shikibu in the capital. They talked of various things until the break of dawn, at which time Dōmyō set about his sutra recitations. After he had been at it for a while, he began to think to himself, "I wonder if that god isn't listening again. I should tell Izumi Shikibu about him and really give her a taste of the fantastic." And so after finishing his routine, Dōmyō called out to the god: "Are you there again tonight?" There was no reply. Dōmyō thought this strange.

In the early morning hours of a certain day Dōmyō chanted a *dharani* with exceptional skill.[15] His tone was exquisite, and as time passed he came to have a feeling in his bones that someone was listening. At that most poignant time of day, when the light of the twilight moon shines down through the pines at

[15]*Dharani* are esoteric Buddhist incantations employed for their practical, magical qualities.

Fig. 55. Izumi Shikibu and Dōmyō. From *Kotohara* (Go-Hanazono Tennō *emaki*). Courtesy of the Archives and Mausolea Department of the Japanese Imperial Household Agency (Kunaichō Shoryōbu).

Suminoe and "moonlit waves of dawn lap against the Golden Shore,"[16] Dōmyō sensed someone moving just beyond his door. He thought that perhaps the god had returned. "Are you there again?" Dōmyō called out after finishing his recitations. In a wondrous voice, the deity replied that he was.

Dōmyō spoke: "The other night when I was with Izumi Shikibu in the capital, I called out to you at dawn and you didn't answer. It seems strange, especially considering how close I was to your shrine. And you say you come here at such a distance every night. How is this?"

"What you say is true," the deity replied. "The closer you are to the capital the better. But when you stay with Izumi Shikibu, the impurity of your wanton deeds is repugnant to me. I do not approach when you engage in such acts, be they ever so infrequent."

Such miraculous events are said to have occurred in the past, and stories of them are told to this day.

[16]This is a slight misquotation of the first two lines of the "Late-night Praise" (*Goyasan*) section of *Gokuraku rokujisan*, a Pure Land hymn attributed to Genshin (942–1017). Takano Tatsuyuki, ed., *Nihon kayō shūsei*, vol. 4 (Tokyo: Tōkyōdō, 1942), 100c. The same two lines are used as the headnote to *Shinkokin wakashū* 1969. "The Golden Shore" (*kogane no kishi*) is the shore of the seven-jeweled lake in Amida Buddha's Pure Land Paradise.

Little Shikibu[1]

There was once an emperor named Ichijō.[2] As his was a most excellent reign, he was served by only the very best of men, from the highest to the lowest of the nobility. Among his women, too, there were many exceptional persons, not only within the ranks of His Majesty's consorts and concubines, but among those holding such positions as Handmaid and Lesser Counselor as well. One of these was a lady by the name of Koshikibu no Naishi. She was a daughter of Lord Michisada of the Senior Fourth Rank, governor of Izumi Province and an eleventh generation descendant of Lord Tachibana no Moroe. Her mother was Izumi Shikibu, daughter of a certain Lord Ōe no Masamune.

Izumi Shikibu was an exceedingly kind-hearted woman. Because her daughter was born to her as a result of her constant faith in the Hase Kannon and her prayers to the Sumiyoshi Deity, Koshikibu was beautiful beyond compare. She had glossy black eyebrows and a richly alluring fragrance, an elegant flush to her complexion and a hundred female charms. Of those who saw or heard of her, there was not one whose heart was not overcome. She was also clever from when she was a baby, like sandalwood, fragrant from when it is but two small leaves, and like a rose that stands undiminished in the midst of a glorious garden.

Koshikibu's father, Lord Michisada, passed away when she was a child, and she and her mother were left utterly without support. Clutching her little daughter to her breast, Izumi Shikibu wandered from place to place. It is the way of the world that a market will spring up at the foot of a majestic city gate, and though Izumi Shikibu too had enjoyed a flourishing social life, those who visited her in her poverty became increasingly few. The creeping weeds of desolation grew up around her door. Left only with the cries of insects to keep her company, Izumi Shikibu felt all things to be most wretched. But although she was forlorn, the flower in her heart remained unfaded,

[1]*Little Shikibu* (*Koshikibu [beppon]*, "The Other *Koshikibu*") survives in a single manuscript, a two-volume *nara ehon* dating from the late seventeenth or early eighteenth century, typeset in Yoshida Kōichi, ed., *Izumi Shikibu zenshū: honbun hen* (Tokyo: Koten Bunko, 1959), 738–50.

[2]Ichijō (980–1011) was the son on Emperor En'yū and Higashi Sanjōin Fujiwara no Senshi.

Fig. 56. Koshikibu with her parents. From *Koshikibu [beppon]*. Courtesy of Tōyō University Library.

and the moon of her mind shone bright. Those acquaintances who were of a more sensitive disposition came to feel pity, and they did not abandon her entirely.

At that time there was a man known as Yasumasa something-or-other, a grandchild of Lord Munetada, Major Controller of the Right.[3] He had been the governor of Tango Province for several years, and he had a compassionate heart. He now learned that Izumi Shikibu had come down in the world. Because she was an exceptional lady, reputed for her fine bearing and appearance, and for her erudition as well, it was only natural that someone as gentle as he should be attracted to her. Yasumasa began to make advances. "What a rare opportunity!" he thought, and upon consulting with a matchmaker, he began to correspond.

Izumi Shikibu's heart was at first extremely chaste, but the matchmaker sought to persuade her with various comforting words. "What would be so wrong if it were for the sake of the child?" she pressed. Overcome with grief at the wretchedness of her plight, Izumi Shikibu softly intoned:

inafune no	Though the rice boats decline,
ina ni wa arade	I shall not say no.
yo wo umi no	For does not the water invite
wataru bakari wo	across the sea of sorrow—
sasou mizu ka wa	this loathsome world?[4]

Taking up with Yasumasa, Izumi Shikibu left the capital for the province of Tango. Reluctantly untying her sash for a second man—with what dreamlike unreality did this heartless world appear to her then! In keeping with the ever-changing nature of things, she soon found herself in a newly spread bed, unsoftened by the accumulation of months or days. As she shed tears for the past, Yasumasa's pillow beside her own, she could only pretend to have forgotten. Hers was the unfamiliar berth of a loathsome mountain village, and so the misery in her heart exceeded any physical hardship she may have had to endure.

The years and months went by like a swift-footed charger, and before long three years had elapsed. Koshikibu was now nine years old. Once recalling the past as she dozed in the night, Izumi Shikibu quietly chanted:

[3]Fujiwara no Yasumasa (958–1036) was actually Munetada's son rather than his grandson. Munetada did not hold the position of Major Controller of the Right; he seems to have been confused here with a later Fujiwara no Munetada (1062–1141) who did.

[4]*Ina* has a double meaning of "rice" and "no." Somewhat more literally translated, the first two lines might read, "[I give] not the no of the naysaying rice boats."

yamazato mo	So the mountain village
neraretsuru ka na	was able to sleep soundly too—
yomosugara	unstartled by
matsu fuku kaze ni	the wind in the pines
odorokasarede	all through the night.

After listening to her mother's poem, Koshikibu spoke: "Why don't you try saying it like this?"

yamazato wa	The mountain village
nerarezarikeri	was unable to sleep—
yomosugara	startled by
matsu fuku kaze ni	the wind in the pines
odorokasarete	all through the night.

Izumi Shikibu chanted the new poem to herself several times. To sleep such that one may not be easily disturbed is truly a mark of the dullest sensitivity. How much more moving is the person who lies awake through the night, frightened by the wind in the pines! Though still but a child, Koshikibu improved her mother's poem by imbuing it with a sentiment as profound as this. As Koshikibu was a gift of the Gods and Buddhas, her mother should not have been surprised, but thinking to herself what a clever little girl she had, she drenched her sleeves in a dew of tears. And so the years passed.[5]

At the age of sixteen Koshikibu was summoned to the capital, where she took service in the jeweled palace of our emperor. Pursuing the ways of poetry and music, she displayed an uncommonly refined aesthetic sense. For this reason she came to serve under Jōtōmon'in, Junior Consort at the time.[6] Spending her days in recreation and her nights in unfailing attendance upon her lady, she was soon designated Principal Handmaid. Named after her mother, she came to be called Koshikibu no Naishi, "Little Shikibu the Handmaid."

It was decided at about this time that a poetry contest would be held at court. All senior nobles, courtiers, and high-ranking ladies-in-waiting were to compete. As each person anxiously pondered how he or she might prevail, it occurred to some that Koshikibu had always been able to string together tolerably good verses because her mother was such a fine poet. Left to her own devices, they said, Koshikibu would never come out with a very good poem, because her mother wrote them all for her. Thus people spoke

[5]Related *setsuwa* are contained in *Koshikibu* and *Sangoku denki* (6:21).

[6]Jōtōmon'in (Fujiwara no Shōshi; 988–1074) was made Junior Consort (*nyōgo*) in 999. She was appointed empress (*chūgū*) in 1000.

Fig. 57. Koshikibu corrects her mother's poem. From *Koshikibu [beppon]*. Courtesy of Toyo University Library.

of her with the utmost contempt. But as there were no grounds for having her excluded from the competition, the days simply passed, and people went on saying that she would probably get her mother to compose a verse for her this time, too.

Middle Counselor Sadayori came by Koshikibu's quarters.[7] "How will you come up with a poem for the contest this time?" he teased, standing before her bamboo blind. "Did you send someone to Tango to ask your mother? You must be awfully anxious if your messenger hasn't yet returned." Gathering up the train of her crimson robes and covering her face with a twelve-layered sleeve, Koshikibu leaned out from behind her blind. She took hold of the startled Middle Counselor's robe, and without a moment for thought, replied:

Ōe-yama	The road to Mount Ōe
Ikuno no michi no	and Ikuno is long—
tōkereba	I have neither crossed the bridge
mada fumi mo mizu	of Ama no Hashidate,
Ama no Hashidate	nor have I heard from my mother.[8]

Taken by surprise, the Middle Counselor was suddenly flustered. Muttering in consternation, humiliated and unable to reply to such an excellent verse, he pulled back his sleeve and ran away. From then on everyone said that Koshikibu could compose fine poems, even without her mother's help.

Now Koshikibu surpassed all others in beauty. She had the lilting hair of a willow and the face of a flower, and even without cosmetics, just as heaven made her, she needed only to smile to display her hundred charms. There were few who could compare, even among the Six Palaces of China, and before long a person known as the Nijō Lord fell in love with her.[9] He pledged his devotion with a thousand brocade spindle branches,[10] and under shared covers, as roosters cried out the break of dawn, he and Koshikibu promised one thousand nights together. As a result, they soon became a subject of court gossip.

A man known as the Horikawa Minister of the Right also loved Koshikibu,[11] and hearing that the Nijō Lord was paying her visits, he sent a mes-

[7]Fujiwara no Sadayori (995–1045), son of the eminent Fujiwara no Kintō.

[8]This is *Kinyō wakashū* 550, attributed to Koshikibu no Naishi. For the headnote, see *Koshikibu*, fn. 38, above.

[9]The Nijō Lord (Fujiwara no Norimichi; 996–1075) was a son of Fujiwara no Michinaga by Minamoto no Rinshi. He was a brother of Jōtōmon'in, in whose salon Koshikibu served.

[10]According to the Japanese poetic tradition, a man could court a woman by leaving up to a thousand *nishikigi* branches in front of her house. See SNKBT 8:213, notes for poem 651.

[11]The Horikawa Minister of the Right (Fujiwara no Yorimune; 993–1065) was a son of Michinaga by Minamoto no Akiko. He was thus Norimichi's half-brother.

sage to her mother:

hito shirade	How vexing
netasa mo netashi	that no one should know!
murasaki no	Perhaps I'll wear that
nezuri no koromo	purple printed robe
uwagi ni mo sen	for everyone to see.[12]

"I have feelings for your daughter," he wrote, "but she is taken by another." Izumi Shikibu replied:

nureginu to	I'll tell everyone
hito ni wa iwan	your sleeves are damp
murasaki no	with lies—
nezuri no koromo	even should you wear a
uwagi nari to mo	purple printed robe for all to see.[13]

"People are sure to say the most awful things," Izumi Shikibu wrote in her reply, "though, like your under-robe, they're unlikely to be true." Koshikibu continued to give her full attention to the Nijō Lord, and she later bore him a son, the archbishop Jōen.

One time the former Kamo Priestess Rokujō was to host a poetry contest. Hearing that the lady-in-waiting Koben was to be on the same Team of the Right,[14] Koshikibu copied her contest poem onto a thin sheet of crimson

[12]This is a slightly alternate version of *Goshūi wakashū* 911, attributed to the Horikawa Minister of the Right. The headnote reads: "Sent upon hearing that the former Nijō Prime Minister had begun visiting Koshikibu no Naishi in her quarters." The "purple printed robe" of his poem is suggestive of hidden love as a result of the anonymous *Kokinshū* 652:

koishiku wa	Hide them deep inside,
shita ni wo omoe	those feelings of love—
murasaki no	the color of a
nezuri no koromo	purple printed robe,
iro ni izu na yume	never let them show through.

Yorimune employs the image of a purple printed robe to refer to Norimichi and Koshikibu's secret affair; his threat to make it public is a threat to Koshikibu's reputation. In his poem, if *hito* is taken to be an allusion to Norimichi, the first two lines could be alternately translated, "How vexing that he [my brother] would not know [of my feelings for her]."

[13]This is *Goshūi wakashū* 912, attributed to Izumi Shikibu. The headnote simply reads, "reply." *Nureginu* signifies both "damp sleeves" and "groundless rumors."

[14]It is obvious from the following poem that Koshikibu was to be on the Team of the Left, and so to whom or what the "same" refers is unclear. This may be a mistaken recounting of the headnote to *Goshūi wakashū* 873 (below), which merely suggests that Koben was cheering for the Right—possibly as a non-contestant.

paper. "Somehow one of my lines isn't right," she said, "and I'll surely be criticized for it." At the bottom she wrote:

arawarete	Should I openly resent
urami ya semashi	those waves of your heart,
kakurenu no	drawing to the shore
migiwa ni yoseshi	of the hidden marsh,
nami no kokoro wo	secretly favoring the right?[15]

"Please, by no means let anyone see my poem," she appended, and she sent it to Koben for advice. Koben replied:

kishi takami	The bank is high
tadayou nami wa	and the wandering waves
nakazora ni	lap against the open sky.
yoru kata mo naki	To which shore shall I tend?
nageki wo zo seshi	I sigh with indecision.[16]

"I hadn't favored either side," Koben wrote back warmly, "but now I'm certain that you'll present a marvelous verse." As it turned out, Koshikibu won her round of the poetry contest this time too, and her fame as a poet grew all the more. Her success was due entirely to the blessings of the Sumiyoshi Deity. She must have been in his eye the entire time.

Now the Nijō Lord maintained a grand estate in a place called Shirakawa. It was there that he kept his wife, a daughter of the Shijō Major Counselor Kintō,[17] and it was there that he spent most of his time. Nevertheless, the Nijō Lord was terribly fond of Koshikibu, and he was unfailing in his devotion to her. Toward the end of the second month, when spring mists hung heavy in the mountains of the four directions and blossoms bloomed at their full-blown peak, such that one might mistake them for clouds or snow, the Shirakawa estate was awash in eight and ninefold cherry blossoms in rows of flowering trees. The Nijō Lord had a taste for rockeries, sculpted gardens and the like, so he sent a message to Koshikibu inviting her to Shirakawa to

[15]This is *Goshūi wakashū* 873, attributed to "Koshikibu." The headnote reads: "Sent to Koben upon hearing that she favored [the Team of] the Right, when the former Kamo Priestess Rokujō was to host a poetry contest." The Koshikibu to whom this poem is attributed is apparently not Koshikibu no Naishi. According to *Chokusen sakusha burui* (ca. 1337), this Koshikibu was a daughter of Fujiwara no Yoshitada, and a lady-in-waiting in the salon of Princess Yūshi (1038–1105), elder half-sister of Princess Baishi (the former Kamo Priestess Rokujō). SNKBT 8:32 (roman numeral pagination beginning from the back of the book).

[16]This is a slightly alternate version of *Goshūi wakashū* 874, attributed to Koben.

[17]Norimichi was married to Fujiwara no Kintō's eldest daughter, who bore him four sons and three daughters before her death in 1024.

Fig. 58. Koshikibu composes a poem. From *Koshikibu [beppon]*. Courtesy of Tōyō University Library.

view the blossoms. Later informing him of her wish to decline, she sent the following poem:

haru no konu	There is no place
tokoro wa naki wo	to which spring has not come,
Shirakawa no	yet do you suppose that
watari ni nomi ya	blossoms bloom
hana wa sakuran	at Shirakawa alone?[18]

The Nijō Lord was deeply touched. Like birds that fly with wings as one, they shared a love of a sort unknown in heaven, and though earthly distance may have held them apart, their converse was as that of trees with branches entwined. How, then, might they have forgotten the moon as it traversed the sky? Saying that nothing could cheer him on those cloudy occasions when Koshikibu was not by his side, the Nijō Lord left Shirakawa for the capital. He took with him a ladies' pink and gold five-layered under-robe, which he presented to Koshikibu in response to her poem.

So the year drew to a close. At some time or other the Nijō Lord's appetite disappeared and his heart came to feel strangely unsettled. Koshikibu was busy in the service of her mistress, and thus unable to visit. But as time passed, she came to miss him more and more. Taking time off from her duties, she went to see him and inquire after his health. The Nijō Lord was elated, but he was bitter, too. "I've been ill all this time," he said. "Why did you wait so long?" Without lengthy excuses or explanations, Koshikibu tearfully took hold of his sleeve and intoned:

shinu bakari	I too was near death
nageki ni koso wa	with sorrow—
nageki shika	for though living,
ikite toubeki	my position is not such
mi ni shi araneba	that I am free to visit.[19]

The Nijō Lord was wonderfully glad, and in a labored voice he replied:

omoiki ya	Did I really think
nageki no mori no	to weep for the dew

[18]This is *Shika wakashū* 280, attributed to Koshikibu no Naishi. The headnote reads: "Composed after having been told by the Nijō Chancellor to come and see the blossoms at Shirakawa."

[19]This is *Goshūi wakashū* 1001, attributed to Koshikibu no Naishi. The headnote reads: "The Nijō Lord once suffered a prolonged illness. After having recovered, he asked, 'Why didn't you come to see me?' [Koshikibu] composed the following [reply]." In the poem, *ikite* has a double meaning of "to live" and "to go." It stands in opposition to *shinu*, "to die."

Fig. 59. The Nijō Lord at Shirakawa. From *Koshikibu [beppon]*. Courtesy of Tōyō University Library.

shitatsuyu no	in the Forest of Sorrows—
okuresakidatsu	for that single drop that
nageki sen to wa	might vanish before the other?[20]

Koshikibu further spoke:

wakareji wa	Though final partings
ari mo suramedo	there may be,
shitatsuyu no	hearing only that the dew
oku to shi kikeba	has formed at all,
nani nagekuran	for what is there to sorrow?

The Nijō Lord took medicines, prayed, and performed numerous pious acts. Koshikibu visited various shrines, presenting poems and prayer slips and praying at each and every one. Before long the Nijō Lord felt improved. Truly, it was thanks to Koshikibu's poems that the Gods and Buddhas deigned to accept her prayers and save his life. Everyone praised

[20]The Forest of Sorrows (*nageki no mori*) is in Ōsumi Province in Kyūshū.

Fig. 60. Koshikibu and the Nijō Lord. From *Koshikibu [beppon]*. Courtesy of Tōyō University Library.

Koshikibu, from the Nijō Lord and his children to all the various nobles at court.

In those days the Nijō Lord spent most of his time with Koshikibu, but for some unknown reason he once failed to visit for a long while. Later, when he came to see her again, Koshikibu was angry. "You must have been on Mount Tatsuta," she said, "'when blowing autumn winds lashed up white-crested waves.'"[21] The Nijō Lord simply replied:

aki kaze wa	Into what sky
izuko no sora ni	would autumn winds blow?
Tatsuta-yama	And to say such things as I wade
momiji fumiwake	through Mount Tatsuta's crimson leaves,
kotosara ni koso	on my way to see you!

Koshikibu replied:

Tatsutagawa	Tatsuta River—
momiji no nishiki	would your color
naka naka ni	not reveal it,
taeteshi iro ni	should your brocade
idezarame ya wa	of autumn leaves run out?[22]

Later taking to their lovebird nest,[23] they retired to the bedchamber, where they passed the long autumn nights in whispers of intimate affection. Though at times resenting one another and voicing their complaints, the tenderness of their cradling arms was of a truly extraordinary sort. A thousand nights were as one,[24] and their sorrow at the dreadful, incessant tolling of dawn's temple bell was quite beyond expression.

As he would receive messages and summons from time to time, the Nijō Lord once again let four or five days pass without a visit. Imagining Koshikibu's ire at his heartless behavior, he sent a messenger with fine wooden

[21]Koshikibu alludes to *Kokinshū* 994, accusing the Nijō Lord of infidelity. See *Koshikibu*, p. 288, above.

[22]Koshikibu's question is rhetorical. *Iro*, "color," has a secondary meaning of "love." In her poem, Koshikibu acknowledges the unchanging nature of Norimichi's feelings.

[23]Actually, the nest of a rooster (*yūtsukedori*). The rooster is suggestive of love as a result of its poetic associations with Meeting-Hill Barrier. See *Kokin wakashū* 536.

[24]This may be an allusion to *Kokin rokujō* 1987 (or to a variant in *Ise monogatari, dan* 22):

aki no yo no	These autumn nights,
chiyo wo hito yo ni	a thousand nights are as one.
nazuraete	Even a full
yachiyo shi nenaba	eight thousand together
koi wa samenan	and my love would never cool.

Fig. 61. Koshikibu and Koben before the gate of Taira no Sanmi. From *Koshikibu [beppon]*. Courtesy of Tōyō University Library.

boxes and a silken summer robe. Koshikibu carefully composed her reply, and at the bottom she wrote:

omohiide	Thinking back—
tare wo ka hito no	what others
tazunemashi	might be visiting,
uki ni taetaru	were my life not spent
inochi narazu wa	enduring your cruelty?[25]

She gave the messenger boy a token of her appreciation and sent him home.

In the days of her service at the palace, Koshikibu was especially close with a person named Koben no Omoto. Koben was a woman of refinement, and as she was also accomplished in the Way of Poetry, people spoke of her as a lady of the very first rank. Koshikibu and Koben once went on an excursion, but they were caught in a downpour when they returned in the evening. As they were standing around outside the house of a certain Taira no Sanmi, a voice called out from inside the gate, punning on the two women's names: "Ah, what torment, these short summer nights!" ["Ah, what torment—Koshikibu and Koben have come!"].[26] Koshikibu replied that "there seem to be geese landing on the sandy plain,"[27] thus herself calling out that person's name.

Around that time Koshikibu began to feel unusually out of sorts. At first she thought it to be a passing illness, but one after another her prayers went unanswered, and the director of the Medical Bureau, Wake no Tanba, was at a loss for a remedy. Her mother, Izumi Shikibu, was distraught, and she rushed about doing various things. Messengers arrived day and night, and not only from the Nijō Lord. Koshikibu's son, Archbishop Jōen of Kohata, as well as Jōkaku Hōin of Nagatani,[28] took up a fearsome invocation of sacred prayers and incantations for the sake of her recovery. Whether with

[25]This is *Senzai wakashū* 843, attributed to Koshikibu. The headnote reads: "Sent in reply to a message from a person who had not visited in a long time."

[26]The person plays on the words *shōshō* and *yoru*. The first, meaning "short" or "brief," is written with the first character of each of Koshikibu's and Koben's names. The second is used in this case to mean both "night" and "visit."

[27]"Geese landing on the sandy plain" (*heisa no rakugan*) is one of the Eight Scenic Views at the Confluence of the Xiao and Xiang Rivers (*Shōshō no hakkei*) in Hunan Province in China. Koshikibu manages to pun on the word *heisa* ("sandy plain," and the first two characters of Taira no Sanmi's name), while making a second implied pun on *Shōshō* (the Xiao and Xiang rivers, and Koshikibu's and Koben's names).

[28]Jōkaku (1024–83) was Norimichi's fourth son by Kintō's eldest daughter. He was a half-brother of Koshikibu's son Jōen, who served as an intendant of Kohata Jōmyōji Temple.

Fig. 62. Koshikibu lies ill. From *Koshikibu [beppon]*. Courtesy of Tōyō University Library.

medicine or prayer, everyone did all they could, but their efforts were for naught.

One evening Koshikibu appeared to suffer most severely. No longer able to distinguish clearly among the faces of those around her, she had weakened beyond the point of taking medicine. Izumi Shikibu was overcome with anguish and despair. Staying by her daughter's side, not leaving for a moment, she pressed her hand to her daughter's forehead and wept. Koshikibu opened her eyes slightly, and gazing up at her mother's face, whispered in a dying voice:

ika ni semu	What shall I do?
yuku beki kata mo	Not knowing the path
omohoezu	one takes before a parent,
oya ni sakidatsu	I cannot imagine
michi wo shiraneba	the way I am to go.[29]

A voice like a yawn sounded from above the ceiling. Koshikibu's inescapable destiny was then at hand, but in having spoken such powerful prayers—having voiced a poem so filial in intent—how could the Buddhas and Gods not have shown their grace? "How moving, how moving," the voice was heard to say. Everyone in the room was struck with such fear and awe that their hair stood on end. At the break of day Koshikibu's fever receded and she felt somewhat better. She began eating again, and gradually she improved.

That Koshikibu returned to her former condition was thanks to the powers of Japanese Poetry. It is poetry that moves Gods and Buddhas to hear our prayers and keep us in their sight. In leading, instructing, and bringing together all people, high and low, lay and ordained, nothing equals the Way of Poetry. Although one may say that it was medicine and prayer that saved Koshikibu's life, the deity declared that he was moved by her single verse, and it was this in particular that brought about her very happy end.

Calligraphy and illustrations by the daughter of Isome.[30]

[29]This is a variant of *Shoku shika wakashū* 439. See *Koshikibu*, fn. 10, above.

[30]Shimizu Yutaka identifies "the daughter of Isome" as Isome Tsune, an eminent female calligrapher active in the Jōkyō and Genroku periods, 1684–1704. In addition to *Little Shikibu*, Isome is the attributed painter and calligrapher of the Shimizu manuscript of *Sagoromo*. Shimizu Yutaka, *Nihon bungaku ronkō* (Kyoto: Hatsune Shobō, 1960), 197 and 200; Yutaka Shimizu, *Nara Picture Books*, trans. Richard Zumwinkle (Los Angeles: Dawson's Book Shop, 1960), 34 and 37.

Appendix
Extant Texts and Textual Lines

Izumi Shikibu

Izumi Shikibu is known to survive in at least six manuscripts:

1. The former Shimizu Yutaka text. A one-vol. *nara ehon* dating from the late Muromachi period (sixteenth century); now in the possession of Yoshida Kōichi. Typeset and annotated with all nine of its illustrations in SNKBZ 63:226–42. Also typeset with four of its illustrations in Yoshida Kōichi, ed., *Izumi Shikibu zenshū: honbun hen* (Tokyo: Koten Bunko, 1959), 720–28.

2. The Yoshida Kogorō text. A one-vol. *tanrokubon* (a woodblock-printed book with distinctive red and green illustrations), dating from ca. 1655–58. Typeset in MJMT 2:342–47. Three of its five illustrations are reproduced in color in Yoshida Kogorō, *Tanrokubon: Rare Books of Seventeenth-century Japan*, trans. Mark A. Harbison (Tokyo: Kodansha International, 1984), 160–62.

3. The Shibukawa text. A one-vol. woodblock-printed manuscript with uncolored illustrations; closely based upon the *Izumi Shikibu tanrokubon*. Also known as the *Otogi bunko* or *Otogizōshi* text because of its inclusion in Shibukawa Seiemon's box-set anthology of medieval prose fiction from ca. 1716–29. Typeset and annotated with all five of its illustrations in NKBT 38:312–18 and NKBZ 36:384–93.

4. The former Akagi Bunko text. Cited in Nara Ehon Kokusai Kenkyū Kaigi, ed., *Otogizōshi no sekai* (Tokyo: Sanseidō, 1982), 62, as an unillustrated hand-copied manuscript in the *tanrokubon* textual line.

5. The Seikadō Bunko text, also known as the Matsui text. An unillustrated, hand-copied manuscript titled *Dōmei no sōshi* (The Book of Dōmei), cited in Ichiko Teiji's annotations to the NKBT Shibukawa *Izumi Shikibu* text.

6. The Kure Fumiaki text. Cited in Nara Ehon Kokusai Kenkyū Kaigi, ed., *Otogizōshi no sekai*, 62, as an unillustrated hand-copied manuscript.

Izumi Shikibu engi (A History of Izumi Shikibu)

Izumi Shikibu engi survives in two known manuscripts, the second of which is incomplete:

1. Seishin'in text. A two-scroll *emaki* titled *Izumi Shikibu engi*; bears a

colophon signed by Kaijuan (Prince Ryōjun; 1604–69), dated the tenth month of 1643. In the possession of Seishin'in (Jōshin'in) Temple in Kyoto. Typeset with all thirteen of its illustrations in Ōhashi Kiyohide, *Izumi Shikibu nikki no kenkyū* (Tokyo: Shoon Shobō, 1961), 529–41.

2. Tōhokuin text. An unillustrated hand-copied manuscript in one scroll, titled *Ippen Shōnin Izumi Shikibu monogatari* (The Tale of Ippen Shōnin and Izumi Shikibu), corresponding to the second scroll of the Seishin'in text. In the possession of Tōhokuin Temple in Kyoto. Umetani Shigeki speculates that it dates from either 1692–93, when Tōhokuin moved to its present location, or from around 1560, when Tōhokuin converted to the Ji sect of Pure Land Buddhism. Umetani Shigeki, "Kyōto Tōhokuin-zō *Ippen Shōnin Izumi Shikibu monogatari* ni tsuite," in *Chūsei yūgyō hijiri to bungaku* (Tokyo: Ōfūsha, 1988), 328 (the Tōhokuin text is typeset on pages 306–21).

Jippon ōgi (Ten Fans)

Jippon ōgi survives in at least five manuscripts, which Fujii Takashi has divided into two main textual lines:

1. Line One. Represented by the Ichiko Teiji text, an unillustrated hand-copied manuscript in one vol., typeset in Ichiko Teiji, ed., *Mikan chūsei shōsetsu*, Koten bunko 12 (Tokyo: Koten Bunko, 1946), 39–55. Lost in a fire during the Pacific War.

2. Line Two. Derived from Line One, and represented by:

> A. The Seikadō Bunko text, also known as the Matsui text. The first vol. of a two-vol. *nara ehon*, typeset in "*Jippon ōgi* kaisetsu," in Ichiko Teiji, ed., *Mikan chūsei shōsetsu*, Koten bunko 12, 6–12.
>
> B. 1. The Honokuni Bunko text. A one-vol. *nara ehon* typeset in MJMT 7:232–42 and photographically reproduced in *Muromachi monogatari shū* (Tokyo: Nihon Koten Bungakukai, 1990), 31–98. Derived from 2A and dated by Fujii to around the Kanbun/Enpō eras (1661–81). Contains twelve illustrations. 2. The Fujii Takashi text. An unillustrated, hand-copied manuscript in two small scrolls. Derived from 2A and dated by Fujii to around the mid-nineteenth century.
>
> C. The Tokuda Kazuo text. A fragmentary work, originally comprising the second vol. of a two-vol. *nara ehon*. The manuscript was disassembled and the pages mounted upon two six-panel *byōbu* screens, now in the possession of Tokuda Kazuo. Tokuda dates the pages to around the Kanbun/Enpō eras (1661–81), and he identifies them as being from the Honokuni Bunko and Seikadō Bunko textual line. The text is typeset and all sixteen illustrations are reproduced

in Tokuda Kazuo, "Shōkai: otogizōshi *Jippon ōgi* no shinshutsu-bon," *Koten shiryō kenkyū* 3 (June 2001): 1–17.

Fujii Takashi, "*Jippon ōgi*" (first published in 1972), in *Chūsei koten no shoshigakuteki kenkyū: otogizōshi hen* (Ōsaka: Izumi Shoin, 1996), 325–40.

Koshikibu

Koshikibu is known to survive in at least seven manuscripts in three textual lines:

1. Line One. Represented by the unillustrated Tenri Library text, hand-copied in one vol.; formerly in the collection of Fujii Otoo. Typeset in MJMT 5:20–38, and in Shimazu Hisamoto, *Kinko shōsetsu shinsan* (Tokyo: Chūkōkan, 1928; republished by Yūseidō in 1983), 233–54.

2. Line Two. Represented by the following five *nara ehon*:

A. The Ono Hisashi (Ichiji?) text. Formerly in the collection of Maeda Yoshiko; two vols. from around the Kan'ei-Kanbun eras (1624–73), according to Yokoyama Shigeru and Matsumoto Ryūshin in MJMT supp. 1:505a. Illustrations lost. Typeset in MJMT supp. 1:505–22.

B. The Taku Library text. Two vols. dating from the eighteenth century, perhaps. Contains a total of twelve illustrations. See Gotō Akiko, "Takubon *Koshikibu* no kōsatsu," *Bungaku ronshū* (Saga Daigaku) 5 (1963): 30–33.

C. The Gifu University Library text. Formerly in the collection of Sorimachi Shigeo; two vols. with a total of sixteen illustrations. Dated to around the Kanbun era (1661–73) by Yuge Shigeru in "Gifu Daigaku Fuzoku Toshokan-zō *Koshikibu*: honkoku to kaidai," *Gifu Daigaku kokugo kokubungaku* 25 (March 1998), 63b (typeset on pages 68–80).

D. The Fujii Takashi text. Dated to around the Kan'ei/Shōhō eras (1624–48) by Fujii Takashi in *Chūsei koten no shoshigakuteki kenkyū: otogizōshi hen* (Ōsaka: Izumi Shoin, 1996), 103.

E. The former Akagi Bunko text. Two vols.; second vol. lost. Cited in Nara Ehon Kokusai Kenkyū Kaigi, ed., *Otogizōshi no sekai*, 78b.

3. Line Three. Represented by the former Togawa Hamao text, an unillustrated manuscript in one scroll titled *Izumi Shikibu no monogatari* (The Tale of Izumi Shikibu); corresponds to the second half of *Koshikibu*. Dated to the late Muromachi period (sixteenth century) by Yokoyama Shigeru and

Matsumoto Ryūshin in MJMT 5:20a, and to the early Muromachi period by Yoshida Kōichi in *Izumi Shikibu zenshū: honbun hen* (Tokyo: Koten Bunko, 1959), 707. Closer to Line Two (the five *nara ehon*) than to Line One (the Tenri Library text). Typeset in MJMT 2:347–56, and in Yoshida, ed., *Izumi Shikibu zenshū: honbun hen*, 709–19.

Seiganji engi (A History of Seiganji)

Seiganji engi survives in at least four textual lines:

1. Line One. Represented by *Seiganji shin engi* (A True History of Seiganji), a one-scroll manuscript in the possession of Seiganji. Internal evidence suggests that it dates from between 1209 and 1288 (there is a reference in the text to a "present Buddha hall" which was constructed in 1209 and is known to have burned in 1288). Typeset and photographically reproduced in Yutani Yūzō, "*Seiganji engi* kankei shiryō," *Fukakusa kyōgaku* 19 (1999), 318–25 (on the dating of the work, see page 303).

2. Line Two. Represented by the Sonkeikaku Bunko text, an eleven-scroll *Seiganji engi* manuscript in the possession of the Sonkeikaku Bunko archive. Although transcribed ca. 1680, Yoshida Kōichi classifies this as the sole surviving manuscript in his first textual line (Yoshida was unaware of *Seiganji shin engi*), which he dates to ca. 1477, when Seiganji was rebuilt after a fire in 1467. Because it contains an account from 1442, the *engi* must date from after that time. Yoshida transcribes the Sei Shōnagon section in "*Seiganji engi* to *Izumi Shikibu engi*," *Bungaku ronsō* (May 1966), 4–5.

3. Line Three. The *Sankan-bon* (three scroll) textual line, named by Yutani Yūzō after the three scrolls of the *Seiganji engi emaki*. Yoshida Kōichi classifies this group of manuscripts as his second textual line, which he dates to sometime between 1565, when Yamashina Tokitsugu (1507–79) records having been shown a single-scroll *Seiganji engi* manuscript corresponding to an older version of the *engi* (*Tokitsugu-kyō ki*, tenth day of the twelfth month of 1565), and 1595, when Tokitsugu's son Tokitsune (1543–1611) alludes to a section from the *Sankan-bon* textual line in an entry on the noh play *Seiganji* in the noh commentary *Utaishō* (Notes on the Noh). Yoshida argues that the *Sankan-bon* was likely composed between 1574, after Seiganji was destroyed by fire, and 1591, when it was reconstructed at its present location. Yoshida, "*Seiganji engi* to *Izumi Shikibu engi*," 8a and 13a. *Sankan-bon* manuscripts include:

A. The Jingū Bunko manuscript, hand-copied in 1751 and typeset in ZGR 27:1:206–43 and DNBZ 117:340–72 (83:148–62); titled *Rakuyō Seiganji engi* (A History of Seiganji in the Capital).

B. The six-scroll *Seiganji engi*, hand-copied in thirty-six parts by thirty-six calligraphers in the late seventeenth century; in the possession of Seiganji. Yutani argues that this six-scroll manuscript constitutes its own textual line; however, it is so close to other works in the *Sankan-bon* textual line that I count it as one of them. This six-scroll text is typeset in Yutani Yūzō, "*Seiganji engi* rokkanbon no kaidai to honkoku," *Dōhō Daigaku Bukkyō bunka kenkyūjo kiyō* 18 (1998), 79–100.

C. *Rakuyō Seiganji honzon engi* (A History of the Principal Image at Seiganji in the Capital), hand-copied in 1723 and typeset in Kikuchi Masakazu, "Kyōhō hachinen-sha *Rakuyō Seiganji honzon engi*," in *Shōdō bungaku kenkyū: dai san shū*, ed. Fukuda Akira and Hirota Tetsumichi (Tokyo: Miyai Shoten, 2001), 352–96.

D. *Seiganji engi emaki*, a three-scroll picture scroll on permanent loan from Seiganji to the Kyoto National Museum. The *Seiganji engi emaki* is described and outlined in Nara Kokuritsu Hakubutsukan, ed., *Shaji engi-e* (Tokyo: Kadokawa Shoten, 1975), 137–38, which dates it to the seventeenth century. Except for *Ekotoba yōryaku Seiganji engi* (below), the *Seiganji engi emaki* is the only illustrated *Seiganji engi* manuscript known to survive today. Yoshida Kōichi notes that the Naikaku Bunko manuscript (in the *Sankan-bon* textual line) is said to have been copied from a three-part picture scroll with a total of thirty illustrations, while the related Tanaka Jūtarō manuscript, in three volumes, is said to have been copied from a work with only twenty-four illustrations ("*Seiganji engi* to *Izumi Shikibu engi*," 3a). However, the *Seiganji engi emaki* contains a total of thirty-two illustrations, indicating that it is probably not the parent text of either the Naikaku Bunko or Tanaka Jūtarō manuscripts. Furthermore, the *Seiganji engi emaki* contains an illustration of the ghosts of Izumi Shikibu and Chūjōhime, yet lacks their story, which is present in the unillustrated Jingū Bunko text. This suggests that the *emaki* was copied from an earlier illustrated work, the Izumi Shikibu/Chūjōhime painting of which was reproduced while the relevant prose section was not.

4. Line Four. Represented by *Ekotoba yōryaku Seiganji engi* (An Abridged History of Seiganji in Pictures and Words), an illustrated, woodblock-printed text from 1792, produced for use in a fund-raising campaign authorized in 1791 after a fire in 1788. Yoshida Kōichi classifies this as his third textual line (Yoshida, "*Seiganji engi* to *Izumi Shikibu engi*," 5b). The illustrations are by Hokkyō Tōshū (Murakami Nariaki; fl. ca. 1800), and at least one copy of the text remains in the possession of Seiganji. Typeset in DNBZ 117:373–85 (83:163–68).

Character List

Agongyō 阿含経
Agui 安居院
ajari 阿闍梨
Akagi Bunko 赤木文庫
Akazome Emon 赤染衛門
Akazome Emon shū 赤染衛門集
ama 尼
Amida 阿弥陀
Amidakyō 阿弥陀経
Ariwara no Narihira 在原業平
Asagao no tsuyu 朝顔の露
Asai Ryōi 浅井了意
Ashikaga Yoshimitsu 足利義満
Ashuku Nyorai 阿閦如来
asobi 遊女
Atsumichi 敦道
Bai Juyi 白居易
Ban Kōkei 伴蒿蹊
Benkei monogatari 弁慶物語
Benzaiten 弁財天
bettō 別当
Bifukumon'in no Kaga 美福門院加賀
bikuni 比丘尼
Bishamon no honji 毘沙門の本地
Bishamonten 毘沙門天
Bishamon Tennō no honji 毘沙門天王之本地
biwa 琵琶
biwa hōshi 琵琶法師
Bongobō 梵語坊
Bunki mandala 文亀曼荼羅
Bussetsu Yakushi rurikō nyorai hongan kudoku kyō 仏説薬師琉璃光如来本願功徳経
byōdōshōchi 平等性智
Chang hen ge 長恨歌
Chihō yōbunshō 地方用文章
Chikanaga-kyō ki 親長卿記
Chingen 鎮源
Chinsō Kashō 珎増和尚
Chion'in 知恩院
Chōhōji yomigaeri no sōshi 長宝寺よみがへりの草紙
Chōjū gi-uta-awase monogatari 鳥獣戯歌合物語
Chōya gunsai 朝野群載
chūgū 中宮
Chūjōhime emaki 中将姫絵巻
Chūjōhime no honji 中将姫の本地
Chōken 澄憲
Chokusen sakusha burui 勅撰作者部類
chūsei 中世
Daiaidō 大愛道
dai-bosatsu 大菩薩
Daibutsu engi 大仏縁起
Daibutsu kuyō 大仏供養
Daibutsu kuyō monogatari 大仏供養物語
Daigoji 醍醐寺
Daihannyakyō 大般若経
Daihatsu nehangyō 大般涅槃経
Daijōin jisha zōjiki 大乗院寺社雑事記
Daikoku-mai 大黒舞
dainagon 大納言
Dainichikyōsho 大日経疏
Dainichi Nyorai 大日如来
daisōjō 大僧正
Daitsūchishō Nyorai 大通智勝如来
dangisho 談義所
darani 陀羅尼
Denkai 伝海
Dōkō 道公
Dokyō kuden myōkyōshū 読経口伝明鏡集
Dōmyō Ajari 道命阿闍梨
Dōmyō Hōshi 道命法師
dōsojin 道祖神
eboshi 烏帽子

Eguchi 江口
Eiga monogatari 栄華物語
Eikai 叡海
Eikaku 永覚
Eishin 栄心
Eizan Bunko 叡山文庫
Ejima Kiseki 江島其磧
Ekotoba yōryaku Seiganji engi 絵詞要略誓願寺縁起
Enkū Shōnin 円空上人
Enkyōji 円教寺
Enkyokushō 宴曲抄
Ennō 円能
Enryakuji 延暦寺
En'yū Tennō 円融天皇
Eon 恵隠
Eshi 恵資
Eshin Sōzu 恵心僧都
etoki 絵解き
etoki bikuni 絵解比丘尼
Etsumokushō 悦目抄
Fahuajing yaojie 法華経要解
Fuboku wakashō 夫木和歌抄
fuda 札
Fūga wakashū 風雅和歌集
Fugen Bosatsu 普賢菩薩
Fuji no hitoana sōshi 富士の人穴草子
Fujiwara no Ishi 藤原威子
Fujiwara no Kamatari 藤原鎌足
Fujiwara no Kaneie 藤原兼家
Fujiwara no Kanesuke 藤原兼輔
Fujiwara no Kintō 藤原公任
Fujiwara no Kishi 藤原嬉子
Fujiwara no Kiyosuke 藤原清輔
Fujiwara no Michinaga 藤原道長
Fujiwara no Michitsuna 藤原道綱
Fujiwara no Mototoshi 藤原基俊
Fujiwara no Nagakiyo 藤原長清
Fujiwara no Nobuzane 藤原信実
Fujiwara no Norimichi 藤原教通
Fujiwara no Sadayori 藤原定頼
Fujiwara no Sanesuke 藤原実資
Fujiwara no Shōshi 藤原彰子
Fujiwara no Sukemi 藤原輔相
Fujiwara no Tadatoshi 藤原斉敏
Fujiwara no Tameaki 藤原為顕
Fujiwara no Tameie 藤原為家
Fujiwara no Teika 藤原定家
Fujiwara no Teishi 藤原定子
Fujiwara no Yasumasa 藤原保昌
Fujiwara no Yorimichi 藤原頼通
Fujiwara no Yorimune 藤原頼宗
Fujiwara no Yoshitada 藤原義忠
fujōkan 不浄観
Fujo shinbun 婦女新聞
Fukakusa no Shii no Shōshō 深草四位少将
Fukūkenjaku Kannon 不空羂索観音
Fukurozōshi 袋草紙
Fushimi Tokiwa 伏見常盤
Fusō ryakki 扶桑略記
Fūyō wakashū 風葉和歌集
gaki 餓鬼
Genji ipponkyō 源氏一品経
Genji kuyō 源氏供養
Genji monogatari 源氏物語
Genkō shakusho 元亨釈書
Genkū Shōnin 源空上人
Gen'ōji 玄応寺
Genpei jōsuiki 源平盛衰記
Genshin 源信
Genshin Sōzu shijūikkajō kishō 源信僧都四十一箇条起請
Gentō 玄棟
giya 祇夜
Go-Hanazono 後花園
Go-Ichijō 後一条
gojin 五塵
Gojōten Jinja 五条天神社
goku 五苦
Gokuraku rokujisan 極楽六時讃
gongen 権現
Go-Reizei 後冷泉
Gosen wakashū 後撰和歌集
Go-Shirakawa 後白河
Go-Suzaku 後朱雀
goshō 五障
Goshūi ōjōden 後拾遺往生伝
Goshūi wakashū 後拾遺和歌集
Go-Suzaku 後朱雀
Goya-san 後夜讃
goze 瞽女
Guan jing shu 観経疏
Guanki hensatsu 愚闇記返札
Gūji enjishō 宮寺縁事抄
gunki mono 軍記物

Gunsho ichiran 群書一覧
Gyōganji 行願寺
Gyokuden jinpi 玉伝深秘
Gyokuyō wakashū 玉葉和歌集
Gyōkyō 行教
hachisu 蓮
Haifū yanagidaru 誹風柳多留
hakubyō 白描
Hakusan 白山
Hamamatsu Chūnagon monogatari 浜松中納言物語
Hamochi Chūjō はもち中将
Hanazono Tennō 花園天皇
Hanyū no monogatari はにふの物語
happū 八風
Harima 播磨
Hase-dera engi 長谷寺縁起
Hase-dera Kannon genki 長谷寺観音験記
Hase-dera reigenki 長谷寺霊験記
Hayashi Jiken 林自見
Heian 平安
Heike monogatari 平家物語
Heike nōkyō 平家納経
heisa no rakugan 平沙落雁
Hibariyama 雲雀山
Hiei-zan 比叡山
Hie Taisha 日吉大社
Higashi Sanjōin Fujiwara no Senshi 東三条院藤原詮子
hijiri 聖
Hirai Yasumasa 平井保昌
Hirano yomigaeri no sōshi 平野よみがへりの草子
Hirota Jinja 広田神社
hishaku 柄杓
Hitomaro 人麻呂
Hitori Musha 一人武者
hōben 方便
Hōbutsushū 宝物集
Hōjōji 法成寺
Hōjō Tokiyori 北条時頼
Hokekyō jikidanshō 法華経直談鈔
Hokekyō jurin shūyōshō 法華経鷲林拾葉鈔
Hokishō 簠簋抄
Hokke genki 法華験記
Hokke hakkō 法華八講
Hokke jikidan 法華直談
Hokkejiku 法花竹
Hokke yakuwashū 法華訳和集
hokkyō 法橋
hōkyōintō 宝篋印塔
Honchō shinsenden 本朝神仙伝
Honchō shinshū ōjōden 本朝新修往生伝
Honda Wake no Mikoto 誉田別命
Hōnen 法然
hongaku 本覚
hongan 本願
honji 本地
Honokuni Bunko 穂久邇文庫
honzon 本尊
Hōrinji 法輪寺
Hōshō 保昌
Hosshinshū 発心集
Huike 慧可
Hyakudayū 百大夫
hyakuhachi bonnō 百八煩悩
Hyakurenshō 百錬抄
Ibuki Dōji 伊吹童子
Ichijō Tennō 一条天皇
Ichijō Kaneyoshi 一条兼良
Ichijō shūgyokushō 一乗拾玉抄
Idaike 韋提希
Ihara Saikaku 井原西鶴
Ikuta Atsumori 生田敦盛
Ima kagami 今鏡
Ima monogatari 今物語
imayō 今様
Inari 稲荷 (noh)
Inryōken nichiroku 蔭涼軒日録
Iōzan engi 医王山縁起
Ippen gishū 一遍儀集
Ippen hijiri e 一遍聖絵
Ippen Shōnin 一遍上人
Ippen Shōnin eden 一遍上人絵伝
Ippen Shōnin eshiden 一遍上人絵詞伝
Ippen Shōnin goroku 一遍上人語録
Ippen Shōnin Izumi Shikibu monogatari 一遍上人和泉式部物語
Ippen Shōnin nenpuryaku 一遍上人年譜略
Iroha jiruishō 色葉字類抄
Ise monogatari 伊勢物語
Ise monogatari chū 伊勢物語注
Ise monogatari kuden shidai 伊勢物語口伝次第
Ise monogatari shō 伊勢物語抄

Ise monogatari shūindan 伊勢物語宗印談
Ise no Taifu 伊勢大輔
Ishiyama-dera engi 石山寺縁起
Ishiyama monogatari 石山物語
Isome Tsune 居初都音
Isozaki 磯崎
itsutsu no sawari 五つの障り
Iwase Bunko 岩瀬文庫
Iwashimizu Hachimangū 石清水八幡宮
Iwashimizu Hachimangū Gokokuji ryakki 石清水八幡宮護国寺略記
Iwashimizu Hachimangū narabi ni Gokurakuji engi no koto 石清水八幡宮並極楽寺縁起之事
Izumi Shikibu 和泉式部
Izumi Shikibu engi 和泉式部縁起
Izumi Shikibu nikki 和泉式部日記
Izumi Shikibu no monogatari いつみしきふの物かたり
Izumi Shikibu ōjō no koto 和泉式部往生事
Izumi Shikibu sennin otoko いづみ式部千人男
Izumi Shikibu shū 和泉式部集
Izumoji Dōso Jinja 出雲路道祖神社
Jie 慈恵
Jiehuan 戒環
Jigenshō 慈元抄
jigoku hensō e 地獄変相絵
jikidan 直談
Jikidan innenshū 直談因縁集
jikishin soku jōdo 直心即浄土
Jikkai 実海
Jikkinshō 十訓抄
Jingū Bunko 神宮文庫
Jinpi kushō 深秘九章
Jippon ōgi 十本扇
jiriki 自力
jisha engi 寺社縁起
Jishū 時衆
jissō 実相
Jizō Bosatsu 地蔵菩薩
Jizō Bosatsu hongankyō 地蔵菩薩本願経
Jōbodai'in 成菩提院
Jōchō 定朝
Jōdo sanbukyō 浄土三部経
Jōkaku 承覚
Jōkaku Hōin 静覚法印
jorō 女郎
jōruri 浄瑠璃
Jōruri-gozen monogatari 浄瑠璃御前物語
Jōruri-hime 浄瑠璃姫
Jōruri monogatari 浄瑠璃物語
jōsan no ki 定散之機
Jōshin'in 誠心院
Jōtōmon'in 上東門院
Jōwa gonen Kasuga rinji saireiki 貞和五年春日臨時祭礼記
Jōwa gonen nigatsu tōka haiden rinjisai shidai 貞和五年二月十日拝殿臨時祭次第
Jūgen 重賢
Jūichimen Kannon 十一面観音
Jūkoku Shamon 十穀沙門
Jūnidan sōshi 十二段草子
Jūzenji 十禅師
Kabu no Bosatsu 歌舞菩薩
kabuki 歌舞伎
Kachō Fūgetsu 花鳥風月
kada 伽陀
Kagerō nikki 蜻蛉日記
Kaihō Yūsetsu 海北友雪
Kaijuan 戒受庵
Kairaishiki 傀儡子記
Kakaishō 河海抄
kakekotoba 掛詞
Kakitsubata 杜若
Kakunyo 覚如
Kamakura 鎌倉
Kan'ami 観阿弥
Kanazawa Bunko 金沢文庫
kanazōshi 仮名草子
kanbun 漢文
Kanden kōhitsu 閑田耕筆
kanjin 観心
kanjin-chō 勧進帳
Kanjin honzon shō 観心本尊鈔
Kanjirō 漢字郎
Kankyo no tomo 閑居友
Kanmon gyoki 看聞御記
Kanmon nikki 看聞日記
Kanmuryōjukyō 観無量寿経
Kannon Bosatsu 観音菩薩
Kanō Eitoku 狩野永徳
Kanō Takanobu 狩野孝信
kanpaku 関白
Kanzaki 神崎

Kanze Nobumitsu 観世信光
Karukaya かるかや (sekkyō-bushi)
Karukaya 苅萱 (noh)
kasen-e 歌仙絵
Kashiwabara 柏原
Kashiwara-ya 柏原屋
Kasuga Daimyōjin 春日大明神
Kawasaki Kannondō 河崎観音堂
Kayoi Komachi 通小町
Kazan Tennō 花山天皇
kazoeuta 数え歌
Kegonkyō 華厳経
Keiran shūyōshū 渓嵐拾葉集
kenju jigoku 剣樹地獄
Kenkyū gojunreiki 建久御巡礼記
Kenmonshi 賢問子
Kenshō 顕昭
kesa 袈裟
Keshikoku 芥子国
Ketsubonkyō 血盆経
Kibitsu Jinja 吉備津神社
Kibune 貴布祢 (noh)
Kichijōten 吉祥天
Kikei Shinzui 季瓊真蘂
Kinbu-sen 金峰山
Kingyoku yōshū 金玉要集
Ki no Tomonori 紀友則
Ki no Tsurayuki 紀貫之
Kinyō wakashū 金葉和歌集
Kitamura Kigin 北村季吟
Kitano tsuya monogatari no koto
 北野通夜物語事
Kiyohara no Fukayabu 清原深養父
Kiyohara no Motosuke 清原元輔
Kiyomizu-dera 清水寺
Kiyomizu Kannon 清水観音
Ko-Atsumori 小敦盛
Koben 小弁
Kōbun'in 弘文院
Kōfukuji 興福寺
kōgō 皇后
Kōgon'in 光厳院
Kohata Jōmyōji 木幡浄妙寺
Kohon setsuwa shū 古本説話集
Kojidan 古事談
Kojiki 古事記
Kokan Shiren 虎関師錬
kokatsuji hanpon 古活字版本
kokige 孤起頌
Kokin joshō 古今序抄
Kokin rokujō 古今六帖
Kokin wakashū 古今和歌集
Kokin wakashū jo kikigaki sanryūshō
 古今和歌集序聞書三流抄
Kokin wakashū Ton'a jochū
 古今和歌集頓阿序注
Kokon chomonjū 古今著聞集
Kokūzō Bosatsu 虚空蔵菩薩
Komachi monogatari 小町物語
Komachi no sōshi 小町草子
Komachi shū 小町集
Komidō 小御堂
Kōmyō Kōgō 光明皇后
Kondaiin 金台院
Kongō Zōō Bosatsu 金剛蔵王菩薩
Konjaku monogatari shū 今昔物語集
Konparu Zenpō 金春禅鳳
konpon 根本
Konrenji 金蓮寺
Korai fūteishō 古来風躰抄
Kōryūji 広隆寺
Kōryūji 興隆寺
Koshikibu 小式部
Koshikibu beppon 小式部別本
Koshikibu no Naishi 小式部内侍
kōshin 庚申
Kōshoku ichidai otoko 好色一代男
kōshokurui 好色類
Kōsō 光宗
kosode 小袖
kotodama 言霊
Kotohara 琴腹
Kotohara ekotoba ことはら絵詞
kōwakamai 幸若舞
Kōya hijiri 高野聖
Kōya-san 高野山
Koyasu monogatari 子やす物語
Koyasu no Tō 子安の塔
kozō 小僧
kugutsu 傀儡
Kuin bukkakushō 九院佛閣抄
Kujō Michiie 九条道家
Kūkai 空海
Kumano bikuni 熊野比丘尼
Kumano kanjin jikkai mandara
 熊野観心十界曼荼羅

Kumano sōsō yurai zasshō
熊野草創由来雑抄
Kunaichō Shoryōbu 宮内庁書陵部
Kurama-dera 鞍馬寺
kusemai 曲舞
Kusenoto 九世戸
kusō-e 九相絵
Kusōshi emaki 九相詩絵巻
kyakubutsu 客仏
Kyōgoku-dono 京極殿
Kyōgoku Tamekane 京極為兼
Kyōjō 敬清
Kyōsen 慶宣
Kyō warabe 京童
Kyō warabe atooi 京童跡追
Lie xian zhuan 列仙伝
Li Furen 李夫人
Maeda-ke-bon 前田家本
makura kotoba 枕詞
Makura no sōshi 枕草子
Mandai wakashū 万代和歌集
mangyō rinen 万行離念
mappō 末法
masugatabon 枡形本
Matsui-bon 松井本
Matsuo Taisha 松尾大社
Matsushima nikki 松島日記
meido 冥土
Menoto no sōshi めのとのさうし
Mibu no Tadami 壬生忠見
Mibu no Tadamine 壬生忠岑
Midō Kanpaku 御堂関白
mikkyō 密教
miko 巫女
Mimuro Kakuyū 三室覚宥
Minamoto no Akiko 源明子
Minamoto no Akikane 源顕兼
Minamoto no Masanobu 源雅信
Minamoto no Rinshi 源倫子
Minamoto no Tokinobu 源時叙
Minamoto no Tsunenobu 源経信
Minamoto no Tsuneyori 源経頼
Minamoto no Yoritomo 源頼朝
Minamoto no Yoshitsune 源義経
miraiki 未来記
Miroku Bosatsu 弥勒菩薩
Miyako meisho zue 都名所図会
Miyoshi Tameyasu 三善為康
mondō 問答
Mongu ryaku taikō shikenmon
文句略大綱私見聞
Monju 文殊
mono no na 物の名
Motoori Norinaga 本居宣長
Mujū Dōgyō 無住道暁
Mujū Ichien 無住一円
Mukanki hanpon 無刊記版本
Mukashi nyōbō no hitokuchi monogatari
むかし女房の一口ものがたり
mukenchō-sō 無見頂相
Mumyōshō 無名抄
Mumyōzōshi 無名草子
Murakami Bunko 村上文庫
Murasaki Shikibu nikki 紫式部日記
Murasaki Shikibu no maki 紫式部の巻
Muromachi 室町
Muro no Tomari 室の泊
Muryōjukyō 無量寿経
Muryōjukyō shaku 無量寿経釈
mushabetsu 無差別
Myōhōin 妙法院
Myōhō rengekyō 妙法蓮華経
Myōkū 明空
Nabiki Tokiwa 靡常盤
Nachi sankei mandara 那智参詣曼荼羅
nadeshiko 撫子
Nagaoki-sukune ki 長興宿禰記
Naikaku Bunko 内閣文庫
Nakamikado Nobutane 中御門宣胤
Nanto daibutsu kuyō monogatari
南都大仏供養物語
Nara daibutsu kuyō 奈良大仏供養
nara ehon 奈良絵本
Nasenbikukyō 那先比丘経
nenbutsu 念仏
nenbutsu rinen 念仏離念
nenbutsu-zanmai 念仏三昧
Nichiren 日蓮
Nihon kiryaku 日本紀略
Nihon ōjō gokuraku ki 日本往生極楽記
Nihon ryōiki 日本霊異記
Nihon shoki 日本書紀
Nihyakujūban utai mokuroku
二百拾番謡目録
Nijō Tamesada 二条為定
nijū happon no uta 二十八品の歌

nikkei 肉髻
nikkeishu 肉髻珠
nishikigi 錦木
Nishinotōin Matsuhara 西洞院松原
Nobutane-kyō ki 宣胤卿記
Nōhon sakusha chūmon 能本作者注文
Nōin-bon 能因本
Nōin utamakura 能因歌枕
Nomori no kagami 野守鏡
Nōyo 能誉
nyōbō 女房
Nyodō 如導
Nyoirin Kannon 如意輪観音
nyonin kinsei 女人禁制
Nyonin ōjō kikigaki 女人往生聞書
Oda Nobunaga 織田信長
odori nenbutsu 踊念仏
Ōe no Masafusa 大江匡房
Ōe no Masamune 大江雅致
Ōe-yama 大江山 (noh)
Ōgishō 奥義抄
Ogura hyakunin isshu 小倉百人一首
ōjōden 往生伝
Ōjō yōshū 往生要集
Ōkagami 大鏡
Okudō 奥堂
Ōmi 近江
ominaeshi 女郎花
Ōmine-san 大峰山
Ōmiya Nagaoki 大宮長興
Ōnen sōdan 往年相談
Onna bunshō takamakie 女文章高蒔絵
Onna-yō bunshō kōmoku 女用文章綱目
Onna-yō chie kagami 女用智恵鏡
Ono no Komachi 小野小町
Ōshajō Bijutsu Hōbutsukan 王舎城美術宝物館
Otogi bunko 御伽文庫
otogizōshi お伽草子
Ōuchi Masahiro 大内政弘
Ozaki Masayoshi 尾崎雅嘉
Ozuki Nagaoki 小槻長興
raigō 来迎
Rakuchū rakugai-zu 洛中洛外図
Rakuyō Seiganji engi 洛陽誓願寺縁起
Rakuyō Seiganji honzon engi 洛陽誓願寺本尊縁起
renga 連歌
Risshō ankoku ron 立正安国論
rokudō 六道
Rokudō Chinnōji 六道珍皇寺
rokudō-e 六道絵
rokushu 六趣
rokuyoku 六欲
Ryōgen 良源
Ryōjin hishō 梁塵秘抄
Ryōjin hishō kuden shū 梁塵秘抄口伝集
Ryōnin Shōnin 良忍上人
Ryūshin 立信
sadaijin 左大臣
Saga 嵯峨
Saga Shakadō 嵯峨釈迦堂
Sagoromo 狭衣
Saichō 最澄
Saigū no Nyōgo 斎宮女御
Saigyō 西行
Saigyō Shōnin danshō 西行上人談抄
Saikō danshō 西公談抄
Sakai-bon 堺本
Sakata 坂田
Sakei ki 左経記
Sanetaka-kō ki 実隆公記
sangai 三界
Sangoki 三五記
Sangoku denki 三国伝記
Sanjōnishi Sanetaka 三条西実隆
sanjū 三従
sanjūni-sō 三十二相
Sanjūrokkasen 三十六歌仙
Sankan-bon 三巻本
sanku 三苦
sannetsu 三熱
Sannō Gongen 山王権現
sarugaku 猿楽
Sarugaku dangi 猿楽談儀
Saru Genji sōshi 猿源氏草紙
Sarumaru Dayū 猿丸大夫
sasara 簓
Seiganji 誓願寺
Seiganji Amida no koto 誓願寺阿弥陀事
Seiganji engi 誓願寺縁起
Seiganji engi emaki 誓願寺縁起絵巻
Seiganji shin engi 誓願寺真縁起
Seikadō Bunko 静嘉堂文庫
Seiryōji 清涼寺
Seiryōji engi 清涼寺縁起

Seishi Bosatsu 勢至菩薩
Seishin'in 誠心院
Sei Shōnagon 清少納言
Sei Shōnagon shū 清少納言集
seishū 正集
Seiwain 清和院
Seizan Fukakusa 西山深草
Seken musume katagi 世間娘気質
sekkyō 説経
sekkyō-bushi 説経節
sekkyō jōruri 説経浄瑠璃
Senchaku hongan nenbutsu shū 選択本願念仏集
Senchakushū 選択集
Senjū hyakuenkyō 撰集百縁経
senju nenbutsu 専修念仏
Senjūshō 撰集抄
senjutsu 仙術
Senmyōji 千妙寺
sennin 仙人
Sennyūji 泉涌寺
Senshi Naishinnō 選子内親王
Senzai wakashū 千載和歌集
sesshō 摂政
setsuwa 説話
Shakadō engi 釈迦堂縁起
Shandao 善導
Shasekishū 沙石集
Shibukawa Seiemon 渋川清右衛門
Shichijūichi-ban shokunin utaawase 七十一番職人歌合
shichū 尸虫
shiigi 四威儀
Shiju hyaku innenshū 私聚百因縁集
shikaku 始覚
Shinbutsu 真仏
Shinkokin wakashū 新古今和歌集
Shinkyōgoku 新京極
shinnyo 真如
Shinnyo kan 真如観
Shinran muki 親鸞夢記
Shinsen rōeishū 新撰朗詠集
Shinsenzai wakashū 新千載和歌集
Shintokumaru しんとく丸
Shintō shū 神道集
shirabyōshi 白拍子
Shisei zōtanshū 市井雑談集
Shitamoe monogatari 下燃物語
Shitennōji 四天王寺
shōen 荘園
Shōgakuji 正覚寺
Shōjōshin'in 清浄心院
Shoku shika wakashū 続詞花和歌集
Shōkū Shōnin 性空上人
Shōkū Shōnin 証空上人 (Zennebō Shōkū)
Shōmu Tennō 聖武天皇
Shōren'in 青蓮院
Shōrin'in 勝林院
Shōsan jōdokyō 称讃浄土経
Shosha-zan 書写山
Shosha-zan engi 書写山縁起
Shosha-zan Enkyōji kyūki 書写山円教寺旧記
Shōshō Hijiri 少将聖
Shōshō no hakkei 瀟湘の八景
Shōtatsu 性達／聖達
Shōtoku Taishi 聖徳太子
Shōyūki 小右記
Shūgaishō 拾芥抄
shugendō 修験道
Shūi kotokuden ekotoba 拾遺古徳伝絵詞
Shūi ōjōden 拾遺往生伝
Shūi wakashū 拾遺和歌集
Shun'yū 舜雄
Shunzei 俊成
Shuryōgon'in 首楞厳院
Shuten Dōji 酒呑童子
Sochiku Bunko 疎竹文庫
Soga monogatari 曾我物語
sōgō 相好
Sōgyō Hachiman 僧形八幡
Sōjiin 総持院
sōmoku jōbutsu 草木成仏
Sonkeikaku Bunko 尊経閣文庫
Sonshun 尊舜
Sotoba Komachi 卒都婆小町
Sotoori-hime 衣通姫
Sudatsu 須達
Sugaoji 菅生寺
Suke no Ajari 亮阿闍梨
Sukunahikona-no-kami 少彦名神
Sumiyoshi Jinja 住吉神社
Sumiyoshi Jinja sairei-zu 住吉神社祭礼図
Suzuriwari 硯破
Taa Chiren 他阿知蓮

Taamidabutsu Shinkyō 他阿弥陀仏真教
Tachibana no Michisada 橘道貞
Tachibana no Narisue 橘成季
Tadasugawara kanjin sarugaku nikki 糺河原勧進猿楽日記
Taema 当麻 (noh)
Taietsu monogatari 大悦物語
Taiheiki 太平記
Taima-dera engi 当麻寺縁起
Taima mandara 当麻曼荼羅
Taima mandara chū 当麻曼荼羅註
Taima mandara engi emaki 当麻曼荼羅縁起絵巻
Taima mandara sho 当麻曼荼羅疏
taimitsu 台密
Taira no Sanmi 平三位
Taira no Yasuyori 平康頼
Taisanji 泰産寺
Taishakuten 帝釈天
Taishi yō 太子用
Taizō mandara 胎蔵曼荼羅
Takakura Tennō 高倉天皇
Takasago 高砂
Takehisa 武久
Taku Toshokan 多久図書館
Tamadasuki 玉だすき
Tamagatsuma 玉勝間
Tamatsukuri Komachi shi sōsuisho 玉造小町子壮衰書
Tamatsushima Jinja 玉津島神社
Tametaka 為尊
Tamonten 多聞天
tanka 短歌
tanrokubon 丹緑本
tariki 他力
Tateyama 立山
teikyoku 鄭曲
Tendai-shū 天台宗
Tendai zasu 天台座主
tengu 天狗
Tengu no dairi 天狗の内裏
Tengu zōshi 天狗草紙
Tennōji 天王寺
Tennōji bettō shidai 天王寺別当次第
Tenpōrin hiden (seppō hijō) 転法輪秘伝(説法秘条)
Tenri Toshokan 天理図書館
Tetsujinshō 轍塵抄
Tōboku 東北
Tōdaiji 東大寺
Tōdaiji engi 東大寺縁起
Tōden gyōhitsu 榻鴫暁筆
tōgū no fu 東宮傅
Tōhokuin 東北院
Tōin Kinkata 洞院公賢
Tōji 東寺
Tōkaidō meishoki 東海道名所記
Tokitsugu-kyō ki 言継卿記
Tokiwa-gozen 常盤御前
Tokiwa mondō 常盤問答
Tomonori shū 友則集
Toran-ni 都藍尼
Tōsai zuihitsu 東斎随筆
Tosa Mitsunobu 土佐光信
Toshiyori zuinō 俊頼髄脳
Tosotsu-ten 兜率天
Toyotomi Hideyoshi 豊臣秀吉
Tsuchigumo 土蜘蛛
Tsuki no karu moshū 月刈藻集
tsuki no sawari 月の障り
udonge 優曇華
Uesugi Kenshin 上杉謙信
Uji shūi monogatari 宇治拾遺物語
Ukiyogara hiyoku no inazuma 浮世柄比翼稲妻
Umezu no chōja 梅津長者
Usuyuki monogatari 薄雪物語
Utaishō 謡鈔
Uta Yakushi 歌薬師
Wa'ami 和阿弥
Wada sakamori 和田宴／和田酒盛
waka 和歌
Waka chikenshū 和歌知顕集
Wakan rōeishū wadanshō 和漢朗詠集和談鈔
Watanabe no Tsuna 渡辺綱
Xiang Zhong 湘中
Xi Wangmu 西王母
Xuanzang 玄奘
Yakuōin 薬王院
Yakushi Nyorai 薬師如来
yamabushi 山伏
Yamanaka Tokiwa 山中常盤
Yama no i 山の井
Yamashina Tokitsugu 山科言継
Yamashina Tokitsune 山科言経

Yamato-kuni Taima-dera engi 大和国当麻寺縁起
Yamato monogatari 大和物語
Yanagita Kunio 柳田国男
Yang Guifei 楊貴妃
Yasuyori hōbutsushū 康頼宝物集
Yichu liutie 義楚六帖
Yōmei Bunko 陽明文庫
Yoshishige no Yasutane 慶慈保胤
Yotsugi monogatari 世継物語
Yotsutsuji Yoshinari 四辻善成
Yugyō Shōnin 遊行上人
Yuishikiron 唯識論
yūjo 遊女
Yūjoki 遊女記
yūkun 遊君
yuyaku kangi 踊躍歓喜
Yūyo Shōsō 酉誉聖聡
Yūzankaku Bunko 雄山閣文庫
Yūzū nenbutsu 融通念仏
Zeami 世阿弥
zenchishiki 善知識
Zenjō bikuni 禅定比丘尼
Zenmui 善無畏
Zennebō Shōkū 善慧房証空
Zoku honchō ōjōden 続本朝往生伝
Zoku kojidan 続古事談
Zonkaku 存覚
Zōshun Shōnin 蔵舜[蔵俊]上人
Zōtanshū 雑談集
zuien shinnyo 随縁真如

Bibliography

Abbreviations

DNBZ	Bussho Kankōkai 仏書刊行会, ed. *Dai Nihon Bukkyō zensho*. 150 vols. Tokyo: Bussho Kankōkai, 1912–22. Also published in 100 vols. by the Suzuki Research Foundation, 1970–73. All DNBZ entries refer to both of these editions.
GR	Hanawa Hokiichi 塙保己一, ed. *Gunsho ruijū*. 19 vols. Tokyo: Keizai Zasshisha, 1898–1902.
MJMT	Yokoyama Shigeru 横山重 and Matsumoto Ryūshin 松本隆信, eds. *Muromachi jidai monogatari taisei*. 13 vols. Tokyo: Kadokawa Shoten, 1973–85. Also 2 supp. vols. ed. by Matsumoto Ryūshin, 1987–88.
NKBT	*Nihon koten bungaku taikei*. 100 vols. Tokyo: Iwanami Shoten, 1958–68.
NKBZ	*Nihon koten bungaku zenshū*. 51 vols. Tokyo: Shōgakukan, 1970–76.
NKT	Sasaki Nobutsuna 佐々木信綱, ed. *Nihon kagaku taikei*. 10 vols. Tokyo: Fūkan Shobō, 1956–63.
NST	*Nihon shisō taikei*. 67 vols. Tokyo: Iwanami Shoten, 1970–82.
SKT	Shinpen Kokka Taikan Henshū Iinkai 新編国歌大観編集委員会, ed. *Shinpen kokka taikan*. 10 vols. in 20 bks. Tokyo: Kadokawa Shoten, 1983–92.
SNKBT	*Shin Nihon koten bungaku taikei*. 100 vols. Tokyo: Iwanami Shoten, 1989–2005.
SNKBZ	*Shinpen Nihon koten bungaku zenshū*. 88 vols. Tokyo: Shōgakukan, 1994–2002.
SNKS	*Shinchō Nihon koten shūsei*. 82 vols. in 97 bks. Tokyo: Shinchōsha, 1976–89.
TSD	Takakusu Junjirō 高楠順次郎 and Watanabe Kaigyoku 渡邊海旭, eds. *Taishō shinshū daizōkyō*. 85 vols. Tokyo: Taishō Issaikyō Kankōkai, 1924–32.
ZGR	Hanawa Hokiichi 塙保己一 et al., eds. *Zoku gunsho ruijū*. 34 vols. Tokyo: Zoku Gunsho Ruijū Kanseikai, 1929–33.

References

Abe, Ryuichi. *The Weaving of Mantra: Kūkai and the Construction of Esoteric Buddhist Discourse*. New York: Columbia University Press, 1999.

Abe Yasurō 阿部泰郎. "Chūjōhime monogatari no seiritsu." In *Chūjōhime setsuwa no chōsa kenkyū hōkoku sho*, ed. Gankōji Bunkazai Kenkyūjo, 49–78. Nara: Gankōji Bunkazai Kenkyūjo, 1983.

———. "Yuya no kōgō: Kōmyō Kōgō yusegyō no monogatari wo megurite." *Bungaku* 54–55, nos. 11 and 1 (1986 and 1987): 76–87 and 79–92.

———— et al., eds. *Nikkō tenkaizō Jikidan innenshū: honkoku to sakuin*. Kenkyū sōsho, no. 225. Osaka: Izumi Shoin, 1998.

Agō Toranoshin 吾郷寅之進, ed. *Kōwaka bukyoku kenkyū*. Vol. 1. Tokyo: Miyai Shoten, 1979.

Akamatsu Toshihide 赤松俊秀 et al., eds. *Sennyūji shi: honbun hen*. Kyoto: Hōzōkan, 1984.

Amino Yoshihiko 網野善彦 and Gotō Toshihiko 後藤紀彦, eds. "Yūjo, kugutsu, shirabyōshi." *Shūkan Asahi hyakka: Nihon no rekishi* 4 (Chūsei 1), no. 3 (April 1986).

————. "Yūjo to hinin/kawaramono." In *Sei to mibun*, ed. Miyata Noboru, 93–128. Tokyo: Shunshūsha, 1989.

Araki, James T. *The Ballad-Drama of Medieval Japan*. Berkeley and Los Angeles: University of California Press, 1964.

Asakura Haruhiko 朝倉治彦, ed. *Tōkaidō meishoki*. Vol. 1. Tōyō bunko 346. Tokyo: Heibonsha, 1979.

Asano Kenji 浅野建二. "Kazoeuta no keifu." *Gengo seikatsu* 266 (November 1973): 25–33.

Aston, W.G. *Nihongi: Chronicles of Japan from the Earliest Times to A.D. 697*. 2 vols. in 1. Tokyo: Charles E. Tuttle, 1972 (first published in 1896).

Bettelheim, Bruno. *The Uses of Enchantment: The Meaning and Importance of Fairy Tales*. New York: Alfred A. Knopf, 1976.

Bowring, Richard. *The Diary of Lady Murasaki*. New York: Penguin Books, 1996.

Brown, W. Norman. "The Metaphysics of the Truth Act (*Satyakriyā*)." In *Melanges d'Indianisme à la Memoire de Louis Renou*, 171–77. Paris: Editions E. de Boccard, 1968.

Childs, Margaret. *Rethinking Sorrow: Revelatory Tales of Late Medieval Japan*. Ann Arbor: University of Michigan Center for Japanese Studies, 1991.

Chimoto Hideshi 千本英史, ed. *Nihon koten gisho sōkan*. Vol. 2. Tokyo: Gendai Shichōshinsha, 2004.

Cogan, Thomas J. *The Tale of the Soga Brothers*. Tokyo: University of Tokyo Press, 1987.

Cooper, Michael, ed. *They Came To Japan*. Ann Arbor: University of Michigan Center for Japanese Studies, 1995.

Cranston, Edwin. *The Izumi Shikibu Diary*. Harvard-Yenching Monograph Series, no. 19. Cambridge: Harvard University Press, 1969.

Czaja, Michael. *Gods of Myth and Stone: Phallicism in Japanese Folk Religion*. New York: Weatherhill, 1974.

Deal, William E. "Women and Japanese Buddhism: Tales of Birth in the Pure Land." In *Religions of Japan in Practice*, ed. George J. Tanabe, Jr., 176–84. Princeton: Princeton University Press, 1999.

Dix, Monika. "Writing Women into Religious Histories: Re-reading Representations of Chūjōhime in Medieval Japanese Buddhist Narratives." Ph.D. diss., University of British Columbia (2006).

Dobbins, James. *Jōdo Shinshū: Shin Buddhism in Medieval Japan*. Bloomington and Indianapolis: Indiana University Press, 1989.

Dykstra, Yoshiko K. *Miraculous Tales of the Lotus Sutra from Ancient Japan: The Dainihonkoku Hokekyōkenki of Priest Chingen*. Honolulu: University of Hawaii Press, 1983.

Endō, Hajime. "The Original Bōmori: Husband and Wife Congregations in Early

Shin Buddhism," trans. James Dobbins. In *Engendering Faith: Women and Buddhism in Premodern Japan*, ed. Barbara Ruch, 501–35. Ann Arbor: University of Michigan Center for Japanese Studies, 2002.

Fabricand-Person, Nicole. "Demonic Female Guardians of the Faith: The *Fugen Jūrasetsunyo* Iconography in Japanese Buddhist Art." In *Engendering Faith: Women and Buddhism in Premodern Japan*, ed. Barbara Ruch, 343–82. Ann Arbor: University of Michigan Center for Japanese Studies, 2002.

Farmer, Sharon. "The Beggar's Body: Intersections of Gender and Social Status in High Medieval Paris." In *Monks & Nuns, Saints & Outcastes: Religion in Medieval Society*, ed. Sharon Farmer and Barbara H. Rosenwein, 153–71. Ithaca and London: Cornell University Press, 2000.

Faure, Bernard. *The Power of Denial: Buddhism, Purity, and Gender*. Princeton and Oxford: Princeton University Press, 2003.

Fischer, Felice Renee. "Ono no Komachi: A Ninth-century Poetess of Heian Japan." Ph.D. diss., Columbia University, 1972.

Foard, James. "*Seiganji*: The Buddhist Orientation of a Noh Play." *Monumenta Nipponica* 35, no. 4 (1980): 437–56.

————. "Prefiguration and Narrative in Medieval Hagiography: The *Ippen Hijiri-e*." In *Flowing Traces: Buddhism in the Literary and Visual Arts of Japan*, ed. James Sanford, William LaFleur, and Masatoshi Nagatomi, 76–92. Princeton: Princeton University Press, 1992.

Foulke, William Dudley, trans. *History of the Langobards*. Philadelphia: Department of History, University of Pennsylvania, 1907.

Freud, Sigmund. *Totem and Taboo: Some Points of Agreement Between the Mental Lives of Savages and Neurotics*, trans. James Strachey. London: Routledge and Kegan Paul, 1950.

Fujii Takashi 藤井隆. "Otogizōshi *Jippon ōgi* no kōsatsu." *Nagoya shiritsu daigaku kyōyōbu kiyō—ninbun shakai kenkyū* 16 (March 1972). Reprinted as "Jippon ōgi," in *Chūsei koten no shoshigakuteki kenkyū: otogizōshi hen*, 325–40. Osaka: Izumi Shoin, 1996.

Fukuda Akira 福田晃 and Manabe Masahiro 真鍋昌弘, eds. *Kōwaka bukyoku kenkyū*. Vol. 8. Tokyo: Miyai Shoten, 1994.

Fukuda Hideichi 福田秀一. "*Nomori no kagami* ni tsuite no kōsatsu." In *Chūsei waka shi no kenkyū*. Tokyo: Kadokawa Shoten, 1972.

Glassman, Hank. "The Nude Jizō at Denkōji: Notes on Women's Salvation in Kamakura Buddhism." In *Engendering Faith: Women and Buddhism in Premodern Japan*, ed. Barbara Ruch, 383–413. Ann Arbor: University of Michigan Center for Japanese Studies, 2002.

————. "'Show Me the Place Where My Mother Is!' Chūjōhime, Preaching, and Relics in Late Medieval and Early Modern Japan." In *Approaching the Land of Bliss: Religious Praxis in the Cult of Amitābha*, ed. Richard K. Payne and Kenneth K. Tanaka, 139–68. Honolulu: University of Hawaii Press, 2004.

Goff, Janet. *Noh Drama and The Tale of Genji*. Princeton: Princeton University Press, 1991.

Goodwin, Janet R. *Alms and Vagabonds: Buddhist Temples and Popular Patronage in Medieval Japan*. Honolulu: University of Hawaii Press, 1994.

————. "Shadows of Transgression: Heian and Kamakura Constructions of Prostitution." *Monumenta Nipponica* 55, no. 3 (Autumn 2000): 327–68.

Gorai Shigeru 五来重. *Jisha engi kara otogibanashi e*. Shūkyō minzoku shūsei 6. Tokyo: Kadokawa Shoten, 1995.

Gotō Akiko 後藤明子. "Takubon *Koshikibu* no kōsatsu." *Bungaku ronshū* (Saga Daigaku) 5 (1963): 30–33.

Gotō Tanji 後藤丹治. "*Genji ipponkyō* to *Genji hyōbyaku*." *Kokugo kokubun no kenkyū* 48 (September 1930): 30–50.

Groner, Paul. *Saichō: The Establishment of the Japanese Tendai School*. Berkeley: University of California at Berkeley, 1984.

———. "Vicissitudes in the Ordination of Japanese 'Nuns' during the Eighth through the Tenth Centuries." In *Engendering Faith: Women and Buddhism in Premodern Japan*, ed. Barbara Ruch, 65–108. Ann Arbor: University of Michigan Center for Japanese Studies, 2002.

Hagiwara Tatsuo 萩原龍夫. *Miko to Bukkyō shi: Kumano bikuni no shimei to tenkai*. Tokyo: Yoshikawa Kōbunkan, 1983.

Hamanaka Osamu 濱中修. "Chūsei no Izumi Shikibu: Eizan no denshō yori." *Bukkyō bungaku* 12 (1988): 53–60.

———. "Otogizōshi *Izumi Shikibu*/*Koshikibu* ron." *Kokubungaku: kaishaku to kanshō* 60, no. 8 (August 1995): 119–24.

———. "Komachi no sōshi." *Kokubungaku: kaishaku to kanshō* 61, no. 5 (May 1996): 56–60.

———. *Muromachi monogatari ronkō*. Shintensha kenkyū sōsho, no. 95. Tokyo: Shintensha, 1996.

Harper, Thomas. "Motoori Norinaga's Criticism of the *Genji monogatari*: A Study of the Background and Critical Content of his *Genji monogatari tama no ogushi*." Ph.D. diss., University of Michigan, 1971.

Hayashi Masahiko 林雅彦. "Shōkū Shōnin setsuwa kō: kitan, kitokudan wo chūshin ni." *Kokugo kokubungaku ronshū* (Gakushūin Joshi Tanki Daigaku) 3 (1974): 35–55.

———. *Zōho Nihon no etoki: shiryō to kenkyū*. Tokyo: Miyai Shoten, 1984.

Heibonsha Chihō Shiryō Sentā 平凡社地方資料センター, ed. *Jiin jinja daijiten: Kyōto, Yamashiro*. Tokyo: Heibonsha, 1997.

———, ed. *Jiin jinja daijiten: Yamato, Kii*. Tokyo: Heibonsha, 1997.

Heidegger, Martin. *Poetry, Language, Thought*, trans. Albert Hofstadter. New York: Harper and Row, 1971.

Henderson, Gregory, and Leon Hurvitz. "The Buddha of Seiryōji: New Finds and New Theory." *Artibus Asiae* 19, no. 1 (1956): 5–55.

Hibbett, Howard. *The Floating World in Japanese Fiction*. London: Oxford University Press, 1959.

Hirota, Dennis. "The Illustrated Biography of Ippen." In *Buddhism in Practice*, ed. Donald Lopez, 563–77. Princeton: Princeton University Press, 1995.

———. *No Abode: The Record of Ippen*. Honolulu: University of Hawaii Press, 1986 (revised ed. 1997).

Hirota Tetsumichi 廣田哲通. *Chūsei Bukkyō setsuwa no kenkyū*. Tokyo: Benseisha, 1987.

———. *Chūsei Hokekyō chūshakusho no kenkyū*. Tokyo: Kasama Shoin, 1993.

———. *Tendai danjo de Hokekyō wo yomu*. Tokyo: Kanrin Shobō, 1997.

———. *Chūsei Bukkyō bungaku no kenkyū*. Osaka: Izumi Shoin, 2000.

Hisamatsu Sen'ichi 久松潜一, ed. *Karonshū*. Chūsei no bungaku. Tokyo: Miyai Shoten, 1971.

Hokekyō jikidanshō. 3 vols. Kyoto: Rinsen Shoten, 1979.

Hokekyō jurin shūyōshō. 4 vols. Kyoto: Rinsen Shoten, 1991.

Hokekyō jikidanshō: koshahon shūsei. 14 vols. Kyoto: Rinsen Shoten, 1989.

Horner, I.B. *Milinda's Questions*. Vol. 1. London: Luzac & Company, 1969.

Hosokawa Ryōichi 細川涼一. *Onna no chūsei*. Tokyo: Nihon Editā Sukūru Shuppanbu, 1989.

Ichijō shūgyokushō: eiin. Kyoto: Rinsen Shoten, 1998.

Ichiko Teiji 市古貞次. *Mikan chūsei shōsetsu kaidai*. Tokyo: Rakurō Shoin, 1942.

———, ed. *Mikan chūsei shōsetsu*. Koten bunko 12. Tokyo: Koten Bunko, 1946.

———. *Chūsei shōsetsu no kenkyū*. Tokyo: Tokyo Daigaku Shuppankai, 1955.

——— et al., eds. *Nihon bunka sōgō nenpyō*. Tokyo: Iwanami Shoten, 1990.

———, ed. *Tōden gyōhitsu*. Chūsei no bungaku. Tokyo: Miyai Shoten, 1992.

Ii Haruki 伊井春樹. *Genji monogatari no densetsu*. Tokyo: Shōwa Shuppan, 1976.

———. *Genji monogatari chūshakusho, kyōjushi jiten*. Tokyo: Tōkyōdō Shuppan, 2001.

Ikeda Kikan 池田亀鑑. *Monogatari bungaku 1*. Tokyo: Shibundō, 1968.

Ikegami Jun'ichi 池上洵一, ed. *Sangoku denki*. 2 vols. Tokyo: Miyai Shoten, 1976 and 1982.

Ikeyama Issaien 池山一切圓. "Kaidai." In *Hokekyō jikidanshō*, vol. 1. Kyoto: Rinsen Shoten, 1979.

Imai Masaharu 今井雅晴. *Ippen jiten*. Tokyo: Tōkyōdō Shuppan, 1989.

Inagaki, Hisao. *The Three Pure Land Sutras*. Kyoto: Nagata Bunshodō, 1995.

Ishida Mizumaro 石田瑞麿. *Reibun Bukkyōgo daijiten*. Tokyo: Shōgakukan, 1997.

Ishiguro Kichijirō 石黒吉次郎. "Yōkyoku to Izumi Shikibu." *Kokubungaku: kaishaku to kyōzai no kenkyū* 35, no. 12 (October 1990): 103–5.

Ishihara Shōhei 石原昭平. "Musashino no Narihira/Komachi setsuwa." In *Setsuwa denshō no Nihon, Ajia, sekai*, ed. Setsuwa Denshō Gakkai, 158–71. Tokyo: Ōfūsha, 1983.

Ishikawa Jun'ichirō 石川純一郎. "Izumi Shikibu setsuwa no tenkai." *Tokoha Gakuen Tanki Daigaku kiyō* 12 (1980): 29–45.

Ishikawa Tōru 石川透. *Muromachi monogatari to kochūshaku*. Tokyo: Miyai Shoten, 2002.

Ishizuka Kazuo 石塚一雄. "Shiryō shōkai: *Mukashi nyōbō no hitokuchi monogatari*." *Shoryōbu kiyō* 30 (1978): 55–64.

———. "Go-Hanazono Tennō shinkan *Kotohara ekotoba*." In *Nihon bungakushi no shin kenkyū*, ed. Kamiya Yoshiyuki, 112–22. Tokyo: Miyai Shoten, 1984.

Iura Yoshinobu 井浦芳信. *Nihon engeki shi*. Tokyo: Shibundō, 1963.

Iwashimizu Hachimangū shiryō sōsho. Vol. 2. Kyoto: Iwashimizu Hachimangū Shamusho, 1976.

Jōdo-shū zensho. 20 vols. Tokyo: Jōdo-shū Shūten Kankōkai, 1908–14.

Kadokawa Shoten Henshūbu 角川書店編集部, ed. *Ippen hijiri e*. Nihon emaki-mono zenshū, vol. 10. Tokyo: Kadokawa Shoten, 1960.

———, ed. *Ishiyama-dera engi-e*. Nihon emaki-mono zenshū, vol. 22. Tokyo: Kadokawa Shoten, 1966.

Kakitani Yūzō 柿谷雄三. "Sei Shōnagon densetsu." *Kokubungaku* 12, no. 6 (June 1967): 70–78.

Kamens, Edward. *The Buddhist Poetry of the Great Kamo Priestess: Daisaiin Senshi and Hosshin Wakashū*. Ann Arbor: University of Michigan Center for Japanese Studies, 1990.

———. "Dragon-Girl, Maidenflower, Buddha: The Transformation of a Waka Topos, 'The Five Obstructions.'" *Harvard Journal of Asiatic Studies* 53, no. 2 (December 1993): 389–442.

———. *Utamakura, Allusion, and Intertextuality in Traditional Japanese Poetry*. New Haven and London: Yale University Press, 1997.

Kaminishi, Ikumi. *Explaining Pictures: Buddhist Propaganda and Etoki Storytelling in Japan*. Honolulu: University of Hawaii Press, 2006.

Kamioka Yūji 上岡勇司. *Waka setsuwa no kenkyū: chūko hen*. Kasama sōsho, no. 196. Tokyo: Kasama Shoin, 1986.

Kanagawa Kenritsu Kanazawa Bunko 神奈川県立金沢文庫, ed. *Bukkyō setsuwa*. Yokohama: Kanazawa Bunko, 1997.

Kanda, Christine Guth. *Shinzō: Hachiman Imagery and Its Development*. Harvard East Asian Monographs, no. 119. Cambridge: Harvard University Press, 1985.

Kanda, Fusae. "Behind the Sensationalism: Images of a Decaying Corpse in Japanese Buddhist Art." *The Art Bulletin* 87, no. 1 (March 2005): 24–49.

Kasahara Kazuo 笠原一男. *Nyonin ōjō shisō no keifu*. Tokyo: Yoshikawa Kōbunkan, 1975.

Katagiri Yōichi 片桐洋一. *Ise monogatari no kenkyū: shiryō hen*. Tokyo: Meiji Shoin, 1969.

———. *Ono no Komachi tsuiseki*. Tokyo: Kasama Shoin, 1975.

———. *Utamakura utakotoba jiten*. Tokyo: Kadokawa Shoten, 1983.

Katō, Hilda. "The *Mumyōshō*." *Monumenta Nipponica* 23, nos. 3–4 (1968): 351–430.

Katsumine Fufū 勝峯晋風, ed. *Nihon haisho taikei*. Vol. 14. Tokyo: Shunshūsha, 1971.

Kawashima, Terry. *Writing Margins: The Textual Construction of Gender in Heian and Kamakura Japan*. Cambridge: Harvard University Asia Center, 2001.

Keene, Donald, ed. *Twenty Plays of the Nō Theatre*. New York: Columbia University Press, 1970.

Khoroche, Peter. *Once the Buddha Was a Monkey: Ārya Śūra's Jātakamālā*. Chicago: University of Chicago Press, 1989.

Kikuchi Hitoshi 菊地仁. "Sekkyō *Karukaya* to 'Kōya no maki.'" *Denshō bungaku kenkyū* 21 (March 1978): 23–35.

———. "Setsuwa denshō to Izumi Shikibu." *Kokubungaku: kaishaku to kyōzai no kenkyū* 35, no. 12 (October 1990): 100–102.

Kikuchi Masakazu 菊池政和. "Kyōhō hachinen-sha *Rakuyō Seiganji honzon engi*." In *Shōdō bungaku kenkyū: dai san shū*, ed. Fukuda Akira 福田晃 and Hirota Tetsumichi 廣田哲通, 352–96. Tokyo: Miyai Shoten, 2001.

Kim, Yung-Hee. *Songs to Make the Dust Dance: The Ryōjin hishō of Twelfth-Century Japan*. Berkeley: University of California Press, 1994.

Kimbrough, R. Keller. "Voices from the Feminine Margin: Izumi Shikibu and the Nuns of Kumano and Seiganji." *Women and Performance* 12, no. 1 (2001): 59–78.

———. "Apocryphal Texts and Literary Identity: Sei Shōnagon and *The Matsushima Diary*." *Monumenta Nipponica* 57, no. 2 (Summer 2002): 133–71.

———. "*Nomori no kagami* and the Perils of Poetic Heresy." *Proceedings of the Association for Japanese Literary Studies* 4 (Summer 2003): 99–114.

———. "*Little Atsumori* and *The Tale of the Heike*: Fiction as Commentary, and the Significance of a Name." *Proceedings of the Association for Japanese Literary Studies* 5 (Summer 2004): 325–36.

———. "Reading the Miraculous Powers of Japanese Poetry: Spells, Truth Acts, and a Medieval Buddhist Poetics of the Supernatural." *Japanese Journal of Religious Studies* 32, no. 1 (Spring 2005): 1–33.

————. "Tourists in Paradise: Writing the Pure Land in Medieval Japanese Fiction." *Japanese Journal of Religious Studies* 33, no. 2 (Autumn 2006): 269–96.

————. "Translation: The Tale of the Fuji Cave." *Japanese Journal of Religious Studies* 33, no. 2 (online supplement, 2006): 1–22.

————. "Preaching the Animal Realm in Late-Medieval Japan." *Asian Folklore Studies* 65, no. 2 (Autumn 2006): 179–204.

Kinoshita Motoichi 木下資一. "Yōkyoku to denshō no Saigyō." *Kanze* 51, no. 12 (1984): 4–11.

Kishi Shōzō 貴志正造. "Kaisetsu." In *Shintōshū*. Tōyō bunko 94, 293–329. Tokyo: Heibonsha, 1967.

Kiyama, Lorinda. "Performative Preaching: The Art and Politics of Persuasion in Medieval Japan." Ph.D. diss., Stanford University (forthcoming).

Klein, Susan Blakeley. *Allegories of Desire: Esoteric Literary Commentaries of Medieval Japan*. Cambridge: Harvard University Asia Center, 2002.

Kobayashi Chishō 小林智昭. "*Nomori no kagami* kō." In *Hōgo bungaku no sekai*, 176–213. Tokyo: Kasama Shoin, 1975.

Kobayashi Naoki 小林直樹. "*Sangoku denki* no seiritsu kiban: *Hokke* jikidan no sekai to no kōshō." In *Chūsei setsuwashū to sono kiban*, 121–65. Osaka: Izumi Shoin, 2004.

Kobayashi Yasuharu 小林保治, ed. *Kojidan*. 2 vols. Koten bunko. Tokyo: Gendai Shichōsha, 1981.

Kōdate, Naomi. "Aspects of *Ketsubonkyō* Belief." In *Practicing the Afterlife: Perspectives from Japan*, ed. Susanne Formanek and William R. LaFleur, 121–43. Vienna: Osterreichische Akademie der Wissenschaften, 2004.

Kokushi Daijiten Henshū Iinkai 国史大辞典編集委員会, ed. *Kokushi daijiten*. 17 vols. Tokyo: Yoshikawa Kōbunkan, 1979–97.

Kokusho sōmokuroku (Hotei-ban). 8 vols. Tokyo: Iwanami Shoten, 1989–90.

Komatsu Shigemi 小松茂美, ed. *Gaki zōshi, Jigoku zōshi, Yamai no sōshi, Kusōshi emaki*. Nihon emaki taisei, vol. 7. Tokyo: Chūō Kōronsha, 1977.

————, ed. *Tsuchigumo sōshi, Tengu zōshi, Ōeyama ekotoba*. Zoku Nihon emaki taisei, vol. 19. Tokyo: Chūō Kōronsha, 1984.

————, ed. *Ippen Shōnin eden*. Nihon no emaki, vol. 20. Tokyo: Chūō Kōronsha, 1988.

————, ed. *Taima mandara engi, Chigo Kannon engi*. Nihon emaki taisei, vol. 24. Tokyo: Chūō Kōronsha, 1979.

Komine Kazuaki 小峯和明. "Chūsei setsuwa no Komachi." *Kokubungaku: kaishaku to kanshō* 60, no. 8 (August 1995): 46–52.

Kondō Keizō 近藤圭造, ed. *Kaitei shiseki shūran*. Vol. 24. Tokyo: Kondō Shuppanbu, 1903 (3rd ed. 1932).

Kotas, Frederic. "Ōjōden: Accounts of Rebirth in the Pure Land." Ph.D. diss., University of Washington, 1987.

Koyama Issei 小山一成. *Fuji no hitoana sōshi: kenkyū to shiryō*. Tokyo: Bunka Shobō Hakubunsha, 1983.

Kubota Jun 久保田淳 et al., eds. *Ima monogatari, Takafusashū, Tōsai zuihitsu*. Chūsei no bungaku. Tokyo: Miyai Shoten, 1979.

Kubukihara Rei 久富木原玲. "Izumi Shikibu to Bukkyō." *Kokubungaku: kaishaku to kanshō* 56 (May 1991): 80–84.

Kuroda Akira 黒田彰. "*Sangoku denki* to *Wakan rōeishū wadanshō*, pt. 2." *Kokubungaku* (Kansai Daigaku) 59 (1982): 1–10.

Kuroda Hideo 黒田日出男. "*Kumano kanjin jikkai mandara* no uchū." In *Bukkyō to Nihonjin, vol. 8: sei to mibun*, ed. Miyata Noboru, 206–73. Tokyo: Shunjūsha, 1989.

————. "The *Kumano kanshin jikkai mandara* and the Lives of the People in Early Modern Japan." In *Practicing the Afterlife: Perspectives from Japan*, ed. Susanne Formanek and William R. LaFleur, 101–20. Vienna: Osterreichische Akademie der Wissenschaften, 2004.

Kuroda, Toshio. "The Discourse of the 'Land of Kami' (*Shinkoku*) in Medieval Japan," trans. Fabio Rambelli. *Japanese Journal of Religious Studies* 23, nos. 3–4 (1996): 353–85.

Kuroita Katsumi 黒板勝美, ed. *Shintei zōho kokushi taikei*. 58 vols. (plus 2 supp. vols.). Tokyo: Yoshikawa Kōbunkan, 1929–62.

Kyōto Daigaku Bungaku-bu Kokugogaku Kokubungaku Kenkyūshitsu 京都大学文学部国語学国文学研究室, ed. *Kyōto Daigaku-zō Muromachi monogatari*. 12 vols. Kyoto: Rinsen Shoten, 2000–2003.

LaFleur, William R. "Saigyō and the Buddhist Value of Nature, Part I." *History of Religions* 13, no. 2 (November 1973): 93–128.

————. *The Karma of Words: Buddhism and the Literary Arts in Medieval Japan*. Berkeley and Los Angeles: University of California Press, 1983.

Lamotte, Etienne. *History of Indian Buddhism: From the Origins to the Śaka Era*, trans. Sara Webb-Boin. Louvain: Peeters Press, 1988.

Law, Jane Marie. "Of Plagues and Puppets: On the Significance of the Name Hyakudayū in Japanese Religion." *Transactions of the Japan Asiatic Society*. Series 4, vol. 8 (1993): 107–31.

Lévi-Strauss, Claude. "The Family." In *Man, Culture, and Society*, ed. Harry Shapiro, 333–57. London: Oxford University Press, 1971 (first edition from 1956).

Mabuchi Kazuo 馬渕和夫 and Taguchi Kazuo 田口和夫. "Honkoku: Daigoji-zō *Tenpōrin hiden (seppō hijō)*." *Daigoji bunkazai kenkyūjo kenkyū kiyō* 18 (2000): 1–13.

Mair, Victor. *Painting and Performance: Chinese Picture Recitation and its Indian Genesis*. Honolulu: University of Hawaii Press, 1988.

Manabe Masahiro 真鍋昌弘. "Fūryū odoriuta kō: katarigusa wo megutte." In *Chūsei/kinsei kayō no kenkyū*. Tokyo: Ōfūsha, 1982.

Matisoff, Susan. "Holy Horrors: The Sermon-Ballads of Medieval and Early Modern Japan." In *Flowing Traces: Buddhism in the Literary and Visual Arts of Japan*, ed. James Sanford, William LaFleur, and Masatoshi Nagatomi, 234–61. Princeton: Princeton University Press, 1992.

————. "Barred from Paradise? Mount Kōya and the *Karukaya* Legend." In *Engendering Faith: Women and Buddhism in Premodern Japan*, ed. Barbara Ruch, 463–500. Ann Arbor: University of Michigan Center for Japanese Studies, 2002.

Matsumoto Kazumi 松本和巳. "Sei Shōnagon no hokora." *Heian bungaku kenkyū* 27 (1961): 130–32.

Matsumoto Ryūshin 松本隆信, ed. *Eiin: Muromachi monogatari*. Vol. 4. Tokyo: Kyūko Shoin, 1971.

Matsuo Ashie 松尾葦江, ed. *Genpei jōsuiki*. Vol. 2. Tokyo: Miyai Shoten, 1993.

Matsuoka Hideaki 松岡秀明. "Waga kuni ni okeru *Ketsubonkyō* shinkō ni tsuite no ichikōsatsu." In *Nihon josei ronshū 5: Josei to shūkyō*, ed. Sōgō Joseishi Kenkyūkai 総合女性史研究会, 257–79. Tokyo: Yoshikawa Kōbunkan, 1998.

Matsuoka Shinpei 松岡心平. "Nō ni egakareta Izumi Shikibu." *Kokubungaku: kaishaku to kanshō* 60, no. 8 (August 1995): 112–18.

Matsushima Ken 松島健 and Kawahara Yoshio 河原由雄. *Taima-dera*. Nihon no koji bijutsu 11. Osaka: Hoikusha, 1988.

McCullough, Helen. *Yoshitsune: A Fifteenth-Century Japanese Chronicle*. Stanford: Stanford University Press, 1966.

————. *Ōkagami: The Great Mirror*. Princeton: Princeton University Press, 1980.

————. *The Tale of the Heike*. Stanford: Stanford University Press, 1988.

McCullough, William and Helen. *A Tale of Flowering Fortunes*. 2 vols. Stanford: Stanford University Press, 1980.

McKelway, Matthew P. "The Partisan View: Rakuchū Rakugai Screens in the Mary and Jackson Burke Collection." *Orientations* 28, no. 2 (February 1997): 48–57.

Mills, D.E. *A Collection of Tales from Uji: A Translation and Study of Uji shūi monogatari*. Cambridge: Cambridge University Press, 1970.

Miya Tsugio 宮次男. "Shaji engi-e no shosō." In *Etoki: shiryō to kenkyū*, ed. Hayashi Masahiko et al., 344–58. Tokyo: Miyai Shoten, 1989.

———— et al., eds. *Kadokawa emakimono sōran*. Tokyo: Kadokawa Shoten, 1995.

Miyakawa Yōko 宮川葉子. *Genji monogatari no bunkashiteki kenkyū*. Tokyo: Kazama Shobō, 1997.

Miyake Hitoshi 宮家準. *Ōmine shugendō no kenkyū*. Tokyo: Kōsei Shuppansha, 1988.

Miyazaki Fumiko. "Female Pilgrims and Mt. Fuji: Changing Perspectives on the Exclusion of Women." *Monumenta Nipponica* 60, no. 3 (Autumn 2005): 339–91.

Mochizuki Shinkō 望月信亨. *Bukkyō daijiten*. 10 vols. Kyoto: Sekai Seiten Kankō Kyōkai, 1954–71.

Moerman, D. Max. *Localizing Paradise: Kumano Pilgrimage and the Religious Landscape of Premodern Japan*. Cambridge and London: Harvard University Asia Center, 2005.

Mori Takenosuke 森武之助. *Jōruri monogatari kenkyū*. Tokyo: Inoue Shobō, 1962.

Morris, Ivan. *The Pillow Book of Sei Shōnagon*. New York: Columbia University Press, 1991.

Murayama Shūichi 村山修一. *Honji suijaku*. Tokyo: Yoshikawa Kōbunkan, 1974.

Muroki Yatarō 室木弥太郎. *Zōtei katarimono (mai, sekkyō, ko-jōruri) no kenkyū*. Tokyo: Fūkan Shobō, 1981 (second revised ed. 1992).

Muromachi monogatari shū. Nihon koten bungaku eiin sōkan, no. 27. Tokyo: Nihon Koten Bungakukai, 1990.

Nagai Yoshinori 永井義憲. "Izumi Shikibu no ko: Eikaku Ajari denkō." *Kokubungaku tōsa* (Taishō Daigaku) 7 (March 1963): 1–9.

————. "Kaidai." In *Hokekyō jurin shūyōshō*, vol. 4. Kyoto: Rinsen Shoten, 1991.

Nagasaki Ken 長崎健. "Kagakusho ni miru Izumi Shikibu." *Kokubungaku: kaishaku to kanshō* 60, no. 8 (August 1995): 100–105.

Nagata, Mizu. "Transitions in Attitudes toward Women in the Buddhist Canon: The Three Obligations, the Five Obstructions, and the Eight Rules of Reverence," trans. and adapted by Paul B. Watt. In *Engendering Faith: Women and Buddhism in Premodern Japan*, ed. Barbara Ruch, 279–95. Ann Arbor: University of Michigan Center for Japanese Studies, 2002.

Nagoya Sangoku Denki Kenkyūkai 名古屋三国伝記研究会, ed. *Sangoku denki*. 3 vols. Koten bunko 434, 436, and 438. Tokyo: Koten Bunko, 1983.

Nakamura Hajime 中村元 et al., eds. *Shin butten kaidai jiten*. Tokyo: Shunjūsha, 1966.

————. *Bukkyōgo daijiten*. 3 vols. Tokyo: Tokyo Shoseki, 1975.

————. *Kōsetsu Bukkyōgo daijiten*. 4 vols. Tokyo: Tokyo Shoseki, 2001.

Nakamura Tanio 中村溪男. "Kusōshi emaki no seiritsu." In *Gaki zōshi, Jigoku zōshi, Yamai no sōshi, Kusōshi emaki*, ed. Komatsu Shigemi, 165–70. Nihon emaki taisei, no. 7. Tokyo: Chūō Kōronsha, 1977.

Nakano Maori 中野真麻理. "*Ichijō shūgyokushō* shoin waka kō." *Kokubungaku kenkyū shiryōkan kiyō* 23 (March 1997): 167–205.

————. "*Hokekyō* chū: ishi wo atsumete tama wo toru." In *Chūsei no chi to gaku: chūshaku wo yomu*, ed. Mitani Kuniaki 三谷邦明 and Komine Kazuaki 小峯和明, 219–46. Tokyo: Shinwasha, 1997.

————. *Ichijō shūgyokushō no kenkyū*. Kyoto: Rinsen Shoten, 1998.

Nakano Tatsue 中野達慧, ed. *Nihon daizōkyō*. Vol. 13. Tokyo: Nihon Daizōkyō Hensankai, 1917.

Nara Ehon Kokusai Kenkyū Kaigi 奈良絵本国際研究会議, ed. *Otogizōshi no sekai*. Tokyo: Sanseidō, 1982.

Nara Kokuritsu Hakubutsukan 奈良国立博物館, ed. *Shaji engi-e*. Tokyo: Kadokawa Shoten, 1975.

————, ed. *Jōdo mandara: Gokuraku Jōdo to raigō no roman*. Special exhibition catalogue. April 24–May 29, 1983.

Nemoto Keizō 根本敬三, ed. *Taikō Ōkagami*. Tokyo: Kasama Shoin, 1984.

Nihon Daijiten Kankōkai 日本大辞典刊行会, ed. *Nihon kokugo daijiten*. 20 vols. Tokyo: Shōgakukan, 1972–76.

Nihon Koten Bungaku Daijiten Henshū Iinkai 日本古典文学大辞典編集委員会, ed. *Nihon koten bungaku daijiten*. 8 vols. Tokyo: Iwanami Shoten, 1983–85.

Nihon Zuihitsu Taisei Henshūbu 日本随筆大成編集部, ed. *Nihon zuihitsu taisei: dai ikki*. 23 vols. Tokyo: Yoshikawa Kōbunkan, 1976.

Nishiguchi Junko 西口順子. *Onna no chikara*. Tokyo: Heibonsha, 1987.

Nishimura Tōru 西村亨. *Uta to minzokugaku*. Minzoku mingei sōsho, no. 6. Tokyo: Iwasaki Bijutsusha, 1966.

O'Flaherty, Wendy Doniger. *Śiva: The Erotic Ascetic*. Oxford: Oxford University Press, 1981.

Ogawa Toyoo 小川豊生. "Katokuron josetsu." *Kagoshima joshi daigaku kenkyū kiyō* 13, no. 1 (March 1992). Reprinted in *Higi to shite no waka*, ed. Watanabe Yasuaki 渡辺泰明, 55–74. Tokyo: Yūseidō, 1995.

————. "Katokuron josetsu 2." In *Uta monogatari to waka setsuwa*, ed. Setsuwa to Setsuwa Bungaku no Kai, 239–73. Setsuwa ronshū, vol. 9. Osaka: Seibundō, 1999.

————, ed. *Nihon koten gisho sōkan*. Vol. 1. Tokyo: Gendai Shichōshinsha, 2005.

Ōgoshi Aiko 大越愛子 and Minamoto Junko 源淳子. *Kaitai suru Bukkyō: sono sekushuaritī kan to shizen kan*. Tokyo: Daitō Shuppanbu, 1994.

Ogurisu Kenji 小栗栖健治. "*Kumano kanjin jikkai mandara* no seiritsu to tenkai." *Hyōgo kenritsu rekishi hakubutsukan kiyō: jinkai* 15 (2004): 129–242.

————. "*Kumano kanjin jikkai mandara* zuzō no seiritsu katei wo megutte: Shiga-ken Kōzenji-bon wo chūshin ni." *Ōmi chihōshi kenkyū* 36 (September 2004): 3–18.

————. "Ise/Shima chihō no *Kumano kanjin jikkai mandara*: Jōganji-bon/Shōkyūji-bon wo chūshin ni." *Mie kenshi kenkyū* 20 (March 2005): 25–41.

Ōhashi Kiyohide 大橋清秀. *Izumi Shikibu nikki no kenkyū*. Tokyo: Shoon Shobō, 1961.

————. *Izumi Shikibu den no kenkyū*. Tokyo: Izumi Shoin, 1994.

Okada Yoshio 岡田希雄. "Izumi Shikibu no ren'ai seikatsu." *Kokugo kokubun no kenkyū* 23, 24, 26 (1928–29): 1–17, 19–34, 31–43.
Okazaki Tomoko 岡崎知子. "Izumi Shikibu to Shōkū Shōnin: 'kuraki yori' no uta wo megutte." 1959. Reprinted in *Heianchō joryū sakka no kenkyū*. Tokyo: Hōzōkan, 1967.
O'Neill, P.G. "The Special Kasuga Wakamiya Festival of 1349." *Monumenta Nipponica* 14, no. 3/4 (October 1958–January 1959): 408–28.
Osaka Shiritsu Hakubutsukan 大阪市立博物館, ed. *Shaji sankei mandara*. Tokyo: Heibonsha, 1987.
Ōshima Tatehiko 大島建彦. *Otogizōshi to minkan bungei*. Minzoku mingei sōsho, no. 12. Tokyo: Iwasaki Bijutsusha, 1967.
———. "Dōsojin no shinkō to setsuwa." In *Chūsei bungaku no kenkyū*, ed. Akiyama Ken 秋山虔, 55–73. Tokyo: Tokyo Daigaku Shuppankai, 1972.
———. "*Uji shūi monogatari* daiichiwa to otogizōshi *Izumi Shikibu*." In *Koten no hen'yō to shinsei*, ed. Kawaguchi Hisao 川口久雄, 251–64. Tokyo: Meiji Shoin, 1984.
Ōshima Yukio 大島由紀夫. "*Izumi Shikibu engi*: Amida shinkō no shujinkō." *Kokubungaku: kaishaku to kanshō* 60, no. 8 (August 1995): 125–30.
Ōsumi Kazuo 大隅和雄. "Josei to Bukkyō: kōsō to sono haha." *Shiron* (Tokyo Joshi Daigaku) 36 (1983): 1–10.
———. "Bukkyō to josei: *Genkō shakusho* no ni'nyoden ni tsuite." *Rekishi hyōron* 395 (1983): 2–11.
Ōta Tōshirō 太田藤四郎, ed. *Sanetaka-kō ki*. Vol. 1. Tokyo: Taiyōsha, 1931.
Ozawa Masao 小沢正夫 et al., eds. *Fukurozōshi chūshaku*. Vol. 1. Tokyo: Hanawa Shobō, 1974.
Pandey, Rajyashree. "Women, Sexuality, and Enlightenment: *Kankyo no tomo*." *Monumenta Nipponica* 50, no. 3 (1995): 325–56.
———. "Poetry, Sex and Salvation: The 'Courtesan' and the Noblewoman in Medieval Japanese Narratives." *Japanese Studies* 24, no. 1 (May 2004): 61–79.
Paul, Diana Y. *Women in Buddhism: Images of the Feminine in Mahāyāna Tradition*. Berkeley: Asian Humanities Press, 1979.
Peyroux, Catherine. "The Leper's Kiss." In *Monks & Nuns, Saints & Outcastes: Religion in Medieval Society*, ed. Sharon Farmer and Barbara H. Rosenwein, 172–88. Ithaca and London: Cornell University Press, 2000.
Philippi, Donald. *Kojiki*. Tokyo: University of Tokyo Press, 1968.
Plutschow, Herbert E. *Chaos and Cosmos: Ritual in Early and Medieval Japanese Literature*. Leiden: E.J. Brill, 1990.
Putzar, Edward D. "The Tale of Monkey Genji." *Monumenta Nipponica* 18, no. 1 (1963): 286–312.
Rhys Davids, T.W. *The Questions of King Milinda*. Vol. 1. Delhi: Motilal Banarsidass, 1965 (first published in 1890).
Ruch, Barbara. "Origins of *The Companion Library*: An Anthology of Medieval Japanese Stories." *The Journal of Asian Studies* 30, no. 3 (May 1971): 593–610.
———. "Medieval Jongleurs and the Making of a National Literature." In *Japan in the Muromachi Age*, ed. John Hall and Toyoda Takeshi, 279–309. Berkeley: University of California Press, 1977.
———. "Woman to Woman: *Kumano bikuni* Proselytizers in Medieval and Early Modern Japan." In *Engendering Faith: Women and Buddhism in Premodern Japan*,

ed. Barbara Ruch, 537–80. Ann Arbor: University of Michigan Center for Japanese Studies, 2002.

Saeki Junko 佐伯順子. *Yūjo no bunkashi*. Chūkō shinsho, no. 853. Tokyo: Chūō Kōronsha, 1987.

Saijō Shizuo 西條静夫. *Izumi Shikibu densetsu to sono koseki*. 3 vols. Tokyo: Kindai Bungeisha, 1992–99.

Sakaguchi Hiroyuki 阪口弘之. "Sekkyō *Karukaya* to Kōya denshō." *Kokugo to kokubungaku* 71, no. 10 (October 1994): 1–18.

Sakaguchi Kōtarō 阪口光太郎. "Jikidan kōkyō ni mieru Shōkū Shōnin Fugen kankendan." *Bungaku ronsō* 67 (February 1993): 86–96.

Sakakibara Kunihiko 榊原邦彦 et al., eds. *Ima kagami: honbun oyobi sōsakuin*. Kasama sakuin sōkan, no. 85. Tokyo: Kasama Shoin, 1984.

Sanari Kentarō 佐成謙太郎, ed. *Yōkyoku taikan*. 7 vols. Tokyo: Meiji Shoin, 1930–31.

Sawa Ryūken 佐和隆研 et al., eds. *Mikkyō jiten*. Kyoto: Hōzōkan, 1975.

Sawai Taizō 沢井耐三. "Otogizōshi *Isozaki* kō: otogizōshi to sekkyō no sekai." In *Koten no hen'yō to shinsei*, ed. Kawaguchi Hisao 川口久雄, 317–28. Tokyo: Meiji Shoin, 1984.

————. "Nara ehon to otogizōshi: Izumi Shikibu." *Kokubungaku: kaishaku to kyōzai no kenkyū* 35, no. 12 (October 1990): 106–9.

Schulenburg, Jane Tibbetts. "The Heroics of Virginity: Brides of Christ and Sacrificial Mutilation." In *Women in the Middle Ages and the Renaissance: Literary and Historical Perspectives*, ed. Mary Beth Rose, 29–72. Syracuse: Syracuse University Press, 1986.

Seidensticker, Edward. *The Tale of Genji*. New York: Alfred A. Knopf, 1991.

Seizan Zenshū Kankōkai 西山全集刊行会, ed. *Seizan zensho*. 5 vols. Kyoto: Bun'eidō Shoten, 1973–74.

Sekimori, Gaynor. "Shugendō: The State of the Field." *Monumenta Nipponica* 57, no. 2 (Summer 2002): 207–21.

Senchakushū English Translation Project, ed. *Hōnen's Senchakushū*. Honolulu: University of Hawaii Press, 1998.

Shiba Kayono 柴佳世乃. "'Dōmyō Izumi Shikibu' kō." *Ryōjin: kenkyū to shiryō* 12 (December 1994): 32–42.

————. "Ono no Komachi to Izumi Shikibu: yūjozō wo megutte." In *Hashi no e: dai yonjū yon kai kōen* (program for a noh performance). Nihon Nōgaku Geijutsu Shinkōkai. Tokyo (December 1994).

————. "Chūsei setsuwashū ni egakareta Izumi Shikibu." *Kokubungaku: kaishaku to kanshō* 60, no. 8 (August 1995): 106–11.

————. "*Izumi Shikibu*: Muromachi ki ni okeru monogatari no hirogari." *Kokubungaku: kaishaku to kanshō* 61, no. 5 (May 1996): 51–55.

————. "Dokyōdō." *Bungaku* 9, no. 1 (Winter 1998): 124–34.

————. "Kyōraku ni okeru Izumi Shikibu zō no fukurami: Seiganji no shūhen." *Tessen* 461 (March 1998): 4–5.

Shibahara Mika 柴原美香. "Chūsei shōsetsu *Chūjōhime* no denbon keitō ni tsuite—*Taima mandarasho* to no hikaku wo chūshin ni." *Kokugo to kyōiku* (Nagasaki Daigaku) 15 (1990): 61–72.

Shigematsu Nobuhiro 重松信弘. *Shinkō Genji monogatari kenkyūshi*. Tokyo: Fūkan Shobō, 1961.

Shimazu Hisamoto 島津久基. *Kinko shōsetsu shinsan*. Tokyo: Chūkōkan, 1928. Republished by Yūseidō in 1983.

Shimizu Yutaka 清水泰. *Nihon bungaku ronkō*. Kyoto: Hatsune Shobō, 1960. Reprinted in *Monogatari bungaku kenkyū sōsho*. Vol. 25. Tokyo: Kuresu Shuppan, 1999.

———. *Nara Picture Books*, trans. Richard Zumwinkle. Los Angeles: Dawson's Book Shop, 1960.

Shimonaka Hiroshi 下中弘, ed. *Nihonshi daijiten*. 7 vols. Tokyo: Heibonsha, 1992–94.

Shimura Kunihiro 志村有弘 et al., eds. *Hachiman jinja kenkyū*. Tokyo: Sōbunsha, 1989.

Shinno Toshikazu 真野俊和. "Kōbō Daishi no haha: Akoya-gozen no denshō to Shikoku reijō engi." In *Kōbō Daishi shinkō*, ed. Hinonishi Shinjō 日野西真定, 89–113. Tokyo: Yūzankaku Shuppan, 1988.

Shintō Taikei Hensankai 神道大系編纂会, ed. *Shintō taikei: bungaku hen 1: Shintōshū*. Tokyo: Shintō Taikei Hensankai, 1988.

Shirane, Haruo, ed. *Traditional Japanese Literature: An Anthology, Beginnings to 1600*. New York: Columbia University Press, 2007.

———, ed. *The Tale of Genji Reader*. New York: Columbia University Press, forthcoming.

Shively, Donald H. "Buddhahood for the Nonsentient: A Theme in *Nō* Plays." *Harvard Journal of Asiatic Studies* 20 (1957): 135–61.

Smith, Henry D., and Matthew P. McKelway. "Digitalizing Japanese Art." *Monumenta Nipponica* 57, no. 4 (Winter 2002): 509–28.

Smyers, Karen. "Women and Shinto: The Relation Between Purity and Pollution." *Japanese Religions* 12, no. 4 (July 1983): 7–18.

Soymié, Michel."Ketsubonkyō no shiryōteki kenkyū." In *Dōkyō kenkyū*, ed. Yoshioka Yoshitoyo and Michel Soymié, 109–66. Tokyo: Shōrinsha, 1965.

Stone, Jacqueline. *Original Enlightenment and the Transformation of Medieval Japanese Buddhism*. Honolulu: University of Hawaii Press, 1999.

———. "The Contemplation of Suchness." In *Religions of Japan in Practice*, ed. George J. Tanabe, Jr. Princeton: Princeton University Press, 1999.

Strong, Sarah M. "The Making of a Femme Fatale: Ono no Komachi in the Early Medieval Commentaries." *Monumenta Nipponica* 49, no. 4 (1994): 391–412.

———. "Komachi at the Crossroads: Elements of Popular Female Performance in Two Nō Plays," *Proceedings of the Midwest Association for Japanese Literary Studies* 3 (Summer 1997): 122–40.

———. "Reading the 'Court' in Courtesan: The Historicization of the Role of Yūjo in Some Muromachi Tales." *Proceedings of the Midwest Association for Japanese Literary Studies* 4 (*The New Historicism and Japanese Literary Studies*) (Summer 1998): 234–53.

———. "Performing the Courtesan: In Search of Ghosts at Zuishin-in Letter Mound." In "Performing Japanese Women," *Women and Performance: A Journal of Feminist Theory* 12:1, no. 23 (2001): 79–95.

Suzuka Sanshichi 鈴鹿三七. *Shinkanshū kaisetsu*. Tokyo: Kunaishō, 1927.

Suzuki Masataka 鈴木正崇. *Nyonin kinsei*. Tokyo: Yoshikawa Kōbunkan, 2002.

Takano Tatsuyuki 高野辰之, ed. *Nihon kayō shūsei*. Vol. 4. Tokyo: Tōkyōdō, 1942.

Takemi, Momoko. "'Menstruation Sutra' Belief in Japan," trans. W. Michael Kelsey. *Japanese Journal of Religious Studies* 10, nos. 2–3 (1983): 229–46.

Takemura Toshinori 竹村俊則, ed. *Kyōto no maki* 1. Vol. 7 of *Nihon meisho fūzoku zue*. Tokyo: Kadokawa Shoten, 1979.

Takigawa Masajirō 滝川政次郎. *Yūjo no rekishi*. Tokyo: Shibundō, 1965.

Tamagami Takuya 玉上琢弥, ed. *Shimeishō, Kakaishō*. Tokyo: Kadokawa Shoten, 1968.

Tanabe, Willa Jane. "The Lotus Lectures: *Hokke hakkō* in the Heian Period." *Monumenta Nipponica* 39 (1984): 393–407.

————. *Paintings of the Lotus Sutra*. New York and Tokyo: Weatherhill, 1988.

Tanaka Jūtarō 田中重太郎. "Ōchō joryū no matsuro." *Kokubungaku* 7, no. 9 (1962): 133–41.

————. *Sei Shōnagon Makura no sōshi kenkyū*. Tokyo: Kasama Shoin, 1971.

————. *Makura no sōshi zen chūshaku*. Vol. 4. Tokyo: Kadokawa Shoten, 1972.

Tanaka Makoto 田中允. "Izumi Shikibu to yōkyoku." *Kokugo to kokubungaku* (April 1946): 12–24.

————, ed. *Mikan yōkyokushū*. Vol. 7. Koten bunko 231. Tokyo: Koten Bunko, 1966.

Tater, Maria. *Off With Their Heads! Fairy Tales and the Culture of Childhood*. Princeton: Princeton University Press, 1992.

ten Grotenhuis, Elizabeth. "Rebirth of an Icon: The Taima Mandala in Medieval Japan." *Archives of Asian Art* 36 (1983): 59–87.

————. *The Revival of the Taima Mandala*. New York: Garland Publishing, 1985.

————. "Chūjōhime: The Weaving of Her Legend." In *Flowing Traces: Buddhism in the Literary and Visual Arts of Japan*, ed. James Sanford, William LaFleur, and Masatoshi Nagatomi, 180–200. Princeton: Princeton University Press, 1992.

————. *Japanese Mandalas: Representations of Sacred Geography*. Honolulu: University of Hawaii Press, 1999.

Thornton, S. A. *Charisma and Community Formation in Medieval Japan: The Case of the Yugyō-ha (1300–1700)*. Cornell East Asia Series, no. 102. Ithaca: Cornell University East Asia Program, 1999.

Thurman, Robert A. F. *The Holy Teaching of Vimalakīrti: A Mahāyāna Scripture*. University Park and London: The Pennsylvania State University Press, 1976.

Tochio Takeshi 栃尾武, ed. *Tamatsukuri Komachi shi sōsuisho*. Iwanami bunko 570. Tokyo: Iwanami Shoten, 1994.

Tokuda Kazuo 徳田和夫. *Otogizōshi kenkyū*. Tokyo: Miyai Shoten, 1988.

————. "*Ōgi no sōshi* emaki wo megutte." *Kokugo kokubun ronshū* (Gakushūin Joshi Tanki Daigaku Kokugo Kokubungakukai) 20 (March 1991): 69–92.

————. "Etoki: toku ni 'Kangyō-hen' to Chūjōhime setsuwa wo megutte." In *Sōden, jisha engi, emaki, eden*, ed. Itō Hiroyuki 伊藤博之 et al., 370–93. Bukkyō bungaku kōza 6. Tokyo: Benseisha, 1995.

————. "Kumano ni mōderu Izumi Shikibu." *Nihon no bigaku* 25 (1997): 74–85.

————. "*Seiganji engi*, soshite kabu no bosatsu-tachi." *Tessen* 492 (April 2001): 6–8.

————. "Shōkai: otogizōshi *Jippon ōgi* no shinshutsu-bon." *Koten shiryō kenkyū* 3 (June 2001): 1–17.

————. "Otogizōshi *Ko-Atsumori* no Kōshōji-bon wo megutte." *Gakushūin Joshi Daigaku kiyō* 4 (2002): 33–50.

————. *Otogizōshi jiten*. Tokyo: Tōkyōdō Shuppan, 2002.

Tokue Gensei 徳江元正. "Otogizōshi: *Izumi Shikibu*." *Kokubungaku: kaishaku to kyōzai no kenkyū* 19, no. 4 (March 1974): 76–77.

————. *Muromachi geinō-shi ronkō*. Tokyo: Miyai Shoten, 1984.

Tonomura, Hitomi. "Re-envisioning Women in the Kamakura Age." In *The Origins of*

Japan's Medieval World, ed. Jeffrey P. Mass, 138–69. Stanford: Stanford University Press, 1997.

Tsugita Kasumi 次田香澄 and Iwasa Miyoko 岩佐美代子, eds. *Fūga wakashū*. Chūsei no bungaku. Tokyo: Miyai Shoten, 1974.

Tsuji Eiko 辻英子. *Zaigai Nihon emaki no kenkyū to shiryō*. Kasama sōsho, no. 328. Tokyo: Kasama Shoin, 1999.

Tsukudo Reikan 筑土鈴寛. *Fukko to jojishi*. In *Tsukudo Reikan chosaku shū*, vol. 1. Tokyo: Serika Shobō, 1976.

Tyler, Susan. *The Cult of Kasuga Seen through its Art*. Ann Arbor: University of Michigan Center for Japanese Studies, 1992.

Uemura Etsuko 上村悦子. *Ōchō joryū sakka no kenkyū*. Tokyo: Kasama Shoin, 1975.

Umetani Shigeki 梅谷繁樹. "Kyōto Tōhokuin zō *Ippen Shōnin Izumi Shikibu monogatari* ni tsuite." In *Chūsei yūgyō hijiri to bungaku*. Tokyo: Ōfūsha, 1988.

Ury, Marian. "*Genkō shakusho*: Japan's First Comprehensive History of Buddhism." Ph.D. diss., University of California at Berkeley, 1971.

———. *Tales of Times Now Past: Sixty-two Stories from a Medieval Japanese Collection*. Berkeley: University of California Press, 1979.

———. "Nuns and Other Female Devotees in *Genkō shakusho* (1322), Japan's First History of Buddhism," revised for publication by Robert Borgen. In *Engendering Faith: Women and Buddhism in Premodern Japan*, ed. Barbara Ruch, 189–207. Ann Arbor: University of Michigan Center for Japanese Studies, 2002.

Waley, Arthur. *The Nō Plays of Japan*. New York: Grove Press, 1957.

Walters, Jonathan. "A Voice from the Silence: The Buddha's Mother's Story." *History of Religions* 33 (1994): 358–79.

Wan xucangjing (*Manji zoku zōkyō*). Vol. 47. Taibei: Xinwenfeng, 1977.

Watanabe Hideo 渡辺秀夫. *Heianchō bungaku to kanbun sekai*. Tokyo: Benseisha, 1991.

Watson, Burton. *The Lotus Sutra*. New York: Columbia University Press, 1993.

Williams, Duncan Ryūken. *The Other Side of Zen: A Social History of Sōtō Zen Buddhism in Tokugawa Japan*. Princeton and Oxford: Princeton University Press, 2005.

Wilson, Liz. *Charming Cadavers: Horrific Figurations of the Feminine in Indian Buddhist Hagiographic Literature*. Chicago and London: University of Chicago Press, 1996.

Yamada Shōzen 山田昭全 and Miki Sumito 三木紀人, eds. *Zōtanshū*. Chūsei no bungaku. Tokyo: Miyai Shoten, 1980.

Yamamoto Isao 山本勇夫, ed. *Kōsō meicho zenshū*. Vol. 10. Tokyo: Heibonsha, 1931.

Yamamoto Takashi 山本節. "Dōmyō to Izumi Shikibu no setsuwa." *Kokugo to kokubungaku* 57, no. 3 (1980): 41–57.

Yampolsky, Philip B., ed. *Selected Writings of Nichiren*. New York: Columbia University Press, 1990.

Yanagita Kunio 柳田国男. "Rōjo kaseki dan." In *Imōto no chikara*. 1916. Reprinted in *Yanagita Kunio zenshū*, vol. 11, 366–79. Tokyo: Chikuma Shobō, 1998.

———. "Izumi Shikibu no tabi." 1931. Reprinted in *Momotarō no tanjō*. 1933. Reprinted in *Teihon Yanagita Kunio shū*, vol. 8. Tokyo: Chikuma Shobō, 1962.

———. *Josei to minkan denshō*. 1932. Reprinted in *Teihon Yanagita Kunio shū*, vol. 8. Tokyo: Chikuma Shobō, 1962.

Yasuda Takako 安田孝子. "Shōkū Shōnin setsuwa: *Senjūshō* wo chūshin to shite." *Sugiyama kokubungaku* (Sugiyama Jogakuen Daigaku) 7 (1983): 15–50.

Yokoyama Shigeru 横山重, ed. *Muromachi jidai monogatari shū*. Vol. 2. Tokyo: Inoue Shobō, 1962.

Yoshida, Kogorō. *Tanrokubon: Rare Books of Seventeenth-century Japan*, trans. Mark A. Harbison. Tokyo: Kodansha International, 1984.

Yoshida Kōichi 吉田幸一, ed. *Izumi Shikibu zenshū: honbun hen*. Tokyo: Koten Bunko, 1959.

———. "Izumi Shikibu no shakkyōka 'kuraki yori' no sakka nendai to *Shūishū* e no nyūshū jijō ni tsuite." *Heian bungaku kenkyū* 28 (June 1962): 35–44.

———. "Izumi Shikibu no shūsseichi: sono koseki wo tazunete." *Bungaku ronsō* (Tōyō Daigaku) 32 (November 1965): 37–45.

———. "*Seiganji engi* to *Izumi Shikibu engi*." *Bungaku ronsō* (May 1966): 1–14.

Yuge Shigeru 弓削繁. "Gifu Daigaku Fuzoku Toshokan-zō *Koshikibu*: honkoku to kaidai." *Gifu Daigaku kokugo kokubungaku* 25 (March 1998): 63–80.

Yutani Yūzō 湯谷祐三. "*Seiganji engi* rokkanbon no kaidai to honkoku." *Dōhō Daigaku Bukkyō bunka kenkyūjo kiyō* 18 (1998): 73–100.

———. "*Seiganji engi* kankei shiryō." *Fukakusa kyōgaku* 19 (1999): 295–355.

Zōho Shiryō Taisei Kankōkai 増補史料大成刊行会, ed. *Zōho shiryō taisei*. 45 vols. Kyoto: Rinsen Shoten, 1965. (Plus 3 supp. vols. from 1968).

Index

ABOUT THE AUTHOR

Keller Kimbrough is an Assistant Professor in the Department of Asian Languages and Civilizations at the University of Colorado, Boulder. He completed his Ph.D. at Yale University in December 1999. He has held teaching positions at the University of Michigan, the University of Virginia, Colby College, and the University of Colorado.